GW00492920

Tolley's Company Law Handbook 2000–2001

by
Robert Wareham BSc(Econ) FCA

Tolley Publishing

Published by Tolley
2 Addiscombe Road
Croydon CR9 5AF England
020-8686 9141

Typeset in Great Britain
by
Interactive Sciences Ltd, Gloucester

Printed in Great Britain
by
The Bath Press, Avon

ISBN 075 450 743–2

About This Book

This is the seventh edition of Tolley's Company Law Handbook. It is intended to be a first book of reference for accountants, solicitors, company secretaries and all those involved in company law.

The book includes the provisions of the Companies Acts and all other relevant company law provisions (excluding insolvency) up to and including 1 January 2000. Relevant case law and other important information, including the Listing Rules and the City Code on Takeovers and Mergers, is also covered.

The chapter on *Directors* includes coverage of directors' duties and directors' service contracts. This text is based on the chapters in *Tolley's Company Law* written respectively by P L R Mitchell and K Dierden. The author is most grateful to them for permission to use their material.

The book follows the same format and style as Tolley's established tax annuals. Chapters are in alphabetical order for ease of reference to a particular subject and cross-references, an index and a table of statutes provide further ways of quickly finding the matter required.

Comments on the publication and suggestions for improvement of future editions are always welcome.

TOLLEY PUBLISHING

Contents

Contents

Abbreviations and References

References throughout the book to numbered sections and schedules are to the Companies Act 1985 unless otherwise indicated.

ABBREVIATIONS

AGM	=	Annual General Meeting
AIM	=	Alternative Investment Market
Art	=	Article
ASL	=	The International Stock Exchange's 'Admission of Securities to Listing' ('Yellow Book')
BNA 1985	=	Business Names Act 1985
CA 1948	=	Companies Act 1948
CA 1967	=	Companies Act 1967
CA 1980	=	Companies Act 1980
CA 1985	=	Companies Act 1985
CA 1989	=	Companies Act 1989
CAO	=	Company Announcements Office
CC(CP)A 1985	=	Companies Consolidation (Consequential Provisions) Act 1985
CDDA 1986	=	Company Directors Disqualification Act 1986
Ch	=	Chapter
CS(ID)A 1985	=	Company Securities (Insider Dealing) Act 1985
EC	=	European Community
ECUs	=	European Currency Units
EEA	=	European Economic Area
EEC	=	European Economic Community
EGM	=	Extraordinary General Meeting
FRS	=	Financial Reporting Standard
FSA 1986	=	Financial Services Act 1986
FTA 1973	=	Fair Trading Act 1973
IA 1985	=	Insolvency Act 1985
IA 1986	=	Insolvency Act 1986
ICTA 1988	=	Income and Corporation Taxes Act 1988
NI	=	Northern Ireland
No	=	Number
Para	=	Paragraph
POS Regulations	=	Public Offers of Securities Regulations 1995
Pt	=	Part
Reg	=	Regulation
s(s)	=	Section(s)
Sec	=	Section
Sch	=	Schedule [*4 Sch 10* = 4th Schedule, paragraph 10]
SFS	=	Summary Financial Statement
SI	=	Statutory Instrument
SSAP	=	Standard Statement of Accounting Practice
STA 1963	=	Stock Transfer Act 1963
STA 1982	=	Stock Transfer Act 1982
VAT	=	Value Added Tax

REFERENCES

AC	=	Law Reports, Appeal Cases
All ER	=	All England Law Reports (1936 onwards)

Abbreviations and References

App Cas	=	Law Reports Appeal Cases (1875–90)
BCC	=	British Company Law Cases (CCH Editions Ltd)
BCLC	=	Butterworths Company Law Cases
[1891] Ch	=	Law Reports, Chancery (1891 onwards)
ChD	=	Law Reports, Chancery Division (1876–90)
CLR	=	Commonwealth Law Reports (1903 onwards)
CPD	=	Common Pleas Division (1875–80)
E & B	=	Ellis and Blackburn's Queen's Bench Reports (1852–58)
Ex D	=	Exchequer Division (1875–80)
Hare	=	Hare's Vice-Chancellor's Reports (1841–53)
HL Cas	=	House of Lords Cases (Clark) (1847–66)
[1901] KB	=	Law Reports, King's Bench (1901 onwards)
Lloyd's Rep	=	Lloyd's List Law Reports
LR CP	=	Law Reports, Common Pleas (1865–75)
LR Eq	=	Law Reports, Equity (1865–75)
LR Ex	=	Law Reports, Exchequer (1865–75)
LR HL	=	Law Reports, English and Irish Appeal Cases (1865–75)
LR QB	=	Law Reports, Queen's Bench (1865–75)
LT	=	Law Times (1843 onwards)
Macq	=	Macqueen's Scotch Appeal Cases (1851–65)
[1891] QB	=	Law Reports, Queen's Bench (1891 onwards)
QBD	=	Law Reports, Queen's Bench Division (1876–90)
[1907] SC	=	Court of Session Cases (1907 onwards)
TLR	=	Times Law Reports (1885 onwards)
WLR	=	Weekly Law Reports
WN	=	Weekly Notes (1886 onwards)

1   Accounting Reference Dates and Periods

1.1   A company must prepare accounts for each financial year. The financial year is determined by the company's 'accounting reference period' (see 1.2 below) which, in turn, is determined by the selection, or imposition, of an 'accounting reference date' (see 1.3 below). [*Sec 224(1); CA 1989, s 3*]. Such a date can then only be altered in certain defined circumstances (see 1.4 below).

1.2   ACCOUNTING REFERENCE PERIODS

Subject to 1.4 below, a company's first accounting reference period is the period of more than six months, but not more than 18 months, from its date of incorporation to its accounting reference date. Subsequent accounting reference periods are successive periods of twelve months from the end of the previous accounting reference period to the accounting reference date. [*Sec 224(4)(5); CA 1989, s 3*].

1.3   ACCOUNTING REFERENCE DATE

The '*accounting reference date*' is the date on which a company's accounting reference period ends in each calendar year.

Companies incorporated on or after 1 April 1996. The accounting reference date of such a company is the last day of the month in which the anniversary of its incorporation falls.

Companies incorporated before 1 April 1996. Such a company could, within nine months of incorporation, give notice in the prescribed form to the Registrar of Companies specifying its accounting reference date. Failing such notice, its accounting reference date is

● 	31 March for a company incorporated before 1 April 1990; and

● 	the last day of the month in which the anniversary of its incorporation falls for a company incorporated after 31 March 1990 and before 1 April 1996.

[*Sec 224(2)(3)(3A); CA 1989, s 3; SI 1990 No 355, 2 Sch 4; SI 1996 No 189, Reg 2*].

1.4   Alteration of an accounting reference date

A company can, by notice to the Registrar of Companies in the prescribed form (Form 225), specify a new accounting reference date which is to have effect in relation to

● 	its current and subsequent accounting reference periods; or

● 	its immediately preceding and subsequent accounting reference periods. This option is not available where the period allowed for laying and delivering of accounts and reports for the immediately preceding period has already expired (normally seven months for public companies and ten months for private companies, see 3.8 ACCOUNTS: GENERAL).

The notice must state whether the current/immediately preceding accounting reference period is to be shortened or extended (i.e. whether it is to end on the first or second occasion on which the new accounting reference date occurs).

Notice to shorten. A company may give notice to shorten the current/immediately preceding accounting reference period as often as it likes.

1.5 Accounting Reference Dates and Periods

Notice to extend. Notice to extend that period is ineffective if given less than five years after the end of an earlier accounting reference period of the company which was extended under these provisions unless

(*a*)   it is given by a company which is a 'subsidiary undertaking' or 'parent undertaking' (see 4.2 ACCOUNTS: GROUPS OF COMPANIES) of another undertaking established in the EEA and the new accounting reference date coincides with that of the EEA undertaking (or, if that undertaking is not a company, the last day of its financial year);

(*b*)   an administration order is in force under *IA 1986, Part II*; or

(*c*)   the Secretary of State allows otherwise.

In any case, unless (*b*) above applies, an accounting period cannot be extended so as to exceed 18 months and any notice attempting to do this is ineffective.

[*Sec 225; CA 1989, s 3; SI 1996 No 189, Reg 3*].

The countries comprising the EEA are Austria, Belgium, Denmark, Finland, France, Germany, Greece, Iceland, Ireland, Italy, Liechtenstein, Luxembourg, Netherlands, Norway, Portugal, Spain, Sweden and the UK.

Listed companies. Where a company which has listed securities changes its accounting reference date, it must notify the Company Announcements Office without delay of the new accounting reference date. (*The Listing Rules, Chapter 12.60*).

1.5   OVERSEA COMPANIES

The provisions in 1.1 to 1.4 above also apply to OVERSEA COMPANIES (38) except that

- for the references to the incorporation of a company there should be substituted references to the company establishing a place of business in Great Britain;

- the restrictions in 1.4 above on the frequency with which the accounting reference period may be extended do not apply; and

- the period allowed for filing accounts under 1.4 above is normally 13 months (see 38.38 OVERSEA COMPANIES).

[*Sec 701; CA 1989, 10 Sch 13*].

2   Accounts: Definitions

2.1   The following definitions apply for the purposes of *Part VII* of *CA 1985* dealt with in ACCOUNTS: GENERAL (3); ACCOUNTS: GROUPS OF COMPANIES (4); ACCOUNTS: INDIVIDUAL COMPANIES (5); ACCOUNTS: INSURANCE AND BANKING COMPANIES (6); ACCOUNTS: SMALL AND MEDIUM-SIZED COMPANIES (7) and DIRECTORS' REPORT (20).

Accounting standards. References to 'accounting standards' are to statements of standard accounting practice issued by prescribed bodies, and references to 'accounting standards applicable to a company's annual accounts' are to such standards as are, in accordance with their terms, relevant to the company's circumstances and to the accounts. [*Sec 256(1)(2); CA 1989, s 19*]. The Accounting Standards Board Ltd is a prescribed body for these purposes. [*SI 1990 No 1667*].

Annual accounts means

- the individual accounts required under 5.2 ACCOUNTS: INDIVIDUAL COMPANIES, or

- the group accounts required under 4.8 ACCOUNTS: GROUPS OF COMPANIES

and includes notes to the accounts giving information required under *CA 1985*. [*Secs 261(2), 262(1); CA 1989, s 22*].

See, however, 4.11 ACCOUNTS: GROUPS OF COMPANIES.

Annual report in relation to a company means the DIRECTORS' REPORT (20). [*Sec 262(1); CA 1989, s 22*].

Associated undertaking. See 4.21 ACCOUNTS: GROUPS OF COMPANIES.

Balance sheet includes notes to the accounts giving information required by *CA 1985* and required or allowed to be given in a note to the company's accounts. [*Sec 261(2); CA 1989, s 22*].

Capitalisation in relation to work or cost means treating that work or those costs as a 'fixed asset'. [*Sec 262(1); CA 1989, s 22*].

Current assets mean assets not intended for use as 'fixed assets'. [*Sec 262(1); CA 1989, s 22*].

Fellow subsidiary undertakings are undertakings which are 'subsidiary undertakings' of the same 'parent undertaking' but are not parent undertakings or subsidiary undertakings of each other. [*Sec 259(4); CA 1989, s 22*].

Financial year. A company's first financial year begins on the date of incorporation and ends, subject to below, on its accounting reference date which is more than six months, but not more than 18 months, after that date. See 1 ACCOUNTING REFERENCE DATES AND PERIODS.

Subsequent financial years begin on the day immediately following the end of the previous financial year and, subject to below, end on the next accounting reference date.

Any financial year may, however, end on such other date, not more than seven days before or after the date as above, as determined by the directors. This allows accounts either to be prepared for a 52-week period or always to end on a specific day of the week. [*Sec 223(1)-(3); CA 1989, s 3*].

In relation to undertakings which are not companies, a reference to its financial year is to any period in respect of which a profit and loss account is required to be made up (by its constitution or by the law under which it is established), whether that period is a year or not. [*Sec 223(4); CA 1989, s 3*].

2.1 Accounts: Definitions

Fixed assets means assets of the company which are intended for use on a continuing basis in the company's activities. [*Sec 262(1); CA 1989, s 22*].

Group means a 'parent undertaking' and its 'subsidiary undertakings' (see 4.2 ACCOUNTS: GROUPS OF COMPANIES).

Group undertaking in relation to an 'undertaking' means an undertaking which is

- a 'parent undertaking' or 'subsidiary undertaking' (see 4.2 ACCOUNTS: GROUPS OF COMPANIES) of that undertaking;

- a subsidiary undertaking of any parent undertaking of that undertaking.

[*Sec 259(5); CA 1989, s 22*].

Historic cost accounting rules. See 5.7 ACCOUNTS: INDIVIDUAL COMPANIES.

Listed investments. See 5.19 ACCOUNTS: INDIVIDUAL COMPANIES.

Parent undertakings. See 4.2 ACCOUNTS: GROUPS OF COMPANIES.

Participating interest means an 'interest in shares' of another 'undertaking' held on a long-term basis for the purpose of exercising control or influence over that undertaking's activities. Unless the contrary is shown, a holding of 20% or more of the 'shares' of an undertaking is presumed to be a participating interest.

'Interest in shares' includes an interest which is convertible into an interest in shares and an option to acquire shares or any such interest (even if the relevant shares are unissued until the conversion or exercise of the option).

An interest held on behalf of an undertaking is to be treated as held by it.

For the purposes of the expression 'participating interest'

- in 4.2(*e*) ACCOUNTS: GROUPS OF COMPANIES (definition of subsidiary undertaking)

  (*a*)   there is to be attributed to an undertaking any interest held by any of its subsidiary undertakings; and

  (*b*)   the references above to 'purpose' and 'activities' of an undertaking include the purpose and activities of any of its subsidiary undertakings and of the group as a whole; and

- in the balance sheet and profit and loss formats in 5.4 and 5.5 ACCOUNTS: INDIVIDUAL COMPANIES and 7.6 and 7.7 ACCOUNTS: SMALL AND MEDIUM-SIZED COMPANIES as they apply in relation to group accounts and the definition of associated companies in 4.21 ACCOUNTS: GROUPS OF COMPANIES, the references above to the 'interest held by', and the 'purpose' and 'activities' of, the undertaking concerned are to be construed as references to the interest held by, and the purposes and activities of, the group.

[*Sec 260; CA 1989, s 22; SI 1997 No 220, Reg 7*].

Profit and loss account includes notes to the accounts giving information required by *CA 1985* and required or allowed to be given in a note to the company's accounts. [*Sec 261(2); CA 1989, s 22*].

Provisions.

- References to provisions for depreciation or diminution in value of assets are to any amount written off by way of providing for depreciation or diminution in value of assets.

4

- References to provisions for liabilities or charges are to amounts retained as reasonably necessary for the purpose of providing for any liability or loss which is either likely to be incurred, or certain to be incurred but uncertain as to amount or as to the date on which it will arise.

[*4 Sch 88, 89*].

See also 6.4 and 6.62 ACCOUNTS: INSURANCE AND BANKING COMPANIES for similar definitions applicable to insurance companies and banking companies respectively.

Qualified in relation to an auditors' report means that the report does not state the auditors' unqualified opinion that the accounts have been properly prepared in accordance with *CA 1985* or, in the case of an 'undertaking' not required to prepare accounts under that Act, under any corresponding legislation. [*Sec 262(1); CA 1989, s 22*].

Realised profit and **realised loss** in relation to a company's accounts are to such profits or losses as fall to be treated as realised in accordance with principles generally accepted, at the time when the accounts are prepared, with respect to their determination. [*Sec 262(3); CA 1989, s 22*].

Shares. References to shares

- in relation to an 'undertaking' with a share capital, are to allotted shares;

- in relation to an undertaking with capital but no share capital, are to rights to share in the capital of the undertaking; and

- in relation to an undertaking without capital, are to interests

    (*a*)   conferring any right to share in the profits, or liability to contribute to the losses, of the undertaking, or

    (*b*)   giving rise to an obligation to contribute to the debts or expenses of the undertaking in the event of a winding up.

[*Sec 259(2); CA 1989, s 22*].

Subsidiary undertakings. See 4.2 ACCOUNTS: GROUPS OF COMPANIES.

Turnover in relation to a company means the amount derived from the provision of goods and services falling within the company's ordinary activities, after deducting trade discounts, VAT and other taxes based on the amounts so derived. [*Sec 262(1); CA 1989, s 22*].

Undertaking means

- a body corporate or partnership; or

- an unincorporated association carrying on a trade or business with or without a view to profit.

Where an undertaking is not a company, expressions appropriate to companies must be construed as references to the corresponding persons, officers, document or organs, as the case may be, appropriate to the undertaking in question.

[*Sec 259(1)(3); CA 1989, s 22*].

3 Accounts: General

Cross–references. See 2 ACCOUNTS: DEFINITIONS; 4 ACCOUNTS: GROUPS OF COMPANIES; 5 ACCOUNTS: INDIVIDUAL COMPANIES; 6 ACCOUNTS: INSURANCE AND BANKING COMPANIES; 7 ACCOUNTS: SMALL AND MEDIUM-SIZED COMPANIES; 45.1 to 45.4 RECORDS for accounting records.

The contents of this chapter are as follows.

3.1 INTRODUCTION

The provisions described in this chapter cover the requirements which relate to accounts generally, whether individual or group. The Secretary of State has power to modify the provisions by Regulations. [*Sec 257; CA 1989, s 20*].

3.2 APPROVAL AND SIGNING OF ACCOUNTS

A company's annual accounts must be approved by the board and signed on its behalf by a director, the signature appearing on the balance sheet. Every issued copy of the balance sheet must state the signatory's name; the copy delivered to the Registrar of Companies (see 3.7 below) must be signed. If a copy of the balance sheet is laid before the company in general meeting, otherwise circulated, published or issued, or delivered to the Registrar, without satisfying these provisions, the company and every officer in default is liable to a fine up to the level in 40.1(*g*) PENALTIES.

Every director who is party to the approval of accounts which do not comply with the requirements of *CA 1985*, and who is aware of their non-compliance or reckless as to whether they comply, is liable to a fine up to the level in 40.1(*d*) PENALTIES. Every director of the company at the time the accounts are approved is regarded as being party to their approval unless he shows that he took all reasonable steps to prevent their being approved.

[*Sec 233, 24 Sch; CA 1989, s 7*].

3.3 PUBLICATION OF ACCOUNTS AND REPORTS

Persons entitled to receive copies. A copy of the annual accounts, directors' report and auditors' report must be sent, at least 21 days (but see below) prior to the general meeting at which copies of those documents are to be laid (see 3.6 below), to

- every member of the company;

- every debenture-holder; and

- every person entitled to receive notice of general meetings.

[*Sec 238(1); CA 1989, s 10*].

Copies need not be sent

- to a person not entitled to receive notices of general meetings and of whose address the company is unaware; or

- to more than one of the joint shareholders or debenture-holders none of whom is entitled to receive notices of general meetings; or

- to those joint shareholders or debenture-holders not entitled to receive notices of general meetings, where some joint holders are, and some are not, so entitled; or

- in the case of a company without a share capital, to anyone not entitled to receive notices of general meetings.

If the accounts etc. are sent out before the meeting but within 21 days thereof, the time limit is regarded as having been complied with if all the members entitled to attend and vote at the meeting so agree.

[*Sec 238(2)-(4); CA 1989, s 10*].

The company and every officer in default of the above provisions is liable to a fine up to the level in 40.1(*d*) PENALTIES. [*Sec 238(5), 24 Sch; CA 1989, s 10*].

Where accounts etc. are sent out over a period of days, they are regarded for the purposes of *CA 1985* as having been sent out on the last of those days. [*Sec 238(6); CA 1989, s 10*].

3.4   **Right to demand copies**

In addition to any copy to which he is entitled under 3.3 above, any member of the company or debenture-holder must be supplied, on demand and free of charge, with a single copy of the last annual accounts, directors' report and auditors' report. This must be supplied within seven days of the demand, the company and every officer in default being liable to a fine up to the level in 40.1(*f*) PENALTIES. The onus of proof that a person has already been supplied with a copy of the relevant document is on the defendant. [*Sec 239, 24 Sch; CA 1989, s 10*].

3.5   **Requirements in connection with publication**

If a company publishes any of its 'statutory accounts', they must be accompanied by the relevant auditors' report (see 12.18 AUDITORS) or, where applicable, the relevant accountants' report (see 12.35 AUDITORS). A company required to prepare group accounts for a financial year must not publish its statutory individual accounts without also publishing with them its statutory group accounts.

A company publishing 'non-statutory accounts' must not publish with them any auditors' report (or accountants' report) but must publish with them a statement indicating

- that they are not the statutory accounts;

- whether statutory accounts for any financial year dealt with by the non-statutory accounts have been delivered to the Registrar of Companies or, in the case of an unlimited company (see 60 UNLIMITED COMPANIES), that the company is exempt from the requirement to deliver statutory accounts;

- whether the auditors (or reporting accountant) have reported on the statutory accounts for any such financial year; and

- whether any such auditors' report was qualified or contained a statement under 12.23(i) or (ii) AUDITORS (or whether any such accountants' report was qualified).

3.6 Accounts: General

In the event of any contravention of the above provisions, the company and any officer in default is liable to a fine up to the level in 40.1(*g*) PENALTIES.

[*Secs 240(1)-(3)(6), 254(4)(a), 24 Sch; CA 1989, ss 10, 17; SI 1994 No 1935, 1 Sch 1*].

'*Statutory accounts*' are a company's individual or group accounts for a financial year as required to be delivered to the Registrar of Companies (see 3.7 below) or, in the case of an unlimited company, as prepared in accordance with *Part VII* and approved by the board. Included are accounts delivered to the Registrar in accordance with the provisions for 'small' and 'medium-sized' companies (see 7.40 and 7.44 ACCOUNTS: SMALL AND MEDIUM-SIZED COMPANIES respectively) and any additional copy of the annual accounts delivered in ECUs (see 3.7 below).

'*Non-statutory accounts*' means any of the following which are published otherwise than as part of the statutory accounts.

- A balance sheet or profit and loss account relating to, or purporting to deal with, a financial year of the company.

- An account in any form purporting to be such a balance sheet or profit and loss account for the group (i.e. the company and its subsidiaries).

[*Secs 240(5), 242B(4), 254(4)(b), 8 Sch 26(1)(2); CA 1989, ss 10, 17, 6 Sch; SI 1992 No 2452*].

As regards 'small' and 'medium-sized' companies delivering accounts to the Registrar of Companies in accordance with the provisions of *Sec 246(5)* or *(6)* or *Sec 246A(3)* (see 7.40 and 7.44 ACCOUNTS: SMALL AND MEDIUM-SIZED COMPANIES), references above to the auditors' report are to be read as references to the special report required under 12.21 AUDITORS. [*Sec 247 B(5); SI 1997 No 220, Reg 5*].

For the purposes of the above provisions, a company is to be regarded as publishing a document if it publishes, issues or circulates it or otherwise makes it available for public inspection in a manner calculated to invite members of the public generally, or any class of such members, to read it. [*Sec 240(4); CA 1989, s 10*].

3.6 LAYING OF ACCOUNTS AND REPORTS BEFORE COMPANY IN GENERAL MEETING

For each financial year, the directors must lay before the company in general meeting (see 33.1 MEETINGS) copies of the annual accounts, directors' report and auditors' report. They must do so before the end of the period allowed for laying and delivering accounts and reports (see 3.8 below). In default, every person who immediately before the end of that period was a director is liable to a fine up to the level in 40.1(*e*) PENALTIES. It is a defence for a person charged under these provisions to prove that he took all reasonable steps to secure compliance with these requirements before the end of the said period; it is not a defence to prove that the documents in question were not in fact prepared. [*Sec 241, 24 Sch; CA 1989, s 11*].

Private companies. A private company may elect (by elective resolution – see 51.3 RESOLUTIONS) to dispense with the above requirements. An election has effect in relation to the accounts and reports for the financial year in which it is made and subsequent financial years. If it ceases to have effect, the above requirements apply in relation to the accounts and reports for the financial year in which it so ceases and subsequent financial years. [*Sec 252(1)(2)(4); CA 1989, s 16*].

Where the election is in force, copies of the accounts and reports sent out in accordance with 3.3 above must be so sent out at least 28 days before the end of the period allowed for laying and delivering accounts and reports (see 3.8 below). Where sent to a member of the company, they must be accompanied by a notice informing him of his right (see below) to require the laying of accounts and reports before a general meeting. The company and every officer in default of this provision is liable to a fine up to the level in 40.1(*d*) PENALTIES.

Any member or auditor of the company may require, by notice in writing deposited at the company's registered office within the period of 28 days beginning with the day on which the accounts and reports are sent out, that a general meeting be held for the purpose of laying the accounts and reports before the company. In the event of the directors failing to proceed to convene such a meeting within 21 days after the deposit of the notice, the person who deposited the notice may do so himself. The meeting must then be held within three months after the date of the said deposit and must be convened, as nearly as possible, in the same manner as meetings are to be convened by directors. Any reasonable expenses incurred by that person due to the failure of the directors to duly convene a meeting (including a failure to convene it for a date within 28 days after the date of the notice convening it) must be made good to him by the company. The company must then recoup the expenses out of any fees or other remuneration due, or to become due, to such of the directors as were in default.

[*Sec 253; CA 1989, s 16*].

Whilst the above election is in force, the following provisions are to be read as if they referred to the sending of accounts and reports to members and others (as in 3.3 above) rather than the laying of such documents before the company in general meeting.

- *Sec 235(1)* (accounts on which auditors are to report, see 12.18 AUDITORS).

- *Sec 270(3)(4)* (accounts by reference to which distributions are justified, see 23.7 DISTRIBUTIONS). A similar modification applies as regards the auditors' statement required under *Sec 271(4)* in connection with these accounts (see 23.7(*a*)(ii) DISTRIBUTIONS).

- *Sec 320(2)* (substantial property transactions with directors, see 19.73 DIRECTORS).

[*Sec 252(3); CA 1989, s 16*].

3.7   DELIVERING OF ACCOUNTS AND REPORTS TO THE REGISTRAR OF COMPANIES

Principal requirements. In respect of each financial year, the directors must deliver to the Registrar of Companies a copy of the company's annual accounts with accompanying directors' report and auditors' report. If any document comprised therein is not in English, the directors must annex thereto an English translation, certified in the prescribed manner (see 28.2 FORMS) to be a correct translation. [*Sec 242(1); CA 1989, s 11*]. See, however, 62.1 WALES for delivery of certain accounts in Welsh only.

Accounts in ECUs. The amounts set out in the annual accounts may also be shown in the same accounts translated into ECUs. Alternatively, when the annual accounts are delivered to the Registrar, the directors may deliver an additional copy of those accounts in which the amounts have been translated into ECUs. In either case, the amounts must have been translated at the rate of exchange used for translating the value of the ECU prevailing at the balance sheet date. That rate must be disclosed in the notes to the accounts. [*Sec 242B(1)-(3); SI 1992 No 2452*].

3.7 Accounts: General

Accounts of oversea or unincorporated subsidiary undertakings. Where, at the end of the financial year, a parent company has, as a subsidiary undertaking (see 4.2 ACCOUNTS: GROUPS OF COMPANIES), either

- a body corporate incorporated outside Great Britain which does not have an established place of business in Great Britain, or

- an unincorporated undertaking,

which is excluded from consolidation under 4.10(*c*) ACCOUNTS: GROUPS OF COMPANIES, the following additional requirements apply.

- A copy of the subsidiary undertaking's latest individual accounts and, if it is itself a parent undertaking (see 4.2 ACCOUNTS: GROUPS OF COMPANIES), of its latest group accounts must be appended to the copy of the company's annual accounts delivered to the Registrar.

- If the accounts so appended are required by law to be audited, a copy of the auditors' report must also be appended.

- The accounts so appended must be for a period ending not more than twelve months before the end of the financial year for which the parent company's accounts are made up.

The requirement for documents to be translated into English (see under *Principal requirements* above) applies equally to documents so appended.

However, no accounts of an undertaking need be prepared for these purposes if none would otherwise be prepared, and if no accounts satisfying the above requirements are prepared, none need be appended. No document need be appended that would not otherwise be required to be published, or made available for public inspection, anywhere in the world, but the reason for not appending it must be stated in a note to the company's accounts. If the undertaking and all its subsidiary undertakings are excluded from consolidation by 4.10(*c*) ACCOUNTS: GROUPS OF COMPANIES, the accounts of any of the subsidiary undertakings (of that undertaking) as are included in its consolidated group accounts need not be appended.

[*Sec 243(1)-(5); CA 1989, s 11; SI 1992 No 1083*].

Penalties. If any of the above requirements are not complied with before the end of the period allowed for laying and delivering accounts and reports under 3.8 below ('the period allowed'), every person who immediately before the end of that period was a director of the company is liable to a fine up to the level in 40.1(*e*) PENALTIES. Also, if the directors fail to make good the default within 14 days after the service of a notice on them requiring compliance, the court may, on the application of the Registrar of Companies or of any member or creditor of the company, order the directors (or any of them) to make good the default within such time as is specified in the order. The order may require the directors to bear all costs of, and incidental to, the application. It is a defence for a person charged under these provisions to prove that he took all reasonable steps for securing compliance with the requirements within the period allowed. [*Secs 242(2)-(4), 243(6), 24 Sch; CA 1989, s 11*].

Civil penalty. In addition, the company is liable to a civil penalty for failure to comply with the principal requirements above within the period allowed. The amount of the penalty depends on the length of the period between the end of the period allowed and the date of eventual compliance and on whether the company is a public or a private company, as follows.

Length of period	Public company £	Private company £
Not more than 3 months	500	100
More than 3 months but not more than 6 months	1,000	250
More than 6 months but not more than 12 months	2,000	500
More than 12 months	5,000	1,000

[*Sec 242A(1)–(3); CA 1989, s 11*].

It is not a defence, in proceedings under either *Sec 242* or *Sec 242A* against non-compliance with the principal requirements, to prove that the documents in question were not in fact prepared. [*Secs 242(5), 242A(4); CA 1989, s 11; SI 1991 No 2945*].

Small and medium-sized companies. See 7.40–7.42 and 7.44 ACCOUNTS: SMALL AND MEDIUM-SIZED COMPANIES for modification to the delivery requirements applicable to 'small' and 'medium-sized' companies respectively. [*Secs 246(5), 246A(3); SI 1997 No 220, Regs 2, 3*].

Quality of accounts sent to the Registrar. See 48.4 REGISTRAR OF COMPANIES.

3.8 PERIOD ALLOWED FOR LAYING AND DELIVERING ACCOUNTS AND REPORTS

Subject to below, the period allowed for laying accounts and reports before the company in general meeting under 3.6 above and for delivering them to the Registrar of Companies under 3.7 above ('the period allowed') is

- for a public company, seven months after the end of the 'relevant accounting reference period';

- for a private company, ten months after the end of the relevant accounting reference period.

The *'relevant accounting reference period'* is the accounting reference period by reference to which the financial year for the accounts in question was determined (see 1.1 ACCOUNTING REFERENCE DATES AND PERIODS).

If the relevant accounting reference period is the company's first and it is of more than twelve months' duration, the period allowed expires at the later of

- seven months (for a public company) or ten months (for a private company) from the first anniversary of the company's incorporation, and

- three months from the end of the accounting reference period.

The directors of a company carrying on business, or with interests, outside the UK, Channel Islands and Isle of Man may, in respect of any financial year, give notice of that fact to the Registrar of Companies in the prescribed form (Form 244) and before the end of what would otherwise be the period allowed (as above), claiming a three-month extension. The period allowed is then extended accordingly.

If, by virtue of the company having given notice under 1.4 ACCOUNTING REFERENCE DATES AND PERIODS, the relevant accounting period is treated as shortened, the period allowed is three months from the date of the notice, where that period expires later than that applicable above.

If for any special reason the Secretary of State thinks fit, he may, on an application by the company before the end of the period otherwise allowed, give written notice to the company extending the period by such further period as may be specified therein. An

3.9   Accounts: General

application for such an extension, giving good reasons why the extension should be granted, should be sent to Companies Administration Branch, PO Box 711, Cardiff, CF4 3YA.

[Sec 244; CA 1989, s 11].

Companies House is rigidly interpreting the seven/ten month period to mean that it expires at midnight on the date in the final month which corresponds with the last day of the relevant accounting period i.e. accounts must be filed as follows.

End of relevant accounting reference period	*Delivery Date* *Private company*	*Public company*
31 January	30 November	31 August
28 February	28 December	28 September
31 March	31 January	31 October
30 April	28 February	30 November
31 May	31 March	31 December
30 June	30 April	30 January
31 July	31 May	28 February
31 August	30 June	31 March
30 September	30 July	30 April
31 October	31 August	31 May
30 November	30 September	30 June
31 December	31 October	31 July

Companies House does not accept accounts until they meet the requirements of *CA 1985*. If, for example, a signature is missing, the accounts will be returned for amendment. The time involved could mean that correct accounts are not delivered on time and it is therefore recommended that accounts are delivered as soon as they are completed and as far in advance as possible of the end of the period allowed for delivery.

(Companies House Notes for Guidance CHN 22).

Listed companies.   Note that such companies are required to publish accounts and reports within six months of the end of the financial year. (*The Listing Rules, Chapter 12.42(e)*).

3.9   **REVISION OF DEFECTIVE ACCOUNTS AND REPORTS: VOLUNTARY REVISION**

If it appears to the directors that any annual accounts of the company (or any directors' report) did not comply with the requirements of *CA 1985*, they may prepare revised accounts (or a revised report). Where copies of the defective accounts etc. have been laid before the company in general meeting under 3.6 above or delivered to the Registrar of Companies under 3.7 above, the revisions must do no more than correct those respects in which the accounts etc. did not comply with the said requirements and make any necessary consequential alterations.

Regulations may make provision as to the application of the provisions of *CA 1985* to revised accounts etc. See *SI 1990 No 2570 (Companies (Revision of Defective Accounts and Report) Regulations 1990)*, the main provisions of which are summarised below.

[Sec 245; CA 1989, s 12; SI 1994 No 1935, 1 Sch 2].

All provisions of *CA 1985* as to the matters to be included in a company's annual accounts apply to revised accounts as if they had been prepared and approved by the directors as at the date of their approval of the original accounts, and in particular the revised accounts must show a true and fair view as at the date of the originals. Where the accounts provisions of *CA 1985* are amended after the date of approval of the original accounts but before the date of approval of the revised accounts, it is the provisions before amendment that apply. [*SI 1990 No 2570, Regs 3(1)(2), 16(1)*]. See 3.13 below for *'true and fair view'*.

The provisions under 3.2 above as regards the approval and signing of accounts applies equally to revised accounts, but if the revision is by way of *'supplementary note'* (i.e. a note indicating corrections to be made to the original accounts and directors' report), it is that note rather than the balance sheet which must be signed. The approved revised accounts (or supplementary note) must state the date of approval. Where copies of the original accounts have been sent out to members etc. under 3.3 above, laid before the company in general meeting under 3.6 above or delivered to the Registrar of Companies under 3.7 above, the matters listed below must be stated in a prominent position in the revised accounts (or supplementary note).

- Where revision is by way of a replacement set of accounts in substitution for the originals:

    (i)   that the revised accounts replace the originals for the specified financial year;

    (ii)   that they are now the company's statutory accounts for that year;

    (iii) that they have been prepared as at the date of the original accounts and thus do not cover events between that date and the date of revision (both dates referring to the date of approval by the directors);

    (iv)   the respects in which the original accounts did not comply with the requirements of *CA 1985*; and

    (v)   any significant amendments made as a consequence of remedying those defects.

- Where revision is by way of supplementary note:

    (i)   that the note revises in certain respects the original annual accounts and forms part of those accounts; and

    (ii)   a similar statement to that in (iii) above.

The penalty provisions in 3.2 above apply in the case of non-compliance.

[*SI 1990 No 2570, Regs 2, 4*].

The revised accounts, from the date of their approval by the directors, become the annual accounts of the company (in place of the originals) for all purposes of *CA 1985*. A copy of the replacement accounts (or supplementary note) (together with the auditors' report on the revised accounts or supplementary note, see 12.22 AUDITORS) must be sent, within 28 days of their approval by the directors, to all persons within 3.3 above to whom the originals were sent. A copy must also be sent, within 28 days of their approval by the directors, to any other person falling within 3.3 above at the date of approval of the revised accounts (with the exception of persons to whom the company would be entitled at that date to send a summary financial statement under *Sec 251*, see 43.23 *et seq.* PUBLIC AND LISTED COMPANIES, and with the same exceptions as in 3.3 above). The penalty provisions in 3.3 above apply equally to the above requirements, but as if the reference to 'the company and every officer in default' were a reference to each of the directors who approved the revised accounts.

References in *CA 1985* to the day on which the accounts are sent out refer to the original accounts (with *Sec 238(6)* – see 3.3 above – applying where necessary) in cases where the sending out of the original accounts has been completed prior to the date of the directors' approval of the revised accounts. In other cases, such references are to the day, or the last day, on which the revised accounts are sent out.

[*SI 1990 No 2570, Regs 8, 10; SI 1992 No 3075, Reg 10(2); SI 1996 No 315*].

Where copies of the original accounts have been laid before the company in general meeting under 3.6 above, a copy of the revised accounts (together with the auditors' report thereon) must be laid at the next general meeting held (after the date of the directors' approval to the revised accounts) at which any annual accounts for a financial year of the company are laid (unless the revised accounts have been laid before an earlier general meeting). The same penalty provisions as in 3.6 above apply, except that the reference to 'the period allowed for delivering accounts and reports' must be read as a reference to the period between the date of approval of the revised accounts and the date of the 'next general meeting' referred to above. [*SI 1990 No 2570, Reg 11*].

Where a copy of the original accounts has been delivered to the Registrar of Companies under 3.7 above, the directors must deliver, within 28 days of their approval of the revised accounts, a copy of the replacement accounts (or supplementary note) together with the auditors' report on the revised accounts. The same penalty provisions as in 3.7 above apply (ignoring those relating to civil penalties), except that the reference to 'the period allowed for delivering accounts and reports' must be read as a reference to the period of 28 days referred to above. [*SI 1990 No 2570, Reg 12*].

For the position where a summary financial statement based on the original accounts has been sent out, see 43.36 PUBLIC AND LISTED COMPANIES.

3.10 Small and medium-sized companies

The following rules apply where the directors have prepared revised accounts and the original accounts (the *'abbreviated accounts'*) delivered to the Registrar of Companies took advantage of the exemptions for 'small' and 'medium-sized' companies under 7.40 and 7.44 ACCOUNTS: SMALL AND MEDIUM-SIZED COMPANIES respectively.

(*a*)   If, in the light of the revised accounts, the abbreviated accounts do not comply with the provisions of *CA 1985* because either the company does not qualify as 'small' or 'medium-sized' or because the revision affects the contents of the abbreviated accounts, the company must either

- deliver to the Registrar a copy of the revised accounts (with directors' report and auditors' report); or

- if appropriate, prepare revised abbreviated accounts and deliver them to the Registrar together with a statement as to the effect of the revisions made.

(*b*)   If the abbreviated accounts as submitted still comply with the requirements of *CA 1985*, the company must deliver to the Registrar a note stating that the annual accounts for the specified financial year have been revised in a respect which has no bearing on the abbreviated accounts already delivered for that year. The note must be accompanied by a copy of the auditors' report on the revised accounts.

If the company has delivered abbreviated accounts which do not comply with the provisions of *CA 1985* for reasons other than under (*a*) above, the company must prepare revised abbreviated accounts and deliver them to the Registrar together with a statement as to the effect of the revisions made.

In every case, delivery of revised accounts etc. must be made within 28 days of the date of the directors' approval of the revised accounts, with the same penalty provisions applying as in 3.7 above (ignoring those relating to civil penalties), except that the reference to 'the period allowed for delivering accounts and reports' must be read as a reference to the period of 28 days referred to above.

Where, after delivery of the original abbreviated accounts but before the date of the directors' approval of the revised accounts, the provisions relating to 'small' and 'medium-sized' companies are amended, reference above to the provisions of *CA 1985* is to the provisions before the said amendments.

[*SI 1990 No 2570, Regs 13, 13A, 16(2); SI 1996 No 315*].

3.11   REVISION OF DEFECTIVE ACCOUNTS AND REPORTS: POWERS OF THE SECRETARY OF STATE

Where copies of a company's annual accounts (or revised annual accounts) have been sent out in accordance with 3.3 above, laid before the company in general meeting under 3.6 above or delivered to the Registrar of Companies under 3.7 above, notice may be given to the directors by the Secretary of State indicating respects in which it appears to him that a question arises, or may arise, as to whether the accounts comply with the requirements of *CA 1985*. If at the end of a period specified in the notice, which must be at least one month, the directors have neither prepared revised accounts nor given him a satisfactory explanation, the Secretary of State (or a person authorised by him for these purposes – see below) may apply to the court for a declaration (or declarator) that the accounts do not comply with the said requirements and for an order requiring the directors to prepare revised accounts.

The applicant must give notice of the application, together with a general statement of the matters at issue, to the Registrar of Companies for registration. At the end of proceedings, he must similarly give the Registrar an office copy of any court order for registration or, where applicable, notice that the application has either failed or been withdrawn.

If the court orders revised accounts to be prepared, it may give directions with respect to

- the auditing of the accounts;

- the revision of any directors' report or summary financial statement (see 43.23 *et seq.* PUBLIC AND LISTED COMPANIES)

- the taking by the directors of steps to bring the order to the notice of those persons likely to rely on the previous accounts; and

- any other matters which it thinks fit.

If the court finds that the accounts did not comply with the requirements of *CA 1985*, it may order that such directors who were party to the approval of those accounts should bear all or part of both the costs (in Scotland, expenses) of, and incidental to, the application and any reasonable expenses incurred by the company in connection with, or in consequence of, the preparing of revised accounts. Every director of the company at the time the accounts were approved is deemed to have been party to their approval unless he shows that he took all reasonable steps to prevent their being approved. The court may, however, take account of whether the directors party to the approval knew, or ought to have known, that the accounts did not comply with the said requirements, and may exclude one or more directors from the order or order the payment of different amounts by different directors.

For the purposes of these provisions, the Secretary of State may authorise, by order made by statutory instrument, any person appearing to him

- to have an interest in, and to have satisfactory procedures directed to securing, compliance with the accounting requirements of *CA 1985*;

3.12 Accounts: General

- to have satisfactory procedures for receiving and investigating complaints about the annual accounts of companies; and

- to be a fit and proper person to be authorised.

A person may be authorised generally or in respect of particular classes of case; different persons may be authorised in respect of different classes of case. The Secretary of State may refuse to authorise any person whose authorisation he considers unnecessary having regard to the fact that there are other persons who have been, or are likely to be, authorised. An order revoking authorisation may make provision with respect to pending proceedings.

Unless the act or omission is shown to have been in bad faith, a person authorised under these provisions (or an officer, servant or member of a governing body of such a person) is not to be liable in damages for anything done (or purporting to have been done) for the purposes of, or in connection with,

(*a*) taking steps to discover whether there are grounds for an application to the Court; or

(*b*) deciding whether or not to make such an application; or

(*c*) publishing the reasons for the decision taken in (*b*) above.

[*Secs 245A, 245B, 245C; CA 1989, s 12*].

The Secretary of State has authorised the Financial Reporting Review Panel Limited for the purposes of the above provisions. [*SI 1991 No 13*].

3.12 ACCOUNTING STANDARDS

Under *CA 1985, 4 Sch 36A* accounts must disclose by way of note that they have been prepared in accordance with applicable accounting standards (see 5.15 ACCOUNTS: INDIVIDUAL COMPANIES). Note that this requirement does not apply to small and medium-sized companies as defined in 7.2 ACCOUNTS: SMALL AND MEDIUM-SIZED COMPANIES.

Prior to 1 August 1990, the Accounting Standards Committee ('ASC') issued a number of Statements of Standard Accounting Practice ('SSAPs'). On that date, the Accounting Standards Board Limited ('ASB') replaced the ASC as the standard-setting body and adopted the 22 SSAPs then extant. Adoption by the ASB gives the SSAPs the status of accounting standards for the purposes of *CA 1985*. The ASB's own accounting standards are called Financial Reporting Standards ('FRSs').

The following accounting standards are currently in issue.

SSAP 2   Disclosure of accounting policies
SSAP 4   The accounting treatment of government grants
SSAP 5   Accounting for value added tax
SSAP 9   Stocks and long-term contracts
SSAP 12   Accounting for depreciation (superseded by FRS 15)
SSAP 13   Accounting for research and development
SSAP 15   Accounting for deferred tax
SSAP 17   Accounting for post balance sheet events
SSAP 18   Accounting for contingencies
SSAP 19   Accounting for investment properties
SSAP 20   Foreign currency translation
SSAP 21   Accounting for leases and hire purchase contracts
SSAP 22   Accounting for goodwill (amended by FRS 6 and FRS 7 below)
SSAP 24   Accounting for pension costs

SSAP 25	Segmental reporting
FRS 1	Cash flow statements
FRS 2	Accounting for subsidiary undertakings
FRS 3	Reporting financial performance
FRS 4	Capital instruments
FRS 5	Reporting the substance of transactions
FRS 6	Acquisitions and mergers
FRS 7	Fair values in acquisition accounting
FRS 8	Related party disclosures
FRS 9	Associates and joint ventures
FRS 10	Goodwill and intangible assets
FRS 11	Impairment of fixed assets and goodwill
FRS 12	Provisions, contingent assets and contingent liabilities
FRS 13	Derivatives and other financial instruments
FRS 14	Earnings per share
FRS 15	Tangible fixed assets
FRS 16	Current Taxation

The ASB has established a sub-committee called the Urgent Issues Task Force (UITF) the main function of which is to resolve deficiencies in accounting standards and which issues its findings in the form of abstracts, which are considered for adoption and publication by the Board.

The following UITF abstracts are currently in issue.

5. Transfers from current assets to fixed assets
6. Accounting for post-retirement benefits other than pensions
7. True and fair view override disclosure
9. Accounting for operations in hyper-inflationary situations
10. Disclosure of directors' share options
12. Lessee accounting for reverse premiums and similar incentives
13. Accounting for ESOP Trusts
14. Disclosure of changes in accounting policy
15. Disclosure of substantial acquisitions
17. Employee share schemes
18. Pension costs following the 1997 tax charges in respect of dividend income
19. Tax on gains and losses on foreign currency borrowings that hedge an investment in a foreign enterprise
20. Year 2000 issues: accounting and disclosure
21. Accounting issues arising from the proposed introduction of the euro

The Secretary of State may make grants to, or for the purposes of, bodies concerned with issuing, or overseeing and directing the issuing of, 'accounting standards' (see 2.1 ACCOUNTS: DEFINITIONS) or with investigating departures from such standards or from the accounting requirements of *CA 1985* and taking steps to secure compliance therewith. [*Sec 256(3)(4); CA 1989, s 19*].

3.13   TRUE AND FAIR VIEW

All accounts prepared in compliance with *CA 1985* must give a 'true and fair view' and auditors are required to state in their report whether, in their opinion, the accounts give such a view. In addition, statements of standard accounting practice apply to all financial statements whose purpose is to give a true and fair view so that, apart from exceptional cases, accounts which do not comply with the standards do not give a true and fair view.

3.13 Accounts: General

There is no definition of 'true and fair view' in *CA 1985* and the courts have never attempted to define it. The Accounting Standards Committee obtained opinion of counsel in November 1983 which concluded, *inter alia*, the following.

- The concept of a true and fair view is dynamic.

- The courts have been wise not to attempt a definition.

- Two of the most common elements which contribute to a true and fair view are accuracy and comprehensiveness but even reasonable businessmen and accountants may differ over the degree to which these are required for particular accounts.

- Cost effectiveness must play a part in deciding the amount of information which is sufficient to make accounts true and fair.

- Ultimately, whether accounts give a true and fair view must be decided on by the courts although judges will look for guidance to the ordinary practices of professional accountants. This is because accounts will not be true and fair unless the information they contain is sufficient in quantity and quality to satisfy the reasonable expectations of the readers to whom they are addressed and these expectations will have been moulded by the practices of accountants. The courts are therefore likely to treat compliance with accepted accounting principles and SSAPs as *prima facie* evidence that the accounts are true and fair and deviation from such principles that they are not. A similar reasoning was given in *Odeon Associated Theatres Ltd v Jones [1971] 1 WLR 442* on the question of whether profit or loss for income tax purposes had been calculated in accordance with the correct principles of commercial accounting.

- Because a SSAP is likely to have an indirect effect on how the courts interpret the true and fair concept, despite the fact that it has no legal effect, a new or revised SSAP may mean that accounts which would previously have been considered true and fair will no longer satisfy the law.

The Institute of Chartered Accountants in Scotland also took counsel's advice which concluded that the above guidance given by English counsel can be accepted as being in accordance with the Scottish approach.

The Accounting Standards Board obtained further opinion of counsel in 1993 in the light of the changes made to *CA 1985* by *CA 1989*, more particularly the statutory weight given to the need for compliance with accounting standards (see 3.12 above). The following is a selection of points made.

- The said changes will affect the way in which the courts approach the question whether compliance with an accounting standard is necessary to satisfy the true and fair view requirement. The courts will infer that statutory policy favours both the issue of accounting standards and compliance with them, and that accounts which meet the true and fair view requirement will follow rather than depart from standards, departure being sufficiently abnormal to warrant justification.

- The status of accounting standards in legal proceedings has been enhanced by changes in the standard-setting process since 1989.

- If a particular standard is generally followed, the courts are very likely to find that compliance with that standard is necessary for accounts to show a true and fair view. This does not mean that non-acceptance of a standard in practice will inevitably lead a court to conclude that compliance with it is not necessary. Whenever a standard is issued, then, irrespective of the lack in some quarters of support for it, the courts are bound to give special weight to the opinion of the Accounting Standards Board in view of its status as the standard-setting body, the process of investigation, discussion and consultation that it will have undertaken before adopting the standard and the evolving nature of accounting standards.

- Although the legislation allows for the possibility of departure from accounting standards where the departure is disclosed and the reasons for it stated (see 5.15 ACCOUNTS: INDIVIDUAL COMPANIES), it does not thereby permit such a departure where not appropriate. If the courts are satisfied that compliance is necessary to meet the true and fair view requirement, departure will breach that requirement even if the statutory disclosure is given.

- The courts are likely to treat abstracts of the Urgent Issues Task Force (UITF) (see 3.12 above) as of considerable standing, which will lead them to a readiness to accept that compliance with such abstracts is also necessary to meet the true and fair view requirement.

- The courts are unlikely to seek to find synonyms for the words 'true' and 'fair' but will instead apply the concepts which those words imply.

- Just as a custom which is upheld by the courts may properly be regarded as a source of law, so, in counsel's view, an accounting standard which the courts hold must be complied with to meet the true and fair view requirement becomes, in applicable cases, a source of law itself in the widest sense of that term.

4 Accounts: Groups of Companies

Cross-references. See 2 ACCOUNTS: DEFINITIONS; 3 ACCOUNTS: GENERAL; 5 ACCOUNTS: INDIVIDUAL COMPANIES; 6 ACCOUNTS: INSURANCE AND BANKING COMPANIES; 7 ACCOUNTS: SUMMARY FINANCIAL STATEMENTS.

The contents of the chapter are as follows.

Sections marked with an asterisk have their own contents list immediately before the first relevant paragraph.

4.1 INTRODUCTION

The provisions described in this chapter relate to the requirements for accounts of groups of companies. The Secretary of State has power to modify the provisions by Regulations. [*Sec 257; CA 1989, s 20*]

'Small' and 'medium-sized' groups. 'Small' and 'medium-sized' groups may be exempt from the requirements to prepare group accounts in certain circumstances. In addition, where a small company is entitled to prepare abbreviated accounts it can prepare any group accounts under the same provisions. See 7.45 to 7.47 ACCOUNTS: SMALL AND MEDIUM-SIZED COMPANIES for full details.

4.2 MEANING OF 'PARENT' AND 'SUBSIDIARY' UNDERTAKING

An 'undertaking' is a *'parent undertaking'* in relation to another undertaking (a *'subsidiary undertaking'*) if

(a) it holds a majority of the 'voting rights' (see 4.3 below) in the undertaking; or

(b) it is a member of the undertaking and has the right to appoint or remove a majority of its board of directors (see 4.4 below); or

(c) it has the right to exercise a dominant influence (see 4.5 below) over the undertaking by virtue either of provisions in the undertaking's memorandum or articles or of a 'control contract' (see 4.5 below); or

(d) it is a member of the undertaking and controls alone, pursuant to an agreement with other shareholders or members, a majority of the 'voting rights' (see 4.3 below); or

(e) it has a 'participating interest' in the undertaking and either

  (i) it actually exercises a dominant influence over it; or

  (ii) the two undertakings in question are managed on a unified basis.

For the above purposes, one undertaking is to be treated as a member of another if

• any of the first undertaking's subsidiary undertakings is a member of the second undertaking; or

- 'shares' in the second undertaking are held by persons acting on behalf of the first undertaking or any of its subsidiary undertakings.

Where a parent undertaking has a subsidiary undertaking which is itself a parent undertaking, the first undertaking is treated as the parent undertaking of the second undertaking's subsidiary undertakings.

See 2.1 ACCOUNTS: DEFINITIONS for '*undertaking*', '*participating interest*' and '*shares*'.

A '*parent company*' means a parent undertaking which is a company.

4.3 to 4.6 below explain expressions used above and cover supplementary provisions.

[*Sec 258; CA 1989, s 21*].

4.3   Voting rights

In 4.2(*a*) and (*d*) above, '*voting rights*' means the rights conferred on shareholders in respect of their shares (or, if the undertaking does not have a share capital, on members) to vote at general meetings on all (or substantially all) matters. In the case of an undertaking which does not have general meetings at which matters are decided by the exercise of voting rights, references to holding 'a majority of the voting rights' should be read as references to having the right, under the constitution of the undertaking, to direct its overall policy or to alter the terms of its constitution. [*10A Sch 2; CA 1989, 9 Sch*]. See also 4.6 below.

4.4   Right to appoint or remove a majority of the directors

In 4.2(*b*) above, the reference to the right to appoint or remove a majority of the board of directors is a reference to the right to appoint or remove directors holding a majority of the voting rights under 4.3 above at board meetings on all (or substantially all) matters.

An undertaking is treated as having the right to appoint to a directorship if either the directorship is held by the undertaking itself or a person's appointment to it follows necessarily from his appointment as director of the said undertaking.

No account is to be taken of a right to appoint (or remove) which can be exercised only with the consent and concurrence of another person, except where, in relation to that directorship, no-one else has the right to appoint (or remove).

[*10A Sch 3; CA 1989, 9 Sch*].

See also 4.6 below.

4.5   Right to exercise dominant influence

For the purposes of 4.2(*c*) above (but with no bearing on 4.2(*e*)(i) above), one undertaking is not to be regarded as having the right to exercise a dominant influence over another unless the first undertaking has the right to give directions, with respect to the second undertaking's operating and financial policies, which the directors of the second undertaking are obliged to carry out regardless of whether they are for the second undertaking's benefit.

In 4.2(*c*) above, a '*control contract*' means a written contract, conferring a right to exercise a dominant influence, which

- is of a kind authorised by the memorandum or articles of the undertaking in relation to which the right is exercisable; and

4.6 Accounts: Groups of Companies

- is permitted by the law under which that undertaking is established.

[*10A Sch 4; CA 1989, 9 Sch*].

See also 4.6 below.

4.6 General rules on 'rights'

The following rules apply for the purposes of 4.2 to 4.5 above.

(*a*) Rights exercisable only in certain circumstances are to be taken into account only

    (i) when the circumstances have arisen and for so long as they persist; or

    (ii) when the circumstances are within the control of the persons having the rights.

(*b*) Rights normally exercisable but temporarily incapable of being exercised must continue to be taken into account.

(*c*) Rights held by a person in a fiduciary capacity are to be treated as not held by him.

(*d*) Rights held by a person as nominee for another (i.e. rights exercisable only on the other's instructions or with his consent or concurrence) are to be treated as held by the other.

(*e*) Rights attached to shares held by way of security are to be treated as held by the person providing the security

    (i) where the rights are exercisable only in accordance with that person's instructions (disregarding any right to exercise them in order to preserve the value of, or realise, the security); and,

    (ii) as regards shares held in connection with the granting of loans as part of normal business activities, where the rights are exercisable only in that person's interests (again disregarding any right to be disregarded under (i) above).

Rights are to be treated as being exercisable in accordance with the instructions of, or in the interests of, an undertaking if they are exercisable in accordance with the instructions of, or in the interests of, any 'group undertaking' (see 2.1 ACCOUNTS: DEFINITIONS).

(*f*) Rights are to be treated as held by a parent undertaking if they are held by any of its subsidiary undertakings.

(*g*) The voting rights in an undertaking must be reduced by any rights held by the undertaking itself.

Nothing in (*d*) or (*e*) above is to be construed as requiring rights held by a parent undertaking to be treated as held by any of its subsidiary undertakings.

References in (*c*) to (*g*) above to rights held by a person include rights falling to be treated as held by him, but exclude rights falling to be treated as not held by him, by virtue of any of these provisions.

[*10A Sch 5-11; CA 1989, 9 Sch*].

4.7 FINANCIAL YEAR

See 2.1 ACCOUNTS: DEFINITIONS for the determination generally of a company's '*financial year*'.

The directors of a parent company must secure that, except where in their opinion there are good reasons against it, the financial year of each of its subsidiary undertakings coincides with that of the company. [*Sec 223(5); CA 1989, s 3*].

4.8   DUTY TO PREPARE GROUP ACCOUNTS

Subject to 4.9 below and exemption for 'small' and 'medium-sized' groups under 7.46 ACCOUNTS: SMALL AND MEDIUM-SIZED COMPANIES, if, at the end of a financial year, a parent undertaking (see 4.2 above) is a company, the directors must, *in addition to* preparing 'individual accounts' (see 5.2 ACCOUNTS: INDIVIDUAL COMPANIES), prepare *'group accounts'* i.e. consolidated accounts comprising

- a consolidated balance sheet dealing with the state of affairs of the parent company and its 'subsidiary undertakings' (see 4.2 above); and

- a consolidated profit and loss account dealing with the profit or loss of the parent company and its subsidiary undertakings.

The accounts must give a true and fair view of the state of affairs as at the end of the financial year, and the profit or loss for the financial year, of the undertakings included in the consolidation as a whole, so far as concerns members of the company.

A company's group accounts must comply with the provisions of *4A Sch* as described in 4.12 to 4.22 below as to the form and content of the consolidated balance sheet and consolidated profit and loss account and additional information to be provided by way of notes to the accounts. If compliance with provisions of *CA 1985* as to matters to be included in group accounts or in notes thereto is insufficient to meet the 'true and fair view' requirement above, such additional information as is necessary must be given in the accounts or notes. If, in special circumstances, compliance with any of those provisions would be inconsistent with the 'true and fair view' requirement, the directors must, to the extent necessary, depart from that provision, but particulars of any such departure, the reasons for it and its effect must be given in a note to the accounts.

[*Sec 227; CA 1989, s 5*]

See 3.13 ACCOUNTS: GENERAL for 'true and fair view'.

'Quasi-subsidiaries'. Sometimes, assets and liabilities are placed in a company, trust, partnership or other vehicle that is effectively controlled by the reporting company or group, but which does not meet the legal definition of a subsidiary undertaking (see 4.2 above). Where the commercial effect is no different from that which would result if the vehicle were a subsidiary, the vehicle is a *'quasi-subsidiary'*.

4.9   Exemption for parent companies included in accounts of larger group

Subject to *all* the conditions in (i) to (vii) below being fulfilled, a company is exempt from the requirement to prepare group accounts if it is itself a subsidiary undertaking, its immediate parent undertaking is established under the law of an EU member state and either

(*a*)   the company is a wholly-owned subsidiary of the said parent undertaking; or

(*b*)   the said parent undertaking holds more than 50% of the company's shares and no notice requesting the preparation of group accounts has been served on the company (within six months after the end of the financial year *before that* to which it relates) by shareholders with aggregate holdings amounting to either more than half the remaining shares in the company or 5% of the total shares in the company.

4.9 Accounts: Groups of Companies

In determining whether the company is a wholly-owned subsidiary for the purposes of (*a*) above, shares held by directors for the purpose of complying with any share qualification requirement are to be disregarded. For the purposes of (*b*) above, shares held by a wholly-owned subsidiary of the parent undertaking are to be attributed to the parent undertaking, as are shares held on behalf of the parent undertaking or a wholly-owned subsidiary of it.

The said conditions are that

(i) the company is included in consolidated accounts for a larger group drawn up to the same date, or an earlier date in the same financial year, by a parent undertaking established under the law of an EU member state;

(ii) those accounts are drawn up and audited, and the parent undertaking's annual report is drawn up, according to that law, in accordance with the *EC 7th Directive (83/349/EEC)* (where applicable as modified by the *Bank Accounts Directive (86/635/EEC)* or the *Insurance Accounts Directive (91/674/EEC)*);

(iii) the company discloses in its individual accounts that it is exempt from the obligation to prepare and deliver group accounts;

(iv) the company states in its individual accounts, in relation to the parent undertaking referred to in (i) above,

- its name;

- if it is incorporated outside Great Britain, the country in which it is incorporated; and

- if it is unincorporated, the address of its principal place of business;

(v) the company delivers to the Registrar of Companies under 3.7 ACCOUNTS: GENERAL, and within the period allowed for delivering its individual accounts under 3.8 ACCOUNTS: GENERAL, copies of the group accounts referred to in (i) above, together with the auditors' report thereon and the parent undertaking's annual report;

(vi) if any document comprised in accounts and reports delivered under (v) above is not in English, there is annexed thereto an English translation, certified in the prescribed manner (see 28.2 FORMS) to be a correct translation; and

(vii) none of the 'securities' of the company are listed on a stock exchange in any EU member state. For these purposes, *'securities'* includes

- shares and stock;

- debentures, including debenture stock, loan stock, bonds, certificates of deposit and other instruments creating or acknowledging indebtedness;

- warrants or other instruments entitling the holder to subscribe for securities within either of the above; and

- certificates or other instruments which confer

  (i) property rights in respect of a security within any of the above; or

  (ii) any right to acquire, dispose of, underwrite or convert a security, being a right to which the holder would be entitled if he held any such security to which the certificate or instrument relates; or

  (iii) a contractual right (other than an option) to acquire any such security otherwise than by subscription.

[*Sec 228; CA 1989, s 5; SI 1992 No 3178, Reg 4; SI 1993 No 3246, 2 Sch; SI 1996 No 189, Reg 4*].

4.10   EXCLUSION OF SUBSIDIARY COMPANIES FROM CONSOLIDATION

All subsidiary undertakings of the parent company must normally be included in the consolidation. There are, however, exclusions, as listed below, and if all its subsidiary undertakings fall within these exclusions, the parent company need not prepare group accounts.

(*a*)   A subsidiary undertaking may be excluded from consolidation if its inclusion is not material for the purpose of giving a true and fair view (see 3.13 ACCOUNTS: GENERAL). Two or more undertakings can be excluded only if they are not material taken together.

(*b*)   A subsidiary undertaking may also be excluded from consolidation where

(i)   severe long-term restrictions substantially hinder the exercise of the parent company's rights over the assets or management of the undertaking; or

(ii)   the information necessary to prepare group accounts cannot be obtained without disproportionate expense or undue delay; or

(iii)   the interest of the parent company is held exclusively with a view to subsequent resale and the undertaking has not previously been included in the parent company's group accounts.

The references in (i) and (iii) above to, respectively, the rights and the interest of the parent company are references to rights and interests held by or attributed to it for the purposes of 4.2 above without which it would not be the parent company.

(*c*)   One or more subsidiary undertakings may be excluded from consolidation if their activities are so different from those of other undertakings to be included that their inclusion would be incompatible with the obligation to give a true and fair view. This does not, however, apply merely because some undertakings are industrial, some commercial and some provide services, or because their activities involve different products or services.

[*Sec 229; CA 1989, s 5*].

4.11   TREATMENT OF INDIVIDUAL PROFIT AND LOSS ACCOUNT WHERE GROUP ACCOUNTS PREPARED

Where a parent company is required to prepare group accounts and does so, and the notes to its individual balance sheet show the company's profit or loss for the financial year (determined in accordance with *CA 1985*), then its individual profit and loss account

•   need not contain the information otherwise required by *4 Sch 52-57* (see 5.24 to 5.29 ACCOUNTS: INDIVIDUAL COMPANIES); and

•   may be omitted from the company's annual accounts although it must still be approved by the board and signed by a director in accordance with 3.2 ACCOUNTS: GENERAL.

The above exemptions apply only if the company's annual accounts disclose the fact that they apply.

[*Sec 230; CA 1989, s 5*].

FORM AND CONTENT OF GROUP ACCOUNTS

4.12   General rules
4.13   Elimination of group transactions

4.12 Accounts: Groups of Companies

4.12 **General rules**

Group accounts must comply, as far as practicable, with the provisions of *Sec 390A(3)* (auditors' remuneration, see 5.44 ACCOUNTS: INDIVIDUAL COMPANIES) and *4 Sch* (see 5.3 to 5.31 ACCOUNTS: INDIVIDUAL COMPANIES) as if the *'group'* (meaning, for these purposes, all the undertakings included in the consolidation) were a single company.

If the parent company falls to be treated as an investment company for the purposes of *4 Sch 71-73* (see 5.31 ACCOUNTS: INDIVIDUAL COMPANIES), the group must be similarly treated.

[*4A Sch 1; CA 1989, 2 Sch; SI 1996 No 189, 2 Sch 2; SI 1997 No 220, Reg 7*].

The consolidated balance sheet and profit and loss account must incorporate in full the information contained in the individual accounts of the undertakings included in the consolidation. This is subject to the adjustments authorised or required by *4A Sch* under this paragraph and 4.13 to 4.22 below and any other adjustments that are appropriate in accordance with generally accepted accounting principles or practice.

If the financial year of a subsidiary undertaking included in the consolidation does not end with that of the parent company, the accounts of the subsidiary to be included in the group accounts are

- its accounts for the financial year last ending before the end of the parent company's financial year, but only if the gap is no more than three months; or

- interim accounts drawn up as at the end of the parent company's financial year.

[*4A Sch 2; CA 1989, 2 Sch; SI 1996 No 189, 2 Sch 3*].

Assets and liabilities. Where assets and liabilities to be included in the group accounts have been valued or otherwise determined by undertakings under accounting rules which differ from those used for the group accounts, the values or amounts must be adjusted in line with the rules used for the group accounts (unless such adjustments are not material for the purpose of giving a true and fair view). If it appears to the parent company's directors that there are special reasons for doing so, they may depart from this requirement, but particulars of the departure, the reasons for it and its effect must be given in a note to the accounts. [*4A Sch 3; CA 1989, 2 Sch*].

Accounting rules. Any differences between accounting rules used for a parent company's individual accounts and those used for its group accounts must be disclosed in a note to the group accounts, and the reasons for the difference given. [*4A Sch 4; CA 1989, 2 Sch*].

Materiality. Amounts which in the particular context of any provision of *4A Sch* (see above and 4.13 to 4.22 below) are not material may be disregarded for the purposes of that provision. [*4A Sch 5; CA 1989, 2 Sch*].

4.13   Elimination of group transactions

In preparing group accounts, the following must be eliminated (unless the amounts concerned are not material for the purpose of giving a true and fair view, see 3.13 ACCOUNTS: GENERAL).

- Debts and claims between undertakings included in the consolidation.

- Income and expenditure relating to transactions between such undertakings.

- Profits and losses included in the book value of assets and resulting from transactions between such undertakings. This may be effected in proportion to the group's interest in the shares of the undertakings concerned.

[*4A Sch 6; CA 1989, 2 Sch*].

4.14   Acquisition and merger accounting

The provisions described in 4.15 to 4.17 below apply where an undertaking becomes a subsidiary undertaking of the parent company, such an event being referred to as an 'acquisition'. An acquisition is to be accounted for by the 'acquisition method of accounting' (see 4.15 below) unless the conditions for accounting for it as a merger are met and the 'merger method of accounting' (see 4.16 below) is adopted. [*4A Sch 7, 8; CA 1989, 2 Sch*].

4.15   *Acquisition method of accounting*

Under the *'acquisition method of accounting'*

- the identifiable assets and liabilities of the undertaking acquired (i.e. those assets and liabilities which are capable of being disposed of or discharged separately, without disposing of a business of the undertaking) must be included in the consolidated balance sheet at their fair values as at the date of acquisition;

- the income and expenditure of the undertaking acquired is to be brought into the group accounts only as from the date of acquisition; and

- the interest of the parent company and its subsidiary undertakings in the 'adjusted capital and reserves' of the undertaking acquired must be set off against the 'acquisition cost' of the interest in the shares of the undertaking held by the parent company and its subsidiary undertakings. The resulting amount, if positive, is to be treated as goodwill and, if negative, as a negative consolidation difference.

  'Adjusted capital and reserves' of the undertaking acquired means its capital and reserves at the date of acquisition after adjusting the identifiable assets and liabilities (see (*a*) above) of the undertaking to fair values as at that date.

  'Acquisition cost' means the amount of cash consideration and fair value of any other consideration, together with such amount (if any) in respect of fees and other expenses of acquisition as the company may determine.

[*4A Sch 9; CA 1989, 2 Sch*].

Where a group is acquired, references above to shares of the undertaking acquired should be read as references to shares of the parent undertaking of the group acquired. Other references to the undertaking acquired are to be read as references to the group acquired. References to assets and liabilities, income and expenditure and capital and reserves of the undertaking acquired are to be read as references to those of the group acquired, after making the set-offs and other adjustments required by *4A Sch* in the case of group accounts. [*4A Sch 12; CA 1989, 2 Sch*].

4.16   Accounts: Groups of Companies

4.16   *Merger method of accounting*

The *'merger method of accounting'* can only be used when the following conditions are satisfied.

- At least 90% of the nominal value of the relevant shares in the undertaking acquired (i.e. those carrying unrestricted rights to participate both in distributions and in the assets of the undertaking upon liquidation) is held by, or on behalf of, the parent company and its subsidiary undertakings.

- The proportion referred to above must have been attained pursuant to an arrangement providing for the issue of equity shares by the parent company or one or more of its subsidiary undertakings.

- The fair value of any consideration other than the issue of equity shares given pursuant to the arrangement by the parent company and its subsidiary undertakings did not exceed 10% of the nominal value of the equity shares issued.

- Adoption of the merger method of accounting accords with generally accepted accounting principles or practice.

[*4A Sch 10; CA 1989, 2 Sch*].

Where the above conditions are satisfied

- the assets and liabilities of the undertaking acquired must be brought into the group accounts at the figures at which they stand in the undertaking's accounts, subject to any adjustment authorised or required by *4A Sch*;

- the income and expenditure of the undertaking acquired is to be included in the group accounts for the entire financial year, including the period before acquisition;

- the group accounts must show comparative figures for the previous financial year as if the undertaking acquired had been included in the consolidation throughout that year; and

- the nominal value of the issued share capital of the undertaking acquired held by the parent company and its subsidiary undertakings must be set off against the aggregate of

  (i)   the appropriate amount in respect of 'qualifying shares' issued by the parent company or its subsidiary undertakings in consideration for the acquisition of shares in the undertaking acquired; and

  (ii) the fair value of any other consideration for the acquisition of shares in the undertaking acquired, determined as at the date they were acquired.

The resulting amount must be shown as an adjustment to the consolidated reserves.

'Qualifying shares' means shares to which *Sec 131* applies (see 56.2 SHARE PREMIUM) in respect of which the appropriate amount is the nominal value or shares to which *Sec 132* applies (see 56.3 SHARE PREMIUM) in respect of which the appropriate amount is the nominal value together with any 'minimum premium value' as there defined.

[*4A Sch 11; CA 1989, 2 Sch*].

Where a group is acquired, references above to shares of the undertaking acquired should be read as references to shares of the parent undertaking of the group acquired. Other references to the undertaking acquired are to be read as references to the group acquired. References to assets and liabilities and to income and expenditure of the undertaking acquired are to be read as references to those of the group acquired, after making the set-offs and other adjustments required by *4A Sch* in the case of group accounts. [*4A Sch 12; CA 1989, 2 Sch*].

4.17 *Information to be given in notes to the accounts*

The information listed below with respect to acquisitions taking place in the financial year must be given in a note to the accounts, although the information specified in (*c*) to (*f*) below need only be given in relation to an acquisition which significantly affects the figures shown in the group accounts.

(*a*)   The name of the undertaking acquired (or, where a group was acquired, the name of the parent undertaking of that group).

(*b*)   Whether the acquisition has been accounted for by the acquisition method of accounting (see 4.15 above) or the merger method of accounting (see 4.16 above).

(*c*)   The composition and fair value of the consideration for the acquisition given by the parent company and its subsidiary undertakings.

(*d*)   Where the acquisition method of accounting (see 4.15 above) has been adopted, the book values immediately before acquisition, and the fair values at the date of acquisition, of each class of assets and liabilities of the undertaking (or group) acquired in tabular form. This must include a statement of the amount of goodwill or negative consolidation difference arising on the acquisition, together with an explanation of any significant adjustments made.

(*e*)   Where the merger method of accounting (see 4.16 above) has been adopted

- an explanation of any significant adjustments made in relation to the amounts of the assets and liabilities of the undertaking or group acquired; and

- a statement of any resulting adjustment to the consolidated reserves, including the restatement of opening consolidated reserves.

Where a group was acquired, the set-offs and adjustments required by *4A Sch* in the case of group accounts must be made in ascertaining, for the purposes of (*d*) or (*e*) above, the group's profit or loss and the amount, book values and fair values of its assets and liabilities.

[*4A Sch 13; CA 1989, 2 Sch; SI 1996 No 189, 2 Sch 4*].

Comparative figures for the previous year (see 5.15 ACCOUNTS: INDIVIDUAL COMPANIES) are not required in respect of the above. [*4 Sch 58(3)(a); CA 1989, 1 Sch 10*].

The following information must also be stated in notes to the accounts.

(i)   The cumulative amount of goodwill resulting from acquisitions in that and earlier financial years which has been written off otherwise than in the consolidated profit and loss account for that or an earlier year. The figure must be shown net of any goodwill attributable to subsidiary undertakings or businesses disposed of prior to the balance sheet date.

(ii)   Where, during the financial year, there has been a disposal of an undertaking or group which significantly affects the figures shown in the group accounts, the name of that undertaking (or parent undertaking of that group) and the extent to which the profit or loss shown in the group accounts is attributable to profit or loss of that undertaking or group.

[*4A Sch 14, 15; CA 1989, 2 Sch; SI 1996 No 189, 2 Sch 5*].

The information required by (*a*) to (*e*) and (i) and (ii) above need not be disclosed with respect to an undertaking which is either established under the law of a country outside the UK or carries on business outside the UK but only if the disclosure would, in the opinion of the directors of the parent company, seriously prejudice the business of the undertaking concerned or that of the parent company or any of its subsidiary undertakings *and* the Secretary of State agrees to the non-disclosure. *[4A Sch 16; CA 1989, 2 Sch]*.

4.18 Minority interests

An item headed 'Minority interests' is added to the balance sheet and profit and loss account formats set out in, respectively, 5.4 and 5.5 ACCOUNTS: INDIVIDUAL COMPANIES.

Balance sheet formats. In format 1, the said item should appear either after item J or at the end (i.e. after item K). In format 2, it should appear, under the general heading 'LIABILITIES', between items A and B. Under this item, there must be shown the amount of capital and reserves attributable to shares (in subsidiary undertakings included in the consolidation) held by, or on behalf of, persons other than the parent company and its subsidiary undertakings.

For the purposes of *4 Sch 3(3)(4)* (see 5.3 ACCOUNTS: INDIVIDUAL COMPANIES), the said item is not to be treated as one to which an Arabic number is assigned.

Profit and loss account formats. The item should appear twice under each format, firstly in respect of profit or loss on ordinary activities and secondly in respect of profit or loss on extraordinary activities.

Ordinary activities. The item should appear as follows:

- in format 1, between items 14 and 15,
- in format 2, between items 16 and 17,
- in format 3, between items 7 and 8 in both A and B, and
- in format 4, between items 9 and 10 in both A and B.

Under this item, there must be shown the amount of any profit or loss on ordinary activities attributable to shares (in subsidiary undertakings included in the consolidation) held by, or on behalf of, persons other than the parent company and its subsidiary undertakings.

Extraordinary activities. The item should appear as follows:

- in format 1, between items 18 and 19,
- in format 2, between items 20 and 21,
- in format 3, between items 9 and 10 in A and between items 8 and 9 in B, and
- in format 4, between items 11 and 12 in A and between items 10 and 11 in B.

Under this item, there must be shown the amount of any profit or loss on extraordinary activities attributable to shares (in subsidiary undertakings included in the consolidation) held by, or on behalf of, persons other than the parent company and its subsidiary undertakings.

For the purposes of *4 Sch 3(3)(4)* (see 5.3 ACCOUNTS: INDIVIDUAL COMPANIES), the said items are to be treated as items to which an Arabic number is assigned.

[4A Sch 17; CA 1989, 2 Sch].

4.19 Interests in subsidiary undertakings excluded from consolidation

Where subsidiary undertakings have been excluded from consolidation under 4.10(*c*) above, the interest of the group in those undertakings and the amount of profit or loss attributable to that interest must be shown in the consolidated balance sheet and consolidated profit and loss account respectively. The equity method of accounting must be used, with any goodwill arising being dealt with in accordance with *4 Sch 21* (see 5.8 ACCOUNTS: INDIVIDUAL COMPANIES). [*4A Sch 18; CA 1989, 2 Sch*].

4.20 Joint ventures

Where an undertaking included in the consolidation manages another undertaking (the 'joint venture') jointly with one or more undertakings not so included, the joint venture, if it is neither a body corporate nor a subsidiary undertaking of the parent company, may be dealt with in the group accounts by the method of proportional consolidation. The provisions of *CA 1985* relating to accounts apply, with any necessary modifications, to such proportional consolidation. [*4A Sch 19; CA 1989, 2 Sch; SI 1997 No 220, Reg 7*].

4.21 Associated undertakings

Definition. For the purposes of 4.22 below, an *'associated undertaking'* means an undertaking in which an undertaking included in the consolidation has a 'participating interest' (see 2.1 ACCOUNTS: DEFINITIONS) and over whose operating and financial policy it exercises a significant influence. However, neither a subsidiary undertaking of the parent company nor a joint venture dealt with as in 4.20 above can be an associated undertaking for these purposes.

If one undertaking holds 20% or more of the voting rights in another, it is presumed to exercise a significant influence over it unless the contrary is shown. The voting rights in an undertaking means the rights conferred on shareholders in respect of their shares (or, if the undertaking does not have a share capital, on members) to vote at general meetings on all (or substantially all) matters. In determining whether 20% or more of the voting rights are held, the provisions of 4.6 above apply.

[*4A Sch 20; CA 1989, 2 Sch*].

4.22 *Disclosure requirements*

The balance sheet and profit and loss account formats in, respectively, 5.4 and 5.5 ACCOUNTS: INDIVIDUAL COMPANIES are modified as described below, in relation to group accounts, to give information in respect of associated undertakings within 4.21 above.

Balance sheet formats. The item 'Participating interests' in each of the two formats (item B.III.3 in format 1 and item B.III.3 under 'ASSETS' in format 2) is replaced by two items, 'Interests in associated undertakings' and 'Other participating interests'.

Profit and loss account formats. The item 'Income from participating interests' in each of the four formats (item 8 in format 1, item 10 in format 2, item B.4 in format 3 and item B.6 in format 4) is replaced by two items, 'Income from interests in associated undertakings' and 'Income from other participating interests'.

The interest of an undertaking in an associated undertaking and the amount of profit or loss attributable thereto are to be shown by the equity method of accounting, with any goodwill arising being dealt with in accordance with *4 Sch 21* (see 5.8 ACCOUNTS: INDIVIDUAL COMPANIES). This method need not be applied if the amounts in question are not material for the purpose of giving a true and fair view.

Where the associated undertaking is itself a parent undertaking, the net assets and profits or losses to be taken into account are those of the parent and its subsidiary undertakings (after making any consolidation adjustments).

[*4A Sch 21, 22; CA 1989, 2 Sch*].

4.23   Accounts: Groups of Companies

DISCLOSURE REQUIRED IN NOTES TO ACCOUNTS: RELATED UNDERTAKINGS

4.23   **General**

The information described in 4.24 to 4.32 below must be given in notes to the annual accounts of a company which is required to prepare group accounts. [*Sec 231(1)(2); CA 1989, s 6*].

The information (other than that in 4.27 and 4.31 below) need not, however, be disclosed with respect to an undertaking which is either established under the law of a country outside the UK or which carries on business outside the UK but only if the disclosure would, in the opinion of the directors of the company, seriously prejudice the business of that undertaking, or that of the company or any of its subsidiary undertakings, *and* the Secretary of State agrees to the non-disclosure. The fact of any non-disclosure must be stated in a note to the accounts. [*Sec 231(3)(4); CA 1989, s 6; SI 1996 No 189, Reg 15*].

The information required under any provision described in 4.24 to 4.32 below need not be given for *all* related undertakings if (in the opinion of the directors of the company) to do so would result in a statement of excessive length. In such a case, the information in question need be given only in respect of

(*a*)   the undertakings whose results or financial position principally affected, in the directors' opinion, the figures shown in the company's annual accounts; and

(*b*)   undertakings excluded from consolidation under *Sec 229(3)* or *(4)* (see 4.10(*b*)(*c*) above).

If advantage is taken of this, both the following apply.

•   The notes to the company's annual accounts must include a statement that the information is given only with respect to undertakings of the type mentioned in (*a*) and (*b*) above.

•   The full information (i.e. that which is disclosed and that which is not) must be annexed to the next annual return delivered to the Registrar of Companies after the accounts in question have been approved by the board (see 3.2 ACCOUNTS: GENERAL). In the event of non-compliance, the company and every officer in default is liable to a penalty up to the level in 40.1(*f*) PENALTIES.

[*Sec 231(5)-(7); CA 1989, s 6; SI 1993 No 1820, Reg 11; SI 1996 No 189, Reg 15*].

In these provisions and in 4.24 to 4.32 below, *'the group'* means the group consisting of the parent company and its subsidiary undertakings. [*5 Sch 14; CA 1989, 3 Sch*]. References to shares held by the group are to any shares held by, or on behalf of, the parent company or any of its subsidiary undertakings. Any shares held on behalf of a person other than the parent company or any of its subsidiary undertakings are to be treated as *not* held by the group. [*5 Sch 32(3); CA 1989, 3 Sch*].

Shares held by way of security are to be treated as held by the person providing the security

- where the rights attached to the shares are exercisable only in accordance with that person's instructions (disregarding any right to exercise them in order to preserve the value of, or realise, the security); and

- as regards shares held in connection with the granting of loans as part of normal business activities, where the rights attached to the shares are exercisable only in that person's interests (disregarding any right to exercise them in order to preserve the value of, or realise, the security).

[*5 Sch 32(4); CA 1989, 3 Sch*].

4.24 Subsidiary undertakings

Subject to 4.23 above, the following information must be given with respect to each undertaking which is a subsidiary undertaking of the parent company at the end of the financial year.

(*a*)　Its name.

(*b*)　If it is incorporated outside Great Britain, the country in which it is incorporated.

(*c*)　If it is unincorporated, the address of its principal place of business.

(*d*)　Whether it is included in the consolidation and, if not, the reasons for its exclusion.

(*e*)　Which of the conditions in 4.2(*a*)–(*e*) above applies to make it a subsidiary undertaking of its immediate parent undertaking.

The information in (*e*) above need not be given if the relevant condition is that in 4.2(*a*) above and the immediate parent undertaking holds the same proportion of the shares in the undertaking as it holds voting rights.

[*5 Sch 15; CA 1989, 3 Sch; SI 1996 No 189, 3 Sch 14*].

4.25 *Shareholdings by the parent company/group*

Subject to 4.23 above, with regard to the shares of a subsidiary undertaking held by the parent company and by the group, there must be stated the identity of each class of shares held and the proportion of the nominal value of the shares of that class represented by those shares. This information must be shown separately as regards the parent company and the group if it is different for each. [*5 Sch 16; CA 1989, 3 Sch*].

For the above purposes, there must be attributed to the parent company shares held on its behalf by any person. Shares held on behalf of a person other than the parent company are to be treated as *not* held by the parent company. [*5 Sch 32(2); CA 1989, 3 Sch*].

Comparative figures for the preceding financial year (see 5.15 ACCOUNTS: INDIVIDUAL COMPANIES) need not be given. [*4 Sch 58(3)(b); CA 1989, 1 Sch 10*].

4.26 *Financial information*

Subject to 4.23 above with respect to each subsidiary undertaking not included in the consolidation, both the aggregate amount of its capital and reserves as at the end of its

4.27   Accounts: Groups of Companies

'relevant financial year' and its profit or loss for that year must be shown. This information need not be given

- if it is not material; or

- if the group's investment in the undertaking concerned is included in the accounts by way of the equity method of valuation; or

- if the group's holding is less than 50% of the nominal value of shares in the undertaking and the latter is not required by any provision of *CA 1985* to deliver to the Registrar of Companies a copy of its balance sheet for its 'relevant financial year' and does not otherwise publish that balance sheet in Great Britain or elsewhere.

The *'relevant financial year'* of a subsidiary undertaking is

- if its financial year ends with that of the company, that year; and

- if not, its financial year ending last before the end of the company's financial year.

[*5 Sch 17; CA 1989, 3 Sch*].

4.27   *Shares and debentures of company held by subsidiary undertakings*

Subject to 4.23 above, the number, description and amount of shares in the company held by, or on behalf of, its subsidiary undertakings must be disclosed. This does not apply to shares in respect of which the subsidiary undertaking is concerned as

- personal representative; or

- trustee unless the company, or any of its subsidiary undertakings, is 'beneficially interested under the trust' otherwise than by way of security only for the purposes of a transaction entered into by it in the ordinary course of a business which includes the lending of money.

In determining whether the company is *'beneficially interested under the trust'* certain interests mentioned in *2 Sch, Part II* are disregarded (residual interests under pension and employee share schemes, company's rights as trustee to expenses, remuneration, etc.).

[*5 Sch 20; CA 1989, 3 Sch; SI 1996 No 189, 3 Sch 17*].

4.28   **Joint ventures**

Subject to 4.23 above, where an undertaking is dealt with in the consolidated accounts by the method of proportional consolidation (in accordance with 4.20 above), the following information must be given in respect of that undertaking.

- Its name.

- The address of its principal place of business.

- The factors on which joint management of it is based.

- The proportion of its capital held by undertakings included in the consolidation. Comparative figures for the preceding financial year (see 5.15 ACCOUNTS: INDIVID-UAL COMPANIES) need not be given. [*4 Sch 58(3)(b); CA 1989, 1 Sch 10*].

- The date on which its financial year ended last before the end of the company's financial year (if the undertaking's financial year did not end with that of the company).

[*5 Sch 21; CA 1989, 3 Sch*].

4.29   **Associated undertakings**

Subject to 4.23 above, identical information to that in 4.24(*a*)–(*c*) above and in 4.25 above (with the same exemption from the need to give comparative figures and the same rules for attributing shares) must be given with respect to each 'associated undertaking' (as defined in 4.21 above) in which an undertaking included in the consolidation has an interest. The information is required notwithstanding that the amounts of net assets, profits or losses attributable to the interest held in the associated undertaking are not material as regards the need for the group accounts to show a true and fair view (see 4.22 above). [*4 Sch 58(3)(b); 5 Sch 22, 32(2); CA 1989, 1 Sch 10, 3 Sch; SI 1996 No 189, 3 Sch 18*].

4.30   **Other significant holdings of parent company or group**

Parent company. Subject to 4.23 above, where at the end of the financial year the parent company has a 'significant holding' in an undertaking which is not one of its subsidiary undertakings and does not fall within 4.28 or 4.29 above, the following must be stated.

(*a*)   The name of the undertaking.

(*b*)   If it is incorporated outside Great Britain, the country in which it is incorporated.

(*c*)   If it is unincorporated, the address of its principal place of business.

(*d*)   The identity of each class of shares of the undertaking held by the parent company.

(*e*)   The proportion of the nominal value of the shares of that class represented by the shares so held.

(*f*)   The aggregate amount of the capital and reserves of the undertaking as at the end of its 'relevant financial year'.

(*g*)   Its profit or loss for that year.

A '*significant holding*' is a holding which amounts to 20% or more of the nominal value of any class of shares in the undertaking *or* the amount of which (as stated or included in the company's accounts) exceeds 20% of the amount of its assets (as so stated).

'*Relevant financial year*' of an undertaking is, if its financial year ends with that of the company, that year. In any other case it is its financial year ending last before the end of the company's financial year.

The information in (*f*) and (*g*) above need not be given if it is not material, and need not be given in respect of an undertaking if the company's holding is less than 50% of the nominal value of shares in the undertaking and the latter is not required by any provision of *CA 1985* to deliver to the Registrar of Companies a copy of its balance sheet for its relevant financial year and does not otherwise publish that balance sheet in Great Britain or elsewhere.

[*5 Sch 23–25; CA 1989, 1 Sch 10, 3 Sch; SI 1996 No 189, 3 Sch 19–21*].

Comparative figures for the preceding year are not required with respect to the information in (*d*) and (*e*) above. [*4 Sch 58(3)(b); CA 1989, 1 Sch 10*].

For the purposes of *5 Sch 23-25*, there must be attributed to the parent company shares held on its behalf by any person. Shares held on behalf of a person other than the parent company are to be treated as *not* held by the parent company. [*5 Sch 32(2); CA 1989, 3 Sch*].

4.31   Accounts: Groups of Companies

Group. Subject to 4.23 above, information similar to that described above (and with the same exemptions) must be given where at the end of the financial year the group has a significant holding in an undertaking which is not a subsidiary undertaking of the parent company and which does not fall within 4.28 or 4.29 above. For these purposes, references above to the company's holding must be read as references to the group's holding and references to the company's assets and to its individual accounts must be read as references to the group's assets and to the group accounts. In the definition of 'relevant financial year', references to the company must be read as references to the parent company. [*4 Sch 58(3)(b), 5 Sch 26-28; CA 1989, 1 Sch 10, 3 Sch; SI 1996 No 189, 3 Sch 19, 21, 22*].

4.31   Membership of certain partnerships and unlimited companies

Where at the end of a financial year the parent company or group is a member of a 'qualifying partnership' (see 39.4 PARTNERSHIPS) or a 'qualifying unlimited company' (see 60.3(*b*) UNLIMITED COMPANIES), the following must be stated.

(*a*)   The name and legal form of the undertaking.

(*b*)   The address of its registered office (wherever situated) or, if it does not have such an office, its head office (wherever situated).

(*c*)   If the undertaking is a qualifying partnership, either

   (i)   a statement that a copy of the latest accounts of the partnership has been or is to be appended to the copy of the company's accounts sent to the Registrar of Companies, or

   (ii)   the name of at least one body corporate (which may be the company itself) in whose group accounts the undertaking has been, or is to be, dealt with on a consolidated basis.

The information required by (*a*) and (*b*) above need not be given if not material and the information required by (*c*)(ii) above need not be given if the notes to the accounts disclose that advantage has been taken of the exemption in 39.4 PARTNERSHIPS.

[*5 Sch 28A; SI 1993 No 1820, Reg 11*].

4.32   Information required where the parent company is itself a subsidiary undertaking

Subject to 4.23 above, where the parent company is itself a subsidiary undertaking, the following information must be given.

(*a*)   Particulars, as follows, with respect to the *'company'* (meaning any body corporate) regarded by the directors as that company's ultimate parent company.

   (i)   Its name.

   (ii)   If it is incorporated outside Great Britain, the country in which it is incorporated.

The information in (ii) is required only if known to the directors.

(*b*)   Particulars, as follows, with respect to that parent undertaking of the company which heads the largest and smallest group of undertakings for which group accounts are drawn up and of which that company is a member.

   (i)   The same information as in (*a*) above (but without the exception for information not known to the directors).

(ii)   If the undertaking is unincorporated, the address of its principal place of business.

(iii)   If copies of the above-mentioned group accounts are available to the public, the addresses from which such copies can be obtained.

[*5 Sch 30, 31; CA 1989, 3 Sch; SI 1996 No 189, 3 Sch 24, 25*].

5 Accounts: Individual Companies

Cross-references. See 2 ACCOUNTS: DEFINITIONS; 3 ACCOUNTS: GENERAL; 4 ACCOUNTS: GROUPS OF COMPANIES; 6 ACCOUNTS: INSURANCE AND BANKING COMPANIES; 7 ACCOUNTS: SUMMARY FINANCIAL STATEMENTS.

The contents of this chapter are as follows.

Sections marked with an asterisk have their own contents list immediately before the first relevant paragraph.

5.1 INTRODUCTION

The provisions described in this chapter relate to the requirements for accounts of individual companies. The Secretary of State has power to modify the provisions by Regulations. [*Sec 257; CA 1989, s 20*].

'Small' companies. Companies which qualify as 'small' in relation to a financial year *may* prepare their individual annual accounts in abbreviated form. In addition, such companies (whether or not they prepare their individual annual accounts in abbreviated form) are entitled to various exemptions with respect to the contents of the individual accounts delivered to the Registrar of Companies.

For the provisions relating to individual accounts of small companies, the reader should refer directly to ACCOUNTS: SMALL AND MEDIUM-SIZED COMPANIES (7) (see 7.2 for the definition of 'small').

'Medium-sized' companies. Companies which qualify as 'medium-sized' in relation to a financial year must prepare their individual annual accounts in accordance with the provisions of this Chapter (i.e. they are not entitled, as are small companies, to prepare such accounts in abbreviated form).

However, medium-sized companies are entitled to various exemptions with respect to the contents of the individual accounts delivered to the Registrar of Companies. See 7.2 and 7.44 ACCOUNTS: SMALL AND MEDIUM-SIZED COMPANIES for the definition of 'medium-sized' and the contents of the accounts submitted to the Registrar of Companies respectively.

5.2 DUTY TO PREPARE ACCOUNTS

The directors of every company must prepare, for each financial year of the company, a balance sheet as at the last day of the year and a profit and loss account. The accounts must respectively give a true and fair view of the state of the company's affairs as at the end of the financial year and of its profit or loss for that year. These accounts are referred to collectively as the company's '*individual accounts*'. See 2.1 ACCOUNTS: DEFINITIONS for '*financial year*'.

A company's individual accounts must comply with the provisions of *4 Sch* as described in 5.3 to 5.31 below as to the form and content of the balance sheet and profit and loss account and additional information to be provided by way of notes to the accounts. If compliance with these provisions and other provisions of *CA 1985* (see 5.32 to 5.53

below) as to matters to be included in individual accounts or in notes thereto is insufficient to meet the 'true and fair view' requirement above, such additional information as is necessary must be given in the accounts or notes. If in special circumstances, compliance with any of those provisions would be inconsistent with the 'true and fair view' requirement, the directors must, to the extent necessary, depart from that provision, but any such departure, the reasons for it and its effect must be given in a note to the accounts.

[*Sec 226; CA 1989, s 4*].

See 3.13 ACCOUNTS: GENERAL for *'true and fair view'*.

FORM AND CONTENT OF COMPANY ACCOUNTS

5.3   **GENERAL RULES**

Every balance sheet of a company must show the items listed in either of the two formats in 5.4 below, and every profit and loss account must show the items listed in any one of the four formats in 5.5 below, in either case in the order and under the headings and sub-headings given in the format adopted, except that no item need be distinguished by any letter or number assigned to that item in the format adopted. Any item required to be shown may be shown in greater detail than required by the format adopted. Any item representing or covering the amount of any asset or liability, income or expenditure, not otherwise covered by any item listed in the format adopted, may be included, except that none of the following items can be treated as assets in the balance sheet.

5.3 Accounts: Individual Companies

- Preliminary expenses.

- Expenses of, and commission on, any issue of shares or debentures.

- Costs of research.

Headings and sub-headings listed in the formats need not be included if there is no amount to be shown, either for the current or the preceding financial year (see below), for items thereunder.

[4 Sch 1, 3(1)(2)(5), 4(3)].

As regards items to which Arabic numbers are assigned in any of the formats in 5.4 and 5.5 below

(a)   the arrangement, headings and sub-headings otherwise required in respect of such items may be adapted if such adaptation is required by the special nature of the company's business;

(b)   such items may be combined in the accounts for any financial year if

    (i)   their individual amounts are not material to assessing the state of affairs or profit or loss of the company; or

    (ii)   the combination facilitates the assessment in (i) above (but in this case the individual items must be disclosed in a note to the accounts).

[4 Sch 3(3)(4)].

Accounts in ECUs. The amounts set out in the annual accounts may also be shown in the same accounts translated into ECUs. Alternatively, when the annual accounts are delivered to the Registrar of Companies, the directors may deliver an additional copy of those accounts in which the amounts have been translated into ECUs. In either case, the amounts must have been translated at the rate of exchange used for translating the value of the ECU prevailing at the balance sheet date. That rate must be disclosed in the notes to the accounts. [Sec 242B(1)-(3); SI 1992 No 2452].

Consistency in use of formats. Where a company's balance sheet or profit and loss account for any financial year has been prepared in accordance with one of the said formats, the same format must be adopted for subsequent financial years unless, in the opinion of the directors, there are special reasons for a change. Any change, and the reasons for it, must be disclosed in a note to the accounts in which the new format is first adopted. [4 Sch 2].

Profit and loss accounts. Every profit and loss account must show the amount of the profit or loss on ordinary activities before taxation, and must show separately as additional items

- any amount set aside to, or withdrawn from, reserves (or proposed to be so set aside or withdrawn);

- the aggregate amount of any dividends paid and proposed; and

- the aggregate amount of any dividends proposed (if not shown in the notes to the accounts).

[4 Sch 3(6)(7); SI 1996 No 189, 1 Sch 2].

Set-offs. Amounts in respect of items representing assets or income may not be set off against amounts representing liabilities or expenditure, or vice versa. [4 Sch 5].

Preceding financial year. For every item in the balance sheet or profit and loss account, the corresponding amount for the immediately preceding financial year must also be shown. Where it is not comparable with that for the current year, the corresponding amount for the preceding year must be adjusted. Particulars of, and the reasons for, the adjustment must be disclosed in a note to the accounts. [*4 Sch 4(1)(2)*].

Materiality. Amounts which in the particular context of any provision of *4 Sch* (see above and 5.4 to 5.31 below) are not material may be disregarded for the purposes of that provision. [*4 Sch 86*].

Provisions. References in *4 Sch* (see above and 5.4 to 5.31 below) to provisions for depreciation or diminution in value of assets are to any amount written off by way of providing for depreciation or diminution in value of assets. [*4 Sch 88(1)*]. References to provisions for liabilities or charges are to any amount retained as reasonably necessary for the purpose of providing for any liability or loss which is either likely to be incurred, or certain to be incurred but uncertain as to amount or as to the date on which it will arise. [*4 Sch 89*].

Listed companies. In addition to the requirements of *CA 1985*, listed companies must also comply with the requirements of the *Listing Rules, Chapter 12.41–12.44* as to content of annual accounts. See 43.15 PUBLIC AND LISTED COMPANIES. The additional requirements may be shown in the directors' report or the notes to the accounts.

Listed companies are also required to prepare half-yearly reports. See 43.17 PUBLIC AND LISTED COMPANIES for contents.

5.4   **BALANCE SHEET FORMATS**

The two balance sheet formats set out in *4 Sch* and referred to in 5.3 above are reproduced below, and are followed by notes to certain of the items listed therein.

Format 1

A.   Called up share capital not paid (see note (1))

B.   Fixed assets

    I   Intangible assets
        1.   Development costs
        2.   Concessions, patents, licences, trade marks and similar rights and assets (see note (2))
        3.   Goodwill (see note (3))
        4.   Payments on account

    II   Tangible assets
        1.   Land and buildings
        2.   Plant and machinery
        3.   Fixtures, fittings, tools and equipment
        4.   Payments on account and assets in course of construction

    III   Investments
        1.   Shares in group undertakings
        2.   Loans to group undertakings
        3.   Participating interests
        4.   Loans to undertakings in which the company has a participating interest
        5.   Other investments other than loans
        6.   Other loans
        7.   Own shares (see note (4))

5.4 Accounts: Individual Companies

C.   Current assets

       I   Stocks
            1.   Raw materials and consumables
            2.   Work in progress
            3.   Finished goods and goods for resale
            4.   Payments on account

       II   Debtors (see note (5))
            1.   Trade debtors
            2.   Amounts owed by group undertakings
            3.   Amounts owed by undertakings in which the company has a partici-
                  pating interest
            4.   Other debtors
            5.   Called up share capital not paid (see note (1))
            6.   Prepayments and accrued income (see note (6))

       III   Investments
            1.   Shares in group undertakings
            2.   Own shares (see note (4))
            3.   Other investments

       IV   Cash at bank and in hand

D.   Prepayments and accrued income (see note (6))

E.   Creditors: amounts falling due within one year
       1.   Debenture loans (see note (7))
       2.   Bank loans and overdrafts
       3.   Payments received on account (see note (8))
       4.   Trade creditors
       5.   Bills of exchange payable
       6.   Amounts owed to group undertakings
       7.   Amounts owed to undertakings in which the company has a participating
            interest
       8.   Other creditors including taxation and social security (see note (9))
       9.   Accruals and deferred income (see note (10))

F.   Net current assets (liabilities) (see note (11))

G.   Total assets less current liabilities

H.   Creditors: amounts falling due after more than one year
       As per list in E. above

I.   Provisions for liabilities and charges
       1.   Pensions and similar obligations
       2.   Taxation, including deferred taxation
       3.   Other provisions

J.   Accruals and deferred income (see note (10))

K.   Capital and reserves

       I   Called up share capital (see note (12))

       II   Share premium account

       III   Revaluation reserve

       IV   Other reserves
            1.   Capital redemption reserve

2.   Reserve for own shares
3.   Reserves provided for by the articles of association
4.   Other reserves

V   Profit and loss account

Format 2

ASSETS

As per A. to D. in format 1 above

LIABILITIES

A.   Capital and reserves

As per K. in format 1 above

B.   Provisions for liabilities and charges

As per list in I. in format 1 above

C.   Creditors (see note (13))

As per list in E. in format 1 above

D.   Accruals and deferred income (see note (10))

Notes

(1)   *Called up share capital not paid.* This item may be shown in either of the two positions given in each format.

(2)   *Concessions etc.* Amounts in respect of assets are to be included under this item only if the assets in question were either acquired for valuable consideration (and are not required to be shown under 'goodwill') or created by the company itself.

(3)   *Goodwill.* Amounts representing goodwill are to be included only to the extent that the goodwill was acquired for valuable consideration.

(4)   *Own shares.* The nominal value of the shares held is to be shown separately.

(5)   *Debtors.* The amount falling due after more than one year is to be shown separately for each item included under debtors.

(6)   *Prepayments and accrued income.* This item may be shown in either of the two positions given in each format.

(7)   *Debenture loans.* The amount of any convertible loans is to be shown separately. (See also FRS 4 *Capital instruments.*)

(8)   *Payments received on account.* Payments to be received on account of orders are to be shown in so far as they are not shown as deductions from stocks.

(9)   *Other creditors including taxation and social security.* The amount for creditors in respect of taxation and social security is to be shown separately from the amount for other creditors.

(10)   *Accruals and deferred income.* The two positions given for this item in format 1 at E.9 and H.9 are an alternative to the position at J., but if the item is not shown in a position corresponding to that at J. it may be shown in either or both of the other two positions (as the case may require). The two positions given for this item in format 2 are alternatives.

5.5 Accounts: Individual Companies

(11) *Net current assets (liabilities).* In determining the amount to be shown for this item, any amounts shown under 'prepayments and accrued income' are to be taken into account wherever shown.

(12) *Called up share capital.* The amount of allotted share capital and the amount of called up share capital which has been paid up are to be shown separately. (See also FRS 4 *Capital instruments*, particularly as regards non-equity share capital.)

(13) *Creditors.* Amounts falling due within one year and after one year are to be shown separately for each of these items and for the aggregate of all of these items.

[*4 Sch Pt I, Section B; SI 1996 No 189, 4 Sch 3*].

5.5 **PROFIT AND LOSS ACCOUNT FORMATS**

The four profit and loss account formats set out in *4 Sch* and referred to in 5.3 above are reproduced below, and are followed by notes to certain of the items listed therein.

Format 1 (see note (4))

1. Turnover
2. Cost of sales (see note (1))
3. Gross profit or loss
4. Distribution costs (see note (1))
5. Administrative expenses (see note (1))
6. Other operating income
7. Income from shares in group undertakings
8. Income from participating interests
9. Income from other fixed asset investments (see note (2))
10. Other interest receivable and similar income (see note (2))
11. Amounts written off investments
12. Interest payable and similar charges (see note (3))
13. Tax on profit or loss on ordinary activities
14. Profit or loss on ordinary activities after taxation
15. Extraordinary income
16. Extraordinary charges
17. Extraordinary profit or loss
18. Tax on extraordinary profit or loss
19. Other taxes not shown under the above items
20. Profit or loss for the financial year

Format 2

1. Turnover
2. Change in stocks of finished goods and in work in progress
3. Own work capitalised
4. Other operating income
5. (*a*) Raw materials and consumables
     (*b*) Other external charges
6. Staff costs:
     (*a*) wages and salaries (see below)
     (*b*) social security costs (see below)
     (*c*) other pension costs (see below)
7. (*a*) Depreciation and other amounts written off tangible and intangible fixed assets
     (*b*) Exceptional amounts written off current assets

8. Other operating charges
9. Income from shares in group undertakings
10. Income from participating interests
11. Income from other fixed asset investments (see note (2))
12. Other interest receivable and similar income (see note (2))
13. Amounts written off investments
14. Interest payable and similar charges (see note (3))
15. Tax on profit or loss on ordinary activities
16. Profit or loss on ordinary activities after taxation
17. Extraordinary income
18. Extraordinary charges
19. Extraordinary profit or loss
20. Tax on extraordinary profit or loss
21. Other taxes not shown under the above items
22. Profit or loss for the financial year

Format 3 (see note (4))

A. Charges
1. Cost of sales (see note (1))
2. Distribution costs (see note (1))
3. Administrative expenses (see note (1))
4. Amounts written off investments
5. Interest payable and similar charges (see note (3))
6. Tax on profit or loss on ordinary activities
7. Profit or loss on ordinary activities after taxation
8. Extraordinary charges
9. Tax on extraordinary profit or loss
10. Other taxes not shown under the above items
11. Profit or loss for the financial year

B. Income
1. Turnover
2. Other operating income
3. Income from shares in group undertakings
4. Income from participating interests
5. Income from other fixed asset investments (see note (2))
6. Other interest receivable and similar income (see note (2))
7. Profit or loss on ordinary activities after taxation
8. Extraordinary income
9. Profit or loss for the financial year

Format 4

A. Charges

1. Reduction in stocks of finished goods and work in progress
2. (*a*) Raw materials and consumables
    (*b*) Other external charges
3. Staff costs:
    (*a*) wages and salaries (see below)
    (*b*) social security costs (see below)
    (*c*) other pension costs (see below)
4. (*a*) Depreciation and other amounts written off tangible and intangible fixed assets
    (*b*) Exceptional amounts written off current assets

45

     5.   Other operating charges
     6.   Amounts written off investments
     7.   Interest payable and similar charges (see note (3))
     8.   Tax on profit or loss on ordinary activities
     9.   Profit or loss on ordinary activities after taxation
   10.   Extraordinary charges
   11.   Tax on extraordinary profit or loss
   12.   Other taxes not shown under the above items
   13.   Profit or loss for the financial year

B.   Income
     1.   Turnover
     2.   Increase in stocks of finished goods and in work in progress
     3.   Own work capitalised
     4.   Other operating income
     5.   Income from shares in group undertakings
     6.   Income from participating interests
     7.   Income from other fixed asset investments (see note (2))
     8.   Other interest receivable and similar income (see note (2))
     9.   Profit or loss on ordinary activities after taxation
   10.   Extraordinary income
   11.   Profit or loss for the financial year

Notes

(1)   *Cost of sales: distribution costs: administrative expenses.* These items are to be stated after taking into account any necessary provisions for depreciation or diminution in value of assets.

(2)   *Income from other fixed asset investments: other interest receivable and similar income.* Income and interest derived from group undertakings are to be shown separately from income and interest derived from other sources.

(3)   *Interest payable and similar charges.* The amount payable to group undertakings is to be shown separately.

(4)   *Formats 1 and 3.* Where either of these formats is used, there is to be disclosed in a note to the accounts the amount of any provisions for depreciation and diminution in value of tangible and intangible fixed assets falling to be shown under items 7(*a*) and A.4(*a*) respectively in formats 2 and 4.

[*4 Sch Pt I, Section B*].

Staff costs. See 5.28 below for the meaning of 'social security costs' and 'pension costs' and for the determination of the amounts to be stated in the profit and loss account in respect of these items and in respect of the item 'wages and salaries'.

Depreciation etc. References in the formats to the depreciation of, or amounts written off, assets of any description are to any provision for depreciation or diminution in value of assets of that description. [*4 Sch 88(2)*].

5.6   ACCOUNTING PRINCIPLES

The amounts to be included in respect of all items shown in the accounts are to be determined in accordance with the principles set out below, except that if it appears to the directors that there are special reasons for departing from any of these principles for a financial year, they may do so, but particulars of the departure, the reasons for it and its effect must be given in a note to the accounts.

(*a*)   The company must be presumed to be carrying on business as a going concern.

(*b*)   Accounting policies must be applied consistently, both within the same accounts and from one financial year to the next.

(*c*)   The amount of any item is to be determined on a prudent basis, and in particular

    (i)   only profits realised at the balance sheet date are to be included in the profit and loss account; and

    (ii)   all liabilities and losses which have arisen, or are likely to arise, in respect of the financial year to which the accounts relate or a previous financial year must be taken into account; this includes any such liabilities and losses which became apparent after the balance sheet date but before the date on which the balance sheet is signed on behalf of the board (see 3.2 ACCOUNTS: GENERAL). Where revised accounts are prepared under *Sec 245* (see 3.9 ACCOUNTS: GENERAL), it is the date on which the original accounts were signed that is taken into account for this purpose.

(*d*)   All income and charges relating to the financial year to which the accounts relate must be taken into account regardless of the date of receipt or payment.

(*e*)   In determining the aggregate amount of any item, the amount of each individual asset or liability that falls to be taken into account must be determined separately.

[*4 Sch 9-15; CA 1989, 1 Sch 5, 10 Sch 20; SI 1990 No 2570, Reg 3(3)*].

5.7   ACCOUNTING RULES: HISTORICAL COST

The rules described in 5.8 to 5.11 below apply to determine the amounts to be included in respect of all items in the accounts, and are known as the historical cost accounting rules, but see 5.12 below for alternative rules. [*4 Sch 16, 29(1)*].

5.8   Fixed assets

General. Fixed assets are to be included at their 'purchase price' or 'production cost' (see 5.11 below). In the case of a fixed asset with a limited useful economic life, that amount (or that amount less any estimated residual value at the end of the asset's useful economic life) is to be reduced by provisions for depreciation calculated to write off the said amount systematically over the asset's useful economic life.

Provisions for diminution in value may be made in respect of any fixed asset investment of a description falling to be included under item B.III of either of the balance sheet formats in 5.4 above, the amount to be included in respect of that asset being reduced accordingly. Such provisions must also be made in respect of any fixed asset which has suffered what is expected to be a permanent reduction in value (whether or not its useful economic life is limited). Where the reasons for any provision for diminution in value have ceased to apply to any extent, it must be written back (to the extent necessary). Any such provisions or amounts written back, where not shown in the profit and loss account, must be disclosed (either separately or in aggregate) in a note to the accounts.

[*4 Sch 17-19*].

Provisions for diminution in value made, by virtue of the above provisions, in the case of an 'investment company' (see 5.31 below) in respect of any fixed asset investments of the above description need not be charged to profit and loss account providing they are either shown as a separate item in the balance sheet under the sub-heading 'other reserves' or charged against a reserve account to which has been credited any amount excluded by *4*

5.9 Accounts: Individual Companies

Sch 71(1) from the 'revaluation reserve' provisions of *4 Sch 34* (see 5.14 below). [*4 Sch 71(2)*].

Goodwill. Where goodwill acquired by a company is treated as an asset, the amount of consideration given must be reduced by provisions for depreciation calculated to write off that amount over a period of the directors' choosing, which must not exceed the useful economic life of that goodwill. Where any amount for goodwill is shown in the balance sheet, the writing-off period chosen, and the reasons for that choice, must be disclosed in a note to the accounts. [*4 Sch 21*].

Development costs. An amount may be included in the balance sheet in respect of development costs only in special circumstances, and if any amount is so included, there must be given in a note to the accounts the reasons for capitalising those costs and the period over which the amount originally capitalised is being, or is to be, written off. [*4 Sch 20*].

5.9 Current assets

The amount to be included for any current asset is its 'purchase price' or 'production cost' (see 5.11 below) or, if lower, its net realisable value. Any provision for diminution in value previously made, i.e. to reduce the asset to its net realisable value, must be written back to the extent that the reasons for it have ceased to apply. [*4 Sch 22, 23*].

5.10 Miscellaneous

Excess of debt over value received. Where the amount repayable on any debt owed by a company is greater than the value of the consideration received in the transaction giving rise to the debt, the amount of the difference may be treated as an asset. It must, however, be written off in reasonable amounts each year and be completely written off before repayment of the debt. If not shown as a separate item in the balance sheet, the current amount must be disclosed in a note to the accounts. [*4 Sch 24*].

Assets included at a fixed amount. Assets which fall to be included either amongst fixed assets under the item 'tangible assets' or amongst current assets under the item 'raw materials and consumables' and are of a kind which are constantly being replaced may be included at a fixed quantity and value, providing

- their overall value is not material in assessing the state of the company's affairs; and

- their quantity, value and composition are not subject to material variation.

[*4 Sch 25*].

5.11 Meaning and determination of 'purchase price' and 'production cost'

The *'purchase price'* of an asset is the actual price paid plus any incidental expenses of acquisition.

The *'production cost'* of an asset is the aggregate of the purchase price of the raw materials and consumables used and the costs incurred by the company which are directly attributable to the production of that asset. In addition, there may be included

- a reasonable proportion of costs so incurred which are only indirectly so attributable, but only to the extent that they relate to the period of production; and

- interest on capital borrowed to finance the production of the asset, to the extent that it accrues in respect of the period of production. The inclusion of interest and the amount so included must be disclosed in a note to the accounts.

The production cost of a current asset is not to include distribution costs.

[*4 Sch 26*].

Where there is no record of the purchase price or production cost (or of any price, expenses or costs relevant to its determination) of any asset, or any such record cannot be obtained without unreasonable expense or delay, then for the purposes of these provisions, the purchase price or production cost of that asset is to be taken to be the value ascribed to it in the earliest available record of its value made on or after its acquisition or production by the company. [*4 Sch 28*].

Stocks and fungible assets. The purchase price or production cost of

- any assets falling to be included under any item in the balance sheet under the general item 'stocks', and

- any 'fungible' assets (including investments)

may be determined by applying any of the following methods in relation to any such assets of the same class (the method chosen being such as appears to the directors to be appropriate in the company's circumstances).

1.   First in, first out (FIFO).

2.   Last in, first out (LIFO).

3.   A weighted average price.

4.   Any other method similar to any of the above.

Where, however, the result of such determination is that the amount shown in respect of any balance sheet item differs materially from the 'relevant alternative amount', the amount of the difference must be disclosed in a note to the accounts.

The *'relevant alternative amount'* is normally that which would have been shown in respect of the said item if assets of any class included under that item at an amount so determined had instead been included at their replacement cost as at the balance sheet date. If, however, the directors consider it a more appropriate standard of comparison in the case of assets of a particular class, the relevant alternative amount may instead be determined by reference to the most recent actual purchase price or production cost (before the balance sheet date) of assets of that class.

Assets of any particular description are to be regarded as *'fungible'* if such assets are substantially indistinguishable from one another.

[*4 Sch 27*].

5.12 ACCOUNTING RULES: ALTERNATIVE TO HISTORICAL COST

Any of the accounting rules set out below may be used (as alternatives to those described in 5.7 to 5.11 above) in determining the amounts to be included in respect of items shown in a company's accounts (as specified).

(*a*)   *Intangible fixed assets*, other than goodwill, may be included at current cost.

(*b*)   *Tangible fixed assets* may be included at market value (as at the date of their last valuation) or at current cost.

(*c*)   *Investments (of any description) falling to be included under item B. III* of either of the balance sheet formats in 5.4 above may be included either at market value (determined as in (*b*) above) or at a value determined on any basis appearing to the directors to be appropriate in the company's circumstances. In the latter case, particulars of, and the reasons for, the method of valuation adopted must be disclosed in a note to the accounts.

(d) *Investments (of any description) falling to be included under item C. III* of either of the balance sheet formats in 5.4 above may be included at current cost.

(e) *Stocks* may be included at current cost.

As regards any asset the value of which is determined on any basis in (a)–(e) above, that value (instead of purchase price, production cost or any value previously so determined) is to be (or is to be the starting point for determining) the amount to be included in the accounts. The value most recently determined is accordingly to be used (instead of purchase price or production cost) for the purpose of applying the rules described in 5.8 and 5.9 above for general fixed assets and current assets.

Where the asset in question is a fixed asset, any provision for depreciation in respect thereof which is either included in the profit and loss account under the appropriate item or taken into account as required by note (1) to the profit and loss account formats in 5.5 above would normally be so included or taken into account at an amount calculated under the above rules. It may, however, be so included etc. at an amount calculated under the historical cost accounting rules described for general fixed assets in 5.8 above, providing any difference between the alternative amounts is separately disclosed either in the profit and loss account or in a note to the accounts.

[*4 Sch 30-32*].

5.13 Additional information to be provided

Where the amount of any asset covered by any item in the accounts has been determined on any basis in 5.12(a)–(e) above, the following additional information must be disclosed in a note to the accounts or alternatively, in the case of (ii) below only, shown separately in the balance sheet.

(i) The item affected and the basis of valuation adopted in determining the amount of the assets in question for each such item.

(ii) For each balance sheet item affected (except stocks), either

- the 'comparable amounts determined under the historical cost accounting rules'; or

- the differences between the amounts in (a) above and the actual amounts shown in the balance sheet in respect of that item.

The *'comparable amounts determined under the historical cost accounting rules'* comprise both

- the aggregate amount which would be required to be shown if the amounts of all assets covered by the item concerned were determined according to the historical cost accounting rules (see 5.7 to 5.11 above); and

- the aggregate amount of the cumulative provisions for depreciation or diminution in value which would be required or permitted in determining those amounts according to those rules.

[*4 Sch 33*].

5.14 Revaluation reserve

Any profit or loss arising from the determination of the value of an asset according to any basis in 5.12(a)–(e) above (after allowing for provisions for depreciation or diminution in value) must be credited or debited to a separate reserve, the *'revaluation reserve'*. The amount of the revaluation reserve must be shown (but not necessarily under that name) in the balance sheet under a separate sub-heading in the position given for the item 'revaluation reserve' in either of the balance sheet formats in 5.4 above.

The revaluation reserve may be reduced to the extent that amounts transferred to it are no longer necessary for the purposes of the valuation method used. In addition, an amount may be transferred

• from the reserve to profit and loss account, if the amount was previously charged to that account or represents realised profit; or

• from the reserve on capitalisation (i.e. by applying the amount in paying up (wholly or partly) unissued shares in the company to be allotted to the members as fully or partly paid shares, see (13) BONUS ISSUES); and

• to or from the revaluation reserve in respect of taxation relating to any profit or loss credited or debited to the reserve.

The revaluation reserve must not be reduced other than as mentioned above.

The treatment for taxation purposes of amounts credited or debited to the revaluation reserve must be disclosed in a note to the accounts.

[*4 Sch 34; CA 1989, 1 Sch 6; SI 1996 No 189, 1 Sch 4*].

These provisions do not apply to any profit or loss arising from a determination of the value of any investments of an 'investment company' (see 5.31 below) on any basis mentioned in 5.12(*c*) above. [*4 Sch 71(1)*].

5.15   **NOTES TO THE ACCOUNTS: GENERAL**

Comparative figures. Except where otherwise stated in this chapter and in 4 ACCOUNTS: GROUPS OF COMPANIES, there must be shown, in respect of each item stated in notes to the accounts, the corresponding amount for the immediately preceding financial year. Where the corresponding amount is not comparable, it must be adjusted and particulars of, and reasons for, the adjustment must be disclosed. [*4 Sch 58(2)*].

Foreign currency translation. Where any item in the profit and loss account or balance sheet includes sums originally denominated in foreign currencies, the basis of translation into sterling must be stated either in the accounts or in the notes. [*4 Sch 58(1)*].

Disclosure of accounting policies. The accounting policies adopted in determining the profit or loss and the amounts of balance sheet items (including policies with respect to depreciation and diminution in value of assets) must be stated either in the accounts or in the notes. [*4 Sch 36; CA 1989, 1 Sch 7*].

Accounting standards. It must also be stated whether the accounts have been prepared in accordance with applicable accounting standards (see 3.12 ACCOUNTS: GENERAL). Particulars of any material departure from those standards, and the reasons for it, must be given. *Medium-sized companies* (see 7.2 ACCOUNTS: SMALL AND MEDIUM-SIZED COMPANIES) are exempt from this requirement. [*Sec 246A(2), 4 Sch 36A; CA 1989, 1 Sch 7; SI 1997 No 220, Reg 3*]. See 3.13 ACCOUNTS: GENERAL for the effect of accounting standards on the requirement for accounts to give a 'true and fair view'.

Listed companies. In addition to the requirements of *CA 1985*, listed companies must also comply with the requirements of the *Listing Rules, Chapter 12.41–12.44* as to content of annual accounts. See 43.15 PUBLIC AND LISTED COMPANIES. The additional requirements may be shown in the directors' report or the notes to the accounts.

5.16   Accounts: Individual Companies

5.16   NOTES TO THE ACCOUNTS: INFORMATION SUPPLEMENTING THE BALANCE SHEET

The information required, as set out in 5.17 to 5.23 below, being information which either supplements that given with respect to particular items in the balance sheet or is otherwise relevant to assessing the state of the company's affairs, must be given by way of notes to the accounts (if not given in the accounts themselves). [*4 Sch 35, 37*].

5.17   Share capital and debentures

Share capital. Both the authorised share capital and, where shares of more than one class have been allotted, the number and aggregate nominal value of shares of each class allotted must be stated.

If any part of the allotted share capital consists of redeemable shares, the following information must be given.

- The earliest and latest dates on which the company has power to redeem those shares.

- Whether the shares must be redeemed in any event or are liable to be redeemed at either the company's or the shareholder's option.

- Whether any premium is payable on redemption, and, if so, the amount thereof.

The following information is required in respect of any shares allotted during the financial year.

(i)   The classes of shares allotted.

(ii)   As regards each class of shares, the number allotted, their aggregate nominal value, and the consideration received by the company for the allotment.

[*4 Sch 38, 39; SI 1996 No 189, 1 Sch 5*].

With respect to any contingent right to the allotment of shares in the company, meaning any option to subscribe for shares and any other right to require the allotment of shares to any person (whether arising on the conversion into shares of securities of any description or otherwise), the following particulars must be given.

- The number, description and amount of shares in respect of which the right may be exercised.

- The period during which the right may be exercised.

- The price to be paid for the shares allotted.

Debentures. Similar information as in (i) and (ii) above is required in respect of any debentures issued during the financial year.

Where any of the company's debentures are held by a nominee or trustee for the company, both their nominal amount and the amount at which they are stated in the company's accounting records (see 45.1 RECORDS) must be stated.

[*4 Sch 40, 41; SI 1996 No 189, 1 Sch 6*].

5.18   Fixed assets

The information set out below is required for each item shown under the general item 'fixed assets' in the balance sheet (or which would be shown there were it not for 5.3(*b*)(ii) above).

(*a*)   The 'appropriate amounts' in respect of that item both at the beginning of the financial year and at the balance sheet date.

(*b*)   The effect on any amount shown in respect of that item of

- any revision of the amount in respect of any assets included under that item made during that year on any basis in 5.12(*a*)–(*e*) above;

- acquisitions and disposals during that year; and

- any transfers of assets of the company to or from that item during that year.

(*c*)   As regards provisions for depreciation or diminution in value of assets

- the cumulative amount of such provisions included under that item at each of the times specified in (*a*) above;

- the amount of any such provisions made in respect of that year; and

- the amounts of any adjustments made to any such provisions during that year, distinguishing between adjustments made in consequence of disposals and other adjustments.

Comparative figures for the preceding year (see 5.15 above) are not required for (*a*)–(*c*) above.

For the purposes of (*a*) above, the *'appropriate amounts'* in respect of any item at either of the times there mentioned are the aggregate amounts determined, as at that time, in respect of assets falling to be included under that item, either on the basis of purchase price or production cost (see 5.11 above) or on any basis in 5.12(*a*)–(*e*) above (but, in either case, leaving out of account any provisions for depreciation or diminution in value).

[*4 Sch 42, 58(3)(d)*].

Assets included at valuation. The following additional information is required where any fixed assets (other than 'listed investments' – see 5.19 below) are included under any balance sheet item at an amount determined on any basis in 5.12(*a*)–(*e*) above.

(i)   The years (so far as known to the directors) in which the assets were severally valued, and the several values.

(ii)   In the case of assets valued during the financial year, the bases of valuation used and either the names or relevant qualifications of the valuers.

[*4 Sch 43*].

Land and buildings. In relation to any amount shown in the balance sheet in respect of the item 'land and buildings' (or which would be shown there were it not for 5.3(*b*)(ii) above) there must be stated how much of that amount is ascribable to freehold land (or Scottish equivalent) and how much to leasehold land (or Scottish equivalent), and, of the latter amount, how much is ascribable to *'long leases'* (i.e. leases with an unexpired term at the end of the financial year of at least 50 years) and how much to *'short leases'* (i.e. any other leases). *'Lease'* includes an agreement for a lease. [*4 Sch 44, 83, 93*].

5.19   Investments

In respect of the amount of each item shown in the balance sheet under the general item 'investments' (whether as fixed or current assets) (or which would be shown there were it not for 5.3(*b*)(ii) above) there must be stated how much is ascribable to 'listed investments'.

5.20 Accounts: Individual Companies

Where the amount of any listed investments is stated (as required above), their aggregate market value, where this differs from the amount so stated, must also be shown. In cases where the market value of any such investments is taken for accounts purposes to be higher than their stock exchange value, both values must be given for those investments.

A *'listed investment'* is an investment which has been granted a listing either on a recognised investment exchange (other than an overseas investment exchange within the meaning of *FSA 1986*) or on any stock exchange of repute outside Great Britain.

[*4 Sch 45, 84; FSA 1986, s 212(2), 16 Sch 23; SI 1996 No 189, 1 Sch 7*].

See also 5.45 to 5.53 below for disclosure of shares in related undertakings.

5.20 Reserves and provisions

Where any amount is transferred

- to or from any reserves,

- to any provisions for liabilities and charges, or

- from any such provision, otherwise than for the purpose for which the provision was set up,

and the reserves or provisions are shown as separate items in the balance sheet (or would be so shown were it not for 5.3(*b*)(ii) above) the following information must be given in respect of the aggregate of reserves or provisions included in the same item.

- The amount of the reserves or provisions at the beginning of the financial year and at the balance sheet date.

- Any amounts transferred thereto or therefrom during the year.

- The source and application of the amounts transferred during the year.

Where the amount of the provision is material, particulars must be given of each provision included in the item 'other provisions' in the balance sheet.

Comparative figures for the preceding year (see 5.15 above) are not required for any of the above information.

[*4 Sch 46, 58(3)*].

Provision for deferred taxation. The amount of any provision for deferred taxation must be stated separately from that of any provision for other taxation. [*4 Sch 47; CA 1989, 1 Sch 8*].

See 2.1 ACCOUNTS: DEFINITIONS for the meaning of *'provision'*.

5.21 Details of indebtedness

In respect of each item shown in the balance sheet under 'creditors' (or which would be shown there were it not for 5.3(*b*)(ii) above) the following information is required.

(*a*)   The aggregate amount of any debts included under that item which are payable or repayable otherwise than by instalments and which fall due for payment or for repayment after the end of a five-year period beginning with the day after the end of the financial year.

(*b*)   In the case of any debts so included which are payable or repayable by instalments, the amount of any instalments which fall due after the end of the period specified in (*a*) above.

(*c*)   The aggregate amount of debts included under that item in respect of which the company has given any security.

(*d*)   An indication of the nature of the securities given.

Where a distinction is made in the balance sheet between amounts falling due to creditors within one year and those falling due after more than one year, (*a*) and (*b*) above apply only to items shown under the latter category and (*c*) above applies to items shown under either category. For each debt falling to be taken into account under (*a*) and (*b*), the terms of payment or repayment and the rate of any interest payable must also be stated. If, however, in the directors' opinion, the number of debts involved is such that this statement would be of excessive length, it is sufficient to generally indicate the terms of payment or repayment and the rates of any interest payable.

[*4 Sch 48; SI 1996 No 189, 1 Sch 8; SI 1997 No 220, Reg 7*].

Fixed cumulative dividends. If any fixed cumulative dividends on the company's shares are in arrears, there must be stated the amount of arrears and the period for which the dividends (or each class of dividends where there is more than one class) are in arrears. [*4 Sch 49*].

5.22   **Guarantees and other financial commitments**

The following information is required.

(*a*)   Particulars of any charge on the company's assets to secure the liabilities of any other person, including, where practicable, the amount secured.

(*b*)   With respect to any other contingent liability not provided for

   (i)   its amount or estimated amount;

   (ii)   its legal nature; and

   (iii)   whether any, and, if so, what, valuable security has been provided by the company in connection with the liability.

(*c*)   Where practicable, the aggregate amount or estimated amount of contracts for capital expenditure, so far as not provided for.

(*d*)   Particulars of any pension commitments included under any provision shown in the balance sheet and of any such commitments for which no provision has been made, giving separate particulars of any commitment to the extent that it relates to pensions payable to past directors.

(*e*)   Particulars of any other financial commitments which have not been provided for and are relevant to assessing the company's state of affairs.

[*4 Sch 50; CA 1989, 24 Sch; SI 1996 No 189, 1 Sch 9*].

Commitments within any of (*a*)–(*e*) above which are undertaken on behalf of or for the benefit of

   (i)   any parent undertaking or fellow subsidiary undertaking, or

   (ii)   any subsidiary undertaking of the company,

must be stated separately from other commitments within each of (*a*)–(*e*) above, distinguishing between commitments within (i) and those within (ii) above. [*4 Sch 59A; CA 1989, 1 Sch 11*].

5.23   Accounts: Individual Companies

5.23   Miscellaneous

The following information must be given.

(*a*)   Particulars of any case where the purchase price or production cost of any asset is for the first time determined under *4 Sch 28* (see 5.11 above).

(*b*)   The aggregate amount, for each item in question, of any outstanding loans authorised by *Sec 153(4)(b), (bb)* or *(c)* or *Sec 155* (see 8.19(*i*), (*j*) and 8.21 ACQUISITION OF OWN SHARES respectively) included under any item shown in the balance sheet.

[*4 Sch 51; CA 1989, 1 Sch 9; SI 1996 No 189, 1 Sch 10*].

5.24   NOTES TO THE ACCOUNTS: INFORMATION SUPPLEMENTING THE PROFIT AND LOSS ACCOUNT

The information required, as set out in 5.25 to 5.29 below, being information which either supplements that given with respect to particular items in the profit and loss account or otherwise provides particulars of income or expenditure or of circumstances affecting items shown in the profit and loss account, must be given by way of notes to the accounts (if not given in the accounts themselves). [*4 Sch 35, 52*].

5.25   Separate statement of loan interest

The amount of interest on (or any similar charges in respect of)

- bank loans and overdrafts, and

- loans of any other kind made to the company

must be stated in the accounts.

The provisions apply to interest and charges on all loans whether or not made on the security of debentures, but do not apply to loans from group undertakings.

[*4 Sch 53(2); CA 1989, 1 Sch 2; SI 1996 No 189, 1 Sch 11*].

5.26   Particulars of tax

Particulars must be given of any special circumstances affecting liability in respect of taxation of profits, income or capital gains for the financial year in question and/or succeeding financial years.

In respect of each of the amounts shown under the items 'tax on profit or loss on ordinary activities' and 'tax on extraordinary profit or loss' in the profit and loss account (or which would be shown there were it not for 5.3(*b*)(ii) above) the following amounts must be stated.

- The amount of the charge for UK corporation tax.

- The amount of any double taxation relief which has reduced that charge.

- The amount of the charge for UK income tax.

- The amount of the charge for taxation imposed outside the UK of profits, income and (so far as charged to revenue) capital gains.

[*4 Sch 54(2)(3)*].

See 5.29 below for taxation on exceptional items and extraordinary items.

5.27   **Particulars of turnover**

If, in the course of the financial year, the company has carried on business of two or more classes that, in the directors' opinion, differ substantially from each other, the following information is required in respect of each class.

- A description of the class concerned.

- The amount of turnover attributable to it.

If, in the course of the financial year, the company has supplied different markets (*'market'* meaning a market delimited by geographical bounds) that, in the directors' opinion, differ substantially from each other, the amount of turnover attributable to each market must be stated.

Where, in the directors' opinion, the disclosure of any of the above information would seriously prejudice the company's interests, that information need not be disclosed, but the fact that it has not been disclosed must be stated.

In analysing for the above purposes the source (in terms of either business or market) of turnover, the directors must have regard to the manner in which the company's activities are organised. Markets and classes of business which, in the directors' opinion, do not differ substantially from each other shall be treated as one market or one class respectively. Any amounts properly attributable to one class of business or one market which are not material may be included in the amount stated in respect of another class or market.

[*4 Sch 55; SI 1996 No 189, 1 Sch 13*].

5.28   **Particulars of staff**

There must be stated

(*a*)   the 'average number of persons employed' by the company in the financial year; and

(*b*)   the average number of persons so employed within each category of persons employed by the company (the categories being such as the directors may select having regard to the manner in which the company's activities are organised).

The *'average number of persons employed'* is calculated by the formula

$$\frac{A}{B}$$

where

A =   the sum of the numbers of persons who, under contracts of service, were employed by the company in each month of the financial year whether throughout it or not (or, where applicable, the numbers so employed within a particular category)

B =   the number of months in the financial year

[*4 Sch 56(1)-(3)(5); SI 1996 No 189, 1 Sch 14*].

In respect of all employees taken into account in arriving at the average number in (*a*) above, there must be stated the aggregate amounts of each of the following.

(i)   Wages and salaries paid or payable in respect of the financial year to those persons.

(ii)   'Social security costs' incurred by the company on their behalf.

(iii)   Other 'pension costs' so incurred.

Any amount stated in respect of any of these items in the profit and loss account must be determined by reference to payments made or costs incurred in respect of those employees.

'Social security costs' means any contributions by the company to any state social security or pension scheme, fund or arrangement.

'Pension costs' includes any costs incurred by the company in respect of any pension scheme set up for current and former employees, any sums set aside for the future payment of pensions directly by the company to current or former employees and any pensions paid directly to such persons without having first been set aside.

[*4 Sch 56(4), 94; SI 1996 No 189, 1 Sch 16*].

5.29   **Miscellaneous**

Prior year adjustments. Where any amount relating to any preceding year is included in any profit and loss account item, the effect must be stated. [*4 Sch 57(1)*].

Exceptional items. The effect of any exceptional (by size or incidence) transactions must be stated, even though they fall within the company's ordinary activities. [*4 Sch 57(3)*].

Extraordinary items. Particulars must be given of any extraordinary income or charges in the financial year. [*4 Sch 57(2)*].

5.30   **PARENT COMPANY OR SUBSIDIARY UNDERTAKING**

See 5.22 above as regards guarantees and other financial commitments in favour of group undertakings.

5.31   **INVESTMENT COMPANIES**

Any distribution made by an 'investment company' which reduces net assets (i.e. total assets less total liabilities including provisions for liabilities or charges) to less than the aggregate of called up share capital and 'undistributable reserves' must be disclosed in a note to the accounts.

A company is to be treated as an *'investment company'* for these purposes in relation to any financial year if during the whole of that year it was an investment company as defined in 23.1 DISTRIBUTIONS and throughout that year it complied with the provisions of 23.6(*c*)(*d*) DISTRIBUTIONS.

[*4 Sch 72, 73*].

See 23.21 DISTRIBUTIONS for *'undistributable reserves'*.

See also 5.8 and 5.14 above (revaluation reserve).

DISCLOSURE REQUIRED IN NOTES TO ACCOUNTS: EMOLUMENTS AND OTHER BENEFITS OF DIRECTORS AND OTHERS

5.32   **GENERAL**

The information required by *6 Sch*, as described in 5.33 to 5.43 below, is to be given in notes to the annual accounts. [*Sec 232(1); CA 1989, s 6*].

Listed companies. In addition to the requirements of *CA 1985*, listed companies must also comply with the requirements of the *Listing Rules*. See 43.15(*r*) PUBLIC AND LISTED COMPANIES and the Appendix to that chapter with details of the Combined Code for additional requirements regarding directors' emoluments.

5.33   **DIRECTORS' EMOLUMENTS ETC.**

The information specified in 5.34 to 5.38 below relates to

- emoluments of directors (including emoluments waived);

- pensions of directors and past directors;

- compensation for loss of office to directors and past directors; and

- sums paid to third parties in respect of directors' services.

Information is to be given only so far as it is contained in the company's books and papers or the company has the right to obtain it from the persons concerned. It is every director's duty, and that of any person who is (or at any time in the previous five years has been) an officer of the company, to give the company notice of such matters relating to himself as may be necessary for the purposes of these provisions. Any person in default is liable to a fine up to the level in 40.1(*g*) PENALTIES.

Where it is necessary, for the purposes of making any distinction required in 5.34 to 5.38 below, to apportion payments between matters in respect of which they have been paid or are receivable, the directors may make the apportionment in such manner as they think appropriate.

[*Sec 232(2)-(4), 6 Sch 12, 14, 24 Sch; CA 1989, s 6, 4 Sch 3*].

Meaning of 'subsidiary undertaking'. Any reference in these provisions to a subsidiary undertaking of the company includes an undertaking (whether or not it would otherwise be a subsidiary undertaking) of which a person who is (or was), while also a director of the company, a director by virtue of the company's direct or indirect nomination. References in 5.34 to 5.36 below to a subsidiary undertaking are to an undertaking which is a subsidiary undertaking at the time the services were rendered, whilst such references in 5.37 below are to an undertaking which was a subsidiary undertaking immediately before the loss of office as a director. [*6 Sch 13(2); CA 1989, 4 Sch 3; SI 1997 No 570, Reg 6*].

5.34   **Aggregate amount of directors' emoluments**

The following must be shown although information, other than that in (*b*) below, is treated as shown if it can be readily ascertained from other information which is shown.

5.34   Accounts: Individual Companies

(*a*)   The aggregate amount of 'emoluments' paid to or receivable by directors in respect of 'qualifying services'.

'*Emoluments*' of a director include

- salary, fees and bonuses;

- sums paid by way of expenses allowances (so far as chargeable to UK income tax); and

- the estimated money value of any other benefits received by him otherwise than in cash

but does not include

- the value of any share options granted to him or the amount of any gains made on the exercise of such options;

- any company contribution paid, or treated as paid, in respect of him under any pension scheme or any benefits to which he is entitled under any such scheme; or

- any money or other assets paid to or received or receivable by him under any 'long term incentive scheme'.

(*b*)   (For listed companies only) the aggregate of the amount of gains made by directors on the exercise of share options in shares of the company or a group undertaking. For this purpose, the amount of any gain is the difference between the market price of the shares on the day the option was exercised and the price actually paid for the shares.

(*c*)   The aggregate of

(i)   the amount of money paid to or receivable by directors under 'long term incentive schemes' in respect of 'qualifying services'; and

(ii)   the 'net value' of assets (other than money and share options and, in the case of unlisted companies, shares in the company or any group undertaking) received or receivable by directors under such schemes in respect of such services. '*Net value*' means the value after deducting any money paid or other value given by the director in respect of those assets.

(*d*)   The aggregate value of any 'company contributions' paid, or treated as paid, to a pension scheme in respect of directors' 'qualifying services', being contributions by reference to which the rate or amount of any 'money purchase benefits' that may become payable will be calculated.

'*Company contributions*' mean any payments (including insurance premiums) made, or treated as made, to the scheme in respect of the director by any person other than the director.

'*Money purchase benefits*' are retirement benefits payable under a pension scheme, the rate or amount of which are calculated by reference to payments made, or treated as made, by the director or by any other person in respect of the director and which are not average salary benefits.

(*e*)   The number of directors (if any) to whom retirement benefits are accruing in respect of 'qualifying services' under each of

(i)   money purchase schemes (i.e. pension schemes under which all of the benefits which may become payable to, or in respect of, the director are 'money purchase benefits', see (*d*) above); and

(ii)   defined benefit schemes (i.e. any pension scheme which is not a money purchase scheme).

(*f*)   (For unlisted companies only) both

   (i)   the number of directors who exercised share options in shares in the company or a group undertaking; and

   (ii)   the number of directors in respect of whose 'qualifying services' shares in the company or any group undertaking were received or receivable under 'long term incentive schemes'.

Small companies (see 7.2 ACCOUNTS: SMALL AND MEDIUM-SIZED COMPANIES) may give the total of the aggregates required by (*a*), (*c*) and (*d*) above instead of giving those aggregates individually and need not give the information required by (*f*) above. [*Sec 246(3); SI 1997 No 570, Reg 6*].

'*Qualifying services*' in respect of any person means

•   his services as director of the company; or

•   his services while director of the company

   (i)   as director of any of its subsidiary undertakings (see 5.33 above); or

   (ii)   otherwise in connection with the management of the company's affairs or those of any of its subsidiary undertakings.

A '*long term incentive scheme*' means any agreement or arrangement under which money or other assets may become receivable by a director and which includes one or more qualifying conditions with respect to service or performance which cannot be fulfilled in a single financial year, but disregarding

•   bonuses determined by reference to service or performance in a single financial year;

•   compensation for loss of office, payments for breach of contract and other termination payments; and

•   retirement benefits.

Notes

(1)   Emoluments paid or receivable or share options granted on a person's accepting office as director are deemed to be emoluments or share options in respect of his services as director.

(2)   For the purpose of determining whether a pension scheme is a money purchase scheme or defined benefit scheme, any death in service benefits provided are to be ignored.

(3)   Where a pension scheme provides for any benefits to be whichever are the greater of money purchase benefits and defined benefits, the company may assume that those benefits will be whichever appears more likely at the end of the financial year.

(4)   Amounts paid to or receivable by a person include amounts paid to or receivable by a connected person or a body corporate controlled by him (both to be construed in accordance with *Sec 346* — see 19.94 DIRECTORS), but not so as to require an amount to be counted twice.

(5)   The amounts to be shown include all relevant sums paid by or receivable from the company, its subsidiary undertakings (see 5.33 above) and any other person. They

do not, however, include sums to be accounted for to the company or any of its subsidiary undertakings or, by virtue of *Sec 314, 315* (payments in connection with takeovers, see 19.54 DIRECTORS), to past or present members of the company or any of its subsidiaries or any class of those members.

(6)   The amounts to be shown for any financial year are the sums receivable in respect of that financial year (whenever paid) or, in the case of sums not payable in respect of a period, the sums paid during the year. However, in either of the two circumstances set out below, the sums in question must be shown (and distinguished as such), to the extent appropriate, in a note to the first accounts in which it is practicable to show them. The said circumstances are where

(i)   any sums are not shown for the relevant financial year because the person receiving them is liable to account for them as mentioned above, but the liability is later released (wholly or partly) or is not enforced within a period of two years; or

(ii)   sums paid by way of expenses allowances are charged to UK income tax after the end of the relevant financial year.

[*6 Sch 1, 10(2)(4), 11, 13(4); CA 1989, 4 Sch 3; SI 1997 No 570, Regs 2, 6*].

5.35   Details of highest paid director's emoluments, etc.

(*Note.* Small companies as defined in 7.2 ACCOUNTS: SMALL AND MEDIUM-SIZED COMPANIES need not give the following information.) Where the aggregate amount to be shown under 5.34(*a*)–(*c*) above is £200,000 or more, the following information must be shown (although information is treated as shown if it can be readily ascertained from other information which is shown).

(*a*)   The total included in the aggregate of 5.34(*a*)–(*c*) above which is attributable to the '*highest paid director*' i.e. the director to whom is attributable the greatest part of that aggregate.

(*b*)   The amount included in 5.34(*d*) above attributable to the highest paid director.

(*c*)   If the highest paid director has performed 'qualifying services' during the financial year by reference to which the rate or amount of any 'defined benefits' that may become payable will be calculated

(i)   the amount of the highest paid director's 'accrued pension' at the end of the year; and

(ii)   where applicable, the amount at the end of the year of his 'accrued lump sum'.

In accounts for financial years ending before 31 March 1998 only, comparative figures for (i) and (ii) above are not required.

'*Accrued pension*' and '*accrued lump sum*' mean respectively the amount of the annual pension and the amount of the lump sum which would be payable under the pension scheme on his attaining normal pension age under the scheme if

●   he had left the company's service at the end of the financial year;

●   there were no increases in the general level of prices in Great Britain from the end of the financial year until his attaining that age;

●   no question arose of any commutation of the pension or inverse commutation of the lump sum; and

- any amounts attributable to voluntary contributions paid by the director to the scheme, and any 'money purchase benefits' which would be payable under the scheme, were disregarded.

(*d*)   In the case of an unlisted company, whether

(i)   the highest paid director exercised any share options in the shares of the company or any group undertaking; and

(ii)   any shares in the company or any group undertaking were received or receivable by that director in respect of 'qualifying services' under a 'long term incentive scheme'.

If the highest paid director has not been involved in any of the transactions in (i) or (ii) above that fact need not be stated.

See 5.34 above for the definitions of '*qualifying services*', '*defined benefits*', '*money purchase benefits*' and '*long term incentive scheme*'.

Notes (1)–(6) in 5.34 above equally apply for the above purposes.

[*6 Sch 2; SI 1997 No 570, Reg 3*].

Listed companies. Details must be given of any arrangements under which emoluments are waived. Where a director has agreed to waive future emoluments, details of such waiver must also be given. (*The Listing Rules, Chapter 12.43(d)*).

[*6 Sch 2–6 as repealed by SI 1997 No 570*].

Listed companies. Details must be given of any arrangements under which emoluments are waived. Where a director has agreed to waive future emoluments, details of such waiver must also be given. (*The Listing Rules, Chapter 12.43(d)*).

5.36   Retirement benefits of directors and past directors

Note. Small companies (see 7.2 ACCOUNTS: SMALL AND MEDIUM-SIZED COMPANIES) do not have to give the following information [*Sec 246(3); SI 1997 No 570*].

Subject to below, there must be shown the aggregate amount of

(a)   so much of 'retirement benefits' paid to, or receivable by, directors under 'pension schemes', and

(b)   so much of retirement benefits paid to, or receivable by, past directors under pension schemes,

as (in each case) is in excess of the retirement benefits to which they were respectively entitled on the date when the benefits first became payable (or 31 March 1997 if later). The amount shown must include the estimated money value of any benefits paid otherwise than in cash, and the nature of any such benefit must be disclosed.

Amounts need not be included in the aggregate if

(i)   the funding of the scheme was such that amounts were or could have been paid without recourse to additional contributions; and

(ii)   amounts were paid or receivable by all pensioners currently entitled to retirement benefits under the scheme on the same basis.

The provisions of *6 Sch 10(2)(4), 11 and 13(4) (see 5.34,* Notes (4)–(6) above) apply equally for the above purposes.

5.37   Accounts: Individual Companies

'Pension scheme' has the meaning assigned to 'retirement benefits scheme' by *ICTA 1988, s 611* and *'Retirement benefits'* has the meaning assigned to 'relevant benefits' by *ICTA 1988, s 612(1)*.

[*6 Sch 7, 13(3); SI 1997 No 570, Regs 5, 6*].

5.37   **Compensation to directors for loss of office**

There must be shown the aggregate amount of any compensation to directors or past directors in respect of loss of office. The amount shown must include the estimated money value of any benefits paid otherwise than in cash, and the nature of any such compensation must be disclosed. The necessary information is treated as shown if it can be readily ascertained from other information which is shown.

There must be included compensation received or receivable for

(*a*)   loss of office as director of the company; and

(*b*)   loss, while director of the company or on (or in connection with) his ceasing to be a director of it, of

    (i)   any other office in connection with the management of the company's affairs; or

    (ii)   any office (as director or otherwise) in connection with the management of the affairs of any subsidiary undertaking (see 5.33 above) of the company.

References to compensation for loss of office include

(i)   compensation in consideration for, or in connection with, a person's retirement from office; and

(ii)   where such retirement is occasioned by a breach of the person's contract with the company or a subsidiary undertaking, payments made by way of damages for breach and settlement or compromise of any claim in respect of the breach.

The provisions of *6 Sch 10(2)(4), 11, 13(4)* (see 5.34, Notes (4)–(6) above) apply equally for the above purposes.

[*6 Sch 8; SI 1997 No 570, Reg 5*].

5.38   **Sums paid to third parties**

There must be shown the aggregate amount of any consideration paid to or receivable by 'third parties' for making available the services of any person

•   as director of the company; or

•   as director (while director of the company) of any of its subsidiary undertakings (see 5.33 above); or

•   otherwise (while director of the company) in connection with the management of the affairs of the company or any of its subsidiary undertakings.

The amount shown must include the estimated money value of any benefits paid otherwise than in cash, and the nature of any such consideration must be disclosed.

A *'third party'* means a person other than

•   the director himself;

•   a person connected with him (construed in accordance with *Sec 346* – see 19.94 DIRECTORS);

- a body corporate controlled by him (construed in accordance with *Sec 346* – see 19.94 DIRECTORS);

- the company;

- any subsidiary undertaking (see 5.33 above) of the company.

[6 Sch 9, 13(4); CA 1989, 4 Sch 3].

The provisions of *6 Sch 10(2)(4), 11, 13(4)* (see 5.34, Notes (4)–(6) above) apply equally for the above purposes.

5.39   LOANS, QUASI-LOANS AND OTHER DEALINGS

The information described below and in 5.40 to 5.42 below relates to loans, quasi-loans and other dealings in favour of directors (including shadow directors, see 19.1 DIRECTORS) and connected persons (see 19.94 DIRECTORS). *[Sec 232(2), 6 Sch 27(1)(d)(2); CA 1989, s 6, 4 Sch 5]*.

Comparative figures for the preceding year are not required in respect of information given under these provisions (including those in 5.41 and 5.42 below). *[4 Sch 58(3)(c), 8 Sch 51(3)(c); CA 1989, 1 Sch 10; SI 1997 No 220, 1 Sch]*.

Subject to the exceptions in 5.40 below, the accounts prepared by a company other than a holding company and the group accounts of a holding company (or, if it is not required to prepare group accounts, its 'individual accounts' – see 5.2 above) must contain particulars (as described in 5.41 below subject to the exclusions in 5.42 below) of

(*a*)   any transaction or arrangement of a kind described in *Sec 330* (see 19.86 to 19.90 DIRECTORS) entered into (by either the company or, if it is a holding company, a subsidiary of it) for a person who at any time in the financial year was a director of the company or of its holding company or was connected with such a director;

(*b*)   an agreement (by either the company or, if applicable, a subsidiary of it) to enter into any such transaction or arrangement for such a person as is described in (*a*) above; and

(*c*)   any other transaction or arrangement (with either the company or, if applicable, a subsidiary of it) in which a person who at any time in the financial year was a director of the company, or of its holding company, had, directly or indirectly, a material interest (see below).

For the purposes of (*c*) above, a transaction or arrangement between a company and a director of it (or of its holding company), or a person connected with such a director, is to be treated (if it would not otherwise be so) as a transaction, arrangement or agreement in which that director is interested.

An interest is not '*material*' if the 'board' have considered the matter and have come to the opinion that it is not so.

The '*board*' means, for this purpose the directors (or a majority of them) of the company preparing the accounts but excludes the director whose interest is under consideration.

[6 Sch 15-17, 27(1); CA 1989, 4 Sch 4].

The above provisions apply whether or not

- the transaction or arrangement was prohibited by *Sec 330*;

- the person for whom it was made was (or was connected with) a director of the company at the time it was made; or

- in the case of a transaction etc. made by a company which at any time in the financial year is a subsidiary of another company, it was such a subsidiary at the time the transaction etc. was made.

[*6 Sch 19*].

5.40 Exceptions

The provisions in 5.39 above do not apply to the following transactions, arrangements and agreements.

- A transaction etc. between one company and another in which a director of the former (or of its subsidiary or holding company) is interested only by virtue of his being a director of the latter.

- A contract of service between a company and a director of it (or of its holding company).

- A contract of service between a director of a company and any of that company's subsidiaries.

- A transaction etc. which was not entered into during the financial year and which did not subsist at any time during that year.

[*6 Sch 18*].

Additionally, 5.39(*c*) above does not apply in relation to any transaction or arrangement if

- (i)   each party to the transaction etc. which is a member of the same group (meaning a holding company and its subsidiaries) as the company entered into the transaction etc. in the ordinary course of business; *and*

  (ii) the terms of the transaction etc. are no less favourable to any such party than would reasonably be expected if the interest mentioned in 5.39(*c*) above had not been an interest of a director of the company or of its holding company; or

- (i)   the company is a member of a group (meaning a holding company and its subsidiaries); *and*

  (ii) either the company is a wholly-owned subsidiary or no body corporate (other than the company or a subsidiary of it) which is a member of the group that includes the company's ultimate holding company was a party to the transaction etc.; *and*

  (iii) the director in question was at some time in the relevant period associated with the company; *and*

  (iv) the material interest of that director would not have arisen if he had not been so associated at any time in the relevant period.

[*6 Sch 20, 21*].

5.41 Particulars required

The particulars required are those of the principal terms of the transaction, arrangement or agreement, and specifically include the following.

(*a*)   A statement of the fact either that the transaction etc. was made or that it subsisted (as the case may be) during the financial year.

(b)   The name of the person for whom it was made and, where that person is a connected person of a director (of the company or its holding company), the name of that director.

(c)   In a case where 5.39(c) above applies, the name of the director with the material interest, and the nature of that interest.

(d)   In the case of a loan, an agreement for a loan or an arrangement within *Sec 330(6)* or *(7)* (see 19.89 and 19.90 DIRECTORS) relating to a loan,

- the liability (of the person to whom the loan was, or was agreed to be, made) in respect of principal and interest, both at the beginning and at the end of the financial year;

- the maximum liability during that year;

- any interest due but not paid; and

- any provision made in respect of any failure (or anticipated failure) by the borrower to repay (in whole or in part) either the loan or any interest on it.

(e)   In the case of a guarantee or security or an arrangement within *Sec 330(6)* (see 19.89 DIRECTORS) relating to a guarantee or security, the following amounts (relating to the company or its subsidiary).

- The liability under the guarantee or in respect of the security at both the beginning and the end of the financial year.

- The maximum potential liability.

- Any amount paid and any liability incurred for the purpose of fulfilling the guarantee or discharging the security (including any loss incurred due to the enforcement of the guarantee or security).

(f)   In the case of any transaction etc. other than those in (d) and (e) above, the value of the transaction or arrangement or, in the case of an agreement, the value of the transaction or arrangement to which it relates.

The provisions in (c)–(f) above do not apply in the case of a loan or quasi-loan made (or agreed to be made) by a company to or for a body corporate which is

- a body corporate (or a wholly-owned subsidiary of a body corporate) of which that company is a wholly-owned subsidiary, or

- a wholly-owned subsidiary of that company

providing that particulars of that loan or quasi-loan (or agreement for it) would not have required to be included in that company's annual accounts if the first-mentioned body corporate had not been associated with a director of that company at any time during the relevant period.

[6 Sch 22, 23].

5.42   Excluded transactions

In relation to a company's accounts for a financial year, compliance with the provisions described in 5.39 to 5.41 above is not required as follows.

(a)   In respect of

- credit transactions,

- guarantees provided or securities entered into in connection with credit transactions,

- arrangements within *Sec 330(6)* or *(7)* (see 19.89 and 19.90 DIRECTORS respectively) relating to credit transactions, and

- agreements to enter into credit transactions

made by the company (or a subsidiary of it) for a person who at any time in the financial year was (or was connected with) a director of the company (or of its holding company) provided that the aggregate of the values of each transaction, arrangement or agreement so made for the director concerned (or any connected person), less the amount (if any) by which the liabilities of the person for whom the transaction or arrangement was made has been reduced, did not at any time in the financial year exceed £5,000. This amount is subject to alteration by statutory instrument.

[*6 Sch 24, 26*].

(*b*) By virtue of 5.39(*c*) above, in the case of any transaction or arrangement (within 5.39(*c*)) in which any particular director had a material interest, if the aggregate of

(i)   the value of each transaction or arrangement in which the director concerned had (directly or indirectly) a material interest and which was made after the start of the financial year with the company or any of its subsidiaries, and

(ii) the value of each such transaction or arrangement which was made before the start of the financial year, less the amount (if any) by which the liabilities of the person for whom the transaction etc. was made have been reduced

did not, at any time during the financial year, exceed the greater of

- £1,000; and

- the lesser of £5,000 and 1% of the value of the 'net assets' (as at the end of the financial year) of the company preparing the accounts in question.

A company's *'net assets'* means, for this purpose, the aggregate of its assets, less the aggregate of its liabilities (including any provision for liabilities or charges within *4 Sch 89, see* 5.3 above).

[*6 Sch 25, 26*].

5.43   TRANSACTIONS ETC. BY OFFICERS OTHER THAN DIRECTORS

The accounts of a company must contain a statement in relation to transactions, arrangements and agreements made by the company or a subsidiary of it for persons who, at any time during the financial year, were officers of the company, but not directors (or shadow directors, see 19.1 DIRECTORS) of it. The statement must show

(*a*) the aggregate 'amounts outstanding' at the end of the financial year under

(i)   loans;

    (ii)   quasi-loans (see 19.87 DIRECTORS);

    (iii)   credit transactions (see 19.88 DIRECTORS); and

(*b*)   the number of officers for whom the transactions, etc. within each of (*a*)(i)–(iii) above were made.

Each of the classes (*a*)(i)–(iii) above includes the following in so far as they relate to that class.

- Guarantees (including indemnities) and securities.

- Arrangements of a kind described in *Sec 330(6)(7)* (see 19.89 and 19.90 DIRECTORS respectively).

- Agreements to enter into any of the said transactions and arrangements.

The above does not apply to transactions, etc. made by the company or any of its subsidiaries for an officer of the company if the aggregate 'amount outstanding' thereunder at the end of the financial year does not exceed £2,500 (this amount being subject to alteration by statutory instrument).

An *'amount outstanding'* means the amount of the outstanding liabilities of the person for whom the transaction, etc. was made, or, in the case of a guarantee or security, the amount guaranteed or secured.

[*Sec 232(2), 6 Sch 28-30; CA 1989, s 6, 4 Sch 6*].

Comparative figures for the preceding year are not required in respect of information given under these provisions. [*4 Sch 58(3)(c)*, *8 Sch 51(3)(c)*; CA 1989, 1 Sch 10; SI 1997 No 220, 1 Sch].

5.44   DISCLOSURE REQUIRED IN NOTES TO ACCOUNTS: AUDITORS' REMUNERATION

Audit work. There must be stated in a note to the annual accounts the amount of the remuneration (including sums payable for expenses) of the company's auditors in their capacity as such.

The amount shown must include, as well as cash payments, the estimated money value of any benefits in kind, and the nature of any such benefit must be disclosed.

[*Sec 390A(3)-(5); CA 1989, s 121*].

Non-audit work. There must also be stated in a note to the annual accounts the aggregate remuneration (including sums payable as expenses), if any, of the auditors and their 'associates' in respect of work carried out in that year for services other than those falling within *Sec 390A* above supplied to the company and any 'associated undertaking' of the company. Where more than one auditor has been appointed in a single financial year, remuneration must be shown separately for each auditor. Comparative figures are also required.

The amount shown must include, as well as cash payments, the estimated money value of any benefits in kind, and the nature of any such benefit must be disclosed.

The auditors must supply the directors of the company with such information as is necessary to enable the relevant associates of the auditors to be identified.

5.44 Accounts: Individual Companies

'Associates' comprise the following.

(*a*) Where the auditors are a body corporate

    (i) any partnership in which the auditors were, at any time in the financial year, a partner;

    (ii) any partnership in which a director of the auditors was, at any time in the financial year, a partner;

    (iii) any body corporate which was, at any time in the financial year, in the same group as the auditors;

    (iv) any body corporate which was an 'associated undertaking' of the auditors, or of a body corporate in the same group as the auditors, at any time in the financial year;

    (v) (subject to the exception below) any body corporate in which any director of the auditors either alone or with any associate of the auditors was, at any time in the financial year, entitled to exercise, or control the exercise of, 20% or more of the voting rights at any general meeting;

    (vi) any body corporate which was, at any time in the financial year, in the same group as any body corporate within (v) above;

    (vii) any director of the auditors; and

    (viii) any person who was, at any time in the financial year, entitled to receive 20% or more of the auditors' profits and any person of whose profits the auditors were, in that financial year, entitled to receive 20% or more.

(*b*) Where the auditors are a partnership

    (i) any other partnership which had, at any time in the financial year, a partner in common with the auditors;

    (ii) any body corporate which was, at any time in the financial year, a partner in the auditors;

    (iii) (subject to the exception below) any body corporate in which, whether alone or with any associate of the auditors, the auditors or any partner in the auditors was, at any time in the financial year, entitled to exercise, or control the exercise of, 20% or more of the voting rights at any general meeting;

    (iv) any body corporate which was, at any time in the financial year, in the same group as any body corporate mentioned under (ii) or (iii) above;

    (v) any partner in the auditors; and

    (vi) any person who was, at any time in the financial year, entitled to receive 20% or more of the auditors' profits and any person of whose profits the auditors were, in that financial year, entitled to receive 20% or more.

(*c*) Where the auditor is an individual

    (i) any partnership in which the auditor was, at any time in the financial year, a partner;

    (ii) (subject to the exception below) any body corporate in which the auditor or any associate of his was, at any time in the financial year, entitled to exercise, or control the exercise of, 20% or more of the voting rights at any general meeting;

    (iii) any body corporate which was, at any time in the financial year, in the same group as any body corporate within (ii) above; and

(iv)   any person who was, at any time in the financial year, entitled to receive 20% or more of the auditor's profits and any person of whose profits the auditor was, in that financial year, entitled to receive 20% or more.

Exception. A body corporate is not to be regarded as an associate of the company's auditors under (*a*)(v), (*b*)(iii) or (*c*)(ii) above where the relevant 20 % control arises solely by virtue of acting as an insolvency practitioner in relation to any person, a receiver (or receiver or manager) of the property of the company, or a judicial factor on the estate of any person.

'*Associated undertaking*' means a subsidiary of the company determined as under *Sec 258* (see 4.2 ACCOUNTS: GROUPS OF COMPANIES) other than a subsidiary formed under the law of a country or territory outside the UK.

[*Sec 390B; SI 1991 No 2128; SI 1995 No 1520*].

DISCLOSURE REQUIRED IN NOTES TO ACCOUNTS: RELATED UNDERTAKINGS

5.45   GENERAL

The information described in 5.46 to 5.53 below must be given in notes to the annual accounts of a company which is not required to prepare group accounts.

The said information (other than that in 5.50 and 5.52 below) need not, however, be disclosed with respect to an undertaking which is established under the law of a country outside the UK or which carries on business outside the UK, but only if the disclosure would, in the opinion of the directors of the company, seriously prejudice the business of that undertaking, or that of the company or any of its subsidiary undertakings *and* the Secretary of State agrees to the non-disclosure. The fact of any non-disclosure must be stated in a note to the accounts.

The information required under any provision described in 5.46 to 5.53 below need not be given for *all* related undertakings if (in the opinion of the directors of the company) to do so would result in a statement of excessive length. In such a case, the information in question need be given only in respect of

(*a*)   the undertakings whose results or financial position, in the directors' opinion, principally affected the figures shown in the company's annual accounts; and

(*b*)   undertakings excluded from consolidation under *Sec 229(3)* or *(4)* (see 4.10(*b*)(*c*) ACCOUNTS: GROUPS OF COMPANIES).

If advantage is taken of this, then both the following apply.

(i)   The notes to the company's annual accounts must include a statement that the information is given only with respect to undertakings of the type mentioned in (*a*) and (*b*) above.

(ii)   The full information (i.e. that which is disclosed and that which is not) must be annexed to the next annual return delivered to the Registrar of Companies after the accounts in question have been approved by the board (see 3.2 ACCOUNTS: GENERAL).

In the event of non-compliance with (ii) above, the company and every officer in default is liable to a penalty up to the level in 40.1(*f*) PENALTIES.

[Sec 231, 24 Sch; CA 1989, s 6; SI 1993 No 1820, Reg 11; SI 1996 No 189, Reg 15].

5.46   **SUBSIDIARY UNDERTAKINGS**

Subject to 5.45 above, where, at the end of the financial year, the company has subsidiary undertakings, there must be stated in respect of each one of them

•   its name;

•   if it is incorporated outside Great Britain, the country in which it is incorporated;

•   if it is unincorporated, the address of its principal place of business.

There must also be stated the reason why the company is not required to prepare group accounts and, if the reason is that all the company's subsidiary undertakings fall within the exclusions in *Sec 229* (see 4.10 ACCOUNTS: GROUPS OF COMPANIES), there must be stated, for each such undertaking, which of those exclusions applies.

[5 Sch 1; CA 1989, 3 Sch; SI 1996 No 189, 3 Sch 2].

5.47   **Shareholdings by the company**

Subject to 5.45 above, for shares of each class 'held by the company' (see below) in a subsidiary undertaking, there must be stated the identity of the class and the proportion of the nominal value of the shares of that class which the shares held represents. A distinction must be made (i.e. in the relevant note to the accounts) between shares held by or on behalf of the company itself and shares attributed to the company (see below) which are held by or on behalf of a subsidiary undertaking. *[5 Sch 2; CA 1989, 3 Sch].*

Comparative figures for the preceding year (see 5.15 above) are not required. *[4 Sch 58(3)(b); CA 1989, 1 Sch 10].*

In ascertaining the shares *'held by the company'*, there must be attributed to the company any shares held by a subsidiary undertaking or by a person acting on behalf of either the company or a subsidiary undertaking. Shares held on behalf of a person other than the company or a subsidiary undertaking (including any that would otherwise be attributed to the company as above) are not to be treated as held by the company. *[5 Sch 13(2); CA 1989, 3 Sch; SI 1996 No 189, 3 Sch 13].* Shares held by way of security must be treated as being held by the person providing the security where

•   the rights attached to the shares are exercisable only in accordance with that person's instructions, and

•   the shares are held in connection with the granting of loans as part of normal business activities and the rights attached to the shares are exercisable only in the said person's interests,

disregarding, in each case, any right to exercise the said rights for the purpose of preserving or realising the value of the security. *[5 Sch 13(4); CA 1989, 3 Sch].*

5.48 **Financial information**

Subject to 5.45 above and the exceptions below, there must be disclosed with respect to each subsidiary undertaking

- the aggregate amount of its capital and reserves as at the end of its 'relevant financial year'; and

- its profit or loss for that year.

For this purpose, the *'relevant financial year'* of a subsidiary undertaking is, if its financial year ends with that of the company, that year and, in any other case, its financial year ending last before the end of the company's financial year.

Exceptions. Information which is not material need not be given. Also, the above information need not be given if

- the company is exempt by virtue of *Sec 228* (see 4.9 ACCOUNTS: GROUPS OF COMPANIES) from the requirement to prepare group accounts;

- the subsidiary undertaking in question is not required by any provision of *CA 1985* to deliver a copy of its balance sheet for its relevant financial year and does not otherwise publish it (in Great Britain or elsewhere), and the shares 'held by the company' (see 5.47 above) are less than 50% of the nominal value of the shares in the undertaking; or

- the company's investment in the subsidiary undertaking is included in the company's accounts by way of the equity method of valuation.

[*5 Sch 3; CA 1989, 3 Sch; SI 1996 No 189, 3 Sch 3*].

5.49 **Financial years**

Where disclosure is made under 5.48 above with respect to a subsidiary undertaking and that undertaking's financial year does not end with that of the company, there must be stated in relation to that subsidiary undertaking the date on which the subsidiary undertaking's last financial year ended (i.e. the last before the end of the company's financial year).

[*5 Sch 4; CA 1989, 3 Sch; SI 1996 No 189, 3 Sch 4*].

5.50 **Shares and debentures of company held by subsidiary undertakings**

Subject to 5.45 above, the number, description and amount of shares in the company held by, or on behalf of, its subsidiary undertakings must be disclosed. This does not apply to shares in respect of which the subsidiary undertaking is concerned as

- personal representative; or

- trustee unless the company, or any of its subsidiary undertakings, is 'beneficially interested under the trust' otherwise than by way of security only for the purposes of a transaction entered into by it in the ordinary course of a business which includes the lending of money.

In determining whether the company is *'beneficially interested under the trust'* certain interests mentioned in *2 Sch Part II* are disregarded (residual interests under pension and employee share schemes, company's rights as trustee to expenses, remuneration, etc.).

[*5 Sch 6; CA 1989, 3 Sch; SI 1996 No 189, 3 Sch 6*].

5.51 Accounts: Individual Companies

5.51 Significant holdings in undertakings other than subsidiary undertakings

Subject to 5.45 above, where at the end of the financial year the company has a 'significant holding' in an undertaking which is not a subsidiary undertaking, the following must be stated.

(*a*)   The name of the undertaking.

(*b*)   If it is incorporated outside Great Britain, the country in which it is incorporated.

(*c*)   If it is unincorporated, the address of its principal place of business.

(*d*)   The identity of each class of shares in the undertaking held by the company.

(*e*)   The proportion of the nominal value of the shares of that class represented by those shares.

(*f*)   The aggregate amount of the capital and reserves of the undertaking as at the end of its 'relevant financial year'.

(*g*)   Its profit or loss for that year.

A *'significant holding'* is a holding which amounts to 20% or more of the nominal value of any class of shares in the undertaking *or* the amount of which (as stated or included in the company's individual accounts) exceeds 20% of the amount of its assets (as so stated).

'Relevant financial year' of an undertaking is, if its financial year ends with that of the company, that year. In any other case it is its financial year ending last before the end of the company's financial year.

The information in (*f*) and (*g*) above need not be given if

● the company is exempt by virtue of *Sec 228* (see 4.9 ACCOUNTS: GROUPS OF COMPANIES) from the requirement to prepare group accounts *and* the investment of the company in all undertakings in which it has a holding of 20% or more is shown, in aggregate, in the notes to the accounts by way of the equity method of valuation; or

● the undertaking in question is not required by any provision of *CA 1985* to deliver a copy of its balance sheet for its relevant financial year and does not otherwise publish it (in Great Britain or elsewhere) *and* the company's holding is less than 50% of the nominal value of the shares in the undertaking.

[*5 Sch 7–9; CA 1989, 3 Sch; SI 1996 No 189, 3 Sch 7–9*].

Comparative figures for the preceding year (see 5.15 above) are not required with respect to the information in (*d*) and (*e*) above. [*4 Sch 58(3)(b); CA 1989, 1 Sch 10*].

In ascertaining, for any of the above purposes, the company's holding, there must be attributed to the company shares held on its behalf by any person. Shares held on behalf of a person other than the company (including any that would otherwise be attributed to the company as above) are not to be treated as held by the company. [*5 Sch 13(3); CA 1989, 3 Sch*]. *5 Sch 13(4)* (see 5.47 above) also applies for these purposes.

5.52 Memberships of certain partnerships and unlimited companies

Subject to 5.45 above, where at the end of a financial year a company is a member of a 'qualifying partnership' (see 39.4 PARTNERSHIPS) or a 'qualifying unlimited company' (see 60.3(*b*) UNLIMITED COMPANIES), the following must be stated.

● The name and legal form of the undertaking (unless not material).

- The address of its registered office or, if it does not have such an office, its head office (unless not material).

- If the undertaking is a qualifying partnership, either

  (i) a statement that a copy of the latest accounts of the partnership has been or is to be appended to the copy of the company's accounts sent to the Registrar of Companies, or

  (ii) the name of at least one body corporate (which may be the company itself) in whose group accounts the undertaking has been, or is to be, dealt with on a consolidated basis. This information need not be given if the notes to the accounts disclose that advantage has been taken of the exemption in 39.4 PARTNERSHIPS.

[5 Sch 9A; SI 1993 No 1820, Reg 11].

5.53 INFORMATION REQUIRED WHERE THE COMPANY IS A SUBSIDIARY UNDERTAKING

Subject to 5.45 above, where the company is a subsidiary undertaking, the following information must be given.

(a) Particulars, as follows, with respect to the 'company' (meaning any body corporate) regarded by the directors as the company's ultimate parent.

  (i) Its name.

  (ii) If it is incorporated outside Great Britain, the country in which it is incorporated (only if known to the directors).

(b) Particulars, as follows, with respect to the parent undertaking of the largest and smallest group of undertakings for which group accounts are drawn up and of which the company is a member.

  (i) The same information as in (a) above (but without the exception for information not known to the directors).

  (ii) If the undertaking is unincorporated, the address of its principal place of business.

  (iii) If copies of the above-mentioned group accounts are available to the public, the addresses from which such copies can be obtained.

[5 Sch 11, 12; CA 1989, 3 Sch; SI 1996 No 189, 3 Sch 11, 12].

6 Accounts: Insurance and Banking Companies

Cross-references. See 2 ACCOUNTS: DEFINITIONS; 3 ACCOUNTS: GENERAL.

The contents of this chapter are as follows:

6.1 INSURANCE COMPANIES AND GROUPS

The Secretary of State has power to modify the provisions of *Part VII*. [*Sec 257; CA 1989, s 20*]. Under these powers, the provisions relating to insurance companies and groups have been recast by *SI 1993 No 3245* and *SI 1993 No 3246* to implement *EC Council Directive 91/674/EEC*. [*SI 1993 No 3246, Reg 7*].

6.2 INSURANCE COMPANIES – INDIVIDUAL ACCOUNTS

An insurance company must prepare its individual accounts in accordance with the special provisions in *Sec 255* and *9A Sch Part I* and the accounts must contain a statement to that effect. [*Sec 255(2)(3); SI 1991 No 2705*].

The provisions of 3 ACCOUNTS: GENERAL apply as for other companies.

6.3 Duty to prepare accounts

The directors of every company must prepare, for each financial year of the company, a balance sheet as at the last day of the year and a profit and loss account. The accounts must respectively give a true and fair view of the state of the company's affairs as at the end of the financial year and of its profit or loss for that year. These accounts are referred to collectively as the company's *'individual accounts'*. See 2.1 ACCOUNTS: DEFINITIONS for *'financial year'*.

An insurance company's individual accounts must comply with the provisions of *9A Sch Part I* as described in 6.4 to 6.40 below as to form and content of the balance sheet and profit and loss account and additional information to be provided by way of notes to the accounts. If compliance with these provisions and other provisions of *CA 1985* (see 6.41 to 6.43 below) as to matters to be included in individual accounts or in the notes to thereto is insufficient to meet the 'true and fair view' requirements above, such additional information as is necessary must be given in the accounts or notes. If in special circumstances, compliance with any of those provisions would be inconsistent with the 'true and fair view' requirement, the directors must, to the extent necessary, depart from that provision, but any such departure, the reason for it and its effect must be given in a note to the accounts.

[*Secs 226, 255(4); CA 1989, s 4; SI 1991 No 2705*].

See 3.13 ACCOUNTS: GENERAL for 'true and fair view'.

6.4   **Form and content – general rules**

Every balance sheet of a company must show the items listed in the format in 6.5 below, and every profit and loss account must show the items listed in the format in 6.8 below, in either case in the order and under the headings and subheadings given in the format, except that no item need be distinguished by any number or letter assigned to it in the format. Any item required to be shown may be shown in greater detail than required. Any item representing or covering the amount of any asset or liability, income or expenditure, not otherwise covered by any item listed in the format, may be included, except that none of the following items can be treated as assets in the balance sheet.

• Preliminary expenses.

• Expenses of, and commission on, any issue of shares or debentures.

• Costs of research.

Headings and subheadings listed in the formats need not be included if there is no amount to be shown, either for the current or the preceding financial year (see below), for the items thereunder.

[*9A Sch Part I, paras 1, 2(1)(2)(4), 3(3); SI 1993 No 3246*].

Preceding financial year. For every item in the balance sheet or profit and loss account, the corresponding amount for the immediately preceding financial year must also be shown. Where it is not comparable with that for the current year, the corresponding amount for the preceding year must be adjusted. Particulars of, and the reasons for, the adjustment must be disclosed in a note to the accounts. [*9A Sch Part I, para 3(1)(2); SI 1993 No 3246*].

Set-offs. Unless otherwise indicated in *9A Sch*, amounts in respect of items representing assets or income may not be set off against amounts representing liabilities or expenditure, or vice versa. [*9A Sch Part I, para 4; SI 1993 No 3246*].

Profit and loss accounts. Every profit and loss account must show separately as additional items

• any amount set aside to, or withdrawn from, reserves (or proposed to be so set aside or withdrawn);

• the aggregate amount of any dividends paid or proposed; and

• the aggregate amount of any dividends proposed (if not shown in the notes to the accounts).

[*9A Sch Part I, para 5; SI 1993 No 3246; SI 1996 No 189 5 Sch 2*].

Long term business. The provisions of *9A Sch* which relate to long term business apply (with necessary modification) to business within Classes 1 and 2 of *Insurance Companies Act 1982, 2 Sch* which is

• transacted exclusively or principally according to the technical principles of long term business; and

• a significant amount of the business of the company.

[*9A Sch Part I, para 6; SI 1993 No 3246*].

Materiality. Amounts which in the particular context of a provision of *9A Sch Part I* (see above and 6.5 to 6.40 below) are not material may be disregarded for the purposes of that provision [*9A Sch Part I, para 83; SI 1993 No 3246*].

6.5 Accounts: Insurance and Banking Companies

Provisions. References in *9A Sch Part I* (see above and 6.5 to 6.40 below) to provisions for depreciation or diminution in the value of assets are to any amount written off by way of providing for depreciation or diminution in value of assets. References to provisions for risks or charges are to any retained as reasonably necessary for the purpose of providing for any liability or loss which is either likely to be incurred, or certain to be incurred but uncertain as to amount or as to the date on which it will arise. [*9A Sch Part I, para 84; SI 1993 No 3246; SI 1996 No 189, 5 Sch 18*].

Listed companies. In addition to the requirement of *CA 1985*, listed companies must comply with the requirements of the *Listing Rules, Chapter 12.41–12.44* as to content of annual accounts. See 43.15 PUBLIC AND LISTED COMPANIES.

6.5 **Balance sheet format**

The balance sheet format set out in *9A Sch Part I* and referred to in 6.4 above is reproduced below, and is followed by notes to certain of the items listed therein.

In respect of items to which Arabic numbers are assigned

(*a*)   (except for items concerning technical provisions and the reinsurers' share of technical provisions) these may be combined in the accounts for any financial year if

   (i)   their individual amounts are not material for the purpose of giving a true and fair view; or

   (ii) the combination facilitates the assessment of the state of affairs of the company for that year (but in this case the individual items must be disclosed in a note to the accounts).

(*b*)   where the gross amount and reinsurance amount or reinsurers' share are required to be shown, a sub-total of those items must also be given.

[*9A Sch Part I, paras 2(3), 7(3); SI 1993 No 3246*].

ASSETS

A.   Called up share capital not paid (note (1))

B.   Intangible assets
   1.   Development costs
   2.   Concessions, patents, licences, trade marks and similar rights and assets (note (2))
   3.   Goodwill (note (3))
   4.   Payments on account

C.   Investments

   I   Land and buildings (note (4))

   II   Investments in group undertakings and participating interests
   1.   Shares in group undertakings
   2.   Debt securities issued by, and loans to, group undertakings
   3.   Participating interests
   4.   Debt securities issued by, and loans to, undertakings in which the company has a participating interest

   III   Other financial investments
   1.   Shares and other variable-yield securities and units in unit trusts
   2.   Debt securities and other fixed income securities (note (5))
   3.   Participation in investment pools (note (6))

        4.   Loans secured by mortgages (note (7))
        5.   Other loans (note (7))
        6.   Deposits with credit institutions (note (8))
        7.   Other (note (9))

    IV   Deposits with ceding undertakings (note (10))

D.   Assets held to cover linked liabilities (note (11))

Da.   Reinsurers' share of technical provisions (note (12))
        1.   Provision for unearned premiums
        2.   Long term business provision
        3.   Claims outstanding
        4.   Provisions for bonuses and rebates
        5.   Other technical provisions
        6.   Technical provisions for unit-linked liabilities

E.   Debtors (note (13))

    I   Debtors arising out of direct insurance operations
        1.   Policy holders
        2.   Intermediaries

    II   Debtors arising out of reinsurance operations

    III   Other debtors

    IV   Called up share capital not paid (note (1))

F.   Other assets

    I   Tangible assets
        1.   Plant and machinery
        2.   Fixtures, fittings, tools and equipment
        3.   Payments on account (other than deposits paid on land and buildings) and assets (other than buildings) in course of construction

    II   Stocks
        1.   Raw materials and consumables
        2.   Work in progress
        3.   Finished goods and goods for resale
        4.   Payments on account

    III   Cash at bank and in hand

    IV   Own shares (note (14))

    V   Other (note (15))

G.   Prepayments and accrued income

    I   Accrued interest and rent (note (16))

    II   Deferred acquisition costs (note (17))

    III   Other prepayments and accrued income

LIABILITIES

A.   Capital and reserves

    I   Called up share capital or equivalent funds

    II   Share premium account

    III   Revaluation reserve

6.5 Accounts: Insurance and Banking Companies

    IV   Reserves
        1.   Capital redemption reserve
        2.   Reserve for own shares
        3.   Reserves provided for by the articles of association
        4.   Other reserves

    V   Profit and loss account

B.   Subordinated liabilities (note (18))

Ba.   Fund for future appropriations (note (19))

C.   Technical provisions

    1.   Provision for unearned premiums (note (20))
        (*a*)   gross amount
        (*b*)   reinsurance amount (note (12))
    2.   Long term business provision (notes (20), (21) and (26))
        (*a*)   gross amount
        (*b*)   reinsurance amount (note (12))
    3.   Claims outstanding (note (22))
        (*a*)   gross amount
        (*b*)   reinsurance amount (note (12))
    4.   Provision for bonuses and rebates (note (23))
        (*a*)   gross amount
        (*b*)   reinsurance amount (note (12))
    5.   Equalisation provision (note (24))
    6.   Other technical provisions (note (25))
        (*a*)   gross amount
        (*b*)   reinsurance amount (note (12))

D.   Technical provisions for linked liabilities (note (26))
    (*a*)   gross amount
    (*b*)   reinsurance amount (note (12))

E.   Provisions for other risks and charges
    1.   Provisions for pensions and similar obligations
    2.   Provisions for taxation
    3.   Other provisions

F.   Deposits received from reinsurers (note (27))

G.   Creditors (note (28))

    I   Creditors arising out of direct insurance operations

    II   Creditors arising out of reinsurance operations

    III   Debenture loans (note (29))

    IV   Amounts owed to credit institutions

    V   Other creditors including taxation and social security

H.   Accruals and deferred income

Notes

(1)   *Called up share capital not paid.* The two positions shown for this item are alternatives.

(2)   *Concessions, patents, licences, trade marks and similar rights and assets* must only be included if either the assets were acquired for valuable consideration and are not

required to be shown as goodwill or the assets in question were created by the company itself.

(3)   *Goodwill* must only be included if acquired for valuable consideration.

(4)   *Land and buildings.* The amount of any land and buildings which the company occupies for its own activities must be shown separately in the notes to the accounts.

(5)   *Debt securities, etc.* This comprises transferable debt securities etc. issued by credit institutions, other undertakings and public bodies if not covered by Assets item C. II.2 or C. II.4. Securities bearing interest rates varying with specific factors (e.g. inter-bank market or Euromarket rates) are to be included.

(6)   *Participation in investment pools.* This item comprises shares held by the company in joint investments constituted by several undertakings or pension funds, the management of which has been entrusted to one of those undertakings or pension funds.

(7)   *Loans secured by mortgages and other loans.* Loans to policy holders for which the policy is the main security must be included under 'Other loans' and their amount disclosed in the notes to the accounts. Loans secured by mortgage must be shown as such even where also secured by insurance policies. Where the amount of 'Other loans' not secured by policies is material, a breakdown must be given in the notes to the accounts.

(8)   *Deposits with credit institutions* comprises sums the withdrawal of which is subject to a time restriction. Sums deposited with no such restriction must be shown under Assets item F. III.

(9)   *Other.* This item comprises those investments not covered by C. III.1 to 6. If significant, they must be disclosed in the notes to the accounts.

(10)   *Deposits with ceding undertakings.* Where the company accepts reinsurance, this item comprises amounts, owed by the ceding undertaking and corresponding to guarantees, which are deposited with those ceding undertakings or with third parties or which are retained by those undertakings. Such amounts cannot be combined with other amounts owed by the ceding insurer to the reinsurer or set off against amounts owed by the reinsurer to the ceding undertakings. Securities deposited with ceding undertakings or third parties which remain the property of the company must be entered in the company's accounts as an investment under the appropriate item.

(11)   *Assets held to cover linked liabilities.* This item includes

   •   in respect of long term business, investments made pursuant to long term policies under which the benefits payable to the policy holder are wholly or partly determined by reference to the value of, an index of the value of, or income from, property of any description (whether or not specified in the contract); and

   •   investments held on behalf of members of a tontine and intended for distribution among them.

(12)   *Reinsurance amounts*, which may be shown under Assets item Da or under the various headings under Liabilities item C, comprise the actual or estimated amounts deducted form the gross amounts of technical provisions under contractual reinsurance arrangements.

(13)   *Debtors.* Amounts owed by group undertakings and undertakings in which the company has a participating interest must be shown separately as sub-items of Assets items E. I, E. II and E. III.

6.5 Accounts: Insurance and Banking Companies

(14) *Own shares.* The nominal value of the shares must be shown separately.

(15) *Other.* This item comprises those assets not covered by Assets items F. I to F. IV. If material they must be disclosed in the notes to the accounts.

(16) *Accrued interest and rent* comprises interest and rent earned up to the balance sheet date but which have not yet become receivable.

(17) *Deferred acquisition costs* (i.e. the cost of acquiring insurance policies which are incurred during a financial year but relate to a subsequent financial year) must be shown at Assets item G. II unless

    (*a*) allowance has been made in the computation of the long term business provision shown under Liabilities item C. 2 or D; or

    (*b*) allowance has been made for such costs in respect of general business policies by a deduction from the provision for unearned premiums under Liabilities item C 1.

Deferred acquisition costs arising in general business must be distinguished for those arising in long term business.

Treatment of such costs, including treatment under (*a*) and (*b*) where applicable, must be shown in the notes to the accounts.

(18) *Subordinated liabilities.* This comprises all liabilities where there is a contractual obligation that, in the event of a winding up or bankruptcy, they are to be repaid only after the claims of other creditors.

(19) *Fund for future appropriation.* This item comprises all funds the allocation of which either to policy holders or shareholders has not been determined by the end of the financial year. Transfers to and from this item must be shown in profit and loss account item II.12a.

(20) *Provision for unearned premiums.* This item comprises an amount representing that part of the gross premiums written which is estimated to be earned in subsequent financial years. In the case of long term business, the provision may alternatively be included in Liabilities item C.2.

(21) *Long term business provision.* This item comprises

    • the actuarially estimated value of the company's liabilities (excluding technical liabilities included in Liabilities item D) including bonuses already declared and after deducting the actuarial value of future premiums); and

    • claims incurred but not reported, plus the estimated cost of settling such claims.

(22) *Claims outstanding* comprises the total estimated ultimate cost of settling all claims arising from events which have occurred up to the end of the financial year (including, in the case of general business, claims incurred but not reported) less any amounts already paid on such claims.

(23) *Provision for bonuses and rebates* comprises amounts intended for policy holders or contract beneficiaries by way of bonuses and rebates and defined in Note (5) to the profit and loss account format (see 6.8 below) to the extent that such amounts have not been credited to policy holders or contract beneficiaries or included in Liabilities items Ba or C.2.

(24) *Equalisation provision* comprises the amount of any reserve maintained by the company under *Insurance Companies Act 1982, s 34A*. It also comprises any amounts which, in accordance with *EC Council Directive 87/343/EEC*, are required

to be set aside to equalise fluctuations in loss ratios in future years or to provide for special risks. If the company constitutes reserves for these purposes in some other way it must disclose that fact in the notes to the accounts.

(25) *Other technical provisions* comprise, *inter alia*, the '*provision for unexpired risks*' (i.e. the amount set aside in addition to unearned premiums in respect of risks to be borne by the company after the end of the financial year, in order to provide for all claims and expenses in connection with insurance contracts in force in excess of the related unearned premiums and any premiums receivable on those contracts). Where this provision is significant, it must be disclosed separately either in the balance sheet or notes to the accounts.

(26) *Technical provisions for linked liabilities.* This item comprises

- technical provisions to cover liabilities relating to investment in the context of long term policies under which the benefits payable to policy holders are wholly or partly to be determined by reference to the value of, an index of the value of, or income from, property of any description (whether or not specified in the contract). Any additional technical provisions to cover death risks, operating expenses or other risks (e.g. benefits payable at maturity or guaranteed surrender values) must be included under Liabilities item C.2; and

- technical provisions representing the obligation of a tontine's organiser in relation to its members.

(27) *Deposits received from reinsurers.* Where the company cedes reinsurance this item comprises

- amounts deposited by or withheld from other insurance undertakings under reinsurance contracts (which amounts must not be merged with other amounts owed to or by those other undertakings); and

- where the company has received as a deposit securities which have been transferred into its ownership, the amount owed by the company by virtue of the deposit.

(28) *Creditors.* Amounts owed to group undertakings and undertakings in which the company has a participating interest must be shown separately as sub-items.

(29) *Debenture loans.* The amount of any convertible loans must be shown separately.

[*9A Sch Part I, Chapter I, Section B, para 81; Insurance Companies Act 1995, s 3; SI 1993 No 3246*].

6.6 *Additional items – long term business*

Where the company carries on long term business

- the aggregate on any amounts included in Liabilities item A (see 6.5 above) which are required not to be treated as realised profits under *Sec 268* (see 23.3 DISTRIBUTIONS) must be shown separately on the balance sheet; and

- the total amount of assets representing the long term fund valued in accordance with *9A Sch* must be shown separately in the balance sheet or the notes to the accounts.

[*9A Sch Part I, para 10; SI 1993 No 3246*].

6.7 Accounts: Insurance and Banking Companies

6.7 *Managed funds*

Where assets and liabilities arising in respect of 'managed funds' fall to be treated as assets and liabilities of the company, they must be included in the company's balance sheet. The notes to the accounts must disclose the total amounts of such assets and liabilities and the amount included under each relevant balance sheet item.

'Managed funds' are funds of a group pension fund falling within *Insurance Companies Act 1982, 1 Sch Class VII* which the company administers in its own name but on behalf of others and to which it has legal title.

[9A Sch Part I, para 11; SI 1993 No 3246].

6.8 Profit and loss account format

The profit and loss format set out in *9A Sch* and referred to in 6.4 above is reproduced below, and is followed by notes to certain of the items listed therein. The headings 'Technical account – General business' and 'Technical account – Long term business' are for business within the classes of insurance specified in *Insurance Companies Act 1982, 2 Sch* and *1 Sch* respectively.

Items to which lower case letters in parentheses are assigned (except for items within items I.1, I.4, II.1, II.5 and II.6) may be combined in the accounts for any financial year if

- their individual amounts are not material for the purpose of giving a true and fair view; or

- the combination facilitates the assessment of the profit or loss of the company for that year (but in this case the individual items must be disclosed in a note to the accounts).

In respect of any item to which an Arabic number is assigned

(*a*)   where the gross amount and reinsurance amount or reinsurers' share are required to be shown, a sub-total of those items must also be given; and

(*b*)   where separate items are required to be shown, then a separate sub-total of those items must also be given in addition to any sub-total under (*a*) above.

[9A Sch Part I, paras 2(3), 7(3)(4), 9; SI 1993 No 3246].

I TECHNICAL ACCOUNT – GENERAL BUSINESS

1.   Earned premiums, net of reinsurance
   (*a*)   gross premiums written (note (1))
   (*b*)   outward reinsurance premiums (note (2))
   (*c*)   change in the gross provision for unearned premiums
   (*d*)   change in the provision for unearned premiums, reinsurers' share

2.   Allocated investment return transferred from the non-technical account (item III.6) (note (10))

2a.   Investment income (notes (8) and (10))
   (*a*)   income from participating interests, with a separate indication of that derived from group undertakings
   (*b*)   income from other investments, with a separate indication of that derived from group undertakings
   (*c*)   value re-adjustments on investments
   (*d*)   gains on the realisation of investments

3.   Other technical income, net of reinsurance

4.   Claims incurred, net of reinsurance (note (4))
     (*a*)   claims paid
           (*aa*)   gross amount
           (*bb*)   reinsurers' share
     (*b*)   change in the provision for claims
           (*aa*)   gross amount
           (*bb*)   reinsurers' share

5.   Changes in other technical provisions, net of reinsurance, not shown under other headings

6.   Bonuses and rebates, net of reinsurance (note (5))

7.   Net operating expenses
     (*a*)   acquisition costs (note (6))
     (*b*)   change in deferred acquisition costs
     (*c*)   administrative expenses (note (7))
     (*d*)   reinsurance commissions and profit participation

8.   Other technical charges, net of reinsurance

8a.   Investment expenses and charges (note (8))
     (*a*)   investment management expenses, including interest
     (*b*)   value adjustments on investments
     (*c*)   losses on the realisation of investments

9.   Change in the equalisation provision

10.   Sub-total (balance on the technical account for general business (item III.1))

II TECHNICAL ACCOUNT – LONG TERM BUSINESS

1.   Earned premiums, net of reinsurance
     (*a*)   gross premiums written (note (1))
     (*b*)   outward reinsurance premiums (note (2))
     (*c*)   change in the provision for unearned premiums, net of reinsurance (note (3))

2.   Investment income (notes (8) and (10))
     (*a*)   income from participating interest, with a separate indication of that derived from group undertakings
     (*b*)   income from other investments, with a separate indication of that derived from group undertakings
     (*c*)   value re-adjustments on investments
     (*d*)   gains on the realisation of investments

3.   Unrealised gains on investments

4.   Other technical income, net of reinsurance

5.   Claims incurred, net of reinsurance (note (4))
     (*a*)   claims paid
           (*aa*)   gross amount
           (*bb*)   reinsurers' share
     (*b*)   change in the provision for claims
           (*aa*)   gross amount
           (*bb*)   reinsurers' share

6.   Changes in other technical provisions, net of reinsurance, not shown under other headings

> (a)   long term business provision, net of reinsurance (note (3))
>   (aa)   gross amount
>   (bb)   reinsurers' share
> (b)   other technical provisions, net of reinsurance

7.   Bonuses and rebates, net of reinsurance (note (5))

8.   Net operating expenses
    (a)   acquisition costs (note (6))
    (b)   change in deferred acquisition costs
    (c)   administrative expenses (note (7))
    (d)   reinsurance commissions and profit participation

9.   Investment expenses and charges (note (8))
    (a)   investment management expenses, including interest
    (b)   value adjustments on investments
    (c)   losses on the realisation of investments

10.   Unrealised losses on investments (note (9))

11.   Other technical charges, net of reinsurance

11a.   Tax attributable to the long term business

12.   Allocated investment return transferred to non-technical account (item III.4)

12a.   Transfers to or from the fund for future appropriations

13.   Sub-total (balance on technical account – long term business) (item III.2)

III NON-TECHNICAL ACCOUNT

1.   Balance on the general business technical account (item I.10)

2.   Balance on the long term business technical account (item II.13)

2a.   Tax credit attributable to balance on the long term business technical account (note (11))

3.   Investment income (note (8))
    (a)   income from participating interests, with a separate indication of that derived from group undertakings
    (b)   income from other investments, with a separate indication of that derived from group undertakings
       (aa)   income from land and buildings
       (bb)   income from other investments
    (c)   value re-adjustments on investments
    (d)   gains on the realisation of investments

3a.   Unrealised gains on investments (note (9))

4.   Allocated investment return transferred from the long term business technical account (item II.12) (note (10))

5.   Investment expenses and charges (note (8))
    (a)   investment management expenses, including interest
    (b)   value adjustments on investments
    (c)   losses on the realisation of investments

5a.   Unrealised losses on investments (note (9))

6.   Allocated investment return transferred to general business technical account (item I.2) (note (10))

7.   Other income

8.   Other charges, including value adjustments

8a. Profit or loss on ordinary activities before tax

9.   Tax on profit or loss on ordinary activities

10. Profit or loss on ordinary activities after tax

11. Extraordinary income

12. Extraordinary charges

13. Extraordinary profit and loss

14. Tax on extraordinary profit or loss

15. Other taxes not shown under the preceding items

16. Profit or loss for the financial year

Notes

(1) *Gross premiums written.* This comprises all amounts due during the financial year in respect of insurance contracts entered into regardless of the fact that such amounts may relate in whole or part to a later financial year. It includes *inter alia*

- premiums yet to be determined where the premium calculation can only be done at the end of the year;

- single premiums, including annuity premiums and, in long term business, single premiums resulting from bonus and rebate provisions in so far as they must be considered as premiums under the terms of the contract;

- additional premiums in the case of half-yearly, quarterly or monthly payments and additional payments from policy holders for expenses borne by the company;

- in the case of co-insurance, the company's portion of the total premiums; and

- reinsurance premiums due from ceding and retroceding insurance undertakings, including portfolio entries

after deduction of cancellations and portfolio withdrawals credited to ceding and retroceding insurance undertakings.

Taxes levied and duties levied with premiums must be excluded.

(2) *Outward reinsurance premiums.* This comprises all premiums paid or payable in respect of outward reinsurance contracts entered into by the company. Portfolio entries payable on the conclusion or amendment of outward reinsurance contracts must be added and portfolio withdrawals receivable must be deducted.

(3) *Change in the provision for unearned premiums, net of reinsurance.* In the case of long term business, the change in unearned premiums may be included either in item II.1(*c*) or II.6(*a*) of the long term business technical account.

(4) *Claims incurred, net of reinsurance.* This comprises all payments made in respect of the financial year with the addition of the provision for claims (but after deducting the provision for claims for the preceding year). Included are annuities, surrenders, entries and withdrawals of loss provisions to and from ceding insurance

6.8 Accounts: Insurance and Banking Companies

undertakings and reinsurers and external and internal claims management costs and charges for claims incurred but not reported (see 6.23 below under the heading *General business*).

Sums recoverable on the basis of subrogation and salvage (see 6.23 below) must be deducted.

Where the difference between

- the loss provision made at the beginning of the year for outstanding claims incurred in previous years, and

- the payments made during the year on account of claims incurred in previous years and the loss provision shown at the end of the year for such outstanding claims,

is material, it must be shown in the notes to the accounts, broken down by category and amount.

(5) *Bonuses and rebates, net of reinsurance.* Bonuses comprise all amounts chargeable for the financial year which are paid or payable to policy holders and other insured parties or provided for their benefit. Included are amounts used to increase technical provisions or applied to the reduction of future premiums, to the extent that such amounts represent an allocation of surplus or profit arising on business as a whole or a section of the business, after deduction of amounts provided in previous years which are no longer required.

Rebates comprise such amounts to the extent that they represent a partial refund of premiums resulting from the experience of individual contracts.

Where material, the amount charged for bonuses and that charged for rebates must be disclosed separately in the notes to the accounts.

(6) *Acquisition costs.* These comprise the costs arising from the conclusion of insurance contracts. They cover both direct costs (e.g. acquisition commissions, the cost of drawing up the insurance document or including the insurance contract in a portfolio) and indirect costs (e.g. advertising costs and administrative expenses connected with the processing of proposals and the issuing of policies).

In the case of long term business, policy renewal commissions must be included under item II.8(c) in the long term business technical account.

(7) *Administration expenses.* This includes

- costs arising from premium collection, portfolio administration, handling of bonuses and rebates, and inward and outward reinsurance, and

- staff costs and depreciation provisions in respect of office furniture and equipment in so far as these need not be shown under acquisition costs, claims incurred or investment charges.

Item II.8(c) must also include policy renewal commissions.

(8) *Investment income, expenses and charges.* To the extent that they arise in the long term fund, these must be disclosed in the long term business technical account. Otherwise they must be disclosed either in the non-technical account or attributed between the appropriate technical and non- technical accounts. Where the company makes such an attribution, it must disclose the basis for it in the notes to the accounts.

(9) *Unrealised gains and losses on investments.* In the case of investments attributed to the long term fund, the difference between the valuation of investments and their

purchase price (or, if previously valued, their valuation at the last balance sheet date) *may* be disclosed (in whole or in part) in item II.3 or II.10 (as the case may be) of the long term business technical account. In the case of investments shown as assets under balance sheet item D (assets held to cover linked liabilities) the difference *must* be so disclosed.

In the case of other investments, the difference as above may be disclosed (in whole or in part) in item III.3(a) or III.5(a) (as the case may require) of the non-technical account.

(10)   *Allocated investment return.* The allocated return may be transferred from one part of the profit and loss account to another.

Where part of the investment return is transferred to the general business technical account, the transfer from the non-technical account must be deducted from item III.6 and added to item I.2.

Where part of the investment return disclosed in the long term business technical account is transferred to the non-technical account, the transfer to the non-technical account must be deducted from item II.12 and added to item III.4.

The reasons for such transfers and the bases on which they are made must be disclosed in a note to the accounts.

(11)   *Tax credit.* This applies only to annual accounts approved by the board after 1 February 1996.

[*9A Sch Part I, Chapter I, Section B; SI 1993 No 3246; SI 1996 No 189, 5 Sch 3; SI 1997 No 2704*].

6.9   Accounting principles

The amounts to be included in respect of all items shown in the accounts are to be determined in accordance with the principles set out below, except that if it appears to the directors that there are special reasons for departing from any of these principles for a financial year, they may do so, but particulars of the departure, the reason for it and its effect must be given in a note to the accounts.

(*a*)   The company must be presumed to be carrying on the business as a going concern.

(*b*)   Accounting policies must be applied consistently, both with the same accounts and from one financial year to the next.

(*c*)   The amount of any item is to be determined on a prudent basis, and in particular

    (i)   subject to Note (9) under 6.8 above, only profits realised at the balance sheet date are to be included in the profit and loss account; and

    (ii)   all liabilities and losses which have arisen, or are likely to arise, in respect of the financial year to which the accounts relate or a previous financial year must be taken into account; this includes any such liabilities and losses which became apparent after the balance sheet date but before the date on which the balance sheet is signed on behalf of the board (see 3.2 ACCOUNTS: GENERAL).

(*d*)   All income and charges relating to the financial year to which the accounts relate must be taken into account regardless of the date of receipt or payment.

6.10   Accounts: Insurance and Banking Companies

(*e*)   In determining the aggregate amount of any item, the amount of each individual asset or liability that falls to be taken into account must be determined separately.

[*9A Sch Part I, paras 13–19; SI 1993 No 3246*].

6.10   Current value accounting rules

The current value accounting rules in 6.11 to 6.16 below must, or as the case may be, may be used to determine the value at which assets are included in the accounts.

6.11   *Valuation of assets*

Subject to 6.14 to 6.16 below, assets are to be valued in the accounts as follows.

(*a*)   Investments falling to be included in the balance sheet under Assets item C *must* be shown at their current value calculated as under 6.13 below or, in the case of securities within 6.12 below, at their amortised value as determined under that paragraph.

(*b*)   Investments falling to be included in the balance sheet under Assets item D (assets held to cover linked liabilities) *must* be shown at their current value under 6.13 below.

(*c*)   Intangible assets (other than goodwill) may be shown at their current cost or as determined under the historical cost accounting rules in 6.17 to 6.21 below.

(*d*)   Assets falling to be included in the balance sheet under Assets items F.I (tangible assets) and F.IV (own shares) may be shown at their current value as under 6.13 below, their current cost or as determined under the historical cost accounting rules in 6.17 to 6.21 below.

(*e*)   Assets falling to be included in the balance sheet under Assets items F.II (stocks) may be shown at current cost or as determined under the historical cost accounting rules in 6.17 to 6.21 below.

For accounts approved by the board before 2 February 1996, under (*c*)–(*e*) above, the same valuation method had to be applied to all investments included in any item in the balance sheet format which was denoted by an Arabic number (see 6.5 above).

[*9A Sch Part I, paras 20–23; SI 1993 No 3246; SI 1996 No 189, 5 Sch 4*].

6.12   *Alternative value of fixed-income securities*

Debt securities and other fixed-income securities shown in the balance sheet under Assets items C.II (investments in group undertakings and participating interests) and C.III (other financial investments) may either be included at their current value as calculated under 6.13 below or at their amortised value in which case the following rules apply.

(*a*)   Where the purchase price of the securities exceeds the amount repayable at maturity, the difference is charged to profit and loss account and shown separately in the balance sheet or notes to the accounts. If the difference is written off in instalments over the period to repayment, the difference between the purchase price (less aggregate amount written off) and the amount repayable at maturity must be shown separately in the balance sheet or notes to the accounts.

(*b*)   Where the purchase price of the securities is less than the amount payable at maturity, the difference must be released to income in instalments over the period to repayment. The difference between the purchase price (plus aggregate amount released to income) and the amount repayable at maturity must be shown separately in the balance sheet or notes to the accounts.

(c)   Where any securities are valued as under (a) or (b) above,

- their purchase price and current value must be disclosed in the notes to the accounts; and

- if they are sold before maturity and the proceeds are used to purchase other securities to which this paragraph applies, the difference between the proceeds of sale and their book value may be spread uniformly over the period remaining until maturity of the original investment.

[9A Sch Part I, para 24; SI 1993 No 3246].

6.13   *Meaning of 'current value'*

Current value is calculated as follows.

(a)   *Assets not falling within (b)–(d) below.* Except where the equity method of accounting is applied, current value means market value calculated on a basis which has prudent regard to the likely realisable value.

(b)   *Listed investments.* Current value means the market value on the balance sheet date or, if not a stock exchange trading day, the last such day before that date. If on the date on which the accounts are prepared, such an investment has been sold or is to be sold within the short term, the market value must be reduced by the actual or estimated realisation costs.

(c)   *Unlisted investments for which a market exists.* Current value means the market value calculated from the average price at which the investments were traded on the balance sheet date or, if not a trading day, the last such day before that date. If on the date on which the accounts are prepared, such an investment has been sold or is to be sold within the short term, the market value must be reduced by the actual or estimated realisation costs.

(d)   *Land and buildings.* Current value means market value i.e. the price at which land and buildings could be sold under private contract between a willing seller and an arm's length buyer on the date of valuation on the assumptions that

- the property is publicly exposed to the market;

- the market conditions permit orderly disposal; and

- a normal period, having regard to the nature of the property, is available for the negotiation of the sale.

Market value must be determined separately for each item of land and buildings and must be carried out at least every five years by a generally recognised method of valuation.

Where the value of land has diminished since the preceding valuation, an appropriate valuation adjustment must be made. This lower value must not be subsequently increased in the balance sheet unless the increase is the result of a new valuation as above.

If on the date on which the accounts are prepared, land and buildings have been sold or are to be sold within the short term, the market value must be reduced by the actual or estimated realisation costs.

Where it is impossible to determine the market value of an item of land and buildings, current value is to be taken as purchase price or production cost.

[9A Sch Part I, para 24; SI 1993 No 3246].

6.14 Accounts: Insurance and Banking Companies

6.14 Depreciation rules

As regards any asset the value of which is determined under 6.11 above, that value (instead of cost or any value previously so determined) is to be (or is to be the starting point for determining) the amount to be included in the accounts. The value most recently determined is accordingly to be used (instead of cost) for the purpose of applying the depreciation rules described in 6.18 and 6.19 below. Where, however, the asset in question falls within 6.18 (*a*) or (*b*) below, any provision for depreciation in respect thereof which is included in the profit and loss account may be calculated on the historic cost amount rather than the current value provided that any difference between the alternative amounts is separately disclosed either in the profit and loss account or notes to the accounts.

[*9A Sch Part I, para 27; SI 1993 No 3246*].

6.15 Additional information to be provided

Where the amount of any asset covered by an item in the accounts has been determined on any basis in 6.11(*a*)–(*e*) above, the following additional information must be disclosed in a note to the accounts or alternatively, in the case of (*c*) below only, shown separately in the balance sheet.

(*a*)   The items affected and the basis of valuation adopted in determining the amount of the assets in question for each such item.

(*b*)   The purchase price of investments valued under 6.11(*a*) or (*b*).

(*c*)   For each balance sheet item affected either

    (i)   the 'comparable amounts determined under the historical cost accounting rules'; or

    (ii)   the differences between the amounts in (i) above and the actual amounts shown in the balance sheet in respect of that item.

The '*comparable amounts determined under the historical cost accounting rules*' comprise both

* the aggregate amount which would be required to be shown if the amounts of all assets covered by the item concerned were determined according to the historical cost rules (see 6.17 to 6.21 below); and

* the aggregate amount of the cumulative provisions for depreciation or diminution in value which would be required or permitted in determining those amounts according to those rules.

[*9A Sch Part I, para 28; SI 1993 No 3246*].

6.16 Revaluation reserve

Subject to the exception below, any profit or loss arising from the determination of the value of an asset according to any basis in 6.11(*a*)–(*e*) above (after allowing for provisions for depreciation or diminution in value) must be credited or debited to a separate reserve, the '*revaluation reserve*'. The amount of the revaluation reserve must be shown (but not necessarily under that name) in the balance sheet under Liabilities item A.III in the format at 6.5 above.

The revaluation reserve may be reduced to the extent that amounts transferred to it are no longer necessary for the purposes of the valuation method used. In addition, an amount may be transferred

- from the reserve to profit and loss account, if the amount was previously charged to that account or represents realised profit; or

- from the reserve on capitalisation, (i.e. by applying the amount in paying up (wholly or partly) unissued shares in the company to be allotted to the members as fully or partly paid shares, see (13) BONUS ISSUES); and

- to or from the revaluation reserve in respect of taxation relating to any profit or loss credited or debited to the reserve.

The revaluation reserve must not be reduced other than as mentioned above.

The treatment for tax purposes of amounts credited or debited to the revaluation reserve must be disclosed in a note to the accounts.

Exception. The above provisions do not apply to the difference between the valuation of investments and their purchase price or previous valuation shown in the long-term business technical account or the non-technical account in accordance with Note (9) on the profit and loss account (see 6.8 above).

[*9A Sch Part I, para 29; SI 1993 No 3246; SI 1996 No 189, 5 Sch 5*].

6.17   Historical cost accounting rules

The rules described in 6.18 to 6.21 below apply to determine the amounts to be included in respect of all items in the accounts, and are known as the historical cost accounting rules, but see 6.10 to 6.16 above for alternative rules. [*9A Sch Part I, para 30; SI 1993 No 3246*].

6.18   *Valuation of assets*

Assets generally. Assets are to be included at their 'cost' (see 6.21 below) subject to provision for depreciation or diminution as follows.

(*a*)   In the case of assets included in the balance sheet under Assets item B (intangible assets), C.I (land and buildings), F.I (tangible assets) or F.II (stocks) which have a limited useful economic life, cost (or cost less any estimated residual value at the end of the asset's useful life) is to be reduced by provisions for depreciation calculated to write off that amount over the asset's useful economic life.

(*b*)   In the case of assets included in the balance sheet under Assets item B (tangible assets), C (investments), F.I (tangible assets) or F.IV (own shares), provisions for any diminution in value *may* be made, the amount to be included in respect of that asset being reduced accordingly. Such provisions *must* also be made in respect of any asset which has suffered what is expected to be a permanent reduction in value (whether or not its useful economic life is limited). Where the reasons for any provision for diminution in value have ceased to apply to any extent, it may be written back (to the extent necessary). Any such provisions or amounts written back, where not shown separately in the profit and loss account, must be disclosed (either separately or in aggregate) in a note to the accounts.

[*9A Sch Part I, paras 31–33; SI 1993 No 3246*].

Debtors and cash. The amount to be included in the balance sheet under Assets items E.I, E.II and E.III (debtors) and F.III (cash at bank and in hand) is their 'cost' (see 6.21 below) or, if lower, their net realisable value. Any provision for diminution in value previously made, i.e. to reduce the asset to its net realisable value, must be written back to the extent that the reasons for it have ceased to apply. [*9A Sch Part I, para 34; SI 1993 No 2346*].

6.19   Accounts: Insurance and Banking Companies

Development costs. An amount may be included in the balance sheet in respect of development costs only in special circumstances (not specified), and if an amount is so included, there must be given in a note to the accounts the reasons for capitalising those costs and the period over which the amount originally capitalised is being, or is to be, written off. [*9A Sch Part I, para 35; SI 1993 No 3246*].

Goodwill. Where goodwill acquired by a company is treated as an asset, the amount of the consideration given must be reduced by provisions for depreciation calculated to write off that amount over a period of the directors' choosing, which must not exceed the useful economic life of that goodwill. Where any amount for goodwill is included as an asset in the balance sheet, the writing-off period chosen, and the reason for that choice, must be disclosed in a note to the accounts. [*9A Sch Part I, para 36; SI 1993 No 3246*].

6.19   *Excess of money owed over value received*

Where the amount repayable on any debt owed by a company is greater than the value of the consideration received in the transaction giving rise to the debt, the amount of the difference may be treated as an asset. It must, however, be written off in reasonable amounts each year and be completely written off before repayment of the debt. If not shown as a separate item in the balance sheet, the current amount must be disclosed in a note to the accounts. [*9A Sch Part I, para 37; SI 1993 No 3246*].

6.20   *Assets included at a fixed amount*

Assets included in the balance sheet under Assets item F.I (tangible assets) which are constantly being replaced may be included at a fixed quantity and value provided

- their overall value is not material to assessing the company's state of affairs; and

- their quantity, value and composition are not subject to material variation.

[*9A Sch Part I, para 38; SI 1993 No 3246*].

6.21   *Meaning and determination of 'cost'*

The *'cost'* of an asset is the actual price paid plus any incidental expenses of acquisition.

The cost of an asset constructed by the company is the aggregate of the purchase price of the raw materials and consumables used and the costs incurred by the company which are directly attributable to the construction of that asset. In addition, there may be included

- a reasonable proportion of costs so incurred which are only indirectly so attributable, but only to the extent that they relate to the period of construction; and

- interest on capital borrowed to finance the construction of the asset, to the extent that it accrues in respect of the period of construction. The inclusion of interest and the amount so included must be disclosed in a note to the accounts.

[*9A Sch Part I, para 39; SI 1993 No 3246*].

Where there are no relevant records of the purchase price (or of any price, expenses or costs relevant to its determination) of any asset, or any such record cannot be obtained without unreasonable expense or delay, then for the purposes of these provisions, the cost of that asset is to be taken to be the value ascribed to it in the earliest available record of its value made on or after its acquisition by the company. [*9A Sch Part I, para 41; SI 1993 No 3246*].

Fungible assets. The cost of any assets which are 'fungible' assets may be determined by applying any of the following methods in relation to any such assets of the same class (the method chosen being such as appears to the directors to be appropriate in the company's circumstances).

- First in, first out (FIFO).

- Last in, first out (LIFO).

- A weighted average price.

- Any other method similar to any of the above.

Where, however, the result of such determination is that the amount shown in respect of any balance sheet item differs materially from the 'relevant alternative amount', the amount of the difference must be disclosed in a note to the accounts.

The *'relevant alternative amount'* is normally determined on the basis of replacement cost as at the balance sheet date. If, however, the directors consider it a more appropriate standard of comparison, the relevant alternative amount may instead be determined by reference to the most recent actual purchase price (before the balance sheet date) of assets of that class.

Assets of any particular description are to be regarded as *'fungible'* if such assets are substantially indistinguishable from one another.

[*9A Sch Part I, paras 40, 81; SI 1993 No 3246*].

6.22 **Determination of provisions**

Provisions shown in the company's accounts must be determined as follows and as in 6.23 below.

(*a*) *Technical provisions* must at all times be sufficient to cover liabilities arising out of insurance contracts as far as can reasonably be foreseen.

(*b*) *Provision for unearned premiums* must in principle be computed separately for each insurance contract except that statistical methods (and in particular proportional and flat rate methods) may be used where they may be expected to give approximately the same results as individual calculations.

Where the pattern of risk varies over the life of a contract, this must be taken into account in the calculation methods.

(*c*) *Provision for unexpired risks* (see 6.5 above at Note (25)) must be computed on the basis of claims and administrative expenses likely to arise after the end of the financial year from contracts concluded before that date, in so far as their estimated value exceeds the provision for unearned premiums and any premiums receivable under those contracts.

(*d*) *Long term business provision* must in principle be computed separately for each long term contract except that statistical or mathematical methods may be used where they may be expected to give approximately the same results as individual calculations.

A summary of the principal assumptions in making the provision must be given in a note to the accounts.

The computation must be made annually by a Fellow of the Institute or Faculty of Actuaries on the basis of recognised actuarial methods, with due regard to the actuarial principles laid down in *EC Council Directive 92/96/EEC*.

[*9A Sch Part I, paras 42–46; SI 1993 No 3246*].

6.23   Accounts: Insurance and Banking Companies

6.23   *Provisions for claims outstanding*

(*a*)   *General business.* A provision must in principle be computed separately for each claim on the basis of the costs still expected to arise except that statistical methods may be used if they result in an adequate provision having regard to the nature of the risks. The following rules apply in calculating the provision.

   (i)   It must also allow for claims incurred but not yet reported by the balance sheet date, the amount of the allowance being determined by past experience as to the number and magnitude of claims reported after previous balance sheet dates.

   (ii)   All claims settlement costs (direct and indirect) must be included in the calculation of the provision.

   (iii)   Recoverable amounts arising out of 'subrogation' or 'salvage' must be estimated on a prudent basis and either deducted from the provision (in which case, if the amounts are material they must be shown in a note to the accounts) or shown as assets.

   '*Subrogation*' means the acquisition of the rights of policy holders with respect to third parties and '*salvage*' means the acquisition of the legal ownership of insured property.

   (iv)   Where benefits resulting from a claim must be paid out in the form of an annuity, the amount to be set aside must be calculated by recognised actuarial methods and (vi) below does not apply to the calculation.

   (v)   Implicit discounting or deductions is prohibited (whether resulting from the placing of a current value on a provision for an outstanding claim which is expected to be settled for a higher figure or otherwise effected).

   (vi)   Explicit discounting or deductions to take account of investment income is permitted subject to the following conditions.

      (A)   The expected average interval between the date for the settlement of claims being discounted and the accounting date must be at least four years.

      (B)   The discounting or deductions must be effected on a recognised prudential basis.

      (C)   When calculating the total cost of settling claims, the company must take account of all factors that could cause increases in that cost.

      (D)   The company must have adequate data at its disposal to construct a reliable model of the rate of claims settlements.

      (E)   The rate of interest used for the calculation of present values must not exceed a rate prudently estimated to be earned by assets of the company which are appropriate in magnitude and nature to cover the provisions for claims being discounted during the period necessary for the payment of such claims. The rate must also not exceed a rate justified by performance of such assets over the preceding five years or during the year preceding the balance sheet date.

      When discounting or effecting deductions, the company must disclose in the notes to the accounts the total amount of provisions (before discounting or deductions); the categories of claims which are discounted and from which deductions have been made; and, for each category of claims, the method used, the rates used for the estimates under (D) and (E) above, and the criteria adopted for estimating the period that will elapse before the claims are settled.

(*b*)   *Long term business.* The amount of the provision must be equal to the sums due to beneficiaries, plus the costs of settling claims.

(*c*)   *Equalisation reserve.* The amount of any reserve maintained under *Insurance Companies Act 1982, s 34A* or *Insurance Companies Regulations 1994, Reg 76 and 14 Sch* must be determined in accordance with *Regulations* made under that *Act* or those *Regulations* (as the case may be).

(*d*)   *Accounting on a non-annual basis.* Either of the following methods may be applied where, because of the nature of the class of insurance in question, information about premiums receivable or claims payable (or both) for the 'underwriting years' is insufficient when the accounts are drawn up for reliable estimates to be made. '*Underwriting year*' means the financial year in which the insurance contracts in the class or type of insurance in question commenced.

   (i)   The excess of the premiums written over the claims and expenses paid in respect of contracts commencing in the underwriting year forms a technical provision included in the technical provision for claims outstanding shown in the balance sheet under Liabilities item C.3. The provision may also be computed on the basis of a given percentage of the premiums written where such a method is appropriate to the type of risk insured. If necessary, the amount of this technical provision must be increased to make it sufficient to meet present and future obligations.

   The technical provision so calculated must be replaced by a provision for claims outstanding estimated as under (*a*) above as soon as sufficient information has been gathered and not later than the end of the third year following the underwriting year. The length of time that elapses before such replacement must be disclosed in a note to the accounts.

   (ii)   The figures shown in the technical account or in certain items within it relate to a year which wholly or partly precedes the financial year (but by not more than 12 months). The length of time by which the earlier year precedes the financial year, and the magnitude of the transactions concerned, must be disclosed in the notes to the accounts. The amounts of the technical provisions shown in the accounts must, if necessary, be increased to make them sufficient to meet present and future obligations.

The use of either method must be disclosed in the notes to the accounts, together with the reason for adopting it. Where one method is adopted, it must be applied systematically in successive years unless circumstances justify a change, in which case the effect on the assets, liabilities, financial position and profit or loss must be stated in the notes to the accounts.

[*9A Sch Part I, paras 47–53; Insurance Companies Act 1995, s 3; SI 1993 No 3246*].

6.24   **Notes to the accounts: general**

Comparative figures. In respect of accounts approved by the board after 1 February 1996, except where otherwise stated in this chapter and in 4 ACCOUNTS: GROUPS OF COMPANIES, there must be shown, in respect of each item stated in a note to the accounts, the corresponding amount for the immediately preceding financial year. Where the corresponding amount is not comparable, it must be adjusted and particulars of, and reasons for, the adjustment must be disclosed. [*9A Sch Part 1, para 54(2); SI 1996 No 189, 5 Sch 6*].

6.25　Accounts: Insurance and Banking Companies

Disclosure of accounting policies. The accounting policies adopted in determining the profit or loss and the amounts of balance sheet items (including policies with respect to depreciation and diminution in value of assets) must be stated in the notes to the accounts. [*9A Sch Part I, para 55; SI 1993 No 3246*].

Accounting standards. It must also be stated whether the accounts have been prepared in accordance with applicable accounting standards (see 3.12 ACCOUNTS: GENERAL). Particulars of any material departure from those standards, and the reasons for it, must be given. [*9A Sch Part I, para 56; SI 1993 No 3246*].

Foreign currency translation. Where any item in the profit and loss account or balance sheet includes sums originally denominated in foreign currencies, the basis of translation into sterling must be stated. [*9A Sch Part I, para 57; SI 1993 No 3246*].

Listed companies. In addition to the requirements of *CA 1985*, listed companies must also comply with the requirements of the *Listing Rules, Chapter 12.41–12.44* as to content of annual accounts. See 43.15 PUBLIC AND LISTED COMPANIES. The additional requirements may be shown in the directors' report or in the notes to the accounts.

6.25　Notes to the accounts: information supplementing the balance sheet

The information required, as set out in 6.26 to 6.33 below must be given by way of a note to the accounts if not given in the company's accounts. [*9A Sch Part I, para 54; SI 1993 No 3246; SI 1996 No 189, 5 Sch 6*].

6.26　*Share capital and debentures*

Both the authorised share capital and, where shares of more than one class have been allotted, the number and aggregate nominal value of shares of each class allotted must be stated.

If any part of the allotted share capital consists of redeemable shares, the following information must be given.

- The earliest and latest dates on which the company has power to redeem these shares.

- Whether the shares must be redeemed in any event or are liable to be redeemed at either the company's or the shareholders' option.

- Whether any premium is payable on redemption and, if so, the amount thereof.

The following information is required in respect of any shares allotted during the financial year.

(i)　The classes of shares allotted.

(ii)　As regards each class of shares, the number allotted, their aggregate nominal value, and the consideration received by the company for the allotment.

[*9A Sch Part I, paras 58, 59; SI 1993 No 3246; SI 1996 No 189, 5 Sch 7*].

With respect to any contingent right to the allotment of shares in the company, meaning any option to subscribe for shares and any other right to require the allotment of shares to any person (whether arising on the conversion into shares of securities of any description or otherwise), the following particulars must be given.

- The number, description and amount of shares in respect of which the right may be exercised.

- The period during which the right may be exercised.

- The price to be paid for the shares allotted.

Debentures. Similar information as in (i) and (ii) above is required of any debentures issued during the financial year.

Where any of the company's debentures are held by a nominee or trustee for the company, both their nominal amount and the amount at which they are stated in the company's accounting records (see 45.1 RECORDS) must be stated.

[9A Sch Part I, paras 60, 61; SI 1993 No 3246; SI 1996 No 189, 5 Sch 8].

6.27   *Assets*

The following information is required for assets of the company included in the balance sheet. Except where otherwise stated, comparative figures for the previous year (see 6.24 above) are not required.

- In respect of assets included in Assets items B (intangible assets), C.I (land and buildings) and C.II (investments in group undertakings and participating interests), the 'appropriate amounts' in respect of those assets both at the beginning of the financial year and at the balance sheet date.

  The *'appropriate amounts'* in respect of any assets at either of those times are the aggregate amounts determined, as at that time, in respect of assets falling to be included under that item, either on the basis of cost (see 6.21 above) or on any basis in 6.11(*a*)–(*e*) above (but, in either case, leaving out of account any provisions for depreciation or diminution in value).

- In respect of assets included in Assets item B (intangible assets), the effect on any amount included in the item in respect of those assets of

  (i)   any determination during the year of the value ascribed to any of those assets under 6.11(*c*) above;

  (ii)   acquisitions and disposals during the year; and

  (iii) any transfers of assets of the company to or from that item during that year.

- In respect of assets included under Assets item C.I (land and buildings), how much of that amount is ascribable to freehold land (or Scottish equivalent) and how much to leasehold land (or Scottish equivalent), and, of the latter amount, how much is ascribable to *'long lease'* (i.e. leases with an unexpired term at the end of the financial year of at least 50 years) and how much to *'short leases'* (i.e. any other lease). Comparative figures for the previous year *are* required. *'Lease'* includes an agreement for a lease.

- In respect of *any* assets included in the balance sheet, as regards provisions for depreciation or diminution in value

  (i)   the cumulative amount of such provisions included under that item at the beginning of the financial year and the balance sheet date;

  (ii)   the amount of any such provision made in respect of the year; and

  (iii) the amounts of any adjustments made to any such provisions during that year, distinguishing between adjustments made in consequence of disposals and other adjustments.

[9A Sch Part I, paras 54(3), 62, 64, 81, 85; SI 1993 No 3246; SI 1996 No 189, 5 Sch 6].

6.28   Accounts: Insurance and Banking Companies

The following additional information is required where any fixed assets (other than listed investments) are included under any balance sheet item at an amount determined on any basis under 6.11(*a*)–(*e*) above.

- The years (so far as known to the directors) in which the assets were severally valued, and the several values.

- In the case of assets valued during the financial year, the bases of valuation used and either the names or relevant qualifications of the valuers.

[*9A Sch Part I, para 63; SI 1993 No 3246*].

6.28   *Investments*

In respect of the amount of each item in the balance sheet under Assets item C (investments) there must be stated how much relates to 'listed investments'.

'Listed investments' are those listed on a recognised stock exchange, or on a stock exchange of repute outside Great Britain.

[*9A Sch Part I, paras 65, 81; SI 1993 No 3246; SI 1996 No 189, 5 Sch 9*].

6.29   *Reserves and provisions*

Where any amount is transferred

- to or from any reserves,

- to any provisions for other risks and charges, or

- from any such provisions, otherwise than for the purposes for which the provision was set up,

and the reserves or provisions are shown as separate items in the balance sheet (or would be so shown were it not for 6.5(*a*) above) the following information must be given in respect of the aggregate of reserves or provisions included in the same item.

- The amount of the reserves or provisions at the beginning of the financial year and at the balance sheet date.

- Any amounts transferred thereto or therefrom during the year.

- The source and application of the amounts transferred during the year.

Where the amount of the provision is material, particulars must be given of each provision included in Liabilities item E.3 (other provisions) in the balance sheet format.

Comparative figures for the preceding year (see 6.24 above) are not required for any of the above information.

[*9A Sch Part I, paras 54(3), 66; SI 1993 No 3246; SI 1996 No 189, 5 Sch 6, 10*].

Provision for deferred taxation. The amount of any provision for deferred taxation must be stated separately from that of any provision for other taxation. [*9A Sch Part I, para 67; SI 1993 No 3246*].

See 2.1 ACCOUNTS: DEFINITIONS for the meaning of '*provision*'.

6.30   *Indebtedness*

Creditors. In respect of each item shown in the balance sheet under 'creditors' (or which would be shown there were it not for 6.5(*a*)(ii) above) the following information is required.

(*a*)   The amount of any debts included under that item which are payable or repayable otherwise than by instalments and which fall due for payment or for repayment after the end of a five-year period beginning with the day after the end of the financial year.

(*b*)   In the case of any debts so included which are payable or repayable by instalments, the amount of any instalments which fall due after the end of the period specified in (*a*) above.

(*c*)   The aggregate amount of debts included under that item in respect of which the company has given any security.

(*d*)   An indication of the nature of the securities given.

Where a distinction is made in the balance sheet between amounts falling due to creditors within one year and those falling due after more than one year, (*a*) and (*b*) above apply only to items shown under the latter category and (*c*) above applies to items shown in either category.

For each debt falling to be taken into account under (*a*) and (*b*) above, the terms of payment and repayment and the rate of any interest payable must also be stated. If, however, in the directors' opinion, the number of debts involved is such that this statement would be of excessive length, it is sufficient to generally indicate the terms of payment or repayment and the rates of any interest payable.

[*9A Sch Part I, para 68; SI 1993 No 3246; SI 1996 No 189, 5 Sch 11; SI 1997 No 220, Reg 7*].

Fixed cumulative dividends. If any fixed cumulative dividends on the company's shares are in arrears, there must be stated the amount of arrears and the period for which the dividends (or each class of dividends if there is more than one) are in arrears. [*9A Sch Part I, para 69; SI 1993 No 3246*].

6.31   *Guarantees and other financial commitments*

The following information is required.

(*a*)   Particulars of any charge on the company's assets to secure the liabilities of any other person including, where practicable, the amount secured.

(*b*)   With respect to any other contingent liability not provided for (other than a contingent liability arising out of an insurance contract)

- its amount or estimated amount;

- its legal nature; and

- whether any, and if so, what valuable security has been provided by the company in connection with the liability.

(*c*)   Where practicable, the aggregate amount or estimated amount of contracts for capital expenditure, so far as not provided for.

(*d*)   Particulars of any pension commitments included under any provision shown in the balance sheet and of any such commitments for which no provision has been made, giving separate particulars of any commitment to the extent that it relates to pensions payable to past directors.

(*e*)   Particulars of any other financial commitments (other than commitments arising out of insurance contracts) which have not been provided for and are relevant to assessing the company's state of affairs.

Commitments within any of (*a*)–(*e*) above which are undertaken on behalf of or for the benefit of

(i)   any parent undertaking or fellow subsidiary undertaking, or

(ii)   any subsidiary undertaking of the company

must be stated separately for other commitments within each of (*a*)–(*e*) above, distinguishing between commitments within (i) and those within (ii) above.

[*9A Sch Part I, para 70; SI 1993 No 3246; SI 1996 No 189, 5 Sch 12*].

6.32   *Dealings with or interests in group undertakings*

For financial years ending before 2 February 1996 only, where a company is a parent company or a subsidiary undertaking, if any item required to be shown in the balance sheet in relation to group undertakings includes amounts attributable to dealings with or interest in

(*a*)   any parent undertaking or fellow subsidiary, or

(*b*)   any subsidiary undertaking of the company,

the aggregate amounts (within each of (*a*) and (*b*)) must be shown as separate items, either by subdivision in the balance sheet or by way of a note to the accounts.

[*9A Sch Part I, para 71; SI 1993 No 3246; SI 1996 No 189, 5 Sch 13*].

6.33   *Miscellaneous*

The following information must be given.

•   Particulars of any case where the cost of any asset is for the first time determined under *9A Sch 41* (see 6.21 above).

•   The aggregate amount, for each item in question, of any outstanding loans authorised by *Sec 153(4)(b), (bb)* or *(c)* or *Sec 155* (see 8.19(*i*), (*j*) and 8.21 ACQUISITION OF OWN SHARES respectively) included under any item shown in the balance sheet.

[*9A Sch Part I, para 72; SI 1993 No 3246; SI 1996 No 189, 5 Sch 14*].

6.34   **Notes to the accounts: information supplementing the profit and loss account**

The information, as set out in 6.35 to 6.40 below must be given by way of notes to the accounts if not given in the company's accounts. [*9A Sch Part I, para 54; SI 1993 No 3246; SI 1996 No 189, 5 Sch 6*].

6.35   *Separate statement of loan interest*

The amount of interest on (or any similar charges in respect of)

•   bank loans and overdrafts, and

•   loans of any other kind made to the company

must be shown separately.

The provisions apply to interest and charges on all loans whether or not made on the security of debentures, but do not apply to loans from group undertakings.

[9A Sch Part I, paras 73(2); SI 1993 No 3246; SI 1996 No 189, 5 Sch 15].

[9A Sch Part I, paras 73(2), 85; SI 1993 No 3246; SI 1996 No 189, 5 Sch 15].

6.36   *Particulars of tax*

Particulars must be given of any special circumstances affecting liability in respect of taxation of profits, income or capital gains for the financial year in question and/or succeeding financial years.

In respect of each of the amounts shown under the items 'tax on [profit][loss] on ordinary activities' and 'tax on extraordinary [profit][loss]' in the profit and loss account the following amounts must be stated.

- The amount of the charge for UK corporation tax.
- The amount of any double taxation relief which has reduced that charge.
- The amount of the charge for UK income tax.
- The amount of the charge for taxation imposed outside the UK of profits, income and (so far as charged to revenue) capital gains.

[9A Sch Part I, para 74; SI 1993 No 3246; SI 1996 No 189, 5 Sch 16].

6.37   *Particulars of business*

(A)   *General business.* A company must disclose

(*a*)   gross premiums written,

(*b*)   gross premiums earned,

(*c*)   gross claims incurred,

(*d*)   gross operating expenses, and

(*e*)   the reinsurance balance.

If reinsurance acceptances amount to 10% or more of gross premiums rewritten, the amounts under (*a*)–(*e*) above must be broken down between direct insurance and reinsurance acceptances.

The amounts required to be disclosed above with respect to direct insurances must be further broken down into the following groups of classes

(i)   accident and health,

(ii)   motor (third party liability),

(iii)   motor (other classes),

(iv)   marine, aviation and transport,

(v)   fire and other damage to property,

(vi)   third-party liability,

(vii)   credit and suretyship,

(viii)   legal expenses,

(ix)   assistance, and

(x)   miscellaneous

where the amount of the gross premiums written for any group exceeds 10 million ECUs. For this purpose the exchange rate between sterling and the ECU to be applied for each financial year is the rate applicable in the last day of the preceding October for which rates of currencies were published in the Official Journal of the Communities.

In any event, the company *must* disclose the amounts relating to the three largest groups of classes in its business under (i)–(x) above.

[*9A Sch Part I, paras 75, 81; SI 1993 No 3246*].

(B)   *Long term business.* A company must disclose

(*a*)   gross premiums written. Subject to below, this must be broken down between direct insurance premiums and reinsurance premiums and the direct insurance premiums must be further broken down between

(i)   individual premiums and premiums under group contracts;

(ii)   periodic premiums and single premiums; and

(iii)   premiums from non-participating contracts, premiums from participating contracts and premiums from contracts where the investment risk is borne by policy holders; and

(*b*)   the reinsurance balance.

Disclosure of any of the break-down figures under (*a*) above is not required if it does not exceed 10% of the gross premiums written or (as the case may be) 10% of the gross premiums written by way of direct insurance.

[*9A Sch Part I, para 76, SI 1993 No 3246*].

(C)   *General and long term business.* A company must disclose the total gross direct insurance premiums resulting from contracts concluded by the company

(*a*)   in the member state of its head office,

(*b*)   in the other member states, and

(*c*)   in other countries

except that any amount within (*a*)–(*c*) above need not be disclosed if it does not exceed 5% of the total gross premiums.

[*9A Sch Part I, para 77; SI 1993 No 3246*].

6.38   *Commissions*

There must be disclosed the total amount of commissions for direct insurance business accounted for in the financial year, including acquisition, renewal, collection and portfolio management commissions. [*9A Sch Part I, para 78; SI 1993 No 3246*].

6.39   *Particulars of staff*

There must be stated

(*a*)   the 'average number of persons employed' by the company in the financial year; and

(*b*)   the average number of persons so employed within each category of persons employed by the company (the categories being such as the directors may select having regard to the manner in which the company's activities are organised).

The '*average number of persons employed*' is calculated by the formula

$$\frac{A}{B}$$

where

A = the sum of the numbers of persons who, under contracts of service, were employed by the company in each month of the financial year whether throughout it or not (or, where applicable, the numbers so employed within a particular category)

B = the number of months in the financial year.

[*9A Sch Part I, para 79(1)–(3)(5); SI 1993 No 3246; SI 1996 No 189, 5 Sch 17*].

In respect of all employees taken into account in arriving at the average number in (*a*) above, there must be stated the aggregate amounts of each of the following.

- Wages and salaries paid or payable in respect of the financial year to those persons.
- 'Social security costs' incurred by the company on their behalf.
- Other 'pension costs' so incurred.

Any amount stated in respect of any of these items in the profit and loss account must be determined by reference to payments made or costs incurred in respect of those employees.

'*Social security costs*' means any contributions by the company to any state social security or pension scheme, fund or arrangement.

'*Pension costs*' includes any costs incurred by the company in respect of any pension scheme set up for current and former employees, any sums set aside for the future payment of pensions directly by the company to current or former employees and any pensions paid directly to such persons without having first been set aside.

[*9A Sch Part I, paras 79(4), 86; SI 1993 No 3246; SI 1996 No 189, 5 Sch 19*].

6.40 *Miscellaneous*

Prior year adjustments. Where any amount relating to any preceding financial year is included in any profit and loss account item, the effect must be stated. [*9A Sch Part I, para 80(1); SI 1993 No 3246*].

Extraordinary items. Particulars must be given of any extraordinary income or charges arising in the financial year. [*9A Sch Part I, para 80(2); SI 1993 No 3246*].

Exceptional items. The effect of any exceptional transactions (by size or incidence) must be stated, even though they fall within the company's ordinary activities. [*9A Sch Part I, para 80(3); SI 1993 No 3246*].

6.41 **Directors' emoluments, loans, quasi-loans and other dealings and transactions by other officers**

The provisions of 5.32 to 5.43 ACCOUNTS: INDIVIDUAL COMPANIES (disclosure of emoluments and other benefits of directors and others) apply to insurance companies as for other companies.

6.42 **Disclosure required in notes to the accounts: auditors' remuneration**

The provisions of 5.44 ACCOUNTS: INDIVIDUAL COMPANIES apply to insurance companies as for other companies.

6.43 Accounts: Insurance and Banking Companies

6.43 Disclosure required in notes to the accounts: related undertakings

The provisions in 5.45 to 5.53 ACCOUNTS: INDIVIDUAL COMPANIES apply to insurance companies as for other companies.

6.44 INSURANCE COMPANIES: GROUP ACCOUNTS

A parent company of an 'insurance group' *must* prepare group accounts in accordance with the special provisions in *9A Sch Part II* and the accounts must contain a statement to the effect.

An *'insurance group'* is a group in which

- the parent company is an insurance company; or

- the parent company does not itself carry on a material business (other than the acquisition of, management of, provision of services to, and disposal of interests in subsidiary undertakings) and its 'principal subsidiary undertakings' are wholly or mainly insurance companies. *'Principal subsidiary undertakings'* are the subsidiary undertakings of the company whose results or financial position would principally affect the figures shown in the group accounts.

[*Sec 255A(2)(3)(5)(5A); SI 1991 No 2705; SI 1993 No 3246, Reg 3*].

6.45 Meaning of 'parent' and 'subsidiary' undertaking and financial year

The provisions of 4.2 to 4.7 ACCOUNTS: GROUPS OF COMPANIES apply as for other groups of companies. [*Sec 255A(2); SI 1991 No 2705*].

6.46 Duty to prepare accounts

The provisions of 4.8 and 4.9 ACCOUNTS: GROUPS OF COMPANIES apply

- ignoring the reference to exemption for 'small' and 'medium-sized' groups in 4.8 (which provisions do not apply to insurance companies); and

- substituting a reference to *4A Sch as modified by 9A Sch Part II* for the reference to *4A Sch* in 4.8.

[*Sec 255A(2)(6); SI 1991 No 2705; SI 1993 No 3246*].

6.47 Exclusion of subsidiary companies from consolidation

The provisions of 4.10 ACCOUNTS: GROUPS OF COMPANIES apply as for other groups of companies. [*Sec 255A(2); SI 1991 No 2705*].

6.48 Treatment of individual profit and loss accounts where group accounts prepared

Where a parent company is required to prepare group accounts and does so, and the notes to its individual balance sheet show the company's profit or loss for the financial year (determined in accordance with *CA 1985*), then its individual profit and loss account

- need not contain the information otherwise required by *9A Sch Part I, paras 73, 74, 79, 80* (see 6.35, 6.36, 6.39 and 6.40 above respectively); and

- may be omitted from the company's annual accounts although it must still be approved by the board and signed by a director in accordance with 3.2 ACCOUNTS: GENERAL.

The above exemptions apply only if the company's annual accounts disclose the fact that they apply.

[*Sec 230, 255A(2)(6); SI 1991 No 2705; SI 1993 No 3246*].

6.49   Form and content of group accounts

Subject to the modifications below, the group accounts of an insurance company must comply, as far as practicable, with the provisions of *Sec 390A(3)* (auditors' remuneration, see 5.44 ACCOUNTS: INDIVIDUAL COMPANIES) and *9A Sch Part I* (see 6.5 to 6.40 above) as if the 'group' (meaning, for these purposes, all the undertakings included in the consolidation) were a single company.

Modifications. For the purposes of group accounts, the provisions of 6.5 to 6.40 above are modified as follows.

- The information required under 6.6 above need not be given.

- In the case of general business, investment income, expenses and charges may be disclosed in the non-technical account rather than the technical account.

- In 6.8 Notes (8) and (9), in the case of subsidiary undertakings not authorised to carry on long term business in Great Britain 'long term business' should be substituted for 'long term fund'.

- In 6.22(*d*), in the case of subsidiary undertakings which do not have a head office in Great Britain, the computation required must be made annually by an actuary or other specialist in the field on the basis of recognised actuarial methods.

- The information required by 6.37 and 6.38 above need not be shown.

[*4A Sch 1, 9A Sch Part II, paras 1(2), 2; SI 1993 No 3246; SI 1996 No 189, 2 Sch 2; SI 1997 No 220, Reg 7*].

The consolidated balance sheet and profit and loss account must incorporate in full the information contained in the individual accounts of the undertakings included in the consolidation. This is subject to the adjustments authorised or required under this paragraph and 6.50 to 6.55 below and any other adjustments that are appropriate in accordance with generally accepted accounting principles or practice.

If the financial year of a subsidiary undertaking included in the consolidation does not end with that of the parent company, the accounts of the subsidiary to be included in the group accounts are

- its accounts for the financial year last ending before the end of the parent company's financial year, but only if the gap is no more than six months; or

- interim accounts drawn up as at the end of the parent company's financial year.

[*4A Sch 2, 9A Sch Part II, para 1(3); CA 1989, 2 Sch; SI 1993 No 3246; SI 1996 No 189, 2 Sch 3*].

Assets and liabilities. Where assets and liabilities to be included in the group accounts have been valued or otherwise determined by undertakings under accounting rules which differ from those used for the group accounts, the values or amounts must be adjusted in line with the rules used for the group accounts (unless such adjustments are not material for the purposes of giving a true and fair view). This does not apply to liabilities valued under provisions applying only to insurance undertakings or asset changes in the value of which also affect or establish policy holders' rights (in either case it only being necessary to disclose that fact in the consolidated accounts).

If it appears to the parent company's directors that there are special reasons for doing so, they may depart from this requirement to adjust, but particulars of the departure, the

6.50 Accounts: Insurance and Banking Companies

reason for it and its effect must be given in a note to the accounts. [*4A Sch 3, 9A Sch Part II, para 1(4); CA 1989, 2 Sch; SI 1993 No 3246*].

Accounting rules. Any differences between accounting rules used for a parent company's individual accounts and those for its group accounts must be disclosed in a note to the group accounts, and the reason for the difference given. [*4A Sch 4; CA 1989, 2 Sch*].

Materiality. Amounts which in the particular context of any provision of *4A Sch* (see above and 6.50 to 6.55 below) are not material may be disregarded for the purposes of that provision. [*4A Sch 5; CA 1989, 2 Sch*].

6.50 *Elimination of group transactions*

Subject to below, in preparing group accounts, the following must be eliminated.

- Debts and claims between undertakings included in the consolidation.

- Income and expenditure relating to transactions between such undertakings.

- Profits and losses included in the book value of assets and resulting from transactions between such undertakings. This elimination may be effected in proportion to the group's interest in the shares of the undertaking concerned.

The above provisions need not be complied with

- where a transaction has been concluded according to normal market conditions and a policy holder has rights in respect of the transaction (in which case that fact must be disclosed in the notes to the accounts, and where the transaction has a material effect on assets, liabilities, financial position and profit and loss of all undertakings included in the consolidation, that fact must also be disclosed); and

- if the amounts concerned are not material for the purpose of giving a true and fair view, see 3.13 ACCOUNTS: GENERAL).

[*4A A Sch 6; 9A Sch Part II, para 1(5); CA 1989, 2 Sch; SI 1993 No 3246*].

6.51 *Acquisition and merger accounting*

The provisions of 4.4 to 4.17 ACCOUNTS: GROUPS OF COMPANIES apply as for other groups of companies.

6.52 *Minority interests*

An item headed 'Minority interests' is added to the balance sheet and profit and loss account formats set out in 6.5 and 6.8 above respectively.

Balance sheet format. The said item should appear under the heading 'LIABILITIES' between items A and B. Under this item, there must be shown the amount of capital and reserves attributable to shares (in subsidiary undertakings included in the consolidation) held by, or on behalf of, persons other than the parent company and its subsidiary undertakings. The power to combine items in the balance sheet under 6.5(*a*) above does not apply in relation to minority interests.

Profit and loss account formats. The said item should appear twice in Section III, between items 10 and 11 in respect of any profit or loss on ordinary activities and between items 14 and 15 in respect of any profit or loss on extraordinary activities. In each case, the profit or loss is that attributable to shares (in subsidiary undertakings included in the consolidation) held by, or on behalf of, persons other than the parent company and its subsidiary undertakings.

[*4A Sch 17, 9A Sch Part II, para 1(6); CA 1989, 2 Sch; SI 1993 No 3246*].

6.53 *Interests in subsidiary undertakings excluded from consolidation*

Where subsidiary undertakings have been excluded from consolidation under 4.10(*c*) ACCOUNTS: GROUPS OF COMPANIES, the interest of the group in those undertakings and the amount of the profit or loss attributable to that interest must be shown in the consolidated balance sheet and consolidated profit and loss account respectively. The equity method of accounting must be used, with any goodwill arising being dealt with in accordance with *9A Sch Part I, paras 31–33, 36* (see 6.18 above). [*4A Sch 18, 9A Sch Part II, para 1(7); CA 1989, 2 Sch; SI 1993 No 3246*].

6.54 *Joint ventures*

The provisions of 4.20 ACCOUNTS: GROUPS OF COMPANIES apply as for other groups of companies.

6.55 *Associated undertakings*

The balance sheet and profit and loss account formats in 6.5 and 6.8 above respectively are modified as described below, in relation to group accounts, to give information in respect of associated undertakings as defined in 4.21 ACCOUNTS: GROUPS OF COMPANIES.

Balance sheet format. Assets item C.II.3 is replaced by two items, 'Interest in associated undertakings' and 'Other participating interests'.

Profit and loss account. Items II.2(a) and III.3(a) are each replaced by two items, 'Income from participating interests other than associated undertakings' and 'Income from associated undertakings'.

The interest of an undertaking in an associated undertaking and the amount of the profit or loss attributable thereto are to be shown by the equity method of accounting, with any goodwill arising being dealt with in accordance with *9A Sch Part I, paras 31–33, 36* (see 6.18 above). [*4A Sch 20, 21, 9A Sch Part II, para 1(8)(9); CA 1989, 2 Sch; SI 1993 No 3246*].

6.56   Disclosures required in the notes to the accounts: related undertakings

The provisions of 4.23 to 4.32 ACCOUNTS: GROUPS OF COMPANIES apply as for other groups of companies.

6.57   MISCELLANEOUS INSURANCE COMPANIES: ACCOUNTS

Special provisions have been introduced by *The Insurance Accounts Directive (Miscellaneous Undertakings) Regulations 1993 (SI 1993 No 3245)* to implement *EC Council Directive 91/674/EEC* in so far as that *Directive* is applicable to insurance undertakings) whether bodies corporate or unincorporate) which are not subject to the *CA 1985* provisions or friendly societies. The *Regulations* also implement the *Directive* in so far as it is applicable to the Council of Lloyd's.

Directors of such bodies must prepare accounts and a directors' report, and obtain an auditors' report thereon, in accordance with the provisions of *CA 1985, Part VII* as they apply to insurance companies and groups, with certain modifications. The accounts prepared must be made available for inspection, without charge, at the body's head office in Great Britain. There are criminal penalties for failure to comply with the provisions.

See SI 1993 No 3245 for full details.

6.58   Accounts: Insurance and Banking Companies

6.58   INSURANCE COMPANIES: REQUIREMENT TO PUBLISH PERIODICAL STATEMENTS

Subject to the exceptions below, every insurance company and every deposit, provident and benefit society must, before it commences business, and on the first Monday in February and the first Tuesday in August in every year in which it carries on business, make a statement in the form set out below. A company which carries on insurance business with any other business(es) is deemed to be an insurance company.

* The share capital of the company is   , divided into   shares of   each.

The number of shares issued is

Calls to the amount of   pounds per share have been made, under which the sum of   pounds has been received.

The liabilities of the company on the first day of January (*or* July) were

Debts owing to sundry persons by the company.
On judgment (in Scotland, in respect of which decree has been granted), £
On speciality, £
On notes or bills, £
On simple contracts, £
On estimated liabilities, £

The assets of the company on that day were

Government securities [*stating them*]
Bills of exchange and promissory notes, £
Cash at the bankers, £
Other securities, £

* If the company has no share capital the portion of the statement relating to capital and shares must be omitted.

A copy of the statement must be put in a conspicuous place in the company's registered office and every branch office or place where the company's business is carried out. Every member and every creditor of the company is entitled to a copy, on payment of a sum not exceeding 2p.

Penalties. If the above provisions are not complied with, the company and every officer of it in default is liable to a fine up to the level in 40.1(*f*) PENALTIES.

[*Sec 720, 23, 24 Schs*].

Exceptions. The above provisions do not apply to

• an insurance company to which *Insurance Companies Act 1982, Part II* applies where the company complies with the provisions of that *Act* as to preparation and deposit of accounts; and

• an EU company which complies with the provisions of law of its home state as to the accounts and balance sheet to be prepared annually and deposited with the supervisory authority in that state.

[*Sec 720(6); SI 1994 No 1696, 8 Sch 9*].

6.59   BANKING COMPANIES AND GROUPS

The Secretary of State has power to modify the provisions of *Part VII*. [*Sec 257; CA 1989, s 20*]. Under these powers, the provisions relating to banking companies and groups were recast by *SI 1991 No 2704* and *SI 1991 No 2705* to implement *EC Council Directive 86/635/EEC*. These provisions came into force on 2 December 1991 and *must* be applied to annual accounts in respect of a financial year beginning on or after 23 December 1992.

Banking partnerships. The Secretary of State may, by regulations, apply the provisions of *Part VII*, modified if appropriate, to a *'banking partnership'* i.e. a partnership which is an authorised institution under *Banking Act 1987*. [*Sec 255D; CA 1989, s 18*].

6.60   BANKING COMPANIES – INDIVIDUAL ACCOUNTS

A banking company must prepare its individual accounts in accordance with the special provisions of *Secs 255, 255A* and *255B* and *9 Sch Parts I, III* and *IV* and the accounts must contain a statement to that effect. [*Sec 255(1)(3); SI 1991 No 2705*].

The provisions of 3 ACCOUNTS: GENERAL apply as for other companies.

6.61   Duty to prepare accounts

The directors of every company must prepare, for each financial year of the company, a balance sheet as at the last day of the year and a profit and loss account. The accounts must respectively give a true and fair view of the state of the company's affairs as at the end of the financial year and of its profit or loss for that year. These accounts are referred to collectively as the company's *'individual accounts'*. See 2.1 ACCOUNTS: DEFINITIONS for *'financial year'*.

A company's individual accounts must comply with the provisions of *9 Sch Part I* as described in 6.62 to 6.105 below as to the form and content of the balance sheet and profit and loss account and additional information to be provided by way of notes to the accounts. If compliance with these provisions and other provisions of *CA 1985* (see 6.106 to 6.108 below) as to matters to be included in individual accounts or in notes thereto is insufficient to meet the 'true and fair view' requirement above, such additional information as is necessary must be given in the accounts or notes. If in special circumstances, compliance with any of those provisions would be inconsistent with the 'true and fair view' requirement, the directors must, to the extent necessary, depart from that provision, but any such departure, the reasons for it and its effect must be given in a note to the accounts.

[*Secs 226, 255(4); CA 1989, s 4; SI 1991 No 2705*].

See 3.13 ACCOUNTS: GENERAL for *'true and fair view'*.

6.62   Form and content – general rules

Every balance sheet of a company must show the items listed in the format in 6.63 below, and every profit and loss account must show the items listed in either of the formats in 6.69 below, in either case in the order and under the headings and sub-headings given in the format adopted, except that no item need be distinguished by any number or letter assigned to that item in the format adopted. Where the heading of any item contains wording in square brackets, that wording may be omitted if not applicable to the company. Any item required to be shown may be shown in greater detail than required by the format adopted. Any item representing or covering the amount of any asset or liability, income or expenditure, not otherwise covered by any item listed in the format adopted, may be included, except that none of the following items can be treated as assets in the balance sheet.

- Preliminary expenses.

- Expenses of, and commission on, any issue of shares or debentures.

- Costs of research.

Headings and sub-headings listed in the formats need not be included if there is no amount to be shown, either for the current or the preceding financial year (see below), for items thereunder.

[*9 Sch Part I, paras 1, 3(1)(2)(4), 4(3); SI 1991 No 2705*].

As regards items to which lower case letters are assigned in any of the formats in 6.63 and 6.69 below, such items may be combined in the accounts for any financial year if

(i)   their individual amounts are not material for the purpose of giving a true and fair view; or

(ii)   the combination facilitates the assessment of the state of affairs or profit or loss of the company for that year (but in this case the individual items must be disclosed in a note to the accounts).

[*9 Sch Part I, para 3(3); SI 1991 No 2705*].

Consistency in use of formats. Where a company's profit and loss account for any financial year has been prepared in accordance with one of the said formats, the same format must be adopted for subsequent financial years unless, in the opinion of the directors, there are special reasons for a change. Any change, and the reasons for it, must be disclosed in a note to the accounts in which the new format is first adopted. [*9 Sch Part I, para 2; SI 1991 No 2705*].

Profit and loss accounts. Every profit and loss account must show separately as additional items

- any amount set aside to, or withdrawn from, reserves (or proposed to be so set aside or withdrawn);

- the aggregate amount of any dividends paid and proposed; and

- the aggregate amount of any dividends proposed (if not shown in the notes to the accounts).

[*9 Sch Part I, para 8; SI 1991 No 2705; SI 1996 No 189, 4 Sch 2*].

Set-offs. Amounts in respect of items representing assets or income may not be set off against amounts representing liabilities or expenditure, or vice versa (except for corresponding items in Profit and Loss Format 1, items 11 and 12 or items 13 and 14 and in Format 2, items A7 and B5 or A8 and B6. [*9 Sch Part I, para 5; SI 1991 No 2705*].

Pledged assets. Assets must be shown under the relevant balance sheet heading even where the company has pledged them as security for its own liabilities or those of a third party or has otherwise assigned them as security to third parties. Assets pledged or otherwise assigned to the company as security must not be included as assets unless in the form of cash in the hands of the company. [*9 Sch Part I, para 6; SI 1991 No 2705*].

Assets acquired in the name of, or on behalf of, third parties must not be shown in the balance sheet. [*9 Sch Part I, para 7; SI 1991 No 2705*].

Preceding financial year. For every item in the balance sheet or profit and loss account, the corresponding amount for the immediately preceding financial year must also be shown. Where it is not comparable with that for the current year, the corresponding amount for the preceding year must be adjusted. Particulars of, and the reasons for, the adjustment must be disclosed in a note to the accounts. [*9 Sch Part I, para 4(1)(2); SI 1991 No 2705*].

Materiality. Amounts which in the particular context of any provision of *9 Sch Part I* (see above and 6.63 to 6.105 below) are not material may be disregarded for the purposes of that provision. [*9 Sch Part I, para 84; SI 1991 No 2705*].

Provisions. References in *9 Sch Part I* (see above and 6.63 to 6.105 below) to provisions for depreciation or diminution in value of assets are to any amount written off by way of providing for depreciation or diminution in value of assets. References to provisions for liabilities or charges are to any retained as reasonably necessary for the purpose of providing for any liability or loss which is either likely to be incurred, or certain to be incurred but uncertain as to amount or as to the date on which it will arise. [*9 Sch Part I, para 85; SI 1991 No 2705*].

Listed companies. In addition to the requirements of *CA 1985*, listed companies must also comply with the requirements of the *Listing Rules, Chapter 12.41–12.44* as to the content of annual accounts. See 43.15 PUBLIC AND LISTED COMPANIES.

6.63   **Balance sheet format**

The balance sheet format set out in *9 Sch Part I* and referred to in 6.62 above is reproduced below, and is followed by notes to certain of the items listed therein.

ASSETS

1.   Cash and balances at central [or post office] banks (note (1))
2.   Treasury bills and other eligible bills (note (20))
     (*a*)   Treasury bills and similar securities (note (2))
     (*b*)   Other eligible bills (note (3))
3.   Loans and advances to banks (notes (4) and (20))
     (*a*)   Repayable on demand
     (*b*)   Other loans and advances
4.   Loans and advances to customers (notes (5) and (20))
5.   Debt securities [and other fixed income securities] (notes (6) and (20))
     (*a*)   Issued by public bodies
     (*b*)   Issued by other issuers
6.   Equity shares [and other variable-yield securities]
7.   Participating interests
8.   Shares in group undertaking
9.   Intangible fixed assets (note (7))
10. Tangible fixed assets (note (8))
11. Called up capital not paid (note (9))
12. Own shares (note (10))
13. Other assets
14. Called up capital not paid (note (9))
15. Prepayments and accrued income

Total assets

LIABILITIES

1.   Deposits by banks (notes (11) and (20))
     (*a*)   Repayable on demand
     (*b*)   With agreed maturity dates or periods of notice
2.   Customer accounts (notes (12) and (20))
     (*a*)   Repayable on demand
     (*b*)   With agreed maturity dates or periods of notice
3.   Debt securities in issue (notes (13) and (20))
     (*a*)   Bonds and medium term notes
     (*b*)   Others

4.   Other liabilities
5.   Accruals and deferred income
6.   Provisions for liabilities and charges
     (*a*)   Provisions for pensions and similar obligations
     (*b*)   Provisions for tax
     (*c*)   Other provisions
7.   Subordinated liabilities (notes (14) and (20))
8.   Called up share capital (note (15))
9.   Share premium account
10.   Reserves
     (*a*)   Capital redemption reserve
     (*b*)   Reserve for own shares
     (*c*)   Reserves provided for by the articles of association
     (*d*)   Other reserves
11.   Revaluation reserve
12.   Profit and loss account

Total liabilities

MEMORANDUM ITEMS

1.   Contingent liabilities (note (16))
     (1)   Acceptances and endorsements
     (2)   Guarantees and assets pledged as collateral security (note (17))
     (3)   Other contingent liabilities
2.   Commitments (note (18))
     (1)   Commitments arising out of sale and option to resell transactions (note (19))
     (2)   Other commitments

Notes

(1)   *Cash and balances at central [or post office] banks.* Cash comprises all currency including foreign notes and coins. Only balances withdrawable without notice and deposited with central banks in the country or countries where the company is established are to be included. Other claims on central banks must be shown under Assets items 3 or 4.

(2)   *Treasury bills etc. (Assets item 2(a)).* This comprises Treasury bills and similar debt instruments issued by public bodies which arc eligible for refinancing with central banks of the country or countries in which the company is established. Treasury bills, etc. not so eligible must be included under Assets item 5(*a*).

(3)   *Treasury bills etc. (Assets item 2(b)).* This comprises all bills eligible under national law for refinancing with central banks of the country or countries in which the company is established.

(4)   *Loans and advances to banks.* These comprise all loans etc. to domestic or foreign credit institutions arising out of transactions entered into in the normal course of deposit-taking business (unless represented by debt or other fixed income securities which must be included under Assets item 5).

(5)   *Loans and advances to customers.* These comprise all types of assets in the form of claims on domestic and foreign customers other than credit institutions (unless represented by debt or other fixed income securities which must be included under Assets item 5).

(6)   *Debt securities, etc.* This comprises transferable debt securities etc. issued by credit institutions, other undertakings and public bodies (in the latter case only if not

shown under Assets item 2). Where a company holds its own debt securities these must not be included here but deducted from Liabilities item 3(*a*) or (*b*) as appropriate. Securities with interest rates varying with specific factors (e.g inter-bank market or Euromarket rates) are regarded as fixed income securities.

(7)   *Intangible fixed assets* comprise

(*a*)   development costs;
(*b*)   concessions, patents, licences, trade marks and similar rights and assets;
(*c*)   goodwill; and
(*d*)   payments on account.

Amounts are included under (*b*) only if the assets in question were either acquired for valuable consideration or created by the company itself. Amounts representing goodwill are to be included only to the extent that the goodwill was acquired for valuable consideration and the amount of goodwill, if any, must be disclosed separately in the notes to the accounts.

(8)   *Tangible fixed assets* comprise

- land and buildings;
- plant and machinery;
- fixtures and fittings, tools and equipment; and
- payments on account and assets in the course of construction.

There must be disclosed in a note to the accounts the amount of any land and buildings included in this item which is occupied by the company for its own activities.

(9)   *Called up capital not paid.* The two positions shown for this item are alternatives.

(10)   *Own shares.* The nominal value of the shares held must be shown separately.

(11)   *Deposits by banks.* This comprises all amounts arising out of bank transactions owed to other domestic or foreign credit institutions (except for liabilities in the form of debt securities or for which transferable certificates have been issued which must be included under Liabilities item 3).

(12)   *Customer accounts.* This comprises all amounts owed to creditors who are not credit institutions (subject to the same exception as in (11) above).

(13)   *Debt securities in issue.* This includes debt securities and debts for which transferable certificates have been issued, including liabilities arising out of own acceptances and promissory notes. (Only acceptances which a company has issued for its own refinancing and in respect of which it is the first party liable are to be treated as acceptances.)

(14)   *Subordinated liabilities.* This comprises all liabilities where there is a contractual obligation that, in the event of a winding up or bankruptcy, they are to be repaid only after the claims of other creditors.

(15)   *Called up share capital.* The amount of allotted share capital and the amount of called up share capital which has been paid up must be shown separately.

(16)   *Contingent liabilities.* This is to include all transactions whereby the company has underwritten the obligations of a third party; liabilities arising out of the endorsement of rediscounted bills; and acceptances other than own acceptances.

(17)   *Contingent liabilities – guarantees etc.* This includes all guarantee obligations incurred and assets pledged as collateral security on behalf of third parties (particularly in respect of sureties and irrevocable letters of credit).

(18) *Commitments.* This must include every irrevocable commitment which could give rise to a credit risk.

(19) *Commitments arising out of sale transactions, etc.* This comprises commitments entered into by the company in the context of sale and option to resell transactions.

(20) *Claims on, and liabilities to, undertakings in which a participating interest is held or group undertakings* must be shown in respect of Assets items 2 to 5 and Liabilities items 1 to 3 and 7. This may be done by sub-dividing the relevant items or by way of note to the accounts.

[*9 Sch Part I, Section B; SI 1991 No 2705*].

6.64 *Subordinated assets*

The amount of any asset 'subordinated' must be shown either as a subdivision of any relevant asset item or in the notes to the accounts. Any assets which must be disclosed under note (20) in 6.63 above must be further subdivided to show the amount of any claims which are subordinated.

Assets are *'subordinated'* for this purpose if there is a contractual obligation that, in the event of a winding up or bankruptcy, they are to be repaid only after the claims of other creditors.

[*9 Sch Part I, para 11; SI 1991 No 2705*].

6.65 *Syndicated loans*

Where the company is party to a syndicated loan transaction

• it must include only that part of the loan which it has funded itself; and

• if it has agreed to reimburse any other party to the syndicate upon the occurrence of any event, any additional liability by reason of such guarantee must be included as a contingent liability in Memorandum item 1(2) (see 6.63 above).

[*9 Sch Part I, para 12; SI 1991 No 2705*].

6.66 *Sale and repurchase transactions*

Where the company is a party to a 'sale and repurchase transaction'

• if it is the transferor of the assets, the assets transferred must (notwithstanding the transfer) be included in the balance sheet, the purchase price received must be included as an amount due to the transferee, and the value of the asset transferred must be disclosed in a note to the accounts; and

• if it is the transferee of the assets, the assets transferred must not be included in the balance sheet but the purchase price must be included as an amount owed by the transferor.

A *'sale and repurchase transaction'* is a transaction which involves the transfer by a credit institution or customer ('the transferor') to another credit institution or customer ('the transferee') of assets subject to an agreement that the same or (in the case of fungible assets) equivalent assets will be transferred back to the transferor at a specified price on a date specified (or to be specified) by the transferor. Forward exchange transactions, options and transactions involving the issue of debt securities with a commitment to repurchase before maturity are specifically excluded.

[*9 Sch Part I, paras 13, 82; SI 1991 No 2705*].

6.67   *Sale and option to resell transactions*

Where the company is party to a 'sale and option to resell transaction'

- if it is the transferor of the assets, the assets transferred must not be included in the balance sheet but the price agreed in the event of a repurchase must be entered under Memorandum item 2 (see 6.63 above); and

- if it is the transferee of the assets, the assets must be included in the balance sheet.

A *'sale and option to resell transaction'* is a transaction which involves the transfer by a credit institution or customer ('the transferor') to another credit institution or customer ('the transferee') of assets subject to an agreement that the transferee is entitled to require the subsequent transfer of the same assets or (in the case of fungible assets) equivalent assets back to the transferor at the purchase price or another price agreed in advance on a date specified (or to be specified).

[9 Sch Part I, paras 14, 82; SI 1991 No 2705].

6.68   *Managed funds*

Where claims and obligations arising in respect of 'managed funds' fall to be treated as claims and obligations of the company, they must be included in the company's balance sheet. The notes to the accounts must disclose the total amounts of such assets and liabilities and the amount included under each relevant balance sheet item.

'Managed funds' are funds which the company administers in its own name but on behalf of others and to which it has legal title.

[9 Sch Part I, para 15; SI 1991 No 2705].

6.69   **Profit and loss account formats**

The two profit and loss account formats set out in *9 Sch* and referred to in 6.62 above are reproduced below, and are followed by notes to certain of the items listed therein.

Format 1 — Vertical layout

1.   Interest receivable (note (1))
     (1)   Interest receivable and similar income arising from debt securities [and other fixed income securities]
     (2)   Other interest receivable and similar income
2.   Interest payable (note (2))
3.   Dividend income
     (*a*)   Income from equity shares [and other variable-yield securities]
     (*b*)   Income from participating interests
     (*c*)   Income from shares in group undertakings
4.   Fees and commissions receivable (note (3))
5.   Fees and commissions payable (note (4))
6.   Dealing [profits][losses] (note (5))
7.   Other operating income
8.   Administrative expenses
     (*a*)   Staff costs
          (i)   Wages and salaries
          (ii)   Social security costs
          (iii) Other pension costs
     (*b*)   Other administrative expenses

9.   Depreciation and amortisation (note (6))
10.   Other operating charges
11.   Provisions
    (*a*)   Provisions for bad and doubtful debts (note (7))
    (*b*)   Provisions for contingent liabilities and commitments (note (8))
12.   Adjustments to provisions
    (*a*)   Adjustments to provisions for bad and doubtful debts (note (9))
    (*b*)   Adjustments to provisions for contingent liabilities and commitments (note (10))
13.   Amounts written off fixed asset investments (note (11))
14.   Adjustments to amounts written off fixed asset investments (note (12))
15.   [Profit][loss] on ordinary activities before tax
16.   Tax on [profit][loss] on ordinary activities
17.   [Profit][loss] on ordinary activities after tax
18.   Extraordinary income
19.   Extraordinary charges
20.   Extraordinary [profit][loss]
21.   Tax on extraordinary [profit][loss]
22.   Extraordinary [profit][loss] after tax
23.   Other taxes not shown under preceding items
24.   [Profit][loss] for the financial year

Format 2 — horizontal layout

A.   Charges
1.   Interest payable (note (2))
2.   Fees and commissions payable (note (4))
3.   Dealing losses (note (5))
4.   Administrative expenses
    (*a*)   Staff costs
        (i)   Wages and salaries
        (ii)   Social security costs
        (iii)   Other pension costs
    (*b*)   Other administrative expenses
5.   Depreciation and amortisation (note (6))
6.   Other operating charges
7.   Provisions
    (*a*)   Provisions for bad and doubtful debts (note (7))
    (*b*)   Provisions for contingent liabilities and commitments (note (8))
8.   Amounts written off fixed asset investments (note (11))
9.   Profit on ordinary activities before tax
10.   Tax on [profit][loss] on ordinary activities
11.   Profit on ordinary activities after tax
12.   Extraordinary charges
13.   Tax on extraordinary [profit][loss]
14.   Extraordinary loss after tax
15.   Other taxes not shown under preceding items
16.   Profit for the financial year

B. Income
1.   Interest receivable (note (1))
    (1)   Interest receivable and similar income arising from debt securities [and other fixed income securities]
    (2)   Other interest receivable and similar income
2.   Dividend income

    (*a*)   Income from equity shares [and other variable-yield securities]
    (*b*)   Income from participating interests
    (*c*)   Income from shares in group undertakings

3.   Fees and commissions receivable (note (3))
4.   Dealing profits (note (5))
5.   Adjustments to provisions
    (*a*)   Adjustments to provisions for bad and doubtful debts (note (9))
    (*b*)   Adjustments to provisions for contingent liabilities and commitments (note (10))
6.   Adjustments to amounts written off fixed asset investments (note (12))
7.   Other operating income
8.   Loss on ordinary activities before tax
9.   Loss on ordinary activities after tax
10.   Extraordinary income
11.   Extraordinary profit after tax
12.   Loss for the financial year

Notes

(1)   *Interest receivable.* This must include all income arising out of banking activities (i.e. activities forming part of a deposit-taking business within *Banking Act 1987*), including

* income from assets in Asset items 1 to 5 in the balance sheet format;

* income resulting from covered forward contracts spread over the actual duration of the contract and similar in nature to interest; and

* fees and commission receivable similar in nature to interest and calculated on a time basis or by reference to the amount of the claim.

(2)   *Interest payable.* This must include all expenditure arising out of banking activities (see (1) above), including

* charges arising out of liabilities included in Liabilities items 1 to 3 and 7 in the balance sheet format;

* charges resulting from covered forward contracts spread over the actual duration of the contract and similar in nature to interest; and

* fees and commission payable similar in nature to interest and calculated on a time basis or by reference to the amount of the liability.

(3)   *Fees and commissions receivable.* These comprise income in respect of all services supplied to third parties (except those within note (1) above) and in particular fees and commissions for

* guarantees, loan administration on behalf of other lenders and securities transactions;

* payment transactions and charges for account administration, safe custody and administration of securities;

* foreign currency transactions and sale and purchase of coin and precious metals; and

* brokerage services in connection with savings and insurance contracts and loans.

(4)   *Fees and commissions payable.* These comprise charges in respect of all services rendered by third parties (except those within note (2) above). Included are fees and commissions payable as listed in note (3) above.

(5)   *Dealing profits and losses.* These comprise the net profit or loss on

- transactions in securities not held as financial fixed assets, together with any amounts written off or back on such securities;

- exchange activities (unless included in interest receivable or payable – see notes (1) and (2) above); and

- other dealing operations involving financial instruments, including precious metals.

(6)   *Depreciation and amortisation* comprises depreciation and other amounts written off balance sheet items 9 and 10.

(7)   *Provisions for bad and doubtful debts* comprise charges for amounts written off and for provisions made in respect of loans and advances under balance sheet items 3 and 4.

(8)   *Provisions for contingent liabilities and commitments.* This comprises charges for such provisions which would, if not provided for, be shown under Memorandum items 1 and 2.

(9)   *Adjustments to provisions for bad debts* includes credits from recovery of loans and advances written off and from the reduction of provisions previously made.

(10)   *Adjustments to provisions for contingent liabilities and commitments* comprises credits from the reduction of provisions previously made.

(11)   *Amounts written off fixed asset investments* comprise amounts written off assets included in Asset items 5 to 8 and which are transferable securities held as financial fixed assets, participating interests or shares in group undertakings.

(12)   *Adjustments to amounts written off fixed asset investments* include amounts written back following earlier write offs and provisions of assets within note (11) above.

[*9 Sch Part I, Section B; SI 1991 No 2705*].

Staff costs. See 6.102 below for meaning of 'social security costs' and 'pension costs' and for the determination of the amounts to be stated in the profit and loss account in respect of these items and in respect of the item 'wages and salaries'.

Depreciation etc. References in the formats to the depreciation of, or amounts written off, assets of any description are to any provision for depreciation or diminution in value of assets of that description. [*9 Sch 85; SI 1991 No 2705*].

6.70   Accounting principles

The amounts to be included in respect of all items shown in the accounts are to be determined in accordance with the principles set out below, except that if it appears to the directors that there are special reasons for departing from any of these principles for a financial year, they may do so, but particulars of the departure, the reasons for it and its effect must be given in a note to the accounts.

(*a*)   The company must be presumed to be carrying on business as a going concern.

(*b*)   Accounting policies must be applied consistently, both within the same accounts and from one financial year to the next.

(*c*)   The amount of any item is to be determined on a prudent basis, and in particular

(i)   only profits realised at the balance sheet date are to be included in the profit and loss account; and

(ii)   all liabilities and losses which have arisen, or are likely to arise, in respect of the financial year to which the accounts relate or a previous financial year must be taken into account; this includes any such liabilities and losses which became apparent after the balance sheet date but before the date on which the balance sheet is signed on behalf of the board (see 3.2 ACCOUNTS: GENERAL). Where revised accounts are prepared under *Sec 245* (see 3.9 ACCOUNTS: GENERAL), it is the date on which the original accounts were signed that is taken into account for this purpose.

(*d*)   All income and charges relating to the financial year to which the accounts relate must be taken into account regardless of the date of receipt or payment.

(*e*)   In determining the aggregate amount of any item, the amount of each individual asset or liability that falls to be taken into account must be determined separately.

[*9 Sch Part I, paras 16-22; SI 1991 No 2705*].

6.71   Accounting rules: historical cost

The rules described in 6.72 to 6.75 below apply to determine the amounts to be included in respect of all items in the accounts, and are known as the historical cost accounting rules, but see 6.76 below for alternative rules. [*9 Sch Part I, para 23; SI 1991 No 2705*].

6.72   *Fixed assets*

General. Fixed assets are to be included at their 'cost' (see 6.75 below). For this purpose, assets included in Assets items 9 (intangible fixed assets) and 10 (tangible fixed assets) in the balance sheet format must be valued as fixed assets. Other assets in the balance sheet must be valued as fixed assets where they are intended for use on a continuing basis in the company's activities. See below for financial fixed assets.

In the case of a fixed asset with a limited useful economic life, cost (or cost less any estimated residual value at the end of the asset's useful economic life) is to be reduced by provisions for depreciation calculated to write off the said amount systematically over the asset's useful economic life.

Provisions for diminution in value may be made in respect of any fixed asset investment of a description falling to be included under Assets items 7 or 8 in the balance sheet format in 6.63 above or any other holding of securities held as a financial fixed asset, the amount to be included in respect of that asset being reduced accordingly. Such provisions must also be made in respect of any fixed asset which has suffered what is expected to be a permanent reduction in value (whether or not its useful economic life is limited). Where the reasons for any provision for diminution in value have ceased to apply to any extent, it may be written back (to the extent necessary). Any such provisions or amounts written back, where not shown in the profit and loss account, must be disclosed (either separately or in aggregate) in a note to the accounts.

[*9 Sch Part I, paras 24-26, 29, 30; SI 1991 No 2705*].

Goodwill. Where goodwill acquired by a company is treated as an asset, the amount of consideration given must be reduced by provisions for depreciation calculated to write off that amount over a period of the directors' choosing, which must not exceed the useful economic life of that goodwill. Where any amount for goodwill is included as an asset in the balance sheet, the writing-off period chosen, and the reasons for that choice, must be disclosed in a note to the accounts. [*9 Sch Part I, para 28; SI 1991 No 2705*].

6.73 Accounts: Insurance and Banking Companies

Development costs. An amount may be included in the balance sheet in respect of development costs only in special circumstances, and if any amount is so included, there must be given in a note to the accounts the reasons for capitalising those costs and the period over which the amount originally capitalised is being, or is to be, written off. [*9 Sch Part I, para 27; SI 1991 No 2705*].

Financial fixed assets. Debts securities (including fixed income securities) held as financial fixed assets must be included in the balance sheet at their maturity value plus any premium/(less any discount) on their purchase. The amount included in the balance sheet in respect of securities purchased at a premium/(discount) must be reduced/(increased) each financial year so as to write the premium off/(extinguish the discount) over the period to maturity. The adjustments must be charged/(credited) to the profit and loss account for the relevant financial years. The amount of any unamortised premium/(discount not extinguished) included in the balance sheet must be disclosed in the notes to the accounts. [*9 Sch Part I, para 31; SI 1991 No 2705*].

6.73 *Current assets*

The amount to be included for

- loans and advances,

- debts or other fixed income securities, and

- equity shares or other variable yield securities not held as financial fixed assets

is their 'cost' (see 6.75 below) or, if lower, their net realisable value. Any provision for diminution in value previously made, i.e. to reduce the asset to its net realisable value, must be written back to the extent that the reasons for it have ceased to apply.

Transferable securities. Subject to the above, the amount to be included in respect of transferable securities not held as financial fixed assets may be the higher of their cost or market value at the balance sheet date, in which case the difference between cost and market value must be shown in aggregate in the notes to the accounts.

[*9 Sch Part I, paras 32-34; SI 1991 No 2705*].

6.74 *Excess of debt owed over value received*

Where the amount repayable on any debt owed by a company is greater than the value of the consideration received in the transaction giving rise to the debt, the amount of the difference may be treated as an asset. It must, however, be written off in reasonable amounts each year and be completely written off before repayment of the debt. If not shown as a separate item in the balance sheet, the current amount must be disclosed in a note to the accounts. [*9 Sch Part I, para 35; SI 1991 No 2705*].

6.75 *Meaning and determination of 'cost'*

The '*cost*' of an asset is the actual price paid plus any incidental expenses of acquisition.

The *cost of an asset constructed by the company* is the aggregate of the purchase price of the raw materials and consumables used and the costs incurred by the company which are directly attributable to the construction of that asset. In addition, there may be included

- a reasonable proportion of costs so incurred which are only indirectly so attributable, but only to the extent that they relate to the period of construction; and

- interest on capital borrowed to finance the construction of the asset, to the extent that it accrues in respect of the period of construction. The inclusion of interest and the amount so included must be disclosed in a note to the accounts.

[*9 Sch Part I, para 36; SI 1991 No 2705*].

Where there is no record of the purchase price (or of any price, expenses or costs relevant to its determination) of any asset, or any such record cannot be obtained without unreasonable expense or delay, then for the purposes of these provisions, the cost of that asset is to be taken to be the value ascribed to it in the earliest available record of its value made on or after its acquisition by the company. [*9 Sch Part I, para 38; SI 1991 No 2705*].

Fungible assets. The cost of any assets which are 'fungible' assets (including investments) may be determined by applying any of the following methods in relation to any such assets of the same class (the method chosen being such as appears to the directors to be appropriate in the company's circumstances).

- First in, first out (FIFO).
- Last in, first out (LIFO).
- A weighted average price.
- Any other method similar to any of the above.

Where, however, the result of such determination is that the amount shown in respect of any balance sheet item differs materially from the 'relevant alternative amount', the amount of the difference must be disclosed in a note to the accounts.

The *'relevant alternative amount'* is normally that which would have been shown in respect of the said item if assets of any class included under that item at an amount so determined had instead been included at their replacement cost as at the balance sheet date. If, however, the directors consider it a more appropriate standard of comparison in the case of assets of a particular class, the relevant alternative amount may instead be determined by reference to the most recent actual purchase price (before the balance sheet date) of assets of that class.

Assets of any particular description are to be regarded as *'fungible'* if such assets are substantially indistinguishable from one another.

[*9 Sch Part I, paras 37, 82; SI 1991 No 2705*].

6.76   Accounting rules: alternative to historical cost

Any of the accounting rules set out below may be used (as alternatives to those described in 6.71 to 6.75 above) in determining the amounts to be included in respect of items shown in a company's accounts (as specified).

(*a*)   *Intangible fixed assets*, other than goodwill, may be included at current cost.

(*b*)   *Tangible fixed assets* may be included at market value (as at the date of their last valuation) or at current cost.

(*c*)   *Investments* (of any description) falling to be included under Assets items 7 (participating interests) or 8 (shares in group undertakings) of the balance sheet format in 6.63 above or any other securities held as financial fixed assets may be included at

- market value (as at the date of their last valuation); or
- a value determined on any basis appearing to the directors to be appropriate in the company's circumstances, in which case particulars of, and the reasons

for, the method of valuation adopted must be disclosed in a note to the accounts.

(*d*)   *Securities* of any description not held as financial fixed assets (if not valued as under 6.73 above) may be included at current cost.

As regards any asset the value of which is determined on any basis in (*a*)-(*d*) above, that value (instead of cost or any value previously so determined) is to be (or is to be the starting point for determining) the amount to be included in the accounts. The value most recently determined is accordingly to be used (instead of cost) for the purpose of applying the rules described in 6.72 and 6.73 above for general fixed assets and current assets.

Where the asset in question is a fixed asset, any provision for depreciation in respect thereof which is included in the profit and loss account under the appropriate item would normally be so included at an amount calculated under the above rules. It may, however, be so included at an amount calculated under the historical cost accounting rules described for general fixed assets in 6.72 above, provided that any difference between the alternative amounts is separately disclosed either in the profit and loss account or in a note to the accounts.

[*9 Sch Part I, paras 40-42; SI 1991 No 2705*].

6.77   *Additional information to be provided*

Where the amount of any asset covered by any item in the accounts has been determined on any basis in 6.76(*a*)–(*d*) above, the following additional information must be disclosed in a note to the accounts or alternatively, in the case of (*b*) below only, shown separately in the balance sheet.

(*a*)   The item affected and the basis of valuation adopted in determining the amount of the assets in question for each such item.

(*b*)   For each balance sheet item affected either

(i)   the 'comparable amounts determined under the historical cost accounting rules'; or

(ii)   the differences between the amounts in (i) above and the actual amounts shown in the balance sheet in respect of that item.

The *'comparable amounts determined under the historical cost accounting rules'* comprise both

•   the aggregate amount which would be required to be shown if the amounts of all assets covered by the item concerned were determined according to the historical cost accounting rules (see 6.71 to 6.75 above); and

•   the aggregate amount of the cumulative provisions for depreciation or diminution in value which would be required or permitted in determining those amounts according to those rules.

[*9 Sch Part I, para 43; SI 1991 No 2705*].

6.78   **Revaluation reserve**

Any profit or loss arising from the determination of the value of an asset according to any basis in 6.76(*a*)-(*d*) above (after allowing for provisions for depreciation or diminution in value) must be credited or debited to a separate reserve, the *'revaluation reserve'*. The amount of the revaluation reserve must be shown (but not necessarily under that name) in the balance sheet under Liabilities item 11 in the balance sheet format in 6.63 above.

The revaluation reserve may be reduced to the extent that amounts transferred to it are no longer necessary for the purposes of the valuation method used. In addition, an amount may be transferred

- from the reserve to profit and loss account, if the amount was previously charged to that account or represents realised profit; or

- from the reserve on capitalisation, (i.e. by applying the amount in paying up (wholly or partly) unissued shares in the company to be allotted to the members as fully or partly paid shares, see BONUS ISSUES (13)); and.

- to or from the revaluation reserve in respect of taxation relating to any profit or loss credited or debited to the reserve.

The revaluation reserve must not be reduced other than as mentioned above.

The treatment for taxation purposes of amounts credited or debited to the revaluation reserve must be disclosed in a note to the accounts.

[*9 Sch Part I, para 44; SI 1991 No 2705; SI 1996 No 189, 4 Sch 3*].

6.79   Assets and liabilities denominated in foreign currencies

Any assets or liabilities denominated in foreign currencies (other than those held for hedging purposes or which are themselves hedged) must be translated into sterling at the appropriate spot rate of exchange prevailing at the balance sheet date with the following exceptions.

(*a*)   An appropriate spot rate at the date of purchase may be used for assets held as financial fixed assets and assets included under Assets items 9 (intangible fixed assets) and 10 (tangible fixed assets) in the balance sheet format (see 6.63 above), if they are not covered (or not specifically covered) in either the spot or forward currency markets.

(*b*)   An appropriate forward rate of exchange prevailing at the balance sheet date must be used for translating uncompleted forward exchange transactions (the spot rate must be used for uncompleted forward exchange transactions).

[*9 Sch Part I, para 45; SI 1991 No 2705*].

Any difference between the amount to be included in respect of an asset or liability under the above provisions and its book value (after translation into sterling) must be credited or debited to the profit and loss account. In the case, however of assets within (*a*) above and transactions undertaken to cover such assets, any difference may be deducted from or credited to any non-distributable reserve available for the purpose.

[*9 Sch Part I, para 46; SI 1991 No 2705*].

6.80   Notes to the accounts: general

Comparative figures. Except where otherwise stated in this chapter and in 4 ACCOUNTS: GROUPS OF COMPANIES, there must be shown, in respect of each item stated in a note to the accounts, the corresponding amount for the immediately preceding financial year. Where the corresponding amount is not comparable, it must be adjusted and particulars of, and reasons for, the adjustment must be disclosed. [*9 Sch Part I, para 47(2); SI 1991 No 2705*].

Foreign currency translation. Where any item in the profit and loss account or balance sheet includes sums originally denominated in foreign currencies, the basis of translation into sterling must be stated. [*9 Sch Part I, para 50; SI 1991 No 2705*].

6.81 Accounts: Insurance and Banking Companies

Disclosure of accounting policies. The accounting policies adopted in determining the profit or loss and the amounts of balance sheet items (including policies with respect to depreciation and diminution in value of assets) must be stated in 'the notes to the accounts. [*9 Sch Part I, para 48; SI 1991 No 2705*].

Accounting standards. It must also be stated whether the accounts have been prepared in accordance with applicable accounting standards (see 3.12 ACCOUNTS: GENERAL). Particulars of any material departure from those standards, and the reasons for it, must be given. [*9 Sch Part I, para 49; SI 1991 No 2705*].

Listed companies. In addition to the requirements of *CA 1985*, listed companies must also comply with the requirements of the *Listing Rules, Chapter 12.41-12.44* as to content of annual accounts. See 43.15 PUBLIC AND LISTED COMPANIES. The additional requirements may be shown in the directors' report or the notes to the accounts.

6.81 Notes to the accounts: information supplementing the balance sheet

The information required, as set out in 6.82 to 6.97 below must be given by way of a note to the accounts if not given in the company's accounts. [*9 Sch Part I, para 47(1); SI 1991 No 2705; SI 1996 No 189, 4 Sch 4*].

6.82 *Share capital and debentures*

Both the authorised share capital and, where shares of more than one class have been allotted, the number and aggregate nominal value of shares of each class allotted must be stated.

If any part of the allotted share capital consists of redeemable shares, the following information must be given.

- The earliest and latest dates on which the company has power to redeem those shares.

- Whether the shares must be redeemed in any event or are liable to be redeemed at either the company's or the shareholder's option.

- Whether any premium is payable on redemption, and, if so, the amount thereof.

The following information is required in respect of any shares allotted during the financial year.

(i) The classes of shares allotted.

(ii) As regards each class of shares, the number allotted, their aggregate nominal value, and the consideration received by the company for the allotment.

[*9 Sch Part I, paras 51, 52; SI 1991 No 2705; SI 1996 No 189, 4 Sch 5*].

With respect to any contingent right to the allotment of shares in the company, meaning any option to subscribe for shares and any other right to require the allotment of shares to any person (whether arising on the conversion into shares of securities of any description or otherwise), the following particulars must be given.

- The number, description and amount of shares in respect of which the right may be exercised.

- The period during which the right may be exercised.

- The price to be paid for the shares allotted.

Debentures. Similar information as in (i) and (ii) above is required in respect of any debentures issued during the financial year.

Where any of the company's debentures are held by a nominee or trustee for the company, both their nominal amount and the amount at which they are stated in the company's accounting records (see 45.1 RECORDS) must be stated.

[*9 Sch Part I, paras 53, 54; SI 1991 No 2705; SI 1996 No 189, 4 Sch 6*].

6.83   *Fixed assets*

The information set out below is required for any fixed assets of the company included in any assets item in the balance sheet.

(*a*)   The 'appropriate amounts' in respect of those assets both at the beginning of the financial year and at the balance sheet date.

(*b*)   The effect on any amount included in the item in respect of those assets of

- any determination during that year of the value ascribed to any of those assets on any basis in 6.76(*a*)–(*d*) above;

- acquisitions and disposals during that year; and

- any transfers of fixed assets of the company to or from that item during that year.

(*c*)   As regards provisions for depreciation or diminution in value of assets

- the cumulative amount of such provisions included under that item at each of the times specified in (*a*) above;

- the amount of any such provisions made in respect of that year; and

- the amounts of any adjustments made to any such provisions during that year, distinguishing between adjustments made in consequence of disposals and other adjustments.

Comparative figures for the preceding year (see 6.80 above) are not required for (*a*)-(*c*) above.

For the purposes of (*a*) above, the *'appropriate amounts'* in respect of any fixed assets at either of the times there mentioned are the aggregate amounts determined, as at that time, in respect of fixed assets falling to be included under that item, either on the basis of cost (see 6.75 above) or on any basis in 6.76(*a*)-(*d*) above (but, in either case, leaving out of account any provisions for depreciation or diminution in value).

[*9 Sch Part I, paras 47(3), 55; SI 1991 No 2705*].

The following additional information is required where any fixed assets (other than 'listed investments' – see 6.92 below) are included under any balance sheet item at an amount determined on any basis in 6.76(*a*)–(*d*) above.

- The years (so far as known to the directors) in which the assets were severally valued, and the several values.

- In the case of assets valued during the financial year, the bases of valuation used and either the names or relevant qualifications of the valuers.

[*9 Sch Part I, para 56; SI 1991 No 2705*].

Land and buildings. In relation to any amount included under Assets item 10 in the balance sheet format (tangible fixed assets) in respect of the land and buildings there must be stated how much of that amount is ascribable to freehold land (or Scottish equivalent) and how much to leasehold land (or Scottish equivalent), and, of the latter amount, how much is ascribable to *'long leases'* (i.e. leases with an unexpired term at the end of the financial year of at least 50 years) and how much to *'short leases'* (i.e. any other leases). *'Lease'* includes an agreement for a lease. [*9 Sch Part I, paras 57, 82, 86; SI 1991 No 2705*].

Participating interests and *shares in group undertakings held by credit institutions* must be disclosed separately. [*9 Sch Part I, para 58; SI 1991 No 2705*].

6.84   *Reserves and provisions*

Where any amount is transferred

● to or from any reserves,

● to any provisions for liabilities and charges, or

● from any such provision, otherwise than for the purpose for which the provision was set up,

and the reserves or provisions are shown as separate items in the balance sheet (or would be so shown were it not for 6.62(i) or (ii) above) the following information must be given in respect of the aggregate of reserves or provisions included in the same item.

● The amount of the reserves or provisions at the beginning of the financial year and at the balance sheet date.

● Any amounts transferred thereto or therefrom during the year.

● The source and application of the amounts transferred during the year.

Where the amount of the provision is material, particulars must be given of each provision included in Liabilities item 6(c) (other provisions) in the balance sheet format.

Comparative figures for the preceding year (see 6.80 above) are not required for any of the above information.

[*9 Sch Part I, paras 47(3), 59; SI 1991 No 2705*].

Provision for deferred taxation. The amount of any provision for deferred taxation must be stated separately from that of any provision for other taxation. [*9 Sch Part I, para 60; SI 1991 No 2705*].

See 2.1 ACCOUNTS: DEFINITIONS for the meaning of *'provision'*.

6.85   *Maturity analysis*

For each of Assets items 3(*b*) and 4 and Liabilities items 1(*b*), 2(*b*) and 3(*b*) in the balance sheet format, there must be disclosed the aggregate amount of loans and advances and liabilities included analysed into those repayable in

● not more than three months,

● more than three months but not more than one year,

● more than one year but less than five years, and

● more than five years

from the balance sheet date. Where the loan or liability is repayable in instalments, each instalment is to be treated as a separate loan or liability.

There must also be disclosed the aggregate amount of loans and advances within Assets item 4 which are repayable on demand or which are, for an indeterminate period, being repaid upon short notice.

[9 Sch Part 1, para 61; SI 1991 No 2705].

6.86 *Debt and other fixed income securities*

There must be disclosed the amount of debt and fixed income securities included in Assets item 5 and Liabilities item 3(*a*) in the balance sheet format becoming due within one year of the balance sheet date. *[9 Sch Part I, para 62; SI 1991 No 2705].*

6.87 *Subordinated investments*

The following information must be given in respect of any borrowing included in Liabilities item 7 in the balance sheet format that exceeds 10% of the total for that item.

- Its amount and the currency in which it is denominated.

- The rate of interest and maturity date (or the fact that it is perpetual).

- The circumstances in which early repayment may be demanded.

- The terms of subordination.

- The existence of any provision whereby it may be converted into capital or some other form of liability and the terms of such provision.

The general terms of any other borrowing included in Liabilities item 7 must also be stated.

[9 Sch Part I, para 63; SI 1991 No 2705].

6.88 *Fixed cumulative dividends*

If any fixed cumulative dividends on the company's shares are in arrears, there must be stated the amount of arrears and the period for which the dividends (or each class of dividends if there is more than one) are in arrears. *[9 Sch Part I, para 64; SI 1991 No 2705].*

6.89 *Details of assets charged*

There must be disclosed in relation to each Liabilities item and Memorandum item of the balance sheet format

- the aggregate amount of any assets of the company charged to secure any liability or potential liability included in that item;

- the aggregate amount of the liabilities or potential liabilities so secured; and

- an indication of the nature of the security given.

There must also be disclosed any other charge on the company's assets to secure the liabilities of any other person including, where practicable, the amount secured.

[9 Sch Part I, para 65; SI 1991 No 2705].

6.90 *Guarantees and other financial commitments*

The following information is required.

(*a*)   Where practicable, the aggregate amount or estimated amount of contracts for capital expenditure, so far as not provided for.

(b)   Particulars of any pension commitments included under any provision shown in the balance sheet and of any such commitments for which no provision has been made, giving separate particulars of any commitment to the extent that it relates to pensions payable to past directors.

(c)   Particulars of any other financial commitments which have not been provided for or included in the Memorandum items in the balance sheet format and which are relevant to assessing the company's state of affairs.

Commitments under (a) to (c) above must be stated separately for

(i)   those undertaken on behalf of, or for the benefit of, any parent company or fellow subsidiary company;

(ii)   those undertaken on behalf of, or for the benefit of, any subsidiary company; and

(iii)   any other commitments.

There must also be disclosed the nature and amount of any contingent liabilities and commitments included in Memorandum items 1 and 2 which are material in relation to the company's activities.

[9 Sch Part I, para 66; SI 1991 No 2705; SI 1996 No 189, 4 Sch 7].

6.91   *Memorandum items – group undertakings*

There must be stated the amount of contingent liabilities and commitments required to be included under Memorandum items 1 and 2 respectively in the balance sheet format incurred on behalf of, or for the benefit of

(a)   any parent company undertaking or fellow subsidiary undertaking, or

(b)   any subsidiary undertaking

of the company, distinguishing between amounts incurred under (a) and (b). [9 Sch Part I, para 67; SI 1992 No 2705].

6.92   *Transferable securities*

There must be disclosed the amount of transferable securities

(a)   included in each of Assets items 5 to 8 in the balance sheet format distinguishing those that are 'listed' and unlisted; and

(b)   included in each of Assets items 5 and 6 in the balance sheet format distinguishing those that are held as financial fixed assets and those that are not so held. The criterion used by the directors to make the distinction must also be disclosed.

The aggregate market value of listed investments within (a) above must also be shown, if different.

A *'listed'* security is one listed on a recognised stock exchange or on any stock exchange of repute outside Great Britain (and *'unlisted'* is construed accordingly).

[9 Sch Part I, paras 68, 82; SI 1991 No 2705; SI 1996 No 189, 4 Sch 8].

6.93   *Leasing transactions*

The aggregate amount of all property (other than land) leased by the company to other persons must be disclosed, broken down to show the aggregate amount included in each relevant balance sheet item. [9 Sch Part I, para 69; SI 1991 No 2705].

6.94 *Assets and liabilities denominated in a currency other than sterling*

The aggregate amounts, in sterling, of such assets and of such liabilities must be disclosed, using an appropriate rate of exchange prevailing at the balance sheet date. [*9 Sch Part I, para 70; SI 1991 No 2705*].

6.95 *Sundry assets and liabilities*

Where any amount shown under Assets item 13 or Liabilities item 4 on the balance sheet format is material, particulars must be given of each type of asset or liability included, together with an explanation of its nature and the amount included with respect to that type. [*9 Sch Part I, para 71; SI 1991 No 2705*].

6.96 *Unmatured forward transactions*

The following must be disclosed in respect of such transactions (including all transactions in relation to which income or expenditure is included in profit and loss format 1, item 6 (format 2, items B4 or A3) or in format 1, items 1 or 2 (format 2, items B1 and A1) by virtue of notes (1)(*b*) or (2)(*b*) under 6.69 above).

- The categories of such transactions by reference to an appropriate system of classification.

- For each category whether they have been made, to any material extent,

  (i)   to hedge the effects of fluctuations in interest rates, exchange rates and market prices; or

  (ii) for dealing purposes.

[*9 Sch Part I, para 72; SI 1991 No 2705*].

6.97 *Miscellaneous*

The following information must be given.

- Particulars of any case where the cost of any asset is for the first time determined under *9 Sch 38* (see 6.75 above).

- The aggregate amount, for each item in question, of any outstanding loans authorised by *Sec 153(4)(b), (bb)* or *(c)* or *Sec 155* (see 8.19(*i*), (*j*) and 8.21 ACQUISITION OF OWN SHARES respectively) included under any item shown in the balance sheet.

[*9 Sch Part I, para 73; SI 1991 No 2705; SI 1996 No 189, 4 Sch 9*].

6.98 **Notes to the accounts: information supplementing the profit and loss account**

The information required, as set out in 6.99 to 6.105 below must be given by way of notes to the accounts if not given in the company's accounts. [*9 Sch Part I, 47; SI 1991 No 2705; SI 1996 No 189, 4 Sch 4*].

6.99 *Separate statement of certain items of income and expenditure*

For financial years ending before 2 February 1996,

  (i)   the amounts respectively set aside for redemption of share capital and for redemption of loans,

  (ii) the amount of income from 'listed investments' (see 6.92 above), and

(iii)   the amount charged to revenue for hire of plant and machinery had to be stated.

[*9 Sch Part I, para 74; SI 1991 No 2705; SI 1996 No 189, 4 Sch 10*].

6.100   *Particulars of tax*

Particulars must be given of any special circumstances affecting liability in respect of taxation of profits, income or capital gains for the financial year in question and/or succeeding financial years.

In respect of each of the amounts shown under the items 'tax on [profit][loss] on ordinary activities' and 'tax on extraordinary [profit][loss]' in the profit and loss account the following amounts must be stated.

• The amount of the charge for UK corporation tax.

• The amount of any double taxation relief which has reduced that charge.

• The amount of the charge for UK income tax.

• The amount of the charge for taxation imposed outside the UK of profits, income and (so far as charged to revenue) capital gains.

[*9 Sch Part I, para 75; SI 1991 No 2705; SI 1996 No 189, 4 Sch 11*].

[*9 Sch Part I, para 75(1) repealed by SI 1996 No 189, 4 Sch 11*].

6.101   *Particulars of income*

If, in the course of the financial year, the company has operated in different geographical markets that differ substantially from each other, the amount of income attributable to each market must be disclosed in respect of profit and loss format 1, items 1, 3, 4, 6 and 7 (format 2, items B1, B2, B3, B4 and B7).

Where, in the directors' opinion, the disclosure of any of the above information would seriously prejudice the company's interests, that information need not be disclosed, but the fact that it has not been disclosed must be stated.

In analysing for the above purposes the source of any income, the directors must have regard to the manner in which the company's activities are organised.

[*9 Sch Part I, para 76; SI 1991 No 2705*].

6.102   *Particulars of staff*

There must be stated

(*a*)   the 'average number of persons employed' by the company in the financial year; and

(*b*)   the average number of persons so employed within each category of persons employed by the company (the categories being such as the directors may select having regard to the manner in which the company's activities are organised).

The '*average number of persons employed*' is calculated by the formula

A
—
B

where

A = the sum of the numbers of persons who, under contracts of service, were employed by the company in each month of the financial year whether throughout it or not (or, where applicable, the numbers so employed within a particular category)

B = the number of months in the financial year

[9 Sch Part I, para 77(1)-(3)(5); SI 1991 No 2705; SI 1996 No 189, 4 Sch 12].

In respect of all employees taken into account in arriving at the average number in (*a*) above, there must be stated the aggregate amounts of each of the following.

- Wages and salaries paid or payable in respect of the financial year to those persons.

- 'Social security costs' incurred by the company on their behalf.

- Other 'pension costs' so incurred.

Any amount stated in respect of any of these items in the profit and loss account must be determined by reference to payments made or costs incurred in respect of those employees.

'Social security costs' means any contributions by the company to any state social security or pension scheme, fund or arrangement.

'Pension costs' includes any costs incurred by the company in respect of any pension scheme set up for current and former employees, any sums set aside for the future payment of pensions directly by the company to current or former employees and any pensions paid directly to such persons without having first been set aside.

[9 Sch Part I, paras 77(4), 87; SI 1991 No 2705; SI 1996 No 189, 4 Sch 13].

See also SSAP 24 *Accounting for pension costs.*

6.103 *Management and agency services*

Where the company provides such services to customers on a scale which is material in the context of the business as a whole, it must disclose that fact. *[9 Sch Part I, para 78; SI 1991 No 2705].*

6.104 *Subordinated liabilities*

Any amounts charged to the profit and loss account representing charges incurred during the year with respect to subordinated liabilities must be disclosed. *[9 Sch Part I, para 79; SI 1991 No 2705].*

6.105 *Miscellaneous*

Other operating income and charges. Particulars, including an explanation of their nature and amount, must be given of any material items included in profit and loss format 1, items 7 and 10 (format 2, items A6 and B7). *[9 Sch Part I, para 80; SI 1991 No 2705].*

Prior year adjustments. Where any amount relating to any preceding financial year is included in any profit and loss account item, the effect must be stated. *[9 Sch Part I, para 81(1); SI 1991 No 2705].*

Extraordinary items. Particulars, including an explanation of their nature and amount, must be given of any material items included in profit and loss format 1, items 18 and 19 (format 2, items A12 and B10). *[9 Sch Part I, para 80; SI 1991 No 2705].*

Exceptional items. The effect of any exceptional (by size or incidence) transactions must be stated, even though they fall within the company's ordinary activities. [*9 Sch Part I, para 81(2); SI 1991 No 2705*].

6.106 Directors' emoluments, loans, quasi-loans and other dealings and transactions by other officers

The provisions of 5.32 to 5.43 ACCOUNTS: INDIVIDUAL COMPANIES (disclosure of emoluments and other benefits of directors and others) apply to a banking company or the holding company of a 'credit institution' with the following modifications.

(*a*) Where such a company prepares annual accounts for a financial year, it need not comply with the provisions of 5.39 to 5.42 (loans, quasi-loans and other dealings) in relation to

- a transaction or arrangement of a kind mentioned in *Sec 330* (see 19.86 to 19.90 DIRECTORS), or

- an agreement to enter into such a transaction or arrangement

to which that company or credit institution is a party.

(*b*) Where such a company takes advantage of the provisions in (*a*) above in its annual accounts, then, in preparing those accounts, it must comply with the provisions of 5.43 (transactions, etc. by officers other than directors) only in relation to a transaction, arrangement or agreement made by that company or credit institution for

- a person who was a director (including a shadow director, see 19.1 DIRECTORS) of the company preparing the accounts or a person 'connected with' such a director; or

- a person who was a chief executive or manager (within the meaning of *Banking Act 1987*) of that company or its holding company.

For these purposes, therefore, references to 'officers' in 5.43 is to be construed as including such persons; and a body corporate which a person does not 'control' is not to be treated as connected with him.

'*Credit institution*' means an undertaking whose business is to receive deposits or other repayable funds from the public and to grant credits for its own account.

See 19.94 DIRECTORS for the meaning of '*connected persons*' and '*control*'.

[*Secs 255B(2), 262, 9 Sch Part IV; CA 1989, 7 Sch 13; SI 1991 No 2705; SI 1994 No 233*].

6.107 Disclosure required in notes to the accounts: auditors' remuneration

The provisions of 5.44 ACCOUNTS: INDIVIDUAL COMPANIES apply to banking companies as for other companies.

6.108 Disclosure required in notes to the accounts: related undertakings

The provisions of 5.45 to 5.53 ACCOUNTS: INDIVIDUAL COMPANIES apply to banking companies as for other companies except that

- for the purposes of 5.51, a significant holding is one which amounts to 20% or more of the nominal value of any class of shares in the undertaking in question; and

- any information required under 5.51 can be omitted if it is not material.

[*Sec 255B(1), 9 Sch Part III; SI 1991 No 2705*].

6.109 BANKING COMPANIES: GROUP ACCOUNTS

A parent company of a 'banking group' *must* prepare group accounts in accordance with the special provisions in *Sec 255B, 9 Sch Part II* and the accounts must contain a statement to that effect.

A '*banking group*' is a group in which

- the parent company is a banking company; or

- the parent company does not itself carry on a material business (other than the acquisition of, management of, provision of services to, and disposal of interests in, subsidiary undertakings) and its 'principal subsidiary undertakings' are wholly or mainly banking companies. '*Principal subsidiary undertakings*' are the subsidiary undertakings of the company whose results or financial position would principally affect the figures shown in the group accounts.

[*Sec 255A(1)(3)(4)(5A); SI 1991 No 2705; SI 1993 No 3246, Reg 3*].

6.110 Meaning of 'parent' and 'subsidiary' undertaking and financial year

The provisions of 4.2 to 4.7 ACCOUNTS: GROUPS OF COMPANIES apply as for other groups of companies. [*Sec 255A(1); SI 1991 No 2705*].

6.111 Duty to prepare accounts

The provisions of 4.8 and 4.9 ACCOUNTS: GROUPS OF COMPANIES apply

- ignoring the reference to exemption for 'small' and 'medium-sized' groups in 4.8 (which provisions do not apply to banking companies); and

- substituting a reference to *4A Sch as modified by 9 Sch Part II* for the reference to *4A Sch* in 4.8.

[*Sec 255A(1)(6); SI 1991 No 2705*].

6.112 Exclusion of subsidiary companies from consolidation

The provisions of 4.10 ACCOUNTS: GROUPS OF COMPANIES apply except that an undertaking (other than a credit institution) whose activities are a direct extension of, or ancillary to, 'banking' business cannot be excluded from consolidation under 4.10(*c*). '*Banking*' means the carrying on of a deposit taking business within the meaning of *Banking Act 1987*. [*Sec 255A(1), 9 Sch Part II, para 1; SI 1991 No 2705*].

6.113 Treatment of individual profit and loss account where group accounts prepared

Where a parent company is required to prepare group accounts and does so, and the notes to its individual balance sheet show the company's profit or loss for the financial year (determined in accordance with *CA 1985*), then its individual profit and loss account

- need not contain the information otherwise required by *9 Sch Part I, paras 74-77, 80, 81* (see 6.99 to 6.102 and 6.105 above); and

- may be omitted from the company's annual accounts although it must still be approved by the board and signed by a director in accordance with 3.2 ACCOUNTS: GENERAL.

6.114   Accounts: Insurance and Banking Companies

The above exemptions apply only if the company's annual accounts disclose the fact that they apply.

[*Secs 230, 255A(1)(6); CA 1989, s 5; SI 1991 No 2705; SI 1996 No 189, Reg 15*].

6.114 Form and content of group accounts

Subject to 6.115 to 6.122 below, the group accounts of a banking company must comply, as far as practicable, with the provisions of *Sec 390A(3)* (auditors' remuneration, see 5.44 ACCOUNTS: INDIVIDUAL COMPANIES) and *9 Sch Part I* (see 6.62 to 6.105 above) as if the 'group' (meaning, for these purposes, all the undertakings included in the consolidation) were a single company.

[*4A Sch, para 1; 9 Sch Part II, para 2; CA 1989, 2 Sch; SI 1991 No 2705; SI 1996 No 189, 2 Sch 2; SI 1997 No 220, Reg 7*].

The consolidated balance sheet and profit and loss account must incorporate in full the information contained in the individual accounts of the undertakings included in the consolidation. This is subject to the adjustments authorised or required under this paragraph and 6.115 to 6.122 below and any other adjustments that are appropriate in accordance with generally accepted accounting principles or practice.

If the financial year of a subsidiary undertaking included in the consolidation does not end with that of the parent company, the accounts of the subsidiary to be included in the group accounts are

*   its accounts for the financial year last ending before the end of the parent company's financial year, but only if the gap is no more than three months; or

*   interim accounts drawn up as at the end of the parent company's financial year.

[*4A Sch 2; CA 1989, 2 Sch; SI 1996 No 189, 2 Sch 3*].

Assets and liabilities. Where assets and liabilities to be included in the group accounts have been valued or otherwise determined by undertakings under accounting rules which differ from those used for the group accounts, the values or amounts must be adjusted in line with the rules used for the group accounts (unless such adjustments are not material for the purpose of giving a true and fair view). If it appears to the parent company's directors that there are special reasons for doing so, they may depart from this requirement, but particulars of the departure, the reasons for it and its effect must be given in a note to the accounts. [*4A Sch 3; CA 1989, 2 Sch*].

Accounting rules. Any differences between accounting rules used for a parent company's individual accounts and those used for its group accounts must be disclosed in a note to the group accounts, and the reasons for the difference given. [*4A Sch 4; CA 1989, 2 Sch*].

Materiality. Amounts which in the particular context of any provision of *4A Sch* (see above and 6.115 to 6.122 below) are not material may be disregarded for the purposes of that provision. [*4A Sch 5; CA 1989, 2 Sch*].

6.115 *Elimination of group transactions*

The provisions of 4.13 ACCOUNTS: GROUPS OF COMPANIES apply as for other groups of companies.

6.116 *Acquisition and merger accounting*

The provisions of 4.14 to 4.17 ACCOUNTS: GROUPS OF COMPANIES apply as for other groups of companies.

6.117 *Minority interests*

An item headed 'Minority interests' is added to the balance sheet and profit and loss account formats set out in 6.63 and 6.69 above respectively.

Balance sheet format. The said item should appear either between Liabilities items 7 and 8 or after Liabilities item 12. Under this item, there must be shown the amount of capital and reserves attributable to shares (in subsidiary undertakings included in the consolidation) held by, or on behalf of, persons other than the parent company and its subsidiary undertakings.

For the purposes of *9 Sch Part I, para 3(3)* (see 6.62 above) the said item is to be treated as an item to which a letter is assigned.

Profit and loss account formats. The item should appear twice under each format, firstly in respect of profit or loss on ordinary activities and secondly in respect of profit or loss on extraordinary activities.

- For ordinary activities, the item should appear

  (i)   in format 1, between items 17 and 18; or

  (ii) in format 2, between items A11 and A12 or between items B9 and B10.

  Under this item, there must be shown the amount of any profit or loss on ordinary activities attributable to shares (in subsidiary undertakings included in the consolidation) held by, or on behalf of, persons other than the parent company and its subsidiary undertakings.

- For extraordinary activities, the item should appear

  (i)   in format 1, between items 22 and 23; or

  (ii) in format 2, between items A14 and A15 or between items B11 and B12.

  Under this item, there must be shown the amount of any profit or loss on extraordinary activities attributable to shares (in subsidiary undertakings included in the consolidation) held by, or on behalf of, persons other than the parent company and its subsidiary undertakings.

For the purposes of *9 Sch Part I, para 3(3)* (see 6.62 above) the said items are to be treated as items to which a letter is assigned.

[4A Sch 17, 9 Sch Part II, para 3; CA 1989, 2 Sch; SI 1991 No 2705].

6.118 *Interests in subsidiary undertakings excluded from consolidation*

Where subsidiary undertakings have been excluded from consolidation under 4.10(*c*) ACCOUNTS: GROUPS OF COMPANIES (note the restriction on that exclusion under 6.112 above), the interest of the group in those undertakings and the amount of profit or loss attributable to that interest must be shown in the consolidated balance sheet and consolidated profit and loss account respectively. The equity method of accounting must be used, with any goodwill arising being dealt with in accordance with *9 Sch Part I, paras 24-26* (see 6.72 above). *[4A Sch 18; 9 Sch Part II, para 4; CA 1989, 2 Sch; SI 1991 No 2705]*.

6.119 *Joint ventures*

The provisions of 4.20 ACCOUNTS: GROUPS OF COMPANIES apply as for other groups of companies.

137

6.120 Accounts: Insurance and Banking Companies

6.120 *Associated undertakings*

The balance sheet and profit and loss account formats in 6.63 and 6.69 above respectively are modified as described below, in relation to group accounts, to give information in respect of associated undertakings as defined in 4.21 ACCOUNTS: GROUPS OF COMPANIES.

Balance sheet format. Assets item 7 is replaced by two items, 'Interests in associated undertakings' and 'Other participating interests'.

Profit and loss account formats. Format 1 item 3(*b*) and format 2 item B2(*b*) are each replaced by 'Income from participating interests other than associated undertakings' and an additional heading of 'Income from associated undertakings' must be shown at an appropriate position.

The interest of an undertaking in an associated undertaking and the amount of profit or loss attributable thereto are to be shown by the equity method of accounting, with any goodwill arising being dealt with in accordance with *9 Sch Part I, paras 24-26* (see 6.72 above).

[*4A Sch 21, 22; 9 Sch Part II, paras 3, 4; CA 1989, 2 Sch; SI 1991 No 2705*].

6.121 *Foreign currency translation*

Any difference between

- the amount included in the consolidated accounts for the previous financial year with respect to any undertaking included in the consolidation or the group's interest in any associated undertaking, together with the amount of any transaction undertaken to cover any such interest, and

- the opening amount for the financial year in respect of those undertakings and in respect of any such transactions

arising as a result of the application of *9 Sch Part I, para 45* (see 6.79 above) may be credited to, or as the case maybe, deducted from consolidated reserves. [*9 Sch Part II, para 5; SI 1991 No 2705*].

Any income and expenditure of undertakings included in the consolidation and associated undertakings in a foreign currency may be translated for consolidation purposes at the average rates of exchange during the financial year. [*9 Sch Part II, para 6; SI 1991 No 2705*].

6.122 *Information as to undertakings in which shares are held as a result of financial assistance*

Where the parent company of a banking group has a subsidiary undertaking which

- is a credit institution of which shares are held as a result of a financial assistance operation with a view to its reorganisation or rescue, and

- is excluded from consolidation under *Sec 229(3)(c)* (interest held with a view to resale, see 4.10(*b*)(iii) ACCOUNTS: GROUPS OF COMPANIES)

then, subject to below, information must be given in a note to the group accounts as to the nature and terms of the operation. A copy of the undertaking's latest individual accounts (and, if a parent undertaking, its latest group accounts) must be appended to the copy of the group accounts delivered to the Registrar of Companies. If the appended accounts are required by law to be audited, a copy of the auditors' report must also be appended. Any appended document in a language other than English must have a certified translation annexed to it.

The accounts of an undertaking need not be appended if

(i)   no accounts would otherwise be prepared if not for these purposes; or

(ii)   they would not otherwise be required to be published, or made available for public inspection, anywhere in the world.

Where a copy of an undertaking's accounts is required to be appended to the copy of the group accounts delivered to the Registrar, that fact must be stated in a note to the group accounts. A note must also be included where (ii) above applies giving the reason for not appending the accounts.

Penalties. If any of the above requirements are not complied with before the end of the period allowed for laying and delivering accounts (see 3.8 ACCOUNTS: GENERAL), every person who immediately before the end of that period was a director of the company is liable to a fine up to the level in 40.1(*e*) PENALTIES. Also, if the directors fail to make good the default within 14 days after the service of a notice on them requiring compliance, the court may, on the application of the Registrar of Companies or of any member or creditor of the company, order the directors (or any of them) to make good the default within such time as is specified in the order. The order may require the directors to bear all costs of, and incidental to, the application. It is a defence for a person charged under these provisions to prove that he took all reasonable steps for securing compliance with the requirements within the period allowed.

[*9 Sch Part II, para 7; CA 1989, 7 Sch 13; SI 1991 No 2705*].

6.123   Disclosures required in the notes to the accounts: related undertakings

The provisions of 4.23 to 4.32 ACCOUNTS: GROUPS OF COMPANIES apply as for other groups of companies except that for the purposes of 4.30

- a significant holding is one which amounts to 20% or more of the nominal value of any class of shares in the undertaking in question; and

- any information required under those paragraphs can be omitted if it is not material.

[*Sec 255B(1), 9 Sch Part III; SI 1991 No 2705*].

6.124   MISCELLANEOUS BANKS: ACCOUNTS

Special provisions have been introduced by *The Bank Accounts Directive (Miscellaneous Banks Order (SI 1991 No 2704)* to implement *EC Council Directive 86/635/EEC* in so far as that Directive is applicable to banking institutions (whether bodies corporate or unincorporate) which are not otherwise subject to the *CA 1985* provisions. In effect, the provisions apply to certain institutions authorised under the *Banking Act 1987* to carry on a deposit taking business which were incorporated or formed by or under Public General Acts which pre-date modern legislation governing the legal forms in which business may be carried on. The provisions are mandatory for accounts with respect to financial years commencing on or after 23 December 1992.

The directors of such bodies must prepare accounts in accordance with the provisions of *CA 1985, Part VII* applicable to banking companies and groups but subject to certain modifications which disapply the provisions of that *Part* which do not derive from the *EC Directives* on accounts. The accounts prepared must be made available for inspection,

6.124   Accounts: Insurance and Banking Companies

without charge, at the body's principal place of business within Great Britain and a copy must be supplied to any person on request at a price not exceeding the administrative cost of making the copy.

There are criminal penalties for failure to comply with the provisions.

See *SI 1991 No 2704* for full details.

7   Accounts: Small and Medium-Sized Companies

Cross-references. See 2 ACCOUNTS: DEFINITIONS; 3 ACCOUNTS: GENERAL; 4 ACCOUNTS: GROUPS OF COMPANIES; 5 ACCOUNTS: INDIVIDUAL COMPANIES.

The contents of this chapter are as follows.

7.1   INTRODUCTION

A company which qualifies as 'small' (see 7.2 below) in relation to a financial year is entitled to various exemptions with respect to

(*a*)   the preparation of individual annual accounts (see 7.5 to 7.39 below);

(*b*)   the individual accounts delivered to the Registrar of Companies (see 7.40 to 7.42 below); .

(*c*)   the requirement to prepare group accounts (see 7.46 below); and

(*d*)   the format of any group accounts prepared (see 7.47 below).

A company which qualifies as 'medium-sized' (see 7.2 below) is similarly entitled to various exemptions as under (*b*) above (see 7.44 below) and as under (*c*) above (see 7.46 below) but *not* as under (*a*) or (*d*) above.

See also

●   20.15 DIRECTORS' REPORT for the contents of the directors' report of a small company;

●   12.21 AUDITORS for the special auditor's report required where small and medium-sized companies take advantage of the exemptions conferred by (*b*) above; and

●   12.32 to 12.40 AUDITORS for the audit exemptions available to small companies satisfying certain conditions.

7.2   MEANING OF 'SMALL' AND 'MEDIUM-SIZED'

Subject to 7.3 below, a company/group qualifies as small or medium-sized in relation to a financial year if the qualifying conditions described below are met

(*a*)   in the case of the company's/parent company's first financial year, in that year; and

(*b*)   in the case of any subsequent financial year, in both that year and the preceding year.

A company/group is *treated* as so qualifying in relation to a financial year

7.2 Accounts: Small and Medium-Sized Companies

(i)   if it so qualified in relation to the previous financial year under (*a*) or (*b*) above (or was treated as so qualifying under (ii) below), or

(ii)   if it was treated as so qualifying in relation to the previous year under (i) above *and* the qualifying conditions are met in the year in question.

The qualifying conditions are met by a company/group in a year in which it satisfies at least two of the three relevant requirements set out below.

Small company

Turnover	£2.8m or less
'Balance sheet total'	£1.4m or less
'Number of employees'	50 or less

Small group

Aggregate turnover	£2.8 million net (or £3.36m gross) or less
Aggregate balance sheet total	£1.4m net (or £1.68m gross) or less
Aggregate number of employees	50 or less

Medium-sized company

Turnover	£11.2m or less
'Balance sheet total'	£5.6m or less
'Number of employees'	250 or less

Medium-sized group

Aggregate turnover	£11.2 million net (or £13.44m gross) or less
Aggregate balance sheet total	£5.6m net (or £6.72m gross) or less
Aggregate number of employees	250 or less

Notes

(1)   Where a company's financial year is not in fact a year, the maximum turnover figure is to be proportionately adjusted.

(2)   For a company, the '*balance sheet total*' means

     (*a*)   where Format 1 of the balance sheet formats in 7.6 below (small companies) or 5.4 ACCOUNTS INDIVIDUAL COMPANIES (medium-sized companies) is adopted, the aggregate of the amounts shown under the headings corresponding to items A to D in that format; and

     (*b*)   where Format 2 of the said formats is adopted, the aggregate of the amounts shown under the general heading 'Assets'.

(3)   For a company, '*number of employees*' means the average number of persons employed by the company in the year, determined on a monthly basis using the formula

$$\frac{A}{B}$$

where

     A =   the sum of the number of person who, under contracts of service, were employed by the company in each month of the financial year whether throughout it or not (or, where applicable, the number so employed within a particular category)

B =   the number of months in the financial year

(4)   For a group, the references above to 'net' figures are to figures net of the set-offs and adjustments required by *4A Sch* (see 4.12 to 4.22 ACCOUNTS: GROUPS OF COMPANIES) in the case of group accounts, and the references to 'gross' figures are to figures before making such set-offs and adjustments. A company may satisfy the relevant requirement on the basis of either the net or the gross figure.

(5)   For a group, the aggregate figures are to be ascertained by aggregating the relevant figures determined under the above provisions for each member of the group. The figures to be included for each subsidiary undertaking are to be those included in its accounts for its financial year ending with the end of the parent company's financial year or, if financial years do not coincide, its financial year ending last before the end of the parent company's financial year. If, however, such figures cannot be obtained without disproportionate expense or undue delay, the latest available figures can be taken.

[*Secs 247, 249, 4 Sch 56; CA 1989, s 13; SI 1992 No 2452; SI 1996 No 189, Reg 8; SI 1997 No 220, Reg 7*].

7.3   Companies not entitled to exemptions for small and medium-sized companies

A company is not entitled to any of the exemptions otherwise available to small and medium-sized companies if it is, or was at any time in the financial year to which the accounts relate,

• a public company;

• a banking or insurance company;

• an authorised person under *FSA 1986*; or

• a member of a group if any of its members is

  (i)   a public company;

  (ii)   a body corporate (other than a company) which has power under its constitution to offer shares or debentures to the public, and may lawfully exercise that power;

  (iii) an authorised institution under *Banking Act 1987*;

  (iv)   an insurance company to which *Insurance Companies Act 1982, Pt II* applies (including an EC company lawfully carrying on insurance business in the UK); or

  (v)   an authorised person under *FSA 1986*.

A parent company does not qualify as a small or medium-sized company in relation to a financial year unless the group headed by it qualifies as, respectively, a small group or a medium-sized group.

[*Sec 247A; SI 1997 No 220, Reg 4*].

7.4   SMALL COMPANIES: DUTY TO PREPARE INDIVIDUAL ACCOUNTS

The directors of any company, including a small company, must prepare, for each financial year of the company, a balance sheet as at the last day of the year and a profit and loss account. The accounts must respectively give a true and fair view of the state of the

7.4   Accounts: Small and Medium-Sized Companies

company's affairs as at the end of the financial year and of its profit or loss for that year. These accounts are referred to collectively as the company's *'individual accounts'*. See 2.1 ACCOUNTS: DEFINITIONS for *'financial year'*.

Where a company qualifies as 'small' in relation to the financial year (see 7.2 above) its accounts may either

(*a*)   be prepared in abbreviated form in compliance with the provisions of *Sec 246(2)(3)* and *8 Sch* (see 7.5 to 7.39 below); or

(*b*)   comply with the fuller provisions as described in 5.3 to 5.54 ACCOUNTS: INDIVIDUAL COMPANIES.

Where abbreviated accounts are prepared under (*a*) above, the balance sheet must contain, in a prominent position above the director's signature, a statement that the accounts have been prepared in accordance with the special provisions relating to small companies.

If compliance with the chosen method under (*a*) or (*b*) above is insufficient to meet the 'true and fair view' requirement, such additional information as is necessary must be given in the accounts or notes. If in special circumstances, compliance with any of those provisions would be inconsistent with the 'true and fair view' requirement, the directors must, to the extent necessary, depart from that provision, but any such departure, the reasons for it and its effect must be given in a note to the accounts.

[*Secs 226, 246(1)(8)(9); CA 1989, s 4; SI 1997 No 220, Reg 2*].

See 3.13 ACCOUNTS: GENERAL for *'true and fair view'*.

SMALL COMPANIES: FORM AND CONTENT OF INDIVIDUAL ACCOUNTS

7.5   **GENERAL RULES**

Every balance sheet of a small company must show the items listed in either of the two formats in 7.6 below, and every profit and loss account must show the items listed in any one of the four formats in 7.7 below, in either case in the order and under the headings and sub-headings given in the format adopted, except that no item need be distinguished by any letter or number assigned to that item in the format adopted. Any item required to be shown may be shown in greater detail than required by the format adopted. Any item representing or covering the amount of any asset or liability, income or expenditure, not otherwise covered by any item listed in the format adopted, may be included, except that none of the following items can be treated as assets in the balance sheet.

- Preliminary expenses.

- Expenses of, and commission on, any issue of shares or debentures.

- Costs of research.

Headings and sub-headings listed in the formats need not be included if there is no amount to be shown, either for the current or the preceding financial year (see below), for items thereunder.

[8 Sch 1, 3(1)(2)(5), 4(4); SI 1997 No 220, 1 Sch].

As regards items to which Arabic numbers are assigned in any of the formats in 7.6 and 7.7 below

(*a*)   the arrangement, headings and sub-headings otherwise required in respect of such items may be adapted if such adaptation is required by the special nature of the company's business;

(*b*)   such items may be combined in the accounts for any financial year if

(i)   their individual amounts are not material to assessing the state of affairs or profit or loss of the company; or

(ii)   the combination facilitates the assessment in (i) above (but in this case the individual items must be disclosed in a note to the accounts).

[8 Sch 3(3)(4); SI 1997 No 220, 1 Sch].

Accounts in ECUs. The amount set out in the annual accounts may also be shown in the same accounts translated into ECUs. Alternatively, when the annual accounts are delivered to the Registrar of Companies, the directors may deliver an additional copy of those accounts in which the amounts have been translated into ECUs. In either case, the amounts must have been translated at the rate of exchange used for translating the value of the ECU prevailing at the balance sheet date. That rate must be disclosed in the notes to the accounts. *[Sec 242B(1)–(3); SI 1992 No 2452].*

7.6 Accounts: Small and Medium-Sized Companies

Consistency in use of formats. Where a small company's balance sheet or profit and loss account for any financial year has been prepared in accordance with one of the said formats, the same format must be adopted for subsequent financial years unless, in the opinion of the directors, there are special reasons for a change. Any change, and the reason for it, must be disclosed in a note to the accounts in which the new format is first adopted. [*8 Sch 2; SI 1997 No 220, 1 Sch*].

Profit and loss accounts. Every profit and loss account must show the amount of the profit or loss on ordinary activities before taxation, and must show separately as additional items

- any amount set aside to, or withdrawn from, reserves (or proposed to be so set aside or withdrawn); and

- the aggregate amount of any dividends paid and proposed.

[*8 Sch 3(6)(7); SI 1997 No 220, 1 Sch*].

Set-offs. Amounts in respect of items representing assets or income may not be set off against amounts representing liabilities or expenditure, or vice versa. [*8 Sch 5; SI 1997 No 220, 1 Sch*].

Preceding financial year. For every item shown in a small company's balance sheet or profit and loss account, the corresponding amount for the immediately preceding financial year must also be shown. Where it is not comparable with that for the current year, the corresponding amount must be adjusted. Particulars of, and the reasons for, the adjustment must be disclosed in a note to the accounts. [*8 Sch 4(1)(2); SI 1997 No 220, 1 Sch*].

Materiality. Amounts which in the particular context of any provision of *8 Sch* (see above and 7.6 to 7.29 below) are not material may be disregarded for the purposes of the provision. [*8 Sch 56; SI 1997 No 220, 1 Sch*].

Provisions. References in *8 Sch* (see above and 7.6 to 7.29 below) to provisions for depreciation or diminution in value of assets are to any amount written off by way of providing for depreciation or diminution in value of assets. [*8 Sch 57(1); SI 1997 No 220, 1 Sch*]. References to provisions for liabilities or charges are to any amount retained as reasonably necessary for the purpose of providing for any liability or loss which is either likely to be incurred, or certain to be incurred but uncertain as to amount or as to the date on which it will arise. [*8 Sch 58; SI 1997 No 220, 1 Sch*].

7.6   **BALANCE SHEET FORMATS**

The two balance sheet formats set out in *8 Sch* and referred to in 7.5 above are reproduced below, and are followed by notes to certain of the items listed therein.

Format 1

A.   Called up share capital not paid (see note (1))

B.   Fixed assets

   I   Intangible assets
   1.   Goodwill (see note (2))
   2.   Other intangible assets (see note(3))

   II   Tangible assets
   1.   Land and buildings
   2.   Plant and machinery etc.

   III   Investments
   1.   Shares in group undertakings and participating interests

      2.   Loans to group undertakings and undertakings in which the company has a participating interest

      3.   Other investments other than loans

      4.   Other investments (see note(4))

C.   Current assets

    I   Stocks
        1.   Stocks
        2.   Payments on account

    II   Debtors (see note(5))
        1.   Trade debtors
        2.   Amounts owed by group undertakings and undertakings in which the company has a participating interest
        3.   Other debtors (see notes (1) and (6))

    III   Investments
        1.   Shares in group undertakings
        2.   Other investments

    IV   Cash at bank and in hand

D.   Prepayments and accrued income (see note(6))

E.   Creditors: amounts falling due within one year
    1.   Bank loans and overdrafts
    2.   Trade creditors
    3.   Amounts owed to group undertakings and undertakings in which the company has a participating interest
    4.   Other creditors (see note(7))

F.   Net current assets (liabilities) (see note(8))

G.   Total assets less current liabilities

H.   Creditors: amounts falling due after more than one year
    As per list in E. above

I.   Provisions for liabilities and charges

J.   Accruals and deferred income (see note(7))

K.   Capital and reserves

    I   Called up share capital (see note(9))

    II   Share premium account

    III   Revaluation reserve

    IV   Other reserves

    V   Profit and loss account

Format 2

ASSETS

As per A. to D. in Format 1 above

LIABILITIES

A.   Capital and reserves
    As per K. in Format 1 above

B.   Provisions for liabilities and charges

C.   Creditors (see note (10))
      As per list in E. in Format 1 above

D.   Accruals and deferred income (see note (7))

Notes

(1)   *Called up share capital not paid.* This item may be shown at item A or included under item C.II.3 in Format 1 or 2.

(2)   *Goodwill.* Amounts representing goodwill are to be included only to the extent that the goodwill was acquired for valuable consideration.

(3)   *Other intangible assets.* Any amounts in respect of concessions, patents, licences, trade marks and similar rights and assets are to be included under this item if the assets in question were either acquired for valuable consideration (and are not required to be shown under 'goodwill') or created by the company itself.

(4)   *Own shares.* Where this item includes own shares, the nominal value of the shares held is to be shown separately.

(5)   *Debtors.* Either

      (*a*)   the amount falling due after more than one year must be shown separately in the balance sheet for each item included under debtors; or

      (*b*)   the aggregate amount included under debtors falling due after more than one year may be disclosed in the notes to the accounts.

(6)   *Prepayments and accrued income.* This may shown at item D or included under item C.II.3 in Format 1 or 2.

(7)   *Other creditors.*

      (*a*)   The amount of any convertible loans must be shown separately.

      (*b*)   The amount for creditors in respect of taxation and social security must be shown separately.

      (*c*)   Payments received on account of orders must be included in so far as they are not shown as deductions from stocks.

      (*d*)   Accruals and deferred income may be shown in Format 1 under item J or included under item E.4 or H.4, or both (as the case may require). In Format 2, accruals and deferred income may be shown under item D or within item C.4 under Liabilities.

(8)   *Net current assets (liabilities).* In determining the amount to be shown under this item, any 'prepayments and accrued income' (see note (6) above) are to be taken into account wherever shown.

(9)   *Called up share capital.* The amount of allotted share capital and the amount of called up share capital which has been paid up are to be shown separately.

(10) *Creditors.* In Format 2, either

      (*a*)   amounts falling due within one year and after one year must be shown separately for each item under this heading and for the aggregate of all these items; or

      (*b*)   the aggregate amounts falling due within one year and after one year must be disclosed in the notes to the accounts.

[*8 Sch Pt 1, Section B; SI 1997 No 220*].

7.7   **PROFIT AND LOSS ACCOUNT FORMATS**

The four profit and loss account formats set out in *8 Sch* and referred to in 7.5 above are reproduced below, and are followed by notes to certain of the items listed therein.

Format 1 (see note (4))

1.   Turnover
2.   Cost of sales (see note(1))
3.   Gross profit or loss
4.   Distribution costs (see note(1))
5.   Administrative expenses (see note(1))
6.   Other operating income
7.   Income from shares in group undertakings
8.   Income from participating interests
9.   Income from other fixed asset investments (see note(2))
10.   Other interest receivable and similar income (see note(2))
11.   Amounts written off investments
12.   Interest payable and similar charges (see note(3))
13.   Tax on profit or loss on ordinary activities
14.   Profit or loss on ordinary activities after taxation
15.   Extraordinary income
16.   Extraordinary charges
17.   Extraordinary profit or loss
18.   Tax on extraordinary profit or loss
19.   Other taxes not shown under the above items
20.   Profit or loss for the financial year

Format 2

1.   Turnover
2.   Change in stocks of finished goods and in work in progress
3.   Own work capitalised
4.   Other operating income
5.   (*a*)   Raw materials and consumables
      (*b*)   Other external charges
6.   Staff costs:
      (*a*)   wages and salaries (see below)
      (*b*)   social security costs (see below)
      (*c*)   other pension costs (see below)
7.   (*a*)   Depreciation and other amounts written off tangible and intangible fixed assets
      (*b*)   Exceptional amounts written off current assets
8.   Other operating charges
9.   Income from shares in group undertakings
10.   Income from participating interests
11.   Income from other fixed asset investments (see note(2))
12.   Other interest receivable and similar income (see note(2))
13.   Amounts written off investments
14.   Interest payable and similar charges (see note(3))
15.   Tax on profit or loss on ordinary activities
16.   Profit or loss on ordinary activities after taxation
17.   Extraordinary income
18.   Extraordinary charges
19.   Extraordinary profit or loss

7.7 Accounts: Small and Medium-Sized Companies

20. Tax on extraordinary profit or loss
21. Other taxes not shown under the above items
22. Profit or loss for the financial year

Format 3 (see note (4))

A. Charges
    1. Cost of sales (see note(1))
    2. Distribution costs (see note(1))
    3. Administrative expenses (see note(1))
    4. Amounts written off investments
    5. Interest payable and similar charges (see note(3))
    6. Tax on profit or loss on ordinary activities
    7. Profit or loss on ordinary activities after taxation
    8. Extraordinary charges
    9. Tax on extraordinary profit or loss
    10. Other taxes not shown under the above items
    11. Profit or loss for the financial year

B. Income
    1. Turnover
    2. Other operating income
    3. Income from shares in group undertakings
    4. Income from participating interests
    5. Income from other fixed asset investments (see note(2))
    6. Other interest receivable and similar income (see note(2))
    7. Profit or loss on ordinary activities after taxation
    8. Extraordinary income
    9. Profit or loss for the financial year

Format 4

A. Charges
    1. Reduction in stocks of finished goods and in work in progress
    2. (a) Raw materials and consumables
       (b) Other external charges
    3. Staff costs:
       (a) wages and salaries (see below)
       (b) social security costs (see below)
       (c) other pension costs (see below)
    4. (a) Depreciation and other amounts written off tangible and intangible fixed assets
       (b) Exceptional amounts written off current assets
    5. Other operating charges
    6. Amounts written off investments
    7. Interest payable and similar charges (see note(3))
    8. Tax on profit or loss on ordinary activities
    9. Profit or loss on ordinary activities after taxation
    10. Extraordinary charges
    11. Tax on extraordinary profit or loss
    12. Other taxes not shown under the above items
    13. Profit or loss for the financial year

B. Income
    1. Turnover

2.   Increase in stocks of finished goods and in work in progress
3.   Own work capitalised
4.   Other operating income
5.   Income from shares in group undertakings
6.   Income from participating interests
7.   Income from other fixed asset investments (see note(2))
8.   Other interest receivable and similar income (see note(2))
9.   Profit or loss on ordinary activities after taxation
10.   Extraordinary income
11.   Profit or loss for the financial year

Notes

(1)   *Cost of sales: distribution costs: administrative expenses.* These items are to be stated after taking into account any necessary provisions for depreciation or diminution in value of assets.

(2)   *Income from other fixed asset investments: other interest receivable and similar income.* Income and interest derived from group undertakings are to be shown separately from income and interest derived from other sources.

(3)   *Interest payable and similar charges.* The amount payable to group undertakings is to be shown separately.

(4)   *Formats 1 and 3.* Where either of these formats is used, there is to be disclosed in a note to the accounts the amount of any provisions for depreciation and diminution in value of tangible and intangible fixed assets falling to be shown under items 7(a) and A.4(*a*) respectively in Formats 2 and 4.

[8 Sch Pt 1, Section B; SI 1997 No 220, 1 Sch].

Wages and salaries. Any amount stated in respect of wages and salaries in the company's profit and loss account is to be determined by reference to payments made or costs incurred in respect of all persons employed by the company during the financial year under contracts of service. *[8 Sch 59(3); SI 1997 No 220, 1 Sch].*

Social security costs. This means any contributions by the company to any state social security or pension scheme, fund or arrangement. Any amount stated in respect of this item in the company's profit and loss account is to be determined by reference to payments made or costs incurred in respect of all persons employed by the company during the financial year under contracts of service. *[8 Sch 59(1)(3); SI 1997 No 220, 1 Sch].*

Pension costs. This includes any costs incurred by the company in respect of any pension scheme established for current and former employees, any sums set aside for the future payment of pensions directly by the company to current or former employees and any pensions paid directly to such persons without having first been set aside. *[8 Sch 59(2); SI 1997 No 220, 1 Sch].*

Depreciation etc. References in the formats to the depreciation of, or amounts written off, assets of any description are to any provisions for depreciation or diminution in value of assets of that description. *[8 Sch 57(2); SI 1997 No 220, 1 Sch].*

7.8   **ACCOUNTING PRINCIPLES**

The amounts to be included in respect of all items shown in a small company's accounts are to be determined in accordance with the principles set out below, except that if it appears to the directors that there are special reasons for departing from any of these principles for a financial year, they may do so, but particulars of the departure, the reasons for it and its effect must be given in a note to the accounts.

7.9   Accounts: Small and Medium-Sized Companies

(*a*)   The company must be presumed to be carrying on business as a going concern.

(*b*)   Accounting policies must be applied consistently, both within the same accounts and from one financial year to the next.

(*c*)   The amount of any item is to be determined on a prudent basis, and in particular

    (i)   only profits realised at the balance sheet date are to be included in the profit and loss account; and

    (ii)   all liabilities and losses which have arisen, or are likely to arise, in respect of the financial year to which the accounts relate or a previous financial year must be taken into account; this includes any such liabilities and losses which become apparent between the balance sheet date and the date on which it is signed on behalf of the board (see 3.2 ACCOUNTS: GENERAL).

(*d*)   All income and charges relating to the financial year to which the accounts relate must be taken into account regardless of the date of receipt or payment.

(*e*)   In determining the aggregate amount of any item, the amount of each individual asset or liability that falls to be taken into account must be determined separately.

[*8 Sch 9–15; SI 1997 No 220, 1 Sch*].

7.9   ACCOUNTING RULES: HISTORIC COST

The rules described in 7.10 to 7.13 below apply to determine the amounts to be included in respect of all items shown in a small company's accounts, and are known as the historical cost accounting rules, but see 7.14 below for alternative rules. [*8 Sch 16, 29(1); SI 1997 No 220, 1 Sch*].

7.10   Fixed assets

General. Fixed asset are to be included at their 'purchase price' or 'production cost' (see 7.13 below). In the case of any fixed asset which has a limited useful economic life, that amount (or that amount less any estimated residual value at the end of asset's useful economic life) is to be reduced by provisions for depreciation calculated to write off the said amount systematically over the asset's useful economic life.

Provisions for diminution in value may be made in respect of any fixed asset investment of a description falling to be included under item B.III of either of the balance sheet formats in 7.6 above, the amount to be included in respect of that asset being reduced accordingly. Such provisions must also be made in respect of any fixed asset which has suffered what is expected to be a permanent reduction in value (whether or not its useful economic life is limited). Where the reasons for which any provision for diminution in value have ceased to apply to any extent, it must be written back (to the extent necessary). Any such provisions or amounts written back, where not shown in the profit and loss account, must be disclosed (either separately or in aggregate) in a note to the accounts.

[*8 Sch 17–19; SI 1997 No 220, 1 Sch*].

Development costs. An amount may be included in a small company's balance sheet in respect of development costs only in special circumstances, and if any amount is so included, there must be given in a note to the accounts the reasons for capitalising those costs and the period over which the amount originally capitalised is being, or is to be, written off. [*8 Sch 20; SI 1997 No 220, 1 Sch*].

Goodwill. Where goodwill acquired by a small company is treated as an asset, the amount of the consideration given must be reduced by provisions for depreciation calculated to write off that amount over a period of the directors' choosing, which must not exceed the useful economic life of that goodwill. Where any amount for goodwill is shown in the balance sheet, the writing-off period chosen, and the reasons for that choice, must be disclosed in a note to the accounts. [*8 Sch 21; SI 1997 No 220, 1 Sch*].

7.11   Current assets

The amount to be included for any current asset is its 'purchase price' or 'production cost' (see 7.13 below) or, if lower, its net realisable value. Any provision for diminution in value previously made, i.e. to reduce the asset to its net realisable value, must be written back to the extent that it is no longer necessary. [*8 Sch 22, 23; SI 1997 No 220, 1 Sch*].

7.12   Miscellaneous

Excess of debt over value received. Where the amount repayable on any debt owed by a small company is greater than the value of the consideration received in the transaction giving rise to the debt, the amount of the difference may be treated as an asset. It must, however, be written off by reasonable amounts each year and be completely written off before repayment of the debt. If not shown as a separate item in the balance sheet, the current amount must be disclosed in a note to the accounts. [*8 Sch 24; SI 1997 No 220, 1 Sch*].

Assets included at a fixed amount. Assets which fall to be included either amongst fixed assets under the item 'tangible assets' or amongst current assets under the item 'raw materials and consumables' and are of a kind which are constantly being replaced may be included at a fixed quantity and value, providing

- their overall value is not material to assessing the company's state of affairs; and

- their quantity, value and composition are not subject to material variation.

[*8 Sch 25; SI 1997 No 220, 1 Sch*].

7.13   Meaning and determination of 'purchase price' and 'production cost'

The '*purchase price*' of an asset is the actual price paid plus any expenses incidental to its acquisition.

The '*production cost*' of an asset is the aggregate of the purchase price of the raw materials and consumables used and the costs incurred by the company which are directly attributable to the production of that asset. In addition, there may be included

- a reasonable proportion of the costs incurred which are only indirectly so attributable, but only to the extent that they relate to the period of production; and

- interest on capital borrowed to finance the production of that asset, to the extent that it accrues in respect of the period of production. The inclusion of the interest and the amount so included must be disclosed in a note to the accounts.

The production cost of a current asset is not to include distribution costs.

[*8 Sch 26; SI 1997 No 220, 1 Sch*].

Where there is no record of the purchase price or production cost (or of any price, expenses or costs relevant to its determination) of any asset, or any such record cannot be obtained without unreasonable expense or delay, then for the purposes of these provisions, the purchase price or production cost of that asset is to be taken to be the value ascribed to it in the earliest available record of its value made on or after its acquisition or production by the company. [*8 Sch 28; SI 1997 No 220, 1 Sch*].

Stocks and fungible assets. The purchase price or production cost of

- any assets falling to be included under any item in the balance sheet under the general item 'stocks', and

- any 'fungible' assets (including investments)

may be determined by applying any of the following methods in relation to any such assets of the same class (the method chosen being such as appears to the directors to be appropriate in the company's circumstances).

1. First in, first out (FIFO).

2. Last in, first out (LIFO).

3. A weighted average price.

4. Any other method similar to any of the above.

Assets of any particular description are to be regarded as '*fungible*' if such assets are substantially indistinguishable from one another.

[*8 Sch 27; SI 1997 No 220, 1 Sch*].

7.14 ACCOUNTING RULES: ALTERNATIVE TO HISTORICAL COST

Any of the accounting rules set out below may be used (as alternatives to those described in 7.9 to 7.13 above) in determining the amounts to be included in respect of items shown in a small company's accounts (as specified).

(*a*) *Intangible fixed assets*, other than goodwill, may be included at their current cost.

(*b*) *Tangible fixed assets* may be included at a market value (as at the date of their last valuation) or at current cost.

(*c*) *Investments (of any description) falling to be included under item B.III* of either of the balance sheet formats in 7.6 above may be included either at market value (determined as in (*b*) above) or at a value determined on any basis appearing to the directors to be appropriate in the company's circumstances. In the latter case, particulars of, and the reasons for, the method of valuation adopted must be disclosed in a note to the accounts.

(*d*) *Investments (of any description) falling to be included under item C.III* of either of the balance sheet formats in 7.6 above may be included at current cost.

(*e*) *Stocks* may be included at their current cost.

As regards any asset of a small company the value of which is determined on any basis in (*a*)–(*e*) above, that value (instead of purchase price, production cost or any value previously so determined) is to be (or is to be the starting point for determining) the amount to be included in the accounts. The value most recently determined is accordingly to be used (instead of purchase price or production cost) for the purpose of applying the rules described in 7.10 and 7.11 above for general fixed assets and current assets.

Where the asset in question is a fixed asset, any provision for depreciation in respect thereof which is either included in the profit and loss account under the appropriate item or taken into account as required by note (1) to the profit and loss account formats in 7.7 above would normally be so included or taken into account at an amount calculated under the above rules. It may, however, be so included etc. at an amount calculated under the historical cost accounting rules described for general fixed assets in 7.10 above, providing any difference between the alternative amounts is separately disclosed either in the profit and loss account or in a note to the accounts.

[8 Sch 30–32; SI 1997 No 220, 1 Sch].

7.15 Additional information to be provided

Where the amount of any asset covered by any item in a small company's accounts has been determined on any basis in 7.14(a)–(e) above, the following additional information must be disclosed in a note to the accounts or alternatively, in the case of (ii) below) only, shown separately in the balance sheet.

(i) The items affected and the basis of valuation adopted in determining the amount of the asset in question for each such item.

(ii) For each balance sheet item affected (except stocks), either

- the 'comparable amounts determined under the historical cost accounting rules'; or

- the differences between the amounts in (a) above and the actual amounts shown in the balance sheet in respect of that item.

The 'comparable amounts determined under the historical cost accounting rules' comprise both

- the aggregate amount which would be required to be shown if the amounts of all assets covered by the item concerned were determined according to the historical cost accounting rules (see 7.9 to 7.13 above); and

- the aggregate amount of the cumulative provisions for depreciation or diminution in value which would be permitted or required in determining those amounts according to those rules.

[8 Sch 33; SI 1997 No 220, 1 Sch].

7.16 Revaluation reserve

Any profit or loss arising from the determination of the value of an asset of a small company according to any basis in 7.14(a)–(e) above (after allowing for provisions for depreciation or diminution in value) must be credited or debited to a separate reserve, the 'revaluation reserve'. The amount of the revaluation reserve must be shown (but not necessarily under that name) in the balance sheet under a separate sub-heading in the position given for the item 'revaluation reserve' in either of the balance sheet formats in 7.6 above.

The revaluation reserve may be reduced to the extent that amounts transferred to it are no longer necessary for the purposes of the valuation method used. In addition, an amount may be transferred

- from the revaluation reserve to profit and loss account, if the amount was previously charged to that account or represents realised profit; or

- from the revaluation reserve on capitalisation (i.e. by applying the amount in paying up (wholly or partly) unissued shares in the company to be allotted to the members as fully or partly paid shares, see BONUS ISSUES (13)); and

- to or from the revaluation reserve in respect of taxation relating to any profit or loss credited or debited to the reserve.

The revaluation reserve must not be reduced other than as mentioned above.

The treatment for taxation purposes of amounts credited or debited to the revaluation reserve must be disclosed in a note to the accounts.

[8 Sch 34; SI 1997 No 220, 1 Sch].

7.17 NOTES TO THE ACCOUNTS: GENERAL

Comparative figures. Except where otherwise stated in this chapter and in 4 ACCOUNTS: GROUPS OF COMPANIES, there must be shown, in respect of each item stated in the notes to the accounts, the corresponding amount for the immediately preceding financial year. Where the corresponding amount is not comparable, it must be adjusted and particulars of, and reasons for, the adjustment must be given. [8 Sch 51(2); SI 1997 No 220, 1 Sch].

Foreign currency translation. Where any items in the balance sheet or profit and loss account includes sums originally denominated in foreign currencies, the basis on which those sums have been translated into sterling must be stated. [8 Sch 51(1); SI 1997 No 220, 1 Sch].

Disclosure of accounting policies. The accounting policies adopted in determining the profit or loss and the amounts of balance sheet items (including policies with respect to depreciation and diminution in value of assets) must be stated either in the accounts or in the notes. [8 Sch 36; SI 1997 No 220, 1 Sch].

7.18 NOTES TO THE ACCOUNTS: INFORMATION SUPPLEMENTING THE BALANCE SHEET

The information required, as set out in 7.19 to 7.25 below, being information which either supplements that given with respect to particular items in the balance sheet or is otherwise relevant to assessing the company's state of affairs, must be given by way of notes to the accounts (if not given in the accounts themselves). [8 Sch 35, 37; SI 1997 No 220, 1 Sch].

7.19 Share capital

Both the authorised share capital and, where shares of more than one class have been allotted, the number and aggregate nominal value of shares of each class allotted must be stated.

If any part of the allotted share capital consists of redeemable shares, the following information shall be given.

- The earliest and latest dates on which the company has power to redeem those shares.

- Whether the shares must be redeemed in any event or are liable to be redeemed at either the company's or the shareholder's option.

- Whether any premium is payable on redemption and, if so, the amount thereof.

The following information must be given in respect of any shares allotted during the financial year.

(i)   The classes of shares allotted.

(ii)   As regards each class of shares, the number allotted, their aggregate nominal value, and the consideration received by the company for the allotment.

[*8 Sch 38, 39; SI 1997 No 220, 1 Sch*].

7.20 Fixed assets

The information set out below is required for each item shown under the general item 'fixed assets' in the balance sheet (or which would be shown there were it not for 7.5(*b*)(ii) above).

(*a*)   The 'appropriate amounts' in respect of that item both at the beginning of the financial year and at the balance sheet date.

(*b*)   The effect on any amount shown in respect of that item of

- any revision of the amount in respect of any assets included under that item made during that year on any basis in 7.14(*a*)–(*e*) above;

- acquisitions and disposals during that year; and

- any transfers of assets of the company to or from that item during that year.

(*c*)   As regards provisions for depreciation or diminution in value of assets

- the cumulative amount of such provisions included under that item as at each of the times specified in (*a*) above;

- the amount of any such provisions made in respect of that year; and

- the amount of any adjustments made to any such provisions during that year, distinguishing between adjustments made in consequence of disposals and other adjustments.

Comparative figures for the preceding year are not required for (*a*)–(*c*) above.

For the purposes of (*a*) above, the '*appropriate amounts*' in respect of any item at either of the times there mentioned are the aggregate amounts determined, as at that time, in respect of assets falling to be included under that item, either on the basis of purchase price or production cost (see 7.13 above) or on any basis mentioned in 7.14(*a*)–(*e*) above (but, in either case, leaving out of account any provisions for depreciation or diminution in value).

[*8 Sch 40, 51(3)(d); SI 1997 No 220, 1 Sch*].

Asset included at valuation. The following additional information is required where any fixed assets (other than 'listed investments' – see 7.21 below) are included under any balance sheet item at an amount determined on any basis in 7.14(*a*)–(*e*) above.

(i)   The years (so far as known to the directors) in which the assets were severally valued, and the several values.

(ii)   In the case of assets valued during the financial year, the bases of valuation used and either the names or relevant qualifications of the valuers.

[*8 Sch 41; SI 1997 No 220, 1 Sch*].

7.21 Investments

In respect of the amount of each item shown in the balance sheet under the general item 'investments' (whether as fixed assets or current assets) (or which would be shown there

7.22 Accounts: Small and Medium-Sized Companies

were it not for 7.5(b)(ii) above) there must be stated how much is ascribable to 'listed investments'.

Where the amount of any listed investments is stated (as required above) their aggregate market value, where this differs from the amount so stated, must also be shown. In cases where the market value of any such investments is taken for accounts purposes to be higher than their stock exchange value, both values must be given for those investments.

A 'listed investment' is an investment which has been granted a listing either on a recognised investment exchange (other than an overseas investment exchange within the meaning of the *FSA 1986*) or on any stock exchange of repute outside Great Britain.

[*8 Sch 42, 54; SI 1997 No 220, 1 Sch*].

See also 7.32 to 7.39 below for disclosure of shares in related undertakings.

7.22 Reserves and provisions

Where any amount is transferred

- to or from any reserves,

- to any provisions for liabilities and charges, or

- from any such provision, otherwise than for the purpose for which the provision was set up,

and the reserves or provisions are shown as separate items in the balance sheet (or would be so shown were it not for 7.5(*b*)(ii) above) the following information must be given in respect of the aggregate of reserves or provisions included in the same item.

- The amount of the reserves or provisions at the beginning of the financial year and at the balance sheet date.

- Any amounts transferred to or from the reserves or provisions during that year.

- The source and application of the amounts transferred during the year.

Where the amount of the provision is material, particulars must be given of each provision included in the item 'other provisions' in the balance sheet.

Comparative figures for the preceding year are not required for any of the above information.

[*8 Sch 43, 51(3)(d); SI 1997 No 220, 1 Sch*].

See 2.1 ACCOUNTS: DEFINITIONS for the meaning of '*provision*'.

7.23 Details of indebtedness

The following information must be disclosed.

(*a*) In respect of the aggregate of all items shown in the balance sheet under 'creditors' (or which would be shown there were it not for 7.5(*b*)(ii) above)

    (i) the aggregate amount of any debts included under 'creditors' which are payable or repayable otherwise than by instalments and which fall due for payment or repayment after the end of the period of five years beginning with the day after the end of the financial year; and

    (ii) the aggregate amount of any debts so included which are payable or repayable by instalments any of which fall due after the end of the period specified in (*a*) above.

(*b*)   In respect of each item shown in the balance sheet under 'creditors' (or which would be shown there were it not for 7.5(*b*)(ii) above) the aggregate amount of any debts included under that item in respect of which the company has given any security.

Where a distinction is made in the balance sheet between amounts falling due to creditors within one year and those falling due after more than one year, (*a*) above applies only to an item shown under the latter category and (*b*) above applies to an item shown under either category.

[*8 Sch 44; SI 1997 No 220, 1 Sch*].

Fixed cumulative dividends. If any fixed cumulative dividends on the company's shares are in arrears, there must be stated the amount of the arrears and the period for which the dividends (or each class of dividends where there is more than one class) are in arrears. [*8 Sch 45; SI 1997 No 220, 1 Sch*].

7.24   **Guarantees and other financial commitments**

The following information is required.

(*a*)   Particulars of any charge on the company's assets to secure the liabilities of any other person, including, where practicable, the amount secured.

(*b*)   With respect to any other contingent liability not provided for

(i)   its amount or estimated amount;

(ii)   its legal nature; and

(iii)   whether any, and if so what, valuable security has been provided by the company in connection with the liability.

(c)   Where practicable, the aggregate amount or estimated amount of contracts for capital expenditure, so far as not provided for.

(*d*)   Particulars of any pension commitments included under any provision shown in the balance sheet and of any such commitments for which no provision has been made, giving separate particulars of any commitment to the extent that it relates to pensions payable to past directors.

(*e*)   Particulars of any other financial commitments which have not been provided for and are relevant to assessing the company's state of affairs.

Commitments within any of (*a*)–(*e*) above which are undertaken on behalf of or for the benefit of

(i)   any parent undertaking or fellow subsidiary undertaking, or

(ii)   any subsidiary undertaking of the company,

must be stated separately from the other commitments within each of (*a*)–(*e*) above, distinguishing between commitments within (i) and those within (ii) above.

[*8 Sch 46; SI 1997 No 220, 1 Sch*].

7.25   **Miscellaneous**

Particulars must be given of any case where the purchase price or production cost of any asset is for the first time determined under *8 Sch 28* (see 7.13 above). [*8 Sch 47; SI 1997 No 220, 1 Sch*].

7.26 NOTES TO THE ACCOUNTS: INFORMATION SUPPLEMENTING THE PROFIT AND LOSS ACCOUNT

The information required, as set out in 7.27 to 7.29 below, being information which either supplements that given with respect to particular items in the profit and loss account or otherwise provides particulars of income or expenditure or of circumstances affecting items shown in the profit and loss account, must be given by way of notes to the accounts (if not given in the accounts themselves). [*8 Sch 35, 48; SI 1997 No 220, 1 Sch*].

7.27 Particulars of turnover

If the company has supplied geographical markets outside the United Kingdom during the financial year in question, the percentage of turnover attributable, in the opinion of the directors, to those markets must be stated. In analysing the source of turnover, the directors must have regard to the manner in which the company's activities are organised. [*8 Sch 49; SI 1997 No 220, 1 Sch*].

7.28 Prior year adjustments.

Where any amount relating to any preceding financial year is included in any profit and loss account item, the effect must be stated. [*8 Sch 50(1); SI 1997 No 220, 1 Sch*].

7.29 Exceptional and extraordinary items

Exceptional items. The effect of any transactions that are exceptional (by virtue of size or incidence) must be stated, even though they fall within the company's ordinary activities. [*8 Sch 50(3); SI 1997 No 220, 1 Sch*].

Extraordinary items. Particulars must be given of any extraordinary income or charges arising in the financial year. [*8 Sch 50(2); SI 1997 No 220, 1 Sch*].

7.30 NOTES TO THE ACCOUNTS: DISCLOSURE OF EMOLUMENTS AND OTHER BENEFITS OF DIRECTORS AND OTHERS

With the following exceptions, the individual accounts of a small company must comply with the provisions of *6 Sch* (emoluments and benefits of directors and others). See 5.32 to 5.43 ACCOUNTS: INDIVIDUAL COMPANIES for full details of *6 Sch*. The exceptions are that small companies

- may give the total of the aggregates required by 5.34(a), (*c*) and (*d*) instead of giving those aggregates individually; and

- need not give the information required by 5.34(*f*) (number of directors exercising share options and receiving shares under long term incentive schemes); 5.35 (highest paid director's emoluments, etc.); or 5.36 (excess retirement benefits of directors and past directors).

[*Sec 246(3); SI 1997 No 220; SI 1997 No 570, Reg 6*].

7.31 NOTES TO THE ACCOUNTS: DISCLOSURE OF AUDITORS' REMUNERATION

The provisions of 5.44 ACCOUNTS: INDIVIDUAL COMPANIES apply to small companies as for other companies.

7.32   NOTES TO THE ACCOUNTS: RELATED UNDERTAKINGS

The information described in 7.33 to 7.39 below must be given in the notes to the annual accounts of a small company which is not required to prepare group accounts. [*Sec 246(3); SI 1997 No 220; SI 1997 No 570, Reg 6*].

The said information (other than that in 7.36 and 7.38 below) need not, however, be disclosed with respect to an undertaking which is established under the law of a country outside the UK or which carries on business outside the UK, but only if the disclosure would, in the opinion of the directors of the company, seriously prejudice the business of that undertaking, or that of the company or any of its subsidiary undertakings *and* the Secretary of State agrees to the non-disclosure. The fact of any non-disclosure must be stated in a note to the accounts.

The information required under any provision described in 7.33 to 7.39 below need not be given for *all* related undertakings if (in the opinion of the directors of the company) to do so would result in a statement of excessive length. In such a case, the information in question need only be given in respect of

(*a*)   the undertakings whose results or financial position, in the directors' opinion, principally affected the figures shown in the company's annual accounts; and

(*b*)   undertakings excluded from consolidation under *Sec 229(3)* or *(4)* (see 4.10(*b*)(*c*) ACCOUNTS: GROUPS OF COMPANIES).

If advantage is taken of this, then both the following apply.

(i)   The notes to the company's annual accounts must include a statement that the information is given only with respect to undertakings of the type mentioned in (*a*) and (*b*) above.

(ii)   The full information (i.e. that which is disclosed and that which is not) must be annexed to the next annual return delivered to the Registrar of Companies after the accounts in question have been approved by the board (see 3.2 ACCOUNTS: GENERAL).

In the event of non-compliance with (ii) above, the company and every officer in default is liable to a penalty up to the level in 40.1(*f*) PENALTIES.

[*Sec 231, 24 Sch; CA 1989, s 6; SI 1993 No 1820, Reg 11; SI 1996 No 189, Reg 15*].

7.33   Details of subsidiary undertakings

Subject to 7.32 above, where, at the end of the financial year, the company has subsidiary undertakings, there must be stated in respect of each one of them

•   its name;

•   if it is incorporated outside Great Britain, the country in which it is incorporated; and

•   if it is unincorporated, the address of its principal place of business.

There must also be stated the reason why the company is not required to prepare group accounts and, if the reason is that all the company's subsidiary undertakings fall within the exclusion in *Sec 229* (see 4.10 ACCOUNTS: GROUPS OF COMPANIES), there must be stated, for each such undertaking, which of those exclusions applies.

[*5 Sch 1; CA 1989, 3 Sch; SI 1996 No 189, 3 Sch 2*].

7.34   Accounts: Small and Medium-Sized Companies

7.34   Shareholdings in subsidiary undertakings

Subject to 7.32 above, for shares of each class 'held by the company' in a subsidiary undertaking, there must be stated the identity of the class and the proportion of the nominal value of the shares of that class which the shares held represents. A distinction must be made (i.e. in the relevant note to the accounts) between shares held by or on behalf of the company itself and shares attributed to the company (see below) which are held by or on behalf of a subsidiary undertaking. [*5 Sch 2; CA 1989, 3 Sch*].

Comparative figures for the preceding year are not required. [*8 Sch 51(3); SI 1997 No 220*].

In ascertaining the shares '*held by the company*', there must be attributed to the company any shares held by a subsidiary undertaking or a person acting on behalf of either the company or a subsidiary undertaking. Shares held on behalf of a person other than the company or a subsidiary undertaking (including any that would otherwise be attributed to the company as above) are not to be treated as held by the company. [*5 Sch 13(2); CA 1989, 3 Sch; SI 1996 No 189, 3 Sch 13*]. Shares held by way of security must be treated as being held by the person providing the security where

- the rights attached to the shares are exercisable only in accordance with that person's instructions, and

- the shares are held in connection with the granting of loans as part of normal business activities and the rights attached to the shares are exercisable only in the said person's interests,

disregarding, in each case, any right to exercise the said rights for the purpose of preserving or realising the value of the security. [*5 Sch 13(4); CA 1989, 3 Sch*].

7.35   Financial information with respect to subsidiary undertakings

Subject to 7.32 above, and the exceptions below, there must be disclosed with respect to every subsidiary undertaking

- the aggregate amount of its capital and reserves as at the end of its 'relevant financial year'; and

- its profit or loss for that year.

For the purpose, the '*relevant financial year*' of a subsidiary undertaking is, if its financial year ends with that of the company, that year and, in any other case, its financial year ending last before the end of the company's financial year.

Exceptions. Information which is not material need not be given. Also, the above information need not be given if

- the company is exempt by virtue of *Sec 228* (see 4.9 ACCOUNTS: GROUPS OF COMPANIES) from the requirement to prepare group accounts;

- the subsidiary undertaking in question is not required by any provision of *CA 1985* to deliver a copy of its balance sheet for the relevant financial year and does not otherwise publish it (in Great Britain or elsewhere), and the shares 'held by the company' (see 7.34 above) are less than 50% of the nominal value of the shares in the undertaking; or

- the company's investment in the subsidiary undertaking is included in the company's accounts by way of the equity method of valuation.

[*5 Sch 3; CA 1989, 3 Sch; SI 1996 No 189, 3 Sch 3*].

7.36   **Shares and debentures of company held by subsidiary undertakings**

Subject to 7.32 above, the number, description and amount of shares in the company held by, or on behalf of, its subsidiary undertakings must be disclosed. This does not apply to shares in respect of which the subsidiary undertaking is concerned as

- personal representative; or

- trustee (unless the company, or any of its subsidiary undertakings, is 'beneficially interested under the trust' otherwise than by way of security only for the purposes of a transaction entered into by it in the ordinary course of a business which includes the lending of money.

In determining whether the company is '*beneficially interested under the trust*' certain interests mentioned in *2 Sch Part II* are disregarded (residual interests under pension and employee share schemes, company's rights as trustee to expenses, remuneration, etc.).

[*5 Sch 6; CA 1989, 3 Sch; SI 1996 No 189, 3 Sch 6*].

7.37   **Significant holdings in undertakings other than subsidiary undertakings**

Subject to 7.32 above, where at the end of the financial year the company has a 'significant holding' in an undertaking which is not a subsidiary undertaking, the following must be stated.

(*a*)   The name of the undertaking.

(*b*)   If it is incorporated outside Great Britain, the country in which it is incorporated.

(*c*)   If it is unincorporated, the address of its principal place of business.

(*d*)   The identity of each class of shares in the undertaking held by the company.

(*e*)   The proportion of the nominal value of the shares of that class represented by those shares.

(*f*)   The aggregate amount of the capital and reserves of the undertaking as at the end of its 'relevant financial year'.

(*g*)   Its profit or loss for that year.

A '*significant holding*' is a holding which amounts to 20% or more of the nominal value of any class of shares in the undertaking *or* the amount of which (as stated or included in the company's individual accounts) exceeds 20% of the amount of its assets (as so stated).

'*Relevant financial year*' of an undertaking is, if its financial year ends with that of the company, that year and, in any other case, its financial year ending last before the end of the company's financial year.

The information in (*f*) and (*g*) above need not be given if

- the company is exempt by virtue of *Sec 228* (see 4.9 ACCOUNTS: GROUPS OF COMPANIES) from the requirement to prepare group accounts *and* the investment of the company in all undertakings in which it has a holding of 20% or more is shown, in aggregate, in the notes to the accounts by way of the equity method of valuation; or

- the undertaking in question is not required by any provision of *CA 1985* to deliver a copy of its balance sheet for its relevant financial year and does not otherwise publish it (in Great Britain or elsewhere) *and* the company's holding is less than 50% of the nominal value of the shares in the undertaking.

7.38   Accounts: Small and Medium-Sized Companies

[*5 Sch 7–9; CA 1989, 3 Sch; SI 1996 No 189, 3 Sch 7–9*].

Comparative figures for the preceding year are not required with respect to the information in (*d*) and (*e*) above. [*8 Sch 51(3)(b); SI 1997 No 220*].

In ascertaining, for any of the above purposes, the company's holding, there must be attributed to the company any shares held on its behalf by any person. Shares held on behalf of a person other than the company (including any that would otherwise be attributed to the company as above) are not to be treated as held by the company. [*5 Sch 13(3); CA 1989, 3 Sch*]. 5 Sch 13(4) (see 7.34 above) also applies for these purposes.

7.38   Membership of certain partnerships and unlimited partnerships

Subject to 7.32 above, where at the end of a financial year a company is a member of a 'qualifying partnership' (see 39.4 PARTNERSHIPS) or a 'qualifying unlimited company' (see 60.3(*b*) UNLIMITED COMPANIES), the following must be stated.

• The name and legal form of the undertaking (unless not material).

• The address of its registered office or, if it does not have such an office, its head office (unless not material).

• If the undertaking is a qualifying partnership, either

   (i)   a statement that a copy of the latest accounts of the partnership has been or is to be appended to a copy of the company's accounts sent to the Registrar of Companies, or

   (ii)   the name of at least one body corporate (which may be the company itself) in whose group accounts the undertaking has been, or is to be, dealt with on a consolidated basis. The information need not be given if the notes to the accounts disclose that advantage has been taken of the exemption in 39.4 PARTNERSHIPS.

[*5 Sch 9A; SI 1993 No 1820, Reg 11*].

7.39   Information required where the company is a subsidiary undertaking

Subject to 7.32 above, where the company is a subsidiary undertaking, the following information must be given.

(*a*)   Particulars, as follows, with respect to the '*company*' (meaning any body corporate) regarded by the directors as the company's ultimate parent.

   (i)   Its name.

   (ii)   If it is incorporated outside Great Britain, the country in which it is incorporated (only if known to the directors).

(*b*)   Particulars, as follows, with respect to the parent undertaking of the largest and smallest group of undertakings for which group accounts are drawn up and of which the company is a member.

   (i)   The same information as in (*a*)(i) and (ii) above (but without the exception for information not known to the directors).

   (ii)   If the undertaking is unincorporated, the address of its principal place of business.

   (iii)   If copies of the above-mentioned group accounts are available to the public, the address from which such copies can be obtained.

[*5 Sch 11, 12; CA 1989, 3 Sch; SI 1996 No 189, 3 Sch 11, 12*].

7.40   **SMALL COMPANIES: ACCOUNTS DELIVERED TO THE REGISTRAR OF COMPANIES**

A small company (see 7.2 above) whether or not it takes advantage of the provisions of 7.5 to 7.39 above with respect to the preparation of its annual accounts generally, may deliver accounts to the Registrar of Companies in an abbreviated form as follows.

(*a*)   It need not deliver a copy of its directors' report for the year (see 20.15 DIRECTORS' REPORT).

(*b*)   It need not deliver a copy of its profit and loss account for the year.

(*c*)   If it delivers a copy of a balance sheet drawn up as at the last day of the financial year in accordance with the requirements in 7.41 below, it need not deliver a copy of the individual balance sheet forming part of its annual accounts.

(*d*)   The notes to the accounts need only comply with the requirements in 7.42 below.

Where the directors take advantage of these provisions, the copy balance sheet delivered to the Registrar of Companies must contain, in a prominent position above the director's signature, a statement that the accounts have been prepared in accordance with the special provisions relating to small companies.

[*Sec 246(5)(8)(9); SI 1997 No 220, Reg 2*].

7.41   **Balance sheet**

A small company may deliver to the Registrar of Companies a copy of the balance sheet abbreviated to show only those items listed in either of the balance sheet formats set out below in the order and under the headings and sub-headings given in the format adopted, but in other respects corresponding to the full balance sheet.

Format 1

A.   Called up share capital not paid

B.   Fixed assets

    I   Intangible assets

    II   Tangible assets

    III   Investments

C.   Current assets

    I   Stocks

    II   Debtors (note (1))

    III   Investments

    IV   Cash at bank and in hand

D.   Prepayments and accrued income

E.   Creditors: amounts falling due within one year

F.   Net current assets (liabilities)

G.   Total assets less current liabilities

H.   Creditors: amounts falling due after more than one year

I.   Provisions for liabilities and charges

7.42 Accounts: Small and Medium-Sized Companies

J. Accruals and deferred income

K. Capital and reserves

    I   Called up share capital

    II   Share premium account

    III   Revaluation reserve

    IV   Other reserves

    V   Profit and loss account

Format 2

ASSETS

As per A. to D. in Format 1 above

LIABILITIES

A. Capital and reserves

    As per K. in Format I above

B. Provisions for liabilities and charges

C. Creditors (note (2))

D. Accruals and deferred income

Notes

(1) *Debtors.* The aggregate amount of debtors falling due after more than one year must be shown separately (unless disclosed in the notes to the accounts).

(2) *Creditors.* The aggregate amount of creditors falling due within one year and after more than one year must be shown separately (unless disclosed in the notes to the accounts).

The provisions of *Sec 233* (see 3.2 ACCOUNTS: GENERAL) as regards the signing of the balance sheet apply equally to an abbreviated balance sheet.

[*Sec 246(7), 8A Sch 1, 2; SI 1997 No 220, Reg 2, 2 Sch*].

7.42 **Notes to the accounts**

The copy of a company's accounts for the year delivered to the Registrar of Companies or a copy of the balance sheet delivered under 7.41 above need only include the following information by way of notes.

(a) *Of the information otherwise required by 8 Sch Part III (4 Sch Part III where advantage is not taken of the small companies provisions)* only the following details need be given.

   • Accounting policies as in *8 Sch 36* (see 7.17 above).

   • Share capital as in *8 Sch 38, 39* (see 7.19 above).

   • Fixed assets as in *8 Sch 40* (see 7.20 above).

   • Indebtedness as in *8 Sch 44* (see 7.23 above).

- Foreign currency translation into sterling as in *8 Sch 51(1)* (see 7.17 above).

Comparative figures for the previous financial year must also be given.

(b)   *Of the information required by 5 Sch* only the following details need be given.

- Details of subsidiary undertakings in *5 Sch 1* (see 7.33 above).

- Shareholdings in subsidiary undertakings in *5 Sch 2* (see 7.34 above).

- Financial information with respect to subsidiary undertakings in *5 Sch 3* (see 7.35 above).

- Significant holdings in undertakings other than subsidiary undertakings in *5 Sch 7–9* (see 7.37 above).

- Membership of certain partnerships and unlimited partnerships in *5 Sch 9A* (see 7.38 above).

- Information required where the company is a subsidiary undertaking in *5 Sch 11, 12* (see 7.39 above).

(c)   *Of the information required by 6 Sch* (emoluments and other benefits of directors and others) only the following details need be given.

- Loans, quasi-loans and other dealings in *6 Sch 15–27* (see 5.39 to 5.42 ACCOUNTS: INDIVIDUAL COMPANIES).

- Transactions etc. by officers other than directors in *6 Sch 28–30* (see 5.43 ACCOUNTS: INDIVIDUAL COMPANIES).

[Sec 246(6), 8A Sch 3–9; SI 1997 No 220].

The company is also exempt from the disclosure requirements for payments to auditors under *Sec 390A* (audit work) and *Sec 390B* (non-audit work), see 5.44 ACCOUNTS: INDIVIDUAL COMPANIES. *[Sec 246(6); SI 1991 No 2128, Reg 4; SI 1997 No 220, Reg 2].*

7.43   MEDIUM-SIZED COMPANIES: FORM AND CONTENT OF INDIVIDUAL ACCOUNTS

With one minor exception, there are no special provisions for the form and content of the individual accounts of 'medium-sized' companies (see 7.2 above). Such companies must prepare individual accounts complying with the full requirements in ACCOUNTS: INDIVIDUAL COMPANIES(5).

The one exception is that a medium-sized company's individual accounts need not comply with the requirements of *4 Sch 36A* (disclosure with respect to compliance with accounting standards, see 5.15 ACCOUNTS: INDIVIDUAL COMPANIES). *[Sec 246A(2); SI 1997 No 220, Reg 3].*

7.44   MEDIUM-SIZED COMPANIES: ACCOUNTS DELIVERED TO THE REGISTRAR OF COMPANIES

A 'medium-sized' company (see 7.2 above) may deliver to the Registrar of Companies a copy of its accounts for the year which vary from its individual accounts as follows.

(a)   In the profit and loss account, the following items listed in the profit and loss account formats set out in 5.5 ACCOUNTS: INDIVIDUAL COMPANIES may be combined as one item under the heading 'gross profit or loss'.

- In Format 1 – items 1, 2, 3 and 6

7.45 Accounts: Small and Medium-Sized Companies

- In Format 2 – items 1 to 5.

- In Format 3 – items A.1, B.1 and B.2.

- In Format 4 – items A.1, A.2 and B1 to B4.

(*b*) In the notes to the accounts, the information required by *4 Sch 55* (particulars of turnover, see 5.27 ACCOUNTS: INDIVIDUAL COMPANIES) need not be given.

Where the directors take advantage of these provisions, the accounts delivered to the Registrar of Companies must contain, in a prominent position on the balance sheet above the director's signature, a statement that the accounts have been prepared in accordance with the special provisions relating to medium-sized companies.

[Sec 246A(3)(4); SI 1997 No 220, Reg 3].

7.45 GROUP ACCOUNTS: EXEMPTIONS FOR SMALL AND MEDIUM-SIZED GROUPS

'Small' and 'medium-sized' groups (see 7.2 above) may be exempt from the requirements to prepare group accounts in certain circumstances. See 7.46 below.

In addition, where a small company is entitled to prepare abbreviated accounts it can prepare any group accounts under the same provisions. See 7.47 below.

7.46 Exemption from requirement to prepare group accounts

A parent company need not prepare group accounts for a financial year in relation to which the group headed by that company qualifies as a 'small' or 'medium-sized' group (see 7.2 above) and is not an 'ineligible' group.

A group is '*ineligible*' if any of its members is

- a public company;

- a body corporate (other than a company) which has power under its constitution to offer shares or debentures to the public, and may lawfully exercise that power;

- an authorised institution under *Banking Act 1987*;

- an insurance company to which *Insurance Companies Act 1982, Pt II* applies (including an EC company lawfully carrying on insurance business in the UK); or

- an authorised person under *FSA 1986*.

[Sec 248(1)(2); CA 1989, s 13; SI 1994 No 1696, 8 Sch 9].

Auditors' report. See 12.21 AUDITORS for the auditors' duty in their report where the company takes advantage of the above exemption.

7.47 SMALL COMPANIES: ABBREVIATED GROUP ACCOUNTS

Where a 'small' company (see 7.2 above) has prepared individual abbreviated accounts for a financial year in accordance with the provisions of 7.5 to 7.39 above and is preparing group accounts in respect of the same year, it may prepare those group accounts under the same rules, subject to the exception below.

The exception referred to above is that in the balance sheet formats, the items under B.III Investments must not be shown as in 7.6 above but as

1. Shares in group undertakings

2.   Interests in associated companies

3.   Other participating interests

4.   Loans to group undertakings and undertakings in which a participating interest is held

5.   Other investments other than loans

6.   Other

Where abbreviated group accounts are prepared under the above provisions, the balance sheet must contain, in a prominent position above the director's signature, a statement that the accounts have been prepared in accordance with the special provisions relating to small companies.

[*Sec 248A; SI 1997 No 220, Reg 6*].

8 Acquisition of Own Shares

Cross-references. See 30.7 INSIDER DEALING for the Stock Exchange Model Code on securities transactions by directors of listed companies which is also to be regarded as applicable to purchases by a listed company of its own shares; 43.7(*d*) and 43.20 PUBLIC AND LISTED COMPANIES for additional requirements of listed companies in connection with own share purchase under the Listing Rules; 59.16 TAKEOVER OFFERS.

The contents of this chapter are as follows.

8.1   INTRODUCTION

As a general rule, a company limited by shares, or limited by guarantee and having a share capital, must not acquire its own shares, whether by purchase, subscription or otherwise. [*Sec 143(1)*]. See *Trevor v Whitworth (1887) 12 App Cas 409*. This does not, however, apply to the following.

(*a*)   The acquisition of own shares otherwise than for valuable consideration. See *Kirby v Wilkins [1929] 2 Ch 444* and *Re Castiglione's Will Trust [1958] Ch 549* for shares acquired by way of gift and bequeathed by will respectively.

(*b*)   The redemption of redeemable shares or the purchase of own shares under *Secs 159-181* (see 8.2 to 8.17 below).

(*c*)   The acquisition of shares in a reduction of share capital duly made (see 58.17 SHARES AND SHARE CAPITAL);

(*d*)   The purchase of shares in pursuance of a court order under

●   *Sec 5* (alteration of objects, see 35.8 MEMORANDUM OF ASSOCIATION);

●   *Sec 54* (objection to re-registration of a public company as a private company, see 49.12 REGISTRATION AND RE-REGISTRATION); or

●   *Secs 459-461* (protection of members against unfair prejudice, see 34.6 and 34.7 MEMBERS).

(*e*)   The forfeiture of shares, or the acceptance of shares surrendered in lieu, for failure to pay any sum payable in respect of the shares (see 58.11 SHARES AND SHARE CAPITAL).

Where a company purports to acquire its own shares in breach of the above provisions it is liable to a fine up to the level in 40.1(*d*) PENALTIES and any officer in default is liable to a penalty up to the level in 40.1(*b*) PENALTIES. The purported acquisition is void.

[*Sec 143(2)(3), 24 Sch*].

The above provisions do not preclude a company from acquiring the shares of another company even in circumstances where the sole asset of the acquired company is shares in the acquiring company (*Acatos & Hutcheson plc v Watson ChD 1994 [1995] 1 BCLC 248*).

See also 8.22 below for restrictions on a subsidiary being a member of its holding company.

In certain circumstances a person can acquire shares in a company with financial assistance from the company. See 8.18 to 8.21 below.

See also 58.26 SHARES AND SHARE CAPITAL where a nominee acquires shares in a company on behalf of the company with or without financial assistance from that company.

8.2   REDEEMABLE SHARES

A company (whether public or private) limited by shares, or limited by guarantee and having a share capital, may, if authorised to do so by its articles, issue redeemable shares whether redemption is at the option of the company or the shareholder. Where *Table A in SI 1985 No 805* has been adopted, the relevant authority is contained in *Art 3*.

Redeemable shares

- must not be issued unless

  (i)   at the time of issue, there are other issued shares which are not redeemable; and

  (ii)   the conditions as to the terms and manner of redemption under 8.3 below are satisfied; and

- must not be redeemed unless they are fully paid and the terms of redemption provide for payment on redemption.

[*Sec 159*].

The provisions of 8.10 to 8.17 below apply both to the redemption of shares under these provisions and the purchase of shares under 8.4 below.

The Secretary of State may, by statutory instrument, modify any of the provisions relating to redeemable shares. [*Sec 179*].

Transitional provisions. Any redeemable shares issued by a company before 15 June 1982 (which before that date could have been redeemed under *CA 1948, s 58*) are now subject to the provisions for redemption under *CA 1985* as described in this chapter. [*Sec 180(1)*].

8.3   Terms and manner of redemption

Shares can be redeemed on such terms and in such manner as the articles provide. [*Sec 160(3)*]. See, however, 43.20 PUBLIC AND LISTED COMPANIES for the maximum price payable by a listed company.

With effect from a date to be appointed, the above provisions are repealed by *CA 1989, s 133* and replaced by a new *Sec 159A*. Redeemable shares could then only be issued if the following conditions were satisfied as regard to their redemption.

- The date on or by which, or dates between which, the shares may be redeemed must be

  (i)   specified in the company's articles; or

  (ii)   if the articles so provide, fixed by the directors (in which case the date or dates must be fixed before the shares are issued).

8.4   Acquisition of Own Shares

- The amount payable on redemption must be specified in, or determined in accordance with, the company's articles (but, in the latter case, not by reference to any person's discretion or opinion).

- Any other circumstances in which the shares may be redeemed, and any other terms and conditions of redemption, must be specified in the company's articles.

However, it is understood that the implementation of *Sec 159A* has been indefinitely postponed.

8.4   PURCHASE OF OWN SHARES

A company limited by shares, or limited by guarantee and having a share capital, may, if authorised by its articles, purchase its own shares (including redeemable shares). Where *Table A in SI 1985 No 805* has been adopted, the relevant authority is contained in *Art 35*. There is no equivalent provision in *Table A in CA 1948*.

A company may not, however, purchase its own shares

- if, as a result of the purchase, there would no longer be any member of the company holding shares other than redeemable shares; and

- unless they are fully paid and the terms of purchase provide for payment on purchase.

The provisions of 8.10 to 8.17 below apply both to the purchase of own shares under these provisions and the redemption of shares under 8.2 above.

[Sec 162].

The Secretary of State may, by statutory instrument, modify any of the provisions relating to purchase of own shares. *[Sec 179]*.

8.5   Authority for off-market purchase

A company may only make an 'off-market purchase' of its own shares if the proposed contract has been authorised, or the proposed 'contingent purchase contract' has been approved in advance, by a special resolution of the company.

An *'off-market purchase'* is one where the shares are either

(i)   not purchased on a 'recognised investment exchange'; or

(ii)   purchased on a recognised investment exchange but neither are the shares listed under *FSA 1986, Part IV* nor has the company been afforded facilities for dealings in those shares to take place on that investment exchange without prior permission for individual transactions from the governing authority and without time limit on the availability of those facilities.

For these purposes *'recognised investment exchange'* means a recognised investment exchange other than an overseas investment exchange within the meaning of *FSA 1986*.

A *'contingent purchase contract'* is one that does not amount to a contract by a company to purchase its own shares but under which, subject to any conditions, the company may become entitled or obliged to purchase those shares.

[Secs 163(1)(2)(4), 164(1)(2), 165; FSA 1986, 16 Sch 1].

See 51 RESOLUTIONS generally for circulating notice and passing etc. of special resolutions. In the case of a public company, the authority conferred by the special resolution and the special resolution itself must specify a date (not later than 18 months after the resolution is passed) on which the authority is to expire.

Further special resolution(s) may vary, revoke or renew the authority given (subject to, in the case of a public company, a similar 18 months' expiry date for any renewed authority).

A special resolution (whether to confer, vary, revoke or renew authority for such a purchase) is not effective unless the following conditions are fulfilled.

(*a*)   Where any member of the company holding shares to which the resolution relates exercises the voting rights of any of those shares in voting on the resolution, the resolution would have been passed if he had not done so. For these purposes

- a member who holds shares to which the resolution relates is regarded as exercising the voting rights on those shares not only if he votes on a poll on whether the resolution should be passed, but also if he votes otherwise than on a poll;

- any member of the company may demand a poll on the question of whether the resolution be passed, notwithstanding anything in the company's articles; and

- a vote and a demand for a poll are the same whether made by a member himself or by his proxy.

(*b*)   A copy of the proposed contract (if it is in writing) or of a written memorandum of its terms (if it is not) is available for inspection by members at the registered office of the company for at least 15 days prior to the meeting and at the meeting itself. A memorandum of contract terms made available must include the names of any members holding shares to which the contract relates and a copy of the contract must have annexed to it a written memorandum specifying any such names not appearing in the contract itself.

The provisions of (*a*) and (*b*) above do not apply for the purposes of *Sec 381A(1)* (written resolutions of private companies, see 51.4 RESOLUTIONS). For those purposes a member holding shares to which the resolution relates is not regarded as a member entitled to attend and vote (and therefore does not need to sign the resolution). Documents referred to under (*b*) must be supplied to each member by whom the resolution has to be signed at or before the time at which the resolution is supplied to him for signature.

A company may agree to a variation to an existing contract which has been properly approved provided the variation is authorised by a special resolution before it is agreed to. All the conditions above apply to the authority for a proposed variation as they apply to the authority for a proposed contract except that under (*b*) above a copy of the original contract (or memorandum of terms) and any variations must be made available for inspection.

[*Sec 164(3)-(7), 15A Sch 5*].

8.6   Authority for market purchase

A company must not make a 'market purchase' of its own shares unless the purchase has first been authorised by the company in general meeting. The authority may be general or limited to the purchase of shares of a particular class or description, and it may be conditional or unconditional. In addition, the authority must

(*a*)   specify the maximum number of shares authorised to be acquired;

(*b*)   determine the maximum and minimum prices which may be paid for the shares. This may be done by specifying a particular sum, or by providing a formula or basis for calculating the price without reference to any person's discretion or opinion; and

(c) specify a date on which the authority is to expire which must be not later than 18 months from the date on which the resolution is passed.

A 'market purchase' is one where the shares are purchased on a 'recognised investment exchange' other than a purchase within 8.5(ii) above. For these purposes, 'recognised investment exchange' means a recognised investment exchange other than an overseas investment exchange within the meaning of *FSA 1986*.

The authority for purchase may be varied, revoked or renewed by the company in general meeting but subject to (a) to (c) above.

A company may make a purchase of its own shares after the expiry of the time limit imposed under (c) above provided

- the contract of purchase was concluded before the authority expired; and

- the terms of the authority permitted the company to make a contract of purchase which would, or might, be executed wholly or partly after its expiry.

A resolution conferring, varying, revoking or renewing authority made under the above provisions must be lodged with the Registrar of Companies for filing within 15 days of it being passed. See 51.9 RESOLUTIONS.

[*Secs 163(3)(4), 166; FSA 1986, 16 Sch 17*].

8.7 Assignment or release of company's right to purchase own shares

The rights of a company under a contract approved under 8.5 above, or a contract for a purchase authorised under 8.6 above, cannot be assigned.

An agreement by a company to release its rights under a contract approved under 8.5 above is void unless the terms of the release agreement are approved in advance by a special resolution before the agreement is entered into. The provisions of *Sec 164(3)-(7)* and *15A Sch 5* (see 8.5 above) apply to approval for a proposed release agreement as to an authority for a proposed variation of an existing contract.

[*Sec 167, 15A Sch 5*].

8.8 Payments to be made out of distributable profits

Apart from the purchase price itself (for which see 8.10 below) any payment made by a company in consideration of

(a) acquiring any right with respect to the purchase of its own shares in pursuance of a contingent purchase contract approved under 8.5 above,

(b) the variation of a contract approved under 8.5 above, or

(c) the release of any of the company's obligations with respect to the purchase of any of its own shares under a contract approved under 8.5 above or authorised under 8.6 above

must be made out of the company's 'distributable profits'. If not, under (a) and (b) above any subsequent purchase of own shares under the contract is unlawful and under (c) above the purported release is void. [*Sec 168*].

'Distributable profits' in relation to the making of any payment by a company means those profits out of which it could lawfully make a distribution (see 23.1 DISTRIBUTIONS). [*Sec 181*].

8.9   Disclosure requirements

Within 28 days from the date shares purchased by a company are delivered to it, the company must deliver to the Registrar of Companies for registration a return in the prescribed form (Form 169) stating, with respect to each class of shares purchased, the number and nominal value of those shares and the date on which they were delivered to the company. For a *public* company the return must also state

(*a*)   the aggregate amount paid for the shares; and

(*b*)   the maximum and minimum prices paid in respect of each class.

Shares delivered to the company on different dates and under different contracts may be included in a single return, in which case the amount under (*a*) above is the aggregate amount for all the shares to which the return relates.

If default is made in delivering any return, every officer of the company in default is liable to a fine up to the level in 40.1(*c*) PENALTIES.

[*Sec 169(1)-(3)(6), 24 Sch*].

Where a company enters into a contract approved under 8.5 above or authorised under 8.6 above the company must keep at its registered office a copy of the contract (if in writing) or a memorandum of its terms (if not) from the conclusion of the contract until ten years from the date on which the purchase of all shares under the contract is completed or (as the case may be) the date on which the contract otherwise determines. This applies to any variation of the contract so long as it applies to the contract. The copy or memorandum required to be kept must be open to inspection without charge by any member or, in the case of a public company, any person for not less than two hours during the period between 9a.m. and 5p.m. every Monday to Friday (other than public and bank holidays). A person inspecting the documents must be permitted to copy any information made available by taking notes or making a transcript but the company is not obliged to provide any additional facilities other than those to facilitate inspection. In default, or if an inspection is refused, the company and every officer in default is liable to a fine up to the level in 40.1(*f*) PENALTIES. For refusal of an inspection the court may compel an immediate inspection. [*Sec 169(4)(5)(7)-(9), 24 Sch; SI 1991 No 1998, Reg 3*].

8.10   FINANCING ETC. OF REDEMPTION OR PURCHASE

Subject to below and the power of *private companies* to redeem or purchase shares out of capital (See 8.12 to 8.16 below)

- shares may only be redeemed or purchased out of 'distributable profits' of the company or out of the proceeds of a fresh issue of shares made especially for the purpose; and

- any premium payable on redemption or purchase must be paid out of distributable profits (but see *Transitional provisions* below).

Where, however, the redeemable shares were issued at a premium, any premium payable on redemption may be paid out of the proceeds of a fresh issue of shares made for the purpose of the redemption, up to an amount equal to

- the aggregate of the premiums received by the company on the issue of the shares redeemed, or

- the current amount of the company's share premium account (including any amount transferred in respect of premiums on the new shares),

whichever is the less. The amount of the company's share premium account must be reduced by an amount (or by an aggregate amount) corresponding to any payment made out of the proceeds of the issue of new shares.

175

8.11 Acquisition of Own Shares

See, also, 8.17(*b*) below for the enforcement of redemption or purchase against the company when shares have not been redeemed or purchased at the commencement of winding up.

'*Distributable profits*' are those profits out of which the company could lawfully make a distribution (see 23.1 DISTRIBUTIONS) equal in value to the payment.

[*Secs 160(1)(2), 162(2), 181*].

On redemption or purchase, the shares must be treated as cancelled and the company's issued share capital (although not its authorised share capital) must be diminished by the nominal value of those shares. [*Sec 160(4)*].

Without prejudice to this, a company about to redeem or purchase shares has power to issue shares up to the nominal value of the shares to be redeemed or purchased as if those shares had never been issued. [*Sec 160(5)*].

Transitional provisions. In the case of redeemable preference shares issued by a company before 15 June 1982, any premium payable on redemption may be paid out of share premium account instead of profits or partly out of each (but subject to the provisions of *CA 1985* as described in this chapter so far as the payment is out of profits). [*Sec 180(2)*].

8.11 THE CAPITAL REDEMPTION RESERVE

Where the purchase or redemption of shares is made wholly out of the company's profits, the amount by which the company's issued share capital is diminished under *Sec 160(4)* (see 8.10 above) on cancellation of the shares must be transferred to a '*capital redemption reserve*'. [*Sec 170(1)*].

Where the purchase or redemption is made wholly or partly out of the proceeds of a fresh issue, and the aggregate amount of those proceeds is less than the aggregate nominal value of the shares purchased or redeemed, the difference in amount must be transferred to the capital redemption reserve; but this does not apply if the proceeds of fresh issue are used to make a redemption or purchase of the company's own shares in addition to a payment out of capital under 8.12 below. [*Sec 170(2)(3)*].

The provisions of *CA 1985* relating to the reduction of a company's share capital (see 58.17 SHARES AND SHARE CAPITAL) apply as if the capital redemption reserve were paid-up share capital except that the reserve may be applied by the company in paying up its unissued shares to be allotted to members as fully paid bonus shares (see 13.4 BONUS ISSUES). [*Sec 170(4)*].

Any capital redemption reserve fund set up before 15 June 1982 under *CA 1948, s 58* is to be treated and construed for all purposes as part of the company's capital redemption reserve. [*Sec 180(3)*].

8.12 PRIVATE COMPANIES: REDEMPTION OR PURCHASE OF OWN SHARES OUT OF CAPITAL

Subject to 8.13 to 8.16 below, a private company limited by shares, or limited by guarantee and having a share capital, may, if authorised by its articles, make a payment in respect of the redemption or purchase of its own shares under 8.10 above other than out of distributable profits or the proceeds of a fresh issue of shares. Where *Table A in SI 1985 No 805* has been adopted, the relevant authority is contained in *Art 35*. There is no equivalent provision in *Table A in CA 1948*.

The payment which may be made out of capital (the '*permissible capital payment*') is such an amount as, taken together with

176

- any available profits of the company (see 8.13 below), and
- the proceeds of any fresh issue of shares made for the purpose of the redemption or purchase

is equal to the redemption or purchase price.

Subject to below, if the permissible capital payment for shares redeemed or purchased

(*a*)   is less than their nominal amount, then the difference must be transferred to the company's capital redemption reserve (see 8.11 above); and

(*b*)   is greater than their nominal amount, then

- the amount of any capital redemption reserve, share premium account (see 56 SHARE PREMIUM) or fully paid share capital of the company, and
- the amount representing unrealised profits standing to the credit of a revaluation reserve under *4 Sch 34* (see 5.14 ACCOUNTS: INDIVIDUAL COMPANIES) or, in the case of small companies, *8 Sch 34* (see 7.16 ACCOUNTS: SMALL AND MEDIUM-SIZED COMPANIES)

may be reduced by a sum (or aggregated sums) not exceeding the amount by which the permissible capital payment exceeds the nominal amount of the shares.

Where the proceeds of a fresh issue are used to make a redemption or purchase of own shares in addition to a payment out of capital, the permissible capital payment for the purposes of (*a*) and (*b*) above is to be taken as referring to the aggregate of that payment and those proceeds.

[*Sec 171; SI 1997 No 220*].

8.13   Availability of profits

Available profits of the company are those which are available for distribution. See generally 23 DISTRIBUTIONS except that, for the purposes of redemption or purchase of own shares out of capital, the question whether a company has any profits so available, and the amount of any such profits, are not determined by reference to 23.7 to 23.9 DISTRIBUTIONS but by reference to

(*a*)   profits, losses, assets and liabilities,

(*b*)   provisions of any kind within *4 Sch 88, 89* (see 5.3 ACCOUNTS: INDIVIDUAL COMPANIES), and

(*c*)   share capital and reserves (including undistributable reserves, see 23.1 DISTRIBUTIONS)

as stated in the 'relevant accounts' for determining the permissible capital payment for the shares.

'Relevant accounts'   means accounts prepared as at any date within the period for determining the permissible capital payment (see below), as are necessary to enable a reasonable judgement to be made on the amounts in (*a*) to (*c*) above.

In determining the permissible capital payment for shares, the company's available profits (if any) as determined above are treated as reduced by any 'distributions lawfully made' by the company after the date of the relevant accounts and before the end of the period for determining the permissible capital payment (see below).

'Distributions lawfully made' by the company include

- financial assistance lawfully given out of distributable profits within *Secs 154* and *155* (see 8.20 and 8.21 below);

8.14   Acquisition of Own Shares

- any payment lawfully made by the company for purchase of its own shares (except a payment lawfully made otherwise than out of distributable profits); and

- any payment within 8.8(*a*)–(*c*) above lawfully made by the company.

For the above purposes, the period for determining the permissible capital payment for the shares is the three months ending with the date when the statutory declaration of the directors purporting to specify the amount of that payment is made (see 8.14(*a*) below).

[*Sec 172*].

8.14   Conditions for payments out of capital

Subject to any court order made under 8.16 below, a payment out of capital by a private company is not lawful unless the following conditions are satisfied.

(*a*)   **Statutory declaration.** The directors must make a statutory declaration specifying the permissible capital payment for the shares and stating that, having made full inquiry into the affairs and prospects of the company, they have formed the opinion that

    (i)   as regards its initial situation immediately after the date on which the payment out of capital is proposed to be made, there will be no grounds on which the company could then be found to be unable to pay its debts (taking into account those liabilities, including prospective and contingent liabilities, which would be relevant in determining whether the company is unable to pay its debts for the purpose of a winding up by the court under *IA 1986, s 122*); and

    (ii)   as regards its prospects for the year following that date (having regard to their intentions with regard to the management of the company's business and the financial resources which will be available), the company will be able to carry on business as a going concern and be able to pay its debts as they fall due throughout the year.

The statutory declarations must be in the prescribed form (Form 173) and contain such information with respect to the nature of the company's business as may be prescribed. It must have annexed to it a report addressed to the directors by the company's auditors stating that they have inquired into the company's state of affairs and

- the amount specified in the declaration as the permissible capital payment for the shares is, in their view, properly determined in accordance with 8.12 and 8.13 above; and

- they are not aware of anything to indicate that the opinion expressed by the directors in the declaration under (i) and (ii) above is unreasonable in all the circumstances.

See *Example 4* under 12.30 AUDITORS for a suggested form of the report.

A director who makes a statutory declaration without having reasonable grounds for the opinion expressed is liable to a penalty up to the level in 40.1(*b*) PENALTIES.

[*Sec 173(3)-(6), 24 Sch; IA 1986, 13 Sch Part I*].

(*b*)   **Special resolution**. The payment must be approved by a special resolution passed on, or within the week immediately following, the date on which the directors make the statutory declaration under (*a*) above. The special resolution is ineffective unless

(i)   the condition in 8.5(*a*) is satisfied; and

(ii)   the statutory declaration and auditors' report under (*a*) above are available for inspection by members of the company at the meeting at which the resolution is passed.

The provisions of (i) and (ii) above do not apply for the purposes of *Sec 381A(1)* (written resolutions of private companies, see 51.4 RESOLUTIONS). For those purposes a member holding shares to which the resolution relates is not regarded as a member entitled to attend and vote (and therefore does not need to sign the resolution). Documents referred to under (ii) above must be supplied to each member by whom the resolution has to be signed at or before the time at which the resolution is supplied to him for signature.

[*Secs 173(2), 174, 15A Sch 6*].

(*c*)   **Timing of payment**. The payment out of capital must be made no earlier than five but no more than seven weeks after the date of the resolution. [*Sec 174(1)*].

For cases on whether the directors and auditors owe a duty of responsibility to individual shareholders who suffer loss, see *Prudential Assurance Co Ltd v Newman Industries Ltd (No 2) [1982] Ch 204*; *Hedley Byrne & Co Ltd v Heller and Partners Ltd [1964] AC 465*; *Caparo Industries plc v Dickman [1990] 1 All ER 568*; and *JEB Fasteners Ltd v Marks, Bloom & Co [1983] 1 All ER 583*.

8.15   Publicity for payments out of capital

Notice in the Gazette, etc. Within a week of the date of the special resolution for payment out of capital under 8.14(*b*) above the company must publish a notice in the *Gazette* and either give notice in writing to each of its creditors or publish a notice in an 'appropriate national newspaper'

- stating that the company has approved a payment out of capital for the purpose of acquiring its own shares by redemption or purchase or both;

- specifying the permissible capital payment for the shares (see 8.12 above) and the date of the resolution;

- stating that the statutory declaration of the directors and auditors' report required under 8.14(*a*) above are available for inspection at the company's registered office; and

- stating that any creditor of the company may, at any time within five weeks of the date of the special resolution, apply to the court under *Sec 176* (see 8.16 below) for an order prohibiting the payment.

An '*appropriate national newspaper*' means, for a company registered in England and Wales, a newspaper circulating throughout England and Wales and, for a company registered in Scotland, a newspaper circulating throughout Scotland.

[*Sec 175(1)-(3)*].

8.16 Acquisition of Own Shares

Copies of the statutory declaration. A copy of the statutory declaration and auditor's report required under 8.14(*a*) above must

- be delivered to the Registrar of Companies not later than the day on which the company first publishes the notice in the *Gazette* or national newspaper or gives notice in writing to its creditors (the *'first notice date'*);

- be kept at the company's registered office from the first notice date until five weeks after the date of the special resolution; and

- be open to the inspection of any member or creditor of the company without charge for not less than two hours during the period between 9a.m. and 5p.m. every Monday to Friday (other than public and bank holidays). A person inspecting the statutory declaration must be permitted to take notes or make a transcript but the company is not obliged to provide any additional facilities other than those to facilitate inspection. If an inspection is refused, the company and every officer in default is liable to a fine up to the level in 40.1(*f*) PENALTIES. The court may also by order compel an immediate inspection.

[Sec 175(4)-(8), 24 Sch; CA 1989, s 143; SI 1991 No 1998, Reg 3].

8.16 Objections by creditors and members

Where a private company passes a special resolution approving any payment out of capital (see 8.14(*b*) above) any creditor and any member who did not consent to, or vote in favour of, the resolution may, within five weeks of it being passed, apply to the court for the resolution to be cancelled. The application may be made on behalf of the persons entitled to make it by one or more of their number as they may appoint in writing.

Where an application is made the company must

- give notice of that fact to the Registrar of Companies in the prescribed form (Form 176); and

- within 15 days of any court order (or such longer period as the court directs) deliver an office copy of the order to the Registrar.

In default, the company and any officer in default is liable to a fine up to the level in 40.1(*f*) PENALTIES.

[Sec 176, 24 Sch].

The court must make an order on such terms and conditions as it thinks fit either confirming or cancelling the special resolution. It may

- adjourn the proceedings in order that an arrangement may be made to purchase the interests of dissentient members or for the protection of dissentient creditors;

- give such directions as it thinks expedient for putting the arrangements into effect;

- if it confirms the resolution, alter or extend any date or period of time applying to the redemption or purchase of the shares;

- provide for the purchase by the company of the shares of any of its members and for the reduction accordingly of the company's capital;

- make such alterations in the company's memorandum and articles as are required in consequence of any such purchase or reduction (any such alteration having effect as if duly made by resolution of the company); and

- require the company not to make any, or any specified, alteration in its memorandum or articles, in which case the company will require leave of the court to make such alteration.

[*Sec 177*].

8.17   EFFECT OF COMPANY'S FAILURE TO PURCHASE OR REDEEM SHARES

The following consequences apply where a company has, after 14 June 1982, either issued shares on terms that they are, or are liable to be, redeemed or agreed to purchase any of its own shares.

(*a*)   It is not liable in damages in respect of any failure on its part to redeem or purchase any of the shares. This is, however, without prejudice to any right of the holder of the shares (e.g. to present a petition for the company to be wound up, see *Re Holders Investment Trust Ltd [1971] 2 All ER 289*) other than his right to sue the company for damages in respect of its failure. The court will not grant an order for specific performance if the company shows it is unable to meet the costs of redeeming or purchasing the shares out of distributable profits. [*Sec 178(1)-(3)*].

(*b*)   If the company is wound up and at the commencement of the winding up any of the shares have not been redeemed or purchased, then, subject to below, the terms of redemption or purchase may be enforced against the company with the shares being treated as cancelled.

This does not apply if

- the terms provide for the redemption or purchase to take place later than the commencement of the winding up; or

- during the period from the date on which the redemption or purchase was to have taken place to the commencement of the winding up, the company could not at any time have lawfully made a distribution equal to the price at which the shares were to have been redeemed or purchased.

All other debts and liabilities (other than any due to members in their character as such) and any amount due in satisfaction of any preferred rights (whether as to capital or income) of other shares must be paid in priority. Subject to that, any liability due under the terms of redemption or purchase must be paid in priority to any amounts due to members in satisfaction of their rights (whether as to capital or income) as members.

[*Sec 178(4)-(6)*].

8.18   FINANCIAL ASSISTANCE FOR ACQUISITION OF OWN SHARES

Subject to the provisions of 8.19 to 8.21 below, there is a general prohibition on a company giving 'financial assistance' to any person (which includes any other company) for the acquisition of its own shares. In particular

(*a*)   where a person *is acquiring or is proposing to acquire* shares in a company, it is not lawful for the company or any of its subsidiaries to give financial assistance directly or indirectly for that purpose before, or at the same time as, the acquisition takes place (see, for example, *Steen v Law [1964] AC 287*); and

(*b*)   where a person *has acquired* shares in a company and any liability has been incurred (by that or any other person) for the purpose of the acquisition, it is not lawful for the company or any of its subsidiaries to give financial assistance directly or indirectly in order to reduce or discharge that liability. For this purpose

8.18   Acquisition of Own Shares

- a person incurs a liability if he changes his financial position by any means including making an agreement or arrangement (whether enforceable or not and whether made on his own account or with another); and

- a company gives financial assistance to reduce or discharge the liability if it does so wholly or partly to restore the financial position of the person acquiring the shares to what it was before the acquisition took place.

Thus, it is not lawful where Company A borrows money from a bank to finance the acquisition of shares in Company B and subsequently the assets of Company B are used to discharge the liability incurred by Company A in acquiring the shares (see, for example, *Selangor United Rubber Estates Ltd v Cradock & Others (No 3) [1968] 2 All ER 1073* and *Wallersteiner v Moir [1974] 3 All ER 217*).

If a company acts in contravention of the above provisions, the company is liable to a fine up to the level in 40.1(*d*) PENALTIES and every officer in default is liable to a penalty up to the level in 40.1(*b*) PENALTIES.

[*Secs 151, 152(3), 24 Sch*].

The above provisions do not prohibit a foreign subsidiary of a UK parent company from giving financial assistance for the acquisition of shares in its parent company (*Arab Bank plc v Mercantile Holdings Ltd and another [1993] BCC 816*).

'*Financial assistance*' means any of the following.

- Financial assistance by way of gift. This may include a sale or transfer at an undervalue (see *Letts v IRC [1957] 1 WLR 201*; *AG v Kitchin [1941] 2 All ER 374*) but possibly only to the extent of the undervalue (*Plant v Steiner (1989) 5 BCC 352*).

- Financial assistance by way of guarantee, security or indemnity in respect of the indemnifier's own neglect or default, or by way of release or waiver.

- Financial assistance by way of a loan or any other agreement under which any of the obligations of the person giving the assistance are to be fulfilled at a time when, in accordance with the agreement, any obligation of another party to the agreement remains unfulfilled, or by way of the novation of, or the assignment of rights arising under, a loan or such other agreement.

- Any other financial assistance by a company the 'net assets' of which are thereby reduced to a material extent or by a company which has no net assets. '*Net assets*' means the aggregate of the company's assets less the aggregate of its liabilities (including any provisions for liabilities or charges reasonably necessary to provide for any liability or loss which is either likely to be incurred, or certain to be incurred but uncertain as to amount or as to the date on which it will arise).

[*Sec 152(1)(a)(2)*].

For a consideration of the meaning of financial assistance, see *Charterhouse Investment Trust Ltd v Tempest Diesels Ltd [1986] BCLC 1* and *Wallersteiner v Moir [1974] 3 All ER 217*. Once assistance has been established, the fact that money is involved in some form will make the assistance financial assistance (*Armour Hick Northern Ltd v Whitehouse [1980] 1 WLR 1520*). It is not necessary that the assistance costs the provider anything. For example, in *Belmont Finance Corporation Ltd v Williams Furniture Ltd [1980] 1 All ER 393* the purchase of an asset for cash at full value from a potential purchaser was held to be financial assistance as it provided the purchaser with cash to buy the shares.

8.19   **Transactions not prohibited**

The following transactions are not prohibited under 8.18 above.

(*a*)   A distribution of a company's assets by way of dividend lawfully made.

(*b*)   A distribution made in the course of the company's winding up.

(*c*)   BONUS ISSUES (13).

(*d*)   A reduction of capital confirmed by court order under *Sec 137*, see 58.18 SHARES AND SHARE CAPITAL.

(*e*)   A redemption or purchase of shares under 8.2 to 8.17 above.

(*f*)   Anything done in pursuance of a court order under *Sec 425* (compromise with creditors and/or members, see 44.1 RECONSTRUCTIONS AND MERGERS).

(*g*)   Anything done under an arrangement made

- in pursuance of *IA 1986, s 110* (acceptance of shares by a liquidator as consideration for sale of property); or

- between a company and its creditors which is binding on the creditors under *IA 1986, Part I*.

(*h*)   Where the lending of money is part of the ordinary business of the company, the lending of money in the ordinary course of its business. A company is not so included merely because it has the power to lend money (*Steen v Law [1963] 3 All ER 770*).

(*i*)   The provision by a company of financial assistance, in good faith in the interests of the company, for an employees' share scheme.

(*j*)   Without prejudice to (*i*) above, the provision of financial assistance by a company or its subsidiaries for the purpose of, or in connection with, anything done by the company (or a company in the same 'group') to enable or facilitate transactions in shares in the first-mentioned company between, and involving the acquisition of beneficial ownership of those shares by,

- the bona fide employees or former employees of that company or a company in the same group; or

- the wives, husbands, widows, widowers, children or step-children under the age of 18 of any such employees or former employees.

For these purposes, a company is in the same *'group'* as another company if it is a holding company or a subsidiary of that company, or a subsidiary of a holding company of that company.

(*k*)   The making by a company of loans to persons (other than directors) employed in good faith by the company to enable those persons to acquire fully paid shares in the company or its holding company to be held beneficially.

(*l*)   Under 8.18(*a*) above, the giving of financial assistance by a company for the purpose of an acquisition of shares in itself or its holding company if

- the company's principal purpose in giving the assistance is not to give it for the purpose of any such acquisition *or* the giving of the assistance is merely an incidental part of some larger purpose of the company; and

- the assistance is given in good faith in the interests of the company.

(*m*)   Under 8.18(*b*) above, the giving of financial assistance by a company if

- the company's principal purpose in giving the assistance is not to reduce or discharge any liability incurred by a person for the purpose acquiring shares in the company or its holding company *or* any reduction or discharge of any such liability is merely an incidental part of some larger purpose of the company; and

- the assistance is given in good faith in the company's interests (see *Brady & Another v Brady & Another (1988) 4 BCC 390*).

[*Sec 153; IA 1986, 13 Sch Part I; FSA 1986, s 196(1)-(3); CA 1989, s 132, 18 Sch 33*].

8.20 Public companies

In the case of a public company, 8.19(*h*)–(*k*) above authorises the giving of financial assistance only if there is no reduction in the company's 'net assets' or, to the extent that those assets are reduced, if the assistance is provided out of 'distributable profits'.

'*Net assets*' means the amount by which the aggregate of the company's assets exceeds the aggregate of its liabilities, in each case as stated in the company's accounting records immediately before the financial assistance is given. Liabilities include any amount retained as reasonably necessary for the purpose of providing for any liability or loss which is either likely to be incurred, or certain to be incurred but uncertain as to amount or as to the date on which it will arise.

'*Distributable profits*' means those profits out of which the company could lawfully make a distribution equal in value to that assistance. It includes, in a case where the financial assistance is or includes a non-cash asset, any profit which, if the company were to make a distribution of that asset, would be available for that purpose under *Sec 276*. See 23 DISTRIBUTIONS generally and particularly 23.1 for the meaning of '*distribution*' and 23.10 for distributions in kind.

[*Secs 152(1)(b), 154*].

8.21 Private companies

A private company is not prohibited under 8.18 above from giving financial assistance where the acquisition of shares is, or was, an acquisition of shares in the company (or, if it is a subsidiary of another private company, in that other company) provided the following conditions are complied with. [*Sec 155(1)*].

(*a*) The 'net assets' of the company must not be reduced or, to the extent that they are reduced, the assistance must be provided out of 'distributable profits'. See 8.20 above for '*net assets*' and '*distributable profits*'. [*Sec 155(2)*].

(*b*) Where the acquisition of shares is, or was, by a subsidiary in its holding company, the subsidiary must not also be a subsidiary of a public company which is itself a subsidiary of that holding company. [*Sec 155(3)*].

(*c*) *Special resolution(s).* Unless the company proposing to give the financial assistance is a wholly-owned subsidiary, the giving of assistance must be approved by special resolution of the company in general meeting passed on, or within the week immediately following, the date on which the directors make the statutory declaration under (*d*) below. Where the acquisition of shares is in its holding company, that holding company and any other company which is both the company's holding company and a subsidiary of that other holding company (except a company which is a wholly-owned subsidiary) must also approve the giving of financial assistance by a special resolution in general meeting.

Where such a special resolution has been passed, application may be made to the court for its cancellation by holders in the aggregate of 10% or more of the nominal value of the company's issued share capital or any class of it (10% of the company's members if the company is not limited by shares). Application must not be made by a person who has consented to or voted in favour of the resolution. The provisions of *Sec 54(3)-(10)* apply to such applications (see 49.12 REGISTRATION AND RE-REGISTRATION).

The special resolution is ineffective

- unless the statutory declaration and auditors' report under (*d*) below are available for inspection by members of the company at the meeting at which the resolution is passed. This does not apply for the purposes of *Sec 381A(1)* (written resolutions of private companies, see 51.4 RESOLUTIONS). For those purposes the documents must be supplied to each member by whom the resolution has to be signed at or before the time at which the resolution is supplied to him for signature; and

- if cancelled on an application to the court as above.

[Secs 155(4)(5), 157, 15A Sch 4].

(*d*)   *Statutory declaration(s).* The directors of the company proposing to give the financial assistance must, before the assistance is given, make a statutory declaration in the prescribed form (Form 155(6)a) containing such particulars of the financial assistance to be given and the business of the company of which they are directors as may be prescribed, and identifying the person to whom the assistance is to be given. Where the shares acquired or to be acquired are in its holding company, the directors of that company and any other company which is both the company's holding company and a subsidiary of that other holding company must also make a similar statutory declaration in the prescribed form (Form 155(6)b).

The declaration must state that the directors have formed the opinion, as regards the company's initial situation immediately after the date the assistance is proposed to be given, that there will be no ground on which the company could then be found to be unable to pay its debts, and either

- if it is intended to commence the winding up of the company within twelve months of that date, the company will be able to pay its debts within the twelve months of commencement of the winding up; or

- in any other case, the company will be able to pay its debts as they fall due during the year following that date.

In forming their opinion the directors must take into account the same liabilities, including contingent and prospective liabilities, as would be relevant in determining whether the company is unable to pay its debts for the purposes of a winding up by the court under *IA 1986, s 122.*

A director of a company who makes a statutory declaration without having reasonable grounds for the opinion expressed in it is liable to a penalty up to the level in 40.1(*b*) PENALTIES.

The statutory declaration must have annexed to it a report addressed to the directors by the company's auditors stating that they have inquired into the company's state of affairs and are not aware of anything to indicate that the directors' opinion on the company's ability to pay its debts is unreasonable in all circumstances. See *Example 5* under 12.30 AUDITORS for a suggested form of the report.

The declaration and report must be delivered to the Registrar of Companies, together with a copy of any special resolution passed under (*c*) above, within 15 days of passing the resolution (or, where no special resolution is required, within 15

185

days of the making of the declaration). In default the company and every officer in default is liable to a fine up to the 'statutory maximum' and, for continued contravention, to a daily default fine of one-fiftieth of the statutory maximum. See 40 PENALTIES for the '*statutory maximum*'.

[*Secs 155(6), 156, 24 Sch; IA 1986, 13 Sch Part I*].

(*e*)   *Timing of financial assistance*. The financial assistance must not be given

- *before* the expiry of the period of four weeks from the date of the special resolution (or, if more than one, the last of them) under (*c*) above unless every member who is entitled to vote at general meetings voted in favour of the resolution (or, if more than one, each of them);

- *before* the final determination of any application to the court for cancellation of any special resolution under (*c*) above (unless the court orders otherwise); or

- *after* the expiry of the period of eight weeks beginning with the date of the statutory declaration under (*d*) above (or, if more than one, the earliest of them) unless the court, on an application under (*c*) above, orders otherwise.

[*Sec 158*].

8.22   MEMBERSHIP OF OWN HOLDING COMPANY

A body corporate (or a nominee acting on its behalf) cannot be a member of its holding company and any allotment or transfer of shares in a company to its subsidiary is void. This is subject to the following exceptions.

(*a*)   Where the subsidiary is only concerned as a personal representative or trustee unless, in the latter case, the holding company, or a subsidiary of it, has a beneficial interest under the trust. In determining whether this is the case, there must be disregarded

- any interest held only by way of security for the purposes of a transaction entered into by the holding company or subsidiary in the ordinary course of a business which includes the lending of money; and

- any interest mentioned in *2 Sch Part I* (residual interests under pension and employees' share schemes, company's right as a trustee to expenses, remuneration, etc.)

(*b*)   The prohibition does not apply where shares in the holding company are held by the subsidiary in the ordinary course of its business as an 'intermediary' (before 20 October 1997, where the subsidiary was only concerned as a market maker).

An '*intermediary*' a person who carries on a *bona fide* business of dealing in securities, is a member of an EEA exchange (or is otherwise approved as a dealer in securities under the laws of an EEA State), and does not carry on an '*excluded business*' i.e.

- wholly or mainly of making or managing investments;

- wholly or mainly in providing services to connected persons (as defined in *ICTA 1988, s 839*);

- insurance business;

- making or acting as trustee in relation to a pension scheme; or

- operating or acting as trustee in relation to a collective investment scheme.

Where a subsidiary which is a dealer in securities has purportedly acquired shares in its holding company in contravention of this prohibition, this does not affect the position of a subsequent purchaser of those shares acting in good faith and without notice of the contravention.

Where the subsidiary became a member

(i) before 1 July 1948, or

(ii) after 30 June 1948 but before 1 November 1990 in circumstances in which the general prohibition above as it then had effect did not apply, or

(iii) after 31 October 1990 in circumstances in which the general provision above did not apply

but subsequently (and after 31 October 1990 in the case of (i) or (ii) above) falls within the general prohibition, the subsidiary may continue to be a member but, so long as that prohibition would otherwise apply, it has no right to vote in respect of those shares at meetings of the company or of any class of its members.

If the subsidiary is so allowed to continue as a member of the holding company, an allotment of fully paid shares may be validly made to it by way of capitalisation of reserves but subject to the same restriction on voting rights.

The above provisions also apply to a company other than a company limited by shares but substituting a reference to the interests of its members as such (in whatever form) for the reference to shares.

[*Sec 23; CA 1989, s 129; SI 1990 No 1392, Art 8; SI 1990 No 1707, Art 8; SI 1997 No 2306*].

Definition of *'subsidiary'* and *'holding company'*. The definition of *'subsidiary'* (and, by implication, *'holding company'*) is amended after 31 October 1990 by *CA 1989, s 144*. See 18.1 DEFINITIONS. Where a body corporate becomes, or ceases to be, a subsidiary of a holding company by reason of the revised definition, the general prohibition above applies (in the absence of exempting circumstances), or ceases to apply, accordingly. [*CA 1989, 18 Sch 32*].

9   Allotment of Shares

Cross-references. See 57.11 SHARE TRANSFERS ETC for issuing of share certificates; 58.8 SHARES AND SHARE CAPITAL for payment of shares.

The contents of this chapter are as follows.

9.1	Introduction
9.2 – 9.4	Allotment of shares
9.5 – 9.10	Pre-emption provisions
9.11 – 9.27	Payment for shares on allotment
9.28	Commissions and discounts

9.1   INTRODUCTION

This chapter deals with the general provisions in *CA 1985* relating to the allotment of shares (see 9.2 to 9.10 below) and payment for the shares allotted (see 9.11 to 9.27 below). See also 9.28 below for the power of a company to pay commission or discount to a person in return for that person subscribing for shares in the company.

Shares are taken to be allotted when a person acquires the unconditional right to be included in the company's register of members in respect of those shares. [*Sec 738(1)*]. See also *Nichol's Case (1885) 29 ChD 421.*

9.2   ALLOTMENT OF SHARES

For cases involving the contractual aspects of application for, and allotment of, shares, see *Jackson v Turquand (1869) LR 4 HL 305* (application for shares is normally the offer with acceptance being the notification of the allotment but a letter of rights from a company is an offer which may be accepted by the shareholder); *Truman's Case [1894] 3 Ch 272, Byrne v Van Tienhoven (1880) 5 CPD 344, Re London and Northern Bank [1900] 1 Ch 220* (revocation of offer); *Household Fire Insurance v Grant (1879) 4 Ex D 216, Holwell Securities Ltd v Hughes [1974] 1 WLR 155* (notification of allotment by post); and *Ramsgate Victoria Hotel v Montefiore (1866) LR 1 Ex D 109* (allotment must be made within a reasonable time of application).

The directors of a company must not exercise any power of the company to allot 'relevant securities' unless they are authorised to do so either by the company in general meeting or by the company's articles. The authority may be given for a particular exercise of the power or for its exercise generally, and may be unconditional or subject to conditions. [*Sec 80(1)(3)*]. Where the directors allot relevant securities without authority, they may be liable to a penalty (see below) although the validity of the allotment is not affected. [*Sec 80(10)*].

'Relevant securities' means

(a)   shares in the company, other than shares shown in the memorandum to have been taken by the subscribers to it or shares allotted in pursuance of an 'employees' share scheme' (see 18.1 DEFINITIONS), and

(b)   any right to subscribe for, or to convert any security into, shares in the company (other than shares so allotted),

and a reference to the allotment of relevant securities includes the grant of, but *not* the allotment of shares pursuant to, such a right. [*Sec 80(2)*].

Maximum amount of securities and time limits. Subject to below, the authority must state the maximum amount of relevant securities that may be allotted under it (or, as the case may be, pursuant to the rights granted under (*b*) above) and the date on which it will expire. Where the authority is contained in the company's articles at the time of its original incorporation, the expiry date will be five years from the date of incorporation; in any other case, the expiry date will be five years from the date on which the resolution is passed by virtue of which the authority is given. The authority may be revoked or varied by the company during the five-year period by ordinary resolution (even if altering the company's articles). [*Sec 80(4)(6)(8)*].

A private company may, however, make an elective resolution under *Sec 379A* (see 51.3 RESOLUTIONS) that the authority is to be given for an indefinite period or a fixed period expiring on a specified date. In either case the authority may be revoked or varied by the company in general meeting. If the *election* subsequently ceases to have effect, any authority then in force (including a renewed authority, see below) expires forthwith if given more than five years previously; otherwise it has effect as if given for a fixed period of five years. [*Sec 80A(1)-(3)(7); CA 1989, s 115*].

Renewal and variation of authority. An authority may be renewed, or further renewed, for a period not exceeding five years (or, in the case of a private company which has made an elective resolution (see above), for an indefinite or fixed period). This may be done by an ordinary resolution of the company (even if altering the company's articles). The renewal resolution must state (or restate) the amount of relevant securities which may be allotted under the authority or, as the case may be, the amount remaining to be so allotted. It must also specify the date on which the renewed authority will expire (in the case of a private company which has made an elective resolution, whether the renewed authority is for an indefinite or fixed period and the date of expiry in the latter case). The provisions of *Sec 380* apply to such a resolution. See 51.9 RESOLUTIONS. [*Secs 80(5)(8), 80A(4)-(6); CA 1989, s 115*].

Allotment after expiration of authority. Notwithstanding that authority has expired, the directors may allot relevant securities if

- they are allotted in pursuance of an offer or agreement made by the company before the authority expired; and

- the authority allowed the company to make an offer or agreement which would or might require relevant securities to be allotted after the authority expired.

[*Sec 80(7)*].

The directors' actions can also be subsequently ratified by the company in general meeting (*Bamford v Bamford [1969] 1 All ER 969*).

Penalties. A director who knowingly and wilfully contravenes, or permits or authorises a contravention of, these provisions is liable to a fine up to the level in 40.1(*d*) PENALTIES. [*Sec 80(9), 24 Sch*].

Restriction on public offers by private companies. A private company (other than a company limited by guarantee and not having a share capital) commits an offence if it offers any shares or debentures to the public or allots (or agrees to allot) them with a view to all or part of them being offered for sale to the public. In default, the company and every officer in default is liable to a fine up to the level in 40.1(*d*) PENALTIES. The commission of such an offence does not however affect the validity of any allotment or agreement. [*Sec 81, 24 Sch*].

9.3   **Allotment where public company issue not fully subscribed**

No allotment must be made of any share capital of a public company offered for subscription unless

9.4 Allotment of Shares

- that capital is subscribed in full; or

- the offer states that, even if the capital is not fully subscribed, the amount of capital subscribed for may be allotted. If this is subject to conditions, all such conditions must be satisfied.

Where 40 days have elapsed since the date of issue of a prospectus and an allotment is prohibited under the above provisions, all money received from applicants must be repaid, initially without interest. If, however, this is not done within 48 days of that date, the directors of the company are jointly and severally liable to repay the money with interest at 5% per annum from the expiration of the 48th day. A director is not liable if he proves that the default in repayment was not due to any misconduct or negligence on his part.

Any condition requiring or binding an applicant to waive compliance with any requirement of these provisions is void.

[Sec 84(1)-(3)(6); FSA 1986, 17 Sch].

Shares offered as wholly or partly payable otherwise than in cash. The above provisions also apply to such shares, the word 'subscribed' being construed accordingly. References to repayment of money received from applicants include the return of any other consideration received or, where this is not practicable, the payment of money equal to the value of such consideration at the time it was so received. *[Sec 84(4)(5)].*

Effect of irregular allotment. Where an allotment is made in contravention of the above provisions, it is voidable at the instance of the applicant within one month after the date of allotment (even if the company is being wound up). Any director of the company who knowingly contravenes, or permits or authorises the contravention of, any of the above provisions is liable to compensate the company and the allottee for any loss, damage or costs provided proceedings for recovery are commenced within two years of the date of allotment. *[Sec 85; FSA 1986, 17 Sch].*

9.4 Returns of allotment

Documents to be delivered to Registrar. A company limited by shares, or a company limited by guarantee and having a share capital which makes an allotment of its shares must, within one month thereafter, deliver the following to the Registrar of Companies for registration.

(*a*) A return of the allotments in the prescribed form (Form 88(2)). The return must state the number and nominal amount of the shares comprised in the allotment, the names and addresses of the allottees, and the amount (if any) paid, or due and payable, on each share, whether on account of the nominal value of the share or by way of premium.

(*b*) Where shares have been allotted as fully or partly paid up otherwise than in cash

    (i) a contract in writing constituting the allottee's title to the allotment, together with any contract of sale, or for services or other consideration, in respect of which that allotment was made (such contracts being duly stamped); and

    (ii) a return stating the number and nominal value of the shares allotted, the extent to which they are to be treated as paid up, and the consideration for which they have been allotted. (In practice, this information may be provided on Form 88(2).)

[Sec 88(1)(2)].

Where such a contract as is mentioned under (*b*)(i) above is not in writing, the company must, within the same time limit, deliver to the Registrar of Companies for registration the prescribed particulars of the contract (on Form 88(3)) stamped with the same stamp duty as would have been payable had the contract been in writing. Form 88(3) is an instrument for stamp duty purposes. [*Sec 88(3)(4)*].

Penalties for default. If default is made in complying with the above provisions, every officer of the company who is in default is liable to a fine up to the level in 40.1(*c*) PENALTIES. However, in the case of default in delivering any document to the Registrar within the time allowed, the company or any officer liable for the default may apply to the court for relief. The court may make an order extending the time for delivery of the document for such period as it thinks proper, if satisfied

(i)   that the omission to deliver the document was accidental or due to inadvertence; or

(ii)   that it is just and equitable to grant relief.

[*Sec 88(5)(6), 24 Sch*].

9.5   **PRE-EMPTION PROVISIONS**

In addition to the general restrictions on the powers of directors of a company to allot shares (see 9.2 and 9.3 above), there are also, subject to 9.8 to 9.10 below, restrictions on their power to allot shares to persons other than existing members of the company as follows.

(*a*)   Subject to the exceptions below, a company must not allot any 'equity securities' on any terms to a person, unless it has made an offer to each 'holder' of 'relevant shares' or 'relevant employee shares' to allot to him a proportion of those shares on the same or more favourable terms. That proportion must, as nearly as practicable, be equal to the proportion in nominal value held by him of the aggregate of relevant shares and relevant employee shares. Furthermore, no such securities may be allotted (other than those which the company has agreed to allot to the holder of the relevant shares or relevant employee shares or anyone in whose favour he has renounced his rights) unless *either* the period during which any such offer may be accepted has expired *or* the company has received notice of the acceptance or refusal of every offer so made. [*Sec 89(1)*].

The above provisions do not apply in the following circumstances.

●   Where the allotment is of equity securities which are, or are to be, wholly or partly paid up otherwise than in cash. [*Sec 89(4)*].

●   Where the allotment of securities would, apart from a renunciation or assignment of the right to their allotment, be held under an employees' share scheme. [*Sec 89(5)*].

(*b*)   Where

●   a company's memorandum or articles contains provisions *requiring* the company not to allot equity securities consisting of relevant securities of any particular 'class' unless it makes an offer as described above to each holder of relevant shares or relevant employee shares of that class, and

●   in accordance with those provisions the company offers to allot securities to such a holder and he, or anyone in whose favour he has renounced his right to their allotment, accepts the offer the company may allot them accordingly but without prejudice to the application of the provisions in (*a*) above in any other case. [*Sec 89(2)(3)*].

An '*equity security*' means a relevant share in a company (other than a share taken by a subscriber or a bonus share), or a right to subscribe for, or to convert securities into, relevant shares in the company. [*Sec 94(2)*]. The allotment of equity securities, or of equity securities consisting of relevant shares of a particular class, includes the grant of a right to subscribe for, or to convert any securities into, relevant shares in the company or (as the case may be) relevant shares of a particular class. It does not include the allotment of any relevant shares pursuant to such a right. [*Sec 94(3)*].

The '*holder*' of shares of any description, in relation to an offer to allot securities, refers to whoever was the holder of shares of that description at close of business on a date to be specified in the offer, which date is to be no earlier than 28 days before the offer date. [*Sec 94(7)*].

'*Relevant shares*' means shares in a company other than

- shares which as respects dividends and capital carry a right to participate only up to a specified amount in a distribution; and

- relevant employee shares, or shares which will be relevant employee shares when allotted.

[*Sec 94(5)*].

'*Relevant employee shares*' means shares in a company which would be relevant shares in it but for the fact that they are held by a person who acquired them pursuant to an employees' share scheme (see 18.1 DEFINITIONS). [*Sec 94(4)*].

A '*class*' of shares refers to shares which carry the same rights as to voting and to participation, as respects both dividends and capital, in a distribution. [*Sec 94(6)*].

9.6 Communication of pre-emption offers

An offer within 9.5(*a*) or (*b*) above must be in writing and made to a shareholder either personally or by pre-paid post to him or to his registered address. If he has no registered address in the UK, the offer is to be sent to the UK address supplied by him for the giving of notices. An offer sent by post is deemed to be made when the letter would be delivered in the normal course of post.

The offer must state a period of not less than 21 days during which it may be accepted, and must not be withdrawn during that period.

Joint holders. Where shares are held jointly, the offer may be made to the joint holder first named in the register of members.

Death or bankruptcy. In the case of a holder's death or bankruptcy, the offer may be made by sending it by pre-paid post to the address in the UK of the persons claiming to be entitled to the shares in consequence of the death or bankruptcy. Until such an address has been supplied, the offer may be made in any manner in which it might have been given if the death or bankruptcy had not occurred.

Publication in Gazette. If the holder

- has no registered address in the UK and has not given the company an address in the UK for the service of notices on him, or

- is the holder of a share warrant

the offer can be made by publishing it, or a notice specifying where a copy of it can be obtained or inspected, in the *London Gazette* (or, in Scotland, the *Edinburgh Gazette*).

[*Sec 90*].

9.7   Consequences of contravening provisions

If there is a contravention of any of the provisions of 9.5 or 9.6 above, the company, and every officer of it who knowingly authorised or permitted the contravention, are jointly and severally liable to compensate any person to whom an offer should have been made for any loss, damage, costs or expenses which the person has sustained or incurred by reason of the contravention. However, no proceedings to recover such loss etc. may be commenced after the expiration of two years

- from the delivery to the Registrar of Companies of the return of the allotments in question; or

- where equity securities other than shares are granted, from the date of the grant.

[*Sec 92*].

9.8   Exclusion of pre-emption rights by private company

A private company may, by a provision contained in its memorandum or articles (or otherwise if imposed before 22 June 1982), exclude the pre-emption provisions in 9.5 and 9.6 above, in relation to all or particular allotments of equity securities. A requirement or authority contained in its memorandum or articles which is inconsistent with any of the provisions has the effect of excluding that provision.

[*Secs 91, 96(3)*].

9.9   Disapplication of pre-emption rights

In addition to the right of a private company to exclude the pre-emption provisions under 9.8 above, both private and public companies have a right to disapply the pre-emption provisions in the following circumstances.

(*a*)   Where the directors have a general authority to allot shares under 9.2 above, they may be given power by the articles, or by a special resolution of the company, to allot equity securities pursuant to that authority as if 9.5(*a*) above either did not apply to the allotment, or applied with such modifications as the directors may determine. Where the directors make such an allotment, the provisions of 9.5 to 9.8 above apply accordingly.

(*b*)   Where the directors have either a general or a specific authority to allot shares, the company may by special resolution resolve that 9.5(*a*) will either

- not apply to a specified allotment of equity securities to be made pursuant to that authority; or

- apply to the allotment with such modifications as may be specified in the resolution.

Where such a resolution is passed, the provisions of 9.5 to 9.8 above apply accordingly.

9.10 Allotment of Shares

The special resolution, or a special resolution to renew such a resolution, must not be proposed unless it is recommended by the directors. In addition, subject to below, there must have been circulated, with the notice of the meeting at which the resolution is to be proposed, a written statement by the directors setting out

- their reasons for making the recommendation;

- the amount to be paid to the company in respect of the equity securities to be allotted; and

- the directors' justification of that amount.

This does not apply for the purposes of *Sec 381A(1)* (written resolutions of private companies, see 51.4 RESOLUTIONS). For those purposes, the statement must be supplied to each member by whom the resolution has to be signed at or before the time at which the resolution is supplied to him for signature.

A person who knowingly or recklessly authorises or permits the inclusion in such a statement of any matter which is misleading, false or deceptive in a material particular is liable to a penalty up to the level in 40.1(*b*) PENALTIES.

The power referred to in (*a*) above, or the special resolution referred to in (*b*) above, ceases to have effect when the authority to which it relates is revoked or would, if not renewed, expire. However, if the authority is renewed, the power or (as the case may be) the resolution may also be renewed, by special resolution, for a period not longer than that for which the authority is renewed. Note that even if any such power or resolution has expired, the directors may allot equity securities pursuant to an offer or agreement previously made by the company, provided that the power or resolution enabled the company to make an offer or agreement which would or might require equity securities to be allotted after it expired.

[*Sec 95, 15A Sch 3, 24 Sch*].

9.10 Saving provisions

The provisions of 9.5 to 9.8 above

- are without prejudice to any enactment whereby a company is prohibited, whether generally or in specified circumstances, from offering or allotting any equity shares to any person [*Sec 93*]; and

- do not apply to the allotment by public companies of equity securities subject to a requirement imposed before 22 June 1982 (whether by the company's memorandum or articles or otherwise) that the company must, when allotting securities, offer to allot them, or some of them, in a manner which (otherwise than because of involving a contravention under 9.6 above) is inconsistent with those provisions. [*Sec 96(1)(2)*].

9.11 PAYMENT FOR SHARES ON ALLOTMENT

Subject to the provisions of 9.12 to 9.27 below, shares allotted by a company, and any premium on them, may be paid up in money or money's worth, including goodwill and know-how. [*Sec 99(1)*]. However, a *public company* must not accept, in payment up of its shares or any premium on them, an undertaking from any person that he or another should do work or perform services for the company or any other person. If it does accept such an undertaking, the 'holder' of the shares, when they or the premium are treated as paid up (in whole or in part) by the undertaking, is liable to pay to the company

- in respect of those shares, an amount equal to their nominal value together with the whole of any premium, or if applicable, such proportion as is treated as paid up by the undertaking; and

- interest at 5% (or such rate specified by statutory instrument) on the amount payable under (*a*) above.

[*Secs 99(2)(3), 107*].

'*Holder*' includes any person who is entitled unconditionally to be included in the company's register of members in respect of those shares or to have an instrument of transfer executed in his favour. [*Sec 99(5)*].

The above provisions do not prevent a company from allotting bonus shares (see 13 BONUS ISSUES) or from paying up with available sums any amounts unpaid on any of its shares (whether on account of their nominal value or by way of premium). [*Sec 99(4)*].

Penalty for contravention. In contravention, the company and any officer who is in default is liable to a fine up to the level in 40.1(*d*) PENALTIES. [*Sec 114, 24 Sch*].

See also 58.8 and 58.9 SHARES AND SHARE CAPITAL for calls on shares.

9.12   Allotment of shares at a discount not permitted

A company's shares must not be allotted at a discount. If shares are so allotted, the allottee is liable to pay the company the full amount of the discount, with interest at 5% (or such rate as specified by statutory instrument). [*Secs 100, 107*]. See *Ooregum Gold Mining Co of India Ltd v Roper [1892] AC 125*. See also *Welton v Saffrey [1897] AC 299* where, although a company being wound up could pay all its creditors, it was held that holders of shares issued at a discount were still liable to account to the company for the discount in order to adjust the rights of the shareholders *inter se*.

A company is permitted in certain circumstances to pay commission (see 9.28 below).

Penalty for contravention. In contravention, the company and any officer who is in default is liable to a fine up to the level in 40.1(*d*) PENALTIES. [*Sec 114, 24 Sch*].

See also 9.23 and 9.25 below.

9.13   Minimum amount to be paid on shares allotted by public company

A public company must not allot a share except as paid up at least as to one-quarter of its nominal value and the whole of any premium on it [*Sec 101(1)*] apart from shares allotted in pursuance of an employees' share scheme (see 18.1 DEFINITIONS). [*Sec 101(2)*].

A share allotted by a company in contravention of this provision is to be treated as if one-quarter of its nominal value, together with the whole of any premium on it, had been received and the allottee is liable to pay the company that minimum amount (less any amount that has actually been applied in paying up the shares and any premium), plus interest at 5% (or such rate as is specified by statutory instrument). This does not, however, apply to the allotment of bonus shares unless the allottee knew, or ought to have known, that the shares were allotted in contravention of the above provision. [*Secs 101(3)-(5), 107*].

9.14 Allotment of Shares

Penalty for contravention. In contravention, the company and any officer who is in default is liable to a fine up to the level in 40.1(*d*) PENALTIES. [*Sec 114, 24 Sch*].

See also 9.23, 9.25 and 9.27 below.

9.14 Restriction on payment to public company by long-term undertaking

A public company must not allot shares as fully or partly paid up (whether as to nominal value or premium) otherwise than in cash if the consideration for the allotment is, or includes, an undertaking which is to be, or *may be*, performed more than five years after the date of the allotment. [*Sec 102(1)*]. See 9.22 below for the meaning of allotted for cash.

If

(*a*)   the company allots shares in contravention of this provision, or

(*b*)   an undertaking which is to be performed within five years of the allotment is not so performed,

the allottee is liable to pay the company an amount equal to the aggregate of the nominal value and any premium (or so much of the aggregate as is treated as paid up by the undertaking), with interest at 5% (or such rate specified by statutory instrument) from the date of allotment under (*a*) or the end of the period allowed for performance under (*b*). [*Secs 102(2)(5)(6), 107*].

Any variation of a contract for the allotment of shares (which includes an ancillary contract relating to payment for them) is void if its effect is that a contract which does not contravene these provisions, would have done so after the variation. Included is a variation of a contract entered into before the company became a public company. [*Sec 102(3)(4)(7)*].

Penalty for contravention. In contravention, the company and any officer who is in default is liable to a fine up to the level in 40.1(*d*) PENALTIES. [*Sec 114, 24 Sch*].

See also 9.23 to 9.27 below.

9.15 Valuation of non-cash consideration in connection with public company allotments

Subject to the exceptions below, a public company must not allot shares as fully or partly paid up (as to their nominal value or any premium) otherwise than in cash unless

(*a*)   the consideration for the allotment has been independently valued under the provisions described in 9.16 below;

(*b*)   a report with respect to its value has been made to the company by a person appointed by the company during the six months immediately preceding the allotment of the shares; and

(*c*)   a copy of the report has been sent to the proposed allottee.

[*Sec 103(1)*].

See 9.22 below for the meaning of allotted for cash.

The company must deliver a copy of the report to the Registrar of Companies at the same time that it files the return of allotments under 9.4 above. See also 9.4 above under the heading *Penalties for default* which also apply to failure to file the valuer's report. [*Sec 111(1)(3), 24 Sch*].

Exceptions. The above provisions do not apply (and it is therefore not necessary to obtain an independent valuation) to the following transactions.

- The payment up by the company of any shares allotted to members of the company or any premiums on such shares (i.e. including bonus shares) from any of the company's reserve accounts or its profit and loss account. This is because such payments do not count as 'consideration for the allotment' for the purposes of (*a*) above. [*Sec 103(2)*].

- An 'arrangement' whereby shares are allotted in a company (Company A) on terms that the whole or part of the consideration for the shares allotted is to be provided by the transfer to Company A (or the cancellation) of some or all of the shares (or shares of a particular class) in another company (Company B), with or without the issue to Company A of shares, or shares of a particular class, in Company B. The arrangement must be open to all of Company B's shareholders (or, where the arrangement applies only to shares of a particular class, to all its shareholders of that class) but disregarding shares held by, or by a nominee of, Company A, its holding company or subsidiary, or a subsidiary of its holding company.

  'Arrangement' means any agreement, scheme or arrangement, including an arrangement pursuant to *Sec 425* (company compromise with creditors and members – see 44.1 RECONSTRUCTIONS AND MERGERS) or *IA 1986, s 110* (liquidator in winding up accepting shares as consideration for sale of company property).

  [*Sec 103(3)(4)(7); IA 1986, 13 Sch*].

- The allotment of shares by a company (Company C) in connection with its proposed merger with another company (Company D); that is, where Company C proposes to acquire the assets and liabilities of Company D in exchange for the issue of shares or other securities of Company C to shareholders of Company D, with or without any cash payment to shareholders. [*Sec 103(5)*].

Effect of contravention. If a company allots shares and either the allottee has not received the valuer's report or there has been some other contravention of these provisions or those in 9.16 or 9.17 below which the allottee knew or ought to have known amounted to a contravention, the allottee is liable to pay the company an amount equal to the aggregate of the nominal value of the shares and the whole of any premium (or, if the case so requires, so much of that aggregate which is treated as paid up by that consideration), with interest at 5% (or such rate specified by statutory instrument). [*Sec 103(6)*].

Penalty for contravention. In contravention, the company and any officer who is in default is liable to a fine up to the level in 40.1(*d*) PENALTIES. [*Sec 114, 24 Sch*].

See also 9.23 to 9.27 below.

9.16 *Valuation and report*

The valuation and report must be made by an independent person ('the valuer'), i.e. a person qualified at the time of the report to be appointed, or continue to be, an auditor of the company. However, in order to make his own report, the valuer may arrange for a valuation and report to be made by another person who appears to him to have the requisite knowledge or experience to make the valuation, where he considers this course of action to be reasonable. That other person must not, however, be

- an officer or servant of the company (excluding an auditor) or any other body corporate which is that company's subsidiary or holding company or a subsidiary of that company's holding company; or

- a partner or employee of such an officer or servant.

9.17   Allotment of Shares

The valuer's report must state

- the nominal value of the shares to be wholly or partly paid for by the consideration in question;

- the amount of any premium payable on the shares;

- the description of the consideration and, as respects so much of the consideration as he himself has valued, a description of that part of the consideration, the method used to value it and the date of the valuation;

- the extent to which the nominal value of the shares and any premium are to be treated as paid up

  (i)   by the consideration; and

  (ii) in cash (see 9.22 below for what constitutes a share being paid up for cash);

- (if applicable) that the consideration or part of it is valued by a person other than the valuer himself plus

  (i)   the other person's name and what knowledge and experience he has to carry out the valuation; and

  (ii) a description of so much of the consideration as was valued by the other person, the method used to value it, and the date of the valuation;

- either in the report itself or an accompanying note that

  (i)   in the case of a valuation made by another person, it appeared to the valuer reasonable to arrange for it to be so made or to accept a valuation so made;

  (ii)   whoever made the valuation, the method of valuation was reasonable in all the circumstances;

  (iii) it appears to the valuer that there has been no material change in the value of the consideration in question since the valuation; and

  (iv)   on the basis of the valuation, the value of the consideration, together with any cash by which the nominal value of the shares or any premium payable on them is to be paid up, is not less than so much of the aggregate of the nominal value and the whole of any such premium as is treated as paid up by the consideration and any such cash.

[Sec 108(1)-(6)].

See *Example 3* under 12.30 AUDITORS for a suggested form of the report.

See also 9.27 below.

9.17   *Position where the consideration accepted is only partly for shares*

Where the consideration to be valued is accepted partly in payment up of the nominal value of the shares and any premium and partly for some other consideration given by the company, the provisions in 9.15 to 9.16 above apply as if references to the consideration accepted by the company included the proportion properly attributable to the payment up of that value and any premium. In such a case

- the valuer must carry out, or arrange for, such other valuations as will enable him to determine that proportion; and

- his report must also state what valuations have been made under (*a*) and also the reason for, and method and date of, any such valuation and any other matters which may be relevant to that determination.

[*Sec 108(7)*].

9.18   *Entitlement of valuer to full disclosure*

A person carrying out a valuation or making a report under 9.16 above with respect to any consideration proposed to be accepted or given by a company, is entitled to require from the company's officers such information and explanation as he thinks necessary to enable him to carry out those tasks.

Where a person knowingly or recklessly makes a statement (whether orally or in writing) to the valuer which conveys, or purports to convey, any information or explanation which he requires and which is misleading, false or deceptive in a material particular, that person is guilty of an offence and is liable to a penalty up to the limit in 40.1(*b*) PENALTIES.

[*Sec 110*].

See also 9.27 below.

9.19   **Transfer of non-cash assets to public company in initial period**

Unless the conditions below are satisfied and subject to the exceptions below, a public company formed as such must not enter into an agreement with a subscriber to the company's memorandum for the transfer by him, to the company or to another, of one or more 'non-cash assets' during the 'initial period' where the consideration for the transfer to be given by the company is equal in value at the time of the agreement to one-tenth or more of the company's nominal share capital issued at that time.

The *'initial period' is* two years beginning with the date on which the company was issued with a certificate under *Sec 117* (see 43.3 PUBLIC AND LISTED COMPANIES) that it was entitled to do business. [*Sec 104(1)(2)*].

See 18.1 DEFINITIONS for *'non-cash assets'*.

A similar restriction applies to a company re-registered as a public company (except one re-registered under *CA 1980, s 8* or *CC(CP)A 1985, s 2*, see 49.14 REGISTRATION AND RE-REGISTRATION) or registered under *Sec 685* (joint stock company, see 15.5 COMPANIES NOT FORMED UNDER CA 1985) or the previous corresponding provision. In such a case, the restrictions apply to the company's dealings with a member of the company at the date of registration or re-registration, and the 'initial period' is two years beginning with that date. [*Sec 104(3)*].

The conditions are as follows.

(*a*)   The consideration to be received by the company (i.e. the asset to be transferred to it or the advantage to the company of the asset's transfer to another person), and any non-cash consideration to be given by the company, must have been independently valued (see 9.20 below). This is without prejudice to any require-ment to value any consideration for purposes of 9.15 above.

(*b*)   A report with respect to the consideration to be so received and given must have been made to the company in accordance with 9.20 below during the six months immediately preceding the date of the agreement.

(*c*)   The terms of the agreement must have been approved by an ordinary resolution of the company.

9.20 Allotment of Shares

(*d*) Not later than the giving of the notice of the meeting at which the resolution is to be proposed, copies of the resolution and report must have been circulated to the members of the company entitled to receive the notice and, if the person with whom the agreement is proposed to be made is not then such a member, to that person.

[*Sec 104(4)(5)*].

Exceptions. The above provisions do not apply to the following agreements.

* Where it is part of a company's ordinary business to acquire, or to arrange for other persons to acquire, assets of a particular description, an agreement entered into by the company in the ordinary course of its business for the transfer of an asset of such a description to it or to such a person, as the case may be.

* An agreement entered into by the company under the supervision of the court, or of an officer authorised by the court for the purpose, for the transfer of an asset to the company or to another.

[*Sec 104(6)*].

Penalty for contravention. In default, the company and any officer who is in default is liable to a fine up to the level in 40.1(*d*) PENALTIES. [*Sec 114, 24 Sch*].

Effect of contravention. If a public company enters into an agreement with a person contravening the above provisions and either that person has not received the valuer's report or there has been some other contravention of these provisions or those in 9.20 below which he knew or ought to have known amounted to a contravention, then the company is entitled to recover from that person any consideration given by it under the agreement, or an amount equal to its value at the time of the agreement. The agreement, so far as not carried out, is void. The person liable may, however, apply to the court for exemption from liability. The court may then exempt him wholly or in part if and to the extent that it appears to the court just and equitable to do so having regard to the benefit accruing to the company by virtue of anything done by him towards the carrying out of the agreement.

However, if the agreement is or includes an agreement for the allotment of shares in the company, then

* whether or not the agreement also contravenes 9.15 above, these provisions do not apply to it in so far as it is for the allotment of shares; and

* the allottee is liable to pay the company an amount equal to the nominal value of the shares and the whole of any premium (or, if the case so requires, so much of that aggregate as is treated as paid up by the consideration), with interest at 5% (or such rate as is specified by statutory instrument).

[*Secs 105, 107, 113(8)*].

See also 9.23 to 9.26 below.

Within 15 days of passing a resolution under (*c*) above, the company must deliver to the Registrar of Companies a copy of the resolution together with a copy of the valuer's report. In default, the company and every officer of it who is in default is liable to a fine up to the level in 40.1(*f*) PENALTIES. [*Sec 111(2)(4), 24 Sch*].

9.20 *Valuation and report*

The valuation and report must be made by an independent person ('the valuer'), i.e. a person qualified at the time of the report to be appointed, or continue to be, an auditor of the company. However, in order to make his own report, the valuer may arrange for a valuation and report to be made by another person who appears to him to have the requisite knowledge or experience to make the valuation, where he considers this course of action to be reasonable. The other person must not, however, be

- an officer or servant of the company (excluding an auditor) or any other body corporate which is that company's subsidiary or holding company or a subsidiary of that company's holding company; or

- a partner or employee of such an officer or servant.

The valuer's report must state

(a)   the consideration to be received by the company, describing the asset in question (specifying the amount to be received in cash) and the consideration to be given by the company (and in respect of each, specifying the amount to be given in cash);

(b)   the method and date of valuation;

(c)   (if applicable) that the consideration or part of it is valued by a person other than the valuer himself plus

- the other person's name and what knowledge and experience he has to carry out the valuation; and

- a description of so much of the consideration as was valued by the other person, the method used to value it, and the date of the valuation;

and

(d)   either in the report itself or an accompanying note, that

- in the case of a valuation made by another person, it appeared to the valuer reasonable to arrange for it to be so made or to accept a valuation so made;

- whoever made the valuation, the method of valuation was reasonable in all the circumstances;

- it appears to the valuer that there has been no material change in the value of the consideration in question since the valuation; and

- the value of the consideration to be received by the company is not less than the value of the consideration to be given by it.

[*Sec 109(1)(2)*].

See *Example 3* under 12.30 AUDITORS for a suggested form of the report.

Entitlement of valuer to full disclosure. The provisions under 9.18 above apply equally to a report under the above provisions. [*Sec 110*].

9.21   *Position where consideration given only partly for transfer of asset*

A reference in 9.19 or 9.20 above to consideration given for the transfer of an asset includes consideration given partly for its transfer; but

- the value of any consideration partly so given is taken as the proportion of the consideration properly attributable to its transfer;

- the valuer must carry out or arrange for such valuations of anything else as will enable him to determine that proportion; and

- his report must state what valuation has been made under this provision, and also the reason for, and method and date of, any such valuation and any other matters which may be relevant to that determination.

[*Sec 109(3)*].

9.22 Allotment of Shares

9.22 Shares issued to subscribers of public companies

Shares issued to a subscriber to the memorandum of a public company in pursuance of an undertaking in the memorandum, together with any premium on them, must be 'paid up in cash'. [*Sec 106*].

For this purpose and the purposes of *CA 1985* generally, a share in a company is deemed to be *'paid up in cash'* or *'allotted for cash'* (the term cash including foreign currency) if the consideration for the payment up or allotment is

- cash received by the company; or
- a cheque received by it in good faith which the directors have no reason for suspecting will not be paid; or
- a release of a liability of the company for a liquidated sum; or
- an undertaking to pay cash to the company at a future date.

[*Sec 738(2)(4)*].

Penalty for contravention. In contravention, the company and any officer who is in default is liable to a fine up to the level in 40.1(*d*) PENALTIES. [*Sec 114, 24 Sch*].

See also 9.27 below.

9.23 Liability of subsequent holders of shares allotted

If a person (A) becomes a 'holder' of shares

- in respect of which there has been a contravention under any of the provisions of 9.11 to 9.15 above (including a failure to carry out an undertaking under 9.14(*b*)), or
- resulting from an agreement for the allotment of shares entered into by a company in contravention of the provisions under 9.19 above

and in either case another person is liable to pay any amount as therein described, then A is also liable to pay that amount (jointly and severally with any other person so liable) unless

- he is a purchaser for value and, at the time of the purchase, he did not have actual notice of the contravention concerned; or
- he derived title to the shares (directly or indirectly) from a person who became a holder of them after the contravention and who was not liable under the above provisions.

'Holder', in relation to shares in a company, includes any person who has an unconditional right to be included in the company's register of members in respect of those shares, or to have an instrument of transfer of the shares executed in his favour.

[*Sec 112*].

See also 9.24, 9.25 and 9.27 below.

9.24 Relief in respect of certain liabilities

Where, under the provisions of paragraphs 9.11, 9.14, 9.15 or 9.19 above (or 9.23 above to the extent that it relates to a contravention under those paragraphs), a person is liable to a company

(*a*) in relation to payment in respect of any shares in the company, or (*b*)   by virtue of an undertaking given to it in, or in connection with, payment for any such shares,

the person so liable may apply to the court to be exempted in whole or in part from the liability.

There are two overriding principles to which the court is directed to have regard in determining whether it should exempt the applicant in whole or in part from any liability. First, a company which has allotted shares should receive money or money's worth at least equal in value to the aggregate of the nominal value of those shares and the whole of any premium or, if the case so requires, so much of that aggregate as is treated as paid up. Subject to this, secondly, where such a company would, if the court did not grant the exemption, have more than one remedy against a particular person, it should be for the company to decide which remedy it should remain entitled to pursue. Because these are 'overriding principles', a court will need very good reasons to accept that it is just and equitable to exempt an applicant from liability where the company has not received sufficient value (*Re Bradford Investments plc (No 2) [1991] BCC 739*).

Otherwise the court may exempt the applicant from the liability only if and to the extent that it appears to the court just and equitable to do so having regard to the following.

- Whether the applicant has paid, or is liable to pay, any amount in respect of any other liability (any liability where (*b*) above applies) arising in relation to those shares under any of the relevant provisions, or, where (*a*) above applies, in respect of any liability arising under (*b*) above.

- Whether any person other than the applicant has paid or is likely to pay (whether in pursuance of an order of the court or otherwise) any such amount.

- Where (*a*) above applies, whether the applicant or any other person has performed, in whole or in part, or is likely so to perform any such undertaking, or has done or is likely to do any other such thing in payment or part payment for the shares.

In addition, if it appears to the court just and equitable to do so, the court may exempt the applicant from liability in respect of any interest which he is liable to pay.

[*Sec 113(1)-(5)*].

See also 9.27 below.

9.25   *Proceedings against a contributor*

Certain powers are conferred on the court in the circumstances where a person brings proceedings against another ('the contributor') for a contribution in respect of liability to a company arising under 9.11 to 9.15, 9.19 or 9.23 above and it appears to the court that the contributor is liable to make such a contribution. The court may, if, and to the extent, that it appears to be just and equitable to do so, having regard to the respective culpability (in respect of liability to the company) of the contributor and the person bringing the proceedings

- exempt the contributor in whole or in part from his liability to make such a contribution; or

- order the contributor to make a larger contribution than, but for this provision, he would be liable to make.

[*Sec 113(6)(7)*].

See also 9.27 below.

9.26 Allotment of Shares

9.26 Enforceability of undertakings

Subject to 9.24 and 9.25 above, where an undertaking to do work or perform services or do any other thing is given by a person to a company in, or in connection with, payment for shares in a company and that undertaking is enforceable by the company apart from *CA 1985*, it is enforceable by the company notwithstanding that

- there has been a contravention in relation to it under 9.11, 9.14 or 9.15 above; or

- it is given in contravention of 9.19 above.

[*Sec 115*].

See also 9.27 below.

9.27 Re-registered public companies and joint stock companies

The provisions of 9.11, 9.13 to 9.16, 9.18 and 9.22 to 9.26 apply

- to a company which has passed, and not revoked, a resolution to be re-registered as a public company under *Sec 43* (see 49.4 REGISTRATION AND RE-REGISTRATION), and

- to a joint stock company which has passed, and not revoked, a resolution that the company be a public company (see 15.5 COMPANIES NOT FORMED UNDER CA 1985)

as they apply to a public company. [*Sec 116; CA 1989, s 131*].

9.28 COMMISSIONS AND DISCOUNTS

A company may lawfully pay a commission to any person in consideration of his subscribing or agreeing to subscribe (whether absolutely or conditionally) for any shares in the company, or procuring or agreeing to procure subscriptions (whether absolute or conditional), provided that the following conditions are satisfied.

- The payment of commission is authorised by the company's articles (see, for example, *SI 1985 No 805, Table A, Art 4*).

- The commission paid or agreed to be paid must not exceed the lesser of

  (i) with effect from a date to be appointed, any limit imposed by rules under *FSA 1986, s 169(2)* or, if none is imposed, 10% of the price at which the shares are issued (before the appointed date 10% of the price at which the shares are issued); or

  (ii) the amount or rate authorised by the articles.

- The disclosure requirements set out below are complied with.

[*Sec 97(1)(2)(a)*].

Disclosure requirements – shares listed or subject to a listing application. The listing rules made under *FSA 1986, Part IV* require the listing particulars to contain details of the name of any promoter and the amount of any payment or other benefit proposed to be paid or which has been paid in the two years preceding publication of the listing particulars. (*The Listing Rules, Chapter 6.C.21, 6.J.15*).

Disclosure requirements – other shares. Before a date to be appointed, the amount or percentage rate of commission paid or agreed to be paid, and the number of shares which persons have agreed for a commission to subscribe absolutely must be disclosed

- in the case of shares offered to the public for subscription, in the prospectus; and

- in the case of shares not so offered in a statement in the prescribed form (Form 97) signed by every director of the company (or his agent authorised in writing) and delivered (before payment of commission) to the Registrar of Companies for registration. In default, the company and every officer in default is liable to a fine up to the level in 40.1(*g*) PENALTIES. Where a circular or notice (not being a prospectus) is issued inviting subscription for the shares, the relevant information must also be disclosed in the circular or notice.

[*Sec 97(2)(b)(3)(4), 24 Sch*].

Except as permitted above, no company may apply any of its shares or capital money either directly or indirectly in payment of any commission, discount or allowance to any person for the consideration stated. This applies whether the shares or money are so applied by being added to the purchase money of any property acquired by the company or to the contract price of any work to be executed by the company, or the money is paid out of the nominal purchase money or contract price, or otherwise. [*Sec 98(1)(2)*].

Brokerage. Nothing in the above provisions affects a company's power to pay such brokerage as has previously been lawful. [*Sec 98(3)*].

Commission paid by other persons. A vendor to, or promoter of, or other person who receives payment in money or shares from, a company has (and is deemed always to have had) power to apply any part of the money or shares so received in payment of any commission, the payment of which would have been lawful under the above provisions if made directly by the company. [*Sec 98(4)*].

10 Annual Returns

10.1 Every company must deliver successive annual returns to the Registrar of Companies containing all the required information and signed by a director or the secretary of the company.

The return must be made up to a date within twelve months of

- the date of the previous return; or

- in the case of a new company, the date of incorporation.

It must be submitted to the Registrar of Companies within 28 days of the date to which it is made up. A filing fee is payable. See 26.1 FEES.

[*Sec 363(1)(2); CA 1989, s 139; SI 1988 No 887*].

10.2 **CONTENTS OF THE ANNUAL RETURN**

The annual return must state the date to which it is made up. An alternative date (but within twelve months) may be shown as the date of the next return. Companies House will automatically send the next return shortly before that date or, where no date is entered, before the anniversary of the current return. The fully completed return sent back to the Registrar must contain the following information.

(*a*) The address of the company's registered office as currently registered.

(*b*) Its principal business activities by reference to one or more codes based on the Standard Industrial Classification of Economic Activities 1992 published by HMSO, see 10.4 below.

(*c*) The type of company, as determined by the memorandum of association, according to the following classification scheme.

T1 Public limited company
T2 Private company limited by shares
T3 Private company limited by guarantee without share capital
T4 Private company limited by shares exempt under *Sec 30* from the requirement to use 'limited' as part of its name
T5 Private company limited by guarantee exempt under *Sec 30* from the requirement to use 'limited' as part of its name
T6 Private unlimited company with share capital
T7 Private unlimited company without share capital

(*d*) The 'name' and 'address' of the company secretary and every 'director' of the company and, additionally, for each director

(i) his nationality, date of birth and business occupation if an individual; and

(ii) (before 13 September 1999) particulars of other directorships and former names as are required to be kept in the register of directors (see 47.3 REGISTERS) or, in the case of corporate directors, would be so required in the case of an individual.

'*Name*' means Christian name (or other forename) and surname. In the case of a peer, or an individual usually known by a title, the title may be stated instead or in addition. In the case of a corporation or Scottish firm, it means its corporate or firm name.

'*Address*' means usual residential address for an individual or principal office for a corporation or Scottish firm.

Where all the partners in a firm are joint secretaries, the name and principal office of the firm may be stated instead of the names and addresses of the partners.

'Director' includes 'shadow director'. See 19.1 DIRECTORS.

(*e*)   If the register of members and/or any register of debenture-holders (or duplicate of any such register or part of it) is not kept at the company's registered office, the address where each is kept.

(*f*)   Before 13 September 1999 only, if a private company has elected to dispense with

(i)   the laying of accounts before the company in general meeting under *Sec 252* (see 3.6 ACCOUNTS: GENERAL), or

(ii)   the holding of annual general meetings under *Sec 366A* (see 33.3 MEET-INGS)

a statement to that effect. This does not apply to *public* companies.

In addition, the annual return of a company having a share capital must contain the following information at the date to which the return is made up.

(*g*)   The total number of issued shares of the company and the aggregate nominal value of those shares.

(*h*)   With respect to each class of shares in the company

(i)   the nature of the class; and

(ii)   the total number and aggregate nominal value of issued shares of that class.

(*j*)   (i)   A list of the names and addresses of every person who is a member of the company or has ceased to be a member of the company since the date to which the last return was made up (or, in the case of the first return, since the incorporation of the company). If the names are not arranged in alphabetical order, an index must be annexed to enable names to be found easily.

(ii)   The number of shares of each class held by each member of the company and the number of shares transferred since the date of the last return (or, in the case of the first return, since the date of incorporation) by each member or person who has ceased to be a member, and the dates of registration of the transfers.

If either of the two immediately preceding returns have given full particulars required by (i) and (ii) above, the return may give only such details as relate to persons ceasing to be or becoming members since the date of the last return and to shares transferred since that date.

See 48.4 REGISTRAR OF COMPANIES for the acceptable quality of the list of members accompanying the annual return.

Overseas branch registers. If copies of entries in any overseas branch register (see 47.6 REGISTERS) are not received at the company's registered office by the date to which a return is made up, those particulars need not be entered on that return but must then be entered on the next annual return.

Conversion of shares into stock. Where the company has converted any of its shares into stock, the return must give the corresponding information in relation to the stock, stating the amount of stock instead of the number or nominal value of shares.

10.3 Annual Returns

Non-disclosure of subsidiaries in the accounts. A company need not disclose full particulars of all its subsidiaries in its annual accounts if it would result in a statement of excessive length. In such a case, it must annex the full information required (i.e. both that which has been disclosed in the notes to the accounts and that which has not) in the next annual return following the approval of the accounts in question. See 5.45 ACCOUNTS: INDIVIDUAL COMPANIES for full details.

[*Secs 231(6), 364, 364A, 365(3); CA 1989, s 139; SI 1990 No 1766; SI 1991 No 1259; SI 1996 No 1105; SI 1999 No 2322*].

10.3 DEFAULT BY COMPANY

If a company fails to deliver an annual return in accordance with the provisions in 10.1 and 10.2 above within the 28 days allowed, the company and every director or secretary is guilty of an offence and liable to a fine up to the level in 40.1(*e*) PENALTIES. It is a defence for a director or secretary to show that he took all reasonable steps to avoid the commission or continuation of the offence. [*Sec 363(3)(4); CA 1989, s 139*]. It is not a defence that another person was required to make the return (*Gibson v Barton (1875) LR 10 QB 329*).

See also 48.2(*h*) REGISTRAR OF COMPANIES for the Registrar's powers of enforcement.

10.4 TRADE CLASSIFICATIONS

The following trade code numbers are required for completion of 10.2(*b*) above.

*Trade
Code*

UK STANDARD INDUSTRIAL CLASSIFICATION

Section A—Agriculture, Hunting and Forestry

Trade Code		Trade Code	
0111	Growing cereals and other crops not classified elsewhere	0130	Growing of crops combined with farming of animals (mixed farming)
0112	Growing vegetables horticultural specialities and nursery products	0141	Agricultural service activities
0113	Growing fruit, nuts, beverage and spice crops	0142	Animal husbandry service activities, except veterinary activities
0121	Farming of cattle, dairy farming	0150	Hunting, trapping and game propagation including related service activities
0122	Farming of sheep, goats, horses, asses, mules and hinnies		
0123	Farming of swine	0201	Forestry and logging
0124	Farming of poultry	0202	Forestry and logging related service activities
0125	Other farming of animals		

Section B—Fishing

0501	Fishing	0502	Operation of fish hatcheries and fish farms

Section C—Mining and Quarrying

CA Mining and Quarrying of Energy Producing Materials

1010	Mining and agglomeration of hard coal	1110	Extraction of crude petroleum and natural gas
1020	Mining and agglomeration of lignite	1120	Service activities incidental to oil and gas extraction including surveying
1030	Extraction and agglomeration of peat	1200	Mining of uranium and thorium ores

Trade
Code

CB Mining and Quarrying except Energy Producing Materials

1310 Mining of iron ores
1320 Mining of non-ferrous metal ores, except uranium and thorium ores
1411 Quarrying of stone for construction
1412 Quarrying of limestone, gypsum and chalk
1413 Quarrying of slate

1421 Operation of gravel and sand pits
1422 Mining of clays and kaolin
1430 Mining of chemical and fertilizer minerals
1440 Production of salt
1450 Other mining and quarrying not elsewhere classified

Section D—Manufacturing
DA Manufacture of Food Products; Beverages and Tobacco

1511 Production and preserving of meat
1512 Production and preserving poultry meat
1513 Production of meat and poultry meat products
1520 Processing and preserving fish and fish products
1531 Processing and preserving of potatoes
1532 Manufacture of fruit and vegetable juice
1533 Processing and preserving of fruit and vegetables not elsewhere classified
1541 Manufacture of crude oils and fats
1542 Manufacture of refined oils and fats
1543 Manufacture of margarine and similar edible fats
1551 Operation of dairies and cheese making
1552 Manufacture of ice cream
1561 Manufacture of grain mill products
1562 Manufacture of starches and starch products
1571 Manufacture of prepared feeds for farm animals
1572 Manufacture of prepared pet foods
1581 Manufacture of bread, fresh pastry goods and cakes

1582 Manufacture of rusks and biscuits, preserved pastry goods and cakes
1583 Manufacture of sugar
1584 Manufacture of cocoa, chocolate and sugar confectionery
1585 Manufacture of macaroni, noodles, couscous and similar farinaceous products
1586 Processing of tea and coffee
1587 Manufacture of condiments and seasonings
1588 Manufacture of homogenised food preparations and dietetic food
1589 Manufacture of other food products not elsewhere classified
1591 Manufacture of distilled potable alcoholic beverages
1592 Production of ethyl alcohol from fermented materials
1593 Manufacture of wines
1594 Manufacture of cider and other fruit wines
1595 Manufacture of other non-distilled fermented beverages
1596 Manufacture of beer
1597 Manufacture of malt
1598 Production of mineral waters and soft drinks
1600 Manufacture of tobacco products

DB Manufacture of Textiles and Textile Products

1711 Preparation and spinning of cotton-type fibres
1712 Preparation and spinning of woollen-type fibres
1713 Preparation and spinning of worsted-type fibres
1714 Preparation and spinning of flax-type fibres

1715 Throwing and preparation of silk including from noils and throwing and texturing of synthetic or artificial filament yarns
1716 Manufacture of sewing threads
1717 Preparation and spinning of other textile fibres
1721 Cotton-type weaving

10.4 Annual Returns

Trade
Code

Section D—Manufacturing – *continued*

DB Manufacture of Textiles and Textile Products – continued

1722 Woollen-type weaving
1723 Worsted-type weaving
1724 Silk-type weaving
1725 Other textile weaving
1730 Finishing of textiles
1740 Manufacture of made-up textile articles, except apparel
1751 Manufacture of carpets and rugs
1752 Manufacture of cordage, rope, twine and netting
1753 Manufacture of nonwovens and articles made from nonwovens, except apparel
1754 Manufacture of other textiles not elsewhere classified
1760 Manufacture of knitted and crocheted fabrics

1771 Manufacture of knitted and crocheted hosiery
1772 Manufacture of knitted and crocheted pullovers, cardigans and similar articles
1810 Manufacture of leather clothes
1821 Manufacture of workwear
1822 Manufacture of other outerwear
1823 Manufacture of underwear
1824 Manufacture of other wearing apparel and accessories not elsewhere defined
1830 Dressing and dyeing of fur; manufacture of articles of fur

DC Manufacture of Leather and Leather Products

1910 Tanning and dressing of leather
1920 Manufacture of luggage, handbags and the like, saddlery and harness

1930 Manufacture of footwear

DD Manufacture of Wood and Wood Products

2010 Sawmilling and planing of wood, impregnation of wood
2020 Manufacture of veneer sheets; manufacture of plywood, laminboard, particle board, fibre board and other panels and boards
2030 Manufacture of builders' carpentry and joinery

2040 Manufacture of wooden containers
2051 Manufacture of other products of wood
2052 Manufacture of articles of cork, straw and plaiting materials

DE Manufacture of Pulp, Paper and Paper Products; Publishing and Printing

2111 Manufacture of pulp
2112 Manufacture of paper and paperboard
2121 Manufacture of corrugated paper and paperboard and of containers of paper and paperboard
2122 Manufacture of household and sanitary goods and of toilet requisites
2123 Manufacture of paper stationery
2124 Manufacture of wallpaper
2125 Manufacture of other articles of paper and paperboard not elsewhere classified

2211 Publishing of books
2212 Publishing of newspapers
2213 Publishing of journals and periodicals
2214 Publishing of sound recordings
2215 Other publishing
2221 Printing of newspapers
2222 Printing not elsewhere classified
2223 Bookbinding and finishing
2224 Composition and plate-making
2225 Other activities related to printing
2231 Reproduction of sound recording
2232 Reproduction of video recording
2233 Reproduction of computer media

Trade
Code

Section D—Manufacturing – *continued*

DF Manufacture of Coke, Refined Petroleum Products and Nuclear Fuel

2310 Manufacture of coke oven products
2320 Manufacture of refined petroleum products

2330 Processing of nuclear fuel

DG Manufacture of Chemicals, Chemical Products and Man-Made Fibres

2411 Manufacture of industrial gases
2412 Manufacture of dyes and pigments
2413 Manufacture of other inorganic basic chemicals
2414 Manufacture of other organic basic chemicals
2415 Manufacture of fertilizers, nitrogen compounds
2416 Manufacture of plastics in primary forms
2417 Manufacture of synthetic rubber primary forms
2420 Manufacture of pesticides and other agro-chemical products
2430 Manufacture of paints, varnishes and similar coatings, printing ink and mastics
2441 Manufacture of basic pharmaceutical products

2442 Manufacture of pharmaceutical preparations
2451 Manufacture of soap and detergents, cleaning and polishing preparations
2452 Manufacture of perfumes and toilet preparations
2461 Manufacture of explosives
2462 Manufacture of glues and gelatine
2463 Manufacture of essential oils
2464 Manufacture of photographic chemical material
2465 Manufacture of prepared unrecorded media
2466 Manufacture of other chemical products not elsewhere classified
2470 Manufacture of man-made fibres

DH Manufacture of Rubber and Plastic Products

2511 Manufacture of rubber tyres and tubes
2512 Retreading and rebuilding of rubber tyres
2513 Manufacture of other rubber products
2521 Manufacture of plastic plates, sheets, tubes and profiles

2522 Manufacture of plastic packing goods
2523 Manufacture of builders' ware of plastic
2524 Manufacture of other plastic products

DI Manufacture Other Non-Metal Mineral Products

2611 Manufacture of flat glass
2612 Shaping and processing of flat glass
2613 Manufacture of hollow glass
2614 Manufacture of glass fibres
2615 Manufacture and processing of other glass including technical glassware
2621 Manufacture of ceramic household and ornamental articles
2622 Manufacture of ceramic sanitary fixtures
2623 Manufacture of ceramic insulators and insulating fittings

2624 Manufacture of other technical ceramic goods
2625 Manufacture of other ceramic products
2626 Manufacture of refractory ceramic products
2630 Manufacture of ceramic tiles and flags
2640 Manufacture of bricks, tiles and construction products, in baked clay
2651 Manufacture of cement
2652 Manufacture of lime
2653 Manufacture of plaster

10.4 Annual Returns

Section D—Manufacturing – *continued*

DI Manufacture Other Non-Metal Mineral Products – continued

2661 Manufacture of concrete products for construction purposes

2662 Manufacture of plaster products for construction purposes

2663 Manufacture of ready-mixed concrete

2664 Manufacture of mortars

2665 Manufacture of fibre cement

2666 Manufacture of other articles of concrete, plaster and cement

2670 Cutting, shaping and finishing of stone

2681 Production of abrasive products

2682 Manufacture of other non-metal mineral products not elsewhere classified

DJ Manufacture of Basic Metals and Fabricated Metal Products

2710 Manufacture of basic iron and steel and of ferro-alloys (ECSC)

2721 Manufacture of cast iron tubes

2722 Manufacture of steel tubes

2731 Cold drawing

2732 Cold rolling of narrow strips

2733 Cold forming or folding

2734 Wire drawing

2735 Other first processing of iron and steel not elsewhere classified; production of non-ECSC ferro-alloys

2741 Precious metals production

2742 Aluminium production

2743 Lead, zinc and tin production

2744 Copper production

2745 Other non-ferrous metal production

2751 Casting of iron

2752 Casting of steel

2753 Casting of light metals

2754 Casting of other non-ferrous metals

2811 Manufacture of metal structures and parts of structures

2812 Manufacture of builders' carpentry and joinery of metal

2821 Manufacture of tanks, reservoirs and containers of metal

2822 Manufacture of central heating radiators and boilers

2830 Manufacture of steam generators, except central heating hot water boilers

2840 Forging, pressing, stamping and roll forming of metal; powder metallurgy

2851 Treatment and coating of metals

2852 General mechanical engineering

2861 Manufacture of cutlery

2862 Manufacture of tools

2863 Manufacture of locks and hinges

2871 Manufacture of steel drums and similar containers

2872 Manufacture of light metal packaging

2873 Manufacture of wire products

2874 Manufacture of fasteners, screw machine products, chain and springs

2875 Manufacture of other fabricated metal products not elsewhere classified

DK Manufacture of Machinery and Equipment Not Elsewhere Classified

2911 Manufacture of engines and turbines, except aircraft, vehicle and cycle engines

2912 Manufacture of pumps and compressors

2913 Manufacture of taps and valves

2914 Manufacture of bearings, gears, gearing and driving elements

2921 Manufacture of furnaces and furnace burners

2922 Manufacture of lifting and handling equipment

2923 Manufacture of non-domestic cooling and ventilation equipment

2924 Manufacture of other general purpose machinery not elsewhere classified

2931 Manufacture of agricultural tractors

2932 Manufacture of other agricultural and forestry machines

2940 Manufacture of machine tools

2951 Manufacture of machinery for metallurgy

Trade
Code

Section D—Manufacturing – *continued*

DK Manufacture of Machinery and Equipment Not Elsewhere Classified – continued

2952 Manufacture of machinery for mining, quarrying and construction

2953 Manufacture of machinery for food, beverage and tobacco processing

2954 Manufacture of machinery for textile, apparel and leather production

2955 Manufacture of machinery for paper and paperboard production

2956 Manufacture of other special purpose machine not elsewhere classified

2960 Manufacture of weapons and ammunition

2971 Manufacture of electric domestic appliances

2972 Manufacture of non-electric domestic appliances

DL Manufacture of Electrical and Optical Equipment

3001 Manufacture of office machinery

3002 Manufacture of computers and other information processing equipment

3110 Manufacture of electric motors, generators and transformers

3120 Manufacture of electricity distribution and control apparatus

3130 Manufacture of insulated wire and cable

3140 Manufacture of accumulators, primary cells and primary batteries

3150 Manufacture of lighting equipment and electric lamps

3161 Manufacture of electrical equipment for engines and vehicles not elsewhere classified

3162 Manufacture of other electrical equipment not elsewhere classified

3210 Manufacture of electronic valves and tubes and other electronic components

3220 Manufacture of TV and radio transmitters and apparatus for line telephony and line telegraphy

3230 Manufacture of TV and radio receivers, sound or video recording or reproducing apparatus and associated goods

3310 Manufacture of medical and surgical equipment and orthopaedic appliances

3320 Manufacture of instruments and appliances for measuring, checking, testing, navigating and other purposes, except industrial process control equipment

3330 Manufacture of industrial process control equipment

3340 Manufacture of optical instruments and photographic equipment

3350 Manufacture of watches and clocks

DM Manufacture of Transport Equipment

3410 Manufacture of motor vehicles

3420 Manufacture of bodies (coachwork) for motor vehicles; manufacture of trailers and semi-trailers

3430 Manufacture of parts and accessories for motor vehicles and their engines

3511 Building and repairing of ships

3512 Building and repairing of pleasure and sporting boats

3520 Manufacture of railway and tramway locomotives and rolling stock

3530 Manufacture of aircraft and spacecraft

3541 Manufacture of motorcycles

3542 Manufacture of bicycles

3543 Manufacture of invalid carriages

3550 Manufacture of other transport equipment not elsewhere classified

DN Manufacturing Not Elsewhere Classified

3611 Manufacture of chairs and seats

3612 Manufacture of other office and shop furniture

3613 Manufacture of other kitchen furniture

3614 Manufacture of other furniture

10.4 Annual Returns

Trade
Code

Section D—Manufacturing – *continued*
DN Manufacturing Not Elsewhere Classified – continued

3615 Manufacture of mattresses
3621 Striking of coins and medals
3622 Manufacture of jewellery and related articles not elsewhere classified
3630 Manufacture of musical instruments
3640 Manufacture of sports goods
3650 Manufacture of games and toys

3661 Manufacture of imitation jewellery
3662 Manufacture of brooms and brushes
3663 Other manufacturing not elsewhere classified
3710 Recycling of metal waste and scrap
3720 Recycling of non-metal waste and scrap

Section E—Electricity, Gas and Water Supply

4010 Production and distribution of electricity
4020 Manufacture of gas; distribution of gaseous fuels through mains

4030 Steam and hot water supply
4100 Collection, purification and distribution of water

Section F—Construction

4511 Demolition and wrecking of buildings; earth moving
4512 Test drilling and boring
4521 General construction of buildings and civil engineering works
4522 Erection of roof covering and frames
4523 Construction of highways, roads, airfields and sport facilities
4524 Construction of water projects
4525 Other construction work involving special trades

4531 Installation of electrical wiring and fitting
4532 Insulation work activities
4533 Plumbing
4534 Other building installation
4541 Plastering
4542 Joinery installation
4543 Floor and wall covering
4544 Painting and glazing
4545 Other building completion
4550 Renting of construction or demolition equipment with operator

Section G—Wholesale and Retail Trade; Repair of Motor Vehicles, Motorcycles and Personal and Household Goods

5010 Sale of motor vehicles
5020 Maintenance and repair of motor vehicles
5030 Sale of motor vehicle parts and accessories
5040 Sale, maintenance and repair of motorcycles and related parts and accessories
5050 Retail sale of automotive fuel
5111 Agents involved in the sale of agricultural raw materials, live animals, textile raw materials and semi-finished goods
5112 Agents involved in the sale of fuels, ores, metals and industrial chemicals
5113 Agents involved in the sale of timber and building materials

5114 Agents involved in the sale of machinery, industrial equipment, ships and aircraft
5115 Agents involved in the sale of furniture, household goods, hardware and ironmongery
5116 Agents involved in the sale of textiles, clothing, footwear and leather goods
5117 Agents involved in the sale of food, beverages and tobacco
5118 Agents specialising in the sale of particular products or ranges of products not elsewhere classified
5119 Agents involved in the sale of a variety of goods
5121 Wholesale of grain, seeds and animal feeds

Trade
Code
**Section G—Wholesale and Retail Trade; Repair of Motor Vehicles, Motorcycles
and Personal and Household Goods** – *continued*

5122 Wholesale of flowers and plants
5123 Wholesale of live animals
5124 Wholesale of hides, skins and leather
5125 Wholesale of unmanufactured tobacco
5131 Wholesale of fruit and vegetables
5132 Wholesale of meat and meat products
5133 Wholesale of dairy produce, eggs and edible oils and fats
5134 Wholesale of alcoholic and other beverages
5135 Wholesale of tobacco products
5136 Wholesale of sugar and chocolate and sugar confectionery
5137 Wholesale of coffee, tea, cocoa and spices
5138 Wholesale of other food including fish, crustaceans and molluscs
5139 Non-specialised wholesale of food, beverages and tobacco
5141 Wholesale of textiles
5142 Wholesale of clothing and footwear
5143 Wholesale of electric household appliances and radio and TV goods
5144 Wholesale of china and glassware, wallpaper and cleaning materials
5145 Wholesale of perfumes and cosmetics
5146 Wholesale of pharmaceutical goods
5147 Wholesale of other household goods
5151 Wholesale of solid, liquid and gaseous fuels and related products
5152 Wholesale of metals and metal ores
5153 Wholesale of wood, construction materials and sanitary equipment
5154 Wholesale of hardware, plumbing and heating equipment and supplies
5155 Wholesale of chemical products
5156 Wholesale of other intermediate products
5157 Wholesale of waste and scrap
5161 Wholesale of machine tools
5162 Wholesale of construction machinery
5163 Wholesale of machinery for the textile industry, and of sewing and knitting machines

5164 Wholesale of office machinery and equipment
5165 Wholesale of machinery for use in industry, trade and navigation
5166 Wholesale of agricultural machinery and accessories and implements, including tractors
5170 Other wholesale
5211 Retail sale in non-specialised stores with food, beverages or tobacco
5212 Other retail sale in non-specialised stores
5221 Retail sale of fruit and vegetables
5222 Retail sale of meat and meat products
5223 Retail sale of fish, crustaceans and molluscs
5224 Retail sale of bread, cakes, flour confectionery and sugar confectionery
5225 Retail sale of alcoholic and other beverages
5226 Retail sale of tobacco products
5227 Other retail sale of food, beverages and tobacco in specialised stores
5231 Dispensing chemists
5232 Retail sale of medical and orthopaedic goods
5233 Retail sale of cosmetic and toilet articles
5241 Retail sale of textiles
5242 Retail sale of clothing
5243 Retail sale of footwear and leather goods
5244 Retail sale of furniture, lighting equipment and household articles not elsewhere classified
5245 Retail sale of electrical household appliances and radio and TV goods
5246 Retail sale of hardware, paints and glass
5247 Retail sale of books, newspapers and stationery
5248 Other retail sale in specialised stores
5250 Retail sale of second-hand goods in stores
5261 Retail sale via mail order houses
5262 Retail sale via stalls and markets
5263 Other non-store retail sale

10.4 Annual Returns

Trade
Code
Section G—Wholesale and Retail Trade; Repair of Motor Vehicles, Motorcycles and Personal and Household Goods – *continued*

5271 Repair of boots, shoes and other articles of leather
5272 Repair of electrical household goods

5273 Repair of watches, clocks and jewellery
5274 Repair not elsewhere classified

Section H—Hotels and Restaurants

5511 Hotels and motels, with restaurant
5512 Hotels and motels, without restaurant
5521 Youth hostels and mountain refuges
5522 Camp sites, including caravan sites

5523 Other provision of lodgings not elsewhere classified
5530 Restaurants
5540 Bars
5551 Canteens
5552 Catering

Section I—Transport, Storage and Communications

6010 Transport via railways
6021 Other scheduled passenger land transport
6022 Taxi operation
6023 Other passenger land transport
6024 Freight transport by road
6030 Transport via pipelines
6110 Sea and coastal water transport
6120 Inland water transport
6210 Scheduled air transport
6220 Non-scheduled air transport
6230 Space transport
6331 Cargo handling
6312 Storage and warehousing

6321 Other supporting land transport activities
6322 Other supporting water transport activities
6323 Other supporting air transport activities
6330 Activities of travel agencies and tour operators; tourist assistance activities not elsewhere classified
6340 Activities of other transport agencies
6411 National post activities
6412 Courier activities other than national post activities
6420 Telecommunications

Section J—Financial Intermediation

6511 Central banking
6512 Other monetary intermediation
6521 Financial leasing
6522 Other credit granting
6523 Other financial intermediation not elsewhere classified
6601 Life insurance
6602 Pension funding
6603 Non-life insurance

6711 Administration of financial markets
6712 Security broking and fund management
6713 Activities auxiliary to financial intermediation not elsewhere classified
6720 Activities auxiliary to insurance and pension funding

Section K—Real Estate, Renting and Business Activities

7011 Development and selling of real estate
7012 Buying and selling of own real estate
7020 Letting of own property
7031 Real estate agencies

7032 Management of real estate on a fee or contract basis
7110 Renting of automobiles
7121 Renting of other land transport equipment
7122 Renting water transport equipment

Trade
Code

Section K—Real Estate, Renting and Business Activities – *continued*

7123 Renting of air transport equipment
7131 Renting of agricultural machinery and equipment
7132 Renting of construction and civil engineering machinery and equipment
7133 Renting of office machinery and equipment including computers
7134 Renting of other machinery and equipment not elsewhere classified
7140 Renting of personal and household goods not elsewhere classified
7210 Hardware consultancy
7220 Software consultancy and supply
7230 Data processing
7240 Data base activities
7250 Maintenance and repair of office, accounting and computing machinery
7260 Other computer-related activities
7310 Research and experimental development on natural sciences and engineering
7320 Research and experimental development on social sciences and humanities

7411 Legal activities
7412 Accounting, book-keeping and auditing activities; tax consultancy
7413 Market research and public opinion polling
7414 Business and management consultancy activities
7415 Management activities of holding companies
7420 Architectural and engineering activities and related technical consultancy
7430 Technical testing and analysis
7440 Advertising
7450 Labour recruitment and provision of personnel
7460 Investigation and security activities
7470 Industrial cleaning
7481 Photographic activities
7482 Packaging activities
7483 Secretarial and translation activities
7484 Other business activities not elsewhere classified
7499 Non-trading company

Section L—Public Administration and Defence; Compulsory Social Service

7511 General (overall) public service activities
7512 Regulation of the activities of agencies that provide health care, education, cultural services and other social services excluding social security
7513 Regulation of and contribution to more efficient operation of business

7514 Supporting service activities for the government as a whole
7521 Foreign affairs
7522 Defence activities
7523 Justice and judicial activities
7524 Public security, law and order activities
7525 Fire service activities
7530 Compulsory social security activities

Section M—Education

8010 Primary education
8021 General secondary education
8022 Technical and vocational secondary education

8030 Higher education
8041 Driving school activities
8042 Adult and other education not elsewhere classified

Section N—Health and Social Work

8511 Hospital activities
8512 Medical practice activities
8513 Dental practice activities
8514 Other human health activities
8520 Veterinary activities

8531 Social work activities with accommodation
8532 Social work activities without accommodation

217

10.4 Annual Returns

Section O—Other Social and Person Service Activities

9000 Sewage and refuse disposal, sanitation and similar services

9111 Activities of business and employers organisations

9112 Activities of professional organisations

9120 Activities of trade unions

9131 Activities of religious organisations

9132 Activities of political organisations

9133 Activities of other membership organisations not elsewhere classified

9211 Motion picture and video production

9212 Motion picture and video distribution

9213 Motion picture projection

9220 Radio and television activities

9231 Artistic and literary creation and interpretation

9232 Operation of arts facilities

9233 Fair and amusement park activities

9234 Other entertainment activities not elsewhere classified

9240 News agency activities

9251 Library and archives activities

9252 Museum activities and preservation of historical sites and buildings

9253 Botanical and zoological gardens and nature reserves activities

9261 Operation of sports arenas and stadiums

9262 Other sporting activities

9271 Gambling and betting activities

9272 Other recreational activities not elsewhere classified

9301 Washing and dry cleaning of textile and fur products

9302 Hairdressing and other beauty treatment

9303 Funeral and related activities

9304 Physical well-being activities

9305 Other service activities not elsewhere classified

Section P—Private Households with Employed Persons

9500 Private households with employed persons

Miscellaneous

9600 Residents Property Management

Group Q—Extra-Territorial Organisations and Bodies

9900 Extra-territorial organisations and bodies

11   Articles of Association

Cross-references. See 35 MEMORANDUM OF ASSOCIATION.

The contents of this chapter are as follows

11.1   REGISTRATION OF ARTICLES

A company limited by shares may register, together with its MEMORANDUM OF ASSOCIATION (35), articles of association signed by the subscribers to the memorandum and prescribing regulations for the internal management of the company. In the case of UNLIMITED COMPANIES (60) and GUARANTEE COMPANIES (29), articles must be registered. [*Sec 7(1)*]. The articles of an unlimited company having a share capital must state the amount of share capital with which the company proposes to be registered. [*Sec 7(2)*].

Articles must be printed, be divided into paragraphs numbered consecutively, and be signed by each subscriber to the memorandum in the presence of at least one witness who must attest the signature (which attestation is sufficient in Scotland as well as in England and Wales). [*Sec 7(3)*]. See 48.4 REGISTRAR OF COMPANIES for the quality of document to be filed with the Registrar.

11.2   FORM AND CONTENTS OF ARTICLES

A company may for its articles adopt the whole or any part of *Table A*. [*Sec 8(1)*]. The current Table A is set out in *SI 1985 No 805* (as amended). If a company limited by shares does not register articles, or in so far as the articles registered do not exclude or modify *Table A* (see 11.4 below), that *Table* will, so far as applicable and as in force at the date of the company's registration (see 11.3 below), constitute the company's articles as if they were contained in duly registered articles. [*Sec 8(2)*].

The form of the articles in the case of

- a company limited by guarantee and not having a share capital,

- a company limited by guarantee and having a share capital, and

- an unlimited company having a share capital,

must be respectively in accordance with *Table C, D,* or *E* set out in *SI 1985 No 805* or as near as circumstances permit. [*Sec 8(4)*].

From a date to be appointed, the Secretary of State has powers to prescribe a *Table G* setting out articles for a 'partnership company' i.e. a company limited by shares whose shares are intended to be held to a substantial extent by or on behalf of its employees. [*Sec 8A; CA 1989, s 128*].

Listed companies. The articles of listed companies must contain certain provisions laid down in the *Listing Rules*. See 43.18 PUBLIC AND LISTED COMPANIES.

11.3   Which form of Table A applies

The *Table A* which applies to a company limited by shares is, to the extent that it has been adopted by the company, that *Table* which, as previously altered, is in force at the date of

11.4 Articles of Association

the company's registration. [*Sec 8(2)*]. If the form of *Table A* is subsequently altered, the alteration does not affect a company registered before the alteration takes effect, nor does it repeal any portion of that *Table* as respects that company. [*Sec 8(3)*].

As regards a company incorporated on or after 2 November 1862, the following form of *Table A* will apply to it (unless disapplied), according to the date on which the company was incorporated.

Date of incorporation	Relevant Table A
2.11.1862–30.9.1906	*CA 1862, 1 Sch, Table A*
1.10.06–31.3.09	*Table A, as substituted by [1906] WN Misc 233*
1.4.09–31.10.29	*CA 1908, 1 Sch, Table A*
1.11.29–30.6.48	*CA 1929, 1 Sch, Table A*
1.7.48–21.12.80	*CA 1948, 1 Sch, Table A*
	—Part I public company
	—Part II private company
22.12.80–30.8.85	*CA 1948, 1 Sch, Table A, Part I*
1.7.85–	*SI 1985 No 805*

11.4 **Scope of Table A**

The articles in *Table A* cover

- **Shares** – share capital, share certificates, lien, calls on shares and forfeiture, transfer of shares, transmission of shares, alteration of share capital, and purchase of own shares.

- **Meetings** – general meetings, notice of general meetings, proceedings at general meetings, and votes of members.

- **Directors** – number, alternate, powers, delegation of powers, appointment and retirement, disqualification and removal, remuneration, expenses, appointments and interests, gratuities and pensions, and proceedings of directors.

- **General administration** – secretary, minutes, the seal, dividends, accounts, capitalisation of profits, notices, winding up, and indemnity.

The detailed provisions are dealt with in the appropriate chapters. A company limited by shares may exclude or modify *Table A* (see 11.2 above), and this occurs frequently in practice.

11.5 **CONTRACTUAL EFFECT OF ARTICLES**

Subject to the provisions of *CA 1985*, the 'articles' (and memorandum), when registered, bind the company and its members to the same extent as if they had been signed and sealed by each member, and contained covenants on the part of each member to observe all the provisions of the articles. [*Sec 14(1)*]. '*Articles*' means the articles as originally framed or as later altered or varied (*Malleson v National Insurance and Guarantee Corporation [1894] 1 Ch 200*).

The wording of *Sec 14(1)* does not make very clear the nature of the relationship which it creates between one member and another and between a member and the company. As a result, there have been numerous court cases on the relationships.

Between members. The cases seem to indicate that, even if the articles do constitute a contract between the members of a company, generally the rights bestowed by the articles can only be enforced through the company or, where the company is being wound up, through the liquidator (*Welton v Saffery [1897] AC 299*).

However, in some cases, the court has adopted a different approach, most notably in *Rayfield v Hands [1960] Ch 1* where the company's articles required the directors to be members of the company, and also required any member proposing to transfer shares in the company to inform the directors 'who will take the shares equally between them at a fair value'. It was held that a member could compel the directors to purchase his shares in accordance with this provision as the relationship was between the plaintiff as a member and the defendants not as directors but as members.

Nevertheless, the general view appears to be that *Welton v Saffery* still represents the principle which will normally be applied and the reasoning in *Rayfield v Hands* is probably only applicable where the articles give one member a personal right as against another member.

Between the company and its members. The general principle is that the articles constitute a contract between the company and its members in relation to their rights and obligations as members. In *Hickman v Kent or Romney Marsh Sheep-Breeders Association [1915] 1 Ch 881* the court granted the company a stay of proceedings brought against it by a member who was disputing his expulsion from the company. The articles provided that disputes between the company and its members were to go to arbitration, and by bringing the action, the member was acting contrary to the articles. Similarly, in *Wood v Odessa Waterworks Co [1889] 42 ChD 636*, a member was granted an injunction restraining the company from acting on a resolution which was contrary to the articles.

However, the general principle applies only where the articles confer a right on a member in his capacity as a member. Thus, in *Eley v Positive Government Security Life Assurance Co (1876) 1 Ex D 88*, the articles stated that the plaintiff was to be employed for life as the company's solicitor. When the company ceased to employ him, the plaintiff was held not to be entitled to damages for breach of contract, because the articles did not constitute a contract between the company and the plaintiff in a capacity other than as a member. (See also *Beattie v Beattie [1938] Ch 708*.)

11.6   INTERPRETATION OF ARTICLES

From the wording of *Sec 14(1)* (see 11.5 above), it is clear that the memorandum and articles are to be read together, but no article is valid or binding upon a shareholder if in conflict with the memorandum (*Welton v Saffery [1897] AC 299*; *Re Duncan Gilmour and Co Ltd [1952] 2 All ER 871*; and *Guinness v Land Corporation of Ireland (1882) 22 ChD 349*). Where possible, the articles should be construed so as to give them reasonable business efficacy (*Holmes v Keyes [1959] Ch 199*).

11.7   ALTERATION OF ARTICLES

A company may alter its articles by special resolution (see 51.2 RESOLUTIONS), subject to the provisions of *CA 1985* and to the conditions contained in its memorandum. Alterations so made are (again subject to *CA 1985*) as valid as if originally contained in the articles, and are similarly subject to alteration by special resolution. [*Sec 9*].

Private companies may also alter their articles without a special resolution by means of a written resolution signed by all the members. See 51.4 RESOLUTIONS.

11.8   Articles of Association

Listed companies may need the approval of the Stock Exchange for certain alterations. See 43.18 PUBLIC AND LISTED COMPANIES.

Apart from the above restrictions, a company is free to alter its articles as it wishes, and it must not nullify or restrict its ability to alter them. See *Allen v Gold Reefs of West Africa Ltd [1900] 1 Ch 656* and *Russell v Northern Bank Development Corporation Ltd and Others [1992] 1 WLR 588.* This applies even if to do so would involve a breach of contract with a third party. Such a third party would, however, be entitled to damages for the breach (*Southern Foundries (1926) Ltd v Shirlaw [1940] AC 701*).

Any alteration must be made bona fide for the benefit of the company as a whole. See *Allen v Gold Reefs of West Africa Ltd supra* (creation of a lien on fully paid shares); *Brown v British Abrasive Wheel Co Ltd [1919] 1 Ch 290* (compulsory purchase of minority shares); and *Sidebottom v Kershaw, Leese and Co Ltd [1920] 1 Ch 154* (forced sale of shares by shareholders carrying on business in direct competition). Whether such an alteration is for the company's benefit is for the shareholders to decide, and the court will intervene only if it considers the alteration to be such that no reasonable person would consider it to be in the interests of the company (*Shuttleworth v Cox Bros and Co (Maidenhead) Ltd [1927] 2 KB 9*). As to the meaning of 'bona fide for the benefit of the company as a whole', see *Greenhalgh v Arderne Cinemas Ltd [1951] Ch 286.*

See also generally *Peter's American Delicacy Co Ltd v Heath (1939) 61 CLR 457.*

Even where there has been no formal alteration of the articles, an alteration can be proved by a long period of acquiescence by the members (*Ho Tung v Man On Insurance Co [1902] AC 232*) and the court has upheld an agreement by all the members of a company to alter the articles (*Cane v Jones [1981] 1 All ER 533*).

Example of special resolution altering the articles

'That regulation [insert number] in the existing articles of association be and hereby is deleted and that the following regulation be and hereby is inserted in its place.

New regulation [insert number]
[Text of new regulation]'

Example of special resolution adopting new articles

'That the existing articles of association be and hereby are deleted in their entirety and that new articles of association as initialled by the chairman and presented to the meeting be and hereby are adopted in their place.'

11.8   Filing requirements, etc.

See 51.9 RESOLUTIONS for filing a special resolution with the Registrar of Companies and issuing copies of the articles after a resolution has been passed.

Where a company is required to send to the Registrar any documents making or evidencing an alteration in the company's articles, it must send a *printed* copy of the articles as altered at the same time.

Where a company's articles are altered by any statutory provision, whether an Act or an instrument made under an Act, a printed copy of the Act or instrument must (together with a printed copy of the articles as altered) be forwarded to the Registrar, not later than 15 days after that provision comes into force, and recorded by him. In default, the company and every officer in default is liable to a fine up to the level in 40.1(*f*) PENALTIES.

[*Sec 18, 24 Sch*].

Companies House are, however, prepared to accept amendments to the articles (or memorandum) in the following form provided that they are validated by the seal or official stamp of the company.

- Where the amendment is small (e.g. a change of name or a change in the nominal share capital), a copy of the original document can be amended by rubber stamp, 'top copy' typing or in some other permanent manner (but not by a hand-written amendment).

- An alteration of a few lines or a complete short page may be similarly dealt with if the new version is permanently fixed to the original, covering the words as amended.

- If more substantial amendments are involved, the amended pages can be removed from a copy of the original, the amended text inserted and the pages securely fixed. The inserted material *must* be printed but need not be produced by the same process as the original.

The Registrar of Companies must ensure that notice of the receipt of any document making or evidencing an alteration in the company's articles is published in the *Gazette*. [*Sec 711*]. See 48.2(*g*) REGISTRAR OF COMPANIES. A company cannot rely on any alteration in its articles as against a third party if, at the material time, this notice has not been published in the *Gazette* or the *Gazette* has been published for less than 15 days and the person concerned was unavoidably prevented from knowing of the alteration. See 16.13 DEALINGS WITH THIRD PARTIES.

Listed companies. See 43.18 PUBLIC AND LISTED COMPANIES for the requirement to lodge copies with the Listing Department of the Stock Exchange.

11.9 Alterations affecting liability of members

Unless he agrees in writing, a member is not bound by an alteration made in the articles after the date on which he becomes a member if the alteration

- requires him to take or subscribe for more shares than the number held at the date of the alteration; or

- in any way increases his liability as at that date to contribute to the company's share capital or otherwise pay money to the company.

[*Sec 16*].

11.10 COPIES OF ARTICLES

A company must, on demand, send a copy of the articles to a member, subject to a payment of 5 pence or less. In default, the company and every officer in default is liable to a fine up to the level in 40.1(*g*) PENALTIES. [*Sec 19, 24 Sch*].

Any person may inspect a copy of the articles at Companies House and may obtain a certified copy of the articles on payment of the prescribed fees. See 26.1 FEES.

12 Auditors

Cross-references. See 8.14 ACQUISITION OF OWN SHARES for report when a private company wishes to redeem or purchase its own shares out of capital; 8.21 ACQUISITION OF OWN SHARES for report when a private company wishes to provide financial assistance for purchase of its own shares or those of its holding company; 9.16 ALLOTMENT OF SHARES for report when a public company wishes to allot shares otherwise than for cash; 9.20 ALLOTMENT OF SHARES for report when a public company purchases non-cash assets from certain of its members; 19.68 DIRECTORS for report on disclosure of loans, etc. by banking company to directors; 23.7 DISTRIBUTIONS for report where qualified accounts are relevant for the purposes of a proposed distribution; 43.28(*c*) PUBLIC AND LISTED COMPANIES for auditors' report on summary financial statements; 47.13 REGISTERS for register of auditors; 49.4 REGISTRATION AND RE-REGISTRATION for report when a private company wishes to re-register as a public company.

The contents of this chapter are as follows.

12.1 APPOINTMENT

Every company must appoint an auditor or auditors (except where the small companies audit exemptions apply (see 12.31 to 12.40 below) and except for certain DORMANT COMPANIES (24)). [*Secs 384(1), 388A(1); CA 1989, s 119; SI 1994 No 1935, Reg 3, 1 Sch 4*].

Subject to 12.2 below, auditors must be appointed at the following times.

(*a*) *All public companies and any private company which has not made an election within (b) below.* The first auditors may be appointed by the directors (or, if they fail to exercise this power, by the company in general meeting) at any time before the first general meeting of the company at which accounts are laid. The auditors so appointed hold office until the conclusion of that meeting. Thereafter a company must make the appointment at each general meeting at which accounts are laid and the auditors so appointed then hold office from the conclusion of that meeting until the conclusion of the next such general meeting. [*Sec 385; CA 1989, s 119*].

Example of resolution for appointment of first auditor

'That [insert name(s)] be and hereby is/are appointed auditor(s) of the company to hold office until the conclusion of the first general meeting at which accounts are laid before the company.'

Example of a resolution to re-appoint existing auditors

'That [insert name(s)] be and hereby is/are re-appointed auditor(s) of the company to hold office until the conclusion of the next general meeting at which accounts are laid before the company and that the directors be and hereby are authorised to fix their/his remuneration.'

(*b*)   *Private companies which have elected under Sec 252 to dispense with the laying of accounts before the company in general meeting* (see 3.6 ACCOUNTS: GENERAL). Unless a member or auditor has given notice under *Sec 253* (see 3.6 ACCOUNTS: GENERAL) requiring a meeting to be held at which accounts are laid (in which case the normal rules under (*a*) apply) the first auditors may be appointed by the directors (or, if they fail to exercise this power, by the company in general meeting) at any time before the end of the period of 28 days beginning with the day on which copies of the company's first annual accounts are sent to members. The auditors so appointed hold office until the end of that period. Thereafter, the company must make the appointment in general meeting before the end of the period of 28 days beginning with the date on which copies of the company's accounts for the previous financial year are sent to members and the auditors so appointed hold office from the end of that period until the end of the time for appointing auditors for the next financial year.

Auditors holding office *when an election is made*, unless the company in general meeting determines otherwise, continue to hold office until the end of the time for appointing auditors for the next financial year. Auditors holding office *when an election ceases* continue to hold office until the conclusion of the next general meeting of the company at which accounts are laid.

[*Sec 385A; CA 1989, s 119*].

12.2   Election by a private company to dispense with annual appointment

A private company may elect by resolution under *Sec 379A* (see 51.3 RESOLUTIONS) to dispense with the obligation to appoint auditors annually. The auditors are then deemed to have been re-appointed for each succeeding financial year on the expiry of the time limit for appointing auditors for that year unless a resolution has been passed

● exempting the company from the obligation to appoint auditors (see 24.2 DORMANT COMPANIES); or

● under the provisions in 12.13 below.

If the election ceases to be in force, the auditors then holding office continue to hold office until the conclusion of the next general meeting of the company at which accounts are laid or, where 12.1(*b*) above applies, until the end of the time for appointing auditors for the next financial year under those provisions.

No account must be taken of any loss of the opportunity of further deemed re-appointment under these provisions in ascertaining the amount of any compensation or damages payable to an auditor on ceasing to hold office.

[*Sec 386; CA 1989, s 119*].

12.3   Appointment by the Secretary of State

Where no auditors are appointed, re-appointed or deemed to be re-appointed under the provisions of 12.1 and 12.2 above, the company must give notice of the fact to the Secretary of State within one week of the end of the time for appointing auditors and he may then appoint a person to fill the vacancy. If the company fails to give notice, the company and every officer who is in default is guilty of an offence and liable to a fine up to the level in 40.1(*f*) PENALTIES. [*Sec 387, 24 Sch; CA 1989, s 119*].

12.4 Filling of casual vacancies

The directors, or the company in general meeting, may fill a casual vacancy but while the vacancy continues, any surviving or continuing auditor or auditors may continue to act.

Special notice (see 51.8 RESOLUTIONS) is required for a resolution at a general meeting

- filling a casual vacancy; or

- re-appointing as auditor a retiring auditor who was appointed by the directors to fill a casual vacancy.

A copy of the intended resolution must be sent to the proposed auditor and, if the casual vacancy was caused by a resignation, the auditor who resigned.

[*Sec 388; CA 1989, s 119*].

12.5 ELIGIBILITY FOR APPOINTMENT

A person is only eligible for appointment as a company auditor if he is

(*a*)   a member of a recognised 'supervisory body'; *and*

(*b*)   eligible for the appointment under the rules of that body. Although more stringent requirements may be imposed by the body, a person cannot be eligible for appointment unless

    (i)   in the case of an individual, he holds an 'appropriate qualification'; and

    (ii)   in the case of a firm, the individuals responsible for company audit work on behalf of the firm hold an appropriate qualification and the firm is controlled by qualified persons.

An individual or a firm may be appointed a company auditor. A firm which has ceased to comply with the conditions in (*b*)(ii) above can only be permitted to remain eligible for appointment as a company auditor for a period of not more than three months.

[*CA 1989, s 25, 11 Sch 4*].

'*Supervisory body*' means a body established in the UK which maintains and enforces binding rules as to eligibility of persons to seek appointment as company auditors and the conduct of company audit work. [*CA 1989, s 30*]. See *CA 1989, 11 Sch* for the rules regarding grant and revocation of recognition of supervisory bodies and rules which the body must have on professional integrity, technical standards, monitoring and enforcement etc. See also 47.13 REGISTERS for the register of firms and individuals eligible for appointment as company auditors to be kept by each supervisory body.

A person holds, or is treated as holding, an '*appropriate qualification*' in the following circumstances.

- He was qualified for appointment as an auditor of a company under *Sec 389(1)(a)* by virtue of membership of a recognised body immediately before 1 January 1990 and immediately before the appointed day.

- He holds a recognised professional qualification obtained in the UK. For a professional qualification to be recognised, it must only be open to persons who have attained university entrance level (or have a sufficient period of professional expertise). It must be restricted to persons who have completed a course of theoretical instruction and passed an examination in certain subjects (or have a sufficient period of professional expertise). The period of professional expertise must be not less than seven years' experience in a professional capacity in the field of finance, law and accountancy. The subjects for theoretical instruction (which are prescribed by statutory instrument) are auditing; analysis and critical assessment of annual accounts; general accounting; cost and management accounting; consolidated accounts; internal control; standards relating to the preparation of annual and consolidated accounts and to methods of valuing balance sheet items and of computing profits and losses; legal and professional standards and professional guidance relating to the statutory auditing of accounting documents and to those carrying out such audits; and aspects of various general subjects which are relevant to auditing including the law (relating to companies, insolvency, tax, civil and commercial matters, social security and employment), computer systems, economics, statistics and financial management. Persons with a university degree (or equivalent qualification) in a particular subject can be exempt from the requirement to take the examination. The qualification must also be restricted to persons who have completed at least three years' practical training, part of which must be spent being trained in company audit work by a fully-qualified auditor.

- He holds an approved overseas qualification under *CA 1989, s 33*.

- He was, immediately before 1 January 1990 and immediately before the appointed day, qualified for appointment as an auditor of a company under *Sec 389 otherwise* than by virtue of membership of a recognised body. In this case he is treated as holding an appropriate qualification for twelve months from the appointed day and continues to be so treated after that time if he notifies the Secretary of State in writing within that twelve-month period (or subsequently if the Secretary of State allows) that he wishes to retain the benefit of his qualification.

- He began before 1 January 1990 a course of study or practical training leading to a professional qualification in accountancy offered by a body established in the UK; he obtains that qualification on or after that date and before 1 January 1996; and the qualification is approved by the Secretary of State.

[*CA 1989, ss 31, 32, 12 Sch; SI 1990 No 1146*].

A person whose only appropriate qualification is that he retains authorisation granted by the Board of Trade or the Secretary of State under *CA 1967, s 13(1)* is eligible only for appointment as auditor of an unquoted company. [*CA 1989, s 34*].

12.6   Effect of appointment of partnership

The appointment of a partnership constituted under the law of England and Wales and Northern Ireland (or any other territory where a partnership is not a legal person) as company auditor is an appointment of the partnership as such and not of the partners. Where the partnership ceases, the appointment is treated as extending to

- any partnership which succeeds to the practice of that partnership provided the membership of the successor partnership is substantially the same as that of the former partnership; and

- any person who succeeds to that practice having previously carried it on in partnership.

In each case, the person or partnership must be eligible for the appointment and are only regarded as succeeding to the practice if succeeding to the whole, or substantially the whole, of the business of the former partnership.

Where a partnership ceases and no person succeeds under the above rules, the appointment may, with the consent of the company, be treated as extending to a partnership or person eligible for appointment who succeeds to the business.

[*CA 1989, s 26*].

12.7 Auditors

12.7 INELIGIBILITY FOR APPOINTMENT

A person is ineligible for appointment as auditor of a company if he is

(*a*)   an officer or employee of the company;

(*b*)   a partner or employee of such a person, or a partnership of which such person is a partner; or

(*c*)   ineligible under (*a*) or (*b*) above for appointment as auditor of any 'associated undertaking' of the company.

'*Associated undertaking*' means a parent undertaking or subsidiary undertaking of the company or a subsidiary undertaking of any parent undertaking of the company.

[*CA 1989, s 27*].

12.8   Effect of ineligibility

If during his term of office a person becomes ineligible for appointment, he must immediately vacate the office and give written notice to the company of that fact. A person who acts when ineligible or fails to give notice is guilty of an offence and liable to a fine up to the level in 40.1(*e*) PENALTIES.

It is a defence for such a person to show that he did not know and had no reason to know that he was, or had become, ineligible for appointment. [*CA 1989, s 28*].

Transitional provisions. Where, on 1 October 1991, a person was ineligible for appointment as a company auditor because he was not a member of a recognised supervisory body under 12.5 above but

•   he was auditor of the company under a valid earlier appointment, and

•   he was not ineligible for appointment to that office under 12.1 above,

he could continue to act, and hold office, as auditor of the company until the normal expiry date of his term of office under 12.1 or 12.2 above or, if earlier, when he became ineligible for appointment under 12.7 above. [*SI 1991 No 1996, Art 4*].

12.9   Power of Secretary of State to require second audit where person ineligible

Where a person was ineligible for appointment at any time when the audit of a company was carried out, the Secretary of State can direct the company to retain a person eligible for appointment to audit the accounts again or review the first audit and report whether a second audit is required. The company must comply with this direction within 21 days. The Secretary of State must send a copy of the direction to the Registrar of Companies and the company must send a copy of any report received to the Registrar within 21 days of receipt.

In default, the company is guilty of an offence and liable to a fine up to the level in 40.1(*e*) PENALTIES.

If a person accepts an appointment or continues to act as a company auditor when he knows that he is ineligible, the company may recover from him any costs incurred in complying with the above requirements.

[*CA 1989, s 29*].

12.10   REMUNERATION

'Remuneration' of auditors appointed by the company in general meeting must be fixed by the company in general meeting or in such manner as the company in general meeting determines. Remuneration of auditors appointed by the directors or the Secretary of State must be fixed by the directors or Secretary of State as the case may be.

'*Remuneration*' includes sums paid in respect of expenses.

[*Sec 390A; CA 1989, s 121*].

See 5.44 ACCOUNTS: INDIVIDUAL COMPANIES for the disclosure of remuneration for audit and non-audit work.

12.11 REMOVAL FROM OFFICE

An auditor can be removed from office at any time by an ordinary resolution of the company. The company must give notice of the fact to the Registrar of Companies within 14 days in the prescribed form. If it fails to do so, the company and every officer in default is guilty of an offence and liable to a fine up to the level in 40.1(*f*) PENALTIES.

The above provisions do not deprive a person removed of compensation or damages in respect of the termination of his appointment.

The removed auditor still has the right under 12.28 below to attend the general meeting of the company at which his term of office would otherwise have expired or at which it is proposed to fill the vacancy caused by his removal.

[*Sec 391, 24 Sch; CA 1989, s 122*].

Example of resolution for removal of auditors

'That [insert name] be and hereby are removed as auditors of the company with immediate effect and that [insert name] be and hereby are appointed as auditors of the company in their stead to hold office until the conclusion of the next general meeting at which accounts are laid before the company and that the directors be and hereby are authorised to fix their remuneration.'

12.12 Rights of auditors who are removed or not re-appointed

Special notice is required for a resolution at a general meeting to remove an auditor before the expiration of his term of office or to appoint a person other than the retiring auditor. On receipt of notice of such an intended resolution, the company must send a copy of it to the existing auditor and, if applicable, to the person proposed to be appointed. The existing auditor may then make written representations, not exceeding a reasonable length, and request their notification to the members. The company must then

(*a*)   unless it is too late to do so, or

(*b*)   unless the court, on application from the company or any aggrieved person, is satisfied that the rights conferred by these provisions are being abused to secure needless publicity for a defamatory matter,

state the fact that representations have been made in the notice of any resolution to the members and send a copy of the representations to every member to whom notice of the meeting has been sent.

Where a copy of the representations are not sent out because of (*a*) above or the company's default, the auditor can, without prejudice to his right to be heard orally, require that the representations be read out at the meeting.

On a successful application under (*b*) above the court may order the whole or part of the company's costs to be paid by the auditor.

[*Sec 391A; CA 1989, s 122*].

12.13   Termination of appointment where auditors not appointed annually

Where an election is in force under 12.2 above, any member may deposit notice in writing at the company's registered office (but not more than once in any financial year) proposing that the appointment of the auditors is brought to an end. The directors must then convene a general meeting of the company within 28 days of the notice to vote on a resolution as to whether the appointment should be brought to an end. If the directors do not, within 14 days of the date of the deposit of the notice, proceed to convene a meeting, the member may convene a meeting for a date within three months of that date. In the latter case, the member must be reimbursed by the company for any reasonable expenses and the company must recoup such sums from the directors in default out of their fees or remuneration.

If the meeting decides that the appointment should be brought to an end, the auditors are not deemed to be re-appointed when next they would be. If the notice was deposited within 14 days of the date on which copies of the company's annual accounts are sent to members, any deemed re-appointment which has already occurred for the financial year following that to which the accounts relate ceases to have effect.

The above provisions apply despite any agreement between the company and its auditors and no compensation or damages are payable by reason only of the auditors' appointment being terminated under these provisions.

[*Sec 393; CA 1989, s 122*].

12.14   RESIGNATION

An auditor may resign his office by depositing a notice in writing to that effect at the company's registered office provided it is accompanied by a statement required under 12.16 below. His term of office then ends on the date of the notice (or such later date as is specified in the notice).

The company must send a copy of the notice to the Registrar of Companies within 14 days of deposit. In default, the company and every officer in default is guilty of an offence and liable to a fine up to the level in 40.1(*c*) PENALTIES.

[*Sec 392; CA 1989, s 122*].

12.15   Rights of resigning auditors

Where an auditor resigns and his notice is accompanied by a statement under 12.16 below of circumstances which he considers should be brought to the attention of the members or creditors of the company, he may also deposit with the notice a signed requisition calling on the directors to convene an extraordinary general meeting for this purpose. He may also request the company to circulate to members

(*a*)   before the meeting convened on his requisition, or

(*b*)   before any general meeting at which his term of office would otherwise have expired or at which it is proposed to fill the casual vacancy caused by his resignation a written statement of reasonable length of the circumstances connected with his resignation.

The company must then

(i)   unless it is too late to do so, or

(ii)   unless the court, on application from the company or any aggrieved person, is satisfied that the rights conferred by these provisions are being abused to secure needless publicity for a defamatory matter,

state the fact that the statement has been made in the notice to the members and send a copy of the statement to every member to whom notice of the meeting has been sent.

Where a copy of the representations are not sent out because of (i) above or the company's default, the auditor can, without prejudice to his right to be heard orally, require that the statement be read out at the meeting.

If the directors do not, within 21 days from the date of deposit of the request for a meeting, proceed to convene a meeting for a day not more than 28 days after the notice convening the meeting is given, every director who failed to take all reasonable steps to secure that a meeting was convened is guilty of an offence and liable to a fine up to the level in 40.1(*d*) PENALTIES.

On a successful application under (ii) above the court may order the whole or part of the company's costs to be paid by the auditor.

An auditor who has resigned still has the right to receive notices of, attend and be heard at, any general meeting mentioned in (*a*) or (*b*) above.

[*Sec 392A, 24 Sch; CA 1989, s 122*].

12.16 STATEMENT BY PERSON CEASING TO HOLD OFFICE AS AUDITOR

An auditor who ceases to hold office for any reason (i.e. whether removed or by resignation) must deposit at the company's registered office

(*a*)   a statement of any circumstances connected with his ceasing to hold office which he considers should be brought to the attention of the members or creditors of the company; or

(*b*)   if he considers that there are no such circumstances, a statement that there are none.

The statement must be deposited

●   in the case of resignation, together with the notice of resignation;

●   in the case of failure to seek re-appointment, not less than 14 days before the end of the time allowed for appointing the next auditors; and

●   in all other cases, not later than 14 days after he ceases to hold office.

If the statement falls within (*a*) above, the company must then within 14 days of receipt either send a copy of it to every person entitled to receive the accounts (see 3.3 ACCOUNTS: GENERAL) or apply to the court and notify the auditor of the application. If the auditor does not receive a notice of application to the court within 21 days of depositing the statement, he must within a further seven days send a copy of the statement to the Registrar of Companies.

If the court is satisfied that the auditor is using the statement to secure needless publicity for a defamatory matter, it must direct that copies of the statement need not be sent out. It may also order the company's costs in connection with the application to be paid in whole or part by the auditor. The company must then, within 14 days of the court's decision, send to every person entitled to receive the accounts as above a statement setting out the effect of the order.

If the court is not satisfied, the company must, within 14 days of the court's decision, send a copy of the statement to every person entitled to receive the accounts and notify the auditors of the court's decision. The auditor must then send a copy of the statement to the Registrar of Companies within seven days of receiving such notification.

[*Sec 394; CA 1989, s 123*].

12.17 Offences for failing to comply with 12.16 above

If a person ceasing to hold office as auditor fails to comply with the provisions of 12.16 above, he is guilty of an offence and liable to a fine up to the level in 40.1(*d*) PENALTIES. It is, however, a defence for the person charged to show that he took all reasonable steps and exercised all due diligence to avoid the commission of the offence. If the company fails to comply with the provisions, the company and every officer of it who is in default is guilty of an offence and liable to a fine up to the level in 40.1(*e*) PENALTIES.

The provisions of *Sec 733* (liability of individuals for corporate default) and *Sec 734* (criminal proceedings against unincorporated bodies) also apply to such an offence. See 32.4 and 32.5 LEGAL PROCEEDINGS respectively.

[*Sec 394A; CA 1989, s 123*].

12.18 AUDITORS' REPORT

A company's auditors must report to the company's members on all annual accounts of the company of which copies are to be laid before the company in general meeting during their tenure of office. [*Sec 235(1); CA 1989, s 9*]. Despite this obligation to report to the *members*, the auditors' obligation is satisfied by forwarding the signed report to the company secretary, leaving him or the directors to convene the meeting and send copies of the account and report to the members (*Re Allen, Craig & Co (London) Ltd [1934] Ch 438*).

The report must state whether, in the auditors' opinion, the accounts have been properly prepared in accordance with *CA 1985* and whether a 'true and fair view' is given

(*a*)   in the case of an individual company, of the state of affairs of the company as at the end of the financial year (as disclosed in the balance sheet) and of its profit and loss for the financial year (as shown in the profit and loss account); and

(*b*)   in the case of group accounts, of the state of affairs as at the end of the financial year, and the profit or loss for the financial year, of the undertakings included in the consolidation as a whole, so far as concerns members of the company.

[*Sec 235(1)(2); CA 1989, s 9*].

See 3.13 ACCOUNTS: GENERAL for 'true and fair view'.

Basic elements of the auditors' report on financial statements. Reports should include the following matters.

(1)   A title identifying the person or persons to whom the report is addressed.

(2)   An introductory paragraph identifying the accounts audited.

(3)   A separate section dealing with the respective responsibilities of directors and auditors.

Auditors should distinguish between their responsibilities and those of the directors by including in their report a statement that the accounts are the responsibility of the company's directors, together with a reference to a description of those responsibilities if set out elsewhere in the accounts. (If this has not been done, the auditors' report should include a description of those responsibilities.)

The report should also include a statement that the auditors' responsibility is to express an opinion on the accounts.

(4)   A separate section dealing with the basis of the auditors' opinion.

This should be explained by including in the report

- a statement as to their compliance or otherwise with Auditing Standards (together with any reason for departure);

- a statement that the audit process includes

    (i)   examining, on a test basis, evidence relevant to the amounts and disclosures in the accounts;

    (ii)   assessing the significant estimates and judgements made by the company's directors in preparing the accounts;

    (iii)   considering whether the accounting policies are appropriate to the company's circumstances, consistently applied and adequately disclosed; and

- a statement that they planned and performed the audit so as to obtain a reasonable assurance that the accounts are free from material misstatement, whether caused by fraud or other irregularity or error, and that they have evaluated the overall presentation of the accounts.

(5)   A separate section dealing with the auditors' opinion on the accounts.

The report should contain a clear expression of opinion on the accounts and on any further matters required by statute or other requirements applicable to the particular engagement.

(6)   The manuscript or printed signature of the auditors.

(7)   The date of the auditors' report.

(*SAS 600 Auditors' Reports on Financial Statements*).

See 12.29 below for examples of audit reports on accounts and example wording of the description of directors' responsibilities for inclusion in the company's accounts or, where this is not done, in the auditors' report.

12.19 Other specific requirements of auditors' report

Directors' remuneration, etc.

(*a*)   *All companies.* If the information to be disclosed under *6 Sch* (emoluments of, loans to, and transactions with, directors, see 5.33 to 5.43 ACCOUNTS: INDIVIDUAL

COMPANIES) is not shown in the accounts, the auditors must include in their report, so far as they are reasonably able to do, a statement giving the required particulars. [*Sec 237(4); CA 1989, s 9*].

(b)   *Listed companies only.* The scope of the auditors' report must cover the disclosures in 43.15(*r*)(ii)(iii)(iv)(ix)(x) PUBLIC AND LISTED COMPANIES. The auditors must state in their report if, in their opinion, the company has not complied with any of these requirements and, in such a case, must include, so far as they are reasonably able to do, a statement giving the required particulars. (*Listing Rules, Chapter 12.43A*).

Combined Code for listed companies. A listed company must include in its accounts a statement on compliance with the Combined Code. See 43.15(*q*) PUBLIC AND LISTED COMPANIES. The auditors must review this statement before publication so far as it relates to Code provisions A.1.2, A.1.3, A.6.1, A.6.2, D.1.1, D.2.1 and D.3.1. See the Appendix at the end of 43 PUBLIC AND LISTED COMPANIES for details of these provisions. (*Listing Rules, Chapter 12.43A*).

12.20 Signature of report

The auditors' report must state the name of the auditors and be signed by them. Where the auditors are a body corporate or a partnership, the report may be signed by a person authorised to sign on its behalf. [*Sec 236(1)(5); CA 1989, s 9*].

Every copy of the auditors' report which is to be laid before the company in general meeting, or which is otherwise circulated, published or issued, must state the names of the auditors. The copy which is delivered to the Registrar of Companies must state the name of the auditors *and* be signed by them. If these requirements are not complied with, the company and every officer in default is guilty of an offence and liable to a fine up to the level in 40.1(*g*) PENALTIES. [*Sec 236(2)-(4), 24 Sch; CA 1989, s 9*].

12.21 Small and medium-sized companies

Individual accounts. Certain small and medium-sized companies may deliver abbreviated versions of accounts to the Registrar of Companies prepared in accordance with *Sec 246(5)* or *(6)* (small companies) or *Sec 246A(3)* (medium-sized companies). See 7.40 and 7.44 ACCOUNTS: SMALL AND MEDIUM-SIZED COMPANIES respectively. In such a case, unless the company is exempt from the requirement to appoint auditors either under *Sec 250* (see 24.2 DORMANT COMPANIES) or under the small companies audit exemption provisions (see 12.31 *et seq.* below), the accounts delivered to the Registrar of Companies must be accompanied by a special auditors' report stating that in their opinion

- the company is entitled to deliver abbreviated accounts in accordance with that provision; and

- the abbreviated accounts delivered to the Registrar are properly prepared in accordance with that provision.

In such a case, a copy of the auditors' report required under 12.18 above need not also be delivered to the Registrar of Companies unless that report

- was qualified, in which case the special report must set out that report in full together with any further material necessary to understand the qualification; or

- contained a statement under *Sec 237(2)* (accounts, records or returns inadequate or accounts not agreeing with records or returns) or *Sec 237(3)* (failure to obtain necessary information and explanations) in which case the special report must set out that report in full.

The provisions of 12.20 above (signature of report) also apply to a special report.

[*Sec 247B; SI 1997 No 220, Reg 5*].

Groups. Where such accounts have taken advantage of the exemption from the requirement to prepare group accounts under *Sec 248* (see 7.46 ACCOUNTS: SMALL AND MEDIUM-SIZED COMPANIES) but, in the auditors' opinion, the company was not entitled to the exemption, the auditors must state that fact in their report. [*Sec 237(4A); SI 1996 No 189, Reg 6*].

12.22 Defective accounts

In certain circumstances, the annual accounts and/or directors' report of a company may be replaced or partially revised because they were originally defective. See 3.9 ACCOUNTS: GENERAL. A special auditors' report is then required unless

• the company is dormant and has passed a resolution not to appoint auditors (see 24.2 DORMANT COMPANIES); or

• the company is a 'small' company which is exempt from audit under 12.32 below (see 12.39 below for the position where a 'small' company is exempt from audit under 12.35 below – cases where accountants' report required).

[*SI 1990 No 2570, Regs 14A(1), 15; SI 1994 No 1935, 2 Sch 3*].

Where the accounts are revised, either through revision by replacement or by supplementary note, the current auditors must make a report or (as the case may be) a further report to the members on the revised accounts. If there has been a change in auditors since the original report, the directors may resolve that the person or persons who made that report should make the further report, provided that he or they are agreeable and still qualify for appointment as auditors of the company.

The provisions of 12.19 and 12.20 above also apply to a further report.

The report must state whether, in the auditors' opinion

• the revised accounts have been properly prepared in accordance with *CA 1985* as relevant to these provisions and in particular whether a true and fair view (see 3.13 ACCOUNTS: GENERAL), seen as at the date the original accounts were approved, is given by the revised accounts with respect to matters in 12.18(*a*) and (*b*) above; and

• the original accounts failed to comply with the requirements of *CA 1985* in the respects identified by the director

(i)   in the case of revision by replacement, in the statement they are required to make in the new accounts; or

(ii)   in the case of revision by supplementary note, in that supplementary note.

The auditors must also consider whether the information contained in the directors' report (whether or not revised) is consistent with the revised accounts. If not, they must state that fact in their report.

From the date of signature by the auditors, the further report prepared under these provisions is the auditors' report on the annual accounts of the company in place of the report on the original defective accounts.

[*SI 1990 No 2570, Reg 6; SI 1996 No 315*].

12.23 Auditors

Where the directors' report only is revised, either through revision by replacement or by supplementary note, the current auditors must make a report or (as the case may be) a further report to the members on the revised directors' report. If there has been a change in auditors since the accounts and original directors' report, the directors may resolve that the person or persons who made the report thereon should also make the further report, provided that he or they are agreeable and still qualify for appointment as auditors of the company.

The auditors' report must state that

- they have considered whether the information given in the revised directors' report is consistent with the annual accounts for the relevant year (specifying it); and

- they are of the opinion, or they are not of the opinion, that it is so consistent.

The provisions of 12.20 above also apply to such a report.

[*SI 1990 No 2570, Reg 7; SI 1996 No 315*].

12.23 DUTIES

The auditors must carry out such investigation as will enable them to form an opinion as to whether

(*a*) proper accounting records have been kept;

(*b*) proper returns adequate for their audit have been received from branches not visited by them; and

(*c*) the company's individual accounts are in agreement with the accounting records.

If the auditors

(i) are of the opinion that (*a*), (*b*) or (*c*) above has not been complied with, or

(ii) fail to obtain all the information and explanations which, to the best of their knowledge and belief, are necessary for the purposes of their audit, or

(iii) are of the opinion that the information given in the DIRECTORS' REPORT (20) is not consistent with the accounts

they must state that fact in their report. Any qualification must clearly state the true state of the company's affairs or the matters of uncertainty or disagreement (*Re London and General Bank (No 2) [1895] 2 Ch 675*).

[*Secs 235(3), 237(1)-(3); CA 1989, s 9*].

An auditor is not bound to do more than exercise reasonable care and skill in making enquiries and investigations. He does not guarantee that the books do correctly show the true position of the company's affairs but he must be honest i.e. he must not certify what he does not believe to be true and must take reasonable care and skill before he believes that what he certifies is true. What is reasonable care in any particular case must depend upon the circumstances of that case (*Re London and General Bank (No 2) supra*). An auditor is a watch-dog not a bloodhound (*Re Kingston Cotton Mill (No 2) [1896] 2 Ch 279*). The standard of skill and care may be more exacting since these earlier cases were decided and where suspicion ought emphatically to be aroused the auditors should take steps to investigate in depth (*Re Thomas Gerrard & Son Ltd [1967] 2 All ER 525*). See also the comments of Lord Denning in *Fomento (Sterling Area) Ltd v Selsdon Fountain Pen Co Ltd [1958] 1 WLR 45*.

In applying the necessary standard of care, the auditors should be aware of the content of the company's memorandum and articles. See *Leeds Estate Building and Investment Co*

Ltd v Shepherd (1887) 36 ChD 787 where dividends were paid out of capital. As to whether auditors should rely on a bank certificate, etc. for verification of ownership of securities, see *Re City Equitable Fire Insurance Co Ltd [1925] Ch 407*.

12.24 Auditing Standards

The Auditing Practices Board (APB) has issued a number of Statements of Auditing Standards ('SASs'). These contain basic principles and essential procedures ('Auditing Standards') which are indicated in bold type and with which auditors are required to comply (except as otherwise stated in the SAS). They also contain explanatory and other material which, rather than being prescriptive, is designed to assist auditors in interpreting and applying Auditing Standards.

The SASs currently in issue are listed below. These include 23 new Statements issued in March 1995. This completes the Auditing Practices Board's project to revise all pre-existing Auditing Standards and Guidelines. Those SASs that take effect for periods ended on or after a date in 1995 are marked accordingly in the list below (the others having taken effect earlier).

Statements of Auditing Standards

010	The scope and authority of APB pronouncements.
100	Objective and general principles governing an audit of financial statements.
110	Fraud and error.
120	Consideration of law and regulations.
130	The going concern basis in financial statements.
140	Engagement letters.
150	Subsequent events.
160	Other information in documents containing audited financial statements.
200	Planning.
210	Knowledge of the business.
220	Materiality and the audit.
230	Working papers.
240	Quality control for audit work.
300	Accounting and internal control systems and audit risk assessments.
400	Audit evidence.
410	Analytical procedures.
420	Audit of accounting estimates.
430	Audit sampling.
440	Management representations.
450	Opening balances and comparatives.
460	Related parties.
470	Overall review of financial statements.
500	Considering the work of internal audit.
510	The relationship between principal auditors and other auditors.
520	Using the work of an expert.
600	Auditors' reports on financial statements.
610	Reports to directors and management.
620	The auditors' right and duty to report to regulators in the financial sector.

12.25 Auditors

See *Lloyd Cheyham & Co Ltd v Littlejohn & Co [1987] BCLC 303* where Auditing Standards were taken to be relevant in determining the standard of skill and care required.

12.25 *Other pronouncements*

The APB also issues Practice Notes and Bulletins. These are persuasive rather than prescriptive but are indicative of good practice and have similar status to the explanatory material in Sass. See 12.30 below for sample audit reports taken from the Practice Note *Reports by auditors under company legislation in the UK*. The predecessor body of the APB, the Auditing Practices Committee, issued Auditing Standards and Auditing Guidelines, the latter having the same status as Practice Notes. These were originally adopted by the APB but have now been superseded by SASs.

12.26 LIABILITIES

See 19.49 and 19.50 DIRECTORS for provisions exempting officers from, and indemnifying them against, liability for negligence, breach of duty, etc. which apply also to auditors.

In addition to the cases listed in 12.23 above, liability of the auditors to the members has been considered in *London Oil Storage Co Ltd v Seear Hasluck & Co (1904) 30 Acct LR 93* (verification of assets); *AE Green & Co v Central Advance and Discount Corporation Ltd (1920) 63 Acct LR 1* (bad debts provision); and *Pendleburys Ltd v Ellis Green & Co (1936) 80 Acct LR 39* (insufficient internal control in a private company where the directors were the sole shareholders).

An auditor has been held to be liable for negligence to third parties (e.g. investors) where he knows, or ought to know, that his work is liable to be relied upon by such a person and that person suffers a financial loss as a result (*Hedley Byrne & Co Ltd v Heller & Partners Ltd [1964] 2 All ER 575*). Subsequent cases have, however, tended to restrict this liability. In *Caparo Industries plc v Dickman [1990] 1 All ER 568* the House of Lords considered the auditors' duty of care to shareholders and potential shareholders. It held that the purpose of the audit report was to enable shareholders to exercise their proprietary powers as shareholders by giving them reliable intelligence on the company's affairs, sufficient to allow them to scrutinise the management's conduct and to exercise their collective powers to control the management through general meetings. To meet the requirements for a duty of care to exist, the report must be used for the purpose for which it was intended and the precise purpose for which the accounts are required must be known to the wrongdoer. In the circumstances of a shareholder (or potential shareholder) simply dealing in the company's shares on the basis of the report, these requirements were not met.

See also 32.7 LEGAL PROCEEDINGS for the power of the court to grant relief in proceedings for negligence, default or breach of duty.

12.27 RIGHT TO INFORMATION

The auditors have a right of access at all times to the company's books, accounts and vouchers and such information and explanations from the company's officers as they think necessary for the performance of their duties as auditors. An officer commits an offence if he knowingly or recklessly makes a written or oral statement to the auditors conveying any information which they are entitled to require and which is misleading, false or deceptive in a material particular. If found guilty, he is liable to a penalty up to the level in 40.1(*b*) PENALTIES. [*Sec 389A(1)(2), 24 Sch; CA 1989, s 120*].

A company cannot rely on any of its regulations which restricts the rights of auditors to information to which they are entitled under these provisions (*Newton v Birmingham Small Arms Co [1906] 2 Ch 378*).

Subsidiary undertakings. A subsidiary which is a body corporate incorporated in Great Britain and its auditors must give such information and explanations to the auditors of the parent company as they reasonably require for their purposes as auditors of that company. If not, the subsidiary and its officers are guilty of an offence and liable to a fine up to the level in 40.1(*g*) PENALTIES. The auditors of the subsidiary are also liable unless they have a reasonable excuse. [*Sec 389A(3), 24 Sch; CA 1989, s 120*]. *Sec 734* (criminal proceedings against unincorporated bodies) applies to such an offence. See 32.5 LEGAL PROCEEDINGS.

Similarly, a parent company with a subsidiary which is not a body corporate incorporated in Great Britain must take all steps as are reasonably open to it to obtain any information which its auditors require concerning that subsidiary, otherwise the parent company and its officers are guilty of an offence and liable to a fine up to the level in 40.1(*g*) PENALTIES. [*Sec 389A(4), 24 Sch; CA 1989, s 120*].

12.28 RIGHT TO ATTEND COMPANY MEETINGS ETC.

A company's auditors are entitled to

- receive all notices of, and other communications relating to, any general meeting of the company which a member is entitled to receive;

- attend any general meeting of the company; and

- be heard at any general meeting on any part of the business which concerns them as auditors.

Where a written resolution has been proposed by a private company under *Sec 381A* (see 51.4 RESOLUTIONS) the auditors are entitled to receive all communications relating to the resolution which must be supplied to members. Additionally, for written resolutions proposed before 19 June 1996, where the auditors had given notice that the resolution concerned them as auditors and should be considered by the company in general meeting (or, as the case may be, by a meeting of the relevant class of members), they could attend any such meeting and be heard on any part of the business which concerned them as auditors.

Where the auditors are a body corporate or a partnership, the right to attend or be heard at a meeting is exercisable by an individual authorised by it in writing to act as its representative at the meeting.

[*Sec 390; CA 1989, s 120; SI 1996 No 1471*].

12.29 AUDIT REPORTS ON ACCOUNTS: EXAMPLES

Auditors are required to comply with the requirements in the statement of auditing standards *SAS 600 Auditors' reports on financial statements*. Although auditors should draft each section of their report to reflect the requirements which apply to the particular audit engagement, the use of a common language in auditors' reports assists readers' understanding. The following examples, taken from *SAS 600*, illustrate wording which meets the auditing standards contained therein.

Example 1 Unqualified opinion: company incorporated in Great Britain

AUDITORS' REPORT TO THE SHAREHOLDERS OF XYZ PLC

We have audited the financial statements on pages . . . to . . . which have been prepared under the historical cost convention [as modified by the revaluation of certain fixed assets] and the accounting policies set out on page . . . .

12.29 Auditors

Respective responsibilities of directors and auditors

As described on page . . . the company's directors are responsible for the preparation of financial statements. It is our responsibility to form an independent opinion, based on our audit, on those statements and to report our opinion to you.

Basis of opinion

We conducted our audit in accordance with Auditing Standards issued by the Auditing Practices Board. An audit includes examination, on a test basis, of evidence relevant to the amounts and disclosures in the financial statements. It also includes an assessment of the significant estimates and judgements made by the directors in the preparation of the financial statements, and of whether the accounting policies are appropriate to the company's circumstances, consistently applied and adequately disclosed.

We planned and performed our audit so as to obtain all the information and explanations which we considered necessary in order to provide us with sufficient evidence to give reasonable assurance that the financial statements are free from material misstatement, whether caused by fraud or other irregularity or error. In forming our opinion we also evaluated the overall adequacy of the presentation of information in the financial statements.

Opinion

In our opinion the financial statements give a true and fair view of the state of the company's affairs as at 31 December 19. . and of its profit [loss] for the year then ended and have been properly prepared in accordance with the Companies Act 1985.

Registered auditors   *Address*

Date

Example 2 Unqualified opinion with explanatory paragraph describing a fundamental uncertainty

AUDITORS' REPORT TO THE SHAREHOLDERS OF XYZ LTD

We have audited the financial statements on pages . . . to . . . which have been prepared under the historical cost convention [as modified by the revaluation of certain fixed assets] and the accounting policies set out on page . . . .

Respective responsibilities of directors and auditors

As described on page . . . the company's directors are responsible for the preparation of financial statements. It is our responsibility to form an independent opinion, based on our audit, on those statements and to report our opinion to you.

Basis of opinion

We conducted our audit in accordance with Auditing Standards issued by the Auditing Practices Board. An audit includes examination, on a test basis, of evidence relevant to the amounts and disclosures in the financial statements. It also includes an assessment of the significant estimates and judgements made by the directors in the preparation of the financial statements, and of whether the accounting policies are appropriate to the company's circumstances, consistently applied and adequately disclosed.

We planned and performed our audit so as to obtain all the information and explanations which we considered necessary in order to provide us with sufficient evidence to give reasonable assurance that the financial statements are free from material misstatement, whether caused by fraud or other irregularity or error. In forming our opinion we also evaluated the overall adequacy of the presentation of information in the financial statements.

Fundamental uncertainty

In forming our opinion, we have considered the adequacy of the disclosures made in the financial statements concerning the possible outcome to litigation against B Limited, a subsidiary undertaking of the company, for an alleged breach of environmental regulations. The future settlement of this litigation could result in additional liabilities and the closure of B Limited's business, whose net assets included in the consolidated balance sheet total £. . . and whose profit before tax for the year is £. . . . Details of the circumstances relating to this fundamental uncertainty are described in note. . . . Our opinion is not qualified in this respect.

Opinion

In our opinion the financial statements give a true and fair view of the state of affairs of the company and of the group as at 31 December 19. . and of the group's profit [loss] for the year then ended and have been properly prepared in accordance with the Companies Act 1985.

Registered auditors   *Address*

Date

Example 3 Company incorporated in Great Britain, using accounting exemptions available for small companies

AUDITORS' REPORT TO THE SHAREHOLDERS OF XYZ LTD

We have audited the financial statements on pages . . . to . . . which have been prepared under the historical cost convention [as modified by the revaluation of certain fixed assets] and the accounting policies set out on page . . . .

Respective responsibilities of directors and auditors

As described on page . . . the company's directors are responsible for the preparation of financial statements. It is our responsibility to form an independent opinion, based on our audit, on those statements and to report our opinion to you.

Basis of opinion

We conducted our audit in accordance with Auditing Standards issued by the Auditing Practices Board. An audit includes examination, on a test basis, of evidence relevant to the amounts and disclosures in the financial statements. It also includes an assessment of the significant estimates and judgements made by the directors in the preparation of the financial statements, and of whether the accounting policies are appropriate to the company's circumstances, consistently applied and adequately disclosed.

We planned and performed our audit so as to obtain all the information and explanations which we considered necessary in order to provide us with sufficient evidence to give reasonable assurance that the financial statements are free from material misstatement, whether caused by fraud or other irregularity or error. In forming our opinion we also evaluated the overall adequacy of the presentation of information in the financial statements.

12.29 Auditors

Opinion

In our opinion the financial statements give a true and fair view of the state of the company's affairs as at 31 December 19. . and of its profit [loss] for the year then ended and have been properly prepared in accordance with the provisions of the Companies Act 1985 applicable to small companies.

Registered auditors   *Address*

Date

Example 4 Auditors' statement on a summary financial statement

AUDITORS' STATEMENT TO THE SHAREHOLDERS OF XYZ PLC

We have audited the summary financial statement set out above/on page . . . .

Respective responsibilities of directors and auditors

The summary financial statement is the responsibility of the directors. Our responsibility is to report to you our opinion as to whether the statement is consistent with the full financial statements and directors' report.

Basis of opinion

We conducted our audit in accordance with Auditing Standards issued by the Auditing Practices Board. The audit of a summary financial statement comprises an assessment of whether the statement contains all information necessary to ensure consistency with the full financial statements and directors' report and of whether the detailed information required by law has been properly extracted from those documents and included in the summary statement.

Our report on the company's full financial statements includes information on the responsibilities of directors and auditors relating to the preparation and audit of financial statements and on the basis of our opinion on the financial statements.

Opinion

In our opinion the summary financial statement above/on page . . . is consistent with the full financial statements and directors' report of XYZ plc for the year ended . . . and complies with the requirements of the Companies Act 1985, and regulations made thereunder, applicable to summary financial statements.

Registered auditors   *Address*

Date

Example paragraphs for inclusion in the basis of opinion section where applicable:

(1) referring to a fundamental uncertainty: Our report on the group's full financial statements included an explanatory paragraph concerning a fundamental uncertainty arising from the outcome of possible litigation against B Ltd, a subsidiary undertaking of the company, for an alleged breach of environmental regulations. Details of the circumstances relating to this fundamental uncertainty are described in note . . . of the summary financial statement. Our opinion on the full financial statements is not qualified in this respect.

(2) referring to a qualified opinion: Our opinion on the company's full financial statements was qualified as a result of a disagreement with the accounting treatment of the company's leased assets. Details of the circumstances giving rise to that opinion are set out in note . . . of the summary financial statement.

Example 5 Qualified opinion: disagreement

AUDITORS' REPORT TO THE SHAREHOLDERS OF XYZ PLC

We have audited the financial statements on pages . . . to . . . which have been prepared under the historical cost convention [as modified by the revaluation of certain fixed assets] and the accounting policies set out on page . . . .

Respective responsibilities of directors and auditors

As described on page . . . the company's directors are responsible for the preparation of financial statements. It is our responsibility to form an independent opinion, based on our audit, on those statements and to report our opinion to you.

Basis of opinion

We conducted our audit in accordance with Auditing Standards issued by the Auditing Practices Board. An audit includes examination, on a test basis, of evidence relevant to the amounts and disclosures in the financial statements. It also includes an assessment of the significant estimates and judgements made by the directors in the preparation of the financial statements, and of whether the accounting policies are appropriate to the company's circumstances, consistently applied and adequately disclosed.

We planned and performed our audit so as to obtain all the information and explanations which we considered necessary in order to provide us with sufficient evidence to give reasonable assurance as to whether the financial statements are free from material misstatement, whether caused by fraud or other irregularity or error. In forming our opinion we also evaluated the overall adequacy of the presentation of information in the financial statements.

Qualified opinion arising from disagreement about accounting treatment

Included in the debtors shown on the balance sheet is an amount of £Y due from a company which has ceased trading. XYZ plc has no security for this debt. In our opinion the company is unlikely to receive any payment and full provision of £Y should have been made, reducing profit before tax and net assets by that amount.

Except for the absence of this provision, in our opinion the financial statements give a true and fair view of the state of the company's affairs as at 31 December 19. . and of its profit [loss] for the year ended and have been properly prepared in accordance with the Companies Act 1985.

Registered auditors   *Address*

Date

Example 6 Qualified opinion: limitation on the auditors' work

AUDITORS' REPORT TO THE SHAREHOLDERS OF XYZ PLC

We have audited the financial statements on pages . . . to . . . which have been prepared under the historical cost convention [as modified by the revaluation of certain fixed assets] and the accounting policies set out on page . . . .

12.29 Auditors

Respective responsibilities of directors and auditors

As described on page . . . the company's directors are responsible for the preparation of financial statements. It is our responsibility to form an independent opinion, based on our audit, on those statements and to report our opinion to you.

Basis of opinion

We conducted our audit in accordance with Auditing Standards issued by the Auditing Practices Board, except that the scope of our work was limited as explained below.

An audit includes examination, on a test basis, of evidence relevant to the amounts and disclosures in the financial statements. It also includes an assessment of the significant estimates and judgements made by the directors in the preparation of the financial statements, and of whether the accounting policies are appropriate to the company's circumstances, consistently applied and adequately disclosed.

We planned our audit so as to obtain all the information and explanations which we considered necessary in order to provide us with sufficient evidence to give reasonable assurance that the financial statements are free from material misstatement, whether caused by fraud or other irregularity or error. However, the evidence available to us was limited because £. . . of the company's recorded turnover comprises cash sales, over which there was no system of control on which we could rely for the purpose of our audit. There were no other satisfactory audit procedures that we could adopt to confirm that cash sales were properly recorded.

In forming our opinion we also evaluated the overall adequacy of the presentation of information in the financial statements.

Qualified opinion arising from limitation in audit scope

Except for any adjustments that might have been found to be necessary had we been able to obtain sufficient evidence concerning cash sales, in our opinion the financial statements give a true and fair view of the state of the company's affairs as at 31 December 19. . and of its profit [loss] for the year then ended and have been properly prepared in accordance with the Companies Act 1985.

In respect alone of the limitation on our work relating to cash sales:

- we have not obtained all the information and explanations that we considered necessary for the purpose of our audit; and

- we were unable to determine whether proper accounting records had been maintained.

Registered auditors   *Address*

Date

Example 7 Disclaimer of opinion

AUDITORS' REPORT TO THE SHAREHOLDERS OF XYZ PLC

We have audited the financial statements on pages . . . to . . . which have been prepared under the historical cost convention [as modified by the revaluation of certain fixed assets] and the accounting policies set out on page . . . .

Respective responsibilities of directors and auditors

As described on page . . . the company's directors are responsible for the preparation of financial statements. It is our responsibility to form an independent opinion, based on our audit, on those statements and to report our opinion to you.

Basis of opinion

We conducted our audit in accordance with Auditing Standards issued by the Auditing Practices Board, except that the scope of our work was limited as explained below.

An audit includes examination, on a test basis, of evidence relevant to the amounts and disclosures in the financial statements. It also includes an assessment of the significant estimates and judgements made by the directors in the preparation of the financial statements, and of whether the accounting policies are appropriate to the company's circumstances, consistently applied and adequately disclosed.

We planned our audit so as to obtain all the information and explanations which we considered necessary in order to provide us with sufficient evidence to give reasonable assurance that the financial statements are free from material misstatement, whether caused by fraud or other irregularity or error. However, the evidence available to us was limited because we were appointed auditors on (date) and in consequence we were unable to carry out auditing procedures necessary to obtain adequate assurance regarding the quantities and conditions of stock and work in progress, appearing in the balance sheet at £. . . . Any adjustment to this figure would have a consequential significant effect on the profit for the year.

In forming our opinion we also evaluated the overall adequacy of the presentation of information in the financial statements.

Opinion: disclaimer on view given by financial statements

Because of the possible effect of the limitation in evidence available to us, we are unable to form an opinion as to whether the financial statements give a true and fair view of the state of the company's affairs as at 31 December 19. . or of its profit [loss] for the year then ended. In all other respects, in our opinion the financial statements have been properly prepared in accordance with the Companies Act 1985.

In respect alone of the limitation on our work relating to stock and work-in-progress:

- we have not obtained all the information and explanations that we considered necessary for the purpose of our audit; and

- we were unable to determine whether proper accounting records had been maintained.

Registered auditors   *Address*

Date

Example 8 Adverse opinion

AUDITORS' REPORT TO THE SHAREHOLDERS OF XYZ PLC

We have audited the financial statements on pages . . . to . . . which have been prepared under the historical cost convention [as modified by the revaluation of certain fixed assets] and the accounting policies set out on page . . . .

12.29   Auditors

Respective responsibilities of directors and auditors

As described on page . . . the company's directors are responsible for the preparation of financial statements. It is our responsibility to form an independent opinion, based on our audit, on those statements and to report our opinion to you.

Basis of opinion

We conducted our audit in accordance with Auditing Standards issued by the Auditing Practices Board. An audit includes examination, on a test basis, of evidence relevant to the amounts and disclosures in the financial statements. It also includes an assessment of the significant estimates and judgements made by the directors in the preparation of the financial statements, and of whether the accounting policies are appropriate to the company's circumstances, consistently applied and adequately disclosed.

We planned and performed our audit so as to obtain all the information and explanations which we considered necessary in order to provide us with sufficient evidence to give reasonable assurance as to whether the financial statements are free from material misstatement, whether caused by fraud or other irregularity or error. In forming our opinion we also evaluated the overall adequacy of the presentation of information in the financial statements.

Adverse opinion

As more fully explained in note . . . no provision has been made for losses expected to arise on certain long-term contracts currently in progress, as the directors consider that such losses should be off-set against amounts recoverable on other long-term contracts. In our opinion, provision should be made for foreseeable losses on individual contracts as required by Statement of Standard Accounting Practice 9. If losses had been so recognised the effect would have been to reduce the profit before and after tax for the year and the contract work in progress at 31 December 19. . by £. . . .

In view of the effect of the failure to provide for the losses referred to above, in our opinion the financial statements do not give a true and fair view of the state of the company's affairs as at 31 December 19. . and of its profit [loss] for the year then ended. In all other respects, in our opinion the financial statements have been properly prepared in accordance with the Companies Act 1985.

Registered auditors   *Address*

Date

Example 9   Qualified opinion and fundamental uncertainty

AUDITORS' REPORT TO THE SHAREHOLDERS OF XYZ PLC

We have audited the financial statements on pages . . . to . . . which have been prepared under the historical cost convention [as modified by the revaluation of certain fixed assets] and the accounting policies set out on page . . . .

Respective responsibilities of directors and auditors

As described on page . . . the company's directors are responsible for the preparation of financial statements. It is our responsibility to form an independent opinion, based on our audit, on those statements and to report our opinion to you.

Basis of opinion

We conducted our audit in accordance with Auditing Standards issued by the Auditing Practices Board. An audit includes examination, on a test basis, of evidence relevant to the amounts and disclosures in the financial statements. It also includes an assessment of the significant estimates and judgements made by the directors in the preparation of the financial statements, and of whether the accounting policies are appropriate to the company's circumstances, consistently applied and adequately disclosed.

We planned and performed our audit so as to obtain all the information and explanations which we considered necessary in order to provide us with sufficient evidence to give reasonable assurance as to whether the financial statements are free from material misstatement, whether caused by fraud or other irregularity or error. In forming our opinion we also evaluated the overall adequacy of the presentation of information in the financial statements.

Fundamental uncertainty

In forming our opinion, we have considered the adequacy of the disclosures made in the financial statements concerning the possible outcome of negotiations for additional finance being made available to replace an existing loan of £. . . which is repayable on 30 April 19. .. The financial statements have been prepared on a going concern basis, the validity of which depends upon future funding being available. The financial statements do not include any adjustments that would result from a failure to obtain funding. Details of the circumstances relating to this fundamental uncertainty are described in note . . . . Our opinion is not qualified in this respect.

Qualified opinion arising from disagreement about accounting treatment

The company leases plant and equipment which have been accounted for in the financial statements as operating leases. In our opinion, these leases should be accounted for as finance leases as required by Statement of Standard Accounting Practice 21. If this accounting treatment were followed, the finance leases would be reflected in the company's balance sheet at £X and the profit for the year would have been reduced by £Y. The financial statements do not include an explanation for this departure from any applicable accounting standard as required by the Companies Act 1985.

Except for the failure to account for the leases referred to above as required by SSAP21, in our opinion the financial statements give a true and fair view of the state of the company's affairs as at 31 December 19. . and of its profit [loss] for the year then ended and have been properly prepared in accordance with the Companies Act 1985.

Registered auditors   *Address*

Date

Example 10 Qualified opinion: disagreement arising from omission of a primary statement required by Financial Reporting Standards

AUDITORS' REPORT TO THE SHAREHOLDERS OF XYZ PLC

We have audited the financial statements on pages . . . to . . . which have been prepared under the historical cost convention [as modified by the revaluation of certain fixed assets] and the accounting policies set out on page . . . .

12.29 Auditors

Respective responsibilities of directors and auditors

As described on page . . . the company's directors are responsible for the preparation of financial statements. It is our responsibility to form an independent opinion, based on our audit, on those statements and to report our opinion to you.

Basis of opinion

We conducted our audit in accordance with Auditing Standards issued by the Auditing Practices Board. An audit includes examination, on a test basis, of evidence relevant to the amounts and disclosures in the financial statements. It also includes an assessment of the significant estimates and judgements made by the directors in the preparation of the financial statements, and of whether the accounting policies are appropriate to the company's circumstances, consistently applied and adequately disclosed.

We planned and performed our audit so as to obtain all the information and explanations which we considered necessary in order to provide us with sufficient evidence to give reasonable assurance as to whether the financial statements are free from material misstatement, whether caused by fraud or other irregularity or error. In forming our opinion we also evaluated the overall adequacy of the presentation of information in the financial statements.

Qualified opinion arising from omission of cash flow statement

As explained in note . . . the financial statements do not contain a statement of cash flows as required by Financial Reporting Standard 1. Net cash flows for the year ended 19. . amounted to £. . . and in our opinion information about the company's cash flows is necessary for a proper understanding of the company's state of affairs and profit [loss].

Except for the failure to provide information about the company's cash flows, in our opinion the financial statements give a true and fair view of the state of the company's affairs as at 31 December 19. . and of its profit [loss] for the year then ended and have been properly prepared in accordance with the Companies Act 1985.

Registered auditors   *Address*

Date

Example 11 Example wording of a description of the directors' responsibilities for inclusion in a company's accounts or, where this is not done, in the auditors' report

Company law requires the directors to prepare financial statements for each financial year which give a true and fair view of the state of affairs of the company and of the profit or loss of the company for that period. In preparing those financial statements, the directors are required to

- select suitable accounting policies and then apply them consistently;

- make judgements and estimates that are reasonable and prudent;

- state whether applicable accounting standards have been followed, subject to any material departures disclosed and explained in the financial statements;

- prepare the financial statements on the going concern basis unless it is inappropriate to presume that the company will continue in business.

The directors are responsible for keeping proper accounting records which disclose with reasonable accuracy at any time the financial position of the company and to enable them to ensure that the financial statements comply with the Companies Act 1985. They are also responsible for safeguarding the assets of the company and hence for taking reasonable steps for the prevention and detection of fraud and other irregularities.

12.30 MISCELLANEOUS AUDIT REPORTS: EXAMPLES

The suggested formats of audit reports on a company's annual accounts in the Auditing Practice Note *Report by auditors under company legislation in the UK* have been superseded by *SAS 600 Auditors' reports on financial statements* (see 12.29 above). However, at the time of publication, the Practice Note has not been withdrawn and no suggested formats have been issued of the other audit reports included in it. These are reproduced below and may still be used, subject to any necessary modification to bring them in line with revised format for reports on accounts.

Example 1 Statement required on a company's ability to make a distribution

AUDITORS' STATEMENT TO THE MEMBERS OF XYZ LIMITED PURSUANT TO SECTION 271(4) OF THE COMPANIES ACT 1985

We have audited the financial statements of XYZ Limited for the year ended 31 December 19. . in accordance with Auditing Standards and have expressed a qualified opinion thereon.

In our opinion the subject matter of that qualification is not material for determining, by reference to those financial statements, whether the distribution (interim dividend for the year ended . . .) of £. . . proposed by the company is permitted under section 270 of the Companies Act 1985.

Auditors

Date

Notes.

1   Where the amount of the dividend has not yet been determined, the auditors' statement should be expressed in terms of the company's ability to make potential distributions up to a specific level. The opinion paragraph will be worded as follows:

'In our opinion the subject matter of that qualification is not material for determining, by reference to those financial statements, whether a distribution of not more than £. . . by the company would be permitted under section 270 of the Companies Act 1985.'

2   This example assumes that a separate report is given regarding the company's ability to make a distribution. This matter is sometimes referred to in the statutory audit report by adding a separate paragraph. That paragraph might be worded as follows:

'In our opinion the subject matter of the foregoing qualification is not material for determining whether the distribution of £. . . proposed by the company is permitted under section 270 of the Act.'

Example 2 Statement required when a private company wishes to re-register as a public company

AUDITORS' STATEMENT TO THE DIRECTORS OF XYZ LIMITED PURSUANT TO SECTION 43(3)(B) OF THE COMPANIES ACT 1985

12.30 Auditors

We have examined the balance sheet of XYZ Limited as at 31 December 19. . which formed part of the financial statements of the year then ended audited by us/ABC and Co. The scope of our work for the purpose of this statement was limited to an examination of the relationship of amounts stated in the audited balance sheet in connection with the company's proposed re-registration as a public company.

In our opinion the balance sheet shows that at 31 December 19. . the amount of the company's net assets was not less than the aggregate of its called-up share capital and undistributable reserves.

*We audited the financial statements of XYZ Limited for the year ended 31 December 19. . in accordance with Auditing Standards and expressed a qualified opinion thereon. The matter giving rise to our qualification is not material for determining by reference to the balance sheet at 31 December 19. . whether at that date the net assets of the company were not less than the aggregate of its called-up share capital and undistributable reserves.

Auditors

Date

*For inclusion as necessary

Example 3 Report required when a public company wishes to allot shares otherwise than for cash

INDEPENDENT ACCOUNTANTS' REPORT TO XYZ PUBLIC LIMITED COMPANY FOR THE PURPOSES OF SECTION 103(1) OF THE COMPANIES ACT 1985

We report on the value of the consideration for the allotment to . . . (name of allottee) of . . . (number) shares, having a nominal value of £1 each, to be issued at a premium of . . . pence per share. The shares and share premium are to be treated as fully paid up.

The consideration for the allotment to . . . (name of allottee) is the freehold building situated at . . . (address) and . . . (number) of shares, having a nominal value of £1 each, in ABC Public Limited Company.

The freehold building was valued on the basis of its open market value by . . . (name of specialist), a fellow of the Royal Institution of Chartered Surveyors, on . . . (date) and in our opinion it is reasonable to accept such a valuation.

The shares in ABC Public Limited Company were valued by us on . . . (date) on the basis of the price shown in The Stock Exchange Daily Official List at . . . (date).

In our opinion, the methods of valuation of the freehold building and of the shares in ABC Public Limited Company were reasonable in all the circumstances. There appears to have been no material change in the value of either part of the consideration since the valuations were made. On the basis of the valuations, in our opinion, the value of the total consideration is not less than £. . . (being the total amount to be treated as paid up on the shares allotted together with the share premium).

Auditors/Independent Accounts

Date

Note
A similar form of report is required pursuant to section 104(4)(b) of the Companies Act 1985 when a public company purchases non-cash assets from certain of its members.

Example 4   Report required when a private company wishes to redeem or purchase its own shares out of capital

AUDITORS' REPORT TO THE DIRECTORS OF XYZ LIMITED PURSUANT TO SECTION 173(5) OF THE COMPANIES ACT 1985

We have examined the attached statutory declaration of the directors dated . . . in connection with the company's proposed purchase of . . . (number) ordinary shares by a payment out of capital and reserves. We have enquired into the state of the company's affairs so far as necessary for us to review the bases for the statutory declaration.

In our opinion, the amount of £. . . specified in the statutory declaration of the directors as the permissible capital payment for the shares to be purchased is properly determined in accordance with sections 171 and 172 of the Companies Act 1985.

We are not aware of anything to indicate that the opinion expressed by the directors in their declaration as to any of the matters mentioned in section 173(3) of the Companies Act 1985 is unreasonable in all the circumstances.

Auditors

Date

Example 5   Report required when a private company wishes to provide financial assistance for the purchase of its own shares or those of its holding company

AUDITORS' REPORT TO THE DIRECTORS OF XYZ LIMITED PURSUANT TO SECTION 156(4) OF THE COMPANIES ACT 1985

We have examined the attached statutory declaration of the directors dated . . . in connection with the proposal that the company should give financial assistance for the purchase of . . . (number) of the company's ordinary shares. We have enquired into the state of the company's affairs so far as necessary for us to review the bases for the statutory declaration.

We are not aware of anything to indicate that the opinion expressed by the directors in their declaration as to any of the matters mentioned in section 156(2) of the Companies Act 1985 is unreasonable in all the circumstances.

Auditors

Date

Example 6   Report required on initial accounts when a public company wishes to make a distribution

AUDITORS' REPORT TO THE DIRECTORS OF XYZ PUBLIC LIMITED COMPANY PURSUANT TO SECTION 273(4) OF THE COMPANIES ACT 1985

We have audited the initial accounts of XYZ Public Limited Company on pages . . . to . . . in accordance with Auditing Standards.

In our opinion the initial accounts for the period from . . . to . . . have been properly prepared within the meaning of section 273 of the Companies Act 1985.

Auditors

Date

12.31 Auditors

SMALL COMPANIES AUDIT EXEMPTIONS

The accounts of certain categories of small companies, as described below, are exempt from audit. [*SI 1994 No 1935, Reg 6; SI 1994 No 2879*].

12.32 **Total exemption**

A company meeting all the conditions set out below in respect of a financial year is exempt in respect of that year from the statutory requirements relating to the audit of accounts, provided the exemption is not excluded under 12.33 below and subject to the further requirement at 12.34 below. The conditions are as follows.

(*a*) The company must qualify as a 'small' company, see 7.2 ACCOUNTS: SMALL AND MEDIUM-SIZED COMPANIES (although it need not take advantage of those provisions).

(*b*) For a company which is a charity,

    (i) its gross income (i.e. its income from all sources as shown in its income and expenditure account) for that year must be not more than £90,000, or a proportionately adjusted figure where the financial year is not in fact a year; and

    (ii) its 'balance sheet total' must be not more than £1.4 million.

(*c*) For any other company not falling within (*b*) above,

    (i) its turnover (see 2.1 ACCOUNTS: DEFINITIONS) in that year must be not more than £350,000 (£90,000 for financial years ending before 15 June 1997), or a proportionately adjusted figure where the financial year is not in fact a year; and

    (ii) its 'balance sheet total' must be not more than £1.4 million.

'*Balance sheet total*' is as defined at 7.2 ACCOUNTS: SMALL AND MEDIUM-SIZED COMPANIES and broadly means the total of assets.

Dormant companies which fall within *Sec 250(1)* (see 24.2 DORMANT COMPANIES) and also satisfy the above conditions may claim exemption from audit under either *Sec 249A* or *Sec 250*.

[*Sec 249A(1)(3)(3A)(6)(6A)(7); SI 1994 No 1935, Reg 2; SI 1997 No 936, Reg 2*].

Where the directors take advantage of the above exemption

● no auditors' report need be laid before the company in general meeting or be delivered to the Registrar of Companies (see 3.6, 3.7 ACCOUNTS: GENERAL);

● the provisions at 3.3, 3.4 ACCOUNTS: GENERAL (entitlement to receive and right to demand copies of accounts and reports) apply with the omission of references to the auditors' report; and

● the requirements at 23.7(*a*)(ii) DISTRIBUTIONS (auditors to have reported on accounts by reference to which a distribution is justified) do not apply.

[*Sec 249E(1); SI 1994 No 1935, Reg 2*].

See 12.41 below as regards guidance for accountants who compile accounts for clients qualifying for this exemption.

12.33 *Cases in which exemption not available*

A company is not entitled to the exemption under 12.32 above if at any time in the financial year in question (*a*)   it was a public company (see 43.1 PUBLIC AND LISTED COMPANIES);

(*b*)   it was a banking or insurance company;

(*c*)   it was enrolled in the list maintained by the Insurance Brokers Registration Council under *Insurance Brokers (Registration) Act 1977, s 4*;

(*d*)   it was an authorised person or an appointed representative under *Financial Services Act 1986*;

(*e*)   it was a special register body or an employers' association as defined by, respectively, *Trade Union and Labour Relations (Consolidation) Act 1992, s 117(1) and s 122*;

(*f*)   it was a parent company (see 4.2 ACCOUNTS: GROUPS OF COMPANIES); or

(*g*)   it was a subsidiary undertaking (see 4.2 ACCOUNTS: GROUPS OF COMPANIES) unless it was dormant throughout the period. See 24.1 DORMANT COMPANIES.

A parent or subsidiary company which would otherwise fall within (*f*) or (*g*) above for any period within a financial year is not treated as so falling if throughout that period it is a member of a group which satisfies the following conditions.

• Throughout the financial year within which the period falls, the group qualifies as a small group under *Sec 249* and is not an ineligible group under *Sec 248(2)* (see 7.2 and 7.3 ACCOUNTS: SMALL AND MEDIUM-SIZED GROUPS).

• The group's aggregate turnover in that year is not more than £350,000 net or £420,000 gross.

• The group's aggregate balance sheet total for that year is not more than £1.4 million net or £1.68 million gross.

The references to 'net' figures are to figures net of set-offs and adjustments required by *4A Sch* (see 4.12 to 4.22 ACCOUNTS: GROUPS OF COMPANIES) and the references to 'gross' figures are to figures before making such set-offs and adjustments.

Notice by members requiring audit. A company loses any right to the exemption for a financial year if one or more of its members holding not less in aggregate than 10% in nominal value of the issued share capital or any class of it (or not less than 10% in number of the members where the company does not have a share capital) require the company to obtain an audit of its accounts for that year. They may do so by depositing written notice to that effect at the company's registered office no later than one month *before* the end of the financial year in question.

[*Sec 249B(1)–(3); SI 1994 No 1935, Reg 2; SI 1996 No 189, Reg 10; SI 1997 No 936, Reg 3*].

12.34   *Statement required from directors*

The company's balance sheet must contain a statement by the directors (in the absence of which the company's entitlement to the exemption lapses) to the effect that

(*a*)   for the financial year in question the company was entitled to exemption under *Sec 249A* (see 12.32 above);

(*b*)   no notice has been deposited by members under *Sec 249B(2)* in relation to the accounts for the financial year (see 12.33 above); and

(*c*)   the directors acknowledge their responsibilities for

    • ensuring that the company keeps accounting records which comply with *Sec 221* (see 45.1 RECORDS); and

- preparing accounts which give a true and fair view of the state of affairs of the company as at the end of the financial year and of its profit or loss for the financial year in accordance with the requirements of *Sec 226* (see 5.2 ACCOUNTS: INDIVIDUAL COMPANIES), and which otherwise comply with the requirements of *CA 1985* relating to accounts so far as applicable to the company.

The statement must appear in the balance sheet above the signature approving the accounts (see 3.2 ACCOUNTS: GENERAL).

[Sec 249B(4)(5); SI 1994 No 1935, Reg 2; SI 1996 No 189, Reg 10].

12.35 Exemption in cases where accountants' report required

A company which is a charity meeting all the conditions set out below in respect of a financial year is exempt in respect of that year from the statutory requirements relating to the audit of accounts, provided the directors cause a report (the accountants' report – see 12.36 below) in respect of the company's individual accounts for the year to be made to the members. The exemption does not apply in the cases mentioned at 12.33 above. The further requirement at 12.34 above also applies, with the necessary modification to 12.34(*a*). The conditions are as follows.

(*a*) The company must qualify as a 'small' company, see 7.2 ACCOUNTS: SMALL AND MEDIUM-SIZED COMPANIES (although it need not take advantage of those provisions).

(*b*) Its gross income (i.e. its income from all sources as shown in its income and expenditure account) in that year must be more than £90,000 but not more than £250,000, or proportionately adjusted figures where the financial year is not in fact a year.

(*c*) Its 'balance sheet total' must be not more than £1.4 million. (*'Balance sheet total'* is defined at 7.2 ACCOUNTS: SMALL AND MEDIUM-SIZED COMPANIES and broadly means the total of assets.)

Dormant companies which fall within *Sec 250(1)* (see 24.2 DORMANT COMPANIES) and also satisfy the above conditions may claim exemption from audit under either *Sec 249A* or *Sec 250*.

[Sec 249A(2)(4)(6)(6A)(7); SI 1994 No 1935, Reg 2; SI 1997 No 936, Reg 2].

Where the directors take advantage of the above exemption,

- the provisions of *Sec 236(2)–(4)* (requiring auditors' report to state name of auditors and be signed – see 12.20 above) apply with necessary modifications to the accountants' report;

- the following provisions apply with the substitution for references to the auditors' report of references to the accountants' report

  (i) *Sec 238* – entitlement to receive copies of accounts and reports (see 3.3 ACCOUNTS: GENERAL);

  (ii) *Sec 239* – right to demand copies of accounts and reports (see 3.4 ACCOUNTS: GENERAL);

  (iii) *Sec 241* – accounts and reports to be laid before company in general meeting (see 3.6 ACCOUNTS: GENERAL);

  (iv) *Sec 242* – accounts and reports to be delivered to the Registrar of Companies (see 3.7 ACCOUNTS: GENERAL);

- the requirements at 23.7(*a*)(ii) DISTRIBUTIONS (auditors to have reported on accounts by reference to which a distribution is justified) do not apply; and

- The provisions of *Sec 389A(1)(2)* (right of auditors to information – see 12.27 above) apply by reference to the reporting accountant.

[*Sec 249E(2); SI 1994 No 1935, Reg 2*].

12.36 *Content of accountants' report*

The accountants' report (also known in practice as a compilation report) must state, in the opinion of the reporting accountant (see 12.37 below) making it,

(*a*)   whether the company's accounts for the financial year in question are in agreement with the accounting records required to be kept by the company (see 45.1 RECORDS);

(*b*)   whether, having regard only to, and on the basis of, the information contained in those records, those accounts have been drawn up in a manner consistent with the following statutory provisions (so far as applicable to the company and modified as appropriate where the company prepares abbreviated accounts (see 7.5 et seq. ACCOUNTS: SMALL AND MEDIUM-SIZED COMPANIES)

- *Sec 226(3)* and *4 Sch* – accounts to comply with requirements of *4 Sch* as to form and content (see 5.2 to 5.31 ACCOUNTS: INDIVIDUAL COMPANIES and note the exemption at 5.15 applicable to 'small' companies in relation to disclosure with respect to compliance with accounting standards);

- *Sec 231* and relevant provisions of *5 Sch* – requirement to give information on related undertakings in notes to accounts (see 5.45–5.53 ACCOUNTS: INDIVIDUAL COMPANIES); and

- *Sec 232* and *6 Sch* – emoluments and benefits of directors and other officers to be disclosed in notes to accounts (see 5.32 to 5.43 ACCOUNTS: INDIVIDUAL COMPANIES);

(*c*)   that, having regard only to, and on the basis of, the information contained in the accounting records, the company met the conditions at 12.35 above, and did not fall within 12.33(*a*)–(*g*) (cases in which small companies audit exemption not available) at any time in the financial year.

The report must state the name of the reporting accountant and be signed by him. Where the reporting accountant is a body corporate or partnership, the report may be signed by a person authorised to sign on its behalf.

[*Sec 249C(2)-(6); SI 1994 No 1935, Reg 2*].

See 12.40 below for examples of accountants' reports.

12.37 *The reporting accountant*

The person preparing the accountant's report (the reporting accountant) must be either

(*a*)   a member of a body listed below who, under that body's rules (as defined and including rules relating to admission and expulsion of members), is entitled to engage in public practice and who would not be ineligible under *CA 1989, s 27* (ineligibility on grounds of lack of independence – see 12.7 above) to be appointed auditor of the company concerned; or

(*b*)   any person (whether or not a member of such a body) who is subject to the rules (as in (*a*) above) of any such body in seeking appointment or acting as a company auditor and who, under those rules, is eligible for appointment as a company auditor.

The bodies in question are the

- Institute of Chartered Accountants in England and Wales;

- Insitute of Chartered Accountants of Scotland;

- Institute of Chartered Accountants in Ireland;

- Association of Chartered Certified Accountants;

- Association of Authorised Public Accountants;

- Association of Accounting Technicians;

- Association of International Accountants; and

- Chartered Institute of Management Accountants.

An individual, body corporate or partnership may be appointed as a reporting accountant. The rules at 12.6 above apply to the appointment as reporting accountant of a partnership constituted under the law of England and Wales or Northern Ireland (or any other territory where a partnership is not a legal person).

[*Secs 249C(1), 249D; SI 1994 No 1935, Reg 2; SI 1995 No 589; SI 1996 No 3080; SI 1997 No 936*].

12.38 **Loss of exemption**

Where a company which has been exempt under 12.32 or 12.35 above ceases to be exempt, auditors must be appointed as follows.

(*a*)   Where (*b*) below does not apply, the auditors may be appointed by the directors (or, if they fail to exercise this power, by the company in general meeting) at any time before the next general meeting of the company at which accounts are to be laid. The auditors so appointed hold office until the conclusion of that meeting.

(*b*)   Where an election has been made by a private company under *Sec 252* to dispense with the laying of accounts before the company in general meeting (see 3.6 ACCOUNTS: GENERAL) then, unless a member or auditor has given notice under *Sec 253* requiring a meeting to be held at which accounts are laid (in which case the normal rules under (*a*) above apply) the auditors may be appointed by the directors (or, if they fail to exercise this power, by the company in general meeting) at any time before the end of the period of 28 days beginning with the day on which copies of the company's annual accounts are next sent to members. The auditors so appointed hold office until the end of that period.

[*Sec 388A(2)-(5); SI 1994 No 1935, Reg 3*].

12.39 **Defective accounts**

In certain circumstances, the annual accounts and/or directors' report of a company may be replaced or partially revised because they were originally defective. See 3.9 ACCOUNTS: GENERAL. See 12.22 above for the provisions applying where the auditors reported on the original accounts.

Where accounts are revised, either by replacement or by supplementary note, and a reporting accountant has, prior to revision, made an accountants' report on the original accounts under 12.35 above, he must make a further report to the members on the revised accounts. The further report may be made by a different reporting accountant, if the directors so resolve, provided he is qualified to act as reporting accountant of the company. From the time of signature by the reporting accountant, the further report is the accountants' report on the annual accounts of the company in place of the report on the original defective accounts.

Where a company was originally exempt from audit under 12.32 above but as a result of revisions to the accounts becomes exempt only by virtue of 12.35 above, it must have an accountants' report prepared on the revised accounts. Where as a result of revisions, a company is no longer within the small companies audit exemptions, it must have an auditor's report prepared on the revised accounts. The accountants' report or auditors' report must be delivered to the Registrar of Companies within 28 days after the date of revision of the accounts. In the event of non-compliance, the penalty provisions of *Sec 242(2)–(5)* (accounts and reports to be delivered to Registrar – see 3.7 ACCOUNTS: GENERAL) apply with suitable modifications.

[*SI 1990 No 2570, Regs 6A, 6B; SI 1994 No 1935, 2 Sch 2*].

Where a company is exempt from audit under 12.35 above, *SI 1990 No 2570, Regs 10–13* (see 3.9, 3.10 ACCOUNTS: GENERAL) apply as if references to the auditors' report were references to the accountants' report, and as if references to the auditors' report on a revised directors' report (see 20.20 to 20.22 DIRECTORS' REPORT) were omitted. [*SI 1990 No 2570, Reg 14A(2); SI 1994 No 1935, 2 Sch 3*].

12.40 **Accountants' report: examples**

The Auditing Practices Board has issued a Statement of Standards for Reporting Accountants entitled 'Audit Exemption Reports', which, in a similar way to Auditing Standards (see 12.24 above), sets out basic principles and essential procedures to be observed by reporting accountants as well as containing explanatory and other material. The Statement includes illustrative examples of the accountants' report required to be prepared under 12.35 above, and these are reproduced below.

Example 1 Affirmative opinion on all matters

ACCOUNTANTS' REPORT TO THE SHAREHOLDERS ON THE UNAUDITED ACCOUNTS OF XYZ LIMITED

We report on the accounts for the year ended . . . set out on pages . . . to . . .

Respective responsibilities of directors and reporting accountants

As described on page . . . the company's directors are responsible for the preparation of the accounts, and they consider that the company is exempt from an audit. It is our responsibility to carry out procedures designed to enable us to report our opinion.

Basis of opinion

Our work was conducted in accordance with the Statement of Standards for Reporting Accountants, and our procedures consisted of comparing the accounts with the accounting records kept by the company, and making such limited enquiries of the officers of the company as we considered necessary for the purposes of this report. These procedures provide only the assurance expressed in our opinion.

Opinion

In our opinion:

(*a*) the accounts are in agreement with the accounting records kept by the company under section 221 of the Companies Act 1985 [see 12.36(*a*) above];

(*b*) having regard only to, and on the basis of, the information contained in those accounting records:

    (i) the accounts have been drawn up in a manner consistent with the accounting requirements specified in section 249C(6) of the Act [see 12.36(*b*) above]; and

    (ii) the company satisfied the conditions for exemption from an audit of the accounts for the year specified in section 249A(4) of the Act* [see 12.35 above] and did not, at any time within that year, fall within any of the categories of companies not entitled to the exemption specified in section 249B(1) [see 12.33(*a*)–(*g*) above].

[*Signature*]

Reporting accountants   *Address*

Date

* Insert 'as modified by section 249A(5)' where the company is a charity (see 12.35 above).

Example 2 Opinion including disagreement

ACCOUNTANTS' REPORT TO THE SHAREHOLDERS ON THE UNAUDITED ACCOUNTS OF XYZ LIMITED

We report on the accounts for the year ended . . . set out on pages . . . to . . .

Respective responsibilities of directors and reporting accountants

[As for Example 1 above]

Basis of opinion

[As for Example 1 above]

Opinion – including disagreement

As stated in note . . ., the directors have made no provision in the accounts for the depreciation of plant and machinery shown in the balance sheet at £ . . . . Paragraph 18 of Schedule 4 to the Companies Act 1985 requires that any fixed asset which has a limited useful economic life be depreciated.

In our opinion:

(*a*) the accounts are in agreement with the accounting records kept by the company under section 221 of the Companies Act 1985;

(*b*) having regard only to, and on the basis of, the information contained in those accounting records:

    (i) because of the absence of the provision for depreciation referred to above, the accounts have not been drawn up in a manner consistent with the accounting requirements specified in section 249C(6) of the Act; and

    (ii) the company satisfed the conditions for exemption from an audit of the accounts for the year specified in section 249A(4) of the Act and did not, at any time within that year, fall within any of the categories of companies not entitled to the exemption specified in section 249B(1).

[Signature]

Reporting accountants   *Address*

Date

Example 3 Opinion including limitation on scope

ACCOUNTANTS' REPORT TO THE SHAREHOLDERS ON THE UNAUDITED ACCOUNTS OF XYZ LIMITED

We report on the accounts for the year ended . . . set out on pages . . . to . . .

Respective responsibilities of directors and reporting accountants

[As for Example 1 above]

Basis of opinion

Our work was conducted in accordance with the Statement of Standards for Reporting Accountants, and so our procedures consisted of comparing the accounts with the accounting records kept by the company, and making such limited enquiries of the officers of the company as we considered necessary for the purpose of this report, except that the scope of our work was limited as explained below. These procedures provide only the assurance expressed in our opinion.

Owing to flood damage, certain accounting records relating to sales for the first month of the year have been destroyed, and so we have been unable to compare the sales shown in the accounts with those accounting records.

Opinion – including limitation on scope

In our opinion:

(*a*)   except for the uncertainty relating to sales which arises from the limitation on the scope of our work described above, the accounts are in agreement with the accounting records kept by the company under section 221 of the Companies Act 1985;

(*b*)   having regard only to, and on the basis of, the information contained in those accounting records:

   (i)   the accounts have been drawn up in a manner consistent with the accounting requirements specified in section 249C(6) of the Act; and

   (ii)   the company satisfied the conditions for exemption from an audit of the accounts for the year specified in section 249A(4) of the Act and did not, at any time within that year, fall within any of the categories of companies not entitled to the exemption specified in section 249B(1).

[Signature]

Reporting accountants   *Address*

Date

Note: In this example the reporting accountants have been able to conclude that the company satisfied the report conditions and that the limitation of scope did not prevent them from forming an opinion as to whether the accounts have been drawn up in a manner consistent with the specified accounting requirements.

12.41 Auditors

Example 4 Including explanatory paragraph

ACCOUNTANTS' REPORT TO THE SHAREHOLDERS ON THE UNAUDITED ACCOUNTS OF XYZ LIMITED

We report on the accounts for the year ended . . . set out on pages . . . to . . .

Respective responsibilities of directors and reporting accountants

[As for Example 1 above]

Basis of opinion

[As for Example 1 above]

Trade debtors

In carrying out our procedures it has come to our attention that the balance sheet total of debtors includes a debt of . . . which has been outstanding for in excess of one year. XYZ Limited has no security for this debt. The directors have made no provision against the debt being irrecoverable and they have informed us that they are satisfied that it will be recovered in full. We are not required to and have not performed any procedures to corroborate the directors' views, and we therefore express no opinion on this matter.

Opinion

[As for Example 1 above]

[*Signature*]

Reporting accountants   *Address*

Date

12.41 Accountants' report where total exemption available

Where a company qualifies for the total exemption from audit at 12.32 above, no accountants' report is required. However, both English and Scottish Institutes of Chartered Accountants have issued guidance on the subject to their members. The ICAEW's Audit Faculty's guidance is contained in its technical release statement 907 'Reports on Accounts Compiled (Prepared) by Accountants'. It states *inter alia* that accountants should ensure that accounts users are aware of the extent of their involvement and do not derive unwarranted assurance or gain comfort from the fact that the accounts have been prepared by a chartered accountant. In particular, if accounts are prepared on paper that can be associated with the firm of accountants involved, a report clarifying their role should be attached. It should be addressed to the directors (not the shareholders, if different) and should state that they (the directors) are responsible for the preparation of the accounts. If it appears that the accounts are misleading and the client refuses to amend them, the accountant may wish to disclose this in his report or in extreme cases resign and not issue a report.

The following is an example given in the guidance notes of a non-mandatory accountants' report.

ACCOUNTANTS' REPORT ON THE UNAUDITED ACCOUNTS OF [ABC LIMITED]

As described on the balance sheet you are responsible for the preparation of the accounts for the year ended . . . , set out on pages . . . to . . . , and you consider that the company is exempt from an audit and a report under Section 249A(2) [see 12.35 above] of the Companies Act 1985. In accordance with your instructions, we have compiled these unaudited accounts in order to assist you to fulfil your statutory responsibilities from the accounting records and information and explanations supplied to us.

[*Signature*]

Chartered Accountants
Address

Date

An example given by the Scottish Institute is very similar but finishes with the phrase 'We have not carried out an audit.'

13   Bonus Issues

Cross-references. See 58 SHARES AND SHARE CAPITAL.

13.1   A company may capitalise its profits by applying them in wholly or partly paying up unissued shares in the company to be allotted to existing shareholders in proportion to their holding. [*Sec 280(2)*]. The procedure is known as a bonus issue or alternatively a scrip issue or capitalisation issue. In practice the bonus shares will generally be fully paid. This is a requirement where *Table A, Art 110* (or *CA 1948, Table A, Art 128*) has been adopted (see 13.2(*c*) below). Any alteration of the articles would require written agreement by a member before he became liable for any unpaid share capital. [*Sec 16*].

13.2   AUTHORITY TO MAKE BONUS ISSUES

A company may make a bonus issue of shares if it is authorised to do so by its articles.

Where *SI 1985 Table A, Art 110* has been adopted by the company, the directors may with the authority of an ordinary resolution of the company

(*a*)   resolve to capitalise certain reserves or profits of the company (see 13.4 below);

(*b*)   appropriate the sum resolved to be capitalised to the members in the proportion that they would have been entitled to it if it were distributed by way of dividend;

(*c*)   apply the sum in paying up in full unissued shares or debentures of the company of a nominal amount equal to that sum; and

(*d*)   allot the shares or debentures, credited as fully paid, to those members, or as they otherwise direct, in those proportions, or partly in one way and partly in the other.

The directors may also make provision, by the issue of fractional certificates or by payment of cash or otherwise, in the case of shares or debentures becoming distributable in fractions. The normal procedure is for all fractional entitlements to be issued to a nominee on trust who sells the shares and divides the proceeds amongst the members *pro rata*.

Where *CA 1948, Table A, Art 128* has been adopted by the company, it may, in general meeting and upon the recommendation of the directors, similarly resolve to make a bonus issue.

Earlier versions of *Table A* (see 11.3 ARTICLES OF ASSOCIATION) contained no authority to make bonus issues.

13.3   Effect of *CA 1985* provisions

The general rule that shares, and any premium payable on them, must be paid up in money or money's worth does not prevent a company from allotting bonus shares to its members. [*Sec 99(1)(4)*]. However, like other shares, bonus shares must not be allotted at a discount (see *Welton v Saffery [1897] AC 299*); if they are, the allottee is liable to repay to the company the amount of the discount, together with interest at 5% (or such rate as specified by statutory instrument). [*Secs 100, 107*].

The provisions in *Sec 103* which require a public company allotting shares otherwise than in cash to have the consideration independently valued do not apply to bonus shares. [*Sec 103(2)*].

13.4 FUNDS AVAILABLE FOR MAKING BONUS ISSUES

A company's profits available for distribution are the excess of its accumulated, realised profits over its accumulated, realised losses. [*Sec 263(3)*]. However, an issue of fully or partly paid bonus shares is not a distribution for this purpose [*Sec 263(2)(a)*] and *unrealised* profits may therefore be utilised for paying up bonus shares although they cannot be applied in paying up bonus *debentures* [*Sec 263(4)*]. In addition, the share premium account [*Sec 130(2)*] and the capital redemption reserve [*Sec 170(4)*] may also be utilised in paying up fully paid bonus shares (but not debentures).

Table A, Art 110 incorporates these statutory rules and, where adopted, empowers the directors to capitalise

(*a*) any undivided profits not required for paying any preferential dividend (whether or not they are available for distribution),

(*b*) any sum standing to the credit of the share premium account, or

(*c*) any sum standing to the credit of the capital redemption reserve

although sums under (*b*) and (*c*) and any profits not available for distribution can only be applied in paying up unissued *shares* to be allotted to members as *fully paid*.

CA 1948, Table A, Arts 128, 128A incorporate similar provisions with effect from 22 December 1980 (when *Art 128A* was inserted) by permitting a company which has adopted those articles to utilise realised and unrealised profits in paying up a bonus issue of shares. Where the version of *Table A* in force before that date applies to a company (i.e. where only *Art 128* applies), there is no power within *Table A* to utilise unrealised profits but where a company was authorised by a provision of its articles to apply its unrealised profits in paying up (in full or in part) a bonus issue of shares, that provision continues as authority after that date (subject to any alteration of the articles). [*Sec 278*].

13.5 OTHER REQUIREMENTS

Listed securities. In a capitalisation issue (other than one in lieu of dividends) if a shareholder's entitlement includes a fraction of a security, that fraction must be sold for the benefit of the holder except that, if its value (net of expenses) does not exceed £3, it may be sold for the company's benefit. Sales of fractions may be made before listing is granted. (*The Listing Rules, Chapter 4.31, 4.32*).

Return of allotments. Where a company makes any allotment of shares (including a bonus issue), it must within one month thereafter deliver to the Registrar of Companies a return in the prescribed form (Form 88(2)). See 9.4 ALLOTMENT OF SHARES.

13.6 PROSPECTUSES

The issue of fully paid bonus shares does not come within the prospectus requirements of *CA 1985* or *FSA 1986*. The definition of prospectus [*Sec 744*] refers to a document offering shares or debentures 'for subscription or purchase', and it has been held that these words indicate a payment in cash (*Governments Stock and Other Securities Investment Co Ltd v Christopher [1956] 1 All ER 490*).

14 Class Rights

14.1 VARIATION OF CLASS RIGHTS

Where a company's share capital is divided into shares of different classes (e.g. ordinary shares and preference shares) there are special provisions concerned with the 'variation' of the rights attached to any class of shares.

'*Variation*' of the rights attached to a class of shares contained in the company's memorandum or articles includes abrogation. [*Sec 125(8)*]. Otherwise the meaning of 'variation' has been strictly construed by the courts, so that where the value of the rights of a class of shareholders has effectively been reduced, but those rights themselves have not been affected as such, this has been held not to be a variation (see *Greenhalgh v Arderne Cinemas Ltd [1946] 1 All ER 512 (CA)*). See also *White v Bristol Aeroplane Co Ltd [1953] 1 All ER 40*; *Re John Smith's Tadcaster Brewery Co Ltd [1953] Ch 308*; *Re Saltdean Estate Co Ltd [1968] 3 All ER 829*; and *House of Fraser plc v ACGE Investments Ltd [1987] AC 387*.

For a right to be a class right, it must be given to members of a class in their capacity as members, although such a right need not be attached to particular shares. See *Cumbrian Newspapers Group Ltd v Cumberland and Westmorland Herald Newspaper and Printing Co Ltd [1986] 3 WLR 26*.

Any alteration of a provision contained in a company's articles for the variation of the rights attached to a class of shares, or the insertion of any such provision into the articles, is itself to be treated as a variation of those rights. [*Sec 125(7)*].

14.2 Conditions for variation

Subject to 14.4 below, the conditions for the variation of class rights depend upon whether the rights are attached to the class of shares by the memorandum or otherwise, and whether the memorandum or articles contain provision for the variation of those rights.

(*a*)   Where the rights are attached to a class of shares otherwise than by the company's memorandum, and its articles do not contain provision for the variation of the rights, those rights may be varied if, but only if

   (i)   the holders of three-quarters in nominal value of the issued shares of that class consent in writing to the variation, or

   (ii)   an extraordinary resolution passed at a separate general meeting of the holders of that class sanctions the variation

   and any other requirement (howsoever imposed) in relation to the variation of those rights is complied with. [*Sec 125(2)*].

(*b*)   Where the memorandum or articles contain provision for the variation of class rights (whether the rights are attached to that class by the memorandum or articles or otherwise) and the variation of those rights is connected with the giving, variation, revocation or renewal of an authority for allotment under *Sec 80* (see 9.2 ALLOTMENT OF SHARES) or with a reduction of the company's share capital under *Sec 135* (see 58.17 SHARES AND SHARE CAPITAL) then those rights may be varied provided that

   (i)   the condition mentioned in (*a*)(i) or (ii) above is satisfied; and

   (ii)   any other requirement of the memorandum or articles in relation to the variation of rights of that class is complied with. [*Sec 125(3)*].

(*c*)   Where

(i)   the rights are attached to a class of shares in the company by the memorandum and the articles contain provision regarding their variation which had been included at the time of the company's original incorporation, or

(ii) the rights are attached otherwise than by the memorandum and the articles contain such provision (whenever first so included),

and in either case the variation is not connected as in (*b*) above, those rights may be varied only in accordance with that provision of the articles. [*Sec 125(4)*].

(*d*) Where the rights are attached to a class of shares by the memorandum, and neither the memorandum nor the articles contain provision regarding the variation of those rights, those rights may be varied if all the members of the company agree to the variation. [*Sec 125(5)*].

14.3   Class meetings

The provisions of *Secs 369* and *370* (notice of meetings and general provisions as to meetings and votes, see 33.5 to 33.11 MEETINGS) and *Secs 376* and *377* (circulation of members' resolutions, see 51.7 RESOLUTIONS) and the provisions of the articles relating to general meetings apply to any shareholders' meeting required to take place in connection with the variation of the rights attached to a class of shares subject to the following modification.

- The necessary quorum at any such meeting (other than an adjourned meeting) is two persons holding or representing by proxy at least one-third in nominal value of the issued shares of the class in question. At an adjourned meeting the quorum is one person holding shares of the class in question or his proxy.

- Any holder of shares of the class in question present in person or by proxy may demand a poll.

[*Sec 125(6)*].

14.4   Powers of the court

Nothing in 14.2(*a*) to (*d*) above derogates from the powers of the court under the following provisions.

- *Secs 4-6* (company resolution to alter objects, see 35.7 to 35.9 MEMORANDUM OF ASSOCIATION).

- *Sec 54* (litigated objection to public company becoming private by re-registration, see 49.12 REGISTRATION AND RE-REGISTRATION).

- *Sec 425* (court control of company compromising with members and creditors) or *Sec 427* (company reconstruction or amalgamation). See 44.1 and 44.3 RECONSTRUCTIONS AND MERGERS respectively.

- *Secs 459-461* (protection of minorities). See 34.6 and 34.7 MEMBERS.

[*Sec 126*].

14.5   Shareholders' rights to object to variation

Where a company has different classes of shares and the rights attached to any class of shares are

- varied in pursuance of a provision in the memorandum or articles authorising such variation, subject to

(i)   the consent of any specified proportion of the holders of the issued shares of that class, or

(ii)   the sanction of a resolution passed at a separate meeting of the holders of those shares,

or

- varied under 14.2(*a*) above,

then within 21 days after the date on which the consent to the variation was given or the resolution for the variation was passed (as the case may be), the holders of not less than 15% of the issued shares of the class in question (being persons who did not consent to, or vote in favour of, the resolution) may apply to the court to have the variation cancelled. Such application may be made, on behalf of the shareholders entitled to make it, by such of their number as they may appoint in writing for the purpose. If an application is made, the variation has no effect unless and until it is confirmed by the court. [*See 127(1)-(3)*].

The court may disallow the variation if satisfied, having regard to all the circumstances of the case, that the variation would unfairly prejudice the shareholders of the class represented by the applicant. If the court is not so satisfied, it must confirm the variation. The court's decision is final. [*Sec 127(4)*].

For an example of what could constitute unfair prejudice in this context, see *Re Holders Investment Trust Ltd [1971] 1 WLR 583*, a case on reduction of capital.

Within 15 days after the court makes an order on such an application, the company must forward a copy of the order to the Registrar of Companies. In default, the company and every officer of it who is in default is liable to a fine up to the level in 40.1(*f*) PENALTIES. [*Sec 127(5), 24 Sch*].

'Variation' includes abrogation. [*Sec 127(6)*].

14.6   REGISTRATION OF PARTICULARS OF SPECIAL RIGHTS

Under certain circumstances, a company is required to provide the Registrar of Companies with particulars relating to those of its shares with special rights.

Allotment of shares. If a company allots shares with rights which are not stated in its memorandum or articles, or in any resolution or agreement which is required by *Sec 380* to be sent to the Registrar of Companies (see 51.9 RESOLUTIONS), the company must, within one month of allotting the shares, deliver to the Registrar of Companies a statement in the prescribed form (Form 128(1)) containing particulars of those rights. This does not apply if the new shares are in all respects uniform with shares previously allotted. For this purpose, the new shares are not to be treated as different merely because they do not carry the same rights to dividends, during the twelve months immediately following their allotment, as do the previously allotted shares. [*Sec 128(1)(2)*].

Variation of rights. Where the rights attached to any shares of a company are varied otherwise than by

(*a*)   amendment of the company's memorandum or articles, or

(*b*)   a resolution or agreement subject to *Sec 380* (see 51.9 RESOLUTIONS),

the company must, within one month from the date on which the variation is made, deliver to the Registrar of Companies a statement in the prescribed form (Form 128(3)) containing particulars of the variation. [*Sec 128(3)*].

Name of class of shares. Where a company (otherwise than by any such amendment, resolution or agreement within (*a*) or (*b*) above) assigns a name or a new name or other designation to any class of its shares, it must, within one month of doing so, deliver to the Registrar of Companies a notice in the prescribed form (Form 128(4)) containing particulars of the name or designation so assigned. [*Sec 128(4)*].

Penalties. If a company fails to comply with the above requirements the company and every officer of it who is in default is liable to a fine up to the level in 40.1(*f*) PENALTIES. [*Secs 128(5), 24 Sch*].

14.7 Companies not having a share capital

Equivalent requirements as under 14.6 above are imposed in relation to companies not having a share capital but in relation to members rather than shares. [*Sec 129, 24 Sch*].

15 Companies not Formed under CA 1985

15.1 The majority of companies currently trading existed before *CA 1985* came into effect, in most cases having been registered and/or formed under *'former Companies Acts'* i.e.

Joint Stock Companies Acts
Companies Act 1862
Companies (Consolidation) Act 1908
Companies Act 1929
Companies Acts 1948 to 1981

The provisions of *CA 1985* apply to such companies as set out in 15.2 below.

Some companies, however, were not formed under companies legislation. These companies may, in certain circumstances, be registered under *CA 1985*. See 15.3 to 15.10 below for registration requirements and consequences.

15.2 **COMPANIES FORMED OR REGISTERED UNDER FORMER COMPANIES ACTS**

CA 1985 applies to such companies registered in Great Britain as follows.

- *Companies formed and registered under former Companies Acts.* Such companies are treated as if they had been formed and registered under *CA 1985* (in the case of a company other than a limited company as if it were an unlimited company).

- *Companies registered but not formed under former Companies Acts. CA 1985* applies to such companies as it does to companies not formed but authorised to register under the provisions in 15.3 *et seq.* below. See 15.9(*e*)-(*h*) below.

- *Companies re-registered with altered status under former Companies Acts. CA 1985* applies to unlimited companies registered or re-registered as limited companies under *former Companies Act*s as it applies to an unlimited company re-registered as limited under that *Act*.

In each case, however, reference to the date of registration (or re-registration) is to be read as the date of registration (or re-registration) under the earlier Act.

Companies registered under *Joint Stock Companies Acts* may allow their shares to be transferred by any method in use before *CA 1985* or in such manner as the company directs. In the case of an unlimited company so formed and registered, it may alter any regulation relating to the amount of capital or its distribution into shares by amending its articles under the powers in 11.7 ARTICLES OF ASSOCIATION even though those regulations are contained in the memorandum.

[*Secs 675-679*].

15.3 **COMPANIES NOT FORMED UNDER COMPANIES LEGISLATION BUT AUTHORISED TO REGISTER**

Subject to the exceptions below any company consisting of two or more members

- existing before 2 November 1862 (including any company registered under the *Joint Stock Companies Acts*), or

- formed after that date (whether before or after 1 July 1985) in pursuance of any Act of Parliament or letters patent or being otherwise duly constituted

may apply for registration under *CA 1985* as a limited or unlimited company or as a company limited by guarantee. Registration is not invalid because it has taken place with a view to the company's being wound up (in fact registration is often sought for this very purpose).

A company is not prevented from registering under *CA 1985* as a private company limited by shares or guarantee solely because it has only one member.

Exceptions. This procedure cannot be used

- by a company registered in any part of the UK under *Companies Acts 1862, 1929* or *1948* or *Companies (Consolidation) Act 1908*;

- by a company having the liability of its members limited by Act of Parliament or letters patent which is either

  (i)   not a 'joint stock company'; or

  (ii)   seeking to register as an unlimited company or a company limited by guarantee; or

- by a company that is not a joint stock company seeking to register as a company limited by shares.

[*Sec 680; SI 1992 No 1699*].

'Joint stock company' means a company having a permanent paid-up or nominal share capital of fixed amount *either* divided into shares of fixed amount *or* held and transferable as stock *or* a combination of both. It must be formed on the principle that its members comprise the holders of those shares or that stock and no other persons. Such a company when registered with limited liability under *CA 1985* is deemed to be a company limited by shares. [*Sec 683*]. The Registrar of Companies can require such evidence as he thinks necessary to satisfy himself whether a company proposing to be registered is, or is not, a joint stock company. [*Sec 686(3)*].

15.4   Requirements for registration

Registration must be agreed to by a majority of members present in person or by proxy at a general meeting summoned for the purpose. Where a company not having the liability of its members limited by Act of Parliament or letter patent is seeking registration as a limited company, such majority must be at least 75%. [*Sec 681(1)-(3)*].

In the case of a company seeking registration as a company limited by guarantee, a resolution must also be agreed to declaring that each member makes the undertaking referred to in 29.2 GUARANTEE COMPANIES under the heading *Liability of members*. [*Sec 681(4)*].

15.5   *Joint stock companies*

A joint stock company must deliver the following to the Registrar of Companies.

- Completed Form 680a with details of name and proposed name following registration (see 15.7 below); situation of the registered office; and share capital (if applicable).

- A list of members (Form 684) with a statutory declaration verifying the list (Form 686). The list must show the members on a date not more than 28 days before the date of registration.

- A copy of the Act of Parliament, Royal Charter, letters patent, deed of settlement or other instrument constituting or regulating the company.

If it is applying for registration as a public company, it must also comply with the following requirements.

15.6 Companies not Formed under CA 1985

(a) Where shares have been recently allotted otherwise than in cash, satisfy the conditions in 49.5 REGISTRATION AND RE-REGISTRATION (but substituting reference to the joint stock company's resolution that it be a public company for the special resolution there referred to).

(b) Satisfy the requirements in 49.6 REGISTRATION AND RE-REGISTRATION (but substituting reference to the joint stock company's resolution that it be a public company for the special resolution there referred to).

(c) Deliver to the Registrar of Companies

  (i) a copy of the resolution that the company be a public company (which resolution may also change the company's name by deleting the word 'company' or the words 'and company' or any abbreviation (or Welsh equivalent));

  (ii) a copy of a written statement by an 'accountant with appropriate qualifications' that in his opinion a 'relevant balance sheet' shows that at the balance sheet date the amount of the company's 'net assets' was not less than the aggregate of its called-up share capital and 'undistributable reserves';

  (iii) a copy of the relevant balance sheet, together with a copy of a report by the accountant in relation to the balance sheet which either has no qualification or a qualification stated as being not material for the purposes of giving his opinion under (ii) above;

  (iv) where (a) above applies, a copy of any valuation report required; and

  (v) a statutory declaration on Form 685 by a director or secretary that conditions (a) (where applicable) and (b) above have been satisfied and that between the balance sheet date under (ii) above and the application, there has been no change in the company's financial position that has resulted in the amount of its net assets becoming less than the aggregate of its called up share capital and undistributable reserves.

'Accountant with appropriate qualifications' means a person who would be eligible for appointment as the company's auditor if the company were registered.

'Relevant balance sheet' means a balance sheet prepared as at a date not more than seven months before the company's application.

'Net assets' means the aggregate of the company's assets less the aggregate of its liabilities (including any amount retained as reasonably necessary to provide for any liability or loss either likely to be incurred or certain to be incurred but uncertain as to amount or as to the date on which it will arise).

'Undistributable reserves' are the share premium account; the capital redemption reserve account; the amount by which the company's accumulated, unrealised profits exceed its accumulated, unrealised losses; and any other reserve which the company is prohibited from distributing.

[Secs 681(5)(6), 684, 685, 686(2), 4 Sch 89; CA 1989, 19 Sch 12; SI 1991 No 1997, Reg 53].

15.6 *Companies other than joint stock companies*

Such a company must deliver to the Registrar of Companies

- completed Form 680b with details of name and proposed name following registration (see 15.7 below) and situation of registered office;

- a list showing name, address, occupation and date of birth of each director or manager who is an individual (in the case of a corporation or Scottish firm, its name and registered or principal office);

- a copy of the Act of Parliament, letters patent or other instrument constituting or regulating the company; and

- in the case of a company intending to be registered as a company limited by guarantee, a copy of the resolution declaring the amount of the guarantee.

[*Secs 681(5)(6), 686(1)(1A); CA 1989, 19 Sch 5*].

15.7   Company name

If the name of the company seeking registration would be prohibited under 36.2 NAMES AND BUSINESS NAMES, the company may change its name with effect from the date of registration but such a change requires similar agreement by members as is required for registration under 15.4 above. [*Sec 682*].

The provisions of 36.1 NAMES AND BUSINESS NAMES also apply to the company's name but substituting 'application for registration' for 'memorandum'. [*Sec 687*].

15.8   Certificate of registration

On compliance with the requirements in 15.4 to 15.7 above, the Registrar of Companies must give a certificate that the company is incorporated under *CA 1985*. The certificate must also state, as appropriate,

- in the case of a limited company, that it is limited; and

- in the case of a joint stock company applying to be a public limited company, that it is a public limited company.

On the issue of the certificate, the company becomes so incorporated (the certificate being conclusive evidence of this fact).

[*Sec 688*].

15.9   Consequences of registration

The consequences of registration under the provisions of 15.3 *et seq.* above are as follows.

(*a*)   All property belonging to or vested in the company at the date of its registration passes to and vests in the company on registration for all the estate and interest of the company in the property.

(*b*)   The company's rights or liabilities in respect of any debt or obligation incurred, or contract entered into, are unaffected.

(*c*)   All legal proceedings etc. pending by or against the company, or any officer of it, may be continued as if registration had not taken place. Execution cannot, however, be issued against the effects of an individual member of the company although an order may be obtained for winding up the company in the event of the company's property being insufficient to satisfy the judgment.

(*d*)   All provisions contained in any Act of Parliament or other instrument constituting or regulating the company are deemed to be conditions contained in the memorandum and articles of the company.

271

15.10   Companies not Formed under CA 1985

   (*e*)   All the provisions of *CA 1985* apply to the company, its members, contributories and creditors as if the company had been formed under the Act except that

- *Table A* does not apply unless adopted by special resolution;

- provisions relating to the numbering of shares do not apply to any joint stock company whose shares are not numbered;

- the company does not have power to alter any provision contained in any Act of Parliament relating to the company;

- the company does not have power to alter any provision contained in letters patent relating to the company without sanction of the Secretary of State and may not alter any provision in letters patent or a Royal Charter with respect to the company's objects; and

- where a company does not have power to alter a provision under (iii) or (iv) above, it does not have power to ratify acts of the directors in contravention of the provision.

   (*f*)   The provisions of *CA 1985* with respect to

- the registration of an unlimited company as limited,

- the powers of an unlimited company on registration as a limited company with regard to reserve capital (see 49.8 REGISTRATION AND RE-REGISTRATION under the heading *Reserve capital*), and

- the power of a limited company to determine that a portion of its share capital shall not be capable of being called up in the event of winding up

apply notwithstanding any provision contained in an Act of Parliament, Royal Charter or other instrument constituting or regulating the company.

   (*g*)   The company is not authorised by (*d*) to (*f*) above to alter any provision contained in an instrument constituting or regulating the company which would have been required to be contained in the memorandum if the company had been originally formed under *CA 1985* and which cannot be altered under that Act.

   (*h*)   The provisions of *CA 1985* (except a court order under 34.7(*e*) MEMBERS regarding the protection of the company's members against unfair prejudice) do not prevent the company altering its constitution or regulations by powers vested in it by any Act of Parliament or other instrument constituting or regulating it.

[*Sec 689, 21 Sch*].

15.10 Power to substitute memorandum and articles for deed of settlement

A company registered under the provisions of 15.3 *et seq.* above may, by special resolution, alter the form of its constitution by substituting a memorandum and articles for a 'deed of settlement'. If it does so, the provisions of *Secs 4* to *6* with respect to application to the court for cancellation of alterations to the company's objects and consequential matters (see 35.7 to 35.9 MEMORANDUM OF ASSOCIATION) apply with certain modifications.

'*Deed of settlement*' includes any instrument constituting or regulating the company other than an Act of Parliament, Royal Charter or letters patent. [*Sec 690*].

16   Dealings with Third Parties

Cross-references. See 54 SEALS.

The contents of this chapter are as follows.

16.1   COMPANY'S CAPACITY

The validity of any act done by a company cannot be called into question on the grounds of lack of capacity by reason of anything in the company's memorandum; and a party to a transaction with a company is not bound to enquire as to whether it is permitted by the company's memorandum. [*Secs 35(1), 35B; CA 1989, s 108*].

Although a member may bring proceedings to restrain the company from doing a certain act which would otherwise be beyond its capacity, no such proceedings can be brought in respect of an act done in fulfilment of a legal obligation arising from a previous action of the company. [*Sec 35(2); CA 1989, s 108*].

Despite the above, it still remains the duty of the directors to observe the limitations on their powers flowing from the company's memorandum. See 35.2(*d*) MEMORANDUM OF ASSOCIATION for the objects clause. Any action by the directors which would otherwise be beyond the company's capacity may be ratified by the company by special resolution although if, by such action, any liability is incurred (by the directors or any other person) relief from such liability must be agreed to separately by special resolution. [*Sec 35(3); CA 1989, s 108*].

See, however, 19.72 DIRECTORS for the invalidity of certain contracts where a director or person connected with him is a party to the contract.

See also 16.3 below for charitable companies.

16.2   Power of directors to bind the company

Where a person 'deals with' a company in good faith, the power of the directors to bind the company, or authorise others to do so, is deemed to be free of any limitation under the company's constitution, including limitation deriving from

- a resolution of the company in general meeting or a meeting of any class of shareholder; or

- any agreement between the members of the company or of any class of shareholder.

[*Sec 35A(1)(3); CA 1989, s 108*].

A person '*deals with*' a company if he is a party to any transaction or other act to which the company is party. He will be presumed to have acted in good faith unless the contrary is proved and is not to be regarded as acting in bad faith only because he knows that an act is beyond the powers of the directors under the company's constitution. [*Sec 35A(2); CA 1989, s 108*]. A person is under no duty to enquire as to whether a particular transaction is beyond the powers of the directors. [*Sec 35B; CA 1989, s 108*].

16.3 Dealings with Third Parties

Although a member may bring proceedings to restrain the doing of an act which would otherwise be beyond the powers of the directors, no such proceedings can be brought in respect of an act done in fulfilment of a legal obligation arising from a previous action of the company. [*Sec 35A(4); CA 1989, s 108*].

The above provisions do not affect any liability incurred by the directors, or any other person, by reason of the directors exceeding their powers. [*Sec 35A(5); CA 1989, s 108*].

See 16.3 below for charitable companies.

16.3 Charitable companies

The provisions in 16.1 and 16.2 above do not apply to the acts of a charitable company unless in favour of a person who

(*a*)   gives full consideration in money or money's worth in relation to the act in question and does not know that the act is not permitted by the company's memorandum or, as the case may be, is beyond the powers of the directors; or

(*b*)   does not know at the time the act is done that the company is a charity.

In any proceedings, the burden of proof that (*a*) or (*b*) above is not satisfied lies with the person making the allegation.

Where, however, a charitable company purports to transfer or grant an interest in property, the title of a person who subsequently acquires the property or an interest and who satisfies the conditions in (*a*) above is not affected by the fact that the act was not so permitted or beyond the directors' powers.

[*Secs 35(4), 35A(6); CA 1989, s 112(3)-(5); Charities Act 1993, s 65(1), 6 Sch 20*].

16.4   CONTRACTS

In England and Wales, a contract may be made

● by a company, by writing under its common seal (or, in the case of a foreign company, in any manner allowed under the laws of the foreign territory); or

● on behalf of the company, by any person acting under its authority, express or implied (in the case of a foreign company, a person so acting in accordance with the laws of the foreign territory).

Unless a contrary intention appears, any formalities required by law in the case of a contract made by an individual also apply to one made by or on behalf of a company.

[*Sec 36; CA 1989, s 130; SI 1994 No 950, Reg 4*].

16.5   Pre-incorporation contracts

Where a contract purports to be made by or on behalf of a company before its formation, then, subject to any agreement to the contrary, it has effect as if made by the person purporting to act for, or as agent for, the company and that person is personally liable on the contract. This also applies to the making of a deed under the law of England and Wales and the undertaking of an obligation under the law of Scotland. [*Sec 36C; CA 1989, s 130*]. It also applies to contracts made by foreign companies. [*SI 1994 No 950*].

For cases involving the enforceability of pre-incorporation contracts by and against the agent or promoter, see *Kelner v Baxter (1866) LR 2 CP 174*; *Newborne v Sensolid (Great Britain) Ltd [1954] 1 QB 45*; *Black v Smallwood (1966) 117 CLR 52*; and *Phonogram Ltd v Lane [1981] 3 WLR 736.* As the company has not yet been formed, it cannot be bound by the contract (*Re English & Colonial Produce Co Ltd [1906] 2 ChD 435*) and cannot sue on it (*Natal Land & Colonisation Co Ltd v Pauline Colliery & Development Syndicate Ltd [1904] AC 120*).

16.6   DOCUMENTS

'Document' includes a summons, notice, order, and other legal process, and registers. [*Sec 744*].

16.7   Execution under law of England and Wales

A document may be executed by a company by

(*a*)   the affixing of the common seal (see 54.1 SEALS) (or, in the case of a foreign company, in any manner allowed under the laws of the foreign territory); or

(*b*)   being signed by a person or persons who, under the laws of the territory where the company is incorporated, is or are acting under the authority of the company and being expressed to be executed by the company.

A document is deemed to have been duly executed in favour of a 'purchaser' in good faith for valuable consideration if it purports to be signed as in (*b*) above. *'Purchaser'* includes a lessee, mortgagee or other person acquiring an interest in property.

A document executed, or deemed to have been executed, by a company which makes it clear on its face that it is intended to be a deed has effect, upon delivery, as a deed; and it is presumed, unless contrary intention is proved, to be delivered upon being executed.

[*Sec 36A; CA 1989, s 130; SI 1994 No 950, Reg 5*].

16.8   Execution under law of Scotland

Except where an enactment provides otherwise, a document is signed by a company if it is signed on its behalf by a director, or by the secretary, or by a person authorised to sign the document on its behalf. [*Requirements of Writing (Scotland) Act 1995, 2 Sch 3*].

A company need not have a seal (see 54.1 SEALS). Where it does not, for the purposes of any enactment providing for a document to be executed under common seal (or referring to a document so executed), any document signed by or on behalf of the company in accordance with the provisions of *Requirements of Writing (Scotland) Act 1995* has effect as if executed under common seal of the company. [*Sec 36B; Requirements of Writing (Scotland) Act 1995, 4 Sch 51*].

16.9   Execution of deeds abroad

In England and Wales, a company may, by writing under its common seal, empower any person as its attorney to execute deeds on its behalf in any place elsewhere than the UK. Such power may be general or for any specified matters. Any deed so executed has the same effect as if it were executed under the company's common seal. [*Sec 38; CA 1989, 17 Sch 1; Law Reform (Miscellaneous Provisions) (Scotland) Act 1990, 8 Sch 33; Requirements of Writing (Scotland) Act 1995, 4 Sch 52*].

16.10   Authentication of documents in England and Wales

A document or proceeding requiring authentication by a company is sufficiently authenticated by the signature of a director, secretary or other authorised officer of the company. [*Sec 41; CA 1989, 17 Sch 4*].

16.11 Dealings with Third Parties

16.11 Exclusion of deemed (constructive) notice

With effect from a date to be appointed, a person is not to be taken to have notice of any matter merely because of its being disclosed in any document or any material containing information

- kept by the Registrar of Companies (and thus available for inspection); or

- made available by the company for inspection.

This does not, however, affect the question of whether a person is affected by notice of any matter by reason of a failure to make such enquiries as ought reasonably to be made. [*Sec 711A; CA 1989, s 142*].

Notice of what is on the file is still relevant to someone who has actually read it or ought to have done so.

See also 16.1 above. The provisions of *Sec 35B* mean that there are no circumstances in which a third party is to enquire into the company's memorandum.

When the above provisions come into effect, they will abolish the doctrine of constructive notice in relation to public documents of a company. Until that time, under common law, a person dealing with a company is deemed to have notice of the contents of its registered memorandum and articles (*Ernest v Nicholls (1857) 6 HL Cas 401*) although, if what the company proposes to do is not inconsistent with anything stated in the articles or memorandum, following the rule in *Royal British Bank v Turquand (1856) 6 E & B 327*, that person can assume that the 'indoor management' of the company has been complied with and the transaction is regular and legitimate. The presumption of regularity does not apply where there is notice of an irregularity or the person has been put on inquiry (see *B Liggett (Liverpool) Ltd v Barclays Bank Ltd [1928] 1 KB 48* and *Rolled Steel Products (Holdings) Ltd v British Steel Corporation [1986] Ch 246*) and cannot be relied upon by persons who should know the internal regulations of the company (*Howard v Patent Ivory Manufacturing Co (1888) 38 ChD 156*).

16.12 BILLS OF EXCHANGE AND PROMISSORY NOTES

Any person may issue, accept or endorse a bill of exchange or promissory note on behalf of a company when acting under its authority. [*Sec 37*].

16.13 NOTIFICATION OF CERTAIN EVENTS TO THIRD PARTIES

A company is not entitled to rely against other persons on

- the making of a winding-up order in respect of the company or the appointment of a liquidator in a voluntary winding up,

- any alteration to the company's memorandum or articles,

- any change in the directors, or

- (as regards the service of any documents) any change in the registered office

if

(i) that event had not been officially notified in the *Gazette* at the material time and is not shown by the company to have been known at that time to the person concerned; or

(ii) the material time fell on or before the 15th day (16th day if that day is a 'non-business' day) after notification in the *Gazette* and it is shown that the person concerned was unavoidably prevented from knowing of the event at that time.

'Non-business day' means a Saturday or Sunday, Christmas Day, Good Friday and any other day which is a bank holiday in the part of Great Britain where the company is registered.

[*Secs 42, 711(2)*].

16.14 FRAUDULENT TRADING

If any business of a company is carried on with 'intent to defraud' creditors (of the company or any other person) or for any fraudulent purpose, every person who is knowingly a 'party' is liable to a penalty up to the level in 40.1(*a*) PENALTIES. This applies whether or not the company has been, or is in the course of being, wound up. [*Sec 458, 24 Sch*].

In addition, if the company is in the course of winding up, the court may, on the application of the liquidator, declare that such a person is liable to make such a contribution to the company's assets as it thinks proper. [*IA 1986, s 213*]. Where the person concerned is a director, he may also be disqualified from acting as a director (see 19.13(*c*)(i) and 19.18 DIRECTORS).

There is *'intent to defraud'* where the company continues to carry on business and to incur debts at a time when there is to the knowledge of the directors no reasonable prospect of the creditors ever receiving payment for those debts (*Re William C Leitch Brothers Ltd [1932] 2 Ch 71*). There must be actual dishonesty involving, according to current notions of fair trading among commercial men, real moral blame (*Re Patrick & Lyon Ltd [1933] Ch 786*).

As to who is a *'party'* see *Re Maidstone Buildings Provisions Ltd [1971] 1 WLR 1085*.

Whether the company was carrying on a business was considered in *Re Gerald Cooper Chemicals Ltd [1978] 2 All ER 49* and *Re Sarflax [1979] Ch 592*.

16.15 INFORMATION TO BE GIVEN IN CORRESPONDENCE ETC.

Company name

Every company must have its name mentioned legibly in all

(*a*)   business letters of the company;

(*b*)   notices and other official publications;

(*c*)   bills of exchange, promissory notes, endorsements, cheques and orders for money or goods purporting to be signed by or on behalf of the company; and

(*d*)   bills of parcels, invoices, receipts and letters of credit.

[*Sec 349(1)*].

If a company fails to comply with these provisions it is liable to a fine up to the level in 40.1(*g*) PENALTIES. Where an officer or a person acting on behalf of the company

(i)   issues, or authorises the issue of, any item within (*a*), (*b*) or (*d*) above, or

(ii)   signs, or authorises the signing of, any item within (*c*) above

in which the company's name in not mentioned, he is personally liable to a fine up to the same level and under (ii) is, additionally, personally liable to the holder of the bill of exchange etc. unless it is duly paid by the company. [*Sec 349(2)-(4), 24 Sch*].

Where a company's cheque misspelt the name of the company, a director who signed the cheque was not personally liable under the above provisions. Despite the error, the

16.16 Dealings with Third Parties

company's name was mentioned for the purpose of (*c*) above. Such misspelling was distinguishable from the omission of a whole word, the transposition of words or an unacceptable abbreviation (*Jenice Ltd and others v Dan [1994] BCC 43*).

See also 16.18 below for a company trading under a business name and 36.7 NAMES AND BUSINESS NAMES for display of name outside any place of business.

Charitable companies. A charitable company registered in England and Wales whose name does not include the word 'charity' or 'charitable' must state the fact that it is a charity in all documents within (*a*) – (*d*) above and all conveyances of land executed by it. [*Charities Act 1993, s 68*]. Similar provisions apply to charitable companies registered in Scotland, see 53.7 SCOTLAND. [*CA 1989, s 112(6)-(8)*].

16.16 Directors' names on correspondence etc.

A company must not state the 'name' of any 'director' (otherwise than in the text or as a signatory) on any business letter on which the company's name appears (see 16.15 above) unless it states legibly the name of *every* director (including 'shadow directors', see 19.1 DIRECTORS). This applies to all companies (including those incorporated outside Great Britain with an established place of business within Great Britain) unless registered (or having an established place of business) before 23 November 1916. In other words a company cannot be selective about which directors' names to show – it must show all or none.

In default, every officer in default is liable to a fine for each offence up to the level in 40.1(*g*) PENALTIES. Where a corporation is an officer of the company, any officer of the corporation is deemed to be an officer of the company.

'Name' means Christian name or other forename (initials or a recognised abbreviation are acceptable) and surname. In the case of a peer or individual usually known by a title, the title may be given instead or in addition.

[*Sec 305, 24 Sch; CA 1989, 19 Sch 4*].

16.17 Other particulars in business letters and order forms

Every company must have the following particulars mentioned in legible characters in all its business letters and order forms.

(*a*)   The company's place of registration and registered number. The place of registration should be indicated by one of the following as appropriate.

  — Registered in Cardiff
  — Registered in England and Wales
  — Registered in England
  — Registered in London
  — Registered in Wales
  — Registered in Scotland
  — Registered in Edinburgh

Where the registered number is changed, the old number may still be used for three years from the date of change.

(*b*)   The address of its registered office.

(*c*)   In the case of an investment company (see 23.1 DISTRIBUTIONS) the fact that it is such a company.

(*d*)   In the case of a limited company exempt from using 'limited' in its name (see 29.4 GUARANTEE COMPANIES) the fact that it is a limited company.

Any reference to the amount of the company's share capital must be to paid up share capital (not authorised capital).

A company which contravenes these provisions or an officer or person on its behalf who issues, or authorises the issue of, a business letter or order form in default of the provisions is liable to a fine up to the level in 40.1(g) PENALTIES.

[*Secs 351(1)(2)(5), 705(4), 24 Sch*]. (Companies House Notes for Guidance CHN7).

16.18 Business names

Where a company trades under a business name which is not its corporate name, it must state its corporate name, and an address in Great Britain where documents may be served, on all

- business letters;

- written orders for goods or services to be supplied to the business;

- invoices and receipts issued in the course of the business; and

- written demands for debts arising in the course of business.

These details must also be given immediately in writing to any person who has business dealings with the company and who requests the information.

A person who, without reasonable excuse, contravenes these provisions is guilty of an offence and liable to a fine up to the level in 40.1(*f*) PENALTIES.

[*BNA 1985, ss 4(1)(2)(6), 7*].

Civil remedies for breach. Any legal proceedings brought by a person to enforce a right arising out of a contract made in the course of a business in respect of which, at the time the contract was made, he was in breach of the above provisions, must be dismissed if the defendant (in Scotland, the defender) shows that, because of the plaintiff's (pursuer's) breach,

- he has a claim against the plaintiff (pursuer) arising out of that contract which he has been unable to pursue; or

- he has suffered some financial loss in connection with the contract.

This does not apply if the court is satisfied that it is just and equitable to permit the proceedings to continue and is without prejudice to the right of any person to enforce such rights as he may have against another person in any proceedings brought by that person.

[*BNA 1985, s 5*].

See also 36.12 NAMES AND BUSINESS NAMES for display of name outside any place of business.

16.19 Oversea companies

See 38.17, 38.18 OVERSEA COMPANIES.

17 Debentures and Other Borrowing

Cross-references. See 3.3 ACCOUNTS: GENERAL for the right of debenture-holders to receive copies of the accounts; 23.5 DISTRIBUTIONS for restriction on paying up debentures out of unrealised profit; 47.12 REGISTERS for the register of debenture holders; 50 REGISTRATION OF CHARGES.

17.1 COMPANY'S POWER TO BORROW GENERALLY

A power to borrow for the purposes of the company's business is implied in the case of a *trading* or *commercial* company as long as the power is not expressly prohibited (see, for example, *Re David Payne and Co Ltd [1904] 2 Ch 608*). A general commercial company has power under *Sec 3A* to do all things incidental or conducive to the carrying on of any trade or business by it. A *non-trading* company will generally include in its memorandum an express power to borrow for the purposes of the business.

Restrictions on borrowing may be

● contained in the articles;

● imposed on the company by special resolution of the members; or

● included in the terms of a contract, loan agreement or trust deed.

Where *CA 1948, Table A, Art 79* applies to the company, the total amount borrowed or secured by the directors remaining undischarged (other than temporary bank loans) must not at any time, without the previous sanction of the company in general meeting, exceed the nominal amount of the issued share capital at that time. There is no similar provision or restriction under *Table A* in *SI 1985 No 805*.

Even where there are limitations on a company's power to borrow, although it is the duty of directors to observe those limitations, any further borrowing cannot be called into question on the grounds of lack of capacity and a third party acting in good faith can enforce the company's obligation. [*Secs 35, 35A; CA 1989, s 108*]. See 16.1 and 16.2 DEALINGS WITH THIRD PARTIES.

17.2 Directors' powers to authorise borrowing

A company's articles will usually contain a regulation permitting the directors to exercise the company's powers to borrow money (but only up to any limit in the articles, see *Irvine v Union Bank of Australia (1877) 2 App Cas 366*). Where the *SI 1985 No 805 Table A, Art 70* has been adopted, directors may borrow money under the general delegation of the management of the business to them. Where *CA 1948, Table A, Art 79* applies, the directors may specifically exercise all the powers of the company to (i) borrow money and to mortgage or charge its undertaking, property and uncalled capital; and (ii) issue debentures and other securities whether outright or as security for a debt or other liability of the company to a third party.

17.3 Valid contracts and legality

The contract for any borrowing must be validly entered into on behalf of the company i.e. the signature(s) and execution must be duly authorised by the directors. (The lender is advised to obtain a certified copy of the minute of any resolution passed at a directors' meeting which authorised the signatures etc.)

The borrowing may be void or unenforceable if the contract is illegal or in contravention of anything which already binds the company. See, for example, 19.85 to 19.93 DIRECTORS for loans to directors and 8.18 to 8.21 ACQUISITION OF OWN SHARES for financial assistance for such acquisitions.

17.4 DEBENTURES

A company may raise capital by means of loans evidenced by 'debentures'. *'Debentures'* include debenture stock, bonds and 'other securities' of a company, whether constituting a charge on the assets of the company or not. [*Sec 744*]. The term is thus used to cover a variety of loan transactions depending upon the circumstances and is not confined to a document actually describing itself as a debenture. In *Slavenburg's Bank v Intercontinental Ltd [1980] 1 All ER 955* a debenture was held to be a document which creates or acknowledges an indebtedness. A note by which a company undertook to repay a loan but gave no security was held to be a debenture in *British India Steam Navigation Co v IRS (1881) 7 QBD 165*. The document may need to disclose an agreement to repay the advance (*Topham v Greenside Glazed Fire Brick Co (1887) 37 ChD 281* and *R v Findlater [1939] 1 KB 594*). *'Other securities'* includes a guarantee (*Temperance Loan Fund v Rose [1932] 2 KB 522*; *IRC v Henry Ansbacher & Co [1963] AC 191*).

17.5 Debenture stock and loan stock

Where money is to be borrowed from many lenders, it may be more convenient to issue 'debenture stock' or 'loan stock'.

Debenture stock. The term 'debenture stock' is used for stock which is secured by a mortgage or charge. The lender has a certificate which gives him a right to a certain sum, which is a proportion of a larger sum, and which may be transferred, in whole or in part, subject to the terms of the issue.

The usual charge is a floating charge (i.e. on unascertained assets and property of the company). For cases of debenture stock accompanied by floating charges see, for example, *Robson v Smith [1985] 2 Ch 118* and *George Barker (Transport) Ltd v Eynon [1974] 1 WLR 462*. Where there is a fixed charge on specific assets of the company, once the charge is registered (see 50 REGISTRATION OF CHARGES) the holder has an immediate security over those assets so that the company may not realise them without his consent.

In the event of default by the company, the holder of secured debenture stock has, in addition to the remedies of an unsecured creditor (see below), the power to appoint a receiver or administrator and the power of sale (although in practice these powers will generally be enforced on his behalf by the trustees where there is a trust deed). See, however, 17.11 below for the rights of preferential creditors in the case of a floating charge.

Loan stock. If the stock is unsecured, the term 'loan stock' is generally used. It is usual for the loan stock to be constituted by a trust deed which contains a covenant by the company for the payment of capital (either at a fixed date or on the happening of a certain event e.g. a winding up) and interest. In the event of default by the company, the holder may sue for his money and present a petition for winding up.

17.6 Convertible debentures

A convertible debenture contains an option entitling the holder to convert into ordinary or preference shares of the company at stated times and in stated proportions.

17.7 Irredeemable and perpetual debentures

A condition imposed in debentures, or a deed for securing debentures, is not invalid by reason only that the debentures are thereby made irredeemable or redeemable only on the happening of a contingency (however remote) or on the expiration of a period (however long). This applies to debentures whenever issued and to deeds whenever executed. [*Sec 193*]. This is an exception to the rule that the 'equity of redemption should not be clogged' (see *Samuel Jarrah Timber & Wood Paving Corporation Ltd [1904] AC 323* and *Bradley v Carritt [1903] AC 253* where a condition that the mortgagee should *always* be a broker for the company's products was held to be such a clog).

The company must be authorised by its memorandum to issue irredeemable debentures but where it has issued such stock, the stock is irredeemable only as long as the company is a going concern (*Re Southern Brazilian Rio Grande do Sul Railway Co Ltd [1905] 2 Ch 78*).

17.8 Issue of debentures

The provisions of 42 PROSPECTUSES AND PUBLIC ISSUES apply to the procedure for offering debentures to the public as they apply to shares.

Debentures, unlike shares (see 9.12 ALLOTMENT OF SHARES), can be issued at a discount. There must, however, be no possibility that *shares* could be issued at a discount as a result, e.g. because debentures are, or will be, convertible into shares (see *Moseley v Koffyfontein Mines Ltd [1904] 2 Ch 108*).

Debentures may also be issued (or redeemed) at a premium.

A contract with a company to take up and pay for debentures may be enforced by an order for specific performance. [*Sec 195*]. In *Kuala Palhi Rubber Estates Ltd v Mowbray (1914) 111 LT 1072* it was held that where a company had forfeited debentures it was not in a position to ask for specific performance on calls made to a shareholder and not paid.

17.9 Transfers and issue of certificates

For the provisions relating to the transfers of debentures and the company's duty to issue certificates, see 57 SHARE TRANSFERS ETC.

17.10 Power to re-issue redeemable debentures

Where a company has at any time redeemed debentures previously issued, it has, and is always deemed to have had, power to re-issue the debentures (either by re-issuing the same debentures or issuing other debentures in their place) provided that

- there is no expressed or implied provision to the contrary contained in the company's articles or in any contract entered into by the company; and

- the company has not passed a resolution or done some act showing an intention that the debentures are to be cancelled.

On the re-issue, the person entitled to the debentures has the same priorities (and is deemed always to have had them) as if the debentures had never been redeemed except that, in the case of debentures redeemed before but re-issued after 1 November 1929, the re-issue does not prejudice (and is deemed never to have prejudiced) the right or priority of persons under mortgages and charges created before that date.

The re-issue (whenever made) is to be treated as the issue of a new debenture for stamp duty purposes but not for the purposes of any provision limiting the amount or number of debentures to be issued.

[*Sec 194(1)(2)(4); CC(CP)A 1985, s 13*].

Where a company has deposited any of its debentures to secure advances from time to time on current account or otherwise, the debentures are not deemed to have been redeemed by reason only of the account ceasing to be in debit while the debentures remain deposited. [*Sec 194(3)*].

A person lending money on the security of a re-issued debenture which appears to be duly stamped may give the debenture in evidence in any proceedings to enforce his security unless

(*a*)   he had notice that the debenture was not duly stamped; or

(*b*)   but for his negligence he might have discovered that fact.

Even where (*a*) or (*b*) above applies, the company is liable for the stamp duty and penalty.

[*Sec 194(5)*].

17.11 Payment of debts out of assets subject to a floating charge in England and Wales

Where debentures of a company registered in England and Wales are secured by a charge which, as created, was a floating charge, then if

- possession is taken, by or on behalf of the holders of any of the debentures, of any property comprised in or subject to the charge, and

- the company is not then being wound up,

the company's preferential debts must be paid out of assets coming into the hands of the person taking possession in priority to any claims for principal or interest in respect of the debentures. Payment made must be recouped, as far as possible, out of the assets of the company available for payment of general creditors.

Preferential creditors are

- deductions of PAYE and NIC, and tax from payments to subcontractors in the construction industry, for the twelve months before the date of taking possession (the '*relevant date*');

- VAT, insurance premium tax, air passenger duty and excise duty on beer referable to the six months before the relevant date;

- car tax, general betting duty, bingo duty, pool betting duty, gaming licence duty and lottery duty due twelve months before the relevant date;

- contributions to occupational pension schemes and state scheme premiums; and

- remuneration due to employees for the four months before the relevant date up to a maximum (currently £800), accrued holiday pay in respect of any period of employment before the relevant date and advances to the company to cover remuneration or holiday pay which would otherwise have been preferential.

[*Sec 196; IA 1986, 6 Sch, 13 Sch Part I*].

17.12 Liabilities of trustees of debentures

Subject to below, any provision in the trust deed securing the issue of debentures (or any contract with the holders secured by it) is void if it purports to exempt a trustee from, or indemnify him against, liability for breach of trust where he fails to show the degree of care and diligence required of him as a trustee. This does not, however,

(*a*)   invalidate a release validly given in respect of anything done or omitted to be done by a trustee before the release is given;

283

(*b*) invalidate any provision allowing such a release to be given

  (i) on the agreement of a majority of not less than 75% in value of the debenture-holders present and voting in person or by proxy at a meeting summoned for the purpose; and

  (ii) either with respect to specific acts or omissions or on the trustee dying or ceasing to act;

(*c*) invalidate any provision in force on 1 July 1948 so long as any person then entitled to the benefit of that provision remains a trustee;

(*d*) deprive any person of any exemption or right to be indemnified in respect of anything done or omitted to be done by him while any provision within (*c*) above was in force.

While *any* trustee remains entitled to the benefit of a provision under (*c*) or (*d*) above, the benefit may also be given to

● all the trustees (present and future), or

● any named trustees or proposed trustees

by a resolution passed as under (*b*)(i) above.

[*Sec 192*].

17.13 Debentures to bearer (Scotland)

Debentures to bearer in Scotland are valid and binding according to the terms of their issue despite anything in the statute of the Scots Parliament of 1696, chapter 25. [*Sec 197*].

18   Definitions

Cross-references. See also 2 ACCOUNTS: DEFINITIONS.

18.1   The following definitions are of general relevance.

Accounting reference date. See 1.2 ACCOUNTING REFERENCE DATES AND PERIODS.

Body corporate includes a company incorporated elsewhere than in Great Britain but does not include a corporation sole or a Scottish firm. [*Sec 740*].

Books and papers include accounts, deeds, writings and documents. [*Sec 744*].

Called-up share capital means so much of the capital of a company as equals

- the aggregate amount of calls made on its shares (whether or not these calls have been paid);

- any share capital paid up without being called; and

- any share capital to be paid on a specified future date whether under the articles, the terms of allotment of the relevant shares or any other arrangements for payment of those shares.

[*Sec 737*].

Debenture includes debenture stock, bonds and any other securities of a company, whether constituting a charge on the assets of the company or not. [*Sec 744*]. See 17 DEBENTURES AND OTHER BORROWING.

Director. See 19.1 DIRECTORS.

Document includes a summons, notice, order, and other legal process, and registers. [*Sec 744*].

Dormant company. See 24.1 DORMANT COMPANIES.

Employees' share scheme is a scheme for encouraging or facilitating the holding of shares or debentures in a company by or for the benefit of

- bona fide employees or former employees of the company, its subsidiary or holding company or a subsidiary of the company's holding company; or

- the wives, husbands, widows, widowers or children or step-children under the age of 18 of such employees or former employees.

For these purposes, the revised definition of 'subsidiary company' which applies after 31 October 1990 (see below) does not affect the position of a company which was treated as a subsidiary under the old rules but is not under the revised provisions.

[*Sec 743; CA 1989, 18 Sch 37*].

Equity share capital means a company's issued share capital excluding any part which, neither as respects dividends nor capital, carries a right to participate beyond a specified amount in a distribution. [*Sec 744*].

Holding company. See, by implication, under definition of 'subsidiary' below.

Non-cash assets means any property or interest in property other than cash and foreign currency. A reference to the transfer or acquisition of a non-cash asset includes the creation or extinction of an estate or interest in, or right over, any property and also the discharge of any person's liability, other than a liability for a liquidated sum. [*Sec 739*].

285

18.1 Definitions

Officer in relation to a body corporate includes a director, manager or secretary. [*Sec 744*].

Officer who is in default means any officer of the company or other body who knowingly and wilfully authorises or permits the default, refusal or contravention. [*Sec 730(5); CA 1989, 19 Sch 17*].

Old public company is a company limited by shares or by guarantee and having a share capital which

- existed on 22 December 1980 (or was incorporated after that date but had applied for incorporation before that date);

- was not a private company within *CA 1948, s 28* on that date (or the date of incorporation if later); and

- has not since that date (or the date of incorporation if later) either been re-registered as a public company or become a private company.

[*CC(CP)A 1985, s 1(1)*].

Oversea company. See 38.1 OVERSEA COMPANIES.

Place of business includes a share transfer or share registration office. [*Sec 744*].

Shadow director. See 19.1 DIRECTORS.

Subsidiary

A company is a subsidiary of another company, its 'holding company' in any of the following circumstances.

- If that other company holds a majority of the 'voting rights' in it.

- If that other company is a member of it and has the right to appoint or remove a majority of its board of directors i.e. the right to appoint or remove directors holding a majority of the voting rights at meetings of the board on all, or substantially all, matters. For these purposes, a company is treated as having the right to appoint to a directorship if

    (i) a person's appointment to it follows necessarily from his appointment as director of the company; or

    (ii) the directorship is held by the company itself.

    A right to appoint which is exercisable only with the consent or concurrence of another person is left out of account unless no other person has a right to appoint or, as the case may be, remove in relation to that directorship.

- If that other company is a member of it and controls alone, pursuant to an agreement with other shareholders or members, a majority of the voting rights in it.

- If it is a subsidiary of a company which is itself a subsidiary of that other company.

'Voting rights' are rights conferred on shareholders in respect of their shares (or, in the case of a company not having a share capital, on members) to vote at general meetings of the company on all, or substantially all, matters.

For the above purposes,

    (i) rights which are exercisable only in certain circumstances are taken into account only

- when the circumstances have arisen, and for so long as they continue to obtain, or

- when the circumstances are within the control of the person having the rights

and rights which are normally exercisable but are temporarily incapable of exercise continue to be taken into account;

(ii)   rights held by a person in a fiduciary capacity are treated as not held by him;

(iii)   rights held by a person as nominee for another are treated as held by the other; and rights are regarded as held as nominee if they are exercisable only on that other person's instructions or with his consent or concurrence;

(iv)   rights attached to shares held by way of security are treated as held by the person providing the security where, apart from the right to exercise them to preserve the value of, or realise, the security

- the rights are exercisable only in accordance with his instructions;

- the shares are held in connection with the granting of loans as part of normal business activities and the rights are exercisable only in his interests.

For these purposes, rights are treated as being exercisable in accordance with the instructions of, or in the interests of, a company if they are exercisable in accordance with the instructions of, or in the interests of, any subsidiary or holding company of that company or any subsidiary of a holding company of that company;

(v)   rights are treated as held by a company if they are held by any of its subsidiaries and nothing in (iii) or (iv) above is to be construed as requiring rights held by a company to be treated as held by any of its subsidiaries; and

(vi)   voting rights in a company are reduced by any rights held by the company itself.

References in the provisions of (ii) to (vi) above to rights held by a person include rights falling to be treated as held by him by virtue of any other of those provisions but not rights which by virtue of any such provision are to be treated as not held by him.

[*Secs 736, 736A; CA 1989, s 144*].

Wholly-owned subsidiary. A company is a wholly-owned subsidiary of another company if it has no members except that other company and that other company's wholly-owned subsidiaries or persons acting on behalf of that other company or its wholly-owned subsidiaries. [*Sec 736(2); CA 1989, s 144*].

19 Directors

Cross-references. See 16.2 DEALINGS WITH THIRD PARTIES for the power of directors to bind the company.

The contents of this chapter are as follows.

19.1 DEFINITIONS

Director includes any person occupying the position of a director, by whatever name called. [*Sec 741(1)*]. In *Re Lo-Line Electric Motors Ltd [1988] BCLC 698*, Browne-Wilkinson V-C regarded that subsection as dealing with nomenclature; for example where the company's articles provide that the conduct of the company is committed to 'governors' or 'managers'. However, in *Re Eurostem Maritime Ltd [1987] PCC 190* Mervyn Davies J thought that the words 'occupying the position of director' covered any person who *de facto* acted as a director despite his appointment being invalid or without having been appointed at all.

This is the only definition given in *CA 1985*. In practice, it is necessary to examine the function of the person, the constitution of the company, the terms of any contract between the company and the person etc. to decide whether a person is occupying the position of director.

The *chairman* is a member of the board (either an executive or non-executive director) who is usually elected to that position by the Board. Strictly the chairman is chairman of the board and not chairman of the company.

The *managing director* is an executive director whose duties may be prescribed by the articles and who is presumed to have authority to deal with all areas of the business.

Executive director is a member of the board authorised to carry out certain day-to-day functions including entering into contracts, managing staff and assets, etc.

Non-executive director is a director who sits as part of the decision-making board but without executive authority.

An *alternate director* acts as a proxy for the appointee and has the right to receive all matters sent to the other directors (see 19.23 below).

Shadow director means a person in accordance with whose directions or instructions the directors of the company are 'accustomed to act', except that

(*a*)   a person is not deemed to be a director merely because the directors act on his professional advice; and

(*b*)   a body corporate is not to be treated as a shadow director of any of its subsidiaries merely because the directors of the subsidiary are accustomed to act in accordance with its directions or instructions in relation to

- *Sec 309* (directors' duty to have regard to interests of employees, see 19.26 below);

- *Sec 319* (directors' long term contracts of employment, see 19.60 below);

- *Secs 320-322* (substantial property transactions involving directors, see 19.73 and 19.74 below);

- *Sec 322B* (contracts with sole members who are directors, see 19.71 below); and

- *Secs 330-346* (loans to directors etc., see 19.85 *et seq.* below).

[*Sec 741(2)(3)*].

The acts of any one of several directors in complying with the directions of an outsider cannot make that outsider a shadow director of the company. Such an outsider cannot be a shadow director unless the whole of the board, or at very least a governing majority of it, are accustomed to act on that outsider's directions. '*Accustomed to act*' refers to acts on more than one occasion, over a period of time and as a regular course of conduct (*In Re Unisoft Group Ltd (No 2) [1994] BCC 766*).

19.2 NUMBER OF DIRECTORS

Every private company must have at least one director. Every other company must have at least two directors unless registered before 1 November 1929 when it must have at least one director. [*Sec 282*]. Where *SI 1985 No 805, Table A, Art 64* has been adopted, the number of directors (excluding alternate directors, see 19.23 below) must not be less than two and must not be subject to any maximum. Under *CA 1948, Table A* the number of directors is to be determined by the subscribers to the memorandum [*Art 75*] but the company may by ordinary resolution increase or reduce that number [*Art 94*].

Where a company has only one director, that person cannot also be

- the company secretary; or

- a corporation whose sole director is the company secretary.

[*Sec 283(2)(4)(b)*].

19.3 DIRECTOR ALSO ACTING AS SECRETARY

A director may also act as secretary subject to the restrictions on sole directors under 19.2 above.

Acts done in a dual capacity. A provision requiring or authorising a thing to be done by or to a director *and* the secretary is not satisfied by its being done by or to the same person in the dual capacity as director and as, or in the place of, the secretary. [*Sec 284*].

19.4 Directors

CHANGES IN DIRECTORS

The appointment of a new director or the departure of an existing director must be notified to the Registrar of Companies on the prescribed form (Form 288) within 14 days. A consent to act signed by a new director must be on the form.

In default, the company and every officer in default is liable to a fine up to the level in 40.1(*e*) PENALTIES.

[*Sec 288(2)(4), 24 Sch; SI 1990 No 1766*].

Listed companies. Changes in directors must be notified to the Stock Exchange immediately.

19.5 **Appointment and retirement**

The first directors of a company are appointed at the time of registration of the company (see 49.1 REGISTRATION AND RE-REGISTRATION). Thereafter the appointment and retirement of directors is determined by the company's articles and the following provisions assume that the company has adopted the relevant provisions of *SI 1985 No 805, Table A* or *CA 1948, Table A*.

Appointment by the directors. The directors may appoint a person either

(*a*) to fill a casual vacancy (including a vacancy created by the removal of a director under 19.11 below if not filled at the meeting at which he is removed); or

(*b*) as an additional director provided this does not cause the number of directors to exceed any maximum permitted by the articles.

A director so appointed holds office until the following annual general meeting. If not then re-appointed, he must vacate office at the end of that meeting. Note that directors of listed companies appointed as under (*a*) or (*b*) above *must* present themselves for re-election at the next annual general meeting, see 43.18(*p*) PUBLIC AND LISTED COMPANIES.

[*Sec 303(3); Table A, Art 79*].

Example of minute for the appointment of a director

'It was resolved that pursuant to Article [insert number] of the Articles of Association of the company [insert name of new director] be and hereby is elected a director of the company with immediate effect.'

Appointment by the company. A director may also be appointed by ordinary resolution at a general meeting of the company but no person other than one retiring by rotation (see 19.6 below) can be appointed unless

• he is recommended by the directors; or

• a voting member has given notice to the company of intention to propose him. Notice must be given not less than 14 days nor more than 35 days before the meeting. The person proposed must give notice of willingness to be appointed. [*Arts 76, 78*]. Under *CA 1948, Table A, Art 93* the time limits are 3 and 21 days respectively.

Notice of the proposed appointment must be given to all the persons entitled to notice of the meeting not less than seven days nor more than 28 days before the date of the meeting. The notice must give full particulars of that person which would be required to be included in the register of directors (see 47.3 REGISTERS). [*Art 77*]. Special notice (see 51.8

RESOLUTIONS) is required to appoint somebody instead of a director removed from office under 19.11 below at the meeting at which he is removed.

Where it is proposed to appoint two or more directors at a general meeting of a public company, this cannot be done by a single resolution unless a unanimous resolution has first been passed at the meeting approving such a resolution. A resolution moved in contravention of this provision is void, whether or not objected to at the time, unless it is a resolution altering the company's articles. [*Sec 292*].

19.6   *Retirement by rotation*

The retirement of directors by rotation is determined by the company's articles and the following provisions assume that the company has adopted the relevant provisions of *SI 1985 No 805, Table A* or *CA 1948, Table A*.

All directors must retire from office at the first annual general meeting.

At every subsequent such meeting one-third of the directors subject to retirement by rotation must retire. Where their number is not divisible by three, the nearest number to one-third must retire; but if there is only one director subject to such retirement by rotation, he must retire. The directors to retire are those who have been longest in office since their last appointment. Unless otherwise agreed among themselves, lots are to be drawn where two or more directors were last appointed on the same day. [*Arts 73, 74*].

For the purposes of determining which directors retire by rotation

*   where *Table A, Art 84* applies, the managing director and a director holding any other executive office are ignored;

*   (i)   a director re-appointed following retirement for age reasons (see 19.8 below) or another person appointed in his place, or

    (ii)   a person appointed a director in place of a person removed from office under 19.11 below

    is deemed to have been appointed on the day on which the retiring director under (i) or the director removed under (ii) was last appointed.

[*Secs 293(6), 303(4); Table A, Art 84*].

At the relevant meeting, if the company does not fill the vacancy, the director retiring by rotation, if willing to act, is deemed to have been appointed unless it is resolved not to fill the vacancy or the resolution for re-appointment is lost. [*Art 75*]. If not re-appointed, he retains office until the meeting appoints someone else in his place or, if it does not do so, until the end of the meeting. [*Art 80*].

Examples of resolutions for re-election of directors retiring by rotation

'That [insert name], who was appointed since the last annual general meeting and in accordance with the company's Articles of Association is now retiring, be and hereby is re-elected as a director of the company.'

'That [insert name] who retires by rotation in accordance with the company's Articles of Association, be and hereby is re-elected as a director of the company.'

19.7   *Share qualification*

Where the company's articles require a director to hold a special share qualification (see, for example *CA 1948, Table A, Art 77*), he must obtain it within two months after his appointment or such shorter time as fixed by the articles. For these purposes, share warrants are ignored. If he fails to do so, or if he ceases at any subsequent time to hold his share qualification, the office of director is vacated and he cannot be re-appointed until he has obtained his qualification. Where a person acts as a director in default, he is liable to a fine up to the level in 40.1(*f*) PENALTIES. [*Sec 291, 24 Sch*].

Where the director must hold shares 'in his own right' this does not necessarily mean beneficially but that he is on the register as a member i.e. with a power to vote (*Bainbridge v Smith (1889) 41 ChD 462*).

19.8 *Restrictions on appointments*

Upper age limit. Subject to below, in the case of a public company or a private company which is a subsidiary of a public company (or NI equivalent)

- no person is capable of being appointed a director if at the time of his appointment he is aged 70 or over; and

- a director must vacate his office at the end of the annual general meeting next after he reaches the age of 70 and cannot be automatically re-appointed. If his appointment should have been so terminated, any acts done by him as a director are still valid.

The above provisions do not, however, apply where

- the company in general meeting approves the appointment or re-appointment by ordinary resolution requiring special notice (see 51.8 RESOLUTIONS) and the notice states the age of the person concerned;

- the articles provide otherwise; or

- the person attained the age of 70 before 1 November 1990 and the company only became a subsidiary of a public company by reason of the revised definition of subsidiary in *Sec 736* (see 18.1 DEFINITIONS).

[*Sec 293(1)-(5)(7); CA 1989, 18 Sch 34*].

A person must give notice to a company within these provisions where he is appointed, or to his knowledge is proposed to be appointed, a director of that company at a time when he has obtained the upper age limit. This does not apply in relation to a re-appointment on the termination of a previous appointment but does apply whether or not the provisions are excluded by the company's articles and whether the age limit applicable is 70 or such other age specified by the articles. [*Sec 294(1)-(3)*]. A person who fails to give the required notice of age, or acts as a director under any appointment which is invalid or has terminated by reason of age, is liable to a fine up to the level in 40.1(*f*) PENALTIES. For this purpose, a person who has acted as a director under an appointment which is invalid or has terminated is deemed to have continued to act throughout the period from the invalid appointment or from the date on which the appointment was terminated (as the case may be) until the last day on which he is shown to have acted thereunder. [*Sec 294(4)(5), 24 Sch*].

Lower age limit. There is no minimum age limit in *CA 1985* for a director to be appointed in England and Wales (although a director must be able to consent to his/her appointment). In Scotland, the Registrar of Companies will refuse to accept the appointment of a director who is under the age of 16 years on the grounds that a child below that age does not have the legal capacity to accept a directorship under *Age of Legal Capacity (Scotland) Act 1991*. (Companies House Notes for Guidance CHN1).

Bankruptcy. A person cannot be appointed a director of a company if he is an undischarged bankrupt (unless the court has given him leave to act).

Disqualification order. A person cannot be appointed a director of a company if he has been disqualified by the court from holding a directorship. See 19.12 *et seq.* below.

Certain non-British nationals. Some persons not of British nationality are under restrictions as to the employment they may undertake whilst in the UK. Further information can be obtained from

Home Office Immigration and Nationality Department
Lunar House
Wellesley Road
Croydon CR2 2BY
Tel: 0181 686 0688
(Companies House Notes for Guidance CHNI).

19.9 *Validity of acts of directors*

The acts of a director are valid despite any defect subsequently discovered in his appointment or qualification. [*Sec 285*]. See *Morris v Kanssen [1946] AC 459* where a distinction is drawn between a defective appointment and no appointment at all.

19.10 *Appointment of managing directors etc.*

The directors may, as they think fit, appoint one or more of their number as managing director or as any other executive officer but such office must terminate if that person ceases to be a director. [*Table A, Art 84*].

19.11 **Removal of directors**

A company may remove a director by ordinary resolution requiring special notice (see 51.8 RESOLUTIONS) despite anything in its articles or any other agreement between it and the director. (Special notice is also required to appoint somebody at the same meeting instead of the director so removed.) [*Sec 303(1)(2)*]. This does not, however, authorise the removal of a director of a private company holding office for life on 18 July 1945. [*CC(CP)A 1985, s 14*]. Although, therefore, any provision in the articles requiring a special or extraordinary resolution to remove a director is overridden by *Sec 303* above, a company is not prevented from 'weighting' votes attached to shares even if the effect is to nullify that section. See, for example, *Bushell v Faith [1970] AC 1099* where the articles stated that, in the event of a resolution to remove a director, any shares held by that director carried three votes per share. This effectively increased each director's share of the votes on such a resolution from one-third to 60% so that a director could not be removed by an ordinary resolution supported by the other directors.

On receipt of notice of an intended resolution to remove a director, the company must immediately send a copy of the notice to the director who is entitled to be heard on the resolution at the meeting (whether or not he is a member of the company). He may also make written representations of reasonable length to the company and, unless received too late, the company must send a copy to every member to whom notice of the meeting is sent. Where it is received too late or not sent through the default of the company, the director may require the representations to be read out at the meeting (without affecting his right to be heard orally). The statement need not be sent out or read at the meeting if, on application by the company or any aggrieved party, the court is satisfied that the rights conferred by these provisions are being abused to secure needless publicity for defamatory matter. The court may order the company's costs on the application to be paid, in whole or in part, by the director even if he is not a party to the application. [*Sec 304*].

19.12   Directors

See also 19.22 below for the possible removal of a director under the provisions of the company's articles where he is bankrupt, suffering mental disorder or absent without permission for over six months.

19.12 DISQUALIFICATION OF DIRECTORS

A court may make a disqualification order against a person if there is established one of the grounds in 19.13 to 19.18 below. The effect of an order being made is that, for the period specified in the order, that person must not, without the leave of the court,

- be a director, liquidator or administrator of a company;

- be a receiver or manager of a company's property; or

- in any way, directly or indirectly, be concerned or take part in the promotion, formation or management of a company. In *R v Campbell [1984] BCLC 83* the Court of Appeal held that a person subject to a disqualification order who, as a management consultant, advised on the financial management and restructuring of a company, could be (and, on the facts of the case, was) 'concerned . . . in the management' of that company, and thereby in breach of the order.

Where a disqualification order is made against a person who is already subject to such an order, the periods specified in the orders run concurrently.

[CDDA 1986, s 1(1)(3)].

Where a court contemplates making a compensation order against a director, it must be careful not to reduce or inhibit his means to pay such an order. See *R v Holmes [1991] BCC 394* where the Court of Appeal held that a compensation order made against a director in the Crown Court was inconsistent with the disqualification order also made since the latter order would seriously diminish his ability to earn the means with which to pay the compensation.

In addition to the above, a person is automatically disqualified, without a disqualification order, in the circumstances in 19.19 below and may be disqualified under the provisions of the company's articles where 19.22 below applies.

Building societies and friendly societies. The provisions apply to a building society or an incorporated friendly society (with effect from 1 February 1993) as they apply to a company. References to a company, or to a director or officer of a company, are accordingly to be construed as including references (as the case may be) to

- a building society, or to a director or officer of it, within the meaning of *Building Societies Act 1986*; or

- an incorporated friendly society, or a member of the committee of management or officer of it, within the meaning of *Friendly Societies Act 1992*.

The term 'shadow director' is applicable in the case of a building society but not in the case of an incorporated friendly society.

[CDDA 1986, ss 22A, 22B; CA 1989, s 211; Friendly Societies Act 1992, 21 Sch 8].

19.13   Disqualification for general misconduct

A court may make a disqualification order against a person in the following circumstances.

(*a*)   *He is convicted of an indictable offence* (whether on indictment or summarily) in connection with promotion, formation, management, liquidation or striking off of

294

a company, or with the receivership or management of a company's property. The maximum period of disqualification is five years where the disqualification order is made by a court of summary jurisdiction and 15 years in any other case. For the wide interpretation given to 'in connection with the management of the company' see *R v Goodman [1992] BCC 625, [1994] 1 BCLC 349.*

An order under this provision may be made by

(i)   any court having jurisdiction to wind up the company involved;

(ii)   the court by or before which the person is convicted of the offence; or

(iii)   in the case of a summary conviction in England and Wales, any other magistrates' court acting for the same petty sessions area.

[*CDDA 1986, s 2; Deregulation and Contracting Out Act 1994, 11 Sch 6*].

(*b*)   He has been *'persistently in default'* in relation to provisions of the companies *legislation* requiring the filing of any return, account or other document with, or the giving of notice of any matter to, the Registrar of Companies.

'Persistently in default' may (without prejudice to its proof in any other matter) be conclusively proved by showing that, in the five years ending with the date of the application to the court, he has been 'adjudged guilty' (whether or not on the same occasion) of three or more defaults in relation to such provisions. See also *Re Arctic Engineering Ltd and Others (No 2) [1986] BCLC 253.*

A person is treated as being *'adjudged guilty'* of a default in relation to any such provision if he is convicted of an offence for contravention or failure to comply with that provision or a default order is made against him under

(i)   *Sec 242(4)* (order requiring delivery of company's accounts, see 3.7 ACCOUNTS: GENERAL under the heading *Penalties*);

(ii)   *Sec 245B* (order requiring preparation of revised accounts, see 3.11 ACCOUNTS: GENERAL);

(iii)   *Sec 713* (enforcement by the Registrar of Companies of company's duty to make returns);

(iv)   *IA 1986, s 41* (enforcement of receiver's or manager's duty to make returns); or

(v)   *IA 1986, s 170* (corresponding provision for liquidator in winding up).

The maximum period of disqualification is five years.

An order may be made by any court having jurisdiction to wind up any of the companies involved.

[*CDDA 1986, s 3*].

(*c*)   *In the course of the winding up of a company* it appears that he has

(i)   been guilty of an offence for which he is liable (whether he has been convicted or not) under *Sec 458* (fraudulent trading, see 16.14 DEALINGS WITH THIRD PARTIES); or

(ii)   otherwise been guilty, while an officer or liquidator of the company or receiver or manager of its property, of any fraud in relation to the company or any breach of duty.

The maximum period of disqualification is 15 years.

An order may be made by any court having jurisdiction to wind up any of the companies involved.

19.14 Directors

[*CDDA 1986, s 4*].

(*d*)   He is convicted of a '*summary offence*' in consequence of a contravention of one of the provisions of the companies legislation requiring the filing of any return, account or other document with, or the giving of any notice to, the Registrar of Companies where

    (i)   during the five years ending with the date of the conviction, he has been convicted (whether on indictment or summarily) of a similar offence or offences or has had made against him one or more default orders under the provisions listed in (*b*)(i)–(v) above; and

    (ii)   the number of convictions and/or default orders made against him (including the current summary conviction) totals three or more.

The maximum period of disqualification is five years.

[*CDDA 1986, s 5*].

An application (to a court with jurisdiction to wind up companies) for the making against any person of a disqualification order under (*a*) to (*d*) above may be made by the Secretary of State; the official receiver; the liquidator; or any past or present member or creditor of any company in relation to which that person has committed, or is alleged to have committed, an offence or other default. [*CDDA 1986, s 16(2)*].

19.14 Disqualification for unfitness

There are both mandatory grounds (19.15 below) and discretionary grounds (19.16 below) whereby a court can make a disqualification order against a person as being unfit to act as a director. In either case the court must have regard to the provisions of 19.17 below in determining his unfitness.

19.15 *Mandatory grounds*

A court *must* make a disqualification order against a person if it is satisfied that

(*a*)   he is or has been a director (or shadow director, see 19.1 above) of a company which has at any time become insolvent (whether while he was a director or subsequently); and

(*b*)   his conduct as a director of that company (whether taken alone or taken together with his conduct as a director of any other company or companies) makes him unfit to be concerned in the management of a company. References to a person's conduct as a director of any company include, where that company has become insolvent, that person's conduct in relation to the insolvency.

A person may be included under (*a*) above where he has acted as a director even though not validly appointed or not appointed at all. To be disqualified as a *de facto* director, there must be clear evidence that either he had been the sole person directing the affairs of the company or, if there were others who were true directors, he acted on an equal footing with them in directing the affairs of the company. Where it is unclear whether his actions are referable to an assumed directorship or some other capacity (e.g. shareholder or consultant) the person must be given the benefit of doubt (*Re Richborough Furniture Ltd [1996] 1 BCLC 507*).

The minimum period of disqualification is two years and the maximum is 15 years.

A company becomes insolvent for these purposes if it goes into liquidation at a time when its assets are insufficient for the payment of its debts and other liabilities and the expenses of winding up; *or* an administration order is made in relation to the company; *or* an administrative receiver of the company is appointed.

An application for the making of a disqualification order against any person may be made by the Secretary of State or, if he so directs, the official receiver in the case of a director or former director of a company which is being wound up by the court in England and Wales. Except with the leave of the court, such an application cannot be made more than two years from the date on which the company became insolvent. In deciding whether an application can be made out of time, the court will consider the length of, and reasons for, the delay, the strength of the case against the director and the degree of prejudice caused to the director by the delay (*Re Probe Data Systems Ltd (No 3) [1992] BCC 110*). See also, *inter alia, Re Lo-Line Electric Motors Ltd [1988] BCLC 698, [1988] 2 All ER 692* and *Re Crestjoy Products Ltd [1990] BCLC 677*.

If it appears, as the case may be, to the official receiver, liquidator, administrator or administrative receiver that the conditions for making an order under these provisions are satisfied, he must report that fact to the Secretary of State. See *Insolvent Companies (Reports on Conduct of Directors) Rules 1996 (SI 1996 No 1909)* and the *Insolvent Companies (Reports on Conduct of Directors) (Scotland) Rules 1996 (SI 1996 No 1910)* for the form and content of such a report.

An order may be made

- in the case of a director or former director of a company which is being wound up by the court, by that court;

- in the case of a director or former director of a company which is being wound up voluntarily, by any court having jurisdiction to wind up the company;

- in the case of any director or former director of a company in relation to which an administration order is in force, by the court which made that order; and

- in any other case, by the High Court or, in Scotland, the Court of Sessions.

[*CDDA 1986, ss 6, 7*].

As to the detailed procedure in England and Wales for applications for disqualification orders under these provisions, see the *Insolvent Companies (Disqualification of Unfit Directors) Proceedings Rules 1987 (SI 1987 No 2023)* (as amended). See also the Practice Direction issued by Sir Richard Scott V-C on 14 December 1995 (set out in *[1996] 1 All ER 445*). For the procedure in Scotland, see the *Act of Sederunt (Company Directors Disqualification) 1986 (SI 1986 No 2296)* (sheriff court) and the *Act of Sederunt (Rules of Court Amendment No 11) (Companies) 1986 (SI 1986 No 2298)* (Court of Sessions).

19.16 *Discretionary ground*

If it appears to the Secretary of State from

- a report made by inspectors under *Sec 437* (see 31.3 INVESTIGATIONS) or *FSA 1986, s 94* or *FSA 1986, s 177* (see 30.6 INSIDER DEALING), or

- from information or documents obtained under *Sec 447* or *448* (see 31.11 INVESTIGATIONS), *FSA 1986, s 105, Criminal Justice Act 1987, s 2, Criminal Law (Consolidation) (Scotland) Act 1995, s 28* or *CA 1989, s 83*

that it is expedient in the public interest for a disqualification order to be made against any director, former director or shadow director of the company, he may apply to the High Court (in Scotland, the Court of Sessions) for such an order to be made against that person. The court may make a disqualification order where it is satisfied that the person's conduct in relation to the company makes him unfit to be concerned in the management of the company.

The maximum period of disqualification is 15 years.

[*CDDA 1986, s 8; FSA 1986, s 198; Criminal Justice (Scotland) Act 1987, s 55; Criminal Justice Act 1988, s 145; CA 1989, s 79; Criminal Procedures (Consequential Provisions) (Scotland) Act 1995, 4 Sch 62*].

As to the detailed procedure in England and Wales for applications for disqualification orders under these provisions, see the *Insolvent Companies (Disqualification of Unfit Directors) Proceedings Rules 1987 (SI 1987 No 2023)* (as amended). For the procedure in Scotland, see the *Act of Sederunt (Company Directors Disqualification) 1986 (SI 1986 No 2296)* (sheriff court) and the *Act of Sederunt (Rules of Court Amendment No 11) (Companies) 1986 (SI 1986 No 2298)* (Court of Sessions).

19.17 Matters for determining unfitness of directors

In determining whether a person's conduct as a director or shadow director of any particular company or companies makes him unfit to be concerned in the management of a company, the court must have regard 'in particular' to the following matters.

Matters applicable in all cases

- Any misfeasance or breach of any fiduciary or other duty by the director in relation to the company.

- Any misapplication or retention by the director of, or any conduct by the director giving rise to an obligation to account for, any money or other property of the company.

- The extent of the director's responsibility for the company entering into any transaction liable to be set aside under *IA 1986, Part XVI* (provisions against debt avoidance).

- The extent of the director's responsibility for any failure by the company to comply with any of the requirements of:

  Sec 221 (companies to keep accounting records, see 45.1 RECORDS);

  Sec 222 (where and for how long records to be kept, see 45.2 RECORDS);

  Sec 288 (register of directors and secretaries, see 47.3 REGISTERS);

  Sec 352 (obligation to keep and enter up register of members, see 47.4 REGISTERS);

  Sec 353 (location of register of members, see 47.5 REGISTERS);

  Sec 363 (duty of company to make annual return, see 10.1 ANNUAL RETURNS); or

  Secs 399 and *415* (company's duty to register the charges it creates, see 50.1 and 50.14 REGISTRATION OF CHARGES).

- The extent of the director's responsibility for any failure by the directors of the company to comply with

(i)   *Sec 226* or *227* (duty to prepare annual accounts, see 5.2 ACCOUNTS: INDIVIDUAL COMPANIES and 4.8 ACCOUNTS: GROUPS OF COMPANIES respectively); or

(ii)   *Sec 233* (approval and signature of accounts, see 3.2 ACCOUNTS: GENERAL).

In relation to a person who is a director of an investment company with variable capital, references to provisions of *CA 1985* above are taken to be references to the corresponding provisions of the *Open-ended Investment Companies (Investment Companies with Variable Capital) Regulations 1996 (SI 1996 No 2827)*.

Matters applicable where company has become insolvent

- The extent of the director's responsibility for the causes of the company becoming insolvent.

- The extent of the director's responsibility for any failure by the company to supply goods or services which have been paid for (in whole or part).

- The extent of the director's responsibility for the company entering into any transaction or giving any preference liable to be set aside under *Sec 127* (see 14.5 CLASS RIGHTS) or *IA 1986, ss 238-240* or challenged under *IA 1986, ss 242, 243* or under any rule of law in Scotland.

- The extent of the director's responsibility for any failure by the directors of the company to comply with *IA 1986, s 98* (duty to call creditors' meeting in creditors' voluntary winding up).

- Any failure by the director to comply with any obligation imposed on him by or under

IA 1986, s 22 (company's statement of affairs in administration);

IA 1986, s 47 (statement of affairs to administrative receiver);

IA 1986, s 66 (statement of affairs in Scottish receivership);

IA 1986, s 99 (directors' duty to attend meetings; statement of affairs in creditors' voluntary winding up);

IA 1986, s 131 (statement of affairs in winding up by court);

IA 1986, s 234 (duty of anyone with company property to deliver it up); or

IA 1986, s 235 (duty to co-operate with the liquidator, etc.).

[*CDDA 1986, s 9, 1 Sch; CA 1989, s 139, 10 Sch 35; SI 1996 No 2827, 8 Sch 10*].

In considering the question of unfitness, the court is concerned with the director's conduct generally and is not restricted in making a finding of unfitness to cases where the director could be disqualified on some other ground. The words *'in particular'* suggest that the court is not confined to looking at the matters set out in the legislation (*Re Bath Glass Ltd [1988] BCLC 329*).

The court is required to have regard to a person's conduct as a director regardless of whether he has been validly appointed or is merely assuming to act as a director. The conduct relevant to his future suitability to act depends on his past record irrespective of the circumstances in which he came to act as a director (*Re Lo-Line Electric Motors Ltd [1988] 2 All ER 692*).

19.18 Directors

19.18 Disqualification for participation in wrongful trading

Where the court makes a declaration under *IA 1986, s 213* (fraudulent trading) or *IA 1986, s 214* (wrongful trading) that a person is liable to contribute to a company's assets, then the court may also make a disqualification order against the person to whom the declaration relates. This applies whether or not an application for such an order is made by any person.

The maximum period of disqualification is 15 years.

[*CDDA 1986, s 10*].

19.19 Automatic disqualification for bankruptcy etc.

A person may not act as a director of, or directly or indirectly take part in or be concerned in the promotion, formation or management of, a company where

(*a*) he is an undischarged bankrupt and the court by which he was adjudged bankrupt (or, in Scotland, by which sequestration of his estates was awarded) has not given leave for him so to act etc. See *R v Brockley [1994] BCC 131*. In England and Wales, the court must not give leave unless notice of intention to apply for it has been served on the official receiver, who has a duty to attend the hearing and oppose the application if he considers that it is contrary to the public interest that the application should be granted. [*CDDA 1986, s 11*]; or

(*b*) he fails to make any payment which he is required to make by virtue of an administration order under *County Courts Act 1984, Part VI* and the court which is administering his estate makes an order revoking the administration order and directing that (*inter alia*) he shall not so act etc. without leave of the court for a specified period not exceeding two years. [*CDDA 1986, s 12*].

19.20 *Consequences of contravention*

Criminal penalties. A person who acts in contravention of a disqualification order under 19.13 to 19.18 above or the provisions of 19.19 above is guilty of an offence and liable, on conviction, to a penalty up to the level in 40.1(*b*) PENALTIES. [*CDDA 1986, s 13*].

Where a body corporate is guilty of an offence of acting in contravention of a disqualification order, a director, manager, secretary, or other similar official of the body corporate is also guilty of the offence if it is proved that the offence occurred with the consent or connivance of, or was attributable to any neglect on the part of, that person. [*CDDA 1986, s 14(1)*]. Similarly, where the affairs of a body corporate are managed by its members, a member will be liable for his acts and defaults in connection with his functions of management as if he were a director of the body corporate. [*CDDA 1986, s 14(2)*].

Personal liability. Where a person, in contravention of a disqualification order or of 19.19(*a*) above, is a director of, or is concerned or takes part in the management of, a company, he is personally responsible for such debts and other liabilities of the company as are incurred while he is so involved.

In addition, where a person (A) involved in the management of a company acts (or is willing to act) on instructions given, without leave of the court, by another person (B) whom A knows to be a disqualified person or undischarged bankrupt, then A is personally responsible for such debts and other liabilities of the company as are incurred while he is acting (or willing to act) on such instructions. For these purposes, where A has at any time acted on instructions given, without the leave of the court, by B, and A knew at that time that B was a disqualified person or undischarged bankrupt, then A is presumed to have been willing to act on B's instructions at any time thereafter, unless the contrary is shown.

Where a person is personally responsible, he is jointly and severally liable for the debts referred to above with

- the company; and

- any other person who is so liable, whether under these provisions or otherwise.

[*CDDA 1986, s 15*].

19.21 *Supplementary provisions*

Applications. See *CDDA 1986, s 16* for provisions relating to the application for disqualification orders and *CDDA 1986, s 17* for provisions relating to applications for leave under a disqualification order.

Register of orders. The Secretary of State is required to keep a register of disqualification orders and can require court officers to furnish him with certain particulars. See *CDDA 1986, s 18* and *The Companies (Disqualification Orders) Regulations 1986 (SI 1986 No 2067; SI 1995 No 1509)*. The register is open to inspection at

- Companies House, Crown Way, Cardiff CF4 3UZ;

- The Insolvency Service, Atlantic House, Holborn Viaduct, London EC1N 2HD;

- London Search Room, Companies House, 55/71 City Road, London EC1Y 1BB; and

- Companies House, 100/102 George Street, Edinburgh EH2 3DJ.

19.22 **Disqualification under the company's articles**

Generally, a company's articles will contain provisions requiring a director to vacate office on grounds additional to those set out in 19.13 to 19.19 above. *SI 1985 No 805, Table A, Art 81* sets out the following additional grounds.

- He becomes bankrupt or makes any arrangement or composition with his creditors generally.

- He is, or may be, suffering from mental disorder and either

    (i) he is admitted to hospital in pursuance of an application for admission for treatment under *Mental Health Act 1983* or, in Scotland, an application for admission under the *Mental Health (Scotland) Act 1984*; or

    (ii) an order is made by a court having jurisdiction (whether in the UK or elsewhere) in matters concerning mental disorder for his detention or for the appointment of a receiver, *curator bonis* or other person to exercise powers with respect to his property or affairs.

- He is absent from directors' meetings for more than six consecutive months without permission of the board.

19.23 Directors

19.23 ALTERNATE DIRECTORS

A company may make provision under its articles for directors to appoint alternates to act on their behalf. The following provisions apply to a company where the appropriate articles of *SI 1985 No 805, Table A* have been adopted.

Appointment. Any director (other than an alternate director) may appoint as his alternate a director or any other person willing to act who is approved by resolution of the directors. [*Art 65*]. The appointment must be by written notice signed by the appointor or in any other manner approved by the directors. [*Art 68*].

Powers and duties. An alternate director is entitled to

- receive notice of all meetings of directors and committees thereof of which his appointor is a member (unless the alternate is absent from the UK);

- attend and vote at any such meeting at which his appointor is not personally present; and

- generally perform all functions of his appointor as a director in his absence.

He is not entitled to receive any remuneration for his services as an alternate. [*Art 66*].

Unless the articles provide otherwise, an alternate director is deemed for all purposes to be a director. He is alone responsible for all his own acts and defaults and is not deemed to be the agent for his appointor. [*Art 69*].

Cessation of appointment. The alternate director may be removed from office at any time by his appointor. [*Art 65*]. The removal must be by written notice signed by the appointor or in any manner approved by the directors. [*Art 68*]. In any case, he ceases to hold office if his appointor ceases to be a director but where a director retires by rotation (or otherwise) and is re-appointed at the same meeting, any appointment of an alternate director made by him in force before his retirement continues after his re-appointment. [*Art 67*].

19.24 POWERS OF DIRECTORS

Subject to any provision to the contrary in *CA 1985* or the company's memorandum or articles, the directors are responsible for the management of the company and they may exercise all the powers of the company. Although the memorandum or articles may be changed to restrict this power, no alteration can invalidate any prior act of the directors which would have been valid but for the alteration. Any special power given to the directors by the articles does not limit this overall power.

The directors may regulate their proceedings as they think fit. See 33.14 MEETINGS for directors' meetings. Any such meeting at which a quorum is present may exercise all powers exercisable by the directors. [*SI 1985 No 805, Table A, Art 70*]. Where such an article has been adopted by the company, the shareholders cannot, by ordinary resolution, give directions to the board or overrule its decision without first altering the articles (*Automatic Self-Cleansing Filter Syndicate Co Ltd v Cunninghame [1906] 2 Ch 34* and *John Shaw & Sons (Salford) Ltd v Shaw [1935] 2 KB 113*).

Delegation of powers. Where *SI 1985 No 805, Table A, Art 72* has been adopted, the directors may delegate

(*a*)   any of their powers to a committee consisting of one or more directors; and

(*b*)   such powers as they consider desirable to be exercised by him to a managing director or any other executive director.

Such delegation may be subject to any conditions the directors impose and may be revoked or altered. Where (*a*) applies, if the committee has two or more members it is subject to the same articles as govern directors' meetings generally. See 33.14 MEET-INGS.

Assignment of office. A director or manager of a company may be empowered, by a provision in the articles or an agreement, to assign his office to another person. If so, any assignment in pursuance of that provision must be approved by a special resolution of the company; otherwise the assignment has no effect despite anything to the contrary in the provision. [*Sec 308*].

Appointment of agents. Where *SI 1985 No 805, Table A, Art 71* has been adopted, the directors may, by power of attorney or otherwise, appoint any person to be the agent of the company for such purposes and on such conditions as they determine. The agent may also be given authority to delegate all or any of his powers.

19.25 DIRECTOR'S DUTIES

Despite *CDDA 1986, 1 Sch* (matters for determining unfitness of directors, see 19.17 above), the law does not present a coherent code of conduct for directors. Directors' duties can be considered under the following broad headings although conduct may be impugned under more than one of the categories.

- Fiduciary duties (see 19.26 to 19.31 below).

- Statutory duties (see 19.32 below).

- Duties of skill and care (see 19.33 below).

Remedies for breach of duty are considered in 19.34 below. Relief from liability is considered in 19.35 below.

Additionally, directors have a considerable number of duties under *CA 1985* relating to the internal management of the company (see 19.36 below) and duties to third parties (see 19.37 below).

Directors' duties are owed by each director individually. But the duty to act in the company's interests is a requirement that directors make corporate decisions properly and this typically affects directors as a body. Where several directors are liable for a default they are jointly and severally liable. See, for example, *Re Englefield Colliery Co (1878) 8 ChD 388.*

To whom are the duties owed? Orthodoxy has it that directors' duties are owed to the company and not to its shareholders. (*Percival v Wright [1902] 2 Ch 421*) but see 19.37 below. The practical point of this analysis is that a minority shareholder can only exceptionally sue to enforce a company's rights (*Foss v Harbottle (1843) 2 Hare 461*, see 34.5 MEMBERS). It also means that the directors of a company do not owe any duties to a subsidiary, at least if the subsidiary has different and independent directors (*Lindgren v L & P Estates Limited [1968] Ch 572*).

Alternate directors. Where a director has appointed an alternate director to act for him in his absence, that alternate director is a director for 'all purposes' (see 19.23 above). The alternate will be subject to all the duties, both statutory and common law, while he retains his appointment.

19.26 Fiduciary duties

The relationship of a director to his company is sometimes described as that of trustee, particularly in the older cases. But unlike a trustee in the strict sense, a director will rarely have the property of the company vested in him as legal owner. A director, too, will be expected to take commercial risks on behalf of the company which would be a breach of duty in a trustee. In these and other respects a director is not strictly a trustee. It is better to describe his relationship with the company as that of a fiduciary.

The duties and disabilities imposed by equity on directors as fiduciaries are described in numerous different ways but fall into three main areas.

(*a*)   A director must not put himself in a position where the interests of the company conflict with his personal interest or his duty to a third party.

It seems that a fiduciary will not commit a breach of any of the duties arising out of this rule merely by getting into a position of potential conflict, but that if he is in such a position, he is obliged by it to prefer the interest of the beneficiary (*Swain v Law Society [1981] 3 All ER 797* at *813*). Thus, a director of a company is not necessarily prevented from becoming a director of another company even where the companies compete (*London and Mashonaland Exploration Co v New Mashonaland Exploration Co [1891] WN 165*) but he may then find himself with conflicting duties to two separate beneficiaries, each of whom can insist on a claim to be preferred. Executive directors with service contracts are anyway precluded from competing (*Hivac Ltd v Park Royal Scientific Instruments Ltd [1946] Ch 169*).

A mere intention by a director to set up in competition with the company after he resigns his directorship does not create an interest which conflicts with his fiduciary duty. He is not under a duty to disclose his intention, nor is he prevented from taking preliminary steps to forward his intention so long as he does not engage in any actual competition while a director nor divert any maturing business opportunity from the company to himself (*Balston Ltd v Headline Filters Ltd [1990] FSR 385*).

(*b*)   A director must not make a profit out of his position as director unless the company permits him to do so. Such permission will not be inferred, and the onus is on the director to obtain it (*British Racing Drivers' Club Ltd v Hextall Erskine [1996] 3 All ER 667*).

(*c*)   Directors must act *bona fide* in what they consider is in the interests of the company as a whole, and not for any collateral purpose (*Re Smith & Fawcett Ltd [1942] Ch 304*).

The court will consider the substantial or principal purpose for which the directors exercised their powers and whether that was a proper purpose. However, the court is not concerned with the merits of the decision from a commercial point of view. See *Howard Smith Ltd v Ampol Petroleum Ltd [1974] AC 821.*

Shareholders' interests. The interests of the company as such need not be the same as those of its shareholders. On the other hand, it could, in some circumstances, amount to a failure to act in the company's interests for directors to accumulate profits for the benefit of the company as a corporate body if that meant failing to pay shareholders' dividends (*Re a Company (No 00370 of 1987), ex parte Glossop [1988] BCLC 570*). See also *Greenhalgh v Arderne Cinemas [1951] Ch 286* at *291* where Lord Evershed MR stated that the phrase 'the company as a whole' did not mean the company as a commercial entity distinct from the corporators but the corporators as a general body.

Directors may, therefore, have to balance fairly the different interests of the company as a going concern, of different classes of present shareholders, and those of present and future shareholders.

Creditors' interests. A company also owes a duty to its creditors, present and future to keep its property inviolate and available for the repayment of its debts. In this respect, a duty is owed by the directors to the company and to the creditors of the company to ensure that the affairs of the company are properly administered and that its property is not dissipated to the prejudice of the creditors (*Winkworth v Edward Baron Development Co Ltd [1987] BCLC 193*). Once a company is insolvent or in danger of becoming so, the interests of the creditors as a general body take the place of the interests of the 'corporators as a general body'. Further, as a consequence of *IA 1986, s 214* (see 19.46 below), directors will, if insolvency looms, be well advised to put creditors' interests (which include the interests of employees) before shareholders' interests to avoid personal liability for wrongful trading.

Employees' interests. The directors (including shadow directors) must have regard to the interests of the company's employees in general. The duty imposed by this provision on the directors is owed by them to the company (and the company alone) and is enforceable in the same way as any other fiduciary duty owed to a company by its directors. [*Sec 309*].

The directors may make provision for the benefit of the company's employees and former employees (or those of any of its subsidiaries) in connection with the cessation, or transfer to any person, of the whole or part of the undertaking of the company (or that subsidiary), even if the exercise of the power is not in the best interests of the company. The power must be exercised in compliance with any requirements of the memorandum or articles and sanctioned by ordinary resolution of the company unless the memorandum or articles allow or require otherwise (e.g. resolution of the directors or company resolution requiring more than a simple majority). Any payments made before the commencement of any winding up of the company may be made out of the profits available for dividend. [*Sec 719*]. For these purposes, the revised definition of 'subsidiary company' which applies after 31 October 1990 (see 18.1 DEFINITIONS) does not affect the position of a company which was treated as a subsidiary under the old rules but is not under the revised provisions. [*CA 1989, 18 Sch 36*].

Other interests (including own). It is permissible for directors to promote their own interests (*Hirsche v Sims [1894] AC 654*) or those of anybody else (*Parke v Daily News [1962] Ch 927*), where to do so is in the company's interest. This permits the promoting of employees' interests (see also above) or those of a group of companies of which the directors' is one (*Charterbridge Corporation v Lloyds Bank [1970] Ch 62*).

Customers and the general public. Strictly from the point of view of company law, directors should not consider the interests of customers or the general public, except insofar as consideration of those interests advance the interests of the company. But there are a number of areas of legislation, e.g Health & Safety at Work, where duties are imposed on the company and its directors, the performance of which may not be in the direct economic interests of the company or of shareholders present or future.

19.27 *Intervention of court to invalidate directors' decisions*

The court will not normally interfere with the acts or decisions of directors save for one of the following reasons:

- They have not acted *bona fide* (i.e. honestly and in good faith). Dishonesty or bad faith is not an independent requirement of directors' liability or of the invalidity of their actions. In *Re W & M Roith Ltd [1967] 1 WLR 432* the director acted in good faith on the advice of a solicitor, but his action was invalidated nonetheless.

19.27 Directors

- They have caused the company to act *ultra vires* (in the sense of beyond its corporate capacity) or illegally. To do so is a misfeasance and directors will be personally liable for any resulting loss to the company.

- They have exceeded the powers delegated to them, although acting within the powers of the company. In such a case, they may have acted outside the powers conferred on the directors by the articles of association or one or more individual directors may have exceeded the authority to act conferred on him or them by a resolution of the board (see 19.24 above). This too is a misfeasance for which the directors so acting will be personally responsible.

- They have acted *intra vires* (in the sense of within the corporate capacity of the company and also within the powers delegated to them) but in breach of the so-called *Wednesbury* principles. These derive from the decision of Lord Greene MR in *Associated Provincial Picture Houses Ltd v Wednesbury Corporation [1948] 1 KB 223*, a case of the judicial review of the exercise of a public duty by a local licensing authority.

The Wednesbury principles have been expressly applied to decisions of directors in *Byng v London Life Association [1989] 1 All ER 561* and *Re a Company (No 00370 of 1987) ex parte Glossop [1988] BCLC 570*. Directors act in breach of the *Wednesbury* principles by acting as follows.

(i)   Taking into account matters which they ought not to take into account. They will do so if they act in their own or some third party's interest or if they have acted for a collateral or improper purpose. If directors act in order to maintain the control of themselves or their friends over the company, they will not be able to assert that they are acting *bona fide* in the company's interests (*Piercy v Mills & Co [1920] 1 Ch 77*). For further cases on collateral or improper purpose see *Howard Smith v Ampol Petroleum Limited [1974] 1 All ER 1126* and *Re a Company (No 00370 of 1987), ex parte Glossop* above.

(ii) Refusing or neglecting to take into account matters which they ought to have taken into account. This would be the case if they did not give their mind to the matters at all, either because such matters never occurred to them or because they acted unthinkingly on another's instruction or advice. It would also be the case if they have prevented themselves from making an unprejudiced decision by either promising an outsider, co-director or shareholder to do something (e.g. to vote in a certain way) or being or getting into a position of actual or potential conflict.

(iii) Doing something which no reasonable board of directors could have reasonably considered to be in the company's interests (see *Gething v Kilner [1972] 1 WLR 337* at *342* and *Charterbridge Corporation v Lloyds Bank [1970] Ch 62* at *74*) or which they actually thought would be injurious to its interests (see *Rolled Steel Products v BSC [1985] 3 All ER 52*).

The *Wednesbury* principles, however, do not give the court overriding power to decide what is reasonable and what is unreasonable. If the directors have asked themselves all the right questions and not been influenced by matters which should not have influenced them, the court will not, even if it disagrees with the decision, invalidate it, unless satisfied that it was so unreasonable that no reasonable board of directors could have reached it (see, for example, *Heron International Ltd v Lord Grade [1982] 1 FTLR 503*).

To safeguard their decisions, particularly those that they can expect may be challenged, directors should ensure that full minutes be made showing their reasons and the factors which they took into account, not least the arguments against the proposed course of action.

19.28 Liability for causing loss to the company

As fiduciaries, directors are liable to compensate those to whom their duties are owed for loss resulting from their defaults (see *Knot v Cottee (1852) 16 Beav 77*). In these circumstances, directors will usually be acting as individuals rather than as a board. The most conspicuous example of loss that may be caused by directors acting as such is the misapplication of corporate property. There is misapplication whenever corporate assets are applied by the directors in breach of their duties i.e. not *bona fide* in the interests of the company, or for purposes not authorised by the memorandum or in breach of the articles (e.g. pursuant to a board resolution passed at an inquorate meeting of the directors). For an example of a director misusing company property, see *International Sales and Agencies Ltd v Marcus [1982] 3 All ER 551* where it was held that the recipient of the misapplied property held it as constructive trustee. See also 19.44 below for enforcing the right to compensation if the company is in liquidation.

19.29 Liability for profits made

Like all fiduciaries, directors are not as such entitled to any remuneration for their services or any allowance for their time and trouble. Nor are they allowed to make a profit from their position. The articles must therefore specifically provide for their remuneration (see 19.52 below) and for the situations where they are allowed to be interested in contracts with their companies and to keep profits (see 19.70 below). Where a director wrongly profits personally from his position, the courts will often give a remedy to a company on the basis that, by reason of his fiduciary position as a director, he is not allowed to derive any remuneration or profit from it without complying with the requirements of the articles. For an example of the operation of, and the relationship between, the requirement as to entitlement to remuneration and that as to keeping profits, see *Guinness plc v Saunders and another [1990] 1 All ER 652*.

Many abuses of position are attributable to use of corporate information, but the way in which a profit is made is irrelevant in establishing liability. The basis of liability is that the director has enriched himself without the knowledge and consent of the shareholders by abusing his fiduciary position as a director. The liability arises from the mere fact of a profit having been made. It in no way depends on fraud or absence of *bona fides*; or upon such questions or considerations as whether the profit would or should otherwise have gone to the plaintiff, or whether he took a risk or acted as he did for the benefit of the plaintiff, or whether the plaintiff has in fact been damaged or benefited by his action (*Regal (Hastings) Limited v Gulliver [1942] 1 All ER 378*).

A director is also liable for any unauthorised or undisclosed profit which he makes out of a transaction which also benefits his company, even if he does so at his own risk and expense. See *Phipps v Boardman [1964] 2 All ER 187*, a case concerning the liability of trustees to a beneficiary. In that case the trustees were allowed by Wilberforce J a generous allowance (subsequently affirmed by the House of Lords: *[1967] 2 AC 46*) for their work and trouble in calculating the undeserved profit for which they had to account to the estate. However, in *Guinness plc v Saunders* (see above), Lord Templeman said he was unable to envisage circumstances in which a court of equity would exercise a power to award remuneration to a director on a *quantum meruit* basis, when the company's articles of association conferred that power on the board of directors.

Thus a director's enrichment need not be at the company's expense. If directors attract a contract to themselves by virtue of their position (and profit thereby), they are liable even though the other party had refused to contract with the company (*Industrial Development*

Consultants Limited v Cooley [1972] 2 All ER 162). Furthermore it does not matter that the company was financially or legally unable to acquire the benefit in question (*Boston Deep Sea Fishing and Ice Co v Ansell (1888) 39 ChD 339*). Another area in which a director may make an unjustifiable profit otherwise than at the company's expense is by INSIDER DEALING (30).

The duty of a director not to usurp for himself, or divert to another person or company with whom or with which he is associated, a maturing business opportunity which his company is actively pursuing, survives his resignation where the resignation may fairly be said to have been prompted or influenced by a wish to acquire for himself the opportunity sought by the company (*Canadian Aero Service Limited v O'Malley (1973) 40 DLR (3d) 371*, and approved in *Island Export Finance ltd v Umunna and another [1986] BCLC 460*). However, in itself, this does not restrict directors from exploiting, after they have ceased to be directors, every opportunity of which they had acquired knowledge while they were directors. Such a restriction would offend the principles relating to contracts in restraint of trade. Whether directors are so restricted will depend on a range of factors, including the nature of the information and whether it was confidential, the nature of the corporate opportunity and how far it had matured, the directors' duty in relation to it, and the length of time which has elapsed since the director left the company, and the reasons for his leaving.

To fix directors with liability to disgorge their profit, the company has to establish that 'what the directors did was so related to the affairs of the company that it can properly be said to have been done in the course of their management and in utilisation of their opportunities and special knowledge as directors' (*Regal (Hastings) Limited v Gulliver [1942]* above). But if they can show that they made full disclosure of the transaction and obtained the consent of the shareholders, or, if the articles so permit, of the board of directors in accordance with the articles, directors can retain their profit.

In principle, a director can also escape liability if the impugned action was performed as an individual not as a director, but, in practice, this may be hard to establish. A director has 'one capacity and one capacity only' in which to carry on business and that is as a director-fiduciary (*Industrial Development Consultants Limited v Cooley [1972] 2 All ER 162*).

19.30 *Liability for non-disclosure of interests in the company's contracts*

A director has a statutory duty to disclose interests in company contracts at a meeting of the directors of the company. See 19.71 below.

Under the general law, where a director makes a contract with the company or is personally interested in a contract to which the company is a party, and has not fully disclosed the contract or the interest to the shareholders in general meeting or they do not sanction it at the meeting, the company will be entitled to any profit made under the rule of avoidance of conflict of interest and duty (see 19.26(*a*) above). The company may also discontinue the source of the director's enrichment by setting aside the contract, as it is voidable at the company's option against all but *bona fide* third parties without notice of the breach (*Transvaal Land Co v New Belgium etc. Co [1914] 2 Ch 488*). But the right of avoidance will probably be subject to Sec 35A (see 16.2 DEALING WITH THIRD PARTIES), and anyway will be lost if such time elapses or such events occur as to prevent rescission of the contract (*Hely-Hutchinson v Brayhead Limited [1967] 3 All ER at 109*).

In practice, virtually all companies include a provision in their articles allowing a director to be interested in a contract with the company provided he has disclosed to the board the nature and extent of his interest (see 19.70 below where *Table A, Art 85* is adopted).

An initial failure to disclose the interest can be cured by a general meeting of the shareholders. The director may vote his shares in his favour (*Northern Counties Securities Limited v Jackson and Steeple Ltd [1974] 1 WLR 1133*).

19.31 *Misuse of information*

A trust will be imposed on profits or other kinds of benefit (e.g. shares or contractual rights) where directors use information in breach of fiduciary duty to make profits. It is not clear whether all information to which a director has access is fixed with a trust or only either that which is confidential or that which is of value to the company or that which is of concern to the company to know. Probably the true test is no more than that the information from which the profit was made derived from the director's special position and knowledge as director.

19.32 **Statutory duties**

Statutory provisions have extended or modified the general principles that directors must not abuse their positions and must deal fairly in certain transactions with the company or in its shares. Notably, these arise in connection with the following.

- Compensation for loss of office (see 19.53 below).
- Service contracts (see 19.55 *et seq.* below).
- Disclosure of interests in contracts (see 19.71 below).
- Invalidity of certain contracts (see 19.72 below).
- Substantial property transactions (see 19.73 below).
- Disclosure of shareholdings in the company (see 19.76 below).
- Dealings in share options (see 19.83 below).
- Loans to directors (see 19.85 below).
- INSIDER DEALING (30).

19.33 **Duties of skill and care**

The classic statement of the duty's nature and extent is Romer J's in *Re City Equitable Fire Insurance Co [1925] Ch 407* at *427*.

'. . . a director need not exhibit in the performance of his duties a greater degree of skill than may reasonably be expected from a person of his knowledge and experience. A director of a life insurance company . . . does not guarantee that he has the skill of an actuary or of a physician . . . a director is not bound to give continuous attention to the affairs of his company. His duties are of an intermittent nature to be performed at periodical board meetings . . . He is not, however, bound to attend such meetings, though he ought to attend whenever he is reasonably able to do so . . . In respect of duties that, having regard to the exigencies of business and the articles . . . may properly be left to some official, a director is, in the absence of grounds for suspicion, justified in trusting that official.'

These *dicta* are often and mistakenly given the status of statutory words, and are now to be regarded as outmoded. Cases in point are few and old, and deal mainly with the obligations of directors who are now called 'non-executive'. They give the impression that these obligations are not very onerous. However, in *Dorchester Finance Co Limited v Stebbing [1989] BCLC 498*, Foster J suggests that there ought to be no difference between

19.33 Directors

the skill demanded of an executive and a non-executive director, at least where the latter is professionally qualified.

The three limbs of Romer J's test may be stated as follows.

- *Skill.* The subjective formulation of required skill means that directors must display such skill as their personal qualifications warrant. More is expected of experienced men of business (*Dorchester Finance Co Limited v Stebbing* above) than the amateur (*Re Denham & Co Ltd (1883) 25 ChD 752*). However, there are indications that an objective standard has been introduced by statute in certain circumstances and has begun to be recognised by the judiciary as applying more broadly. See, for example, 19.46 below for the standard of skill and care required for wrongful trading under *IA 1986, s 214*. The effect of this is to put directors or shadow directors into a quasi-professional or skilled class. In *Norman v Theodore Goddard [1991] BCLC 1028* it was held that the standard of skill stated in *IA 1986, s 214* was the standard required by the duty of care in cases of negligence generally although this appears to be at odds with the standard laid down by Romer J.

- *Diligence.* The degree of diligence required of a director depends on the facts of each particular case. Broadly, he must exhibit in the performance of his duties such care as an ordinary man might be expected to take on his own behalf. One director among many (*Marquis of Bute's Case [1892] 2 Ch 100*), or a director who is not vested by the articles with much, or any, effective power (*Re Denham & Co Ltd* above), need not be as diligent as one on whom the company relies, though it may be that an executive director (or experienced or professionally qualified non-executive director) must show appropriate diligence and give some attention to the affairs of the company (*Dorchester Finance Co Limited v Stebbing* above). However, each director, whether executive or non-executive, is responsible for the proper management of the company's affairs (*Euro RSCG v Conran, The Times, 2 November 1992*). The duty of the director to participate in the management of the company was stated by Romer J in very undemanding terms. However, the law may be evolving in response to changes in attitude to corporate governance. See the *obiter* comments in *Maxwell v Bishopsgate Investment Management Ltd [1993] BCC 120*.

- *Liability for others' acts.* A director is not liable for the acts of co-directors or company officers solely by virtue of his position. But he will be if he participates in the wrong and it takes little to establish participation. Merely signing minutes approving a misapplication of property attracts liability (*Re Lands Allotment Co [1894] 1 Ch 616*). So does unquestioningly signing a cheque for what turns out to be an unauthorised payment (*Re City Equitable Fire Insurance Co* above), though a director is not liable for signing a cheque for an authorised payment put to an unauthorised use. It may not be enough to escape liability that an executive or experienced non-executive director missed a board meeting (*Dorchester Finance Co Limited v Stebbing* above). A director is liable though actually ignorant of another's wrong where he ought to have supervised the activity or ought to have known that it was wrong (*Selangor United Rubber Estates Limited v Cradock (No 3) [1968] 1 WLR 1555*). Signing share transfer forms having the effect of disposing of the company's property for a purpose outside the powers of the board also constitutes a breach of fiduciary duty, even if the director signing had made reasonable enquiries as to the purpose of the transfer and had received reassuring answers from other directors whom he was reasonably entitled to trust. The director will be liable even if he is subsequently entitled to relief under *Sec 727*, see 32.7 LEGAL PROCEEDINGS (*Bishopsgate Investment Management Ltd v Maxwell [1994] 1 All ER 261*).

19.34 Remedies

A number of remedies are available to the company.

- A director has a duty to account for secret profits or other unjust enrichment, and to restore the company's property. Where remedies for the breach of fiduciary duty are sought, these can take the form of personal remedies against the fiduciary or, in certain circumstances, proprietary remedies. A personal remedy is always available, but will be ineffective if the director is unable to pay. Proprietary remedies, however, will be available in most cases involving directors, but not all. When the profit made by the director represents or derives from property which never belonged to the company, only a personal remedy is likely to be available (see *Lister v Stubbs (1890) 45 ChD 1* in relation to a dishonest commission or bribe).

  Availability of proprietary relief allows recovery of misapplied property or its product, not merely from a defaulting director but by way of tracing from third parties who hold the property (other than as *bona fide* purchasers for value). It allows recovery not merely of the property but of any profits flowing from its use which are said to belong in equity to the company (*Keech v Sandford (1726) Sel Cas Ch 61; Cook v Deeks [1916] 1 AC 554*). Where a proprietary remedy is available, the property is held by the director or third party as a constructive trustee for the company.

  A person dealing with the company into or through whose hands the company's property passes on completion of a transaction which amounts to a breach of fiduciary duty on the part of the directors may himself be liable as a constructive trustee if he was aware of the breach. The property may also be traceable into third parties' hands, unless the defence of *bona fide* purchaser without notice is available to them (see *Selangor United Rubber Estates Limited v Cradock (No 3) [1968] 1 WLR 1555; Belmont Finance Corporation v Williams Furniture Limited (No 2) [1980] 1 All ER 393* and *International Sales and Agencies Limited v Marcus [1982] 3 All ER 551*), or the more general defence of 'change of position' (see *Lipkin Gorman v Karpnale Ltd [1991] 3 WLR 10 (HL)*).

  However, as a result of *Secs 35* and *35A* (see 16.1, 16.2 DEALINGS WITH THIRD PARTIES), to make a person who as a result of a transaction with a company receives its property liable as constructive trustee, it will not be sufficient to show that such a person was aware merely that the original transaction was a breach by the directors of a limitation on their powers under the company's constitution. It will be necessary to prove that the person himself was not acting *bona fide*.

  Where a third party has not received the misapplied property, but to his knowledge the breach by the directors was dishonest or fraudulent and he assisted in it, he can be personally liable as a constructive trustee or for damages for conspiracy (*Belmont Finance Corporation v Williams Furniture Limited (No 2)* above). *Secs 35* and *35A* (see 16.1, 16.2 DEALINGS WITH THIRD PARTIES) will not give any additional protection to third parties who assist a dishonest or fraudulent misapplication. The level of awareness required to make a person liable as a constructive trustee is often crucial. Full knowledge may not be necessary. It may be sufficient for the company to establish that the person was aware of facts which ought to have led him to make enquiries, which he failed to do.

- Damages in negligence for breach of the duty of skill or care.

- An injunction or declaration, chiefly to prevent a threatened breach.

- Rescission of a contract with the company, subject normally to the rights of third parties acting *bona fide* without notice and provided that *restitutio in integrum* (restoration to the original position) is still possible.

19.35 Directors

- Removal of the director by the company in general meeting (and dismissal from any executive office).

Actions against delinquent directors must be instituted by the company, but exceptionally a minority shareholder may do so (see 34.5 *et seq.* MEMBERS for minority actions). If the company is in liquidation, the liquidator will cause the company to bring the action.

See also 19.44 below for a remedy against a past or present director who has misapplied or retained any money or other property of the company.

19.35 Relief from liability

A director may be relieved of liability in the following ways.

- **Honesty and reasonableness.** If a director is or will be liable for negligence, default, breach of a duty or breach of trust to his company (but not to a third party, see *Customs and Excise Commissioners v Hedon Alpha Limited [1981] 2 All ER 697*) a court may relieve him wholly or partly from liability under *Sec 727*. See 32.7 LEGAL PROCEEDINGS.

- **Indemnity against liability.** With certain exceptions, any provision exempting a director from, or indemnifying him against, any liability for negligence, default or breach of duty or trust in relation to the company is void. This does not, however, prevent a company from insuring a director against any such liability. See 19.50 below.

- **Ratification.** The shareholders might wish to ratify what a director has done. In *Rolled Steel Products Limited v BSC [1985] 3 All ER 52* at *86* Slade LJ observed (*obiter*) that if an act is beyond the corporate capacity of a company, it cannot be ratified. However, any act which falls within the corporate capacity of a company will bind it if it is done with the unanimous consents of all the shareholders or is subsequently ratified by such consents (see *Salomon v A Salomon & Co Ltd [1897] AC 22* at *47*; *Re Horsley & Weight Ltd [1982] 3 All ER 1045* at *1055*; and *Multinational Gas and Petrochemical Co v Multinational Gas and Petrochemical Services Ltd [1983] 2 All ER 563*). This last-mentioned principle certainly is not however an unqualified one and, in particular, will not enable the shareholders of a company to bind the company to a transaction which constitutes a fraud on its creditors (see, e.g. *Re Halt Garage (1964) Ltd [1982] 3 All ER 1016* at *1037*).

In some cases acts of directors will be ratifiable merely by an ordinary resolution passed by a majority in general meeting, provided full disclosure has been made. But the following acts are not ratifiable by this method.

(i) Breaches of duty involving the abridgement of the rights of individual shareholders (e.g. a refusal to register a share transfer in *Re Smith & Fawcett [1942] Ch 304*), or a class of shareholders (e.g. cases of a fraud on the minority). The principle may prevent ratification of acts involving misapplication of corporate property or information (as it did in *Cook v Deeks [1916] 1 AC 554*). The rights of individual shareholders to bring an action in such a case will depend on whether it comes within the exceptions to the rule in *Foss v Harbottle* (see 34.5 MEMBERS).

(ii) Acts which are fraudulent or dishonest.

(iii) Acts for which the articles establish a procedure (e.g. obtaining a special resolution) which is not followed.

The making of a secret profit (*Regal (Hastings) Limited v Gulliver [1942] 1 All ER 378*) or a transaction involving a failure in skill and care (*Pavlides v Jensen [1956] Ch 565*) are ratifiable.

Directors may normally vote their shares in favour of ratification save for any shares acquired as a result of the breach of duty to be ratified. But in cases where family companies are concerned, the court may hold that equitable considerations arising out of the relationship between the shareholders make it wrong for directors to do so.

19.36 Duties of internal management under the Companies Act 1985

Apart from the statutory duties (see 19.32 above) which amplify the equitable rules concerning abuse of position and fair dealing, a director has a considerable number of duties under the *CA 1985* which he must perform or ensure are performed. To a large extent they relate to matters of internal management and are dealt with in the appropriate chapters of this book. They include provisions relating to the keeping of accounting records, the preparation of annual accounts, the filing of documents with the Registrar of Companies, and the keeping of the statutory books of the company. The company is punishable for failure by a fine and in some cases a daily default fine; directors suffer fines, daily default fines, and, in some cases, imprisonment. Failure to secure compliance by the company may also amount to breach by directors of their duty of skill and care.

A director may, in addition, be disqualified from acting as such

- for conviction of an indictable offence in connection with the promotion, formation, management or liquidation of a company (see 19.13(*a*) above);

- for persistent default in the various duties under *CA 1985* to submit documents to the Registrar of Companies (see 19.13(*b*) above); or

- on the grounds that he is unfit to be concerned in the management of a company through failure to comply with statutory provisions, particularly those relating to the keeping of books of account and the preparation of annual accounts (see 19.15 and 19.17 above).

19.37 Duties to third parties

Although a director in his capacity as such owes his duties only to the company, he may in the course of carrying out those duties find that he has put himself in a position where he also owes duties to other persons.

- **Shareholders.** In *Gething v Kilner [1972] 1 WLR 337* at *341* Brightman J accepted, in connection with a dispute regarding a take-over, that the directors of an offeree company had a duty towards their own shareholders, which clearly included a duty to be honest and not to mislead.

  Further, if directors have put themselves in a position in which they can be considered as agents of some of their shareholders, they incur fiduciary duties towards those shareholders (*Allen v Hyatt (1914) 30 TLR 444*).

  Where, in such cases, the directors owe a duty to an individual shareholder, the recoverable damages are limited to the loss suffered personally by him without reference to any loss suffered by the company itself (*Prudential Assurance Co Limited v Newman Industries Limited (No 2) [1980] 2 All ER 841*).

- **Subscribers for and purchasers of securities.** Subscribers for securities which are listed on the Official List are now protected by *FSA 1986, s 150*. This provides that the persons responsible for any listing particulars shall be liable to pay compensation to any person who has acquired any of the securities in question and suffered loss in respect of them as a result of any untrue or misleading statement in them or the omission of any matter required to be included in them.

19.37   Directors

- **Customers, suppliers and other contracting parties.** Directors are not normally liable on contracts made between their company and third parties (*Ferguson v Wilson (1866) LR 2 Ch 77*).

  As agents, they are not liable for the tort of procuring their company to break a contract (*Said v Butt [1920] 3 KB 497*) except possibly in cases where equitable interests in property acquired by third parties under a contract with their company are adversely affected by the breach (see *Telemetrix plc v Modern Engineers of Bristol (Holdings) plc [1985] BCLC 213*). Furthermore, they are not liable if the company cannot or fails to perform a contract due to some other default, such as negligence, on their part, unless they have assumed a special responsibility (*Williams v Natural Life Health Foods Ltd [1997] 1 BCLC 131; [1998] 1 BCLC 689*).

  However, a director may be personally liable in the following circumstances.

  (i)   On bills of exchange, promissory notes, cheques or orders for money or goods signed by him or on his authority, unless the document mentions the name of the company in legible characters [*Sec 349(4)*]. The account number of the company without the name is not sufficient (*Rafsanjan Pistachio Producers Co-operative v Reiss [1990] BCLC 352*).

  (ii) On any contract if the director does not make it clear during negotiations or in the contract itself that he is contracting as an agent of the company and not personally.

  (iii) For damages if he makes fraudulent (*Edgington v Fitzmaurice (1885) 29 ChD 459*) or negligent (*Hedley Byrne & Co Limited v Heller & Partners Ltd [1964] AC 465*) misrepresentations in the course of negotiating a contract between his company and a third party.

  (iv) For damages if he guarantees that his company will perform a contract, and the company does not do so.

  (v)   For damages for breach of his implied warranty of authority if he concludes a contract on behalf of the company but exceeds his authority in so doing and the company is therefore able to set it aside (*West London Commercial Bank v Kitson (1884) 13 QBD 360*).

  (vi) On contracts signed by him purportedly on behalf of a company before its incorporation. [*Sec 36C*]. See also *Kelner v Baxter (1866) LR 2 CP 174*).

  Directors may also be liable to the company for any loss or damage suffered by it.

- **To third parties in tort.** Directors are not liable for a tort committed by their company or its servants or agents unless they committed, authorised, directed or procured its commission, or because it occurred due to their own negligence. See, for example, *Performing Right Society Limited v Ciryl Theatrical Syndicate Limited [1924] 1 KB 1*. Trespasses, copyright and patent infringement and negligence are common examples of torts committed by a company, for which directors can, if they initiated or participated in the commission, be personally responsible.

  Directors have a liability under the principles in *Hedley Byrne & Co Limited v Heller & Partners Ltd* above for negligent misstatements made by them on behalf of the company. The House of Lords in *Caparo Industries Plc v Dickman & others [1990] 1 All ER 568* held that the three criteria for imposing a duty of care are foreseeability of damage, proximity of relationship and the reasonableness or otherwise of imposing a duty of care. They also held that if a statement was put into general circulation which might be relied on by any number of third parties for any number of different purposes which the maker of the statement had no specific reason to anticipate, there was no relationship of proximity between the maker of the statement and any person relying on it unless it was shown that

(i)   the maker knew his statement would be communicated to the person relying on it, either as an individual or as a member of an identifiable class, specifically in connection with a particular transaction or a transaction of a particular kind, and

(ii)   that person would be very likely to rely on it for the purpose of deciding whether to enter into that transaction.

This decision may have considerably reduced the range of persons to whom directors owe a duty of care in respect of public documents issued by companies, such as audited accounts, interim statements, take-over documents and statements issued through The Stock Exchange. Because, for example, audited accounts are prepared for the shareholders as a body for the purpose of reviewing the directors' stewardship of that company and not to enable persons (including existing shareholders) to decide whether or not to buy or sell shares in or to give credit to the company, it may well be that there is not a sufficient degree of proximity between the directors and members of the investing public or lenders or suppliers to the company on which to base a duty of care, even if in fact those persons have relied on the accounts.

Directors are not liable for the fraud of their co-directors, unless they are in some way a party to it (*Cargill v Bower (1878) 10 ChD 502*).

If a director himself commits a tort in the course of the performance of his duties for the company, he is personally liable for it jointly and severally with the company. He may also be liable to the company for breach of duty.

- **Constructive trustees.** Persons who receive moneys or property for their own benefit in circumstances which call for inquiry, and who fail to make the inquiries which would have to be made to satisfy themselves that they were not engaged in furthering a fraud or breach of trust, will be liable to account as constructive trustees to the true owners.

Further, persons who use their own companies or provide nominee companies or act as directors of such companies to enable fraudsters' activities to be kept secret, have themselves acted dishonestly, if they are on notice that fraud might be involved and, from indifference to the possibility of fraud, fail to make enquiries. They will have personally to account accordingly for funds which have passed through those companies (*Agip (Africa) Ltd v Jackson & others [1991] 3 WLR 116 (CA)*).

19.38 LIABILITY OF DIRECTORS

A director is not liable for the acts of co-directors and company officers solely by virtue of his position, although he will be if he participates in the wrong. Merely signing minutes approving a misapplication of property attracts liability (*Re Lands Allotment Co [1894] 1 Ch 616*) as does unquestioningly signing a cheque for an unauthorised payment (*Re City Equitable* above). A director is liable for, though actually ignorant of, another's wrong where he ought to have supervised the activity or ought to have known that it was wrong (*Selangor United Rubber Estates Limited v Cradock (No 3) [1968] 1 WLR 1555*).

19.39 Directors

19.39 Liabilities and offences under *CA 1985* provisions

There are a large number of offences for failure to comply with the requirements of the *Companies Acts*. These are dealt with in the appropriate part of the text. See also 40 PENALTIES and 32.4 LEGAL PROCEEDINGS for directors' liabilities where a body corporate is guilty of certain offences.

19.40 Liabilities and offences under *IA 1986*

In addition to offences under the *Companies Acts*, *IA 1986* contains a number of other offences for malpractice before and during liquidation. These are considered in 19.41 to 19.47 below.

19.41 *Fraud in anticipation of winding up*

Any past or present officer (including a shadow director) is deemed to have committed an offence if, within twelve months of the commencement of winding up or at any time thereafter, he has

(*a*)   concealed or fraudulently removed company property valued at £500 or more;

(*b*)   concealed any debt due to or from the company;

(*c*)   concealed, destroyed, mutilated or falsified any books or papers relating to the company;

(*d*)   fraudulently parted with, altered or made an omission in any document relating to the company;

(*e*)   pawned, pledged or disposed of property of the company obtained on credit and not paid for (unless done in the normal course of business); or

(*f*)   been privy to the doing by others of any act within (*c*) or (*d*) above.

Where appropriate, it is a defence to prove there was no intent to defraud or conceal.

A person guilty of an offence under these provisions is liable to a penalty up to the level in 40.1(*a*) PENALTIES.

[*IA 1986, s 206, 10 Sch*].

19.42 *Transactions in fraud of creditors*

An officer of the company is deemed to have committed an offence if he has

● made any gift or transfer of, or charge on, or has connived at the levying of any execution against, the company's property in the five years before winding up; or

● concealed or removed any part of the company's property since, or in the two months before, the date an unsatisfied judgment or order for payment of money has been obtained against the company.

It is a defence to prove that there was no intent to defraud the company's creditors.

A person guilty of an offence under these provisions is liable to a penalty up to the level in 40.1(*b*) PENALTIES.

[*IA 1986, s 207, 10 Sch*].

19.43 *Misconduct in the course of winding up*

When a company is being wound up, an officer of the company commits an offence if he

(a)   does not to the best of his knowledge give the liquidator details of all the company's property and any disposals of that property not in the ordinary course of business;

(b)   does not deliver up to the liquidator any of the company's property or books in his possession;

(c)   fails to inform the liquidator as soon as practicable if he knows that a false debt has been proved;

(d)   prevents the production of any books or papers relating to the company's property;

(e)   attempts to account for any of the company's property by fictitious losses or expenses;

(f)   destroys, mutilates, alters or falsifies any of the company's books or papers or is privy to the making of a false entry therein;

(g)   makes any material omission in any statement relating to the company's affairs; or

(h)   makes any false representation or commits any other fraud (whether before or after the date of winding up) to obtain the consent of any of the company's creditors to an agreement in connection with the company's affairs or the winding up.

The provisions also apply, except for (f), to past officers and shadow directors (see 19.1 above).

It is a defence under (a), (b), (d) and (g) to prove that there was no intent to defraud or conceal.

A person guilty of an offence under these provisions is liable to a penalty up to the level in 40.1(a) PENALTIES.

[*IA 1986, ss 208-211, 10 Sch*].

19.44 *Summary remedy against delinquent officers*

If in the course of winding up it appears that a past or present officer of the company has misapplied or retained any money or other property of the company, or been guilty of any misfeasance or breach of fiduciary or other duty in relation to the company, the court may examine the conduct of the person concerned and compel him to

•   repay, restore or account for the money or property with interest; or

•   contribute such sum to the company's assets by way of compensation as the court thinks fit.

[*IA 1986, s 212*].

The above is a procedural remedy only and does not give any additional right of action so that it cannot be invoked where the director has been negligent only (*Re B Johnson & Co (Builders) Ltd [1955] Ch 634*). However, 'misfeasance' comprehends any breach of duty involving a misapplication or wrongful retention of the company's assets and does not necessarily involve moral turpitude (see *Selangor United Rubber Estates Limited v Cradock [1967] 1 WLR 1168*).

19.45 *Fraudulent trading*

If in the course of the winding up of a company it appears that any business has been carried on 'with intent to defraud creditors' (whether of the company or any other person) or for any fraudulent purpose, the court may declare that any persons knowingly involved are liable to make such contributions to the company's assets as the court thinks proper. [*IA 1986, s 213*]. For a consideration of the phrase *'with intent to defraud creditors'* see *Re William C Leitch Bros Ltd [1932] 2 Ch 71* and for *'fraudulent purposes'* see *Re Patrick and Lyon Ltd [1933] Ch 786*. It does not matter that only one creditor was defrauded (*Re Gerald Cooper Chemicals Ltd [1978] Ch 262*).

19.46 *Wrongful trading*

If a company has gone into insolvent liquidation and before that time a director (or shadow director) knew, or ought to have concluded, that there was no reasonable prospect that the company would avoid such liquidation, the court may declare that that person is liable to make such contribution to the company's assets as the court thinks proper. The court must not make such a declaration if satisfied that, once the director knew etc., he took every step which a reasonably diligent person having both

• the general knowledge, skill and experience that may be reasonably expected of a person carrying out his functions, and

• the general knowledge, skill and experience that the director himself has

would have taken to minimise the potential loss to the company's creditors.

[*IA 1986, s 214*].

19.47 *Re-use of company name*

Where a company goes into insolvent liquidation, a director or shadow director of that company is prohibited from

• being a director of another company, or

• in any way being involved in the promotion, formation or management of another company, or

• in any way being concerned in the carrying on of a business

using the same, or a similar, name. Subject to certain exceptions (see *The Insolvency Rules (SI 1986 No 1925, r 4.226-230)*), the prohibition applies to any person who was a director or shadow director within the twelve months before the date of winding up and any name used by the company in that period.

A person guilty of an offence under these provisions is liable to a penalty up to the level in 40.1(*b*) PENALTIES. If a person is involved in the *management* of a company re-using the name, he is personally responsible for the debts of the company incurred when so involved. Additionally, any other person involved in the management who acts, or is willing to act, on that person's instructions is also personally responsible for debts incurred when so acting.

[*IA 1986, ss 216, 217*].

19.48 **Criminal liability**

Where any officer of a company (or person purporting to act as such) publishes or concurs in publishing a written statement which to his knowledge is or may be misleading, false or deceptive in a material particular, he is liable on conviction on indictment, to imprisonment for up to seven years if he acted with intent to deceive the members or creditors about the company's affairs. [*Theft Act 1968, s 19*].

Malpractice discovered during winding up. If it appears in the course of a winding up that any past or present officer of the company has been guilty of an offence in relation to the company for which he is criminally liable, then the liquidator must report the matter to the official receiver in a winding up by the court or the prosecuting authority in a voluntary liquidation. [*IA 1986, ss 218, 219*].

19.49 Relief from liability by court

If a director is or will be liable for negligence, default, breach of duty or breach of trust to his company (but not a third party, see *Customs and Excise Commissioners v Hedon Alpha Limited [1981] 2 All ER 697*) a court may relieve him wholly or partly from liability. See 32.7 LEGAL PROCEEDINGS.

19.50 Exemption from, or indemnity against, liability

Any provision (whether contained in the company's articles or in any contract with the company or otherwise) which purports to exempt from, or indemnify against, liability

(i)   any officer of the company, or

(ii)   any person (whether an officer or not) employed by the company as auditor

is, subject to below, void. This applies to any liability which by virtue of any rule of law would otherwise attach to that person in respect of any negligence, default, breach of duty or breach of trust of which he may be guilty in relation to the company. [*Sec 310(1)(2)*].

The above provision does not, however, prevent a company from

(*a*)   insuring a person within (i) or (ii) above against any such liability; or

(*b*)   indemnifying any such person against any liability incurred by him

- in defending any civil or criminal proceedings in which judgment is given in his favour or he is acquitted; or

- in connection with any application under *Sec 144(3)(4)* (acquisition of shares by innocent nominee – see 58.26 SHARES AND SHARE CAPITAL) or *Sec 727* (general power to grant relief in case of honest and reasonable conduct, see 32.7 LEGAL PROCEEDINGS) in which relief is granted to him by the court.

[*Sec 310(3); CA 1989, s 137*].

Where *SI 1985 No 805, Table A, Art 118* has been adopted by the company, all officers and auditors are indemnified as under (*b*) above.

19.51 Unlimited liability of directors

Although there are restrictions on exempting directors from liability (see 19.50 above) the liability of directors and managers of a limited company may be unlimited if so provided by the memorandum. In such a case, any proposal to appoint a director of the company must include a statement that his liability will be unlimited and he must be given written notice of this fact by either the promoters, directors or managers of the company or the company secretary. In default, any person responsible is liable

- to a fine up to the level in 40.1(*d*) PENALTIES; and

- for any damages which the person so appointed sustains from the default.

However, the liability of the person appointed is not affected by the default.

19.52   Directors

[*Sec 306*].

Where the articles permit, the memorandum of a limited company may be altered by special resolution so as to make the liability of its directors or managers unlimited. Once passed, the provisions of such a resolution are as valid as if originally contained in the memorandum. [*Sec 307*].

19.52 EMPLOYMENT, REMUNERATION, ETC.

Remuneration. The directors are entitled to such remuneration as the company determines by ordinary resolution. Unless the resolution provides otherwise, the remuneration accrues from day to day. [*SI 1985 No 805, Table A, Art 82*].

Subject to below, a director's remuneration cannot be paid free of income tax or otherwise calculated by reference to, or varying with, the amount of his income tax or the rate of income tax. Any provision in the articles, in any contract or in any resolution of the company or its directors which seeks to do this is not lawful and has effect as if it provided for payment, as a gross sum subject to income tax, of the net sum for which it actually provides. [*Sec 311*]. This does not apply to remuneration under a contract in force on 18 July 1945 which provided expressly (and not by reference to the articles) for payment of remuneration free of income tax etc. [*CC(CP)A 1985, s 15*].

Pensions etc. The directors may provide benefits by means of payment of pensions, insurance, gratuities etc. for former directors of the company or any of its subsidiaries and for his family and dependants. They may also (before and after he ceases to hold office) contribute to any fund and pay premiums for the purchase or provision of any benefit. [*SI 1985 No 805, Table A, Art 87*].

Expenses. The directors may be paid all travelling, hotel and other expenses properly incurred by them in attending directors' meetings, general meetings, class meetings or otherwise in connection with the carrying out of their duties. [*SI 1985 No 805, Table A, Art 83*].

19.53 Payments to director for loss of or retirement from office

Subject to below, a company is prohibited from making any payment to a director of the company by way of compensation for loss of office, or as consideration for or in connection with his retirement from office unless particulars of the proposed payment (including its amount) have been disclosed to members of the company and the proposal has been approved by the company [*Sec 312*].

If such a payment is made without the requirements being complied with, the director receiving it can be compelled to refund it and the directors responsible for the payments being made are also liable for the amount of the payment (*Re Duomatic [1969] 2 Ch 365*).

A payment will not fall within the above provisions if it is a *bona fide* payment as follows.

(*a*)   By way of damages for breach of contract. This covers the situation where a service contract has been terminated prematurely without justification by the company and the payment made to the director is an amount which is considered to represent the director's loss arising from the breach by the company. See 19.68 below.

(*b*)   By way of pension (including a superannuation allowance, superannuation gratuity or similar payment) in respect of past service.

[*Sec 316(3)*].

It has also been held in *Taupo Totara Timber Company v Rowe [1977] 3 WLR 466*, that the making of a payment by a company to a director which it is obliged to make and which he is entitled to receive under his service contract on termination of the contract (e.g. a 'golden parachute') would not require prior shareholder approval under *Sec 312* above. This is consistent with the exclusion under (*a*) above. An *ex gratia* payment to a director for loss of office as a director would be caught by *Sec 312*.

The fact that a director has been removed from office by a resolution of the company does not necessarily deprive him of compensation or damages in respect of the termination of his appointment. [*Sec 303(5)*].

Payments in connection with the transfer of the company's undertaking or property. A similar requirement for shareholder consent applies where, in connection with the transfer of the whole or any part of the undertaking or property of a company, a 'payment' is to be made by the company, or any other person, to a director for loss of office or as consideration in connection with his retirement from office. Any unlawful payment is to be held by the director in trust for the company. [*Sec 313*]. '*Payment*' includes the excess of the price paid for any of the director's shares over that which could have been obtained by any other holder of like shares and any other valuable consideration given to the director. [*Sec 316(2)*].

19.54 *Disclosure of payments in connection with take-overs, etc.*

Where, following an offer for the company's shares, and in connection with the subsequent transfer of shares, a 'payment' by way of compensation for loss of office, or as consideration for or in connection with his retirement from office, is made to a director (as in 19.53 above and subject to the same exceptions), he must take all reasonable steps to secure that particulars of the proposed payment (including the amount) are included in, or sent with, any notice of the offer given to shareholders. If not

- the director, or any person properly required by him to do so, is in default and liable to a fine up to the level in 40.1(*g*) PENALTIES; and

- unless the proposed payment has been approved by a meeting (summoned for the purpose) of holders of the shares to which the offer relates, any sum received by the director on account of the payment is deemed to have been received in trust for the persons who have sold their shares as a result of the offer. Any expenses incurred by the director distributing that sum amongst the shareholders must be borne by him and not retained out of that sum.

  Where no quorum is present at the meeting, or at an adjourned meeting called for a later date, the payment is deemed to have been approved.

'*Payment*' includes the excess of the price paid for any of the director's shares over that which could have been obtained by any other holder of like shares and any other valuable consideration given to the director.

[*Secs 314, 315, 316(2)*].

19.55 **DIRECTORS' SERVICE CONTRACTS**

In considering directors' service contracts, two points should be borne in mind.

(*a*)   Where a director of a company is also an employee of the company, his directorship and his rights in respect of that directorship are quite separate from his rights as an employee. The former are primarily governed by the company's articles of association and the latter by the director's service contract.

19.55 Directors

(b)   It follows from (a) that an individual can hold the office of director and not have a service contract. Examples include the numerous non-executive directors on the boards of many public and larger private companies, who generally serve on a part-time basis and receive only directors' fees for their services.

The director as an employee. Whether a director is also an employee is of significance in three main instances.

- It determines whether he can claim the right under the *Employment Rights Act 1996* (*'ERA 1996'*) not to be unfairly dismissed and/or the right to a redundancy payment.

- Benefits may in certain situations be made available only to employees of a company. Examples include the right to participate in a company's pension scheme and/or profit sharing/share option scheme (although eligibility under approved profit sharing schemes, SAYE-related schemes and share option schemes under *ICTA 1988* can include directors who are not employees, subject to certain restrictions) and the right to receive preferential share allocations when shares in the company are offered to the public pursuant to a flotation.

- In a receivership or winding up, the remuneration of employees may obtain priority in payment as a preferential debt.

The question as to whether a director is an employee is one of fact. In practice the question arises most frequently in relation to managing or working directors. Managing directors were held to be employees in *Anderson v James Sutherland (Peterhead) Limited 1941 SC 203* and more recently in the case of *Folami v Nigerline (UK) Ltd [1978] ICR 277* where Phillips J said: 'It seems to us that where it is established that a person has been appointed managing director of a company, that his duties include effective management of the affairs of the company in all respects, that he has discharged those duties and that he has been remunerated by the company in the sense that he has received a salary from the hands of that company, the *prima facie* conclusion to be drawn is that he is an employee of the company.'

However, the decision of the Court of Appeal in *Parsons v Albert J Parsons & Sons Ltd [1979] ICR 271* indicates that a full-time working director will not necessarily be held to be an employee. In that case, there were three factors which appear to have influenced the decision of Lord Denning MR. First, no written service contract was drawn up and there was no evidence of an oral contract; in particular, no contract or memorandum of a contract was filed or made available for inspection in accordance with what is now *Sec 318*. Secondly, no wages or salaries were shown in the company's accounts for the director: at the end of each year remuneration was voted to him by way of director's emoluments. Thirdly, the applicant was treated as self-employed for national insurance purposes.

From the above cases the position seems to be that it is generally open to the parties to agree that a director will also be an employee. In the *Parsons* case there was no oral or written service contract and the sole question which had to be decided was whether a service contract was to be implied. The court refused to do so on the basis of the evidence available to it.

The position of a director who is also the majority shareholder in the company was considered in *Fleming v Secretary of State for Trade and Industry [1997] IRLR 682*. The managing director of a company had no written service agreement but his remuneration was paid under the PAYE system, he worked the same hours as other company employees and had no other employment. However, he owned 65% of the company's shares, had issued personal guarantees to company suppliers and had elected not to take his salary in a month when the company had a cash flow problem. When the company went into liquidation, the managing director claimed a redundancy payment from the Secretary of State for Trade and Industry. On the facts, the Court of Session upheld the industrial tribunal's view that the managing director was not an 'employee' and therefore was not entitled to a redundancy payment. However, on the issue of the director's majority shareholding, the Court of Session stated that 'the fact that the claimant is a majority shareholder is always a relevant factor. Normally it will be an important factor and there may well be cases in which it is decisive. We are not, however, convinced that it would be proper to lay down any rule of law to the effect that the fact that a person is a majority shareholder necessarily and in all circumstances implies that that person cannot be regarded as an employee, for the purposes of the employment protection legislation.' This *dictum* was followed in *Secretary of State for Trade and Industry v Bottrill [1998] IRLR 120*, where a director who temporarily held 100% of a company's shares was held to be an employee of the company.

Where the parties have expressly made their intentions clear, the courts are generally prepared to presume an employment relationship if the director is required to work full-time in return for a salary. But, as the *Parsons* case shows, much will depend upon the actual evidence in each case. The courts will decline to infer a service contract if, notwithstanding that the director works full-time, the other available evidence points against there being an employment or, possibly, because the court feels the company is in the nature of a quasi-partnership.

19.56 **The service contract**

Where a director is an employee, *ERA 1996* will apply to his service contract and, to comply with that Act, the director should receive a written statement of the terms and conditions of his employment which complies with *ERA 1996, s 1.*

In broad terms this can be done in one of three ways.

- The director can be treated in the same manner as other employees. Practice varies widely but commonly an employee will receive an offer letter together with a subsequent statement containing the details required by *ERA 1996* or, possibly, a reference to an employee handbook.

- The provisions relating to his employment which *ERA 1996* requires to be confirmed in writing may be incorporated, together with other terms, into a written service contract.

- The terms which the parties regard as the most fundamental provisions covering the employment relationship can be inserted in a service contract whilst *ERA 1996* requirements are covered in a separate statement or, possibly, in a schedule to the service contract.

The option chosen, and the extent to which provisions additional to those required by *ERA 1996* are inserted, is very much a question of personal preference of the parties and the type of company involved. In the case of a small family company informality is more common, whereas, at the other extreme, a quoted company will generally be concerned to ensure certainty as to the terms, and the extent of the terms, of the service contract.

It should be stressed that there is no single correct form of director's service contract. The matters to be dealt with in any particular case depend upon the facts of the case. However, if it is accepted that certainty is always preferable, a service contract should clearly deal with such matters as the director's duties and responsibilities, pay and other benefits (including pensions), holidays, sickness, working hours, termination and dismissal. Other clauses commonly included provide that the director will

- devote the whole of his time and attention to the business of the company and its subsidiaries (if any);

- not, without the previous consent of the company, engage or be interested in any other business during the employment (this is normally subject to a right of the director to hold shares in certain categories of companies up to a modest percentage); and

- neither during nor after the employment disclose to third parties the company's trade secrets, business methods and other confidential information concerning the business and affairs of the company.

Also, depending upon the nature of the company's business and the director's position and responsibilities, a restriction may be sought by the company that the director will not for a specified period following termination of the employment solicit business from any customer of the company or entice away its employees or, possibly, engage in any business similar to or competing with that carried on by the company.

In the case of listed companies, regard should be had to the principles and provisions of the Combined Code annexed to the *Listing Rules*. See 19.61 below.

The Institute of Directors makes available to its members on request a form of director's service contract.

See 19.69 below for a checklist of information commonly required for the preparation of a service contract.

19.57 Notice

The provisions relating to termination of a service contract otherwise than for 'good cause' (e.g. for gross misconduct) can take a variety of forms. The contract may provide simply for the giving of a specified period of notice by either party (which may be different). The contract may be for a fixed period. A third possibility is the so-called 'rolling' or 'evergreen' contract which, in broad terms, is a contract for a fixed term which contains a clause whereby it is renewed on the same terms at a specified date in the future unless contrary notice is given. This device ensures that in the case of, say, a four-year contract which is renewed annually, the unexpired portion of the contract cannot at any time be less than three years. (The same level of security can be provided for the director by inserting a clause in the service contract requiring the company to give three (or four) years' notice.) In practice, the primary significance of the provisions relating to termination in a service contract is that they determine the potential cost to the company if it wishes to terminate the director's employment otherwise than in accordance with the terms of the service contract.

The directors of the company are under a duty to act *bona fide* in what they consider to be the interests of the company. It is therefore important that any action taken by the directors in relation to the formulation of service contracts should be for the benefit of the company as a whole, rather than merely for the benefit of a particular director.

19.58 *Employees' notice*

It is sometimes suggested that a long notice period or fixed term is of benefit to the company because it restricts the employee's freedom of action. However, the conventional wisdom has always been that there is very little that an employer can do if an employee leaves having failed to give the notice which he is obliged to give under his contract. A court will not generally order an employee to comply with his obligations under his service contract. Neither will it grant an injunction to enforce a negative covenant (e.g. not to work for anybody else) if the consequences of that injunction would be to put the employee in a position whereby he would either have to go on working for his former employer or not work at all (see *Trade Union and Labour Relations (Consolidation) Act*

1992, s 236 and *Lumley v Wagner (1852) 1 De GM & G 604; Warner Bros Pictures Inc v Nelson [1937] 1 KB 209; Hill v C A Parsons & Co Ltd [1972] Ch 305; C H Giles & Co Ltd v Morris [1972] 1 All ER 960* and *Irani v Southampton & South West Hampshire Health Authority [1985] IRLR 203*). Further, whilst the company could have a right to seek damages for breach of contract equal to the loss arising to the company from the breach, in practice it can be difficult (or even impossible) to quantify and prove such loss.

However, following the case of *Evening Standard Co Ltd v Henderson [1987] IRLR 64* the use of so-called 'gardening leave' clauses (whereby the employer is entitled to suspend the employee from work whilst continuing to provide his salary and other benefits) have become more common, particularly in the case of senior executives. If such a clause is combined with a clause in the service contract preventing the executive from working for a third party whilst his employment continues, there is scope for stopping the executive who has given notice from starting work with somebody else until the notice expires, while at the same time preventing him from remaining on the employer's premises.

Although there is merit in including a 'gardening leave' clause in an employee's contract of employment, care is needed in drafting such a provision. Among other things, the notice period should not be excessive if the provision is to be effective. See, for example, *Provident Financial Group plc v Hayward [1989] IRLR 84.*

19.59 *Employers' notice*

If the company wishes to terminate a service contract in breach of its provisions then, in broad terms, the company is obliged to pay to the employee a sum which, after deduction of any taxation for which the employee would be liable in respect of the payment, equals the value to the employee of the salary and other benefits which he would have received under his contract during the remainder of the term or a valid notice period (as appropriate). This is subject to any allowance to be made to take account of the employee's duty to mitigate (i.e. the principle whereby the employee is under a duty to seek reasonable alternative employment and is not entitled to be compensated for any period in respect of which he has not suffered loss).

Given the above, a long fixed-term contract, or a contract which the employer can only lawfully terminate on the giving of long notice, may be seen as being of significantly greater benefit to the employee than the company. See also 19.61 and 19.68 below for provisions of the Combined Code in the *Listing Rules* on directors' notice periods and compensation. However, it may be that a director of the right calibre cannot in practice be recruited unless he is given a contract for a lengthy fixed term or with a long notice period. It may also be in the interests of the company to grant a long fixed-term contract to an existing director whom the other directors have a genuine desire to retain and whom they have reason to believe might leave the company unless such a contract is granted.

A company wishing to secure a director's service for a specified period should also consider other means of achieving the same objective e.g. share options which are only capable of exercise after, say, three years, and beneficial pension rights.

19.60 *Contracts for more than five years*

Unless first approved by a resolution of the company in general meeting, a company other than a wholly-owned subsidiary, must not incorporate into a contract of employment of a director or shadow director any term whereby his employment with the company

- is to, or may, be continued for a period of more than five years otherwise than at the instance of the company (whether under the original agreement or a new agreement entered into in pursuance of it); and

- cannot be terminated by the company by notice during that period or can only be terminated in specific circumstances.

[*Sec 319(1)(3)(4)*].

Similar provisions apply where a person is a director of a holding company and his employment is within the group. Such a term must be approved by a resolution of the holding company in general meeting. [*Sec 319(1)(3)*].

As an anti-avoidance measure, where a director is employed under a contract which cannot be terminated by the company by notice or can only be terminated in specific circumstances and, more than six months before its expiration, the company enters into a further such agreement with the director, the unexpired period of the original agreement is added to the period of the further agreement for the purposes of the above provisions. [*Sec 319(2)*]. This is clearly intended to cover the situation where, for example, at the end of the first year of a four-year contract, a director enters into another four-year contract commencing on the expiry of the original four-year contract. In these circumstances the period for which he is to be employed would be seven years.

Where a resolution to approve such a term in a contract is proposed, a written memorandum setting out the proposed agreement incorporating the relevant term must be made available for inspection by members both at the registered office for at least 15 days before the meeting and at the meeting itself; otherwise the resolution cannot be passed. [*Sec 319(5)*]. This is not necessary where a private company can pass a written resolution without a meeting (see 51.4 RESOLUTIONS) but the memorandum must be supplied to each relevant member at or before the time the resolution is passed to him for signature. [*15A Sch 7*].

Thus, shareholders can agree to a term that would otherwise be prohibited by these provisions. Once the shareholders have given their approval, the contract will be fully binding on the company.

If an agreement contains a clause which contravenes the above provisions, the effect is to render the *term* (not the agreement) void to the extent that it contravenes those provisions. In addition, the agreement and, in a case where *Sec 319(2)* applies, the original agreement is deemed to contain a term entitling the company to terminate it at any time by the giving of reasonable notice. [*Sec 319(6)*].

Where a company is a charity in England and Wales, any ratification by the company for the purposes of *Sec 319* is ineffective without the prior written consent of the Charity Commissioners. [*Charities Act 1993, s 66*].

19.61 *Listed companies: further limitations on notice*

Listed companies must also consider the provisions of the Combined Code in the *Listing Rules*. Boards should aim to set notice or contract periods at, or reduce them to, one year or less. If it is necessary to offer longer periods of notice to new directors recruited from outside, such periods should be reduced after the initial period. (Combined Code paras B.1.7, B.1.8).

See 43.15 PUBLIC AND LISTED COMPANIES for the details which UK companies with listed equity securities must give in their accounts and the contents of the report to the shareholders by the remuneration committee.

19.62 **'Golden parachutes'**

The aim of a 'golden parachute' is generally to ensure that, on termination of an executive's service contract, he is entitled to receive a substantial and clearly determined payment of compensation which is generally calculated by reference to his salary (and, possibly, the value of other benefits to which he is entitled) on termination of the contract. The arrangement is sometimes seen where, for example, a take-over is anticipated. The effect in such cases can be to discourage the bidder, if successful, from dismissing the executive but, if it does not do so, to make the dismissal less financially onerous for the executive. Alternatively, an executive who is being encouraged to leave his existing employment and accept a new post may, if he is uncertain as to his future with his new employer, seek financial protection for the giving up of his existing position and from the future uncertainty.

Such clauses can take a variety of forms. They may provide that an obligation by the company to make a payment may arise automatically if

- notice of termination of employment is given by it to the executive at any time;

- the executive gives notice at any time;

- his contract is terminated by either party only following a successful bid for the company's shares; or

- the executive is not, following such a bid, provided with a post of similar status on the board of directors of the acquiring company.

Provision may also be made to cover the possibility of dismissal in cases of gross misconduct or sickness.

In considering the use of such clauses the potential pitfalls should be borne in mind.

- As in the case of long fixed-term contracts, the directors of the company must act in the best interests of the company and the introduction of such a clause into a service contract may be challenged on this basis.

- The sum payable on termination of the service contract may, depending upon the facts, be a penalty (and, as such, irrecoverable) rather than liquidated damages. See *Dunlop Pneumatic Tyre Company Limited v New Garage and Motor Company Limited [1915] AC 79*, the leading case on penalties.

- The impact of taxation should be borne in mind. In particular, where a sum is payable pursuant to the terms of the director's service contract, it will generally be treated by the Inland Revenue as an emolument arising from his employment. Accordingly, it will be taxed under the normal Schedule E rules as deferred remuneration in respect of the year in which it is paid, not under the more beneficial 'golden handshake' provisions in *ICTA 1988, ss 148* and *188*.

19.63 Directorships

The termination of a director's employment does not of itself affect his position as a director of a company. This is generally governed by the company's articles (and possibly memorandum) of association. If the directorship is also to be terminated (which will often be the case) this can in principle be achieved by the passing of a resolution under *Sec 303* (see 19.11 above) at a shareholders' meeting. However, it may not be convenient or practical to convene such a meeting, particularly in the case of a quoted company or a company with a number of institutional shareholders.

From the company's point of view it is useful to provide in the service contract that the director will resign his directorship on termination of his employment for any reason. A director, on the other hand, may have reservations about agreeing to this. If, for example, he feels that he is being dismissed for opposing a course of action which he considered was not in the company's interests, he may feel that he should be removed as a director

19.64 Directors

by a shareholders' resolution under *Sec 303* (as opposed to resigning) because this would entitle him to be heard at any meeting called to consider his removal (*Sec 304*, see 19.11 above).

19.64 Execution formalities

It is essential that, prior to the execution of a director's service contract on behalf of the company, the correct formalities are followed.

The effect of *Sec 35* (see 16.1 DEALINGS WITH THIRD PARTIES) is that there should be no question of entry into the contract being beyond the company's capacity. However, the articles of association of the company should be checked to ascertain whether or not the matter requires the approval of shareholders.

On the basis that Table A has been adopted, the directors may enter into an agreement or arrangement with any director for his employment by the company or for the provision of services by him outside the scope of ordinary duties of a director [*SI 1985 No 805, Table A, Art 84*] and will be empowered to authorise the execution of the agreement on behalf of the company. [*Art 70*]. However, it is not uncommon for companies incorporated for purposes other than trading activities to have specialised articles which require the consent of shareholders and, sometimes, third parties.

Where the board of directors does have sufficient authority and the employee under the service contract is already a director, the quorum and voting requirements of the articles in respect of directors' meetings should be checked. See 33.14 MEETINGS for the provisions of Table A in *SI 1985 No 805*. However, these provisions may have been excluded by the articles. It should also be noted that these articles are different from the comparable provisions contained in the old Table A in *CA 1948* which will still apply to a great many companies.

If approval is to be delegated to a committee (e.g. a remuneration committee) the implications of the decision in *Guinness v Saunders [1990] 2 WLR 324* should also be considered. The House of Lords held that Guinness' articles did not permit the board to delegate its power to determine directors' remuneration. The implications of this are that where a company has a remuneration committee then, depending upon the wording of the articles under which it operates, it may be appropriate for decisions of that committee to be ratified or approved by the whole board.

In addition, the provisions in *Sec 317* should be complied with. See 19.71 below. In the case of *Runciman v Walter Runciman plc [1992] BCLC 1084* Simon Brown J confirmed that *Sec 317* applies to service contracts between a company and its directors and to their subsequent variation. He concluded, in that case, that failure to comply with *Sec 317* would not automatically render the contract or variation in question invalid (he had discretion whether or not to permit rescission) and it was not appropriate, having regard to the facts, to allow the company to avoid the contract. But clearly it is inadvisable to be forced to rely on the exercise of judicial discretion.

19.65 The service contract and the articles

Some of the terms on which a director is to be employed by a company can be contained in the company's articles of association. It is also possible that a company may employ a director on terms which conflict with its articles at the time of appointment or as subsequently varied.

The main case in this area is *Southern Foundries (1926) Limited v Shirlaw [1940] AC 701* which was followed in *Shindler v Northern Raincoat Company Limited [1960] 1 WLR 1038*. It may be contrasted, however, with the decision in *Read v Astoria Garage (Streatham) Limited [1952] Ch 637*. On the basis of these decisions it appears that if a director has an express contract of service, the terms of which would be breached by the exercise by the company of powers granted to it in the articles, such exercise will not prevent the director from successfully claiming damages for breach of contract. However, if the service contract incorporates the terms of the articles (either by providing expressly that the director shall be employed on those terms or because it can be implied that the contract shall embody the terms of the articles) a termination of the director's service contract pursuant to the articles will not be a breach of the service contract.

19.66 Inspection of directors' service contracts

In relation to service contracts of directors or shadow directors (see 19.1 above) or any variation therein, every company must keep the following available for inspection, free of charge, by members for not less than two hours during the period 9 a.m. to 5 p.m. every Monday to Friday (other than public and bank holidays).

- **For service contracts under which the work is performed wholly or mainly outside the UK,** a memorandum giving the director's name and setting out the provisions of the contract relating to its duration. Where the contract is with a subsidiary company, the name and place of incorporation of the subsidiary must also be given.

- **For all other service contracts,** a copy of that contract (whether with the company or a subsidiary) if it is in writing or, if not, a written memorandum setting out its terms.

A person inspecting the contract must be permitted to copy any information made available by taking notes or making a transcript but the company is not obliged to provide any additional facilities other than those to facilitate inspection.

It is not necessary to keep a copy of, or a memorandum setting out the terms of, any contract (or its variation) which has less than twelve months to run or which can be terminated within the next twelve months without payment of any compensation.

All such copies and memorandum must be kept at the same place and at either

- the company's registered office;

- the place where the register of members is kept, if different (see 47.5 REGISTERS) or

- the company's principal place of business, provided that it is situated in the same part of Great Britain in which the company is registered.

The company must notify the Registrar of Companies on the prescribed form (Form 318) within 14 days of the place where the copies and memorandum are kept and any changes in that place unless they have always been kept at the company's registered office.

If default is made in complying with any of the above provisions or an inspection is refused, the company and every officer in default is liable to a fine up to the level in 40.1(*f*) PENALTIES. In the case of a refusal of inspection, the court may compel an immediate inspection.

19.67 Directors

[Sec 318; SI 1991 No 1998].

Listed companies. See 43.21(*c*) PUBLIC AND LISTED COMPANIES for additional requirements regarding inspection of directors' service contracts.

19.67 Variation of service contracts

Frequently the parties to a service contract will wish to alter some of its terms during the subsistence of the contract. The most common changes are to

• improve the salary and/or other benefits of the director;

• alter the termination provisions; or

• incorporate formally into the service contract provisions which have been operated by the company on an informal basis in such a way that they are viewed in practice, if not in law, as part of the terms of employment.

In approving any such changes, the board of directors must act in the best interests of the company as a whole and the correct formalities under the company's articles of association must be followed. If any changes vary the terms of employment to be included, or referred to, in the written statement to be given to the employee under *ERA 1996, s 1* (see 19.56 above), the employer is required to inform the employee of the nature of the changes by a written statement at the earliest opportunity and, in any event, no later than one month after the change. [*ERA 1996, s 4*]. In practice, though, where the change is properly documented, this requirement will automatically have been complied with. In addition, the copy of the director's service contract made available for inspection under *Sec 318* must be updated (see 19.66 above).

The City Code. The provisions of the City Code on Take-overs and Mergers must be considered in the case of, broadly speaking, listed and unlisted public companies. *Rule 21* (restrictions on frustrating action, see 59.9 TAKEOVER OFFERS) restricts entering into contracts otherwise than in the normal course of business. The notes on *Rule 21* make clear that the Panel will regard this as including amending or entering into a service contract with, or creating or varying the terms of employment of, a director if the new or amended contract or terms constitute an abnormal increase in his emoluments or a significant improvement in his terms of service. *Rule 25* (offeree board circulars, see 59.10 TAKEOVER OFFERS) requires the first major circular from the offeree board to contain particulars of all service contracts of any director or proposed director of the offeree company with the company or any subsidiary where the contracts have more than twelve months to run. Where any such service contract has been entered into or amended within six months prior to the date of the circular, particulars must be given of any earlier contract replaced by the current contract or of the contract prior to its amendment. Details disclosed must include the director's name, the expiry date of the contract and fixed or variable remuneration. (*Rule 25.4, Note 1*).

19.68 Termination

A service contract may be terminated either in accordance with its terms or prematurely without good cause. The latter case will generally require a payment to be made by the company to the director by way of damages for wrongful dismissal (this is not required where the premature termination is for 'good cause' e.g. gross misconduct). Where no such payment is required, a company may nevertheless wish to make an *ex gratia* payment to the director.

Corporate capacity. *Sec 35* (see 16.1 DEALING WITH THIRD PARTIES) provides that the validity of an act done by a company shall not be called into question on the ground of lack of capacity by reason of the fact that it is beyond the objects of the company stated in the memorandum of association. Accordingly, there should be no question of a payment on termination of employment going beyond the company's capacity.

Powers of the board. *Sec 35A* (see 16.2 DEALINGS WITH THIRD PARTIES) provides that, in favour of a person dealing with a company in good faith, the power of the board of directors to bind the company, or authorise others to do so, shall be deemed to be free of any limitations under the company's constitution. However, this is subject to *Sec 322A* (see 19.72 below) which, *inter alia*, applies where a company enters into a transaction with a director of the company and the board of directors exceed any limitation on their powers under the company's constitution. In these circumstances the transaction is voidable at the instance of the company. Also, whether or not it is avoided, the director with whom the transaction is entered into and any director of the company who authorised the transaction is liable to account to the company for any gain which he has made directly or indirectly by the transaction and to indemnify the company for any loss or damage resulting from the transaction.

Directors must also not exceed their authority and must exercise their powers in the best interests of the company. In this context a distinction can be drawn between a *bona fide* payment by way of damages for breach of contract and any other payment, such as an *ex gratia* payment. Subject to the point mentioned below, the former will generally satisfy the above requirements, unless it can be construed as a fraud on creditors (e.g. where the company's business is to close down). The payment will by definition be one which the company can be compelled to pay. However, where such a payment is to be made it should be considered whether the entering into of the contract by the company can be challenged. For example, where in anticipation of a take-over of the company the directors vote each other long-term service agreements with the predominant purpose of protecting their own interests, the service contracts may be set aside as not being made *bona fide* in the interests of the company and not being for a proper purpose.

In the case of an *ex gratia* payment, if the directors are exercising the relevant power for purposes other than the purposes of the company and the director in receipt of the payment has notice of this, he cannot rely on the authority of the directors to bind the company and the company will not be bound. However, the company will (subject to an exception if the transaction constitutes a fraud on creditors) be bound by an act if it is done with the unanimous consent of all the shareholders or is susbequently ratified by such consent.

On the basis that the above requirements are complied with, any approval by the board of directors of a payment should be given in accordance with the company's articles of association.

Listed companies. Remuneration committees should consider what compensation commitments (including pension contributions) their directors' contracts of service would entail in the event of early termination. They should, in particular, consider the advantage of providing explicitly in the initial contract for such compensation commitments (except in the case of removal for misconduct). Where the initial contract does not explicitly provide for compensation commitments, the remuneration committee should, within legal constraints, tailor their approach in individual early termination cases to the wide variety of circumstances. The broad aim should be to avoid rewarding poor performance while dealing fairly with cases where departure is not due to poor performance and take a robust line on reducing compensation to reflect departing directors' obligations to mitigate loss. (Combined Code, paras B.1.9 and B.1.10).

See 43.15 PUBLIC AND LISTED COMPANIES for details to be given in the report to the shareholders by the remuneration committee.

19.69   Directors

Shareholder approval. See 19.53 and 19.54 above for approval by shareholders of payments to directors for loss of, or retirement from, office.

19.69   Checklist of information commonly required in preparing a service contract

1.   *Parties*

Names and addresses.

2.   *Term*

- (i)   Is the contract to be for a fixed term and, if so, for how long?

   (ii)   Is there any right of termination by notice during that term?

- Is the contract to be for an initial fixed period, followed by continuation until terminated by notice? If so, what is the length of the initial period?

- Is the contract to continue until terminated by notice?

- If notice provisions are to be included, what is the length of the notice periods?

- Is automatic termination at a certain age appropriate?

3.   *Details of the job*

- Job title.

- Any specific duties of the executive.

- Is it appropriate that the executive should be obliged to do work for other group companies?

- To whom is the executive to be responsible?

4.   *Commencement*

- Is the executive already employed by the employer? If so, since when has he been employed and what are the current terms of his employment?

- Is employment with any other employer to be counted as part of the executive's continuous period of employment with the employer? If so, on what date did the executive's continuous period of employment begin?

- From what date should the service agreement be effective?

5.   *Remuneration*

- Salary

   (i)   What is the amount and when is it payable?

   (ii)   Is it to be subject to review and, if so, what are the review provisions?

- Is any form of commission or bonus payable? If so, on what terms?

- (i)   Will a car be provided for the executive? If so, on what terms? In particular, which party will pay the costs of running the car, and are the costs of private motoring to be paid by the employer?

   (ii)   Will the executive be entitled to have the car changed during his employment? If so, on what terms?

- What other expenses of the executive will be met by the employer? In particular, will the employer make any credit cards available to the executive and how will payment of expenses be made (e.g. by way of an advance or by reimbursement)?

6.   *Hours and place of work*

- What are the normal hours of work, if any?

- Is work in excess of normal hours to be expected?

- What will be the normal place of work?

- Will the employer require the right to move the executive to a different place of work? If so, might that requirement extend to moving the executive outside the United Kingdom?

- Will the employer pay relocation expenses?

- Will the executive be required to travel abroad?

7.   *Holiday and sickness*

- What is the executive's entitlement to holiday?

- Will the executive have to obtain approval for the timing of his holidays? If so, from whom must approval be obtained?

- Is the executive to be entitled to accrued holiday pay on termination of employment?

- Is the executive entitled to be paid during absence from work due to sickness or injury over and above the requirements of Statutory Sick Pay?

- Are national insurance benefits received or receivable by the executive during absence from work, to be deducted from his pay? (This will only apply after Statutory Sick Pay ceases to be payable.)

8.   *Termination and suspension*

- Does the employer require the right to suspend the executive? If so, would suspension be with or without pay?

- Does the employer require the right to transfer the executive to another job rather than dismissing him?

- Does the employer wish to be able to send an employee on 'garden leave', if notice of termination is given by either the employer or employee?

9.   *Grievance and disciplinary procedure*

- If the executive has a grievance relating to his employment, to whom should he first refer it? To whom should he refer the matter if dissatisfied thereafter?

- Does the employer have a set of disciplinary rules and procedures? Where can the executive obtain a copy during his employment?

10.   *Pension and other benefits*

- Will the executive join the employer's pension scheme? If so, where are particulars of the scheme available?

- Is a national insurance contracting-out certificate in force in respect of the executive's employment?

- Will the executive be entitled to:

    (i)   participate in a permanent disability and/or accident or similar scheme;

(ii)   private medical insurance?

(iii)   other such benefits?

11.   *Restraint on activities of executive*

(*Note*: Any restrictions are only enforceable to the extent that they can be proved to be reasonable to protect the legitimate interests of the employer. It will be necessary to consider carefully the extent of any restriction.)

- Is the executive to be entitled to be engaged or interested in any business, trade or occupation outside his employment during the term of the contract? If so, on what terms?

- Does the employer require a prohibition on the executive's soliciting customers, suppliers etc. from the employer after termination of the contract? If so, for how long is the prohibition to last, and how recently and how frequently must the customer or other party have dealt with the employer?

- Are any restrictions to be imposed on the carrying on by the executive of activities in competition with the employer after termination of the contract?

12.   *Directorships*

- Is the executive to receive director's fees in addition to his salary?

- Is the directorship to cease automatically on termination of the employment?

- Is it possible that the executive will continue to be employed while no longer a director?

- Will any qualifying shares be required to be held by the executive?

13.   *Inventions and designs*

Is it possible that the executive will develop any invention or copyright work during his employment? If so, in whom is ownership of any intellectual or industrial property rights to vest?

19.70 **INTERESTS IN CONTRACTS**

Subject to the provisions of *CA 1985* and provided he has disclosed his interests under 19.71 below, a director may have an interest in contracts with the company. [*Sec 317(9)*]. In particular, where *SI 1985 No 805, Table A, Art 85* has been adopted

- a director may be a party to, or otherwise interested in, any transaction or arrangement with the company or in which it is interested;

- he may be

(i)   a director or other officer of,

(ii)   employed by,

(iii)   a party to any transaction with, or

(iv)   otherwise interested in

another company in which the company is interested;

- he is not accountable to the company for any benefit he derives in this way; and

- no such transaction or arrangement is liable to be avoided on the grounds of his interest or benefit.

Where there are no specific provisions in the articles, any such contract is voidable at the instance of the company (*Aberdeen Rly Co v Blackie Bros (1854) 1 Macq 461*) but may be ratified by the company in general meeting (*North-West Transportation Co Ltd v Beatty (1887) 12 App Cas 589*).

19.71 **Disclosure of interest in contracts**

General. A director must declare, at a directors' meeting, the nature of any direct or indirect interest he has in any 'contract' or proposed contract of the company. *'Contract'* includes any transaction or arrangement (whether or not constituting a contract) entered into after 21 December 1980. A loan etc. within 19.85 below is specifically included.

Specific notice. The declaration must be made at the first meeting at which the proposed contract is considered or, if later, the first meeting at which he was interested in the contract or proposed contract.

General notice may be given to the directors that the director is to be regarded as interested in any contract which may be made with a specific company or firm of which he is a member or with a specific person who is connected with him (see 19.94 below). Such notice does not have effect unless either it is given at a meeting of directors or the director takes reasonable steps to secure that it is brought up and read at the next such meeting after it is given.

[*Sec 317(1)-(6)*].

Penalties. A director who fails to comply with these provisions is guilty of an offence and liable to a fine up to the level in 40.1(*d*) PENALTIES. [*Sec 317(7), 24 Sch*].

Shadow directors. The above provisions also apply to shadow directors (see 19.1 above) except that a shadow director must declare his interest in writing to the directors either by specific notice before the meeting at which a director would be required to give such notice or by general notice. [*Sec 317(8)*].

Sole directors. When holding the meeting alone, the sole director must make the declaration to himself (not necessarily out loud) and record the declaration in the minutes (otherwise the court may find it difficult to accept that the declaration has been made). If the meeting is attended by anyone else (e.g. the company secretary) the declaration must be made out loud and in the hearing of those attending and again should be recorded. In this case, if it was proved that the declaration had been made, the fact that the minutes did not record its making would not preclude proof that it had been made (*Neptune (Vehicle Washing Equipment) Ltd v Fitzgerald [1995] BCC 474*).

Non-compliance with the above provisions does not make the contract void only voidable (*Hely-Hutchinson v Brayhead Ltd [1968] 1 QB 549*).

Listed companies. See 43.15(*j*) PUBLIC AND LISTED COMPANIES for disclosure of significant contracts in the annual accounts.

Contracts with sole members who are directors. Unless a contract is entered into in the ordinary course of business or is in writing, where a private company limited by shares or guarantee has one member who is also a director, the company must ensure that the terms of the contract are either set out in a written memorandum or recorded in the minutes of the first meeting of directors following the making of the contract. [*Sec 322B(1)(2); SI 1992 No 1699*].

Shadow directors. A sole member who is a shadow director is treated as a director. [*Sec 322B(3); SI 1992 No 1699*].

19.72 Directors

Penalties. In default, the company and every officer in default is liable, on summary conviction, to a fine up to the level of the statutory maximum (see 40.1 PENALTIES). [*Sec 322B(4), 24 Sch; SI 1992 No 1699*].

Non-compliance with the above provisions does not affect the validity of the contract. [*Sec 322B(6); SI 1992 No 1699*].

19.72 INVALIDITY OF CERTAIN CONTRACTS

Despite the provisions of *Sec 35* (see 16.1 DEALINGS WITH THIRD PARTIES) a transaction is *voidable* at the instance of the company where it enters into a transaction to which the parties include

(*a*)   a director of the company or its holding company, or

(*b*)   a person connected with such a director or a company with whom such a director is associated

and the board of directors, in connection with the transaction, exceeds any limitation in their powers under the company's constitution. This applies whether the limitation derives from a company resolution in general meeting or meeting of any class of shareholders or from any agreement between the members or any class of shareholders.

See 19.94 below for connected and associated persons.

Whether or not the transaction is avoided, any person within (*a*) or (*b*) above and any director of the company who authorised the transaction is liable to account for any gain he has made and indemnify the company for any loss or damage resulting. However, a person other than a director of the company is not liable if he shows that, at the time of the transaction, he did not know that the directors were exceeding their powers.

The transaction ceases to be voidable if

•   restitution of any money or other asset the subject matter of the transaction is no longer possible;

•   the company is indemnified for any loss or damage resulting from the transaction;

•   rights acquired bona fide for value, and without actual notice of the directors' exceeding their powers, by a person not party to the transaction would be affected by the avoidance; or

•   the transaction is ratified by the company in general meeting.

Where a transaction is voidable by virtue of the above but valid by virtue of *Sec 35A* (see 16.2 DEALINGS WITH THIRD PARTIES) in relation to a party not within (*a*) or (*b*) above, that party or the company may apply to the court to affirm, sever or set aside the transaction on such terms as appears to the court to be just.

[*Sec 322A; CA 1989, s 109*].

19.73 SUBSTANTIAL PROPERTY TRANSACTIONS

Subject to the exception below, a company must not enter into an agreement whereby

(i)   a director of the company or its holding company, or a person connected with such a director, acquires 'non-cash assets' of 'requisite value' from the company, or

(ii)   the company acquires non-cash assets of requisite value from such a director or a person so connected unless the arrangement is first approved by a resolution of the company in general meeting. Where the director or connected person is a director of its holding company or a person connected with such a director, the arrangement must also be approved by a resolution of the holding company in general meeting. [*Sec 320(1)*].

Director includes a shadow director (see 19.1 above). [*Sec 320(3)*].

See 19.94 below for connected persons and 18.1 DEFINITIONS for '*non-cash assets*'.

'*Requisite value*' means in excess of £100,000 or 10% of the company's asset value, subject to a *de minimis* value of £2,000. The company's asset value is taken as its net assets shown in the accounts for the last preceding financial year or, where no accounts have been prepared, the company's called-up share capital. [*Sec 320(2); SI 1990 No 1393*].

Exceptions to the above are as follows.

- No approval is required to be given by a wholly-owned subsidiary.

- The provisions do not apply to an arrangement for the acquisition of non-cash assets

  (i) by a holding company from a wholly-owned subsidiary or vice versa or by one wholly-owned subsidiary from another; or

  (ii) entered into by a company being wound up unless it is a members' voluntary winding up.

- Where a person acquires an asset from a company of which he is a member, then (i) above does not apply to the arrangement if it is made with that person in his character as a member.

- The provisions do not apply to a transaction on a recognised investment exchange effected by a director, or a person connected with him, through an '*independent broker*' i.e. a person who independently selects the person with whom the transaction is to be effected.

[*Sec 321; CA 1989, 19 Sch 8*].

Listed companies. In addition to the requirements of *CA 1985*, listed companies must also comply with the requirements of the *Listing Rules, Chapter 11* as to transactions with related parties. See 43.13 PUBLIC AND LISTED COMPANIES.

19.74 Liabilities arising from contravention

Any arrangement entered into by a company in contravention of the provisions of 19.73 above and any transaction entered into in pursuance of the arrangement (whether by the company or any other person) is *voidable* at the instance of the company unless

- restitution of any money or other asset the subject matter of the transaction is no longer possible;

- the company has been indemnified by any other person for the loss or damage suffered by it;

- any rights acquired bona fide for value and without actual notice of the contravention by any person not party to the arrangement or transaction would be affected by its avoidance; or

- the arrangement is, within a reasonable period, affirmed by the company in general meeting, and also, where it is an arrangement for the transfer of an asset to or by

19.75 Directors

a director of its holding company or a connected person, is so affirmed with the approval of the holding company by a resolution in general meeting.

[*Sec 322(1)(2)*].

Whether or not the arrangement has been avoided, any person within 19.73(i) above, and any other director of the company who authorised it, is liable to account to the company for any gain he has made and (jointly and severally with any other person liable) to indemnify the company for any loss or damage resulting from it, except that

- if the arrangement is entered into by a company and a person connected with a director of the company or its holding company, the director is not liable if he shows that he took all reasonable steps to secure the company's compliance with the provisions of 19.73 above; and

- a connected person and any other director of the company is not liable if he shows that, at the time of the arrangement, he did not know the relevant circumstances constituting the contravention.

[*Sec 322(3)-(6)*].

19.75 SHARE DEALING

A director may hold shares or debentures in the company of which he is a director. In certain circumstances he may be obliged to hold qualifying shares as a condition of being a director (see 19.7 above). He must, however, notify the company of his holdings and any changes therein. This is extended to certain family members. See 19.76 to 19.81 below for full details. Listed companies must in turn notify The Stock Exchange of any share dealings by its directors. See 19.82 below.

Directors are prohibited from dealing in share options. See 19.83 below.

19.76 Disclosure of shareholdings by a director to the company

Subject to the exceptions in 19.78 below, a director of a company or shadow director (see 19.1 above) must notify the company in writing of the following. Notification must state, in addition to the specific information listed, the number or amount, and class, of shares or debentures involved. It must also indicate that the information is being given in fulfilment of the obligation under these provisions; otherwise the obligation is treated as not discharged.

(*a*)   His interests, at the time of becoming a director, in the shares and debentures of the company, its holding company, any subsidiary company or any subsidiary of its holding company.

(*b*)   Any event in consequence of which he becomes, or ceases to become, interested in such shares while a director. If this event is the entering into a contract to purchase shares or debentures, the notification must include the price to be paid under the contract.

(*c*)   His entering into a contract to sell any such shares while a director. Notification must include the price received under the contract.

(*d*)   The assignment by him of a right granted by the company to subscribe for shares or debentures of the company. Notification must include the consideration for the assignment or, if there is no consideration, that fact.

(*e*)   The grant to him by the company's holding company or subsidiary company, or by a subsidiary company of its holding company, of a right to subscribe for shares or debentures in that company. Notification must include details of the

- date on which the right was granted;

- period during which, or the time at which, the right is exercisable;

- consideration for the grant or, if there is no consideration, that fact; and

- price to be paid for the shares or debentures.

(f) The exercise of a right granted within (e) above. Notification must include details of the

- number of shares or amount of debentures in respect of which the right was exercised; and

- name or names in which they were registered (and the number or amount in each name if applicable).

(g) The assignment by him of a right granted within (e) above. Notification must include the consideration for the assignment or, if there is no consideration, that fact.

[*Sec 324(1)(2)(5), 13 Sch 17-20*].

See 19.77 below for the interpretation of 'interest'.

The company is obliged to keep a register of directors' interests (see 47.7 REGISTERS). It is also obliged to disclose the information to The Stock Exchange (see 19.82 below).

19.77 *Interpretation of 'interests in shares or debentures'*

A reference to an interest in shares or debentures includes any interest of any kind whatsoever and there are to be disregarded any restraints or restrictions to which the exercise of any right attached to the interest is or may be subject. [*13 Sch 1*]. It is immaterial that shares or debentures in which a person has an interest are unidentifiable. [*13 Sch 8*].

A person is to be taken as having an interest in shares or debentures in the following circumstances.

(a) He enters into a contract for their purchase.

(b) Not being the registered holder, he is entitled to exercise any right conferred by the holding of the shares or debentures or is entitled to control the exercise of any such right. *Included* is a person who has a right or is under an obligation, the exercise or the fulfilment of which would make him so entitled. *Excluded* is a person who has been appointed a proxy to vote at a specific meeting or has been appointed by a corporation as its representative at any meeting.

(c) A company is interested in the shares or debentures and either

(i) that company or its directors are accustomed to act in accordance with his directions or instructions; or

(ii) he is entitled to exercise or control the exercise of one-third or more of the voting power of the company at general meetings.

Where a person is entitled as under (ii) above and that company is entitled to exercise, or control the exercise of, any voting power of another company at general meetings (the 'effective voting power') then, for the purposes of (ii) above, the effective voting power is taken to be exercisable by that person.

(d) Otherwise than by having an interest under a trust,

(i) he has a right to call for delivery of the shares or debentures to himself or his order, or

(ii)   he has a right to acquire an interest in the shares or debentures or is under an obligation to take an interest in them

whether the right or obligation is conditional or absolute. Rights or obligations to subscribe for shares or debentures are not included under (ii) above.

[*13 Sch 2-6*].

There is to be disregarded any interest

(i)   arising to a person by virtue of any authorised unit trust scheme within *FSA 1986* or any scheme under *Charities Act 1960, ss 22, 22A* or *Charities Act 1993, ss 24, 25, Trustees Investment Act 1961, s 11, Administration of Justice Act 1965, s 1* or the *Schedule* to the *Church Funds Investment Measure 1958*; or

(ii)   of the Church of Scotland General Trustees or of the Church of Scotland Trust in shares or debentures held by them; or

(iii)   of any other person in shares or debentures held by the Trustees or Trust within (ii) above otherwise than as simple trustees.

[*13 Sch 11, 12; FSA 1986, 16 Sch 25; Charities Act 1992, 6 Sch 11; Charities Act 1993, 6 Sch 20*].

Joint interest. Persons having a joint interest are each deemed to have that interest. [*13 Sch 7*].

Trusts. Where trust property includes any interest in shares or debentures, any beneficiary of the trust is taken as having such an interest. However, where a person is entitled to receive, during the lifetime of himself or another, the income from the trust, an interest in the shares or debentures in reversion or remainder (or, in Scotland, in fee) is to be disregarded. [*13 Sch 2, 9*].

Bare trustees etc. A person is not treated as interested in shares or debentures if, and so long as, he holds them under the law in force in England and Wales as bare trustee or custodian trustee, or under the law in force in Scotland as a simple trustee. [*13 Sch 10*].

19.78 *Exceptions*

The provisions of 19.76 above do not require notification of the following.

• Events coming to the knowledge of the person after he ceased to be a director. [*Sec 324(4)*].

• Shares in a company which is the wholly-owned subsidiary of another company. [*Sec 324(6)*].

• Interests in shares or debentures

(i)   held by a person as trustee or personal representative of any trust or estate of which the Public Trustee is also a trustee (otherwise than as custodian trustee) or personal representative;

(ii)   of a society registered, or deemed to be registered, under *Industrial and Provident Societies Act 1965*;

(iii)   held by a person as trustee of, or beneficiary under, an approved retirement benefits scheme or superannuation fund; or

(iv)   held by a company as trustee of an approved retirement benefits scheme or superannuation fund where the person is deemed to be interested in that company under 19.77(*c*) above.

[*SI 1985 No 802, Reg 2(a)-(c)(e)*].

- Any event occurring in relation to a person arising out of his interests in shares or debentures under the above. [*SI 1985 No 802, Reg 2(d)(f)*].

- Interests in shares in a company arising solely on account of any limitation imposed by the memorandum or articles on a person's rights to dispose of a share. [*SI 1985 No 802, Reg 2(g)*].

Overriding exceptions. Even where the provisions would otherwise require it, a person is not required to give notification *to*

- a wholly-owned subsidiary in respect of interests or events within 19.76(*a*)–(*g*) above relating to *any* shares or debentures where the director is also a director of that company's holding company and the holding company is required to keep a register of directors' interests (see 47.7 REGISTERS); or

- a wholly-owned subsidiary of a company incorporated outside Great Britain in respect of interests or events within 19.76(*a*)–(*g*) above relating to the shares or debentures of its holding company or any other company incorporated outside Great Britain.

[*SI 1985 No 802, Reg 3*].

19.79 *Extension to spouses and children*

A director's interest in the shares or debentures of a company is treated as including any interest of

- the wife or husband of the director, and

- an 'infant' son or daughter (including step-child) of the director

unless that person is a director in his or her own right.

'*Infant*', in relation to Scotland, means a pupil or minor.

Subject to the above, a director must also therefore notify information under 19.76(*a*)–(*g*) above relating to his or her spouse and children. *Additionally*, for them alone, he must notify under 19.76(*e*) and (*f*) above details of the grant of a right to subscribe for shares or debentures, or the exercise of that right, in the company of which he is a director.

[*Sec 328*].

19.80 *Time limit for notification*

The obligation to disclose information must be fulfilled within the five days next following

- where 19.76(*a*) above applies, the day he becomes a director or, if later, the day the existence of the interest comes to his knowledge;

- where 19.76(*b*)–(*g*) above applies, the day on which the event occurs or, if later, the day on which the fact that the occurrence of the event gives rise to an obligation comes to his knowledge; and

- where 19.79 above applies, the day on which the occurrence of the event comes to his knowledge.

In calculating the five days, weekends and bank holidays in any part of Great Britain are ignored.

[*Sec 328(5), 13 Sch 14-16*].

19.81 Directors

A person who

- fails to discharge any obligation under 19.76 or 19.80 above within the proper period, or

- in purporting to discharge his obligation makes a statement which he knows to be false or recklessly makes a statement which is false

is guilty of an offence and liable to a penalty up to the level in 40.1(*b*) PENALTIES. [*Secs 324(7), 328(6), 24 Sch*]. Such proceedings can only be brought with the consent of the Secretary of State or the Director of Public Prosecutions. [*Sec 732*]. See 32.3 LEGAL PROCEEDINGS.

19.82 Disclosure of director's shareholding by company to an investment exchange

Whenever a company whose shares or debentures are listed on a recognised investment exchange (other than an overseas investment exchange within the meaning of *FSA 1986*) is notified by a director of any matters under the requirements of 19.76 or 19.79 above in relation to shares so listed, the company must also notify that investment exchange. It must do this before the end of the day next following the receipt of the information, disregarding weekends and bank holidays in any part of Great Britain. In default, the company and every officer in default is guilty of an offence and liable to a fine up to the level in 40.1(*f*) PENALTIES. [*Sec 329, 24 Sch; FSA 1986, 16 Sch 20*]. Such proceedings can only be brought with the consent of the Secretary of State or the Director of Public Prosecutions. [*Sec 732*]. See 32.3 LEGAL PROCEEDINGS.

See also 43.21(*d*) PUBLIC AND LISTED COMPANIES for the disclosure requirements as detailed in the Listing Rules.

19.83 Dealing in share options

It is an offence for a director or shadow director (see 19.1 above) of a company to buy a right

- to call for, or

- to make, or

- as he may elect, to call for or make

delivery at a specified 'price' and within a specified time of a specified number of 'relevant' shares or a specified amount of 'relevant' debentures.

'Price' includes any consideration other than money.

'Relevant' shares or debentures in relation to a director of a company are those of the company, its holding company, any subsidiary company, or any subsidiary company of its holding company, which are listed on a stock exchange (whether in Great Britain or elsewhere).

However the provision does not penalise a person who buys

- a right to *subscribe* for shares or debentures of a company; or

- debentures which confer a right to subscribe for, or to convert the debentures into, shares of that company.

Penalties. A person guilty of an offence under the above provisions is liable to a penalty up to the level in 40.1(*b*) PENALTIES.

[*Sec 323, 24 Sch*].

19.84 *Extension to spouses and children*

The provisions on 19.83 above also apply to

(*a*)   the wife or husband of the director or shadow director, and

(*b*)   an 'infant' son or daughter (including step-child) of the director

unless that person is a director in his or her own right.

'Infant' in relation to Scotland means a pupil or minor.

However, it is a defence for a person within (*a*) or (*b*) above charged with an offence under 19.83 above to prove that he or she had no reason to believe that his or her spouse or, as the case may be, parent was a director of the company in question.

[*Sec 327*].

19.85 LOANS TO DIRECTORS

The restrictions in 19.86 to 19.90 below apply to loans etc. to directors and shadow directors (see 19.1 above) and, where applicable, persons connected with them (see 19.94 below). [*Sec 330(1)(5)*].

19.86 Loans by all companies

Subject to the exceptions below and the general exemptions in 19.91 below, a company must not

(i)   make a loan to a director of the company or its holding company; or

(ii)   enter into any 'guarantee' or provide any security in connection with a loan by any person to a director of the company or its holding company.

'Guarantee' includes indemnity.

Exception for small loans. A company may make a loan within (i) above provided the aggregate of all 'relevant amounts' does not exceed £5,000.

'Relevant amounts' are

(*a*)   the value of the proposed transaction; and

(*b*)   the amount outstanding under any other transactions, or the value of any existing arrangement within 19.89 or 19.90 below, made for the director under the exception for small loans by

●   the company or its subsidiary; or

●   where the proposed transaction is for a director of the company's holding company, that holding company or any of its subsidiaries.

For the purposes of (*b*) above, a previous transaction by a subsidiary or fellow subsidiary of the company making the loan can be ignored if it is no longer such a subsidiary at the time of the current transaction in question.

[*Secs 330(2), 331(2), 334, 339; CA 1989, s 138*].

Value. The value of a loan is the amount of its principal; and the value of a guarantee or security is the amount guaranteed or secured. [*Sec 340(2)(4)*].

19.87 Loans and quasi-loans by relevant companies

Subject to the exceptions below and the general exemptions in 19.91 below, a 'relevant company' must not

19.88 Directors

(*a*)   make a 'quasi-loan' to a director of the company or its holding company;

(*b*)   make a loan or quasi-loan to a person connected with such a director; or

(*c*)   enter into a 'guarantee' or provide any security in connection with a loan or quasi-loan made by any other person for such a director or a person connected with such a director.

See 19.94 below for connected persons.

'Relevant company' means a company which is a public company or a member of a group which contains a public company.

'Quasi-loan' is a transaction under which one party ('the creditor') agrees to pay a sum for another ('the borrower') or agrees to reimburse expenditure incurred by another party for the borrower. The transaction must either be made on terms that the borrower (or a person on his behalf) will reimburse the creditor or in circumstances giving rise to a liability on the borrower to reimburse the creditor.

'Guarantee' includes indemnity.

Exception for short-term quasi-loans. A relevant company may make quasi-loans to a director of the company or its holding company provided that it must be reimbursed within two months of incurring the expenditure and the aggregate amount outstanding on all 'relevant quasi-loans' to the director does not exceed £5,000.

'Relevant quasi-loans' are those made to the director by the company or its subsidiaries or, where the loan is to a director of the holding company, by any subsidiaries of that holding company.

Exception for inter-company loans. Where the relevant company is a member of a group, it is not prevented

● under (*b*) above from making a loan to another group member, or

● under (*c*) above from entering into a guarantee etc. made by any person to another member of the group

by reason only that a director of one member of the group is associated (see 19.94 below) with another.

[Secs 330(3), 331(2)(3)(6), 332, 333; CA 1989, s 138].

Value. The value of a loan is the amount of its principal; the value of a quasi-loan is the amount, or maximum amount, which the person to whom it is made is liable to reimburse the creditor; and the value of a guarantee or security is the amount guaranteed or secured. *[Sec 340(2)-(4)].*

19.88 Credit transactions by relevant companies

Subject to the exceptions below and the general exemptions in 19.91 below, a 'relevant company' must not

(i)   enter into a 'credit transaction' as a creditor for a director of the company or its holding company or a person connected with such a director; or

(ii)   enter into a 'guarantee' or provide any security in connection with a credit transaction made by any other person for such a director or a person so connected.

See 19.94 below for connected persons.

'Relevant company' means a company which is a public company or a member of a group which contains a public company.

'Credit transaction' is a transaction under which one party supplies any goods or sells any land under a hire purchase or conditional sale agreement; leases or hires any land or goods in return for periodic payments; or otherwise disposes of land or supplies goods or 'services' on the understanding that payment is to be deferred. *'Services'* means anything other than goods or land.

'Guarantee' includes indemnity.

Exception for minor transactions. A company may enter into a transaction within (i) or (ii) above for a person if the aggregate of all 'relevant amounts' does not exceed £10,000.

'Relevant amounts' are

(*a*)   the value of the proposed transaction; and

(*b*)   the amount outstanding under any other transactions, or the value of any existing arrangement within 19.89 or 19.90 below, made under the exemption for minor transactions for the director or any person connected with him (or, where the proposed transaction is for a person connected with a director, for that director or any person connected with him) by

- the company or its subsidiary; or

- where the proposed transaction is for a director of the company's holding company or a person connected with such a director, that holding company or any of its subsidiaries.

For the purposes of (*b*) above, a previous transaction by a subsidiary or fellow subsidiary of the company making the loan can be ignored if it is no longer such a subsidiary at the time of the current transaction in question.

Exception for business transactions. A company may enter into a transaction within (i) or (ii) above for a person if it is entered into in the ordinary course of its business and the value and terms of the transaction are no more favourable than those which would have been offered to an unconnected person of the same financial standing.

[Secs 330(4), 331(2)(6)-(8), 335, 339; SI 1990 No 1393].

Value. The value of a credit transaction is the price which it is reasonable to expect could be obtained for the goods, land or services to which the transaction relates if they had been supplied in the ordinary course of business and on the same terms (apart from price) as they are under the transaction. If the value cannot be ascertained, it is assumed to exceed £100,000. *[Sec 340(6)(7); SI 1990 No 1393].*

19.89   Assignment and assumption of rights and obligations by companies

Subject to the general exemptions in 19.91 below, a company must not arrange for the assignment to it, or the assumption by it, of any rights, obligations or liabilities under a transaction which, if it had been entered into by the company, would have contravened the provisions of 19.86 to 19.88 above. Where it does so, the transaction is treated as having been entered into at the date of the arrangement. *[Sec 330(6)].*

Value. The value of the arrangement is the value of the transaction to which the arrangement relates *less* any amount by which the liabilities under the arrangement of the person for whom the transaction was made have been reduced. If the value cannot be ascertained, it is assumed to exceed £100,000. *[Sec 340(5)(7)].*

19.90   Other arrangements with third parties

Subject to the general exceptions in 19.91 below, a company must not take part in any arrangement whereby

- another person enters into a transaction which, if it had been entered into by the company would have contravened the provisions of 19.86 to 19.89 above; and

- that other person, in pursuance of the arrangement, has obtained any benefit from the company, its holding company or a fellow subsidiary.

[*Sec 330(7)*].

Value. The value of the arrangement is as under 19.89 above.

19.91 General exemptions

The following transactions are exempt from the prohibitions under 19.86 to 19.90 above.

- A company making a loan or quasi-loan to its holding company. [*Sec 336(a)*].

- A company entering into a guarantee or providing security in connection with a loan or quasi-loan made by any person to its holding company. [*Sec 336(a)*].

- A company entering into any credit transaction as creditor for its holding company or entering into a guarantee or providing any security in connection with a credit transaction by any person for its holding company. [*Sec 336(b)*].

- A company providing funds to enable a director to meet expenditure incurred, or to be incurred, by him for company purposes (or to avoid incurring such expenditure) provided that

  (i)   prior approval is given by the company at a general meeting at which details of purpose, amount and extent of liability under any connected transaction are disclosed (if approved by written resolution of a private company, see 51.4 RESOLUTIONS, the information must be disclosed to members before or at the time of signature); or

  (ii) if approval is not given at or before the next annual general meeting, the loan (or any other liability arising) is repaid within six months of that meeting.

In the case of a 'relevant company' the aggregate of the 'relevant amounts' must not exceed £20,000.

Where the company is a charity in England and Wales, any ratification by the company under (i) above is ineffective without the prior written consent of the Charity Commissioners.

[*Sec 337, 15A Sch 8; SI 1990 No 1393; Charities Act 1993, s 66*].

- A money-lending company, in the ordinary course of business, making a loan or quasi-loan to any person or entering into a guarantee in connection with any other loan or quasi-loan. The amount and terms involved must be no more favourable than those which would have been offered to an unconnected person of the same financial standing; this condition does not, however, in itself prevent a company making a loan to one of its directors, or a director of its holding company, in connection with the purchase or improvement of his only or main residence (or a loan in substitution of such a loan) if such loans are ordinarily made by the company to its employees on no *less* favourable terms to the transaction in question and the aggregate of the 'relevant amounts' does not exceed £100,000.

In the case of a 'relevant company' other than a banking company, the aggregate of the 'relevant amounts' must, in all cases, not exceed £100,000 but for this purpose a director is not deemed to be connected with a company which he does not control.

[*Sec 338; CA 1989, 10 Sch 10*].

See 19.94 below for connected persons and control.

'Relevant company' means a company which is a public company or a member of a group which contains a public company. [*Sec 331(6)*].

'Relevant amounts' are

(*a*)   the value of the proposed transaction; and

(*b*)   the amount outstanding under any other transactions, or the value of any existing arrangement within 19.89 or 19.90 above, made under the same exemption for the director or any person connected with him (or where the proposed transaction is for a person connected with a director, for that director or any person connected with him) by

- the company or its subsidiary; or

- where the proposed transaction is for a director of the company's holding company or a person connected with such a director, that holding company or any of its subsidiaries.

For the purposes of (*b*) above, a previous transaction by a subsidiary or fellow subsidiary of the company making the loan can be ignored if it is no longer such a subsidiary at the time of the current transaction in question.

[*Sec 339*].

See 19.94 below for connected persons.

19.92   Consequences of breach

Civil remedies. A transaction or arrangement entered into by a company in contravention of 19.86 to 19.90 above is voidable at the instance of the company unless

- restitution of any money or any asset the subject matter of the transaction is no longer possible;

- the company has been indemnified by any other person for the loss or damage suffered by it; or

- any rights acquired, bona fide for value and without actual notice of the contravention, by a person other than the person for whom the transaction was made would be affected by its avoidance.

Whether or not the transaction has been avoided, the director for whom the transaction was made, any person connected with him and any other director of the company who authorised the transaction is liable to account to the company for any gain he has made and (jointly and severally with any other person liable) to indemnify the company for any loss or damage resulting from it, except that

(i)   where the transaction is entered into by the company with a person connected with a director of the company, or its holding company, that director is not liable if he shows that he took all reasonable steps to secure the company's compliance; and

(ii)   a connected person and any other director is not liable if he shows that at the time of the transaction he did not know the relevant circumstances constituting the contravention.

[*Sec 341*].

As the effect of the above provisions is to make void any loan in contravention of 19.86 to 19.90 above, the company is entitled to recover such a loan irrespective of the terms on which it is made (*Tait Consibee (Oxford) Ltd v Tait, [1997] 1 BCLC 349*).

19.93   Directors

See 19.94 below for connected persons.

Criminal penalties. A director of a 'relevant company' who authorises or permits the company, or any person who procures a relevant company, to enter into a transaction knowing, or having reasonable cause to believe, that it is thereby in contravention of the provisions of 19.86 to 19.90 above is guilty of an offence.

A relevant company which enters into a transaction for one of its directors, or for a director of its holding company, in contravention of the provisions is similarly guilty of an offence unless it shows that, at the time the transaction was entered into, it did not know the relevant circumstances.

A person guilty of an offence is liable to a penalty up to the level in 40.1(*b*) PENALTIES.

'Relevant company' means a company which is a public company or a member of a group which contains a public company.

[*Secs 331(6), 342, 24 Sch*].

19.93 Disclosure of loans etc. by banking companies

By *9 Sch Part IV, para 2*, a banking company or the holding company of a 'credit institution' (before 28 February 1994, the holding company of a banking company) is not obliged to disclose in its accounts details of loans and quasi-loans to directors within 19.86 to 19.90 above. Subject to the exceptions below,

(*a*)   where such a company takes advantage of that provision in relation to a financial year, it must keep a register containing a copy of every transaction, arrangement or agreement of which particulars would, but for that provision, have to be disclosed in the company's accounts or group accounts for that financial year and for each financial year in the preceding ten financial years in which the company has taken advantage of that provision. Where the transaction, etc. is not in writing, the register must contain a memorandum setting out its terms; and

(*b*)   where such a company took advantage of that provision in relation to the last complete financial year preceding its annual general meeting, then (unless it is a wholly-owned subsidiary of a company incorporated in the UK) it must make available for inspection by its members at the registered office, for at least the 15 days before the AGM, a statement containing particulars of the transaction, etc. which the company would, but for that provision, be required to disclose in its accounts or group accounts for the financial year. The statement must also be available for their inspection at the AGM.

'Credit institution' means an undertaking whose business is to receive deposits or other repayable funds for the public and to grant credits for its own transactions.

If the company fails to comply with these provisions, every director at the time of the failure is liable to a fine up to the level in 40.1(*d*) PENALTIES unless he can show that he took all reasonable steps to secure compliance. A person is not guilty of an offence by virtue only of being a shadow director.

Auditors' report. The company's auditors must examine the statement under (*b*) before it is made available to the members and make a report to them indicating whether, in their opinion, the statement contains the required particulars. If in their opinion it does not, they must include in the report, so far as they are reasonably able, a statement giving the required particulars. The report must be annexed to the statement before it is made available.

Exceptions. The above provisions do not apply to

- transactions etc. made or subsisting during a financial year by a company or its subsidiary for a person who, at any time during that year, was a director of that company or its holding company or was connected with such a director, or

- agreements made or subsisting during that year to enter into such transactions etc.

if the aggregate of the values of each such transaction and agreement made for that person, less the amount (if any) by which it is reduced, did not exceed £2,000 at any time during the financial year. See 19.86 to 19.90 above for the determination of value.

[*Secs 262, 343, 344; CA 1989, 10 Sch 10, 11; SI 1990 No 1393; SI 1994 No 233*].

19.94 **CONNECTED PERSONS, ASSOCIATION AND CONTROL**

For the purposes of 19.71 to 19.73, 19.85, 19.87, 19.88 and 19.91 to 19.93 above, the following provisions apply.

(*a*)   **A person is connected with a director of a company** if, but only if, he is not a director himself and is

    (i)   that director's spouse, 'child or step-child';

    (ii)   unless the context requires otherwise, a body corporate with which the director is associated (see (*b*) below);

    (iii)   a person acting in his capacity as a trustee of any trust, the beneficiaries of which include the director or any person within (i) or (ii) above;

    (iv)   a person acting in his capacity as a trustee of any trust whose terms confer a power on the trustees that may be exercised for the benefit of the director or any person within (i) or (ii) above;

    (v)   a partner of the director, or any person connected with the director under (i) to (iv) above, when acting in that capacity;

    (vi)   a Scottish firm in which either that director is a partner or a partner is a person who is connected with that director under (i) to (iv); and

    (vii)   a Scottish firm in which a partner is a Scottish firm falling within (vi) above.

'Child or step-child' of any person includes an illegitimate child of his, but does not include any person who has attained the age of 18.

(*b*)   **A director of a company is 'associated' with a body corporate** if, but only if, he and the persons connected with him are

    (i)   interested in at least 20% of the nominal value of the equity share capital; or

    (ii)   entitled to exercise, or control the exercise of, more than 20% of the voting power at any general meeting. Included is any voting power controlled by a body corporate which is controlled by the director.

(*c*)   **A director of a company is deemed to control a body corporate** if, but only if,

    (i)   he or any person connected with him is interested in the equity share capital or is entitled to exercise, or control the exercise of, any voting power at a general meeting; and

(ii) that director, the persons connected with him and the other directors of that company are interested in more than 50% of that share capital or are entitled to exercise, or control the exercise of, more than 50% of that voting power.

Included is any voting power controlled by a body corporate which is controlled by the director.

For the purposes of (*b*) and (*c*) above, a body corporate is not to be treated as connected with the director in question unless it is also connected with him by virtue of (*a*)(iii)–(v) above. Also the trustees of a trust, the beneficiaries of which include (or may include) a body corporate with which the director is associated is not to be treated as connected with a director by reason only of that fact.

See also 19.77 above on the interpretation of 'interests in shares and debentures' which also applies for the purposes of (*a*) and (*b*) above.

[*Sec 346*].

20   Directors' Report

Cross-references. See 3 ACCOUNTS: GENERAL for publication of directors' report, laying before members and delivery to Registrar of Companies, etc; 12.23 AUDITORS for auditors' duty to consider the directors' report.

The contents of this chapter are as follows

20.1   CONTENTS

The directors of a company must prepare a report for each financial year containing the information in 20.2 to 20.13 below. In the case of any failure, every person who was a director immediately before the end of the period for laying and delivering accounts and reports for the financial year in question (see 3.8 ACCOUNTS: GENERAL) is guilty of an offence and liable to a fine up to the level in 40.1(*d*) PENALTIES. It is a defence against any proceedings to prove that a person took all reasonable steps for securing compliance with the requirements in question. [*Sec 234(1)(5)(6), 24 Sch; CA 1989, s 8*].

20.2   Review of developments

The report must contain a fair review of the development of the business of the company and its subsidiary undertakings during the financial year and their position at the end of it. [*Sec 234(1)(a); CA 1989, s 8*].

20.3   Dividends and reserves

The report must state the amount of dividends (if any) recommended. For financial years ending before 2 February 1996, the report also had to state the amount (if any) proposed to be carried to reserves. [*Sec 234(1)(b); CA 1989, s 8; SI 1996 No 189, Reg 5*].

20.4   Names of directors

The report must state the names of the persons who, at any time during the financial year, were directors of the company. [*Sec 234(2); CA 1989, s 8*].

See also 43.15(*p*) PUBLIC AND LISTED COMPANIES for disclosure of details of independent non-executive directors of a listed company.

20.5   Principal activities

The report must state the principal activities of the company and its subsidiary undertakings in the course of the year and any significant change in those activities in the year. [*Sec 234(2); CA 1989, s 8*].

20.6   Asset values

For fixed assets of the company or any of its subsidiaries consisting of interests in land, the report must indicate the difference (with such degree of precision as is practicable) between the market value at the end of the financial year and the amount at which they are

20.7 Directors' Report

included in the balance sheet where these figures differ substantially and the difference is, in the directors' opinion, of such significance as to require being drawn to the attention of the members or debenture-holders. [*7 Sch 1(2); CA 1989, 5 Sch 2; SI 1996 No 189, Regs 14, 15*].

20.7 Directors' interests

The following information must be given in the directors' report (or in the notes to the accounts) in respect of every person who was a director at the end of the financial year.

(*a*) Whether or not, according to the register of directors' interests (see 47.7 REGISTERS) each director was interested in the shares or debentures of the company, or any other company in the same group, at the end of the financial year and, if he was, the number of shares in, or amount of debentures of, each body (specifying it).

(*b*) If a director had interests as in (*a*) above, similar information must be given as at the beginning of the financial year (or the time when he became (or first became) a director, if later). If a director had no interests as in (*a*) above, there is no requirement to disclose any interests at the beginning of the year unless the company is a listed company when this is required under *ASL, Section 5*.

(*c*) Whether, according to the register of directors' interests, any right to subscribe for shares in, or debentures of, the company, or any other company in the same group, was granted to, or exercised by, the director or a member of his 'immediate family' during the financial year. If so, there must be stated the number of shares in, or amount of debentures of, each body (specifying it) in respect of which the right was granted or exercised.

'Immediate family' means spouse and 'infant' children, including step-children but does not include a person who is himself or herself a director of the company. *'Infant'*, in relation to Scotland, means pupil or minor.

[*7 Sch 2, 2A, 2B; CA 1989, 5 Sch 3; SI 1990 No 355*].

See also 43.15(*e*) PUBLIC AND LISTED COMPANIES for disclosures by listed companies under the Listing Rules.

20.8 Political and charitable gifts

Where a company, other than a wholly-owned subsidiary of a company incorporated in Great Britain, has in the financial year given money exceeding £200 for

(*a*) political purposes i.e. directly or indirectly to a UK political party or to a person who, to the company's knowledge, is carrying on, or intends to carry on, activities which are likely to affect public support for such a party; or

(*b*) exclusively charitable purposes (but leaving out of account any money given to a person ordinarily resident outside the UK),

or both, the directors' report must contain a statement of the amount of money given for each of those purposes for which money has been given. In addition, where money is given for political purposes, the report must state the name of any person or political party given over £200 and the amount given.

In the case of a company which has subsidiaries but is not itself a wholly-owned subsidiary, the £200 limit and the particulars to be given under (*a*) and (*b*) above relate to the combined gifts of the company and its subsidiaries.

[*7 Sch 3-5*].

20.9   Disclosure by company acquiring or charging its own shares

Where shares in the company are

- purchased by the company or acquired by it by forfeiture or surrender in lieu of forfeiture, or

- acquired by a nominee of the company from a third person without financial assistance from the company or by any person with financial assistance from the company, and in either case the company has a beneficial interest in the shares, or

- made subject to a lien or other charge by the company under permitted circumstances (see 58.10 SHARES AND SHARE CAPITAL),

the directors' report for the financial year must state

   (i)   the number and nominal value of the shares so purchased, the aggregate amount of the consideration paid by the company and the reason for the purchase;

  (ii)   the number and nominal value of the shares so acquired or charged during the financial year;

 (iii)   the maximum number and nominal value of shares which, having been so acquired or charged (whether or not during the year) are held at any time by the company or that other person during the year;

 (iv)   the number and nominal value of the shares so acquired or charged (whether or not acquired during the year) which are disposed of by the company or that other person or cancelled by the company during the year;

  (v)   the percentage of called-up share capital represented by the number and nominal value of the shares of any particular description stated within (i) to (iv) above;

 (vi)   where any of the shares have been so charged, the amount of the charge in each case; and

(vii)   where any of the shares have been disposed of by the company or person who acquired them, the consideration in each case.

[*7 Sch 7, 8*].

20.10   Employment of disabled persons

Where, during the financial year, the 'average number of persons employed' exceeded 250, the directors' report must include a statement on the company's policy for that year for

- giving full and fair consideration to applications for employment made by disabled persons;

- continuing employment of, and arranging for appropriate training for, employees who have become disabled during the period when they were employed by the company; and

- the training, career development and promotion of disabled persons (as defined in *Disability Discrimination Act 1995*) employed by the company.

'Average number of persons employed' is calculated by the formula

A

—

B

where

20.11 Directors' Report

A = the sum of the numbers of persons who, under contracts of service, were employed by the company in each week of the financial year (whether throughout it or not)

B = the number of weeks in the financial year

[*7 Sch 9; Disability Discrimination Act 1995, 6 Sch 4*].

20.11 Employee involvement

Where, during the financial year, the average number of persons employed exceeded 250 (calculated as in 20.10 above), the directors' report must contain a statement describing what action has been taken regarding

- providing employees with information on matters concerning them as employees;

- consulting employees or their representatives so that their views can be taken into account in making decisions likely to affect their interests;

- encouraging the involvement of employees through a share scheme or by some other means; and

- achieving a common awareness on the part of all employees of the financial and economic factors affecting the performance of the company.

[*7 Sch 11*].

20.12 Policy and practice on the payment of creditors

The report of a company which at any time in the financial year

- was a public company, or

- did not qualify as a small or medium-sized company (see 7.2 ACCOUNTS: SMALL AND MEDIUM-SIZED COMPANIES) for that year and was a member of a group of which the parent company was a public company

must state the following with respect to the financial year immediately following that covered by the report.

(*a*)   Whether, in respect of some or all of its 'suppliers', it is the company's policy to

- follow any code or standard on payment practice and, if so, the name of the code or standard, and the place where information about it and copies of it can be obtained;

- settle the terms of payment with those suppliers when agreeing the terms of each transaction;

- ensure that those suppliers are made aware of the terms of payment; and

- abide by the terms of payment.

(*b*)   Where the company's policy does not fall within (*a*) above in respect of some or all of its suppliers, what its policy is with respect to payments to those suppliers.

(*c*)   If the company's policy is different for different suppliers or classes of suppliers, the identity of the suppliers or classes of suppliers to which the different policies apply.

(*d*)   For financial years ending after 24 March 1997, the number of days calculated by the formula

$$\frac{F \times Y}{Y}$$

where

F = the number of days in the financial year

X = the aggregate of the amounts which were owed to trade creditors at the end of the year. This is either

    (i)   where the accounts are prepared in accordance with the balance sheet formats in *4 Sch*, the amount shown under the heading corresponding to item E.4 in Format 1 or, as the case may be, item C.4 in Format 2 (see 5.4 ACCOUNTS INDIVIDUAL COMPANIES); or

    (ii)   where the accounts are prepared in accordance with *9 Sch* or *9A Sch* (banking and insurance companies), the amount which would be shown under the heading corresponding to item E.4 in Format 1 if the accounts were prepared in accordance with *4 Sch*.

Y = the aggregate of the amounts invoiced by suppliers to the company during the year.

A '*supplier*' for these purposes is a person who, in respect of goods or services supplied to the company, is owed an amount which would be included under the heading corresponding to item E.4 (trade creditors) if accounts were prepared at that time under balance sheet Format 1 in *4 Sch* (see 5.4: ACCOUNTS INDIVIDUAL COMPANIES). For the purposes of (*a*) to (*c*) above, suppliers include any persons who are or may become its suppliers.

[*7 Sch 12; SI 1997 No 571*].

20.13 Miscellaneous

The directors' report must contain

(*a*)   particulars of all important events affecting the company or any of its subsidiary undertakings which have occurred since the end of the financial year;

(*b*)   an indication of likely future developments in the business of the company and its subsidiary undertakings;

(*c*)   an indication of the activities (if any) of the company and its subsidiary undertakings in the field of research and development; and

(*d*)   (unless the company is an unlimited company) for financial years beginning on or after 1 January 1993 an indication of the existence of branches of the company outside the UK.

[*7 Sch 6; CA 1989, 5 Sch 2; SI 1992 No 3178, Reg 3*].

20.14 LISTED COMPANIES

In addition to the requirements of *CA 1985*, listed companies must also comply with the requirements of the *Listing Rules, Chapter 12.41–12.44* as to content of annual accounts. See 43.15 PUBLIC AND LISTED COMPANIES and the Appendix to that chapter for details of the requirements of the Combined Code. The additional requirements may be shown in the directors' report or the notes to the accounts. See also 43.21(*c*) PUBLIC AND LISTED COMPANIES for disclosure re directors' service contracts.

20.15 Directors' Report

20.15 SMALL COMPANIES

Preparation of an abbreviated report. A company which qualifies as a small company (see 7.2 ACCOUNTS: SMALL AND MEDIUM-SIZED COMPANIES) in relation to any financial year is entitled to prepare an abbreviated report provided the report contains a statement, in a prominent position above the signature of the director or secretary, that the report has been prepared under the special provisions relating to small companies.

The abbreviated report need only contain the following information.

- Names of directors (see 20.4 above).

- Principal activities (see 20.5 above).

- Directors' interests (see 20.7 above).

- Political and charitable gifts (see 20.8 above).

- Disclosure by company acquiring or charging its own shares (see 20.9 above).

- Employment of disabled persons (see 20.10 above).

[*Sec 246(4)(8); SI 1997 No 220, Reg 2*].

Accounts delivered to the Registrar of Companies. A small company (see 7.2 ACCOUNTS: SMALL AND MEDIUM-SIZED COMPANIES), whether or not it prepares an abbreviated report under the above provisions, need not deliver a copy of its report to the Registrar of Companies. [*Sec 246(5); SI 1997 No 220, Reg 2*].

20.16 APPROVAL AND SIGNING OF THE REPORT

The directors' report must be approved by the board of directors and signed on its behalf by a director or the secretary of the company. Every copy of the report laid before the company in general meeting, or otherwise circulated or issued, must then state the name of the person who signed it on behalf of the board.

In addition, the copy of the report delivered to the Registrar of Companies must be signed by a director or the secretary.

In the case of a failure to comply with any of the above requirements, the company and every officer who is in default is guilty of an offence and liable to a fine up to the level in 40.1(*g*) PENALTIES.

[*Sec 234A, 24 Sch; CA 1989, s 8; SI 1990 No 355*].

20.17 DEFECTIVE ACCOUNTS AND REPORT

In certain circumstances, the annual accounts and/or directors' report of a company may be replaced or partially revised because they were originally defective. See 3.9 ACCOUNTS: GENERAL. The provisions of 20.2 to 20.13 above apply to a revised report as if it was prepared and approved by the directors as at the date of the original directors' report. [*SI 1990 No 2570, Reg 3(4)*].

20.18 Approval and signing

The provisions in 20.16 above also apply to any revised directors' report prepared by the directors, either through revision by replacement or revision by supplementary note, except that in the latter case the provisions apply as if they required the signature to be on the supplementary note.

Where the original directors' report has already been sent out to members, laid before the company in general meeting or delivered to the Registrar of Companies, the directors must, before approving the revised report ensure that statements as to the following matters are made in a prominent position in the revised report (or, in the case of revision by supplementary note, in that note).

(*a*)   In the case of revision by replacement

- that the revised report replaces the original report for the financial year (specifying it);

- that it has been prepared as at the date of the original directors' report and not at the date of revision and accordingly does not deal with any events between those dates;

- the respects in which the original directors' report did not comply with the requirements of the Act; and

- any significant amendments made as a result of remedying those defects.

(*b*)   In the case of revision by a supplementary note

- that the note revises in certain respects the original directors' report of the company and is to be treated as forming part of that report; and

- that the directors' report has been revised as at the date of the original directors' report and not as at the date of the revision and accordingly does not deal with events between those dates.

The date of approval of the revised report must be stated on the face of the report (or supplementary note).

The penalty for failure to comply with these provisions is as in 20.1 above.

[*SI 1990 No 2570, Reg 5*].

20.19   Effect of revision

On approval by the directors, the revised report has effect as if it was, as from the date of approval, the directors' report in place of the original report, in particular for the purposes of

- *Sec 239* (right to demand copies of accounts and report, see 3.4 ACCOUNTS: GENERAL); and

- *Sec 238* (persons entitled to receive copies, see 3.3 ACCOUNTS: GENERAL), *Sec 241* (accounts and reports to be laid before company in general meeting, see 3.6 ACCOUNTS: GENERAL) and *Sec 242* (accounts and report to be delivered to Registrar of Companies, see 3.7 ACCOUNTS: GENERAL) if the requirements of these provisions have not been complied with prior to the date of revision.

[*SI 1990 No 2570, Reg 9; SI 1996 No 315*].

20.20   Publication of revised report

Where copies of the original accounts and report have been sent out, a copy of the revised accounts and report (or supplementary note) and the auditors' report thereon (see 12.22 AUDITORS) must be sent, within 28 days of their approval by the directors, to

- any person who has been sent a copy under *Sec 238* (see 3.3 ACCOUNTS: GENERAL); and

- any other person who has not been sent a copy but who would be entitled to receive a copy under *Sec 238* at the date of revision.

20.21   Directors' Report

In default, each director who approved the revised report is liable to a fine up to the level in 40.1(*d*) PENALTIES.

[*SI 1990 No 2570, Reg 10; SI 1996 No 315*].

20.21 Laying of revised report

Where the directors prepare a revised report and the original accounts and report have already been laid before the company in general meeting, a copy of the revised report and auditors' report thereon must be laid before the next general meeting of the company held after the date of revision at which annual accounts for a financial year are laid. In default, every person who is a director of the company immediately before that meeting is liable to a fine up to the level in 40.1(*e*) PENALTIES. It is a defence for a person charged with this offence to prove that he took all reasonable steps to secure compliance with these requirements before that meeting; it is not a defence to prove that the revised report was not in fact prepared. [*SI 1990 No 2570, Reg 11*].

20.22 Delivery of revised report to the Registrar of Companies

Where a copy of the original report has been delivered to the Registrar of Companies, the directors must, within 28 days of the revision, deliver to him a copy of the revised report (or supplementary note) and auditors' report thereon. In default, every director is liable to a fine up to the level in 40.1(*e*) PENALTIES. Also, if the directors fail to make good the default within 14 days after the service of a notice on them requiring compliance, the court may, on application of the Registrar or any member or creditor of the company, order the directors (or any of them) to make good the default within a specified time. The order may require the directors to bear all the costs of, and incidental to, the application. It is a defence for a person charged to prove that he took all reasonable steps for securing compliance within the required period; it is not a defence to prove that the revised report was not prepared. [*SI 1990 No 2570, Reg 12*].

21   Disclosure of Interests in Public Company Shares

Cross-references. See 19.76 DIRECTORS for disclosure of shareholdings by a director to the company; 43.8 PUBLIC AND LISTED COMPANIES for obligations of listed companies to disclose information to the Company Announcement Office.

21.1   OBLIGATION OF DISCLOSURE

An obligation to notify a public company of interests held in its shares arises when a person either

(*a*)   to his knowledge acquires an interest in shares comprised in the company's 'relevant share capital', or ceases to be interested in any such shares (whether or not retaining any other such shares), or

(*b*)   becomes aware that he has acquired or ceased to possess such an interest,

and where that person

(i)   has a 'notifiable interest' immediately after the 'relevant time', not having had such an interest immediately before that time; or

(ii)   had a notifiable interest immediately before the relevant time, but does not have such an interest immediately after that time; or

(iii)   has a notifiable interest both immediately before and immediately after the relevant time, but with differing percentage levels. In determining the percentage levels, the aggregate nominal value of shares comprised in the company's 'relevant share capital' in which the person has a material or other interest is expressed as a percentage of the total nominal value of that share capital and rounded down to the next whole number. If the total nominal value increases at the relevant time, holdings both before and after that time are compared with the higher figure.

[Secs 198(1), 199(4)(5), 200; SI 1993 No 1819, Regs 3, 5].

Such an obligation similarly arises when a person becomes aware of facts relevant to the determination of his interests to be disclosed under these provisions, or when there is a change in circumstances affecting such facts of which he is aware, and where (i) above would apply. *[Secs 198(3), 199(4)].*

As regards (*a*) and (*b*) above, if a person authorises an agent to make acquisitions and disposals on his behalf, he must arrange to be notified immediately of any which may be relevant to an obligation of disclosure. *[Sec 210(1)].*

The 'interests' in shares which may give rise to an obligation of disclosure are widely defined, including the whole of interests held jointly and those where the shares in which the interest is held are unidentifiable. Where an interest in shares is held on trust, a beneficiary is treated as having an interest in the shares (if he would not otherwise be so treated). A person is taken to have an interest in shares if he enters into a contract to purchase them or if, not being the registered holder, he is entitled to exercise, or control the exercise of, any right conferred by the holding of the shares (but not if he has only been appointed a proxy to vote at a specified meeting). A person is also taken to have an interest in shares if he has a right to call for delivery of, or acquire an interest in, the shares or is under an obligation to take an interest in them. *[Sec 208, 209(12); SI 1993 No 1819, Reg 8].* See, however, 21.5 below as regards certain interests which are to be disregarded for these purposes. See also 21.3 below as regards certain family and corporate interests which are to be taken into account.

21.2 Disclosure of Interests in Public Company Shares

'Relevant share capital' is issued share capital carrying rights to vote in general meeting in all circumstances (ignoring temporary suspensions of such rights), and different classes of shares are considered separately for these purposes. [*Sec 198(2)*].

The *'relevant time'* is the time of the event or change in circumstances, or of the person becoming aware of the facts in question, as appropriate. [*Sec 198(4)*].

'Notifiable interests'. A person has a notifiable interest in a company's relevant share capital at any time when, on the basis of facts known to him at that time, he either has 'material interests' in shares representing in aggregate 3% or more of the nominal value of that share capital or has interests (whether or not including material interests) in shares representing in aggregate 10% or more of the nominal value of that share capital. A *'material interest'* is any interest other than

(i) an interest held by a person authorised under *FSA 1986* to manage investments belonging to another;

(ii) an interest which a person has as the operator of an authorised unit trust scheme, a recognised scheme or a UCITS (as defined);

(iii) an interest belonging to an investment company with variable capital;

(iv) an interest in shares in a listed company which would be disregarded under 21.5 below if the company were not listed; and

(v) an interest of another which a person is taken to have under *Sec 203* (see 21.3 below) or *Sec 205* (see 21.4 below) where the interest of that other person falls within (i), (ii) or (iv) above.

[*Sec 199(1)-(3)(6)-(8); SI 1993 No 1819, Reg 4; SI 1996 No 2827, 8 Sch 5*].

The Secretary of State has wide powers to amend the definition of relevant share capital, the percentage giving rise to a notifiable interest and what is to be taken as an interest in shares for the above purposes, and may make different provision for different descriptions of company and for different descriptions of person, interest or capital. [*Sec 210A; CA 1989, s 134*].

21.2 Particulars to be notified

An obligation on a person to give notification under 21.1 above must be performed in writing within two working days after the day on which the obligation arose. [*Secs 202(1), 220(2); CA 1989, s 134, 24 Sch*].

The notification must specify the share capital to which it relates and must state either

- the number of shares comprised in that capital in which he knows he had material interests or was interested immediately after the obligation arose (but without any requirement to state whether or not the interests are material); or

- that he no longer has a notifiable interest in such shares.

If he still has a notifiable interest, the notification must identify

- each registered holder of shares to which it relates and the number of shares held by each of them, and

- the number of shares in which his interest otherwise than through a trust, is

  (i) a right to call for delivery of the shares, or

  (ii) a right to acquire an interest in shares, or

  (iii) an obligation to take an interest in shares

so far as he knows at the date of the notification. [*Secs 202(2)(2A)(2B)(3), 208(5); CA 1989, s 134; SI 1993 No 1819, Reg 6*]. Any particulars, or change in particulars, relating to a notifiable holding, of which he becomes aware before another obligation of disclosure arises in respect of the same share capital, must similarly be notified in writing within two working days. [*Secs 202(4)-(6), 220(2); CA 1989, s 134*].

The Secretary of State has wide powers to amend the time limits within which notifications must be given as above, and may make different provision for different descriptions of company and for different descriptions of person, interest or capital. [*Sec 210A; CA 1989, s 134*].

A notification under these provisions must identify the person on whom the obligation of disclosure falls and give his address. If he is a director of the company concerned, the notice must be expressed to be in fulfilment of such an obligation. [*Sec 210(2)*].

For the register which companies are required to keep of notifications under these provisions, see 47.8 REGISTERS. For the removal of entries, see 47.10 REGISTERS.

21.3   Family and corporate interests

The shares in which a person is taken as having an interest for the purposes of 21.1 and 21.2 above include any in which his spouse, or an infant (in Scotland, pupil or minor) child or step-child of his, is interested, or in which certain bodies corporate are interested. The bodies corporate concerned are any

(*a*)   which, or whose directors, are accustomed to act in accordance with his directions or instructions; or

(*b*)   in relation to which he is entitled to exercise, or control the exercise of, one-third or more of the voting power at general meetings.

Any voting power exercisable or controlled by bodies corporate which are themselves within (*b*) above is treated as exercisable by him in considering whether any other body corporate is within (*b*) above.

Entitlement to exercise, or control the exercise of, voting power for these purposes includes a right or obligation (conditional or otherwise) the exercise or fulfilment of which would give him such an entitlement.

There are detailed provisions to ensure that family and corporate interests are attributed as above in a wide range of circumstances of which the person to whom they are to be attributed has knowledge.

[*Secs 203, 207*].

21.4   Agreement to acquire interests in a company

Subject to below, special obligations to disclose arise from certain agreements between two or more persons which

(*a*)   include provision for the acquisition by any one or more of them of interests in shares comprised in the relevant share capital (see 21.1 above) of a particular public company (the 'target company'); and

(*b*)   impose obligations or restrictions on one or more of the parties with respect to the 'use', retention or disposal of interests in shares in the target company acquired in pursuance of the agreement. The *'use'* of an interest means the exercise of any rights, or of any control or influence arising from those interests.

[*Sec 204(1)-(3)*].

21.5   Disclosure of Interests in Public Company Shares

Where shares in the target company are acquired by any of the parties in pursuance of the agreement, each party is taken (for the purposes of the obligation to disclose) to be interested in all the shares in the target company in which any other party is interested (otherwise than by this provision), including any interest that other party has (or is treated as having) under 21.1 above or under these provisions in relation to any other agreement with respect to shares in the target company to which he is a party. [Sec 205(1)-(3)].

Once any interest in shares in the target company has been acquired in pursuance of such an agreement, the agreement (and any substituted agreement) continues to be within these provisions so long as it continues to include provisions within (b) above. This applies whether or not there are further acquisitions in the target company and irrespective of any changes in the persons who are party to the agreement. [Sec 204(4)].

'Agreement' for these purposes includes any arrangement, and the provisions of an agreement accordingly include undertakings, expectations or understandings operative thereunder, and may be express or implied and absolute or not. [Sec 204(5)].

The provisions do not, however, apply

- to an agreement which is not legally binding, unless it involves mutuality in the undertakings, expectations or understandings of the parties to it; or

- to an agreement confined to the underwriting or sub-underwriting of any offer of shares and matters incidental thereto.

[Sec 204(6)].

A notification under 21.2 above to the target company by a party to such an agreement must state that he is such a party, give the names and (if known) addresses of the other parties, and indicate whether any of the shares to which the notification relates are shares in which his interest arises by virtue of these provisions (and if so how many are such shares). If the notification arises from the cessation of an interest in any shares due to his (or any other person's) ceasing to be a party to the agreement, this must be stated in the notification, together, if appropriate, with the name and (if known) address of the other person leaving the agreement. [Sec 205(4)(5)].

All the parties to such an agreement are obliged to keep all the other parties to the agreement informed by written notice on all matters necessary to comply with the above provisions, the usual time limit of two working days (which may be varied by the Secretary of State by regulations) applying to the giving of notice under such obligation. [Secs 206, 210A, 220(2); CA 1989, s 134; SI 1993 No 1819, Reg 7].

There are detailed provisions to ensure that interests under an agreement are attributed as above in a wide range of circumstances of which the person to whom they are to be attributed has knowledge. [Sec 207].

21.5   Interests to be disregarded

The following interests in shares are disregarded for the purposes of disclosure under 21.1 and 21.2 above.

(a)   Provided the relevant person is not entitled to exercise, or control the exercise of, voting rights in respect of the shares concerned

- where shares are held on trust, an interest of a beneficiary which is discretionary or in reversion or remainder or an interest of a bare trustee (in Scotland, an interest in fee or of a simple trustee);

- an interest which a person has by virtue of holding units in an authorised unit trust scheme, a recognised scheme or a UCITS;

- an *'exempt security interest'* i.e. an interest held by way of security only (with no entitlement to exercise, or control the exercise of, voting rights) for the purposes of a transaction entered into in the ordinary course of business by any of the following: a banking company authorised under *Banking Act 1987*; a person authorised under the law of another member state to accept deposits who would require authorisation under that *Act* if accepting such deposits in the UK; an authorised credit institution or insurance undertaking; a person authorised under the law of any member state to deal in securities or derivatives on a relevant stock exchange or a relevant investment exchange; a relevant stock exchange; a relevant investment exchange; a recognised clearing house; the Bank of England; or the central bank of another member state;

  The interest is also disregarded if the person in question is entitled to exercise, or control the exercise of, voting rights but has not evidenced any intention or taken steps to do so.

- an interest which a person has by being a beneficiary under a retirement benefits scheme as defined in *ICTA 1988, s 611*;

- an interest in share which a person has as the result of a take-over offer made by him for shares where any threshold acceptance condition has not been fulfilled;

- an interest of a person as a custodian (whether under trust or by contract) or under an arrangement pursuant to which he has or will issue depositary receipts in respect of the shares concerned;

- an interest which a person has by virtue of being a personal representative of any estate; and

- an interest which a person has by being (i) the trustee of an authorised unit trust scheme; (ii) entrusted with custody of the shares under a recognised scheme or a UCITS; or (iii) a depositary of an investment company with variable capital.

(b)   An interest held by a market maker in securities for the purpose of his business but only so far as it is not used by him to intervene in the management of the company.

(c)   Certain temporary interests in shares arising from arrangements effected under CREST whereby

- securities of a particular aggregate value are transferred from one person (A) to another (B) under the system;

- the securities are of kinds and amounts determined by the facilities and procedures maintained and operated by Crestco Ltd; and

- those securities, or securities of the same kinds and amounts, are returned from B to A on the next working day.

(d)   Provided the interest is in a public company which is not listed

- an interest which subsists by virtue of certain statutory provisions;

- certain Scottish Church trust interests;

- a life interest in settled property provided the settlement is irrevocable and the settlor has no interest in it;

- certain interests of the President of the Family Division of the High Court or the Accountant General of the Supreme Court;

21.6 Disclosure of Interests in Public Company Shares

- an interest of the Public Trustee; and

- certain interests of the Probate Judge in Northern Ireland.

The Secretary of State has wide powers to amend the categories of interest which are to be disregarded as above, and may make different provision for different descriptions of company and for different descriptions of person, interest or capital.

[*Secs 209, 210A; FSA 1986, s 197, 16 Sch 18; ICTA 1988, 29 Sch 32; CA 1989, s 134, 10 Sch 2, 24 Sch; SI 1993 No 1819, Reg 8; SI 1993 No 2689; SI 1996 No 1560; SI 1996 No 2827, 8 Sch 6*].

21.6 **Penalties**

A person who

(*a*)   fails to fulfil within the time limit an obligation of disclosure within 21.1 above, or

(*b*)   in purporting to fulfil such an obligation makes a statement he knows to be false or recklessly makes a false statement to a company, or

(*c*)   fails to fulfil within the time limit an obligation to give another person notice under 21.4 above, or

(*d*)   fails without reasonable excuse to make arrangements for immediate notification of acquisitions and disposals by an agent (see 21.1 above),

is guilty of an offence and liable to a penalty up to the level in 40.1(*b*) PENALTIES. It is, however, a defence to a charge under (*c*) above to prove that it was not possible to give the required notice within the time limit, and that either it has not since become possible or notice was given as soon as it became possible to do so.

Secs 732 and *733(2)(3)* (see 32.3 and 32.4 LEGAL PROCEEDINGS) apply to such offences.

Where a person has been convicted of an offence as above (other than one relating to his ceasing to be interested in a company's shares), the Secretary of State may by order place restrictions (until further order) on the shares concerned, notwithstanding that the company may under its memorandum or articles itself be able to impose similar restrictions. However, where the Secretary of State is satisfied that such an order may unfairly affect the rights of third parties, he may direct that specified acts by such persons do not constitute a breach of the restrictions. See 21.9 to 21.11 below as regards such orders.

[*Sec 210(3)-(6), 24 Sch; SI 1991 No 1646, Reg 3*].

21.7 **COMPANY INVESTIGATIONS**

Where a public company has reason to believe that a person is or has, within the preceding three years, been interested in shares comprised in its relevant share capital (see 21.1 above), it may give that person written notice requiring him to indicate whether or not that is the case. If it is, the notice may require him, within a reasonable time, to give particulars of such interests, and (so far as lies within his knowledge) of other interests subsisting in the shares concerned currently or within the same period and of the identity of the person to whom any interest previously held was passed. *Secs 203-205* (see 21.3 and 21.4 above) and *Sec 208* (see 21.1 above) apply in relation to persons interested in shares and interests in shares respectively for these purposes.

Notice may similarly be given to a person who has or has had, or is or was entitled to acquire, a right to subscribe for shares in the company which would on issue form part of its relevant share capital.

[*Sec 212*].

The Secretary of State has wide powers to amend the above provisions, and may make different provision for different descriptions of company. He may also, in consultation with the Governor of the Bank of England, exempt persons from the operation of the provisions if he is satisfied that there are special reasons for doing so. [*Secs 210A, 216(5); CA 1989, s 134*].

For the register entries required to be made by the company following receipt of information under these provisions, see 47.9 REGISTERS. For the removal of entries, see 47.10 REGISTERS.

If a notice is served as above on a person who is or was interested in the company's shares, and he fails to give the required information within the time allowed, the company may apply to the court for an order imposing restrictions on the shares (see 21.9 to 21.11 below). Such an order may be made notwithstanding that the company may under its memorandum or articles itself be able to impose similar restrictions. The court may make an interim order and any such order may be made unconditionally or on such terms as it thinks fit. If the court is satisfied that an order may unfairly affect the rights of third parties, it may direct that specified acts by such persons do not constitute a breach of the restrictions.

A person who fails to comply with a notice, or who in purported compliance makes a statement he knows to be materially false or recklessly makes a materially false statement, is guilty of an offence, and liable to a penalty up to the level in 40.1(*b*) PENALTIES, unless he proves that the requirement to give the information with which he failed to comply was frivolous or vexatious. *Sec 733* (see 32.4 LEGAL PROCEEDINGS) applies to such offences.

[*Sec 216(1)-(4), 24 Sch; SI 1991 No 1646, Reg 4*].

See also 43.18(*k*) PUBLIC AND LISTED COMPANIES for sanctions imposed by listed companies on shareholders in default under these provisions.

21.8   **Investigation on requisition by members**

A company may be required to exercise its investigative powers as under 21.7 above on the requisition of members holding at least one-tenth of the paid-up capital carrying voting power in general meeting. The requisition must specify the manner in which they require those powers to be exercised, and give reasonable grounds. It may consist of several documents in like form each signed by one or more requisitionists. It must be signed by the requisitionists and deposited at the company's registered office, and the company must then exercise its powers in the specified manner. Failure to do so renders the company and every officer of it liable to a fine up to the level in 40.1(*d*) PENALTIES.

A report of the information received in pursuance of the investigation must be prepared on its conclusion, and must be made available at the company's registered office within a reasonable period thereafter (which may not exceed 15 working days), the requisitionists being so informed within three working days of its being made available. Three-monthly interim reports must be so prepared and made available if the investigation is not concluded within three months of the deposit of the requisition. The investigation is regarded as concluded when all necessary or expedient enquiries have been made, and either a response to each of them has been received or the time allowed for a response has elapsed.

The report(s) must not include information protected under *Sec 231(3)* i.e. in respect of an undertaking established under the law of a country outside the UK or which carries on business outside the UK if the disclosure would, in the opinion of the directors, seriously prejudice the business of the undertaking, or that of the company or any of its subsidiaries

21.9 Disclosure of Interests in Public Company Shares

and the Secretary of State agrees to the non-disclosure. The fact of omission of such information must be stated. Any reports prepared must be kept at the registered office for six years.

Default in compliance with any of the above reporting requirements renders the company and every officer of it liable to a fine up to the level in 40.1(*d*) PENALTIES.

The report(s) must be available for inspection for so long as they are kept at the registered office. The detailed requirements for inspection and copies, and penalties in default, are the same as those applicable to registers of interests in shares (see 47.8 REGISTERS).

[*Secs 214, 215, 219, 220(2), 24 Sch; CA 1989, s 143, 10 Sch 3; SI 1991 No 1998*].

21.9 ORDERS IMPOSING RESTRICTIONS ON SHARES

Orders may be made under *Sec 210(5)* or *Sec 216* (see 21.6 and 21.7 above) or *Sec 445* (see 31.8 INVESTIGATIONS) imposing restrictions on shares. So long as shares are directed to be subject to such restrictions

(*a*)   any transfer or issue of them, or of the right to be issued with them, is void;

(*b*)   no voting rights are exercisable in respect of them;

(*c*)   no further shares may be issued in right of them or in pursuance of any offer made to their holder; and

(*d*)   (except in a liquidation) no payment may be made of any sums due from the company on them.

[*Sec 454(1); SI 1991 No 1646, Reg 6*].

As regards (*a*) above, any agreement for such a transfer is also void (except as under 21.11 below). [*Sec 454(2); CA 1989, 19 Sch 10; SI 1991 No 1646, Reg 6*].

As regards (*c*) and (*d*) above, an agreement to transfer any right to be issued with other shares in right of those shares (except as under 21.11 below), or to receive any payment on them (other than in a liquidation), is void. [*Sec 454(3); CA 1989, 19 Sch 10; SI 1991 No 1646, Reg 6*].

The Secretary of State may make such amendments by statutory instrument to the provisions relating to the imposition of restrictions on shares as appear to him necessary and expedient to protect the rights of third parties and in relation to the relaxation or removal of restrictions and the making of interim court orders. [*CA 1989, s 135*].

21.10 Punishment for attempted evasion of restrictions

If a person

●   exercises (or purports to exercise) any right to dispose of any shares which, to his knowledge, are for the time being subject to restrictions under 21.9 above, or of any right to be issued with such shares, or

●   votes in respect of any such shares (whether as holder or proxy), or appoints a proxy to vote in respect of them, or

●   being the holder of any such shares, fails to notify the existence of the restrictions to any person whom he knows is entitled (apart from the restrictions) to vote in respect of the shares (whether as holder or proxy) but whom he does not know to be aware of the restrictions, or

●   being the holder of any such shares, or entitled to any right to be issued with other shares in right of them, or to receive any payment on them (other than in a liquidation), enters into any agreement which is void under *Sec 454(2)* or *(3)* (see 21.9 above),

he is liable to a fine up to the level in 40.1(*d*) PENALTIES. If shares in a company are issued in contravention of such restrictions, the company and every officer of it in default is liable to a fine up to the level in 40.1(*d*) PENALTIES. In either case, *Sec 732* (see 32.3 LEGAL PROCEEDINGS) applies to the offence. [*Sec 455, 24 Sch; SI 1991 No 1646, Reg 7*].

21.11   Relaxation and removal of restrictions

Application may be made to the court for the lifting of restrictions on shares in a company imposed as under 21.9 and 21.10 above by any person aggrieved and, in the case of restrictions imposed under *Sec 216* on application to the court by the company, by that company. Where the court is satisfied that the order unfairly affects the rights of third parties, it may direct that specified acts by such persons do not constitute a breach of the restrictions and such an order is not subject to *Sec 456(3)* below. [*Sec 456(1)(1A)(2); SI 1991 No 1646, Reg 8*].

An order of the court or of the Secretary of State lifting the restrictions may (except as below) be made only if

- the relevant facts about the shares have been disclosed to the company and no unfair advantage has accrued to any person as a result of the earlier failure to make that disclosure; or

- the shares are to be transferred for valuable consideration and the court or (where the restrictions were imposed under *Sec 210* or *Sec 445*) the Secretary of State approves the transfer.

[*Sec 456(3); CA 1989, 19 Sch 10*].

An application may also be made to the court by the company or (unless the restrictions were imposed under *Sec 216*) by the Secretary of State for an order that the shares subject to the restrictions be sold, subject to the court's approval, and the court may also direct that the restrictions be lifted. [*Sec 456(4)*]. Following such an order, the court may, on application by the company, or by the person appointed to effect the sale, or by any person interested in the shares, or (unless the restrictions were imposed under *Sec 216*) by the Secretary of State, make such further order relating to the sale or transfer of the shares as it thinks fit. [*Sec 456(5)*].

The proceeds of sale (less costs) of shares sold in pursuance of a court order under *Sec 456(4)* above must be paid into court for the benefit of those beneficially interested in the shares, who may apply to the court for payment (with interest). Costs of a successful application under *Sec 456(4)* or *(5)* above may, if the court so orders, be a prior charge on the sale proceeds. [*Sec 457*].

An order lifting any restrictions under 21.9 above, if it is made under *Sec 456(4)* above or expressed to be made with a view to permitting the transfer of the shares, may continue the restrictions at 21.9(*c*) and (*d*) above, in whole or part, so far as they relate to any right acquired or offer made before the transfer. An order lifting restrictions so continued in force is not subject to the restrictions of *Sec 456(3)* above. [*Sec 456(6)(7)*].

21.12   Transitional provision

Where before 3 December 1981 restrictions were imposed on shares in a company by order of the Secretary of State under *CA 1948, s 174*, and the order remains in force, the order continues to have effect notwithstanding the repeal of that section. [*CC(CP)A 1985, s 23*].

22 Dissolution and Striking Off

22.1 STRIKING OFF DEFUNCT COMPANIES AT INSTIGATION OF THE REGISTRAR

If the Registrar of Companies has reasonable cause to believe that a company is not carrying on business or in operation, he may send to the company by post a letter inquiring whether it is carrying on business or in operation. [*Sec 652(1)*].

He may take this action, for example, because he has not received documents from the company which should have been delivered to him (e.g. annual returns and accounts) or mail sent to the registered office is returned undelivered (Companies House Notes for Guidance CHN 27).

If the Registrar does not, within one month of sending that letter, receive a reply, he must within 14 days send by post a registered letter referring to the first letter and stating that no answer has been received. The letter must also state that if no reply is received to the second letter within one month from its date, a notice will be published in the *London/ Edinburgh Gazette* with a view to striking the company's name off the register.

Where the Registrar

* receives an answer from the company to the effect that the company is not carrying on a business or in operation, or

* does not receive a reply to the second letter above within one month,

he may publish a notice in the *London/Edinburgh Gazette* that, at the expiration of three months from the date of that notice, the company will be struck off the register and dissolved unless cause is shown to the contrary. The Registrar must send a copy of any such notice to the company (and will also place a copy on the company's public file). At the expiration of the three months, unless cause to the contrary has been shown, the Registrar may strike the company name off the register and publish notice of this in the *London/Edinburgh Gazette*. On publication, the company is dissolved (although this does not affect the power of the court to wind up the company).

The Registrar may also take this course of action where *a company is being wound up* and he has reasonable cause to believe that no liquidator is acting, or that the affairs of the company are fully wound up, and the returns required to be made by the liquidator have not been made for a period of six consecutive months.

[*Sec 652(2)-(5)(6)(b)*].

Addresses for notices etc. A letter or notice to be sent to a company may be addressed

* to the company at its registered office, or, if no office has been registered,

* to the care of some officer of the company, or if no officer is known to the Registrar,

* to each of the subscribers to the memorandum at the addresses there mentioned.

A notice to a liquidator may be addressed to him at his last known place of business. [*Sec 652(7)*].

In England and Wales, notices are published in the Company Law Official Notifications Supplement to the *London Gazette*, published weekly on microfiche. Copies are available from HMSO Publications 51, Nine Elms Lane, London SW8 5DR. In Scotland, notices are published in the *Edinburgh Gazette*, published twice weekly. Copies are available from HMSO, 71 Lothian Raod, Edinburgh EH3 9AZ.

22.2 STRIKING OFF PRIVATE COMPANIES ON APPLICATION BY THE COMPANY

Subject to the conditions in 22.3 below being satisfied, a private company may apply to the Registrar for the company's name to be struck off the register. The application must be made on its behalf by the directors (or a majority of them) and be in the prescribed form (Form 652a). [*Sec 652A(1)(2); Deregulation and Contracting Out Act 1994, 5 Sch*].

A filing fee is payable. (see 26.1 FEES) although this will be refunded if the application is rejected or withdrawn after its registration.

Appliction might be made, for example, where a company is no longer required because the active directors wish to retire; the company is a subsidiary whose name is no longer needed; or the company was set up to exploit an idea that turned out not to be feasible. The procedure is not an alternative to formal insolvency proceedings where those are appropriate as creditors must be informed and are likely to object (see 22.5 and 22.6 below).

Following receipt of the Form 652a, the Registrar will publish a notice in the *London/ Edinburgh Gazette* stating that he may exercise his power under these provisions and inviting any person to show cause why he should not do so. If cause to the contrary is not shown and the application has not been withdrawn, the Registrar will strike the company off the register not less than three months after the date of the notice. The company will be formally dissolved when the Registrar publishes a notice to that effect in the *London/ Edinburgh Gazette*. [*Sec 652A(3)–(5); Deregulation and Contracting Out Act 1994, 5 Sch*].

Even where the company is struck off the register and dissolved, creditors and others may apply for the company to be restored to the register (see 22.9 below).

22.3 Conditions for applying

A private company cannot make an application to be struck off under 22. 2 above if

(*a*) at any time in the previous three months, it has

- changed its name;

- traded or otherwise carried on business;

- disposed for value of any property or rights which, immediately before ceasing to trade or carry on business, it held for disposal or gain in the normal course of that business or trade; or

- engaged in any other activity except one necessary or expedient for making a striking off application, concluding the affairs of the company or complying with any statutory requirement; or

(*b*) the company is the subject, or proposed subject, of any insolvency proceedings or compromise or arrangement with its creditors under *Sec 425* (see 44.1 RECONSTRUCTIONS AND MERGERS).

For the purposes of (*a*) above, a company is not treated as trading or carrying on business by virtue only of the fact that it makes a payment in respect of a liability incurred in the course of trading or carrying on business.

[*Sec 652B(1)–(5); Deregulation and Contracting Out Act 1994, 5 Sch*].

22.4 Dissolution and Striking Off

22.4 Withdrawal of application

The directors must withdraw a company's application under 22.2 above (using Form 652c) where, at any time after application has been made and before it is finally dealt with or voluntarily withdrawn, the company

(a)   changes its name;

(b)   trade or otherwise carries on business;

(c)   disposes for value of any property or rights (other than those which it needed to retain to make, or proceed with, the application);

(d)   engages in any other activitity except one necessary or expedient for

- making or proceeding with a striking off application;

- concluding the affairs of the company which are outstanding because of what was necessary or expedient to make or proceed with the application; or

- complying with any statutory requirement; or

(e)   becomes the subject of any insolvency proceedings or makes a compromise or arrangement with its creditors under *Sec 425* (see 44.1 RECONSTRUCTIONS AND MERGERS).

For the purposes of (b) above, a company is not treated as trading or carrying on business by virtue only of the fact that it makes a payment in respect of a liability incurred in the course of trading or carrying on business.

[Sec 652C(4)–(7); Deregulation and Contracting Out Act 1994, 5 Sch].

22.5 Notification

Where an application is made under 22.2 above, a copy of the Form 652a must be given, within seven days of the date of application, to every person who on that date was

(a)   a member of the company;

(b)   an employee of the company;

(c)   a creditor of the company (including a contingent or prospective creditor);

(d)   a director of the company who did not sign the Form 652a; or

(e)   a manager or trustee of any employee pension fund.

[Secs 652B(6)(7), 652D(8); Deregulation and Contracting Out Act 1994, 5 Sch].

A copy of Form 652a must also be given to any person who becomes a member, employee, etc. under (a)–(e) above on a date subsequent to the application (within seven days of so becoming). *[Secs 652C(1)(2), 652D(8); Deregulation and Contracting Out Act 1994, 5 Sch].*

There is no requirement to give notice if the application is withdrawn within the seven day period of notice. *[Secs 652B(8), 652C(3); Deregulation and Contracing Out Act 1994, 5 Sch].*

For the above purposes, a copy of the Form 652a is treated as given to a person if it is delivered to, left at, or posted to his *'proper address'* i.e.

(i)   in the case of an individual, his last known address;

(ii)   in the case of a company or partnership incorporated under the law outside the UK which has a place of business in the UK, its principal office in the UK;

(iii)   in the case of a company or partnership not falling within (ii) above, its registered or principal office.

Where a creditor has more than one place of business, copies of Form 652a must be left at, or sent by post to, each place of business of the creditor which the company has had dealings with in relation to the debt.

[*Sec 652D(1)–(4); Deregulation and Contracting Out Act 1994, 5 Sch*].

22.6 Objections to proposed striking off and dissolution

Any interested party may have grounds to object to the striking off and dissolution of the company. Any objections should be in writing and sent to the Registrar of Companies, together with supporting evidence (e.g. copies of invoices showing that the company is trading). Examples of grounds for objecting are that

- the company has breached any of the conditions of its application under 22.2 above;

- the directors have failed to comply with the requirements for informing interested parties;

- any of the declarations on Form 652a are false;

- some form of action is being taken, or is pending, to recover any moneys owed (e.g. a winding up petition or action in the small claims court);

- other legal action is being taken against the company; or

- the directors have wrongfully traded, perpetrated a tax fraud or committed some other offence.

(Companies House Note for Guidance CHN 27).

22.7 Offences and penalties

The following offences and penalties are imposed for breaches in connection with the provisions in 22.2 to 22.5 above.

- A person who breaches or fails to perform a duty imposed under 22.3 to 22.5 above is guilty of an offence and liable to a fine up to the level in 40.1(*d*) PENALTIES. It is a defence for the accused to prove that

    (i)   in proceedings for an offence of breach of duty under 22.3 above (by making an application when all the conditions were not satisfied) that he did not know, and could not reasonably have known, of the existence of the facts which led to the breach;

    (ii)   in proceedings for an offence consisting of failure to give notice under *Sec 652B(6)* (see 22.5 above) that he took all reasonable steps to perform the duty; and

    (iii) in proceedings for an offence consisting of failure to give notice under *Sec 652C(2)* (see 22.5 above) or failure to withdraw an application under 22.4 above, either that, at the time of the failure, he was not aware that an application had been made or he took all reasonable steps to perform the duty.

- A person who fails to give notification as required under 22.5 above with the intention of concealing the making of the application is guilty of an offence and liable to a penalty up to the level in 40.1(*a*) PENALTIES.

22.8 Dissolution and Striking Off

- Where a company makes an application under 22.2 above, any person who, in connection with the application, knowingly or recklessly furnishes any information to the Registrar of Companies which is false or misleading in a material particular is guilty of an offence and liable to a penalty up to the level in 40.1(*d*) PENALTIES.

- Any person who knowingly or recklessly makes an application to the Registrar of Companies, which purports to be an application under 22.2 above, but which is not, is guilty of an offence and liable to a penalty up to the level in 40.1(*d*) PENALTIES.

[*Secs 652E, 652F, 24 Sch; Deregulation and Contracting Out Act 1994, 5 Sch*].

22.8 EFFECT OF DISSOLUTION

Liability of directors, etc. The liability (if any) of every director, managing officer and member of the company continues and may be enforced as if the company had not been dissolved. [*Secs 652(6)(a), 652A(6); Deregulation and Contracting Out Act 1994, 5 Sch*].

Assets of the company. All property and rights whatsoever vested in or held on trust for the company immediately before its dissolution (including leasehold property, but not property held on trust for any other person) are deemed to be *bona vacantia* and accordingly

- if the company's registered office is in Lancashire, belong to the Duchy of Lancaster;

- if the registered office is in Cornwall, belong to the Duchy of Cornwall; and

- in all other cases, belong to the Crown.

Enquiries regarding *bona vacantia* should be addressed, as appropriate, to

In England and Wales
The Solicitor to the Duchy of Lancaster
66 Lincoln's Inn Fields
London WC2A 3LH

The Solicitor to the Duchy of Cornwall
10 Buckingham Gate
London SW1E 6LA

The Treasury Solicitor (BV)
Queen Anne's Chambers
28 Broadway
London SW1H 9JS

In Scotland
The Queen's and Lord Treasurer's Remembrancer
Crown Office
25 Chambers Street
Edinburgh EH1 1LA

The property vesting as *bona vacantia* may be disclaimed by the Crown or Duchy as the case may be. [*Secs 654, 656*]. See *Sec 657* and *20 Sch* for the effect of Crown disclaimer.

Liability for rentcharge on company's land in England and Wales. Where land in England and Wales vests subject to a rentcharge in the Crown or any other person (the *'proprietor'*) on the dissolution of a company, the proprietor and his successors in title are not subject to any personal liability in respect of any sums becoming due under the rentcharge except sums becoming due after the proprietor, or some person claiming under or through him, has taken possession or control of the land or has entered into occupation of it. [*Sec 658; IA 1985, 6 Sch 47; IA 1986, 13 Sch*].

22.9   **RESTORATION TO THE REGISTER**

Where a company has been struck off the register, the court may, on application within 20 years of dissolution, order the company's name to be restored to the register.

If the company has been struck off at the instigation of the Registrar under 22.1 above, the application may be made by the company (even though it does not legally exist) or any member or creditor. The court may order the company's name to be restored if it was carrying on business or in operation at the time it was struck off or if it is just to do so. For a consideration of these criteria for restoring to the register, see *Re Priceland Ltd [1997] BCC 207*.

If the company was struck off following an application by the company under 22.2 above, the application may be made by any person to whom a copy of the application was required to be given under 22.5 above. The court may order the company's name to be restored to the register if that person was not given a copy of the application, or the application by the company involved a breach of the conditions of the application under 22.3 above, or for some other reason if it is just to do so. The court may also order restoration, on application by the Secretary of State, if satisfied that it is in the public interest to do so.

[*Sec 653(1)–(2D); Deregulation and Contracting Out Act 1994, 5 Sch*].

The application for restoration may be made by any person who was legally prejudiced by the dissolution of the company. This includes a person who wishes to enforce a liability of the company and does not depend on there having been an existing cause of action when the company was struck off. The provisions are also intended to provide a remedy for a person who has a claim, whether against the company or against a third party (such as the company's insurer or guarantor), which can only be enforced if the company is restored to the register (*City of Westminster Assurance Co Ltd v Registrar of Companies, [1997] BCC 960*).

Procedure. The Registrar of Companies will provide information to assist in an application to the court but has no power to register a company without a court order.

In England and Wales, the application can be made to the High Court by originating summons. The Registrar of the Companies Court in London usually hears restoration cases in chambers once a week on Friday afternoons. Cases are also heard in the District Registries. Alternatively, an application can be made to a County Court that has the authority to wind up the company. The originating summons should be served on the solicitor dealing with any *bona vacantia* (see 22.8 above) and the Registrar of Companies, Restoration Section, PO Box 435, Companies House, Crown Way, Cardiff CF14 3YA (tel 01222 380069; fax 01222 380006). The Registrar will accept delivery by post (recorded delivery is recommended) or by hand at Companies House, Cardiff or London. At the hearing the Registrar will be represented by the Treasury Solicitor or his agent.

In Scotland, application may be made to the Court with jurisdiction to wind up the company, i.e. the Court of Sessions or, for a company whose paid up capital does not exceed £120,000, the Sheriff Court in the Sheriffdom in which the company has its registered office. The petition should be served on The Lord Advocate, Crown Office, 25

22.10 Dissolution and Striking Off

Chambers Street, Edinburgh EH1 1LA and the Registrar of Companies, Companies House, 37 Castle Terrace, Edinburgh EH1 2EB. The Registrar will accept service by post (recorded delivery is recommended) or by hand. The Registrar and/or the Lord Advocate may be represented at the hearing by an agent.

Evidence. The Registrar will normally ask for delivery (prior to the hearing) of any statutory documents to bring the public file of the company up to date, and the rectification of any irregularities in the company's structure.

The court will require evidence covering

(*a*)   service of the originating summons/petition

(*b*)   the circumstances of the company, including

- when it was incorporated and the nature of its objects (a copy of the certificate of incorporation and memorandum and articles of association should be exhibited);

- its membership and officers;

- its trading activities and, if applicable, when this ceased;

- an explanation of any failure to deliver accounts, returns or notices to the Registrar;

- details of the striking-off and dissolution (based on information provided by the Registrar);

- comments on the company's solvency; and

- any further information necessary to explain the reason for the application.

The applicant will normally be expected to pay the Registrar's costs in relation to the hearing.

(Companies House Notes for Guidance CHN 27 and CHN 275).

Effect of court order. When an office copy of the order is delivered to the Registrar, the company is deemed to have continued in existence as if its name had not been struck off. The court may, by the order, give such directions and make such provisions as seem just for placing the company and all other persons in the same position (as nearly as possible) as if the company's name had never been struck off. [*Sec 653(3); Deregulation and Contracting Out Act 1994, 5 Sch*].

22.10 POWER OF COURT TO DECLARE DISSOLUTION OF COMPANY VOID

Where a company has been dissolved, the court may, on an application within two years (subject to below) of the date of dissolution by the liquidator or any other interested party, make an order, on such terms as it thinks fit, declaring the dissolution to have been void. Such proceedings may then be taken as if the company had not been dissolved.

The applicant must, within seven days of the order (or such further time as the court allows), deliver an office copy of the order to the Registrar of Companies. In default, he is liable to a fine up to the level in 40.1(*f*) PENALTIES.

For companies dissolved after 15 November 1989, there is no time limit where the application is for the purposes of bringing proceedings against the company for

(*a*)   damages in respect of 'personal injuries' including any funeral expenses claimed by virtue of *Law Reform (Miscellaneous Provisions) Act 1934, s 1(2)(c),* or (*b*)   damages under *Fatal Accidents Act 1976* or the *Damages (Scotland) Act 1976*,

although no order must be made if the proceedings would fail under a time limit in any other enactment. For the interaction of this provision in relation to personal injuries actions with *Limitation Act 1980, s 33*, see *Re Workvale Ltd [1992] BCC 349.*

'Personal injuries' include any disease and any impairment of a person's physical or mental condition.

For companies dissolved before 16 November 1989, no application within (*a*) or (*b*) above can be made in relation to a company dissolved before 16 November 1969.

[*Sec 651; CA 1989, s 141*].

The interest of an applicant under *Sec 651* above in having the company revived does not have to be firmly established or likely to prevail. It is sufficient that it is not 'merely shadowy'. It follows, therefore, that an order may be made to enable a company to meet a liability which would otherwise remain unpaid. Normally a third party should not be entitled to intervene to argue that an order should not be made. However, in cases where the making of an order would directly affect the rights of a third party, irrespective of whether the applicant has any claim against the company or the company has any claim against the third party, the third party is entitled to be joined to argue that such an order should not be made (*Re Forte's (Manufacturing) Ltd, Stanhope Pension Trust Ltd and another v Registrar of Companies [1994] BCC 84*).

22.11 EFFECT OF COMPANY'S REVIVAL AFTER DISSOLUTION

The person in whom any property or right is vested following dissolution (see 22.8 above under the heading *Assets of the company*) may dispose of that property or right, or any interest in it, despite the fact that an order may be made under 22.9 or 22.10 above. Where such an order is then made,

- it does not affect the disposition; and

- the Crown (or Duke of Cornwall) must repay to the company an amount equal to

    (i)   the consideration received; or

    (ii)   the value of any such consideration at the time of the disposition; or

    (iii) if no consideration was received, the value of the property, right or interest disposed of, as at the date of the disposition.

[*Sec 655*].

23 Distributions

Cross-references. See 13 BONUS ISSUES.

The contents of this chapter are as follows

23.1 GENERAL DEFINITIONS

Capitalisation means, in relation to a company's profits, any of the following operations (whenever carried out), i.e.

- applying the profits in wholly or partly paying up unissued shares to be allotted to members of the company as fully or partly paid bonus shares; or

- transferring the profits to capital redemption reserve (see 8.11 ACQUISITION OF OWN SHARES).

[*Sec 280*].

Distribution means every description of distribution of a company's assets to its members, in cash or otherwise, except

- an issue of shares as fully or partly paid bonus shares;

- the redemption or purchase of any of the company's own shares out of capital (including the proceeds from the fresh issue of shares) or out of unrealised profits under *Secs 159-181* (see 8.2 to 8.17 ACQUISITION OF OWN SHARES);

- the reduction of share capital by extinguishing or reducing the liability of any of the members on company shares in respect of unpaid share capital, or by paying off paid up share capital; and

- a distribution of assets to members of the company on its winding up.

[*Sec 263(2)*].

Investment company within 23.6 below means a *public company* which has given (and not revoked) requisite notice in the prescribed form to the Registrar of Companies of its intention to carry on business as an investment company, and since the date of that notice has complied with the following requirements, namely that

- the business of the company consists of investing its funds mainly in securities, with the aim of spreading investment risk and giving members of the company the benefit of the results of the management of its funds;

- none of the company's holdings in companies (other than in investment companies) are more than 15% by value of the investing company's investments (for interpretation, see *ICTA 1988, s 842(1A)-(3)*);

- distribution of the company's capital profits is prohibited by its memorandum or articles (except that, with effect from 8 November 1999, an investment company need not be prohibited from redeeming or purchasing its own shares under *Sec 160* or *162*, see 8.10 and 8.4 ACQUISITION OF OWN SHARES respectively); and

- the company has not retained (otherwise than in compliance with the provisions of this chapter) more than 15% of the income derived from securities in respect of any accounting reference period.

[*Sec 266; SI 1999 No 2770*].

Profits and **losses** of any description are references (respectively) to profits and losses of that description made at any time and, except where the context otherwise requires, are to revenue and capital profits and revenue and capital losses. [*Sec 280(3)*].

Undistributable reserves are

- the share premium account, see 56 SHARE PREMIUM;

- the capital redemption reserve (see 8.13 ACQUISITION OF OWN SHARES);

- the amount by which the company's accumulated, unrealised profits (so far as not previously utilised by capitalisation other than a transfer to capital redemption reserve after 21 December 1980) exceeds its accumulated, unrealised losses (so far as not previously written off in a reduction or reorganisation of capital); and

- any other reserve which the company is prohibited from distributing by any other enactment or by its memorandum or articles.

[*Sec 264(3)*].

23.2   PROFITS AVAILABLE FOR DISTRIBUTION

Profits available for distribution are, subject to the provisions for investment companies in 23.6 below, accumulated, realised profits (so far as not previously utilised by distribution or capitalisation) less accumulated, realised losses (so far as not previously written off in a reduction or reorganisation of capital).

Where directors, after making reasonable enquiries, are unable to determine whether a particular profit or loss made before 22 December 1980 is realised or unrealised, they may treat the profit as realised and the loss as unrealised.

[*Sec 263(3)(5)*].

Where, before 22 December 1980 under *CA 1980*, a company was authorised by its articles to apply its *unrealised* profits to pay up unissued shares as fully or partly paid bonus shares, that provision continues (subject to any alteration of the articles) as authority after that date. [*Sec 278*].

23.3   Realised profits of insurance companies

Where an insurance company as defined by *Insurance Companies Act 1982, Part II* carries on *long-term business*

- any amount included in the 'relevant part of the balance sheet' of the company which represents a 'surplus' in the fund or funds maintained by it in respect of that business and which has not been allocated to policy holders in accordance with *section 30(1)* of that Act or carried forward unappropriated as mentioned in *section 30(7)* of that Act, and

- any 'deficit' in that fund or those funds

are to be treated respectively as a realised profit and a realised loss.

23.4 Distributions

'Relevant part of the balance sheet' is Liabilities item A.V in the balance sheet format in 6.5 ACCOUNTS: INSURANCE AND BANKING COMPANIES.

'Surplus' means the excess of the assets representing that fund or those funds over the liabilities of the company attributable to its 'long term business' as shown by an 'actuarial investigation'.

'Deficit' means the excess of the liabilities over assets.

'Actuarial investigation' means an investigation to which *Insurance Companies Act 1982, s 18* (periodic actuarial investigation) applies or which is made under *section 42* of that Act (actuarial investigation required by the Secretary of State).

'Long term business' means insurance business of any of the classes specified in *Insurance Companies Act 1982, 1 Sch.*

[*Sec 268; SI 1993 No 3246, 2 Sch; SI 1996 No 189, Reg 13*].

See also 23.12 below.

23.4 Treatment of development costs

Where development costs are shown as an asset in the company's accounts, any amount shown in respect of those costs is to be treated as

- a realised loss for the purposes of 23.2 above; and

- a realised revenue loss for the purposes of 23.6 below.

The above does not apply to any part of that amount representing an unrealised profit made on revaluation of those costs. It also does not apply if

(i) there are special circumstances in the company's case justifying the directors in deciding that the amount is not to be so treated; and

(ii) the note to the accounts under *4 Sch 20* or *8 Sch 20* (reasons for showing development costs as an asset, see 5.8 ACCOUNTS: INDIVIDUAL COMPANIES and 7.10 ACCOUNTS: SMALL AND MEDIUM-SIZED COMPANIES) states that the amount is not to be so treated and explains the circumstances relied upon to justify the decision.

[*Sec 269; SI 1997 No 220, Reg 7*].

23.5 RESTRICTIONS ON DISTRIBUTIONS

The following provisions apply without prejudice to any law or any provision of a company's memorandum or articles restricting the sums out of which, or the cases in which, a distribution may be made. [*Sec 281*].

A company must not

- make a distribution except out of profits available for distribution (see 23.2 above) although there is no rule that all profits must be distributed (*Burland v Earle [1902] AC 83*) until the company is wound up; or

- apply an unrealised profit in paying up debentures or unpaid amounts on its issued shares.

[*Sec 263(1)(4)*].

Additionally, subject to 23.6 below, a *public company* may only make a distribution if

- its 'net assets' at the time of the distribution are not less than the aggregate of its called-up share capital and 'undistributable reserves'; and

- the distribution does not reduce the amount of those assets to less than that aggregate.

'Net assets' means the aggregate of the company's assets (excluding any uncalled share capital) less the aggregate of its 'liabilities'.

'Liabilities' includes any provision for liabilities or charges retained as reasonably necessary for the purpose of providing for any liability or loss which is either likely to be incurred, or certain to be incurred but uncertain as to amount or as to date on which it will arise.

See 23.1 above for *'undistributable reserves'*.

[Sec 264(1)(2)(4)].

See 23.7 to 23.10 below for the company's accounts to be considered in determining whether a distribution may be made without contravening the above provisions.

23.6   **Investment companies, etc.**

Subject to below, an investment company (as defined in 23.1 above) may also make a distribution at any time out of its accumulated, realised revenue profits (so far as not previously utilised by distribution or capitalisation) *less* its accumulated revenue losses (whether realised or unrealised and so far as not previously written off in a reduction or reorganisation of capital) if

(*a*)   its assets (excluding any uncalled share capital) at the time of the distribution are at least equal to one and a half times the aggregate of its 'liabilities';

(*b*)   the distribution does not reduce that amount to less than one and a half times that aggregate;

(*c*)   its shares are listed on a recognised investment exchange (other than an overseas investment exchange as defined in *FSA 1986, s 207(1)*);

(*d*)   during the 'relevant period' it has not

- distributed any of its capital profits (otherwise than, with effect from 8 November 1999, by way of redemption or purchase of its own shares under *Sec 160* or *166*, see 8.10 and 8.4 ACQUISITION OF OWN SHARES respectively), or

- applied any unrealised profits or any capital profits (realised or unrealised) in paying up debentures or amounts unpaid on its issued shares; and

(*e*)   it has given the requisite notice under 23.1 above to the Registrar of Companies

- before the beginning of the relevant period under (*d*) above; or

- in the case of a company incorporated after 21 December 1980, as soon as reasonably practical after incorporation.

The *'relevant period'* is the period beginning with

- the first day of the accounting reference period immediately preceding that in which the proposed distribution is to be made, or

- where the distribution is to be made in the company's first accounting reference period, the first day of that period

and ending with the day of the distribution.

See 23.5 above for the definition of *'liabilities'*.

23.7 Distributions

[*Sec 265; FSA 1986, 16 Sch 19; SI 1999 No 2770*].

Regulations may be made by statutory instrument to extend the above provisions to companies whose principal business consists of investing their funds in securities, land or other assets with the aim of spreading investment risk and giving members the benefit of the results of the management of the assets.

See 23.7 to 23.10 below for the company's accounts to be considered in determining whether a distribution may be made without contravening the above provisions.

23.7 ACCOUNTING REQUIREMENTS

A distribution which may be made without contravening the provisions of 23.5 and 23.6 above is determined by reference to

(i) profits, losses, assets and liabilities,

(ii) provisions of a kind defined in 2.1 ACCOUNTS: DEFINITIONS, and

(iii) share capital and reserves (including 'undistributable reserves', see 23.1 above)

as stated in the company's 'relevant accounts'.

The '*relevant accounts*' for these purposes are:

(a) Where (b) or (c) below does not apply, the accounts laid under 3.6 ACCOUNTS: GENERAL in respect of the last preceding accounting reference period (the '*last annual accounts*').

In respect of a distribution of *any company*

(i) the accounts must have been 'properly prepared' or have been so prepared subject only to matters which are not material for determining, by reference to (i)–(iii) above, whether the distribution would contravene the relevant provisions. Subject to this, the accounts must give a true and fair view (see 3.13 ACCOUNTS: GENERAL) of the state of the company's affairs at the balance sheet date and its profit or loss in respect of the period for which they were prepared; and

(ii) the auditors must have reported on the accounts and, if that report is qualified, they must state in writing whether, in their opinion, the qualification is material for determining by reference to (i)–(iii) above, whether the distribution would contravene the relevant provisions. A copy of the statement must have been laid before the company in general meeting. See *Example 1* under 12.30 AUDITORS for a suggested form of the report.

See also *Precision Dippings Ltd v Precision Dippings Marketing Ltd and Others CA [1985] 3 WLR 812.*

(b) Where the distribution would contravene the relevant provisions if reference were made only to the last annual accounts in (a) above, such *interim accounts* as are necessary to enable a reasonable judgement to be made as to the amounts in (i)–(iii) above.

In respect of a proposed distribution by a *public company*

(i) the provisions of (a)(i) above apply (but see below for the meaning of 'properly prepared'); and

(ii) a copy of the accounts must have been delivered to the Registrar of Companies.

(c) Where the distribution is proposed to be declared during the company's first accounting reference period (or before any accounts are laid in respect of that period) such *initial accounts* as are necessary to enable a reasonable judgement to be made as to the amounts in (i)–(iii) above.

In respect of a proposed distribution by a *public company*

   (i)   the provisions of (*a*)(i) above apply (but see below for the meaning of 'properly prepared');

  (ii)   the auditors must have made a report stating whether, in their opinion, the accounts have been properly prepared and, if their report is qualified, they must state in writing whether, in their opinion, the qualification is material for determining, by reference to (i)–(iii) above, whether the distribution would contravene the relevant provisions; and

 (iii)   a copy of the accounts, auditors' report and statement (if any) must have been delivered to the Registrar of Companies.

See *Example 6* under 12.30 AUDITORS for a suggested form of an unqualified report under (ii) above.

'Properly prepared' for the purposes of (*a*)(i) above means prepared in accordance with *CA 1985*. For the purposes of (*b*)(i) and (*c*)(i) above it means that the accounts must comply with *Sec 226* and *4 Sch* (see 5.2 to 5.31 ACCOUNTS: INDIVIDUAL COMPANIES), with necessary modifications where the accounts are prepared otherwise than in respect of an accounting reference period, and any balance sheet must have been signed in accordance with *Sec 233* (see 3.2 ACCOUNTS: GENERAL).

Documents in foreign languages. Where any document within (*b*)(ii) or (*c*)(iii) above is in a language other than English, an English translation, certified as correct, must also have been delivered to the Registrar of Companies. See 28.2 FORMS for the method of certification. (Note that any accounts and auditors' report delivered to the Registrar of Companies under (*a*) above (apart from certain Welsh language accounts) must be accompanied by a certified translation under *Sec 242*, see 3.7 ACCOUNTS: GENERAL.)

[*Secs 270-273; CA 1989, 10 Sch 4-6*].

23.8   Successive distributions

For determining by reference to a particular set of accounts whether a proposed distribution may be made, 23.7 above has effect where one or more distributions have already been made by reference to those accounts as if the proposed distribution was increased by those distributions already made. [*Sec 274(1)*].

This applies to distributions generally and also, if it would not otherwise do so, to

• 'financial assistance' lawfully given by a public or private company out of its distributable profits where assistance is required to be given under *Sec 154* or *155(2)* (see 8.20 and 8.21(*a*) ACQUISITION OF OWN SHARES respectively);

• financial assistance given by a company in contravention of *Sec 151* (see 8.18 ACQUISITION OF OWN SHARES) which reduces the company's 'net assets' or increases its 'net liabilities';

• a payment made by a company for purchase of its own shares (except a payment made lawfully otherwise than out of distributable profits); and

• a payment of any description specified in *Sec 168* (see 8.8 ACQUISITION OF OWN SHARES).

23.9 Distributions

The financial assistance or payments must have been given or made after the relevant accounts were prepared and are treated as if they were distributions already made in pursuance of a determination made by reference to the accounts.

For the meaning of '*financial assistance*' and '*net assets*' see 8.18 and 8.20 ACQUISITION OF OWN SHARES respectively.

'*Net liabilities*' means the amount by which the aggregate of the company's liabilities (including any amount retained as reasonably necessary to provide for any liability or loss which is either likely to be incurred or certain to be incurred but uncertain as to amount and date) exceeds the aggregate amount of its assets, taking the amount of the assets and liabilities to be as stated in the company's accounting records immediately before the financial assistance is given.

The Secretary of State has power to modify the above provisions.

[*Sec 274*].

23.9 Treatment of assets in the relevant accounts

Provisions to be treated as realised losses. For the purposes of 23.5 above

(*a*)   any provision within *4 Sch 88, 89* (see 5.3 ACCOUNTS: INDIVIDUAL COMPANIES) other than one within (*b*) below is treated as a realised loss; and

(*b*)   a provision in respect of a diminution in value of a fixed asset appearing on a revaluation of all the fixed assets (or all the fixed assets other than goodwill) is treated as an unrealised loss.

[*Sec 275(1)*].

Subject to below, for the purpose of (*b*) above, any consideration by the directors of the value of any fixed assets is treated as a revaluation but where such assets have not actually been revalued, the directors must be satisfied that their aggregate value at the time in question is not less than the aggregate amount at which they are for the time being stated in the company's accounts. Where, however, proper accounts are required under 23.7(*a*)(i), (*b*)(i) or (*c*)(i) above, this does not apply in determining whether a revaluation affecting the relevant items in 23.7(i)–(iii) above has taken place unless it is stated in a note to the accounts

* that the directors have considered the value at any time of any fixed assets without actually revaluing those assets;

* that they are satisfied that the aggregate value of those assets at the time in question is or was not less than the aggregate amount at which they are or were for the time being stated in the company's accounts; and

* that the relevant items in question are stated in the relevant accounts on the basis that a revaluation of the company's fixed assets, which by virtue of (*b*) above included the assets in question, took place at that time.

[*Sec 275(4)-(6)*].

Depreciation following revaluation of fixed asset. If an unrealised profit is made on the revaluation of a fixed asset and subsequently a sum is written off or retained for depreciation of that asset, then a *realised* profit is treated as made for the purposes of 23.5 above of the amount by which that depreciation is greater than it would have been but for the revaluation. [*Sec 275(2)*].

Example

	Asset value	Depreciation at 10%
	£	£
1994	10,000	1,000
1995	10,000	1,000
1996	15,000 (revaluation)	1,500
1997	15,000	1,500
1998	15,000	1,500

The increase of £500 in depreciation in 1993 and subsequent years following the revaluation may be treated as a realised profit and available for distribution.

Cost of asset unknown. Where there is no record of the original cost of an asset, or no record can be obtained without unreasonable expense or delay, then in determining whether the company has made a profit or loss on the asset, its cost is taken to be the value given to it in the earliest available record made on or after its acquisition by the company. [*Sec 275(3)*].

23.10 Distribution in kind

Where a company makes a distribution of (or including) a non-cash asset, and any part of the amount at which that asset is stated in the accounts relevant for the purposes of the distribution under 23.7 to 23.9 above represents an *unrealised profit*, this profit is to be treated as *realised* for the purposes of

(*a*)   determining the lawfulness of the distribution in accordance with the provisions of this chapter (whether before or after the distribution takes place); and

(*b*)   the application of *4 Sch 12(a), 34(3)(a) or 8 Sch 12(a), 34(3)(a)* (only realised profits are to be included in or transferred to the profit and loss account).

[*Sec 276; CA 1989, 10 Sch 7; SI 1997 No 220, Reg 7*].

23.11 CONSEQUENCES OF UNLAWFUL DISTRIBUTIONS

Where a distribution, or part of one, made by a company to one of its members is unlawful under the provisions of this chapter and at the time of the distribution the member knows, or has reasonable grounds for believing, it to be unlawful, he must repay it to the company. In the case of a non-cash distribution, he must repay an amount equal to the value of the distribution at the time it was made. [*Sec 277(1)*]. See *Precision Dippings Ltd v Precision Dippings Marketing Ltd and Others CA [1985] 3 WLR 812*.

The above is without prejudice to any obligation otherwise imposed on a member to repay an unlawful distribution, but does not apply to

•   financial assistance given by a company in contravention of *Sec 151* (see 8.18 ACQUISITION OF OWN SHARES); or

•   any payment made by a company in respect of the redemption or purchase of shares in itself.

The Secretary of State may modify these provisions by regulations.

[*Sec 277(2)(3)*].

Directors who are parties to the payment of an unlawful dividend are jointly and severally liable to repay the amount. This applies even if the dividend is approved by a general meeting or the company's articles. See *Flitcroft's Case (1882) 21 ChD 519* and also

23.12 Distributions

Wallerstein v Moir [1974] 3 All ER 217; Selangor United Rubber Estates Ltd v Cradock (No 3) [1968] 1 WLR 1555 and *Belmont Finance Corporation Ltd v Williams Furniture (No 2) [1980] 1 All ER 393.*

23.12 INSURANCE COMPANIES

Where a company's accounts are prepared under the special provisions in *Part VII* relating to insurance companies (see 6 ACCOUNTS: INSURANCE AND BANKING COMPANIES) the provisions in 23.1 to 23.11 above apply with the following modifications.

- In 23.4(ii) above the reference is to *9A Sch Part I, para 35* (see 6.18 ACCOUNTS: INSURANCE AND BANKING COMPANIES).

- in 23.5 above, for distributions made after 1 February 1996, 'liabilities' is defined to include any provision for other risks and charges within *9A Sch Part I, para 84* (see 6.4 ACCOUNTS: INSURANCE AND BANKING COMPANIES) and any amount included under Liabilities Items Ba (fund for future appropriations), C (technical provisions) and D (technical provisions for linked liabilities) in the balance sheet format in 6.5 ACCOUNTS: INSURANCE AND BANKING COMPANIES.

- In 23.7 above, in the definition of 'properly prepared' the references are to *Sec 255* and *9A Sch Part I* instead of *Sec 226* and *4 Sch.*

- In 23.9(*a*) above the reference is to any provision in *9A Sch Part I, para 84* (see 6.4 ACCOUNTS: INSURANCE AND BANKING COMPANIES) and, for distributions made after 1 February 1996, any amount included under Liabilities Items Ba (fund for future appropriations), C (technical provisions) and D (technical provisions for linked liabilities) in the balance sheet format in 6.5 ACCOUNTS: INSURANCE AND BANKING COMPANIES.

- In 23.10(*b*) above the reference is to the application of *9A Sch Part I, paras 16(a), 29(3)(a)* (only realised profits are to be included in or transferred to the profit and loss account).

[*Sec 279, 11 Sch; SI 1993 No 3246; SI 1996 No 189, 6 Sch*].

23.13 BANKING COMPANIES

Where a company's accounts are prepared under the special provisions in *Part VII* relating to banking companies (see 6 ACCOUNTS: SPECIAL CATEGORY COMPANIES) the provisions in 23.1 to 23.11 above apply with the following modifications.

- In 23.4(ii) above the reference is to *9 Sch Part I, para 27* (see 6.72 ACCOUNTS: INSURANCE AND BANKING COMPANIES).

- In 23.7 above in the definition of 'properly prepared' the references are to *Sec 255* and *9 Sch Part I* instead of *Sec 226* and *4 Sch.*

- In 23.9(*a*) above the reference is to any provision in *9 Sch Part I, para 85* (see 6.62 ACCOUNTS: INSURANCE AND BANKING COMPANIES).

- In 23.10(*b*) the reference is to the application of *9 Sch Part I, paras 19(a)* and *44(3)(a)* (only realised profits are to be included in or transferred to the profit and loss account).

[*Sec 279, 11 Sch; SI 1991 No 2705*].

23.14 PROCEDURES ETC. FOR PAYMENT OF DIVIDENDS

1985 Table A. The following provisions apply where a company has adopted the relevant article in *Table A* in *SI 1985 No 805.*

Declaration of dividends. A company may declare a dividend by ordinary resolution but it must not exceed the amount recommended by the directors. [*Art 102*]. Unless otherwise provided in the rights attaching to the shares, any dividend must be declared and paid according to the amounts paid up on the relevant shares. It must be apportioned and paid proportionately in relation to any part period in respect of which it is paid (unless the terms of the issue provide that the shares rank for a dividend as from a particular date). [*Art 104*]. There is no principle which compels a company to divide its profit among its shareholders. Whether the whole or part should be paid as dividend is a question for the directors and shareholders to decide (*Burland v Earle [1902] AC 83*).

Interim dividends. Subject to the provisions of *CA 1985* the directors may pay interim dividends if justified by the company's profits available for distribution. This includes dividends on shares with deferred or non-preferred rights but only if, at the time of payment, any preferential dividend is not in arrears. Provided they act in good faith, the directors do not incur any liability to the preferential shareholders for any loss suffered by the lawful payment of any such interim dividend. The directors may also pay fixed rate dividends at intervals settled by them if justified by the company's profits available for distribution. [*Art 103*].

Non-cash dividends. On the recommendation of the directors, a general meeting declaring a dividend may direct that it is satisfied, in whole or part, by the distribution of assets. The directors may settle any difficulties which arise including valuation of assets, issue of fractional certificates and payment of cash to members to adjust their rights. They may also vest any asset in trustees. [*Art 105*]. Unless a company's articles adopt *Art 105* or a similar article, a distribution must be made in cash (*Wood v Odessa Waterworks Co (1889) 42 ChD 636*).

Payment of dividends. A dividend may be paid by cheque sent by post to the registered address of the person entitled. Where two or more persons are jointly entitled, it may be sent to the registered address of the first-named or to such address as the person or persons entitled elect in writing. Cheques must be made payable to the order of the person/persons entitled (or such other person/persons as directed) and payment of the cheque is a good discharge to the company. [*Art 106*]. See also 43.18(*l*) PUBLIC AND LISTED COMPANIES for powers of listed companies to cease sending dividend warrants to untraceable members.

Interest on dividends. No dividend carries interest against the company unless otherwise provided by the rights attaching to the shares. [*Art 107*].

Unclaimed dividends. Any dividend which has remained unclaimed for twelve years from the date it became due for payment may, if the directors resolve, be forfeited and cease to remain owing by the company. [*Art 108*]. (Listed companies must include such a provision in their articles, see 43.18(*m*) PUBLIC AND LISTED COMPANIES.)

CA 1948, Table A. Similar provisions to the above apply where *Table A* in *CA 1948* has been adopted by the company except that

- there is no article on unclaimed dividends;

- the directors may, before recommending a dividend, set aside out of profits such sums as they think proper as reserves to be employed in the business or invested; and

- the directors may deduct from any dividend payable to a member all money (if any) payable to the company by the member for unpaid calls or otherwise in relation to the company's shares.

[*CA 1948, Table A, Arts 114-122*].

23.15 Distributions

23.15 Stock Exchange requirements

For listed companies decisions by the board on dividends, profits and other matters requiring announcement must be notified to the CAO without delay and not later than 8.30 a.m. on the following business day.

(*The Listing Rules, Chapter 9.35*).

24 Dormant Companies

Cross-references. See 38.35 OVERSEA COMPANIES for dormant oversea companies.

24.1 DEFINITION

A company is dormant during a period in which no significant accounting transaction occurs i.e. no transaction which is required under *Sec 221* to be entered in the company's accounting records. A company ceases to be dormant on the occurrence of such a transaction. For these purposes, payment for shares taken by a subscriber to the memorandum in pursuance of an undertaking of his in the memorandum is disregarded. [*Sec 250(3); CA 1989, s 14*].

24.2 RESOLUTION NOT TO APPOINT AUDITORS

Subject to the exceptions below, a company may exempt itself from the provisions relating to the audit of accounts and the appointment of auditors in the following circumstances.

- *Newly-formed companies.* If the company has been dormant from the time of its formation, it may pass a special resolution at any time. (Before 31 December 1992, the special resolution had to be passed before the first general meeting of the company at which annual accounts are laid.)

- *Other companies.* If the company has been dormant since the end of the previous financial year and

  (i) is entitled in respect of its individual accounts for that year to prepare accounts in accordance with the special provisions for 'small' companies, or would be but for being a public company or a member of an ineligible group (see 7.3 ACCOUNTS: SMALL AND MEDIUM-SIZED COMPANIES), and

  (ii) is not required to prepare group accounts for that year

  it may pass a special resolution at a general meeting of the company at any time after copies of the annual accounts and reports for that year have been sent out in accordance with *Sec 238(1)* (see 3.3 ACCOUNTS: GENERAL). (Before 31 December 1992, the special resolution had to be passed at the general meeting at which annual accounts for that year were laid.)

[*Secs 250(1), 388A(1); CA 1989, s 14; SI 1992 No 3003, Regs 1, 2; SI 1994 No 1935, Reg 3; SI 1997 No 220, Reg 7*].

Exceptions. A company may not pass such a resolution if it is a banking or insurance company or an authorised person under *FSA 1986*. [*Sec 250(2)(b)(c); CA 1989, s 14*]. A public company could not pass such a resolution before 2 February 1996 but the restriction is lifted from that date. [*Sec 250(2)(a) repealed by SI 1996 No 189, Reg 11*].

The resolution must also not contravene the articles of the company. For example, auditors must be appointed where *CA 1948, Table A, Art 130* has been adopted (subject to altering the articles by a further special resolution) although there is no similar provision in the 1985 *Table A*.

24.3 Form of resolution

Dormant Company Resolution   Company No

THE COMPANIES ACT 1985, s 250 (as amended)

24.4 Dormant Companies

SPECIAL RESOLUTION OF   LIMITED

At a general meeting of the above company, held on the   the following resolution was passed.

Either

The company, having been dormant since its formation, resolves to make itself exempt from the provisions of Part VII of the Companies Act 1985 relating to the audit of accounts and from the obligation to appoint auditors.

Or

The accounts of the company for the financial year ending [. . .] having been sent out in accordance with section 238 of the Companies Act 1985, and the company, having been dormant since the end of that year, resolves to make itself exempt from the provisions of Part VII of the Companies Act 1985 relating to the audit of accounts and from the obligation to appoint auditors.

Signed. . . . . .
Director or Secretary

Date. . . . . .

(Companies House Notes for Guidance CHN 21).

24.4 Effect of resolution

Where a company is, at the end of a financial year, exempt from the obligation to appoint auditors, the following provisions apply to it.

- The right to receive or demand copies of accounts under *Secs 238, 239* (see 3.3 and 3.4 ACCOUNTS: GENERAL) applies with the omission of references to the auditors' report.

- Copies of the auditors' report need not be laid before the company in general meeting nor delivered to the Registrar of Companies. In the latter case the copy of the balance sheet delivered must contain a statement by the directors, in a position above their signatures required by *Sec 233(4)*, to the effect that the company was dormant throughout the financial year.

- The company is treated as entitled to prepare accounts in accordance with the special provisions for 'small' companies even if it is a member of an ineligible group (see 7.3 ACCOUNTS: SMALL AND MEDIUM-SIZED COMPANIES).

[*Sec 250(4); SI 1996 No 189, Reg 11; SI 1997 No 220, Reg 7*].

24.5 Loss of exemption

The exemption from the obligation to appoint auditors under 24.2 above is lost if the company ceases to be dormant or, for any other reason, no longer qualifies to make itself exempt by passing a special resolution. [*Sec 250(5)*].

When the exemption ceases, auditors must be appointed. The same rules apply as at 12.38 AUDITORS.

24.6 ANNUAL RETURNS

A dormant company is still obliged to submit ANNUAL RETURNS (10). The payment of the filing fee, if paid by the company, is not excluded from being a significant accounting transaction (see 24.1 above).

25   European Community Legislation

The contents of this chapter are as follows.

25.1   EUROPEAN COMMUNITY INSTITUTIONS

The three European Communities are the European Coal and Steel Community ('ECSC'), the European Economic Community ('EEC') and the European Atomic Energy Community ('EAEC' or 'Euratom').

The EEC is the body principally concerned with company law. It was set up by *The First Treaty of Rome ('EEC Treaty')* with effect from 1 January 1958 and was entered into initially by Belgium, the Federal Republic of Germany, France, Italy, Luxembourg and The Netherlands (who were also the initial members of ECSC and EAEC). By *The Treaty of Accession*, the UK, Ireland and Denmark entered the EC with effect from 1 January 1973. The relevant UK legislation is *European Communities Act 1972*. Greece joined the EC with effect from 1 January 1981, Spain and Portugal with effect from 1 January 1986 and Austria, Finland and Sweden with effect from 1 January 1995.

The *EEC Treaty* is widely drafted and there is emphasis on provisions for the free movement of persons, goods, services and capital as well as powers for the implementation of common policies in many areas of economic and social life.

The *Single European Act*, which came into force on 1 July 1987, prescribed 31 December 1992 as the deadline for the adoption of the necessary measures to set up the internal market of the EC. Many of these measures, including many company law provisions, can be adopted by a qualified majority of the Council of Ministers rather than a unanimous vote. Unanimity is still required for measures involving tax, the free movement of persons and the rights and interests of employed persons.

On 1 November 1993, the Treaty on European Union, signed at Maastricht in December 1992, came into force. The Treaty created a European Union with the so-called three pillars: the European Community, foreign policy co-operation and home affairs.

The *European Commission* consists of Commissioners from the various member states and is divided into various Directorates-General, each of which deals with a different area of activity. Proposals for EC legislation are initially made by the Commission. The Commission is also responsible for EC merger control, see 44.19 RECONSTRUCTIONS AND MERGERS below.

Council of the European Union. The Council consists of representatives from each member state at ministerial level. Now often in conjunction with the European Parliament, it decides on legislation submitted by the European Commission.

The *European Parliament* consists of directly elected members from each member state. The formal opinion of the European Parliament is required on many of the proposals for legislation formulated by the Commission before those prosposals can be adopted by the Council. Many of the proposals for legislation are subject to a 'co-operation procedure' under which the Council must adopt a common position by a qualified majority vote on a legislative proposal of the Commission which has been considered by Parliament. Parliament must then either approve, reject or amend the common position adopted by the

25.2 European Community Legislation

Council. In the event that Parliament rejects the common position, the Council may only adopt the proposal if it has unanimity.

The Maastricht Treaty introduced a procedure known as the 'co-decision procedure' which gives the European Parliament power to veto and propose amendments to Community acts in certain policy areas.

The role of the *European Court of Justice* is to interpret and apply Community law. In this connection, it is the ultimate court of appeal and its judgments are binding on all member states.

25.2 LEGAL INSTRUMENTS OF THE EC

Statements of the Council and the European Commission are graded as follows.

- **Regulations** which are binding in their entirety and have general effect to all member states. They are directly applicable in the legal systems of member states and do not have to be implemented by national legislation.

- **Directives** are binding as to result and their general effect is specific to named member states. The form and methods of compliance are left to individual member states which are normally given a specific period in which to implement the necessary legislation. If a member state fails to enact the necessary legislation, or does so incorrectly, an individual may in certain circumstances, rely on the terms of the directive itself. The directive then has 'direct effect' provided a number of tests are satisfied. First, the time limit for bringing the directive into force must have expired; secondly, the terms of the directive must be clear and precise; and thirdly, the provision relied on must be unconditional. Directives only have direct effect as against a member state and cannot therefore be relied upon as between private parties. However, in *Marleasing SA v La Commercial Internacional de Alimentacion SA (Case 106/89) [1992] 1 CMLR 305* the ECJ ruled that national courts are obliged to interpret national law in the light of the wording and purpose of a directive.

  A member state can be held liable in damages for its failure to implement a directive. Three conditions need to be fulfilled to establish liability. First, the directive must be intended to confer rights on individuals; secondly, the content of the rights must be identifiable; and thirdly, the damage suffered must be caused by the member state's breach of its obligations (*Francovich and Bonifaci v Italian Republic (C6–9/90) [1993] 2 CMLR 66*).

- **Decisions** are binding in their entirety and are specific to a member state, commercial enterprise or private individual. They take effect on notification to the addressee. [*Art 191*].

- **Recommendations and opinions** are not binding and are directed to specific subjects on which the Council's or Commission's advice has been sought.

25.3 EC COMPANY DIRECTIVES

A directive must be read as a whole. The preamble, which sets out the purpose of the legislation, is an essential part of it. Moreover, as distinct from UK law, it is acceptable when determining the purpose of the legislation to consider the discussions, decisions, etc. (*'travaux preparatoires'*) which led to the legislation being drafted in its final form.

The principal directives issued by the Council relating to company law are as follows.

1st Directive. [*68/151/EEC*]. This deals with the protection of certain interests of members and third parties. It was given effect in the UK by *European Communities Act 1972, s 9* and subsequently consolidated in *CA 1985*.

2nd Directive. [*77/91/EEC*]. This deals with the formation of public limited liability companies and the maintenance and alteration of their share capital. It was given effect in the UK by *CA 1980* and subsequently consolidated in *CA 1985*.

3rd Directive. [*78/855/EEC*]. This relates to the mergers of public limited liability companies and was given effect in the UK by *The Companies (Mergers and Divisions) Regulations 1987* (*SI 1987 No 1991*). See 44.4 RECONSTRUCTIONS AND MERGERS.

4th Directive. [*78/660/EEC*]. This is concerned with annual accounts of companies. It was given effect in the UK by *CA 1981* and subsequently consolidated in *CA 1985, Part VII* as amended by *CA 1989*. The directive has been amended to

- cover certain partnerships and limited partnerships and unlimited companies all of whose shareholders are limited companies (implemented in the UK by *SI 1993 No 1820*, see 39.4-39.7 PARTNERSHIPS and 60.3 UNLIMITED COMPANIES); and

- extend the exemptions available to small and medium-sized companies and allow all companies to publish accounts in European Currency Units as well as national currency (implemented in the UK by *SI 1992 No 2452*, see ACCOUNTS: SMALL AND MEDIUM-SIZED COMPANIES (7) and 5.3 ACCOUNTS: INDIVIDUAL COMPANIES).

5th Directive (draft). This Directive has been in various drafts for a number of years and is unlikely to be adopted for several years. It would apply to all public companies and deals with the structure and duties of boards, responsibilities of directors, rights of minority shareholders, powers and conduct of general meetings and independence of auditors.

6th Directive. [*82/891/EEC*]. This is concerned with the division or demerger of public limited liability companies. It was given effect in the UK by *The Companies (Mergers and Divisions) Regulations 1987* (*SI 1987 No 1991*). See 44.4 RECONSTRUCTIONS AND MERGERS.

7th Directive. [*83/349/EEC*]. This is concerned with consolidated accounts of groups and affects public and private companies. It was given effect in the UK by *CA 1989, Part I* which amends *CA 1985*. The directive has been amended to

- cover certain partnerships and limited partnerships and unlimited companies all of whose shareholders are limited companies (implemented in the UK by *SI 1993 No 1820*, see 39.4-39.7 PARTNERSHIPS and 60.3 UNLIMITED COMPANIES); and

- extend the exemptions available to small and medium-sized companies and allow all companies to publish accounts in European Currency Units as well as national currency (implemented in the UK by *SI 1992 No 2452*, see 7.45–7.47 ACCOUNTS: SMALL AND MEDIUM-SIZED COMPANIES).

8th Directive. [*84/253/EEC*]. This relates to the qualification of auditors and was given effect in the UK by *CA 1989, Part II*. See 12.5 to 12.9 AUDITORS.

9th Directive (suspended).

10th Directive (proposed). This would apply to public companies and deals with cross-border mergers where two or more companies are governed by the laws of different countries.

25.3   European Community Legislation

11th Directive. [*89/666/EEC*]. This deals with the disclosure requirements in member states of branches of companies which are registered in another member state or in a non-EC country (i.e. OVERSEA COMPANIES (38)). It was given effect in Great Britain by *The Oversea Companies and Credit and Financial Institutions (Branch Disclosure) Regulations 1992 (SI 1992 No 3179)*.

12th Directive. [*89/667/EEC*]. This Directive requires member states to allow private limited companies to have a single member who may be either a natural person or a legal person. It was given effect in the UK by *The Companies (Single Member Private Limited Companies) Regulations 1992 (SI 1992 No 1699)*. See 34.2 MEMBERS. Any decision taken by the sole member which would have been taken by the company in general meeting must be recorded (see 51.11 RESOLUTIONS). Except for any contracts entered into in the ordinary course of the company's activities, where any contract between the company and a sole member/director is not in writing, the terms of the contract must either be set out in a written memorandum or in the minutes (see 19.71 DIRECTORS).

13th Directive (draft). This deals with takeovers and other general bids and includes an obligation on the bidder to bid for all shares once he has acquired 33.3% of the shares in the target company. All takeovers of public limited companies would have to be supervised and controlled by a competent authority. Currently in the UK control of takeovers lies with the Panel on Takeovers and Mergers and The Stock Exchange. See 59 TAKEOVER OFFERS.

14th Directive (proposed). This would permit companies to transfer their registered offices from one member state to another without the need for winding-up or reincorporation.

In addition, a number of subsidiary directives have been made as follows.

Council Directive of 5.3.79. [*79/279/EEC*]. This co-ordinates the conditions for the admission of securities to official stock exchange listing. It was given effect in the UK by *The Stock Exchange (Listing) Regulations 1984 (SI 1984 No 716)* which were subsequently replaced by *FSA 1986, Part IV*.

Council Directive of 17.3.80.[*80/390/EEC*]. This co-ordinates the requirements for the drawing up, scrutiny and distribution of the listing particulars to be published for the admission of securities to official stock exchange listing. It was given effect in the UK by *The Stock Exchange (Listing) Regulations 1984 (SI 1984 No 716)* which were subsequently replaced by *FSA 1986, Part IV*.

Council Directive of 18.2.82. [*82/121/EEC*]. This deals with the information to be published on a regular basis by companies whose shares have been admitted to official stock exchange listing. It was given effect in the UK by *The Stock Exchange (Listing) Regulations 1984 (SI 1984 No 716)* which were subsequently replaced by *FSA 1986, Part IV*.

Council Regulation of 25.7.85. [*85/2137/EEC*]. This specifies the rules concerning the creation, registration and management of a European Economic Interest Grouping (EEIG). See 25.4 *et seq.* below.

Council Directive of 20.12.85. [*85/611/EEC*]. This deals with the co-ordination of laws, etc. relating to undertakings for collective investment in transferable securities and sets down minimum requirements for the authorisation of unit trusts, etc. in other member states which invest in securities. It was given effect in the UK by *FSA 1986, s 24* which was implemented by *The Financial Services Act 1986 (Commencement No 12) Order 1989 (SI 1989 No 1583)*.

Council Directive of 8.12.86 ('Bank Accounts Directive'). [*86/635/EEC*]. This establishes the minimum financial reporting standards for banks and other financial institutions which are excluded from the *4th* and *7th Directives*. It was given effect in the UK by *SI 1991 No 2705*. See 6.59 ACCOUNTS: INSURANCE AND BANKING COMPANIES.

Council Directive of 22.6.87. [*87/345/EEC*]. This Directive provides for the mutual recognition of listing particulars required to be produced when companies from member states are admitted to an official stock exchange listing. It also makes provisions for the EC to enter into agreements with non-EC countries on recognition of listing particulars. It is given effect in the UK by *SI 1995 No 1537, 4 Sch* (see 42.35 PROSPECTUSES AND PUBLIC ISSUES) and the *Listing Rules, Chapter 17*.

Council Directive of 12.12.88. [*88/627/EEC*]. The Directive requires owners of shares in listed companies to disclose their holdings on reaching any of five thresholds (10%, 20%, 33.3%, 50% and 66.6%). Existing UK legislation implemented many of the requirements but the Directive was fully implemented by *The Disclosure of Interests in Shares (Amendment) Regulations 1993 (SI 1993 No 1819)* and *The Disclosure of Interests in Shares (Amendment) (No 2) Regulations 1993 (SI 1993 No 2689)*. See 21 DISCLOSURE OF INTERESTS IN PUBLIC COMPANY SHARES.

Council Directive of 12.88. [*89/48/EEC*]. Under this Directive, each member state is to recognise professional qualifications gained in other member states as equipping a migrant to practice, in some circumstances subject to completing an adaptation procedure which may consist of a period of supervised practice or an aptitude test. The Directive is a general one which applies to all professions for which a diploma gained after three years' higher education training or equivalent is required and for which there is no special directive. Its coverage includes practice under a professional title regulated by a Chartered professional body. It was given effect in the UK by *The European Communities (Recognition of Professional Qualifications) Regulations 1991*.

Council Directive of 13.2.89 ('Bank Branches Directive'). [*89/117/EEC*]. This pre-scribes for the branches of credit and other financial institutions, as defined in the Bank Accounts Directive (see above), established in a member state and whose head office is outside that member state, the accounting documents that they must file at the relevant local registry. The Directive also requires the branches of such institutions whose head office is established in another member state to file accounts drawn up in accordance with the Bank Accounts Directive, and allows member states the option of requiring additional information relating to the branch itself to be filed. The Directive requires the branches of credit institutions whose head office is outside the EC to file accounts which are 'equivalent' to accounts prepared in accordance with the Bank Accounts Directive. Where 'equivalent' accounts are not available, the Directive allows member states to require the credit institutions to file branch accounts. This Directive was given effect in Great Britain with effect from 1 January 1993 by *The Oversea Companies and Credit and Financial Institutions (Branch Disclosure) Regulations 1992 (SI 1992 No 3179)*.

Council Directive of 17.4.89. [*89/298/EEC*]. This deals with the information to be contained in a prospectus when securities are offered for subscription or sale to the public for the first time. It also provides for the mutual recognition of prospectuses drawn up in accordance with *Directive 80/390/EEC* (see above). See 42.35 PROSPECTUSES AND PUBLIC ISSUES.

Council Directive of 13.11.89. [*89/592/EEC*]. This requires member states to make insider dealing unlawful and to co-operate by exchanging information for enforcement. See 30.1-30.5 INSIDER DEALING.

Council Regulation of 21.12.89.[*89/4064/EEC*]. This regulates the problems arising from cross-border mergers. See 44.19 RECONSTRUCTIONS AND MERGERS.

Council Directive of 19.12.91. [*91/674/EEC*]. This establishes a framework for a common standard of accounting disclosure for insurance companies excluded from the *4th* and *7th Directives*. It was given effect in the UK by *The Companies Act 1985 (Insurance Companies Accounts) Regulations 1993 (SI 1993 No 3246)*.

25.4 European Community Legislation

25.4 EUROPEAN ECONOMIC INTEREST GROUPINGS

Council Regulation 85/2137/EEC provides for a new form of undertaking known as a European Economic Interest Grouping ('EEIG') to encourage businesses in different member states to co-operate. The *Regulations*, which have direct effect in the UK, are supplemented by *The European Economic Interest Grouping Regulations 1989 (SI 1989 No 638)* which contains rules concerning the creation, registration and management of an EEIG.

An EEIG is a form of association between companies or other legal bodies, firms or individuals from different member states who need to operate together across national frontiers. It is formed to carry out particular tasks for its member owners and is quite separate from its owners' businesses. It may be set up in any member state and operate in any part of the EC. It can enter into arrangements with organisations outside the EC. (Companies House Notes for Guidance CHN6).

An EEIG registered in the UK is a body corporate from the date shown on its certificate of registration. [*SI 1989 No 638, Reg 3*].

25.5 Objects and activities

The purpose of an EEIG is to facilitate or develop the economic activities of its members. Its activities must relate to the economic activities of its members and must be ancillary to those activities. Normally it will provide services for its members e.g. scientific research in an area of common concern, joint marketing for a new range of products, pooling technical knowledge.

An EEIG cannot

- be formed with the object of making a profit (although it may do so in the normal course of operations);

- exercise management control over its members' own activities or those of any other undertaking;

- hold shares in any of its members;

- have investment from the public;

- be a member of another EEIG;

- employ more than 500 persons;

- be used to make loans to a company director or any person connected with him where that would be restricted or controlled by national law; or

- be used for the transfer of any property between a company and a director (or any person connected with him) except to the extent allowed by national law.

[*Council Regulation 85/2137/EEC, Arts 3, 23*]. (Companies House Notes for Guidance CHN6).

25.6 Members

An EEIG must comprise at least two members from at least two different member states. To be eligible for membership, companies, firms and other legal bodies governed by public or private law must have their central administration and registered office (where this is required) in the EC. Natural persons may be members if they carry on any industrial, commercial, craft or agricultural activity or provide professional or other services in the EC. Organisations from non-EC countries cannot be members of the EEIG.

Each potential member must have been engaged in an economic activity in the EC prior to becoming a member.

[*Council Regulation 85/2137/EEC, Art 4*].

Access to information, etc. Each member is entitled to obtain information from the managers concerning the EEIG's business and to inspect its books and business records. [*Council Regulation 85/2137/EEC, Art 18*].

Voting. Each member must have one vote. The contract for the formation may, however, give more than one vote to certain members provided that no one member holds a majority of votes. A unanimous decision by members is required to

- alter the object of the grouping, the number of votes for each member or the conditions for making decisions;

- extend the duration of the EEIG beyond any fixed period in the contract for the formation;

- alter the member's contributions or any other obligation of a member; or

- make any alteration to the contract for the formation unless otherwise provided in that contract.

Subject to the above, members are free to decide the voting procedures to be set down in the contract of formation.

[*Council Regulation 85/2137/EEC, Art 17*].

Liability of members. Each member has unlimited joint and several liability for all the EEIG's debts and other liabilities. [*Council Regulation 85/2137/EEC, Art 24*].

New members. New members can be admitted on the unanimous vote of existing members. Unless the contract for the formation provides otherwise, a new member is jointly and severally liable for debts and other liabilities both before and after his admission. [*Council Regulation 85/2137/EEC, Art 26*].

Cessation of membership. A member ceases to be a member

- by assigning his interest (or part) to another member or group (with the unanimous agreement of other members);

- by withdrawing in accordance with conditions laid down in the contract for formation or, in the absence of any such conditions, with the unanimous agreement of the other members;

- by withdrawing on just and proper grounds;

- on expulsion for reasons listed in the contract for formation or for seriously failing his obligations or causing serious disruption to the operation of the EEIG;

- on death or insolvency; or

- if he no longer qualifies as a member.

On cessation, the managers must inform the other members of that fact. The member who ceases to belong to the EEIG remains liable for debts and other liabilities arising before he ceased to be a member for five years after the publication of notice of his cessation (or such shorter period as provided for under the relevant national law).

The EEIG continues to exist for the remaining members (unless the contract for formation provides otherwise).

[*Council Regulation 85/2137/EEC, Arts 22, 27-30, 34, 37; SI 1989 No 638, Reg 6*].

25.7 Managers

The members must appoint one or more managers to operate the EEIG on a day-to-day basis. The contract for the formation of the EEIG must determine their powers. A manager of an EEIG registered in Great Britain may be a natural person or a legal person (e.g. a company) provided that, in the latter case, one or more natural persons are also registered as its representative.

The contract for the formation of the EEIG (or, failing that, a unanimous decision by the members) must determine the conditions for appointment and removal of managers and their powers.

The managers represent the EEIG in respect of dealings with third parties and their actions are binding on the EEIG. The members are jointly liable for those actions. The only limitation which may be applied on the managers by the members in this respect is for the contract for formation to provide that the EEIG is to be validly bound only by two or more managers acting jointly. If this device is used, it will only be effective if its existence is published in the appropriate Gazette (see 25.9 below).

[*Council Regulation 85/2137/EEC, Arts 19, 20; SI 1989 No 638, Reg 5*].

25.8 Contract for formation

The contract for formation of an EEIG must include, at least, the following information.

(*a*)   Its full name proceeded or followed either by the words 'European Economic Interest Grouping' or the initials 'EEIG' (unless already forming part of the name).

If the EEIG is registered in Great Britain, the name cannot include the words 'limited', 'unlimited', 'public limited company' or their Welsh equivalents (or any abbreviations of any of these). Otherwise substantially the same rules and restrictions apply to names of EEIGs as to companies registered under *CA 1985*. See 36 NAMES AND BUSINESS NAMES.

(*b*)   Its official address. This must be situated in the EC and must be fixed either

- where the EEIG has its central administration; or
- where one of the members has its central administration (or, in the case of a natural member, his principal activity) provided the EEIG carried on an activity there.

(*c*)   The objects for which it was formed.

(*d*)   The name, business name, legal form, permanent address or registered office, and the number and place of registration (if any) of each member of the group.

(*e*)   The duration of the EEIG (unless indefinite).

[*Council Regulation 85/2137/EEC, Arts 5, 12; SI 1989 No 638, Regs 10, 11, 17*].

25.9   **Registration and filing requirements**

Registration of an EEIG. An EEIG must be registered at the *'appropriate registry'* in the member state in which it has its official address (see 25.8(*a*) above). In Great Britain this is the Registrar of Companies for England and Wales, Scotland or Northern Ireland (as the case may be) depending upon where the contract of formation states that the EEIG's official address is to be situated. In order to be registered, an EEIG must submit to the Registrar its contract of formation together with Form EEIG 1. Where the contract is in a language other than English, it must be accompanied by a translation certified as under 28.2(*a*) or (*b*) FORMS. If satisfied, the Registrar must register the EEIG and issue a certificate of registration. [*Council Regulation 85/2137/EEC, Arts 6, 7; SI 1989 No 638, Reg 9*]. See 26.1 FEES for the fee for registration.

Registration following change of official address. An EEIG may unanimously propose to transfer its official address. If this results in a change in the law applicable to it (i.e. normally a transfer to another member state) it must draw up a transfer proposal. This must be filed at the registry where it is currently registered (see (*h*) below) and must also be publicised in the appropriate Gazette (see below). If the change is not opposed by a competent authority within two months, the transfer takes effect on the date that the EEIG is registered in the registry for the new official address. Where that new address is in Great Britain, the Registrar of Companies must register it on receipt of Form EEIG 1 together with evidence of the publication of the transfer proposal and a statement that no competent authority has opposed the transfer. [*Council Regulation 85/2137/EEC, Art 14; SI 1989 No 638, Reg 9*].

Registration of an establishment. If an EEIG opens an establishment in a member state other than that in which its official address is situated, that establishment must be registered in the appropriate registry in that state. In Great Britain this is the Registrar of Companies for England and Wales, Scotland or Northern Ireland (as the case may be) depending upon where the establishment is situated. In order to be registered, within one month of setting up the establishment the EEIG must submit to the Registrar Form EEIG 2 together with certified copies of all documents which were submitted to the registering authority in the other member state where the EEIG has its official address. Where any document is in a language other than English, it must be accompanied by a translation certified as under 28.2(*a*) or (*b*) FORMS. [*Council Regulation 85/2137/EEC, Art 10; SI 1989 No 638, Reg 12*].

Other documents to be filed. In addition to the above, the following documents must also be filed with the appropriate registry (on the form indicated where this is the Registrar of Companies).

(*a*)   Any amendment to the contract for formation, including any change in composition (Form EEIG 4).

(*b*)   Notice of the appointment and removal of managers, together with their details (Form EEIG 3 where the official address is in Great Britain and Form EEIG 4 where it is elsewhere).

(*c*)   Any judicial decision nullifying the EEIG (Form EEIG 4).

(*d*)   Notice of a member's assignment of all or part of his participation in the EEIG (Form EEIG 4).

(*e*)   Any judicial or member's decision ordering or establishing the winding up of the EEIG (Form EEIG 4).

(*f*)   Notice of appointment, or termination of appointment, of a liquidator of the EEIG (Form EEIG 4).

(*g*)   Notice of the conclusion of the liquidation of the EEIG (Form EEIG 4).

(*h*) Any proprosal to transfer the official address of the EEIG which results in a change in the law applicable to it (Form EEIG 4).

(*i*) Notice of any provision exempting a new member from the payment of debts and other liabilities which originated prior to his admission (Form EEIG 4).

(*j*) Notice of setting up or closure of any establishment of the grouping (Form EEIG 5 except where Form EEIG 2 is required, see above).

The above documents must be filed with the Registrar of Companies within 15 days (in the case of an EEIG whose address is outside the UK, 30 days) of the event in question. Where any document is in a language other than English, it must be accompanied by a translation certified as under 28.2(*a*) or (*b*) FORMS. If it fails to comply with these provisions, the EEIG and, any officer who intentionally authorises or permits the default, is guilty of an offence and liable on summary conviction to a fine not exceeding level 3 on the standard scale (see 40.1 PENALTIES).

[*Council Regulation 85/2137/EEC, Art 7; SI 1989 No 638, Regs 4, 13*].

Inspection of documents. Any person may inspect any of the documents and particulars kept by the Registrar of Companies under the above provisions. He may also require him to deliver, or send by post, copies or extracts of any document or particulars. [*1989 No 638, Reg 14*]. See 26.1 FEES for fees payable to the Registrar.

Official Gazette. The Registrar must arrange for the following information to be published in the appropriate official gazette (i.e. the London Gazette for EEIGs registered in England and Wales, the Edinburgh Gazette for those registered in Scotland and the Belfast Gazette for those registered in Northern Ireland).

• Full particulars of the information which must be included in the contract for formation (see 25.8 above) and any amendments thereto.

• The number, date and place of registration as well as notice of the termination of that registration.

• In the case of the documents and particulars referred to in (*b*) to (*j*) above, a notice stating the name of the EEIG, a description of the documents, etc. and the date of receipt.

[*Council Regulation 85/2137/EEC, Art 8; SI 1989 No 638, Reg 15*].

Official Journal of the European Communities. The Registrar must also send to the Office for Official Publications of the European Communities, within one month of publication in the appropriate gazette, notice that an EEIG has been formed, or that the liquidation of an EEIG has been concluded, stating the number, date and place of registration. [*Council Regulation 85/2137/EEC, Art 11; SI 1989 No 638, Reg 15*].

25.10 **Information to be given in correspondence, etc.**

Letters, order forms and similar documents issued by an EEIG must indicate the following.

• Its name either preceded or followed by the words 'European Economic Interest Grouping' or the initial 'EEIG' (unless already appearing in the name).

• The location of the registry where the EEIG is registered and its number at that registry.

• Its official address.

• Where applicable, a statement that managers must act jointly.

● Where applicable, that it is in liquidation.

If an EEIG registered in Great Britain fails to comply with the above requirements, it is guilty of an offence and liable on summary conviction to a fine not exceeding level 3 on the standard scale (see 40.1 PENALTIES). If any officer of the EEIG, or person on its behalf, issues or authorises the issue of a letter, etc. not complying with those requirements, he is liable to a similar penalty.

[*Council Regulation 85/2137/EEC, Art 25; SI 1989 No 638, Reg 16*].

25.11 Accounting and taxation

The profits or losses resulting from the EEIG's activities are deemed to be the profits or losses of the members and must be apportioned among them as laid down in the contract for formation (in default, in equal shares). They are taxable only in the hands of the members. [*Council Regulation 85/2137/EEC, Arts 21, 40*].

An EEIG is not subject to any accounting or auditing requirements and does not have to file an annual return with the Registrar of Companies. It must, however, make a return to the Inland Revenue. (Companies House Notes for Guidance CHN 6).

For the provisions relating to the taxation of EEIGs in the UK, see *FA 1990, 11 Sch*.

26 Fees

26.1 FEES PAYABLE TO THE REGISTRAR OF COMPANIES

The following fees are payable to the Registrar of Companies.

General

Registration of a company on formation (see 49.1 REGISTRATION AND RE-REGISTRATION) or under *Part XXII. Ch II* (see 15.3 COMPANIES NOT FORMED UNDER CA 1985) and for re-registration of a company	£20.00
Registration of particulars by an oversea company in respect of the establishment of a place of business (see 38.3 OVERSEA COMPANIES) or a branch (see 38.6 OVERSEA COMPANIES) in Great Britain	£20.00
Registration of an ANNUAL RETURN (10) (unless relating to an oversea company incorporated in the Channel Islands or Isle or Man)	£15.00
Registration of copies of accounts of an oversea company delivered otherwise than at the same time as the registration of a branch of that company (see 38.38 OVERSEA COMPANIES)	£15.00
Entering on the register the name of a company assumed by the passing of a special resolution under *Sec 28* (see 36.6 NAMES AND BUSINESS NAMES)	£10.00
Registration of a change of name of an oversea company (see 38.4 OVERSEA COMPANIES)	£10.00
Inspection of a basic set of microfiche copies	£5.00
Inspection of the 'excluded documents' of a branch or undertaking recorded and kept by the Registrar of Companies in the form of a microfiche copy	£5.00
Inspection of a list of members consisting of more than 10 pages, other than an inspection requested on the same occasion as a request to inspect the basic set of microfiche copies relating to the same company	£5.00
Inspection on any one occasion of one or more original documents relating to one branch or undertaking where the record kept by the Registrar is illegible or unavailable	£6.00
Paper copies of original documents, other than a list of members, delivered at an office of the Registrar relating to one branch or undertaking not recorded and kept by the Registrar in the form of a microfiche copy, per document	£7.00

A 'basic set of microfiche copies':
- delivered at an office of the Registrar — £5.00
- delivered by post pursuant to an on-line request — £8.00
- delivered by post pursuant to another form of request — £8.00

A microfiche copy of the excluded documents of a branch or undertaking a company recorded and kept by the Registrar in the form of a microfiche copy:
- delivered at an office of the Registrar — £5.00
- delivered by post pursuant to an on-line request — £8.00
- delivered by post pursuant to another form of request — £8.00

A microfiche copy of a list of members consisting of more than 10 pages:
- delivered at an office of the Registrar   £5.00
- delivered by post pursuant to any other form of request   £8.00

Paper copies or records relating to a company delivered to the office of the Registrar
- if requested on the same occasion as an inspection of the records relating to that company, or on the same occasion as a request for a basic set of microfiche copies relating to the company, per page   10p
- if requested otherwise, not being a list of members of the company   £5.00 plus £1 for each document supplied

Paper copies of records relating to a company, other than a list of members, recorded and kept by the Registrar in the form of a microfiche copy, delivered by post pursuant to any form of request
- in respect of one document   £9.00
- in respect of each further document relating to the same company requested on the same occasion   £2.50

Paper copies delivered by post of records relating to a branch or undertaking, other than a list of members, not recorded and kept by the Registrar in the form of a microfiche copy, per document   £10.00

Paper copy of a list of members delivered by post
- up to 20 pages   £9.00
- for each additional page   20p

For paper copies of particulars registered in respect of a branch or undertaking
- delivered at an office of the Registrar   10p per screen of information on a computer terminal
- delivered by post   £4 per copy of information available on a computer terminal

Paper copy of the index:
- delivered at an office of the Registrar, per page   £1.00
- delivered by post
  - (i) for the first page   £4.00
  - (ii) for each additional page   £1.00

Microfiche copy of the whole index   £35.00

26.1 Fees

Certified copy of, or extract from, any record:
- where the record is not a list of members consisting of more than 10 pages   £25.00
- where the record is a list of members consisting of more than 10 pages
  - (i) for the first 10 pages   £25.00
  - (ii) for each additional page   £1.00

Certificate of the incorporation of a company:
- for the first certificate supplied on any one occasion   £25.00
- for each additional certificate on the same occasion   £10.00

For the performance by the Registrar of his functions in relation to an application by a private company under *Sec 652A* for the company's name to be struck off the register   £10.00

Registration of a charge under *Part XII, Ch 1 and 2* (see 50.7 REGISTRATION OF CHARGES) per entry on the register of charges kept by the Registrar in respect of a company or overseas company).   £10.00

'*Excluded documents*' means any copy accounts, annual returns or copy annual returns other than the last three received by the Registrar in respect of a branch or undertaking.

'*Basic set of microfiche copies*' means a set of copies of the records relating to one branch or undertaking kept by the Registrar in the form of microfiche copies, other than copies of excluded documents and lists of members with more than 10 pages.

[*SI 1991 No 1206; SI 1992 No 2876; SI 1994 No 2217; SI 1995 No 1423; SI 1996 No 1444; SI 1998 No 3088*]

Open-ended investment companies (OIECs)

Registration of an OIEC following incorporation   £20.00

Registration of a copy annual report of an OIEC   £15.00

Inspection of the microfiche copies of the records of an OIEC   £5.00

A set of microfiche copies of the records of an OIEC
- delivered at an office of the Registrar   £5.00
- delivered by post   £8.00

Paper copies of particulars registered for an OIEC
- delivered at an office of the Registrar   10p per screen of information on a computer terminal
- delivered by post   £4.00 per copy of information available on a computer terminal

Certified copy of, or extract from, any record relating to an OIEC	£25.00
Registration of an altered instrument of incorporation in respect of a change of name of an OIEC	£10.00

Paper copies of records relating to an OIEC delivered at an office of the Registrar
- if requested on the same occasion as an inspection of the records or a request for a set of microfiche copies of the same OIEC is made — 10p per page
- if requested otherwise — £5.00 plus £1.00 per document supplied

Paper copies of records relating to an OIEC kept by the Registrar in the form of microfiche copy, delivered by post
- in respect of one document — £9.00
- for each further document relating to the same OIEG requested on the same occasion — £2.50

[*SI 1999 No 3087*].

European Economic Interest Groupings (EEIGs)

Registration of an EEIG whose official address is in Great Britain	£20.00
Inspection of a basic set of microfiche copies	£5.00

A basic set of microfiche copies
- delivered at an office of the Registrar — £5.00
- delivered by post — £8.00

Paper copies of records relating to an EEIG delivered at an office of the Registrar
- if requested on the same occasion as an inspection of the records, or a request for a set of microfiche copies, relating to the EEIG — 10p per page
- if requested otherwise — £5.00 plus £1.00 per document supplied

Paper copies of records relating to an EEIG recorded and kept by the Registrar in the form of microfiche copy, delivered by post
- in respect of one document — £9.00
- for each further document relating to the same EEIG requested on the same occasion — £2.50

Paper copies of particulars registered in respect of an EEIG
- delivered at an office of the Registrar — 10p per screen of information on a computer terminal

26.2 Fees

<table>
<tr><td>● delivered by post</td><td>£4.00 per copy of information available on a computer terminal</td></tr>
<tr><td>Certified copy of, or extract from, any record</td><td>£25.00</td></tr>
<tr><td>Registration of a charge on the registration of charges kept by the Registrar in respect of an EEIG</td><td>£10.00</td></tr>
</table>

[*SI 1999 No 268*].

26.2 FEES PAYABLE TO COMPANIES

The following *maximum* fees are payable to companies for inspection of, and copies of entries in, registers, etc.

<table>
<tr><td>Inspection by non-members of register of debenture-holders, register of directors and secretaries, register of directors' interests in share and debentures, and registers of members and index.
(Note. Inspection is free to members.)</td><td>£2.50 for each hour (or part) of inspection</td></tr>
<tr><td>Copies of entries in the register of debentures, register of interests in shares (or report under Sec 215), register of directors' interests in shares and debentures, and register of members
● for the first 100 entries
● for the next 1,000 entries (or part)
● for every subsequent 1,000 entries (or part)</td><td>

£2.50
£20.00
£15.00</td></tr>
<tr><td>Copies of trust deeds under Sec 191(3) (see 47.12 REGISTERS) or minutes under Sec 383(3) (see 33.15 MEETINGS)</td><td>10p per 100 words or part</td></tr>
</table>

[*SI 1991 No 1998*].

27 Formation

27.1 Subject to below, any two or more persons associated for a lawful purpose may, by subscribing their names to a MEMORANDUM OF ASSOCIATION (35) and complying with the necessary requirements of registration (see 49.1 REGISTRATION AND RE-REGISTRATION), form an incorporated company with or without limited liability. [*Sec 1(1)*].

Companies so formed may be either

(*a*) *companies limited by shares* i.e. having the liability of their members limited by the memorandum to the amount, if any, unpaid on their shares;

(*b*) *companies limited by guarantee*, see GUARANTEE COMPANIES (29); or

(*c*) UNLIMITED COMPANIES (60).

Companies within (*a*) above can either be PUBLIC COMPANIES (43) or PRIVATE COMPANIES (41).

[*Sec 1(2)(3)*].

Single member private companies. Only one person is required to form a private company limited by share or by guarantee. [*Sec 1(3A); SI 1992 No 1699*].

27.2 PROMOTERS

A *'promoter'* is a person who undertakes to form a company with reference to a given project and to set it going, and who takes the necessary steps to accomplish that purpose (*Twycross v Grant (1877) 2 CPD 469*).

A promoter has duties towards the company before it comes into existence and may continue to be in a fiduciary relation to it after incorporation (*The Emma Silver Mining Co Ltd v Lewis & Son (1879) 4 CPD 396*). If he sells property to the company he is bound to take care that he sells it through the medium of the board of directors who can and do exercise an independent judgement on the transaction (*Emile Erlanger and Others v The New Sombrero Phosphate Company and Others (1878) 3 App Cas 1218*). Where a promoter makes any undisclosed profit, this should be handed over to the company (*Whaley Bridge Calico Printing Co Ltd v Green and Smith (1879) 5 QBD 109*). See also *Gluckstein v Barnes [1900] AC 240*.

For pre-incorporation contracts entered into by promoters, see 16.5 DEALINGS WITH THIRD PARTIES.

27.3 EFFECTS OF FORMATION: COMPANY AS A SEPARATE LEGAL PERSON

Once a company has been validly formed and incorporated, it is a legal person distinct from its members. This applies even where a controlling shareholder effectively owns all the shares in the company (*Salomon v Salomon & Co Ltd [1897] AC 22*). See also *Lee v Lee's Air Farming Ltd [1961] AC 12* where such a person may function in a dual capacity and a contractual relationship may be established between the shareholder and the company.

Once incorporated, the company is bound by the decision of a majority of its members in general meeting and the courts will not normally interfere in the internal management of a company acting within its powers (*Foss v Harbottle (1843) 2 Hare 461*).

Foss v Harbottle also established the fundamental rule that to redress a wrong done to a company or to recover moneys or damages due to it, action must *prima facie* be brought by the company itself. Subsequent case law, however, established exceptions to the rule in *Foss v Harbottle* for the protection of minority interests. See 34.6 MEMBERS.

27.4 Formation

27.4 Lifting the veil

In certain circumstances, the court may pull aside the corporate veil and look through the transactions of the company to see what really lies behind them. See *Wallersteiner v Muir [1974] 1 WLR 991* and *Littlewoods Mail Order Stores Ltd v IRC [1969] 3 All ER 855*. The courts have frequently done this and looked at the personal relationships of the shareholders when deciding if a family company should be wound up (see, for example, *Ebrahimi v Westbourne Galleries Ltd [1973] AC 360*); to determine whether a company is an 'enemy' at time of war (*Daimler Co Ltd v Continental Tyre and Rubber Co (Great Britain) Ltd [1916] 2 AC 307*); where a company is used to carry out a fraud (*Re Darby, ex parte Brougham [1911] 1 KB 95*); and to treat a group of companies as one company (*DHN Food Distributors Ltd v Tower Hamlets London Borough Council [1976] 1 WLR 852*).

28   Forms

28.1   Copies of all statutory forms are available free of charge from the stationery section of Companies House Cardiff and from Companies House Edinburgh (see 48.1 REGISTRAR OF COMPANIES).

See 48.4 REGISTRAR OF COMPANIES for use of own forms and completion of forms generally.

The forms which are currently prescribed are as follows.

6	Cancellation of alteration to the objects of a company
10	First directors and secretary and intended situation of registered office
10CYM	Ditto (Welsh language version)
12	Declaration on application for registration
12CYM	Ditto (Welsh language version)
30(5)(a)	Declaration on application for the registration of a company exempt from the requirement to use the word 'limited' or 'cyfyngedig'
30(5)(a) CYM	Ditto (Welsh language version)
30(5)(b)	Declaration on application for registration under *CA 1985, s 680* of a company exempt from the requirement to use the word 'limited' or 'cyfyngedig'
30(5)(b) CYM	Ditto (Welsh language version)
30(5)(c)	Change of name omitting 'limited' or 'cyfyngedig'
30(5)(c) CYM	Ditto (Welsh language version)
43(3)	Application by a private company for re-registration as a public company
43(3)(e)	Declaration on application by a private company for re-registration as a public company
49(1)	Application by a limited company to be re-registered as unlimited
49(8)(a)	Members' assent to company being re-registered as unlimited
51	Application by an unlimited company to be re-registered as limited
53	Application by a public company for re-registration as a private company
54	Application to the Court for cancellation of resolution for re-registration
88(2)	Return of allotments of shares
88(2)CYM	Ditto (Welsh language version)
88(3)	Particulars of a contract relating to shares allotted as fully or partly paid up otherwise than in cash
97	Statement of the amount or rate per cent of any commission payable in connection with the subscription of shares
117	Application by a public company for certificate to commence business and statutory declaration in support

28.1 Forms

122	Notice of consolidation, division, subdivision, redemption or cancellation of shares, or conversion, reconversion of stocks into shares
123	Notice of increase in nominal capital
128(1)	Statement of rights attached to allotted shares
128(3)	Statement of particulars of variation of rights attached to shares
128(4)	Notice of assignment of name or new name to any class of shares
129(1)	Statement by company without share capital of rights attached to newly created class of members
129(2)	Statement by company without share capital of particulars of variation of members' class rights
129(3)	Notice by a company without share capital of assignment of a name or other designation to a class of members
139	Application by a public company for re-registration as a private company following a court order reducing capital
147	Application by a public company for re-registration as a private company following cancellation of shares and reduction of nominal value of issued capital
155(6)a	Declaration in relation to assistance for the acquisition of shares
155(6)b	Declaration by the directors of a holding company in relation to assistance for the acquisition of shares
157	Notice of application made to the court for the cancellation of a special resolution regarding financial assistance for the acquisition of shares
169	Return by a company purchasing its own shares
173	Declaration in relation to the redemption or purchase of shares out of capital
176	Notice of application to the Court for the cancellation of a resolution for the redemption or purchase of shares out of capital
190	Location of register of debenture holders
190a	Notice of place for inspection of a register of holders of debentures which is kept in a non-legible form, or of any change in that place
225	Change of accounting reference date
225CYM	Ditto (Welsh language version)
244	Notice of claim to extension of period allowed for laying and delivering accounts – overseas business or interest
266(1)	Notice of intention to carry on business as an investment company
266(3)	Notice that a company no longer wishes to be an investment company
287	Change in the situation or address of registered office
287CYM	Ditto (Welsh language version)
287(I)	Change of registered office
288a	Appointment of director or secretary
288aCYM	Ditto (Welsh language version)

288b	Resignation of director or secretary
288bCYM	Ditto (Welsh language version)
288ab(I)	Resignation/appointment of director or secretary
288c	Changes in particulars of director or secretary
288cCYM	Ditto (Welsh language version)
288c(I)	Change in the details of a director or secretary
318	Location of directors' service contracts
325	Location of register of directors' interests in shares etc.
325a	Notice of place for inspection of a register of directors' interests in shares, etc. which is kept in a non-legible form, or of any change in that place
353	Register of members
353a	Notice for place of inspection of a register of members which is kept in non-legible form, or of any change in that place
362	Notice of place where an overseas branch register is kept, of any change in that place, or of any discontinuance of any such register
362a	Notice of place for inspection of an oversea branch register which is kept in a non-legible form, and of any change in that place
363a	Annual return
363CYM	Ditto (Welsh language version)
391	Notice of passing of resolution removing an auditor
395	Particulars of a mortgage or charge (Also for the use of a company incorporated outside Great Britain which has a place of business in England or Wales)
397	Particulars for the registration of a charge to secure a series of debentures (Also for the use of a company incorporated outside Great Britain which has a place of business in England or Wales)
397a	Particulars of an issue of secured debentures in a series (Also for the use of a company incorporated outside Great Britain which has a place of business in England or Wales)
398	Certificate of registration in Scotland or Northern Ireland of a charge comprising property situate there
400	Particulars of a mortgage or charge subject to which property has been acquired (Also for the use of a company incorporated outside Great Britain which has a place of business in England or Wales)
401	Register of charges, memorandum of satisfaction and appointment and cessation of receivers
403a	Declaration of satisfaction in full or in part of mortgage or charge (Also for the use of a company incorporated outside Great Britain which has a place of business in England or Wales)
403b	Declaration that part of the property or undertaking charged (a) has been released from the charge; (b) no longer forms part of the company's property or undertaking (Also for the use of a company incorporated outside Great Britain which has a place of business in England or Wales)

28.1 Forms

405(1)	Notice of appointment of receiver or manager
405(2)	Notice of ceasing to act as receiver or manager
410 (Scot)	Particulars of a charge created by a company registered in Scotland (Also for use of a company incorporated outside Great Britain which has a place of business in Scotland)
413 (Scot)	Particulars for the registration of a charge to secure a series of debentures (Also for use of a company incorporated outside Great Britain which has a place of business in Scotland)
413a (Scot)	Particulars of an issue of debentures out of a series of secured debentures (Also for use of a company incorporated outside Great Britain which has a place of business in Scotland)
416 (Scot)	Particulars of a charge subject to which property has been acquired by a company registered in Scotland (Also for use of a company incorporated outside Great Britain which has a place of business in Scotland)
417 (Scot)	Register of charges, alteration of charges, memorandum of satisfaction and appointments and cessations of receivers
419a (Scot)	Application for registration of a memorandum of satisfaction in full or in part of a registered charge (Also for use of a company incorporated outside Great Britain which has a place of business in Scotland)
419b (Scot)	Application for registration of a memorandum of fact that part of the property charged (a) has been released from the charge; (b) no longer forms part of the company's property (Also for use of a company incorporated outside Great Britain which has a place of business in Scotland)
429(4)	Notice to non-assenting shareholders
429 (dec)	Statutory declaration relating to a notice to non-assenting shareholders
430A	Notice to non-assenting shareholders
466 (Scot)	Particulars of an instrument of alteration to a floating charge created by a company registered in Scotland (Also for use of a company incorporated outside Great Britain which has a place of business in Scotland)
652a	Application for striking off
652aCYM	Ditto (Welsh language version)
652c	Withdrawal of application for striking off
652cCYM	Ditto (Welsh language version)
680a	Application by joint stock company for registration under *Part XXII* of the *Companies Act 1985*, and declaration and related statements
680b	Application by a company which is not a joint stock company for registration under *Part XXII* of the *Companies Act 1985*, and declaration and related statements
684	Registration under *Part XXII* of the *Companies Act 1985*: list of members – existing joint stock company
685	Declaration on application by a joint stock company for registration as a public company
686	Registration under *Part XXII* of the *Companies Act 1985*: statutory declaration verifying list of members

691	Return and declaration delivered for registration by an oversea company
692(1)(a)	Return of alteration in the charter, statutes, etc. of an oversea company
692(1)(b)	Return of alteration in the directors or secretary of an oversea company or in their particulars
692(1)(c)	Return of alteration in the names and addresses of persons resident in Great Britain authorised to accept service on behalf of an oversea company
692(2)	Return of change in the corporate name of an oversea company
694(4)(a)	Statement of name, other than corporate name, under which an oversea company proposes to carry on business in Great Britain
694(4)(b)	Statement of name, other than corporate name, under which an oversea company proposes to carry on business in Great Britain in substitution for name previously registered
703P(1)	Return by oversea company that the company is being wound up
703P(3)	Notice of appointment of liquidator of an oversea company
703P(5)	Notice by the liquidator of an oversea company concerning the termination of liquidation of the company
703Q(1)	Return by an oversea company which becomes subject to insolvency proceedings, etc.
703Q(2)	Return by an oversea company on cessation of insolvency proceedings, etc.
BR1	Return delivered for registration of a branch of an oversea company
BR2	Return by an oversea company subject to branch registration of an alteration to constitutional documents
BR3	Return by an oversea company subject to branch registration, for alteration of company particulars
BR4	Return by an oversea company subject to branch registration of change of directors or secretary or of their particulars
BR5	Return by an oversea company subject to branch registration of change of address or other branch particulars
BR6	Return of change of person authorised to accept service or to represent the branch of an oversea company or of any change in their particulars
BR7	Return by an oversea company of the branch at which the constitutional documents of the company have been registered in substitution for a previous branch
R7	Application by an old public company for re-registration as a public company
R7a	Notice of application made to the court for the cancellation of a special resolution by an old public company not to be re-registered as a public company
R8	Declaration by director or secretary on application by an old public company for re-registration as a public company
R9	Declaration by old public company that it does not meet the requirements of a public company

28.2 Forms

[*SI 1985 No 724; SI 1985 No 854; SI 1986 No 2097; SI 1987 No 752; SI 1988 No 1359; SI 1990 No 572; SI 1990 No 1766; SI 1991 No 879; SI 1992 No 3006; SI 1994 No 117; SI 1995 No 734; SI 1995 No 736; SI 1995 No 1479; SI 1995 No 1480; SI 1995 No 1508; SI 1996 No 594; SI 1996 No 595; SI 1998 No 1702; SI 1999 No 2356; SI 1999 No 2357; SI 1999 No 2678; SI 1999 No 2679*].

28.2 CERTIFIED TRANSLATIONS

For the purposes of the relevant provisions set out below, a 'certified translation' must accompany the document sent to the Registrar of Companies.

A *'certified translation'* is a translation of the document into English certified to be a correct translation by

(*a*)   if the translation was made in the UK

    (i)   a notary public or solicitor;

    (ii)   a person certified by a person within (i) above to be known to him to be competent to translate the document into English; or

    (iii)   in the case of a translation of a Welsh document into English obtained by the Registrar of Companies under *Sec 710B(4)*, the person who translated the document into English; or

(*b*)   if the translation was made outside the UK

    (i)   a notary public;

    (ii)   a person authorised in the place where the translation was made to administer an oath;

    (iii)   any of the British officials mentioned in *Commissioners for Oaths Act 1889, s 6*; or

    (iv)   a person certified by a person within (i) to (iii) above to be known to him to be competent to translate the document into English.

The relevant provisions are

- *Sec 21* (registered documentation of Welsh companies before 1 February 1994, see 62.1 WALES);

- *Sec 228(2)(f)* (exemption for parent company included in accounts of larger groups, see 4.9(vi) ACCOUNTS: GROUPS OF COMPANIES); *Secs 242(1)* and *243(4)* (delivery of accounts to Registrar of Companies, see 3.7 ACCOUNTS: GENERAL); and *Sec 702(1)* (delivery of accounts to Registrar of Companies by oversea companies, see 38.38 OVERSEA COMPANIES);

- *Secs 272(5)* and *273(7)* (relevant accounts for the purposes of a distribution, see 23.7 DISTRIBUTIONS);

- *Secs 691(1)(a)* and *698* (registration of oversea companies, see 38.3(a) OVERSEA COMPANIES);

- *Sec 710B* (documents relating to Welsh companies, see 62.1 WALES);

- *21A Sch 5(b), 6(1)(b)* and *7(1)* (accounting documents to be delivered by overseas credit and financial institutions required to prepare accounts under parent law, see 38.49 OVERSEA COMPANIES); and

- *21D Sch 2(4)* (accounting documents to be delivered by oversea companies with branches in Great Britain where the companies are required to make disclosures

412

under parent law, see 38.41 OVERSEA COMPANIES) and *21D Sch 10(2)* (accounts and reports to be delivered by oversea companies with branches in Great Britain where companies are not required to make disclosure under parent law, see 38.45 OVERSEA COMPANIES).

[*SI 1985 No 854, Reg 6; SI 1990 No 572, Reg 5; SI 1992 No 3006; SI 1994 No 117*].

29 Guarantee Companies

29.1 DEFINITION

A company limited by guarantee is a registered company having the liability of its members limited by the memorandum to such amounts as the members may respectively undertake to contribute to the assets of the company in the event of its being wound up. [*Sec 1(2)(b)*]. Such companies are widely used by schools, professional and trade associations, clubs and management companies for blocks of flats in which all the tenants are members.

A company cannot be formed as, or become, a company limited by guarantee with a share capital. [*Sec 1(4)*]. As the definition of a public company in *Sec 1(3)* only includes companies limited by guarantee which have a share capital, it follows that a guarantee company can only be formed as a private company.

29.2 MEMORANDUM AND ARTICLES OF ASSOCIATION

Model forms of memorandum of association and articles of association are to be found in *SI 1985 No 805, Tables C* and *D*.

Memorandum. The memorandum must state the company's name, situation of registered office, objects and liability of members as detailed below. For companies formed before 22 December 1980, the memorandum must also, if applicable, state that the company is a public company and give details of share capital. See also 35.2 MEMORANDUM OF ASSOCIATION.

Liability of members. The memorandum of a company limited by guarantee must state that the liability of its members is limited. [*Sec 2(3)*]. It must also state that each member undertakes to contribute such amount as may be required (but not exceeding a specified sum) to the company's assets if it should be wound up while he is a member, or within one year after he ceases to be a member, for

- payments of debts and liabilities of the company contracted before he ceases to be a member;

- costs, charges and expenses of winding up; and

- adjustments of the rights of the contributories among themselves.

[*Sec 2(4)*].

Articles *must* be in accordance with *Table C* (companies not having a share capital) or *Table D* (companies having a share capital) or as near to those forms as circumstances permit. [*Sec 8(4)*]. There is no provision, as with *Table A*, for the articles to be adopted or not. [*Secs 7(1), 8(4)*].

29.3 RESTRICTION ON MEMBERS' RIGHTS

In order to prevent members of a company limited by guarantee and not having a share capital being given rights equivalent to those of shareholders, any provision in the memorandum or articles, or in any resolution, of the company which purports to

(*a*)   give any person a right to participate in the divisible profits of the company otherwise than as a member, or

(*b*)   divide the company's undertaking into shares or interests

is void. [*Sec 15(1)*].

The above provisions do not apply to guarantee companies registered before 1 January 1901. [*CC(CP)A 1985, s 10*].

29.4   EXEMPTION FROM INCLUSION OF 'LIMITED' AS PART OF NAME

A private company limited by guarantee may exclude from its name the word 'limited', or its Welsh equivalent ('cyfyngedig'), or any abbreviation meaning the same, provided the following conditions are met. (The provisions also apply to a company which on 25 February 1982 was a private company limited by shares with a name which by virtue of a licence under *CA 1948, s 19*, did not include the word 'limited'.)

(*a*)   The objects of the company are (or, in the case of a company about to be registered, will be) the promotion of commerce, art, science, education, religion, charity or any profession, and anything incidental or conducive to any of those objects.

(*b*)   The company's memorandum or articles

    (i)   require that its profits or other income will be applied only for those purposes;

    (ii)   prohibit the payment of dividends to members; and

    (iii)   require that, upon winding up, its assets otherwise available to members will be transferred to another body with similar objects or to another body the objects of which are the promotion of charity and anything incidental or conducive thereto.

(*c*)   A statutory declaration that the company complies with (*a*) and (*b*) above is delivered to the Registrar of Companies in the prescribed form

    (i)   in the case of a company not yet formed, by a solicitor engaged in its formation or by a person named as director or secretary in the statement delivered under *Sec 10(2)* (see 49.1(*c*) REGISTRATION AND RE-REGISTRATION) (Form 30(5)(a)); and

    (ii)   in the case of an existing company proposing to change its name so that it ceases to have the word 'limited' as part of its name, by a director or secretary (Form 30(5)(c)).

There is no fee under (i) above apart from the normal incorporation fee. Under (ii) the normal fee for change of name is payable. See 26.1 FEES.

(*d*)   In the case of a company which already exists, a special resolution to change its name by omitting the word 'limited' is passed and sent to the Registrar of Companies with the statutory declaration under (*c*) above.

A company which is exempt from the requirement to use 'limited' and does not use the word as part of its name

• is also exempt from the requirements of *CA 1985* relating to the publication of its name (see 16.5 DEALINGS WITH THIRD PARTIES and 36.7 NAMES AND BUSINESS NAMES) and the sending of lists of members to the Registrar of Companies; and

• must not alter its memorandum or articles so that it ceases to comply with the requirements of (*a*) or (*b*) above. If it does, then any officer in default is liable to a fine up to the level in 40.1(*e*) PENALTIES.

Additionally, the Secretary of State may direct the company to change its name by resolution of the directors so that its name ends with 'limited'. A copy of the resolution must be sent to the Registrar of Companies within 15 days of passing. If the company fails

29.4 Guarantee Companies

to comply with this requirement, any officer of the company in default is liable to a fine up to the level in 40.1(*f*) PENALTIES. Once a company has received such a direction, it can only be registered thereafter by a name excluding 'limited' with the approval of the Secretary of State.

[*Secs 30, 31, 24 Sch*].

30 Insider Dealing

Cross-references. See 19.76 DIRECTORS for disclosure of shareholdings by a director to the company; 19.83 DIRECTORS for dealing in options; 47.7 REGISTERS for register of directors' interests; and 59.5 TAKEOVER OFFERS.

30.1 INTRODUCTION

The *Criminal Justice Act 1993* implemented the provisions of *EC Directive 89/592/EEC* on insider dealing and, in doing so, amended and restated the law on the subject, repealing in full the *CS(ID)A 1985*. The provisions in the *CJA 1993*, as implemented by *SI 1994 No 242*, are considered in 30.2 to 30.4 below.

See 30.6 below for the power of the Secretary of State to order investigations into insider dealing and 30.7 below for the provisions of the Stock Exchange Model Code which must also be observed by directors of listed companies.

A person guilty of the offence of insider dealing under 30.3 below is liable on conviction to a penalty up to the level in 40.1(*a*) PENALTIES. The consent of the Secretary of State or the Director of Public Prosecutions (in Northern Ireland, the Director of Public Prosecutions for Northern Ireland) must be obtained for proceedings to be instituted. [*CJA 1993, s 61*].

The fact that a person has been found guilty of the offence of insider dealing does not, in itself, make any contract void or unenforceable. [*CJA 1993, s 63(2)*].

30.2 Definitions

Acquire, in relation to a security, includes agreeing to acquire the security and entering into a contract which creates the security. [*CJA 1993, s 55(2)*].

Company means any body (whether or not incorporated and wherever incorporated or constituted) which is not a 'public sector body'. [*CJA 1993, s 60(3)*].

Dealing in securities. A person deals in securities if he

- 'acquires' or 'disposes' of the securities (as principal or agent); or

- procures (directly or indirectly) an acquisition or disposal of the securities by any other person (including his agent, his nominee or a person acting at his direction).

[*CJA 1993, s 55(1)(4)(5)*].

Dispose, in relation to a security, includes agreeing to disposal of the security and bringing to an end a contract which created the security. [*CJA 1993, s 55(3)*].

Information as an insider. A person has information as an insider if (and only if)

- it is, and he knows that it is, 'inside information'; and

- he has it, and knows that he has it, from an inside source i.e.

  (i) through being a director, employee or shareholder of an issuer of securities or through having access to the information by virtue of his employment, office or profession; or

  (ii) the direct or indirect source of his information is a person within (i) above.

[*CJA 1993, s 57*].

30.2   Insider Dealing

Inside information means information which

(*a*)   relates to particular securities or issuer(s) and not to securities or issuers generally;

(*b*)   is specific or precise;

(*c*)   has not been 'made public'; and

(*d*)   if it were made public would be likely to have a significant effect on the price of any securities.

Information is '*made public*' if it is published under the rules of a regulated market to inform investors and professional advisers; it is contained in public records; it can readily be obtained by those likely to 'deal in any securities'; or it is derived from information which has been made public. Information may be treated as made public even though it can be acquired only by exercising diligence or expertise; it is communicated only to a section of the public or for payment of a fee; it can be acquired only by observation; or it is only published outside the UK.

[*CJA 1993, ss 56(1), 58*].

As regards (*b*) above, information such as 'our results will be much better than the market expects or knows' is not precise (as the actual results are not disclosed) but it is specific because it gives information about the results which has obviously not been made available to the public. A statement such as 'our profit will be at a certain level and the market does not know that', without stating whether they would be better or worse than the market expected, is precise information. It would be up to the recipient to judge whether the information is likely to be price-sensitive. (Hansard, Standing Committee B, col 175, 10 June 1993).

Market information is information consisting of one or more of the following facts.

(*a*)   That securities of a particular kind have been, or are to be, acquired or disposed of (or such acquisition or disposal is under consideration or the subject of negotiation).

(*b*)   That securities of a particular kind have not been, or are to be, acquired or disposed of.

(*c*)   The number or price (or range of prices) of securities involved in a transaction within (*a*).

(*d*)   The identity of the persons involved or likely to be involved in any capacity in an acquisition or disposal.

[*CJA 1993, 1 Sch 4*].

Price-sensitive information in relation to securities means 'inside information' which would, if made public, be likely to have a significant effect on the price of the securities. [*CJA 1993, s 56(2)*]. The London Stock Exchange have issued a booklet *Guidance on the dissemination of price sensitive information*. This indicates that it is not possible to give any precise definition of 'price-sensitive' or to define any theoretical percentage movement in a share price which will make a piece of information price-sensitive. This is because it is generally necessary to take into account a number of factors specific to the particular case, in addition to the information itself, including the price and volatility of the share and the prevailing market conditions. The *Listing Rules* indicate many events which may have to be announced to the market because they may be price-sensitive (e.g. dividend announcements, board appointments or departures, profit warnings, share dealings by directors or substantial shareholders, acquisitions and disposals above certain sizes, annual and interim results, preliminary results, rights issues and other offers of securities).

Public sector body means the government of any country or territory; any local authority (in the UK or elsewhere); any international organisation of which any member state is a member; and the Bank of England and the central bank of any sovereign state. [*CJA 1993, s 60(3)*].

Securities. The insider dealing provisions apply to any of the following securities which satisfy the conditions set out below.

(*a*)   Shares and stock in the share capital of a 'company'.

(*b*)   Debt securities (i.e. any instrument creating or acknowledging indebtedness which is issued by a 'company' or 'public sector body' and including, in particular, debentures, loan stock, bonds and certificates of deposit).

(*c*)   Warrants (i.e. any right to subscribe for shares or debt securities).

(*d*)   Depositary receipts (i.e. any certificate or other record which is issued by, or on behalf of, a person who holds securities within (*a*)–(*c*) above of a particular issuer and which acknowledges that another person is entitled to rights in relation to those securities or such securities of the same kind).

(*e*)   Options to acquire or dispose of any security within (*a*)–(*d*) above or (*f*) or (*g*) below.

(*f*)   Futures (i.e. rights under a contract for the acquisition or disposal of any securities within (*a*)–(*e*) above or (*g*) below under which delivery is to be made at a future date and at a price agreed when the contract is made).

(*g*)   Contracts for differences (i.e. rights under a contract which does not provide for the delivery of securities but whose purpose is to secure a profit (or avoid a loss) by reference to fluctuations in a share index connected with securities within (*a*)–(*f*) above or the price of such securities or the interest rate offered on money placed on deposit).

The conditions are

(i)   for any security within (*a*) or (*b*) above, that it is officially listed in a state within the European Economic Area (i.e. any member state of the EC or Iceland, Norway or Liechtenstein) or is admitted to dealing on, or has its price quoted on or under the rules of, a 'regulated market';

(ii)   for a warrant within (*c*) above, that *either* it satisfies the condition in (i) above *or* the right under it is a right to subscribe for any share or debt security of the same class as the share or debt security which satisfies the conditions in (i) above;

(iii)   for a depositary receipt within (*d*) above, that *either* it satisfies the condition in (i) above *or* the rights under it are in respect of any share or debt security which satisfies the condition in (i) above;

(iv)   for an option within (*e*) above or a future within (*f*) above, that *either* it satisfied the condition in (i) above *or* the option/rights under the future are in respect of any share or debt security which satisfies the condition in (i) above or any depositary receipt which satisfies that condition or the alternative condition in (iii) above); and

(v)   for a contract for differences within (*g*) above, that *either* it satisfies the condition in (i) above *or* that the purpose (or pretended purpose) of the contract is to secure a profit or avoid a loss by reference to the fluctuations in the price (or an index of the price) of any shares or debt securities which satisfy the condition in (i) above.

A '*regulated market*' is any market established under the rules of

30.3 Insider Dealing

- The London Stock Exchange Ltd
- LIFFE Administration & Management
- OMLX, the London Securities and Derivatives Exchange Ltd
- Tradepoint Financial Networks plc
- The Irish Stock Exchange Ltd
- The exchange known as NASDAQ
- The exchange known as the Nouveau Marché
- Securities Exchange of Iceland
- The stock exchanges of Amsterdam, Antwerp, Athens, Barcelona, Bavarin, Berlin, Bilbao, Bologna, Bremen, Brussels, Copenhagen, Dusseldorf, Florence, Frankfurt, Genoa, Hamburg, Hanover, Helsinki, Iceland, Lisbon, Luxembourg, Lyon, Madrid, Milan, Naples, Oporto, Oslo, Palermo, Paris, Rome, Stockholm, Stuttgart, Trieste, Turin, Valencia, Venice or Vienna.

[*CJA 1993, 2 Sch; SI 1994 No 187; SI 1996 No 1561*].

30.3 The offence of insider dealing

Subject to the defences in 30.4 below, an individual who has 'information as an insider' is guilty of the offence of insider dealing in the following circumstances.

(*a*)   He 'deals in securities' that are price-affected in relation to the 'inside information' in either of the following circumstances, namely

    (i)   the acquisition or disposal in question occurs on a regulated market; or

    (ii)   the person dealing relies on, or is himself acting as, a 'professional intermediary'.

A *'professional intermediary'* is a person who carries on a business (or is employed in a business) which, other than on an incidental or occasional basis, acquires and disposes of securities (as principal or agent) or acts as an intermediary between other persons dealing in securities.

(*b*)   He encourages another person to 'deal in securities' that are (whether or not he knows it) price-affected securities in relation to the 'inside information' and he knows (or has reasonable cause to believe) that dealing will take place in the securities under one of the circumstances as in (*a*)(i) or (ii) above.

(*c*)   He discloses the information (otherwise than in the proper performance of the functions of his employment, office or profession) to another person.

[*CJA 1993, ss 52, 59*].

Territorial scope. An individual is not guilty of an offence under (*a*) above unless *either* he was in the UK when the alleged deal took place *or* the regulated market is identified (by order) as being regulated in the UK *or* the professional intermediary was in the UK at the time he is alleged to have done anything by means of which the offence is alleged to have been committed.

An individual is not guilty of an offence under (*b*) or (*c*) above unless *either* he was in the UK when he is alleged to have encouraged the dealing or disclosed the information *or* the alleged recipient of the encouragement or disclosure was in the UK at the time of the alleged receipt.

[*CJA 1993, s 62*].

Public sector bodies. The above offences do not apply to anything done by an individual acting on behalf of a 'public sector body' in pursuit of monetary policies or policies with respect to exchange rates or the management of public debt or foreign exchange reserves. [*CJA 1993, s 63(1)*].

30.4   **Defences**

An individual is not guilty of insider dealing under 30.3(*a*) or (*b*) above if he can show any of the following.

- He did not at the time expect the dealing to result in a profit (or avoidance or loss) attributable to the fact that the information in question was 'price-sensitive information' in relation to the securities.

- At the time he believed on reasonable grounds that the information had been (or, where 30.3(*b*) applies, would be) disclosed widely enough to ensure that none of those taking part in the dealing would be prejudiced by not having the information.

- He would have done what he did even if he had not had the information.

- He acted in good faith in the course of his business as a 'market maker' or his employment in the business of a market maker. A *'market maker'* is a person who holds himself out at all normal times (in compliance with the rules of a regulated market or an approved international securities self-regulating organisation) as willing to acquire or dispose of securities and who is recognised as doing so under those rules.

- The information which he had as an insider was 'market information' and it was reasonable for an individual in his position to have acted as he did with that information at that time. In determining whether his actions were reasonable (despite having market information) there is, in particular, to be taken into account

  (i)   the contents of the information;

  (ii)   the circumstances in which he first had the information and in what capacity; and

  (iii) the capacity in which he now acts.

- He acted in connection with, and with a view to facilitating, an acquisition or disposal which was under consideration or the subject of negotiation (or a series of such acquisitions or disposals). The information which he had as an insider must have been 'market information' arising directly out of his involvement in that acquisition, etc.

- He acted in conformity with the price stabilisation rules under *FSA 1986, s 48(2)(i)*.

[*CJA 1993, s 53(1)(2)(6), 1 Sch 1–3, 5*].

An individual is not guilty of insider dealing under 30.3(*c*) above if he can show that

- he did not at the time expect any person, because of the disclosure, to 'deal in securities' under one of the circumstances as in 30.3(*a*)(i) or (ii) above; or

- although he had such an expectation at that time, he did not expect the dealing to result in a profit (or avoidance of loss) attributable to the fact that the information was 'price-sensitive information' in relation to the securities.

[*CJA 1993, s 53(3)(6)*].

30.5 Insider Dealing

30.5 Disclosure of information which may affect the price of securities

EC Directive 89/592/EEC, Art 7 requires all undertakings whose securities are admitted to trading on a market to publish certain information which may affect the price of its securities. The provisions have been implemented in the UK by *SI 1994 No 188*.

With effect from 1 March 1994, a company or undertaking which is an issuer of 'securities' admitted to trading on a 'regulated market' must, subject to below, inform the public as soon as possible of any major new developments in its sphere of activity which are not public knowledge and which may, because of the effect on its assets and liabilities or financial position or on the general course of its business, lead to substantial movements in the price of that security.

'Securities' are defined as in 30.2(*a*)–(*g*) above but, under (*a*), substituting 'undertaking' for 'public sector body' and, under (*g*), omitting the reference to 'the interest rate offered on money placed on deposit'.

'Regulated market' for these purposes means any market in the UK on which securities are admitted to trading being a market which is regulated and supervised by a recognised investment exchange and which operates regularly and which is accessible directly or indirectly to the public.

The provisions do not apply

- to listed securities (because similar obligations are imposed on such securities under the *Listing Rules*, see 43.6 PUBLIC AND LISTED COMPANIES); or

- where the relevant investment exchange exempts the issuer from the obligation to disclose because it is satisfied that disclosure of particular information would prejudice the legitimate interests of the issuer.

The rules of a recognised investment exchange must *at least*, in the event of failure by the issuer to disclose, enable it to

- discontinue the admission of the securities to trading;

- suspend trading in the securities;

- publish the fact that the issuer has failed to comply with the obligation; and

- itself make public any information which the issuer has failed to publish.

[*SI 1994 No 188*].

30.6 INVESTIGATIONS INTO INSIDER DEALING

The Secretary of State may appoint inspectors to carry out investigations to establish whether or not offences have been committed under the insider dealing provisions. The inspectors have power to require a person to produce documents or attend before them for examination under oath. Any person convicted on a prosecution instituted as a result of such an investigation may be ordered to pay the expenses of the investigation, including reasonable sums for general staff cost and overheads. [*FSA 1986, s 177; CA 1989, s 74; CJA 1993, 5 Sch 9*]. There are also penalties for failure to co-operate with the investigation. [*FSA 1986, s 178; CJA 1993, 5 Sch 10; SI 1992 No 1315*].

30.7 STOCK EXCHANGE MODEL CODE FOR LISTED COMPANIES

A listed company must adopt by board resolution, and take all reasonable steps to secure compliance with, a code of dealing in its listed securities in terms no less exacting than those of the Model Code. This Code imposes restrictions on dealings beyond those imposed by the legislation. Its purpose is to ensure that directors and 'relevant employees' do not abuse price sensitive information that they have, especially in periods leading up to an announcement of results.

A '*relevant employee*' is any employee of the listed company or a director or employee of a subsidiary or parent undertaking of the listed company, who, because of his office or employment is likely to be in possession of unpublished price sensitive information in relation to the listed company.

'*Dealings*' include any sale or purchase of, or agreement to sell or purchase, any securities and the grant, acceptance, acquisition, disposal, exercise or discharge of an option or other right to acquire or dispose of securities or any interest in securities. *Specifically included* are 'bed and breakfast' arrangements; dealings between directors and/or relevant employees; transfer of shares already held into a personal equity plan by means of a matched sale and purchase; off-market dealings; and transfers for no consideration by a director unless retaining a beneficial interest. *Specifically excluded* are the taking up of entitlements under a rights issue or other offer (including an offer of shares in lieu of cash dividend); allowing such rights etc. to lapse; sale of sufficient entitlements under a rights issue to allow for the balance to be taken up; the acceptance of a takeover offer; dealings by a director with a person whose interests in securities is to be treated as the director's interest under *Sec 328* (see 19.79 DIRECTORS); transfers of shares arising out of the operation of an employees' share scheme into a personal equity plan investing only in the securities of the listed company within 90 days of the exercise of the option or release of shares; and the grant, termination and exercise of an option under an approved SAYE share option scheme.

Subject to the special circumstances below, a director or relevant employee must not deal in any securities of the listed company as follows.

(*a*)   On considerations of a short-term nature. A director must also take reasonable steps to prevent any dealings by or on behalf of persons connected with him in any securities of the company on consideration of a short-term nature.

(*b*)   During a '*close period*' i.e. the period of two months immediately preceding the preliminary announcement of the company's annual results and half-yearly results (or one month before the announcement of quarterly results where the company reports on a quarterly basis). In each case the period from the end of the relevant financial year/period up to the time of the announcement is substituted, if shorter.

(*c*)   At any time when he is in possession of 'unpublished price sensitive information' in relation to those securities (see 30.2 above).

(*d*)   Without advising the chairman (or other director or directors designated for the purpose) and receiving clearance. (The chairman or any sole director designated should advise the board.) The procedure should be in writing. Clearance must not be given during

(i)   any close period (see (*b*) above) except in exceptional circumstances (e.g. the sale of securities for a pressing financial commitment);

(ii)   any period where unpublished price sensitive information exists (whether or not the director in question has knowledge of it) and where the proposed dealing would take place after the time when it had become reasonably probable that an announcement would be required in relation to that information; or

(iii)   any period when the person responsible for clearance has reason to believe that the proposed dealing is in breach of the Model Code.

30.7 Insider Dealing

Directors acting as trustees. Where a director is a sole trustee (other than a bare trustee), the provisions of the Code apply as if he were dealing for his own account. Where a director is a co-trustee, he must advise the other trustees of the names of the listed companies of which he is a director. Provided he is not a beneficiary, any dealings by the trustees will be outside the Code where the decision to deal is taken by the other trustees acting independently of the director or by investment managers.

Connected persons. A director must also seek to prohibit any dealings in the listed company's securities by a person connected with him (see 19.94 DIRECTORS) during a close period (see (*b*) above) or at a time when the director is in possession of unpublished price sensitive information and would be prevented from dealing under (*d*)(ii) above. He should do this by advising the connected person of the names of the listed companies of which he is a director, together with the close or other periods during which they cannot deal. They must also be advised to tell the director immediately after they have dealt in securities.

Investment managers. Similar rules apply as for connected persons to dealings by an investment manager on behalf of a director (or any person connected with him) where the director (or connected person) has funds under management with that investment manager.

Record of dealings. A list of dealings in the company's securities by directors and connected persons (or investment managers on their behalf) since the date of the last such list should be circulated to board members before each meeting.

Special circumstances. The provisions above are overridden in the following circumstances.

(i)   *Exercise of options.* The chairman or designated director may allow

- the exercise of an option or right under an employees' share scheme, or

- the conversion of a convertible security

where the final date for the exercise or conversion falls during a prohibited period and the director could not reasonably have been expected to act at an earlier time when he was free to deal.

The chairman, etc. cannot, however, give clearance for the sales of the securities so acquired.

(ii) *Personal equity plans and authorised unit trust.* A director or relevant employee may enter into a discretionary personal equity plan or deal in units of an authorised unit trust without regard to the provisions of the Code. However, if it is a personal equity plan involving regular payments by standing order or direct debit for investment in the listed company only, he must not enter into the plan, carry out the first purchase, cancel or vary his terms or participation or sell any securities during a prohibited period. He must also obtain clearance from the chairman, etc. before doing any of those things.

(iii) *Saving Schemes, etc.* A director or relevant employee may enter into a scheme under which his company's securities are purchased by regular standing orders or direct debits or acquired by way of a standing election to reinvest dividends, subject to the same provisions as for personal equity plans investing in the listed company only under (ii) above.

(*The Listing Rules, Chapter 16, Appendix*).

31 Investigations

The contents of this chapter are as follows.

31.1 INVESTIGATIONS INTO THE AFFAIRS OF THE COMPANY GENERALLY

The Secretary of State *may* appoint inspector(s) to investigate and report on the affairs of a company either

(*a*) on the application of

   (i)   at least 200 members (or members holding at least 10% of the shares issued) of a company having a share capital; or

   (ii) at least 20% of the registered members of a company not having a share capital; or

   (iii) the company itself; or

(*b*) (whether or not the company is in the course of being voluntarily wound up) if it appears to the Secretary of State that

   (i)   the company's affairs are being or have been conducted with intent to defraud creditors (of the company or of any other person) or otherwise for a fraudulent or unlawful purpose, or in a manner unfairly prejudicial to some members (or to other persons to whom shares have been transferred or transmitted by operation of law); or

   (ii) any actual or proposed act or omission of the company or on its behalf is or would be so prejudicial; or

   (iii) the company was formed for any fraudulent or unlawful purpose; or

   (iv) persons concerned with the company's formation or management have in that connection been guilty of fraud, misfeasance or other misconduct towards the company or its members; or

   (v)   the company's members have not been given all the information with respect to its affairs which they might reasonably expect.

The Secretary of State is *required* to appoint inspector(s) if a court having jurisdiction to wind up the company by order declares that the company's affairs ought to be so investigated.

[*Secs 431(1)(2), 432(1)-(4), 744*].

The Secretary of State may require from applicant(s) under (*a*) above supporting evidence demonstrating good reason for their requiring the investigation, and security (not exceeding £5,000) for payment of the costs of the investigation. (The figure of £5,000 may be altered by order made by statutory instrument by the Secretary of State.) [*Sec 431(3)(4)*].

As regards (*b*) above the appointment may be on terms that any report is not for publication, notwithstanding *Sec 437(3)* (see 31.3 below). [*Sec 432(2A); CA 1989, s 55; SI 1990 No 142*].

31.2 Investigations

Inspectors appointed as above have power, if they consider it necessary, to extend their investigation to the affairs of certain other bodies corporate with a holding or subsidiary relationship to the company under investigation. Their report will then include a report on the affairs of such bodies corporate, so far as relevant to their investigation. [*Sec 433*].

31.2 Production of documents and evidence

Officers and 'agents' (past and present) of a company or body corporate under investigation are under a duty to

- produce to the inspectors all 'documents' in their custody or power of or relating to the company or body corporate;

- attend before the inspectors as required; and

- otherwise give them all reasonable assistance in connection with the investigation.

They are under a similar duty in relation to a requirement by the inspectors concerning information on matters they believe to be relevant to their investigation.

An inspector may examine any person on oath, and an answer given by a person to a question put under any of the above powers may be used in evidence against him. In *R v Saunders and others [1996] 1 CR App R 463* the Court of Appeal held that there was a clear intention in these provisions to override any privilege against self-incrimination in the context of interviews by inspectors. By way of contrast, in *Saunders v United Kingdom (Case 43/1994/490/572) [1997] BCC 872* the European Court of Human Rights accepted that the use made of certain statements to inspectors was unfair and in violation of the European Convention on Human Rights, stating that the *CA 1985* provisions could not properly override an individual's rights not to be required to incriminate himself. The incorporation into English law of the European Convention on Human Rights by the *Human Rights Act 1998* will also have an impact on this complex area.

'**Agents**' includes bankers, solicitors and auditors, whether or not they are officers but see 31.16 below for privileged information.

'*Documents*' for these purposes includes any recorded information (in legible form). [*Sec 434; CA 1989, s 56*].

Failure or refusal by any person to comply with any of the above requirements, or to answer any of the inspectors' questions, may be certified in writing by the inspector to the court, and may be treated as contempt of court. [*Sec 436; CA 1989, s 56*].

31.3 Inspectors' reports

Final (and, if required, interim) reports are made by the inspectors to the Secretary of State, who is kept informed of any matters coming to the inspectors' knowledge as a result of their investigations. If matters that come to light, suggesting that a criminal offence has been committed, have been referred to the appropriate prosecuting authority, the Secretary of State may direct the inspectors to take no further steps in the investigation, or to take only specified further steps. Following such a direction, a final report is made only where the inspectors were appointed following a declaration by order of the court (see 31.1 above) or the Secretary of State so directs. [*Sec 437(1)-(1C); FSA 1986, 13 Sch 7; CA 1989, s 57*].

A copy of any report must be furnished to the court where the inspectors were so appointed. In any case, if he thinks fit, the Secretary of State may forward a copy to the registered office of the company under investigation and, on request and on payment of a fee prescribed by him by statutory instrument, he may furnish a copy to:

- any member of the company or other body corporate which is the subject of the report;

- the auditors of that company or body corporate;

- any person whose conduct is referred to in the report;

- the applicants for the investigation (see 31.1 above); and

- any other person whose financial interests appear to him to be affected by the matters dealt with in the report.

He may also cause any report to be printed and published (but see 31.1 above for certain reports excluded from publication under the terms of appointment of the inspectors). [*Secs 437(2)(3), 744*].

See, however, 31.7 below as regards omission of certain parts of inspectors' reports from disclosure under these provisions.

A copy of the report is admissible in any legal proceedings as evidence of the inspectors' opinion in relation to any matter in the report, and in proceedings on an application under *CDDA 1986, s 8* (see 19.16 DIRECTORS) as evidence of any fact stated therein. The copy must be certified a true copy by the Secretary of State, and a document purporting to be such a certificate will be received in evidence as such unless the contrary is proved. [*Sec 441; IA 1985, 6 Sch 3; IA 1986, 13 Sch Part I; CA 1989, s 61*].

31.4   Civil proceedings on company's behalf

If it appears to the Secretary of State from any report or information under 31.1 to 31.3 above that civil proceedings should in the public interest be brought by any body corporate, he may bring such proceedings in the name and on behalf of the body corporate. He must indemnify the body corporate against costs or expenses it incurs in or in connection with such proceedings. [*Sec 438; CA 1989, s 58*].

31.5   Investigation expenses

The expenses of an investigation under 31.1 above (including reasonable general costs and overheads as determined by the Secretary of State) are defrayed in the first place by the Secretary of State. He may, however, recover them as follows.

(*a*)   A person convicted on a prosecution instituted as a result of the investigation, or ordered to pay any of the costs of proceedings under *Sec 438* (see 31.4 above), may in those proceedings be ordered to pay investigation expenses to a specified extent.

(*b*)   A body corporate in whose name proceedings are brought under *Sec 438* (see 31.4 above) is liable for investigation expenses to the amount or value of any sums or property recovered by it as a result of those proceedings, as a first charge on such sums or property.

(*c*)   Except where the inspectors were appointed of the Secretary of State's own motion (see 31.1 above), a body corporate dealt with by an inspectors' report is liable for investigation expenses, unless it was the applicant for the investigation, except so far as the Secretary of State otherwise directs.

(*d*)   Where inspectors were appointed as under 31.1(*a*) above or on an application as under 31.7 below, the applicant(s) for the investigation is(are) liable for investigation expenses to such extent as the Secretary of State may direct.

31.6 Investigations

Except where the inspectors were appointed of the Secretary of State's own motion (see 31.1 above), their report may, and may be required by the Secretary of State to, include a recommendation as to any appropriate direction(s) under (*c*) and (*d*) above in the light of their investigations.

Investigation expenses include costs or expenses incurred by the Secretary of State in or in connection with proceedings brought under *Sec 438* (see 31.4 above) (including under the indemnity referred to therein) to which the investigation gave rise.

A liability under (*a*) above is, subject to the Secretary of State's right to repayment, also a liability to indemnify all persons against liability under (*b*), (*c*) and (*d*) above, and a liability under (*b*) is similarly a liability to indemnify all persons against liability under (*c*) and (*d*). A person liable under any of (*a*) to (*d*) above is entitled to contribution from any other person liable under the same sub-paragraph, according to the amount of their respective liabilities under the sub-paragraph.

[*Sec 439; CA 1989, s 59*].

31.6 OTHER POWERS OF INVESTIGATION

Various powers of investigation are available to the Secretary of State, in addition to those described at 31.1 to 31.5 above, under *Secs 442-446*.

31.7 Power to investigate company ownership

If there appears to be good reason to do so, the Secretary of State may appoint inspector(s) to investigate and report on the membership of any company, and otherwise with respect to the company, to determine the true persons financially interested in the success or failure (real or apparent) of the company, or able to control or materially to influence its policy. Subject to the terms of their appointment, the inspectors' powers extend to the investigation of any circumstances suggesting the existence of a relevant arrangement or understanding which, though not legally binding, is or was observed or likely to be observed in practice.

The appointment may define the scope of the investigation, and in particular may limit it to matters connected with particular shares or debentures. If an application is made to the Secretary of State by members of a company for such a limited investigation, and the applicants would meet the requirements in 31.1(*a*)(i) or (ii) above as regards numbers or shares, the Secretary of State must (except as below) appoint inspectors to conduct the investigation, unless he is satisfied that the application is vexatious. The terms of appointment will, however, exclude any matter in so far as he is satisfied that it is unreasonable for it to be investigated. He may, before appointing inspectors, require security (not exceeding £5,000) from the applicant(s) for payment of the costs of the investigation. (The figure of £5,000 may be altered by order made by statutory instrument by the Secretary of State.)

Where it appears to the Secretary of State that his powers under *Sec 444* (see 31.8 below) are sufficient for the investigation of matters which inspectors would otherwise be appointed to investigate on an application as above, he may instead conduct the investigation under *Sec 444*.

[*Sec 442; CA 1989, s 62*].

The provisions of *Sec 433* (see 31.1 above), *Secs 434, 436* (see 31.2 above) and *Sec 437* (see 31.3 above) apply to an investigation under *Sec 442* above with appropriate modification. In addition, they apply to

- all persons who are or have been (or whom the inspector has reasonable cause to believe to be or have been)

(i)   financially interested in the success or failure (real or apparent) of the company or any other body corporate whose membership is investigated with that of the company, or

(ii) able to control or materially influence its policy (including persons concerned only on behalf of others), and

- any other person whom the inspector has reasonable cause to believe possesses relevant information,

as they apply in relation to officers or agents of the company or other body corporate.

The Secretary of State may by order impose restrictions on shares and debentures under *Secs 454-457* (see 21.9 to 21.12 DISCLOSURE OF INTERESTS IN PUBLIC COMPANY SHARES) where there is difficulty in ascertaining the relevant facts about them in connection with an investigation under these provisions. However, where he is satisfied that such on order may unfairly affect the rights of third parties, he may direct that specified acts by such persons do not constitute a breach of the restrictions.

If the Secretary of State considers there is good reason for not divulging any part of a report under these provisions, he may omit that part from the disclosure of the report under *Sec 437* (see 31.3 above). He may cause a copy of any report to be kept by the Registrar of Companies, again with the omission of any part not disclosed under *Sec 437*.

[*Secs 443, 445; CA 1989, 24 Sch; SI 1991 No 1646, Reg 5*].

31.8   Power to obtain information as to those interested in shares, etc.

The Secretary of State may act without the appointment of inspectors if there appears to be good reason to investigate the ownership of any shares or debentures of a company, and he considers their appointment unnecessary. He may require any person he has reasonable cause to believe to have, or to be able to obtain,

- any information as to the present and past interests in those shares, etc., and

- the names and addresses of the persons interested and of any persons who act or have acted on their behalf in relation to those shares, etc.,

to deliver such information to him.

A person has an interest for this purpose if

- he has any right to acquire or dispose of the shares, etc. (or of an interest in them);

- he has any right to vote in respect of them;

- his consent is necessary for the exercise of any rights of other persons interested in them; or

- other persons interested in them can be required to, or are accustomed to, exercise their rights in accordance with his instructions.

Any person who fails to give information required as above, or who knowingly gives materially false information, or who recklessly makes materially false statements, is liable to a penalty up to the level in 40.1(*b*) PENALTIES. See, however, 31.16 below for privileged information.

[*Sec 444, 24 Sch*].

The Secretary of State may by order impose restrictions on shares, etc. under *Secs 454-457* (see 21.9 to 21.12 DISCLOSURE OF INTERESTS IN PUBLIC COMPANY SHARES) where there is

31.9 Investigations

difficulty in ascertaining the relevant facts about them in connection with an investigation under these provisions. [*Sec 445*].

31.9 Investigation of share dealings

If it appears to the Secretary of State that, in relation to a company's shares or debentures, contraventions may have occurred of *Sec 323* (directors dealing in share options, see 19.83 DIRECTORS) or *Sec 324* and *13 Sch* or *Sec 328(3)-(5)* (disclosure of shareholdings by a director, see 19.76 to 19.81 DIRECTORS), he may appoint inspector(s) to investigate and report on whether such contraventions have occurred. The terms of the appointment may limit the period to which the investigation is to extend and/or confine it to a particular class of shares or debentures. *Secs 434-437* (see 31.2 and 31.3 above), modified as necessary, apply to such an investigation, but the duties (and penalties) imposed on company officers under those sections apply also to

- an individual,

- an officer (past or present) of a body corporate,

- a partner (past or present) of a partnership, or

- a member of the governing body or officer (past or present) of an unincorporated association,

where the individual, body corporate, partnership or unincorporated association is an authorised person within *FSA 1986*, holds a permission granted under *FSA 1986, 1 Sch 23* or is a European institution carrying on home-regulated investment business in the UK. [*Sec 446; FSA 1986, 13 Sch 8, 16 Sch 21, 17 Sch Part I; CA 1989, 24 Sch; SI 1992 No 3218, 10 Sch 16*].

31.10 REQUISITION AND SEIZURE OF BOOKS AND PAPERS

Various powers are available to the Secretary of State under *Secs 447-451A* to require the production of documents, etc. and to seize books and papers.

31.11 Power to require production of documents

If he thinks there is good reason to do so, the Secretary of State may at any time

- direct a company to produce specified 'documents' at a specified time and place; or

- authorise an officer of his or any other competent person to require a company to produce to him forthwith any specified documents.

'Documents' for these purposes includes any recorded information (in legible form).

Such powers also extend to require production of the specified documents from any other person who appears to be in possession of them, but any such production is without prejudice to any lien claimed by such a person on the documents. See also 31.16 below for privileged information.

The power to require production of documents includes power to take copies and obtain an explanation of them, and, if the documents are not produced, to require the person required to produce them to state, to the best of his knowledge and belief, where they are. Statements made by a person in compliance with these requirements may be used in evidence against him.

Failure to comply with any of the above requirements renders the person in default guilty of an offence and liable to a fine up to the level in 40.1(*d*) PENALTIES. It is, however, a defence against such a charge to prove that the documents in question were not in that person's possession or under his control, and that it was not reasonably practicable for him to comply with the requirement. *Secs 732-734* (see 32.3 to 32.5 LEGAL PROCEEDINGS) apply to such an offence.

[*Sec 447, 24 Sch; CA 1989, s 63*].

The circumstances in which information or a document relating to a company, obtained under the above provisions, may be published or disclosed (other than to a competent authority, as defined) without the prior consent in writing of the company are set out in *Sec 449*. These relate mainly to publication or disclosure required in relation to various proceedings and the discharge of various statutory functions. A person who publishes or discloses any information or document other than as permitted under *Sec 449* is guilty of an offence (to which *Secs 732-734*, see 32.3 to 32.5 LEGAL PROCEEDINGS, apply) and liable to a penalty up to the level in 40.1(*b*) PENALTIES. [*Sec 449, 24 Sch; IA 1985, 6 Sch 4; FSA 1986, 13 Sch 9; IA 1986, 13 Sch Part I; Banking Act 1987, 6 Sch 18; CA 1989, s 65, 24 Sch; Friendly Societies Act 1992, 21 Sch 7; Criminal Justice Act 1993, 5 Sch 4; Pensions Act 1995, 3 Sch 12; Bank of England Act 1998, 5 Sch 62; SI 1988 No 1334; SI 1992 No 1315, 4 Sch 1*]. Similar protection applies to documents obtained under a warrant under *Sec 448* (see 31.12 below) whose production was, or could have been, required under *Sec 447*. [*Sec 448(8)*].

31.12 Entry and search of premises

A justice of the peace (or, in Scotland, a sheriff) may issue a warrant if satisfied, on information on oath (in Scotland, on evidence on oath), that

(*a*)   there are reasonable grounds for believing that there are, on any premises, 'documents' whose production has been required under any of the provisions dealt with in this chapter but which have not been produced in compliance therewith; or

(*b*)   • there are reasonable grounds for believing that an offence has been committed for which the penalty on conviction on indictment is imprisonment for a term of not less than two years, and that there are on any premises documents relating to whether the offence has been committed; and

   • the Secretary of State (or an authorised person) has power under the provisions in this chapter to require their production; and

   • there are reasonable grounds for believing that if production was so required the documents would not be produced but would be removed from the premises, hidden, tampered with or destroyed.

'Document' for these purposes includes information recorded in any form.

The warrant continues in force for one month beginning with the day on which it is issued. It will authorise a constable, and any other named persons and any other constables, to enter specified premises (using reasonable force if necessary), to search the premises and take possession of any documents appearing to be those referred to in (*a*) or (*b*) above (or to take steps necessary to protect them), to take copies, and to require any person named in the warrant to provide an explanation of them or state where they may be found. See, however, 31.16 below for privileged information.

A warrant issued under (*b*) above may also authorise such action in respect of other documents relevant to the investigation.

Documents obtained under these provisions may be retained for three months or, if within that period any proceedings to which the documents are relevant are commenced against any person for a criminal offence, until the conclusion of those proceedings.

31.13 Investigations

Any person intentionally obstructing the exercise of rights under these provisions, or failing (without reasonable excuse) to provide an explanation of a document or state where it may be found when required to do so, is guilty of an offence and liable to a fine up to the level in 40.1(*d*) PENALTIES. *Secs 732-734* (see 32.3 to 32.5 LEGAL PROCEEDINGS) apply to such an offence.

[*Sec 448, 24 Sch; CA 1989, s 64*].

31.13 Punishment for destroying, mutilating etc. company documents

An officer of a company (which for this purpose includes an insurance company to which *Insurance Companies Act 1982, Pt II* applies and an EC company lawfully carrying out insurance business in the UK) who

(*a*) destroys, mutilates or falsifies a 'document' affecting or relating to the company's property or affairs, or makes a false entry in such a document, or is privy to any such act, or

(*b*) fraudulently either parts with, alters or makes an omission in any such document, or is privy to any such fraudulent act or omission,

is guilty of an offence and liable to a penalty up to the level in 40.1(*a*) PENALTIES unless (in the case of acts within (*a*)) he proves that he had no intention to conceal the company's state of affairs or to defeat the law. *Secs 732-734* (see 32.3 to 32.5 LEGAL PROCEEDINGS) apply to such an offence.

'*Document*' for these purposes includes information recorded in any form.

[*Sec 450, 24 Sch; CA 1989, s 66*].

31.14 Punishment for publishing false information

A person who, in purporting to comply with a requirement under *Sec 447* (see 31.11 above) to explain a document or state its whereabouts, provides an explanation or makes a statement which he knows to be materially false, or recklessly provides or makes such a false explanation or statement, is guilty of an offence and liable to a penalty up to the level in 40.1(*b*) PENALTIES. *Secs 732-734* (see 32.3 to 32.5 LEGAL PROCEEDINGS) apply to such an offence.

[*Sec 451, 24 Sch; CA 1989, s 67*].

31.15 Disclosure of information by Secretary of State or inspector

Information obtained under *Secs 434-446* (see 31.2 to 31.9 above) may be disclosed, as permitted by *Sec 449*, by the Secretary of State or by an inspector authorised by him to do so. It may also be disclosed by the inspector to certain other persons appointed or authorised under statutory powers. In either case it may be disclosed to any officer or servant of the person to whom disclosure is permitted as above. [*Sec 451A(1)-(4)*]. Disclosure is similarly permitted of documents obtained under a warrant under *Sec 448* (see 31.12 above) whose production was, or could have been, required under *Sec 434* (see 31.2 above). [*Sec 448(8)*].

Information obtained under *Sec 444* (see 31.8 above) may also be disclosed by the Secretary of State to the company whose ownership was under investigation, any member of that company, any person whose conduct was investigated in the course of the investigation, the company's auditors, and any person whose financial interests appear to the Secretary of State to be affected by matters covered by the investigation. [*Sec 451A(5); CA 1989, s 68*].

31.16 PRIVILEGED INFORMATION

There are two categories of privileged information under the provisions described at 31.1 to 31.15 above.

Legal professional privilege. Nothing in *Secs 431-446* (see 31.2 to 31.9 above) requires the disclosure by any person to the Secretary of State or to an inspector of information which that person would be entitled to refuse to disclose in a High Court (or Court of Session) action on grounds of legal professional privilege, except that a lawyer may be required to disclose the name and address of his client. Similarly, nothing in *Secs 447-451* (31.10 to 31.14 above) compels the production by any person of a document similarly covered by legal professional privilege, or authorises the taking of possession of any such document in the person's possession.

Obligation of confidence. Unless the making of the requirement is authorised by the Secretary of State, nothing in *Secs 434, 443* or *446* (see 31.2, 31.7 and 31.9 above) requires a person to disclose information or produce documents in respect of which he owes an obligation of confidence by virtue of carrying on a banking business, unless either

- that person, or the person to whom the obligation is owed is the company or other body corporate under investigation, or

- the person to whom the obligation is owed consents to the disclosure or production.

Similarly, under *Sec 447* (see 31.11 above), the Secretary of State may not (and may not authorise any other person to) require the production by a person carrying on a banking business of a document relating to a customer's affairs unless either

- it is necessary to do so in investigating the affairs of the person carrying on the banking business; or

- the customer is a person on whom a requirement has been imposed under *Sec 447* or under the corresponding provisions of the *Insurance Companies Act 1982*.

[*Sec 452; CA 1989, s 69*].

31.17 INVESTIGATION OF OVERSEA COMPANIES

The provisions of 31.1(*b*), 31.2, 31.3, 31.5 and 31.10 to 31.16 above apply to bodies corporate incorporated outside Great Britain which carry on, or have carried on, business in Great Britain subject to such modifications and adaptations as the Secretary of State may specify by regulations made by statutory instrument. [*Sec 453; CA 1989, s 70*].

32 Legal Proceedings

32.1 OFFENCES UNDER THE COMPANIES ACTS

There are a large number of offences for failure to comply with the requirements of the *Companies Acts*. These are dealt with in the appropriate part of the text. See also 40 PENALTIES.

32.2 Summary proceedings

Summary proceedings for an offence under the *Companies Acts* (including *BNA 1985*) may be taken

- against a company at any place at which it has a place of business; and

- against any other person at any place at which he is for the time being.

In England and Wales, proceedings which are triable by a magistrates' court must be brought within three years of the commission of the offence and within twelve months of the date on which evidence sufficient, in the opinion of the Director of Public Prosecutions or the Secretary of State (as the case may be), to justify the proceedings comes to his knowledge.

In Scotland, summary proceedings must be commenced within three years of the commission of the offence. Subject to this, proceedings may be commenced within twelve months of the date on which evidence sufficient, in the Lord Advocate's opinion, to justify the proceedings came to his knowledge or, where the evidence was reported to him by the Secretary of State, within twelve months of the date on which it came to the notice of the latter.

[*Sec 731; BNA 1985, s 7(6); Criminal Procedures (Consequential Provisions) Scotland Act 1995, 4 Sch 56*].

32.3 Prosecution by public authorities

Proceedings for offences under the following provisions can only be instituted in England and Wales by, or with the consent of the appropriate authority indicated.

- *Sec 210* (see 21.6 DISCLOSURE OF INTERESTS IN PUBLIC COMPANY SHARES); *Sec 324* (duty of directors to disclose shareholdings in own company, see 19.76 DIRECTORS); and *Sec 329* (duty of listed company to notify stock exchange of certain share transactions by directors, see 19.82 DIRECTORS) – the Secretary of State or the Director of Public Prosecutions.

- *Secs 447-451* (production of documents and seizure of books and papers, see 31.11 to 31.14 INVESTIGATIONS) – the Secretary of State, the Director of Public Prosecutions or the Industrial Assurance Commissioner.

- *Sec 455* (punishment for attempted evasion of restrictions on shares, see 21.10 DISCLOSURE OF INTERESTS IN PUBLIC COMPANY SHARES) – the Secretary of State.

In any proceedings instituted under the *Companies Acts* (including *BNA 1985*) by the Director of Public Prosecutions, the Secretary of State or the Lord Advocate, nothing in those Acts is to be taken as requiring any person to disclose any information which he is entitled to refuse to disclose on the grounds of legal professional privilege.

[*Sec 732; BNA 1985, s 7(6)*].

32.4   Offences by bodies corporate

Where a body corporate is guilty of an offence under the provisions listed below and it is proved that the offence occurred with the consent or connivance of, or was attributable to any neglect on the part of, any director, manager, secretary or other similar officer (or any person purporting to act in such a capacity) he, as well as the body corporate, is guilty of that offence and is liable to be proceeded against and punished accordingly. If the affairs of the company are managed by the members, this also applies in relation to any act or default of a member in connection with his functions of management as if he were a director.

The relevant provisions are as follows.

(*a*)   *Sec 210* (see 21.6 DISCLOSURE OF INTERESTS IN PUBLIC COMPANY SHARES).

(*b*)   *Sec 216(3)* (failure to comply with notice requiring details of interests, see 21.7 DISCLOSURE OF INTERESTS IN PUBLIC COMPANY SHARES).

(*c*)   *Sec 394A(1)* (statement by person ceasing to hold office as auditor, see 12.16 AUDITORS).

(*d*)   *Secs 447-451* (production of documents and seizure of books and papers, see 31.11 to 31.14 INVESTIGATIONS). For these purposes, director includes shadow director (see 19.1 DIRECTORS).

[*Sec 733; CA 1989, s 123*].

32.5   Criminal proceedings against unincorporated bodies

Proceedings for an offence alleged to have been committed by an unincorporated body under

(*a*)   *Sec 389A(3)* (right of auditors to information, see 12.25 AUDITORS),

(*b*)   *Sec 394A(1)* (statement by person ceasing to hold office as auditor, see 12.16 AUDITORS), or

(*c*)   *Secs 447-451* (production of documents and seizure of books and papers, see 31.11 to 31.14 INVESTIGATIONS)

must be brought in the name of that body (and not any of its members). For the purposes of such proceedings, any rules of court relating to the service of documents apply as if that body were a corporation.

Any fine imposed on an unincorporated body on conviction of such an offence must be paid out of the funds of the body.

Where an offence within (*a*) to (*c*) above is proved to have been committed with the consent or connivance of, or to be attributable to any neglect on the part of,

• in the case of a partnership, a partner, or

• in the case of any other unincorporated body, an officer of the body or a member of its governing body,

that person, as well as the body, is guilty of the offence and liable to be proceeded against and punished accordingly.

[*Sec 734; CA 1989, ss 120, 123, 19 Sch 18; Criminal Procedures (Consequential Provisions) (Scotland) Act 1995, 4 Sch 56*].

32.6　Legal Proceedings

32.6　SERVICE OF DOCUMENTS

A document may be served on a company by leaving it at, or sending it by post to, the company's registered office. [*Sec 725(1)*]. See also *JC Houghton & Co v Nothard, Lowe and Wills [1928] AC 1*.

Where a company registered in Scotland carries on business in England and Wales, the process of any court in England and Wales may be served on the company by leaving it at, or sending it by post to, the company's principal place of business in England and Wales. It should be addressed to the manager or other head officer of the company in England and Wales. The person issuing out the process must send a copy by post to the company's registered office. [*Sec 725(2)(3)*].

32.7　POWER OF COURT TO GRANT RELIEF

If in any proceedings for negligence, default, breach of duty or breach of trust against an officer of a company or auditor it appears to the court that that person, although liable, acted honestly and reasonably and ought fairly to be excused, the court may relieve him, wholly or partly, from liability on such terms as it thinks fit. If the case is being tried by a judge with a jury, the judge may, after hearing the evidence, withdraw the case in whole or part from the jury and direct judgment to be entered for the defendant. [*Sec 727(1)(3)*].

Where an officer of a company or auditor has reason to believe that a claim will or might be made against him for negligence etc., he may apply to the court for relief. The court has the same powers of relief on such an application as it does above in actual proceedings for negligence, etc. [*Sec 727(2)*].

32.8　SECURITY FOR COSTS AND EXPENSES IN CERTAIN ACTIONS

Where a limited company is plaintiff (in Scotland, pursuer) in legal proceedings and there is reason to believe that the company will be unable to pay the defendant's costs (in Scotland, the defender's expenses) if defence is successful, the court may require security to be given for those costs (in Scotland, order the company to find caution) and may determine not to proceed until such condition is satisfied. [*Sec 726*].

33   Meetings

Cross-references. See 3.6 ACCOUNTS: GENERAL for laying of accounts and reports before company in general meeting; 12.28 AUDITORS for rights of auditors to attend company meetings.

The contents of this chapter are as follows.

33.1   ANNUAL GENERAL MEETINGS

A company must hold an annual general meeting (AGM) each year in addition to any other meetings held. The notice calling the meeting must specify it as such. Successive AGMs must not be more than 15 months apart. [*Sec 366(1)(3)*]. See *Gibson v Barton (1875) LR 10 QB 329.*

First AGM. Provided the first AGM is held within 18 months of incorporation, a company need not hold an AGM in the year of incorporation or the following year. [*Sec 366(2)*].

Register of directors' interests. The register (see 47.7 REGISTERS) must be produced at the start of the AGM and remain open and available for inspection throughout to any person attending. [*13 Sch 29*].

Business of the meeting. There is no set business which must be held at the AGM but it is usual to consider the annual accounts, declare the final dividend based thereon (if any), deal with the election of directors, approve directors' remuneration and re-appoint the auditors, fixing the level of their remuneration.

Listed companies. See Section C.2 in the Appendix at the end of 43 PUBLIC AND LISTED COMPANIES for recommendations in the combined Code for constructive use of the AGM by listed companies.

33.2   Default in holding AGM

If default is made in holding a meeting under the provisions in 33.1 above, the company and every officer in default is liable to a fine up to the level in 40.1(*d*) PENALTIES. [*Sec 366(4), 24 Sch*].

Powers of the Secretary of State. Where there is default, the Secretary of State may, on the application of any member, call a meeting or direct that one be called. His directions may modify or supplement the company's articles and may include a direction that one member of the company (present in person or by proxy) constitutes a meeting. If default is made in complying with the direction, the company and every officer in default is liable to a fine up to the level in 40.1(*d*) PENALTIES. [*Sec 367(1)-(3), 24 Sch*].

A meeting thus called is deemed to be an AGM but if it is not held in the year of default it will only be the AGM for the actual year in which it is held if the company so resolves at the meeting. If it does so resolve, a copy of the resolution must be forwarded to the Registrar of Companies within 15 days of passing; otherwise the company and every officer in default is liable to a fine up to the level in 40.1(*f*) PENALTIES. [*Sec 367(4)(5), 24*

33.3 Meetings

Sch]. Voting rights at such a meeting are determined as at the date of the actual meeting (*Musselwhite v CH Musselwhite & Son Ltd [1962] Ch 964*).

33.3 Election by private company to dispense with AGM

A private company may by elective resolution (see 51.3 RESOLUTIONS) elect to dispense with the holding of AGMs. An election has effect for the year in which it is made and subsequent years but does not affect any liability already incurred to hold an AGM by reason of default.

In any year in which an AGM would be required but for the election, a member may, by notice not later than three months before the end of the year, require the holding of an AGM in which case the normal provisions in 33.1 and 33.2 above apply.

If the election ceases to have effect, the company need not hold an AGM in that year if, at that time, less than three months of the year remains (unless an AGM has already been requested by a member).

[*Sec 366A; CA 1989, s 115*].

33.4 EXTRAORDINARY GENERAL MEETINGS

All general meetings other than annual general meetings are called extraordinary general meetings. [*SI 1985 No 805, Table A, Art 36*].

The directors *may* call an EGM whenever they think fit. If there are insufficient directors in the UK to call such a meeting, any director or any member may call it [*SI 1985 No 805, Table A, Art 37*] or, where *CA 1948, Table A, Art 49* applies, any director or any two members may call it. Where there are no provisions in the company's articles with regard to the calling of an EGM, a meeting may be called by two or more members holding not less than one-tenth of the issued share capital (or not less than 5% in number of the members where the company does not have a share capital). [*Sec 370(3)*].

The directors *must* convene an EGM, notwithstanding the articles, when requested to do so by members of the company

- holding at least one-tenth of the paid-up capital carrying the right to vote at a general meeting; or

- in the case of a company not having a share capital, representing at least one-tenth of the total voting rights of all members having the right to vote at a general meeting.

In each case, the requirement must be fulfilled at the date the request is deposited with the directors. The request must state the object of the meeting, be signed by the requisitionists and deposited at the company's registered office. It may consist of several similar documents each signed by one or more requisitionists.

[*Sec 368(1)-(3)*].

If the directors

- do not proceed duly to convene a meeting within 21 days of the deposit of the request, or

- in the case of a meeting at which a special resolution is to be proposed, do not give the 21 days' notice required for such a resolution, or

- convene a meeting for a date more than 28 days after the date of notice convening the meeting the requisitionists (or any of them representing more than one-half of the total voting rights of them all) may convene a meeting themselves provided it is held within three months of the date of the original request. Any reasonable expenses incurred must be repaid to them by the company and recovered by the company from the directors in default. [*Sec 368(4)-(8); CA 1989, 19 Sch 9*].

Resigning auditors may request an EGM in certain circumstances. See 12.15 AUDI-TORS.

Serious loss of capital. Directors of a public company must call an EGM on becoming aware that the value of the company's net assets are half or less of its called-up share capital. See 58.30 SHARES AND SHARE CAPITAL.

Power of court to order meeting. The court, of its own motion or on the application of either any member who would be entitled to vote at the meeting or any director, may order a meeting of the company to be called. This power exists if for any reason it is impracticable to call or conduct a meeting in the normal manner. Ancillary directions may be given e.g. so that one member (whether in person or by proxy) is deemed to constitute a meeting. A meeting thus convened is deemed duly called etc. for all purposes. [*Sec 371*]. The power of the court, on application, to call a meeting cannot be used by one group of shareholders to defeat the class rights of another group. See *BML Group Ltd v Harman, The Times, 8 April 1994.*

For a case where the court exercised its discretion under these provisions, see *Re Sticky Fingers Restaurant Ltd [1991] BCC 754* where the only two directors and members of the company were in dispute and one was refusing to attend meetings so that the company was effectively deadlocked. The court stipulated that any director appointed at the meeting would not be allowed to act unless he gave specified undertakings designed to protect the existing directors (e.g. not to vote for their dismissal).

33.5 **NOTICE OF MEETING**

Apart from adjourned meetings, at least 21 days' notice must be given of an AGM or a meeting for the passing of a special resolution; other meetings require at least 14 days' notice (seven days' notice in the case of an unlimited company). Any provision for shorter notice in the articles is void. However, a meeting is deemed to have been duly called by shorter notice if it is agreed to by,

• in the case of an AGM, all members entitled to attend and vote at it; and

• in the case of any other meeting, a majority in number of the members having a right to attend and vote who together hold at least 95% in nominal value of the shares giving such a right (or, if the company has no share capital, 95% of the total voting rights).

A private company may, by elective resolution, substitute a lesser percentage for 95% (but not less than 90%). See 51.3 RESOLUTIONS.

[*Sec 369; CA 1989, s 115*].

Example of consent to short notice

'We, the undersigned, being all the members for the time being of the company having the right to attend and vote at the Extraordinary/Annual General Meeting of the company convened to be held at [insert place] on [insert date] at [insert time] (the attached notice being the notice convening the meeting), hereby agree

(*a*)   in accordance with section 369(3)(a) of the Companies Act 1985, to the holding of such meeting notwithstanding that less than the statutory period of notice thereof has been given; and

33.5 Meetings

(b) to accept service of documents in accordance with section 238(4) of the Companies Act 1985 notwithstanding that the said documents were sent less than 21 days before the meeting.

Dated this   day of   19

[name of member]   [name of member]'

The following provisions apply where a company has adopted the relevant articles in *Table A* in *SI 1985 No 805* or earlier equivalent.

- **Details to be given.** The notice should specify the time and place of the meeting and the general nature of the business to be transacted. See *Tiessen v Henderson [1899] 1 Ch 861*. The time and place of the meeting are at the discretion of the directors but this must be exercised in good faith. See *Cannon v Trask (1875) LR 20 Eq 669* where the company was restrained from bringing forward the date of a meeting before share transfers were registered to persons opposed to the board. Subject to the provisions of the articles and any restrictions imposed on any shares, the notice should be given to

  (i) all members;

  (ii) all persons entitled to a share in consequence of the death or bankruptcy of a member; and

  (iii) the directors and auditors.

  [*Table A, Art 38*].

- **Service of notice.** Notice of the meeting must be served on every member in the manner in which notices are required to be served by *Table A*. [*Sec 370(2)*]. It must therefore be in writing (other than notice calling a meeting of directors) and may be given personally, by prepaid post to the member's registered address, or by leaving it at that address. Proof of posting is conclusive evidence that the notice was given and a notice is deemed to be given 48 hours after the envelope containing it was posted. [*Table A, Arts 111, 112, 115*]. Under *CA 1948, Table A, Art 131*, notice is deemed to be given 24 hours after posting.

  Notice may be given to a *deceased member's personal representative* or *bankrupt member's trustee* by sending it to the address supplied by such person. Until such an address is supplied, notice may be given in any way as if the death or bankruptcy had not occurred. [*Table A, Art 116*].

  In the case of *joint shareholders*, notice must be given to the first-named holder in the register of members. [*Table A, Art 112*].

  A member whose registered address is not in the UK is only entitled to receive notice if he gives an address within the UK at which notices may be given to him. [*Table A, Art 112*].

  A member present at a meeting (in person or by proxy) is deemed to have received notice of the meeting and the purposes for which it is called. [*Table A, Art 113*].

  A shareholder is bound by any notice in respect of that share given to the previous holder before his name has been entered in the register of members. [*Table A, Art 114*].

  Accidental omission to give notice, or non-receipt of notice by any person, does not invalidate the proceedings at the meeting. [*Table A, Art 39*]. See *Re West Canadian Collieries Ltd [1962] Ch 370*. Failure to give notice under the mistaken belief that a person is not a shareholder for the purpose of a particular meeting is not an accidental omission (*Musselwhite and Another v CH Musselwhite & Son Ltd and Others [1962] Ch 964*).

Example of a notice for an annual general meeting

'Notice is hereby given that the Annual General Meeting of [insert name of company] will be held at [insert place of meeting] on [insert date] at [insert time].

BUSINESS

1   To receive and adopt the Directors' Report and the audited Accounts for the year/ period ended [insert date].

2   To re-elect [insert name] a director.

3   To confirm the directors' remuneration.

4   To declare a dividend.

5   To re-appoint the retiring auditors and authorise the directors to fix their remuneration.

Dated this   day of   19

By order of the Board

Secretary

Note. A member entitled to attend and vote is entitled to appoint a proxy to attend and on a poll vote in his/her place. Such proxy need not also be a member of the company.'

33.6   GENERAL PROVISIONS RELATING TO MEETINGS

The following provisions and those in 33.7 to 33.13 below apply in relation to meetings. Where *Table A* is given as the statutory reference, the provisions only apply to a company which has adopted the relevant articles in *SI 1985 No 805* or earlier equivalent.

33.7   Quorum

Unless the articles make other provision, two members personally present are a quorum. [*Sec 370(4)*]. Where, however, *Table A* has been adopted, two persons entitled to vote upon the business, each being a member, a proxy for a member or a duly authorised representative of a corporation, are a quorum. [*Table A, Art 40*].

If such a quorum is not present within half an hour of the appointed time for the meeting, or if during a meeting such a quorum is not present, the meeting must be adjourned. [*Table A, Art 41*]. Note that where *CA 1948, Table A, Art 53* applies, the quorum is only required to be present at the time when the meeting proceeds to business. If the subsequent departure of a member reduces the meeting below the necessary quorum this does not invalidate the proceedings after his departure (*In re Hartley Baird [1955] Ch 143*) unless only one shareholder remains (*Re London Flats Ltd [1969] 1 WLR 711*).

A meeting cannot be constituted by one person (*Sharp v Dawes (1876) 2 QBD 26*) even where that one person holds proxies (see 33.12 below) from other members (*Re Sanitary Carbon Co (1877) WN 223* where the shareholder present held proxies from all the other shareholders). See, however, *East v Bennett Bros Ltd [1911] 1 Ch 163* where there was only one shareholder of a particular class.

Single member private companies. Notwithstanding any of the above (including any provisions in the company's articles) where, after 14 July 1992, a private company limited by shares or guarantee has only one member, that member present in person or by proxy is a quorum. [*Sec 370A; SI 1992 No 1699*].

33.8 Meetings

33.8 Chairman and directors

Chairman. Unless the articles make other provision, any member elected by the members present at a meeting may be chairman of it. [*Sec 370(5)*]. Where, however, *Table A* has been adopted, the chairman, if any, of the board of directors or in his absence some other director nominated or elected by the directors presides as chairman of the meeting. If no director is willing to act or is present within 15 minutes of the appointed time for the meeting, the members present and entitled to vote must chose one of their number to be chairman. [*Table A, Arts 42, 43*].

Directors. A director, even if not a member, is entitled to attend and speak at any general meeting and any separate meeting of the holders of any class of shares. [*Table A, Art 44*].

33.9 Adjournment of meeting

The chairman may adjourn the meeting but no business can be transacted at an adjourned meeting other than business which might properly have been transacted at the meeting had no adjournment taken place. Where a meeting is adjourned for 14 days or more, at least seven clear days' notice must be given of the adjourned meeting. Otherwise it is not necessary to give any such notice. [*Table A, Art 45*]. Where *CA 1948, Table A, Art 57* applies, notice is only required if the meeting is adjourned for 30 days or more, in which case notice must be given as for the original meeting.

A chairman cannot adjourn a meeting at his own will and pleasure. If he no longer wishes to take part, the meeting itself can resolve to go on and appoint a new chairman (*National Dwellings Society v Sykes [1894] 3 Ch 159*).

33.10 Votes of members

Unless the articles make other provision, in the case of a company originally having a share capital, every member has one vote in respect of each share or each £10 of stock he holds; and in any other case every member has one vote. [*Sec 370(6)*].

Where, however, *Table A* has been adopted, subject to any restrictions attached to any shares, on a show of hands every member who (being an individual) is *present in person* and every duly represented corporation (see 33.13 below) has one vote. On a poll (see 33.11 below), every member has one vote for every share of which he is the holder [*Table A, Art 54*] and votes may be given personally or by proxy (see 33.12 below). [*Table A, Art 59*]. Where a member has more than one vote, he need not use all the votes or cast all the votes he uses in the same way. [*Sec 374*].

Joint holders. The vote of the senior holder who tenders a vote (in person or by proxy) must be accepted to the exclusion of other joint holders. Seniority is decided by the order in which names stand in the register of members. [*Table A, Art 55*].

Mental disorder. A member in respect of whom a court order has been made concerning mental disorder may vote by his receiver, *curator bonis* or other person authorised by the court. Evidence of authority must be deposited at least 48 hours before the meeting at the registered office or such other place as is specified. [*Table A, Art 56*].

Unpaid calls. No member can vote at a meeting in respect of any share unless all moneys presently payable by him on that share have been fully paid. [*Table A, Art 57*].

Objections to voters. An objection to the qualification of a voter may only be raised at the meeting in question. Any vote not disallowed at the meeting is valid. The chairman's decision on any objection is final and conclusive. [*Table A, Art 58*]. See also *Wall v London and Northern Assets Corporation [1899] 2 Ch 550* and *Wall v Exchange Investment Corporation [1926] Ch 143*.

Bankruptcy. Unless there is any contrary provision in the articles, a bankrupt still remains a member of the company as long as his name appears on the register and his trustee in bankruptcy has not secured registration in his own name (*Morgan and Another v Gray and Others [1953] Ch 83*).

33.11 Voting procedure

Unless a poll is demanded, a resolution put to the vote is decided on a show of hands. The declaration by the chairman that the resolution has been carried or lost and an entry to that effect in the minutes is then conclusive evidence of the fact, without proof of the number of votes recorded. [*Table A, Arts 46, 47*]. Where no poll is demanded, a resolution is passed on a show of hands even if, on a poll, a different result would have been obtained (*Re Horbury Bridge Coal, Iron and Waggon Co (1879) 11 ChD 109*).

A poll may be demanded on any question, other than the election of the chairman or the adjournment of the meeting, by

(*a*)   at least five members having the right to vote at the meeting,

(*b*)   by a member or members representing at least one-tenth of the total voting rights of all members having the right to vote at the meeting, or

(*c*)   by a member or members holding shares conferring a right to vote at the meeting being shares on which an aggregate sum has been paid up equal to at least one-tenth of the total sum paid up on all such shares,

and any provision in the company's articles which excludes this right is void. [*Sec 373(1)*]. Where *Table A, Art 46* has been adopted, a poll may be demanded on *any* resolution put to the meeting and the number of members required under (*a*) above is reduced to two. The chairman may also demand a poll.

The instrument appointing a proxy to vote (see 33.12 below) is deemed also to confer authority to demand a poll. [*Sec 373(2)*].

The demand may be withdrawn before the poll with the consent of the chairman. If withdrawn, this does not affect the result of any previous show of hands. [*Table A, Art 48*].

The demand does not prevent the continuation of the meeting for any other business. [*Table A, Art 51*].

A poll is taken as the chairman directs. [*Table A, Art 49*]. It must be held directly on the election of a chairman or on a question of adjournment. Otherwise it may be taken as the chairman directs but not more than 30 days after it is demanded. [*Table A, Art 51*]. If the time and place for the poll is announced at the meeting, no further notice is required. Otherwise, seven clear days' notice must be given. [*Table A, Art 52*]. Where *CA 1948, Table A, Art 61* applies, there is no 30 days' time limit or requirement for seven days' notice.

Equality of votes. In such a case, whether on a show of hands or a poll, the chairman has a casting vote in addition to any other vote he may have. [*Table A, Art 50*].

33.12 Proxies

Any member entitled to attend and vote at a meeting (whether a general meeting or a meeting of any class of members) is entitled to appoint another person (whether a member or not) to attend and vote for him as his proxy. In the case of a private company, the proxy has the same right as the member to speak at the meeting. [*Sec 372(1)(7)*].

Unless, however, the articles provide otherwise,

● this does not apply to a company not having a share capital;

33.12 Meetings

- a member of a private company is not entitled to appoint more than one proxy to attend on the same occasion (where *Table A, Art 59* is adopted this is specifically allowed); and

- a proxy is not entitled to vote except upon a poll.

[Sec 372(2)].

Notice calling a meeting must state with reasonable prominence that a member is entitled to appoint a proxy or proxies and that a proxy need not also be a member. If not, the company and every officer in default is liable to a fine up to the level in 40.1(g) PENALTIES. *[Sec 372(3)(4), 24 Sch]*.

Any provision in the articles requiring a proxy form to be lodged more than 48 hours before the meeting is void. *[Sec 372(5)]*. Where *Table A, Art 62* has been adopted, it must be deposited not less than 48 hours before the meeting or, where a poll is demanded but not taken immediately

- if taken more than 48 hours after it is demanded, not less than 24 hours before the poll; and

- if taken 48 hours or less after it was demanded, at the meeting at which the poll was demanded.

A company may, at its own expense, issue proxy forms inviting members to appoint a person, or one of a number of persons, as their proxy. Unless it does this at the written request of a member and the form is available on request to every member, it must send the forms to *all* members otherwise every officer who knowingly and wilfully authorised or permits their issues is liable to a fine up to the level in 40.1(g) PENALTIES.

[Sec 372(6), 24 Sch].

Where *Table A, Arts 60, 61* have been adopted, the instrument appointing the proxy must be in writing, executed by the appointor and in the following form (or as near thereto as circumstances allow).

Examples of proxy forms

General proxy
ABC plc/Limited

I/We,   of
being a member/members of the above-named company, hereby appoint
                                    of
, or failing him,·
                                    of
as my/our proxy to vote in my/our name[s] and on my/our behalf at the annual/ extraordinary general meeting of the company to be held on   19   , and at any adjournment thereof.

Signed on   19

Specific proxy
ABC plc/Limited

I/We,   of
being a member/members of the above-named company, hereby appoint
                                    of
, or failing him,
                                    of
as my/our proxy to vote in my/our name[s] and on my/our behalf at the annual/ extraordinary general meeting of the company to be held on   19   , and at any adjournment thereof.

This form is to be used in respect of the resolutions mentioned below as follows.

Resolution No 1 *for *against
Resolution No 2 *for *against

*Strike out whichever is not desired.

Unless otherwise instructed, the proxy may vote as he thinks fit or abstain from voting.

Signed this   day of   19

Withdrawal of proxies. An authority to vote by proxy at a meeting can be withdrawn by serving notice of determination on the company at its registered office, or the same place as the proxy was deposited, before the relevant meeting or poll. Otherwise, a vote given or poll demanded by proxy is valid despite any previous (unreceived) determination. [*Table A, Art 63*]. Where a shareholder has given a proxy, in the absence of any special circumstances or any special contract expressly excluding the right to vote in person, his right to vote at a meeting is paramount to the right of the proxy to vote (*Cousins v International Brick Co Ltd [1931] 2 Ch 90*).

Listed companies. A proxy form must be sent with the notice convening a meeting of holders of the listed securities to each person entitled to vote at the meeting. The proxy form must provide for two-way voting on all resolutions (except procedural resolutions) and must state that a shareholder is entitled to appoint a proxy of his choice (providing a space for the insertion of the name of such proxy). The proxy form must also state that if it is returned without an indication as to how the proxy shall vote on any particular matter, the proxy will exercise his discretion as to whether, and if so how, he votes. Where the resolutions to be proposed include the re-election of retiring directors and if the number of retiring directors standing for re-election exceeds five, the proxy must give each shareholder the opportunity to vote for or against the re-election of the retiring directors as a whole but must also allow votes to be cast for or against the re-election of them individually. (*The Listing Rules, Chapter 13.28, 13.29*).

33.13 Representation of corporations at meetings

A corporation (whether a company or not) which is a member of a company may, by resolution of the directors or governing body, authorise any person to act as its representative at any general or class meeting of the company. The person so authorised is entitled to exercise the same powers as the corporation could exercise if it were an individual shareholder. [*Sec 375*].

Example of resolution appointing a representative

'That pursuant to section 375 of the Companies Act 1985 [insert name of representative] be and hereby is appointed to act as the company's representative at any general or class meeting of the members of [insert name of company]. The appointment shall remain in force until the company shall resolve otherwise or until [insert name of representative] ceases to be an officer of the company.'

33.14 DIRECTORS' MEETINGS

There are no provisions in *CA 1985* with regard to the holding of directors' meetings and, subject to the terms of the articles, the directors may regulate their proceedings as they think fit. The provisions in *Table A* relating to proceedings of directors outlined below may or may not be incorporated into a company's articles.

33.14 Meetings

A director may (and the secretary at the request of a director must) call a meeting of directors. Notice need not be given to a director who is outside the UK.

[*Table A, Art 88*].

Quorum. The quorum may be fixed by the directors and unless so fixed is two. A person who holds office only as an alternate director (see 19.23 DIRECTORS) is counted in the quorum if his appointor is not present but a director is not to be counted in the quorum in relation to any resolution on which he is not entitled to vote (see below). If the number of continuing directors is less than the quorum, they may act only for the purpose of filling vacancies or calling a general meeting. [*Table A, Arts 89, 90, 95*].

Chairman. The directors may appoint a chairman and remove him from office at any time. The director so appointed presides at the meetings at which he is present. If no director holds that office, or if he is unwilling to preside or is not present within five minutes of the appointed time of any meeting, the directors present may appoint one of their number to be chairman for the meeting. [*Table A, Art 91*].

Voting. Questions arising at the meeting are decided by a majority of votes, with the chairman having a second and casting vote if required. A director who is an alternate director (see 19.23 DIRECTORS), in the absence of his appointor, is entitled to a vote on behalf of his appointor in addition to his own vote. If a question arises during a meeting as to the right of a director to vote, the matter may be referred to the chairman before the conclusion of the meeting and his ruling in relation to any director other than himself is final and conclusive. [*Table A, Arts 88, 98*].

A director must not vote at a meeting on any resolution concerning a matter in which he, or a person connected with him, has, directly or indirectly, a material interest or duty which conflicts with the interests of the company. This does not apply in the following cases.

- Where the resolution relates to the giving to him of a guarantee, security or indemnity in respect of money lent to him, or an obligation incurred by him, for the benefit of the company or any of its subsidiaries.

- Where the resolution relates to the giving to a third party of a guarantee, security or indemnity in respect of an obligation of the company or any of its subsidiaries for which the director has assumed responsibility in whole or part.

- Where his interest arises by virtue of his agreeing to subscribe for any shares, debentures or securities of the company or its subsidiaries or by virtue of his underwriting an offer of any such shares etc.

- Where the resolution relates in any way to an approved retirement benefits scheme.

In the case of an alternate director, the interest of the appointor is treated as his interest.

[*Table A, Art 94*].

A company may by ordinary resolution suspend or relax, either generally or in respect of a particular matter, any provision of the articles prohibiting a director from voting at a meeting of directors. [*Table A, Art 96*].

Acts done by directors' meetings. Where following a meeting of directors it is discovered that there was a defect in the appointment of a director or that any of them were disqualified from holding office or had vacated office or were not entitled to vote, all acts done by that meeting are as valid as if there was no defect etc. [*Table A, Art 92*].

Written resolutions signed by all directors entitled to receive notice of a directors' meeting are as valid as if passed at a duly convened meeting. [*Table A, Art 93*]. This, however, does not override the requirement that a quorum exists for board meetings (see above). For example, where the quorum to conduct business is two directors, a written resolution signed by one director is invalid even if the only other director is outside the UK and not entitled to receive notice of the meeting (see *Hood Sailmakers Ltd v Axford and another [1996] 4 All ER 830*).

Listed companies. See 43.11(*b*) PUBLIC AND LISTED COMPANIES for the obligation to notify the Company Announcements Office of certain dates of, and decisions at, board meetings and 43 Appendix for provisions of the Combined Code relating to board meetings.

33.15 MINUTES OF MEETINGS

Every company must keep minutes of all general meetings, directors' meetings and, where there are managers, all managers' meetings in books kept for those purposes. If it does not, the company and every officer in default is liable to a fine up to the level in 40.1(*f*) PENALTIES.

Any such minutes, if purported to be signed by the chairman (either of the actual or next succeeding meeting), is evidence of the proceedings and, until the contrary is proved, the meeting is deemed duly held and convened and all proceedings and appointments are deemed valid.

[*Sec 382, 24 Sch*].

A company which has adopted *Table A, Art 100* similarly has an obligation to keep minutes of all appointments of officers made by the company and all proceedings at meetings of the company, holders of any class of shares, directors and committees of directors. The names of directors present at each such meeting must also be recorded.

Form of minute book. See 45.5 RECORDS.

Inspection of minute book. The minute books containing the minutes of proceedings of general meetings held after 31 October 1929 must be kept at the company's registered office and must be open to inspection by any member free of charge for not less than two hours during the period 9a.m. to 5p.m. every Monday to Friday (other than public and bank holidays). A person inspecting the minutes must be permitted to copy any information made available by taking notes or making a transcript but the company is not obliged to provide any additional facilities other than those to facilitate inspection. Any member is entitled to a copy of any such minutes within seven days of request on payment of a maximum fee (see 26.2 FEES).

If inspection is refused or a copy not sent within the proper time, the company and every officer in default is liable in respect of each offence to a fine up to the limit in 40.1(*g*) PENALTIES. The court may also enforce the provisions.

[*Sec 383, 24 Sch; SI 1991 No 1998*].

Single-member private companies. Where the sole member takes any decision which may be taken by the company in general meeting, he must provide the company with a written record of the decision. See 51.11 RESOLUTIONS.

34 Members

Cross-references. See 14 CLASS RIGHTS; 57 SHARE TRANSFERS ETC.; 58 SHARES AND SHARE CAPITAL.

34.1 DEFINITION AND GENERAL

The *'members'* of a company are

- the subscribers to the company's memorandum (who are deemed to have agreed to become members), and

- all other persons who agree to become members of the company

and whose names are entered in the register of members (see 47.4 REGISTERS). [*Sec 22*].

Except in relation to share qualifications for directors (see 19.7 DIRECTORS) the bearer of a share warrant may, if the articles so provide, be deemed a member of the company, either to the full extent or for any purposes defined in the articles. [*Sec 355(5)*].

Who may be members.

- A *company* may hold shares in *another* company if authorised to do so in its memorandum of association (*Re Barned's Banking Co (1867) LR 3 Ch App 105*). See ACQUISITION OF OWN SHARES (8) for restrictions on a company subscribing for or purchasing its own shares and 8.22 for prohibition of a company being a member of its own holding company.

- In England and Wales, *minors* (i.e. persons under the age of 18) may become shareholders unless the articles forbid this. On reaching majority, the minor may repudiate the contract and avoid liability for future calls but cannot recover money paid for the allotment of the shares as there has not been a total failure of consideration (*Steinberg v Scala (Leeds) Ltd [1923] 2 Ch 452*). In Scotland, under *Age of Legal Capacity (Scotland) Act 1991*, with effect from 25 September 1991, a person has full legal capacity from the age of 16 subject to the right, while under the age of 21, to apply to the court for the setting aside of a 'prejudicial transaction' which was entered into between the ages of 16 and 18. Prior to the age of 16, contracts made will be void subject to an exception where the terms of the contract are not unreasonable and the subject matter is of a kind commonly entered into by someone of his or her age and circumstances.

- A *bankrupt* may continue to be a shareholder even after his beneficial interest has vested in the trustee in bankruptcy, unless the articles provide otherwise. He must, however vote as directed by the trustee.

- *Personal representatives and trustees in bankruptcy.* See 57.15 SHARE TRANSFERS.

- *Partnerships*, even though not legal persons in England and Wales, may be registered as members under the partnership name (*Weikerheim's Case (1873) 8 Ch App 831*).

Trustees. In the case of companies registered in England and Wales, no notice of any trust (express, implied or constructive) must be entered on the register of members. [*Sec 360*]. Where *Table A* has been adopted, there is a more general rule that, except as required by law, no person must be recognised by the company as holding shares upon trust and, except as required by law or as provided by the articles, the company is not bound by (and must not recognise) any interest in any share except an absolute right to the entirety thereof in the holder. [*SI 1985 No 805, Table A, Art 5*]. The company is not therefore required to enquire as to whether any transfer is within the powers of the trustees and is not liable for registering a transfer which is in breach of trust (*Simpson v Molson's Bank [1895] AC 270*). Equally, as the company cannot recognise any interest of a beneficiary in the shares, it has no lien on shares held by trustees for a debt due to it by a beneficiary (*Re Perkins (1890) 24 QBD 613*).

34.2 MINIMUM AND MAXIMUM MEMBERSHIP

A private company limited by shares or by guarantee may have one member and any enactment or rule of law which applies in relation to such a company applies, in the absence of any express provision to the contrary, with such modification as is necessary. [*Sec 1(3A); SI 1992 No 1699*]. Any other company must have at least two members [*Sec 1(1)*] and if it carries on business without having at least two members for more than six months, a person who is a member of the company and knows that it is carrying on a business with only one member is liable (jointly and severally with the company) for the payment of the company's debts contracted after that period and whilst a member of the company. [*Sec 24; SI 1992 No 1699*]. A person who, before 15 July 1992, was liable for the debts of a private company limited by shares or guarantee under this provision is not liable for any debts contracted for on or after that date. [*SI 1992 No 1699*].

There is no maximum number of members except that where a private company has adopted *CA 1948, Table A, Part II, Art 2*, there is an upper limit of 50 members (excluding employees and past employees who held when employed, and have continued to hold, shares in the company). For these purposes, joint holders are treated as a single member. There is no equivalent article in *Table A* in *SI 1985 No 805*.

34.3 MEMBERS' RIGHTS

No member has any right to any item of property owned by the company for he has no legal or equitable interest in it. The company's assets are its own property not the property of its members. See *In Re George Newman & Co [1895] 1 Ch 674* and *Short v Treasury Commissioners [1947] 2 All ER 298* where it was held that shareholders are not, in the eye of the law, part owners of the undertaking which is something different from the totality of the shareholding. Neither does a member have an insurable interest in any particular assets which the company holds (*Macaura v Northern Assurance Co Ltd [1925] AC 619*). A member is merely entitled to a *share* in the company and shares are merely a right of participation in the company on the terms of the articles of association (*Prudential Assurance Co Ltd v Newman Industries Ltd (No 2) [1982] 1 All ER 354*). In that case it was held that a shareholder had no personal claim against a person whose actions had reduced the company's profits because the shares themselves were not directly affected and the right of participation remained intact.The correct action is one in the name of the company in respect of the loss or damage caused to it.

See also 27.3 FORMATION for the company as a separate legal person and 11.5 ARTICLES OF ASSOCIATION for the contractual effect of the articles between members and between company and its members.

Members are given many rights under *CA 1985* including the right to

- receive and demand copies of the annual accounts (see 3.3 and 3.4 ACCOUNTS: GENERAL);

- receive notice of, attend, vote at, and in certain circumstances requisition, meetings of the company (see 33 MEETINGS);

- inspect the statutory registers (see 47 REGISTERS), minute books (see 33.15 MEETINGS), and directors' service contracts (see 19.55 DIRECTORS);

- receive copies of the articles (see 11.10 ARTICLES OF ASSOCIATION) and memorandum of association (see 35.11 MEMORANDUM OF ASSOCIATION);

- require the company to circulate resolutions (see 51.7 RESOLUTIONS);

- receive dividends if declared (see 23.14 DISTRIBUTIONS);

- object to the payment for the redemption or purchase of the company's shares out of capital (see 8.16 ACQUISITION OF OWN SHARES);

- object to any alteration in the memorandum (see 35.8 MEMORANDUM OF ASSOCIATION);

- apply to the court for a meeting following a proposed compromise with members and/or creditors (see 44.1 RECONSTRUCTIONS AND MERGERS);

- apply to the court following the re-registration of a public company as a private company (see 49.12 REGISTRATION AND RE-REGISTRATION);

- be bought out following a takeover offer where the offeror holds at least 90% of the shares (see 59.23 TAKEOVER OFFERS);

- petition the court for the winding up of the company under *IA 1986, s 124*; and

- apply to the Secretary of State to appoint an inspector to investigate the company's affairs (see 31 INVESTIGATIONS).

Rights of members to damages, etc. A person is not debarred from obtaining damages or other compensation from a company by reason only that he holds, or has held,

- shares in the company; or

- any right to subscribe for shares or to be included in the company's register in respect of shares.

[*Sec 111A; CA 1989, s 131*].

34.4 MEMBERS' LIABILITIES

Apart from the liability under 34.2 above for carrying on business without the minimum number of members, the principal liabilities of a member are as follows.

- To pay any outstanding amounts or calls on his shares as required by the company (see 58.8 SHARES AND SHARE CAPITAL). If the articles of the company provide, a member's shares may be forfeited for non-payment (see 58.11 SHARES AND SHARE CAPITAL).

- In the event of a winding up, to contribute to the assets of the company in respect of any amounts unpaid on his shares. [*IA 1986, s 74*]. For the liability of members of companies limited by guarantee, see 29.2 GUARANTEE COMPANIES.

34.5 PROTECTION OF MINORITY INTERESTS

Foss v Harbottle (1843) 2 Hare 461 established the fundamental rule that to redress a wrong done to a company or to recover moneys or damages due to it, action must *prima facie* be brought by the company itself. Subsequent case law, however, established exceptions to the rule in *Foss v Harbottle* for the protection of minority interests. These were summarised in *Burland v Earle [1902] AC 83* as applying where the persons against whom the relief is sought themselves control the majority of shares in the company and will not permit an action to be brought in the company's name. In such a case the courts will permit the complaining shareholder to bring an action in the company's name. In such an action, however, the plaintiff cannot have a larger right to relief than the company itself would have if it were the plaintiff, and cannot complain of acts which are valid if done with the approval of the majority of shareholders. The cases in which the minority can maintain such an action are, therefore, confined to the following.

- Where the acts complained of are of a fraudulent character or *ultra vires*. See *Simpson v Westminster Palace Hotel Co (1860) 8 HL Cas 712* and *Russell v Wakefield Waterworks Co (1875) LR 20 Eq 474.*

- Where the matter is one which could only validly be done or sanctioned, not by a simple majority, but only by a special majority, see *Cotter v National Union of Seamen [1929] 2 Ch 58* and *Edwards v Halliwell [1950] 2 All ER 1064.*

- Where the rights of an individual member have been infringed, see *Pender v Lushington (1877) 6 ChD 70.*

- Where the majority are endeavouring to appropriate to themselves money, property or advantage which belongs to the company or in which the other shareholders are entitled to participate i.e. a fraud on the minority. See *Atwool v Merryweather (1867) LR 5 Eq 464* and *Burland v Earle* above.

34.6   Protection of members against unfair prejudice

Application may be made to the court by petition by

(*a*)   a member of a company (including a statutory water company), or

(*b*)   the Secretary of State where he has received a report under *Sec 437* (see 31.3 INVESTIGATIONS) or exercised his powers under *Secs 447* or *448* (see 31.11 and 31.12 INVESTIGATIONS)

on the grounds that

- the company's affairs are being, or have been, conducted in a manner which is unfairly prejudicial to the interests of its members generally or of some part of its members (including under (*a*) above at least the member bringing the petition); or

- any actual or proposed act or omission of the company (including an act or omission on its behalf) is, or would be, so prejudicial.

Included under (*a*) above is a person who is not a member of the company but to whom shares in the company have been transferred or transmitted by operation of the law.

The powers of the Secretary of State to make an application under (*b*) above may be used in addition to, or instead of, the presentation of a winding-up petition against the company.

[*Secs 459, 460; CA 1989, 19 Sch 11, 24 Sch; Water Act 1989, 25 Sch 71*].

See also *Meyer v Scottish Co-operative Wholesale Society CS 1954 SC 381* and *Scottish Co-operative Wholesale Society v Meyer [1959] AC 324; Re HR Harmer Ltd [1959] 1 WLR 62; Re a Company [1983] 2 All ER 36; Re a Company [1983] 2 All ER 854;* and *Re Bird Precision Bellows Ltd [1985] 3 All ER 523.*

The above procedures are not available to a company's majority shareholders, having the power to procure the passing of any resolution of the company, in order to force the minority shareholder to give up his investment (*Morris and others v Hateley and another, The Times, 10 March 1999*).

34.7   Provisions relating to petitions

The petition under 34.6 above must be in the form set out in *The Companies (Unfair Prejudice Applications) Proceedings Rules 1986 (SI 1986 No 2000)* with such variations, if any, as circumstances require. It must specify the grounds on which it is presented and the nature of the relief sought and be delivered to the court for filing with sufficient copies for service as below. The court must fix a hearing for a day (the 'return day') on which the petitioner and any respondent (including the company) must attend before the registrar in chambers for directions to be given in relation to the procedure on the petition. On fixing the return day, the court must return to the petitioner sealed copies of the petition, each endorsed with the return day and the time of the hearing, for service on the company and, in a petition under 34.6(*a*) above, every respondent named in the petition. This must be done at least 14 days before the return day.

The court must give such directions as it thinks appropriate with respect to service and advertisement of the petition; whether particulars of claim and defence are to be delivered; the manner in which evidence is to be given at the hearing; and generally as to the procedure on the petition and the hearing and disposal of the petition.

[*SI 1986 No 2000, Rules 1-5*].

Following the hearing, if the court is satisfied that a petition is well founded, it may make such order as it thinks fit to give relief including

(*a*)　regulating the conduct of the company's future affairs;

(*b*)　requiring a company to refrain from doing an act complained of or to do an act which it has omitted to do;

(*c*)　authorising civil proceedings to be brought in the name and on behalf of the company by such persons as it directs;

(*d*)　providing for the purchase of the shares of any member by other members or the company itself and, in the latter case, the reduction of the company's share capital accordingly;

(*e*)　requiring the company not to make an alteration in its memorandum or articles (in which case the company does not then have the power to make any such alteration in breach of that requirement without leave of the court); or

(*f*)　making an alteration in the company's memorandum or articles (in which case the alteration has effect as if duly made by resolution of the company).

An office copy of any order altering, or giving leave to alter, a company's memorandum or articles must, within 14 days from the making of the order or such longer period as the court allows, be delivered to the Registrar of Companies for registration. In default, the company and every officer in default is liable to a fine up to the level in 40.1(*f*) PENALTIES.

[*Sec 461, 24 Sch*].

When an order has been made, the petitioner and every other person who has appeared at the hearing must, not later than the business day following that on which the order is made, leave at the court all documents required to enable the order to be completed forthwith. The court may also give directions that the order should be advertised. [*SI 1986 No 2000, Rule 6*].

35   Memorandum of Association

Cross-references. See 11 ARTICLES OF ASSOCIATION; 49.1 and 49.2 REGISTRATION AND RE-REGISTRATION for registration of the memorandum.

The contents of this chapter are as follows.

35.1   INTRODUCTION

A company's memorandum of association is its constitution, which regulates its *external* relations, including the objects that it may legitimately pursue. The regulations governing a company's *internal* management are contained in its ARTICLES OF ASSOCIATION (11).

35.2   CONTENTS OF THE MEMORANDUM

The memorandum of a company *must* state the following.

(*a*)   The name of the company. [*Sec 2(1)(a)*]. See 36.1 to 36.8 NAMES AND BUSINESS NAMES.

(*b*)   If applicable, that the company is to be a public company. [*Sec 1(3)*]. Where a private company is to be re-registered as a public company (or vice versa) the special resolution effecting the change must also alter the company's memorandum accordingly. See 49.4 and 49.11 REGISTRATION AND RE-REGISTRATION.

(*c*)   Whether the REGISTERED OFFICE (46) of the company is to be situated in England and Wales or in Scotland. Alternatively, the memorandum may contain a statement that the registered office is to be situated in Wales. A company whose registered office is situated in Wales may alter its memorandum by special resolution so as to provide that its registered office is to be so situated. Apart from this provision, the registered office clause cannot be altered. [*Sec 2(1)(b)(2)*].

(*d*)   The objects of the company. [*Sec 2(1)(c)*]. Broadly, a company's objects clause sets out the business which the company may transact and the powers that the company may exercise in the carrying out of that business. The significance of the objects clause is that it defines the extent of a company's legal capacity. The act of a company outside the scope of its objects has been held to be void as *ultra vires* the company (*Ashbury Railway Carriage and Iron Co v Riche (1875) LR 7 HL 653*). In *Rolled Steel Products (Holdings) Ltd v British Steel Corporation [1985] 3 All ER 52*, a distinction was drawn between an act outside the capacity of the company (*ultra vires* and therefore void) and an act within the capacity of the company but beyond the powers of the directors (not *ultra vires* but possibly unenforceable). *Ultra vires* is a complex subject and a detailed analysis is beyond the scope of this book. For other cases concerning the doctrine of *ultra vires*, see *Cotman v Brougham [1918] AC 514* and *Introductions Ltd v National Provincial Bank Ltd [1970] Ch 199* (powers and objects); *Bell Houses Ltd v City Wall Properties Ltd [1966] 2 QB 656;* and *Re David Payne & Co Ltd [1904] 2 Ch 608* and *Sinclair v Brougham [1914] AC 398* (borrowing powers). In any case, the effects of the doctrine have already been mitigated and reformed by *Secs 35, 35A*. See 16.1 DEALINGS WITH THIRD PARTIES.

Where a company's memorandum states that the object of the company is to carry on business as a general commercial company, then

- the object of the company is to carry on any trade or business whatsoever; and

- the company has power to do all such things as are incidental or conducive to the carrying on of any trade or business by it.

[*Sec 3A; CA 1989, s 110*].

See 35.7 below for alteration of the company's objects.

(*e*)   In the case of a company limited by shares or by guarantee, that the liability of its members is limited. [*Sec 2(3)*]. Where a limited company is to be re-registered as an unlimited company (or vice versa) the necessary alteration must be made to the memorandum (see 49.9 and 49.10 REGISTRATION AND RE-REGISTRATION respectively).

(*f*)   In the case of a company having a share capital, other than an unlimited company, the 'amount' of the share capital with which the company proposes to be registered (not less than £50,000 in the case of a public company) and the division of the share capital into shares of a 'fixed amount'. [*Secs 2(5)(a), 11, 118*]. '*Amount*' means a monetary amount which may be stated in any currency. The amount of a company's share capital does not have to be stated as an aggregate total, but can (for example) be stated as so many pounds sterling, US dollars, and Swiss francs. The '*fixed amount*' of a share cannot be stated in two currencies, but it may be stated in different currencies for different shares (*Re Scandinavian Bank Group plc [1987] 2 All ER 70*).

See 58.14 to 58.16 SHARES AND SHARE CAPITAL for the provisions of *Secs 121* to *123* which enable a company to alter the conditions of its memorandum with respect to share capital. See also 58.17 to 58.22 SHARES AND SHARE CAPITAL for the alteration of the memorandum to allow a reduction in share capital.

See also 29.2 GUARANTEE COMPANIES for a required clause in such a company regarding liability of members for contributions to the company's assets if the company is wound up.

In addition to the above compulsory requirements, the memorandum may include other conditions.

35.3 **FORM OF THE MEMORANDUM**

The memorandum of a company must be in the form specified for that type of company in regulations made by the Secretary of State by statutory instrument, or as near that form as circumstances permit. [*Sec 3*]. The current statutory forms of memoranda are as follows.

Table B   Private company limited by shares
Table C   Company limited by guarantee and not having a share capital
Table D   Part I   Public company limited by guarantee and having a share capital
           Part II Private company limited by guarantee and having a share capital
Table E   Unlimited company having a share capital
Table F   Public company limited by shares

[*SI 1985 No 805*].

35.4   SUBSCRIBERS OF THE MEMORANDUM

There must be at least two subscribers to the memorandum except that, after 14 July 1992, only one person is required to subscribe his name to the memorandum of a company being formed as a private company limited by shares or guarantee. [*Sec 1(1)(3A); SI 1992 No 1699*]. Each subscriber must sign the memorandum in the presence of at least one witness who must attest the signature; such attestation is sufficient in Scotland as well as in England and Wales. [*Sec 2(6)*]. No subscriber to the memorandum may take less than one share, and there must be shown in the memorandum against the name of each subscriber the number of shares he takes. [*Sec 2(5)(b)(c)*].

Each of Tables B to F referred to in 35.3 above contains, at the end of the statutory clauses, a subscription table setting out the name and address of, and the number of shares to be taken by, each subscriber. The format of this table must be followed.

35.5   EFFECT OF THE MEMORANDUM

Subject to the provisions of *CA 1985*, the memorandum, when registered, binds the company and its members to the same extent as if it had been signed and sealed by each member, and contained covenants on the part of each member to observe all the provisions of the memorandum. [*Sec 14(1)*]. This provision also applies to the company's articles. See 11.5 ARTICLES OF ASSOCIATION for a consideration of decided cases on the nature of the relationship created by *Sec 14(1)*, the principles explained being equally applicable to the memorandum of association.

Money payable by a member to the company under the memorandum is a debt due from him to the company and, in England and Wales, is of the nature of a specialty debt i.e. created by deed. [*Sec 14(2)*].

A subscriber to the memorandum is deemed to have agreed to become a member of the company (see 34.1 MEMBERS) and, on registration of the memorandum, must be, and is entitled to be, entered as a member in the register of members. A subscriber is automatically entitled to the number of shares he has agreed to subscribe, even if the company does not allot the shares to him or does not enter his name in the register (*Evans' Case (1867) LR 2 Ch App 427*). He is not, however, liable to take them up if the company does not allot them to him and the whole of the share capital is allotted to other persons (*Mackley's Case (1875) 1 Ch D 247* and *Baytrust Holdings Limited v IRC [1971] 1 WLR 1333*) as the company cannot complete its side of the bargain.

35.6   ALTERATION OF THE MEMORANDUM

A company may only alter its memorandum as provided for by *CA 1985*. [*Sec 2(7)*].

Any condition contained in a company's memorandum which could lawfully have been contained in articles of association instead of in the memorandum may be altered by the company by special resolution except that

- if an application is made to the court for the alteration to be cancelled, the alteration only has effect in so far as the court confirms it;

- any alteration is subject to 35.8 below and *Secs 459-461* (court order protecting minorities, see 34.6 and 34.7 MEMBERS); and

- the provisions do not apply where the memorandum itself provides for or prohibits the alteration of all or any such conditions, and does not authorise any variation or abrogation of the special rights of any class of members.

[*Sec 17(1)(2)*].

35.7 Memorandum of Association

See 35.8 below for the procedure for objecting to alterations and 35.9 below for filing requirements with the Registrar of Companies.

35.7 Alteration of a company's objects

A company may by special resolution alter its memorandum with respect to the statement of its objects.

[Sec 4(1); CA 1989, s 110].

The validity of an alteration in the company's objects can only be questioned, in proceedings taken for that purpose (either under 35.8 below or otherwise) within 21 days of the date of the resolution, on the grounds that it was not authorised under the above provisions. *[Sec 6(4)]*.

If an application is made under 35.8 below for the alteration to be cancelled, then the alteration only has effect to the extent that the court confirms it. *[Sec 4(2); CA 1989, s 110]*.

See 35.9 below for filing requirements with the Registrar of Companies.

Example of a special resolution to change the objects clause

'That the main objects of the memorandum of association of the company be and hereby are altered by the deletion of the existing clause [insert number] and the insertion instead of the following new clause [insert number]:

New clause [insert number]
[Text of new clause]'

35.8 Procedure for objecting to alteration in memorandum

Where a company's memorandum has been altered by special resolution under *Sec 17* (see 35.6 above) or *Sec 4* (see 35.7 above) application may be made to the court for the alteration to be cancelled. Such an application may be made

- by the holders of not less than 15% in nominal value of the company's issued share capital or any class of it or, if the company is not limited by shares, not less than 15% of the company's members, or

- (for an alteration in the company's objects only) by the holders of not less than 15% of the company's debentures entitling the holders to object to such an alteration (i.e. any debentures secured by a floating charge which were issued or first issued before 1 December 1947 or form part of the same series as any debentures so issued),

but an application cannot be made by any person who has consented to, or voted in favour of, the alteration.

The application must be made within 21 days after the date on which the resolution altering the company's objects was passed. It may be made, on behalf of the persons entitled to make it, by one or more of their number appointed in writing for the purpose.

The court may as it thinks fit

- make an order confirming the alteration either wholly or in part on any terms and conditions;

- adjourn the proceedings in order that an arrangement may be made to its satisfaction for the purchase of the interests of dissentient members;

- give directions and make orders for facilitating or carrying into effect any such arrangement; and

- provide for the purchase by the company of the shares of any of the members, and accordingly for the reduction of its capital, and make such consequential alterations in the company's memorandum and articles as may be required.

Any alteration to the memorandum or articles made by virtue of any court order has the same effect as if duly made by resolution of the company. Conversely, if the court's order requires the company *not* to make any, or any specified, alteration in its memorandum or articles, the company does not then have power to make any such alteration in breach of that requirement, without the leave of the court.

[*Secs 5, 17(3)*].

For a successful application see *Re Hampstead Garden Suburb Trust Ltd [1962] Ch 806*.

35.9 Disclosure and filing requirements

See 51.9 RESOLUTIONS for filing a special resolution with the Registrar of Companies.

Where a company passes a special resolution altering its memorandum under *Sec 17* (see 35.6 above) or *Sec 4* (see 35.7 above)

- *if no application is made to the court for the alteration to be cancelled*, the company must, within 15 days from the end of the period for making such an application (i.e. within 36 days of the resolution), deliver to the Registrar of Companies a printed copy of its memorandum as altered. [*Sec 6(1)(a)*]; and

- *where such an application is made*, the company must forthwith give notice of that fact to the Registrar in the prescribed form (Form 6) and then, within 15 days from the date of any order cancelling or confirming the alteration, deliver to the Registrar an office copy of the order and, in the case of an order confirming the alteration, a printed copy of the memorandum as altered. The court may by order at any time extend the 15-day time limit for such period as it thinks proper. [*Sec 6(1)(b)(2)(5)*].

In all other cases where a company is required to send any documents making or evidencing an alteration in the company's memorandum, it must send a printed copy of the memorandum as altered at the same time. [*Sec 18(2)*].

See 11.8 ARTICLES OF ASSOCIATION for the policy of Companies House with regard to amendments to the articles which also apply to the memorandum.

Alteration by statutory provisions. Where a company's memorandum is altered by any statutory provision, whether an Act or an instrument made under an Act, a printed copy of the Act or instrument must be forwarded to the Registrar, not later than 15 days after the provision comes into force, and recorded by him. [*Sec 18(1)*].

Penalties. In default of any of the above requirements, the company and every officer of it who is in default is liable to a fine up to the level in 40.1(*f*) PENALTIES. [*Secs 6(3), 17(3), 18(3), 24 Sch*].

35.10 Effect of alteration on company's members

Unless he agrees in writing, a member is not bound by an alteration made in the memorandum after the date on which he became a member if the alteration

- requires him to take or subscribe for more shares than the number held by him at the date of alteration; or

35.11 Memorandum of Association

- in any way increases his liability as at that date to contribute to the company's share capital or otherwise to pay money to the company.

[*Sec 16*].

35.11 COPIES OF THE MEMORANDUM

A company must, on demand, send to a member a copy of

- the memorandum, subject to payment of 5 pence or less; and
- any Act which alters the memorandum, subject to payment not exceeding its published price.

In default, the company and every officer in default is liable to a fine up to the level in 40.1(*g*) PENALTIES.

[*Sec 19, 24 Sch*].

Every copy of the memorandum issued after the date of an alteration to it must be in accordance with the alteration. If not, the company and every officer in default is liable to a fine up to the limit in 40.1(*g*) PENALTIES for each occasion on which copies are incorrectly issued. [*Sec 20, 24 Sch*].

Companies House. Any person may inspect, and obtain a certified copy of, the memorandum of a company at the companies registration offices in Cardiff, London or Edinburgh, as appropriate, on payment of the prescribed fee. [*Sec 709*]. See 26.1 FEES for the current fees.

36   Names and Business Names

Cross-references. See 16.15 DEALINGS WITH THIRD PARTIES for disclosure of name in correspondence etc.; 19.47 DIRECTORS for re-use of company name following insolvent liquidation.

36.1   NAMES

Subject to the exemption below, the name of a company must end

(*a*)   in the case of a public company, with the words 'public limited company' (or its abbreviated form 'plc'); and

(*b*)   in the case of a company limited by shares or guarantee (other than a public company), with the word 'limited' (or its abbreviated form 'ltd').

If the memorandum states that the registered office is to be in Wales, then the Welsh equivalents of 'cwmni cyfyngedig cyhoeddus' (or abbreviated form 'ccc') under (*a*) or 'cyfyngedig'(abbreviated form 'cyf') under (*b*) may be used instead.

[*Secs 25, 27*].

Exemption. Subject to certain conditions,

• a private company limited by guarantee, and

• a company which on 25 February 1982 was a private company limited by shares with a name which, by virtue of a licence under *CA 1948, s 19*, did not include 'limited'

may be exempt from the requirement to use 'limited' as part of the company name. [*Secs 30, 31*]. See 29.4 GUARANTEE COMPANIES for full details.

36.2   Prohibition on registration of certain names

A company name must not be registered if

(*a*)   it includes in full or abbreviated form, otherwise than at the end of the name, any of the words 'limited', 'unlimited' or 'public limited company' (or their Welsh equivalents 'cyfyngedig', 'anghyfyngedig' or 'cwmni cyfyngedig cyhoeddus');

(*b*)   it includes the expression 'investment company with variable capital' (or its Welsh equivalent 'cwmni buddsoddi â chyfalaf newidiol');

(*c*)   it is 'the same as' a name already appearing in the index of company names maintained by the Registrar of Companies; or

(*d*)   in the opinion of the Secretary of State the use of the word would be offensive or constitute a criminal offence.

In addition, the approval of the Secretary of State is required for a name likely to give the impression that the company is connected in any way with the government or a local authority or which includes specified words or expressions. See 36.3 below.

In determining for the purposes of (*c*) above whether a name is '*the same as*' another, certain words and their abbreviation, together with type and case of letters, accents, spaces between letters and punctuation marks, are disregarded. These words comprise the definite article, the words 'company', 'and company', 'company limited', 'and company limited', 'limited', 'unlimited', 'public company limited' and 'investment company with variable capital' (or their Welsh equivalents). Additionally, 'and' and '&' are taken as the same.

[*Sec 26; SI 1996 No 2827, 8 Sch 4*].

36.3 Names and Business Names

Example

A company is already registered in the name of Hands Limited.

The following names would be refused.

- Hands Public Limited Company (or plc)
- H & S Limited (or Ltd)
- H and S Limited (or Ltd)
- H and S Public Limited Company (or plc)
- any of the above names with the addition of 'Company (or Co)' or 'and (or &) Company (or Co)'.

(Companies House Guidance Notes CHN2).

In considering whether names are similar, it is material to ascertain (i) what business has been or is intended to be carried on by the existing company and what is intended to be carried on by the new company; and (ii) what sort of name has been adopted by the existing company. See *Aerators Ltd v Tollitt [1902] 2 Ch 319*. The use of a name will not be allowed if it is intended to deceive or induce belief that the business is an extension of, or otherwise connected with, another company (*Ewing v Buttercup Margarine Company Ltd [1917] 2 Ch 1*).

36.3 Names requiring approval

Certain words or expressions require approval by the Secretary of State for Trade and Industry (Lists A and B below). In the case of words and expressions in List B, written request must be made to the relevant body. After 11 June 1992, approval is required (and, as the case may be, written request must be made) to use the plural and possessive forms of the words and expressions. This change, and subsequent additions to the list, do not, however, prohibit

- a person carrying on a business under a name which was lawful before the date of change from continuing to carry on the business under the same name after that date; or
- a person to whom a business is transferred after the date of change from continuing to carry on the business, for twelve months after the date of transfer, under the same name which was lawful before the date of change.

[*Sec 29(1); SI 1981 No 1685; SI 1982 No 1653; SI 1992 No 1996; SI 1995 No 3022*].

The use of certain words and expressions is covered by other legislation and their use may constitute a criminal offence. See List C below (which is not exhaustive).

LIST A

Words which imply national or international pre-eminence

British. The use of the word 'British' can vary depending on the way in which it is used in the name. Normally ownership should be British and the company must show pre-eminence in its field preferably by independent support e.g. from a government department or trade association. If 'British' is qualified by words not describing an activity or product (e.g. by a 'made-up' word) pre-eminence is not necessarily essential but the company should still be substantial in relation to its activities or products and eminent within its own field.

National. The criteria are similar to 'British'.

Great Britain or *United Kingdom*. If used as a prefix or preceded by the word 'of', the same comments apply as for 'British'. If the words are used as a suffix, they are normally allowed without difficulty. The use of the initials 'GB' or 'UK' does not require approval.

England, English, Scotland, Scottish, Wales, Welsh, Ireland, Irish. These words will be treated similar to 'British' when used as prefixes. When used as a suffix, the name will normally be approved provided the company is trading in the relevant country. If used as surnames, names will usually be approved if coupled with initials or forenames.

International. If used as a prefix, the company must show that the major part of its activities are in trading overseas. If used as a suffix, it will generally be approved where it can be shown that the company's main activities are exports or it operates in more than one overseas country.

European. Names will not be approved if they unjustifiably imply connection with official bodies of the EC.

Words which imply business pre-eminence or representative status

Association, Federation, Society. The company would normally be expected to be limited by guarantee with each member having one vote under the constitution. Normally, any profits should be used to further the objects of the organisation rather than be paid out to the members as dividends.

Authority, Board, Council. Advice on usage should be requested from Companies House.

Institute, Institution. Such words will normally only be approved to organisations carrying out research at the highest level or to professional bodies of the highest standing. The company must show that there is a need for the proposed institute, it has appropriate examination standards or regulations and it has evidence of support from other representative and independent bodies.

Words which imply specific objects or functions

Insurance words (Assurance, Insurance, Reinsurance, Reassurance, Insurer, Assurer, Re-assurer, Re-insurer). If the name is required for an underwriting company, Companies House will normally seek further advice. If the company is only to provide insurance services, the name should include the appropriate qualification (e.g. agents, consultants or services).

Patent, Patentee. Names will only be approved if they do not contravene the *Copyright, Designs and Patent Act 1988*.

Chamber of Commerce, Chamber of Trade, Chamber of Industry and *Chamber of Commerce, Training and Enterprise.* Before determining whether to approve such a name (or its Welsh equivalent), the Secretary of State must consult at least one 'relevant representative body'. The current '*relevant representative bodies*' are the British Chambers of Commerce and the body known as the Scottish Chambers of Commerce. The Secretary of State may add to or delete a body from the list by statutory instrument. [*Company and Business Names Act 1999*].

Co-operative. Use of this word is more common in (but not restricted to) companies limited by guarantee with each member having one vote and with a non-profit distribution clause in the memorandum of association. More detailed information may be required before names with this word can be approved.

Friendly Society and *Industrial Provident Society.* Names including these words are referred to the Registrar of Friendly Societies for advice.

36.3 Names and Business Names

Group. When used to imply that there are a number of companies under one ownership, then association with one or more British or overseas companies must be shown. If the name clearly shows that the company is to promote the interests of a group of individuals it will be approved.

Holding(s). The company must be a holding company within *CA 1985, s 736.*

Post Office, Giro. The Department is likely to seek advice on applications.

Trust. This word can be used in many senses and different criteria will apply. The following considers the main uses of the word but there may be others which will have to be dealt with on an individual basis. *Financial* and *investment trust* requires a written assurance that substantial paid-up share capital or other funds will be achieved within a reasonable period after incorporation. *Family trust* will usually be approved provided the name as a whole identifies the company as such. The company should be non-profit distributing and the objects reflect the nature of the trust. *Educational* or *artistic trust* requires a non-profit distribution clause in the memorandum of association, the promoters to be of some standing in the field and the name to reflect the nature of the trust. *Charitable trust* requires charitable objects, a non-profit distribution clause in the memorandum of association and confirmation that an application has or will be made for registration with the Charity Commission (Inland Revenue in Scotland). *Pensions* and *staff trust* requires the name of the parent company in the name and the objects of the company to include the operation of pension funds. *Enterprise trust* requires a non-profit distribution clause in the memorandum of association and evidence of recognisable support (e.g. from local authorities, businesses, banks, etc.). For use of the words *Unit trust* advice should be sought from New Companies Section, Companies House, Cardiff or Edinburgh.

Stock Exchange. Permission will normally be refused unless there are special circumstances.

Register, Registered. Generally, if these words are linked with a professional qualification, advice will be sought from the appropriate body. The name should not unjustifiably imply connection with the government or a local authority.

Trade Union. Names including these words will not normally be approved unless they conform to legislation relating to trade unions.

Charter, Chartered. Names including these words will be refused if they give a false impression that the company has a Royal Charter. If used to qualify a profession, advice of the appropriate governing body will be sought.

Sheffield. Companies House will need to establish the location and nature of the business activities unless the name clearly shows that there is no involvement in the manufacture or sale of cutlery. If the name implies connection with the traditional Sheffield industries, advice of the Company of Cutlers will be sought.

Charity. Approval is normally conditional upon the company being registered with the Charity Commission (Inland Revenue in Scotland). The company's objects should be charitable and the memorandum should contain a non-profit distribution clause.

Benevolent, Foundation, Fund. If the name implies charitable status, it will not normally be approved unless the company is limited by guarantee and has a non-proft distribution clause in the memorandum of association.

Chemist, Chemistry. The advice of Companies House should be sought about the use of these words in names.

(Companies House Notes for Guidance CHN3).

LIST B

Word or expression	*Relevant body*
Royal, Royale, Royalty, King, Queen, Prince, Princess, Windsor, Duke, His/Her Majesty	England: Home Office, A Division Room 730 50 Queen Anne's Gate London SW1H 9AT
	Wales: Welsh Office Crown Buildings Cathays Park Cardiff CE1 3NQ
	Scotland: The Scottish Ministers Civil Law and Legal Aid Division Saughton House Broomhouse Drive Edinburgh EH11 3XD
Police	England and Wales: Home Office, Police Dept Strategy Group Room 510 50 Queen Anne's Gate London SW1H 9AT
	Scotland: The Scottish Ministers Police Division St Andrews House Edinburgh EH1 3DG
Special School	Department for Education and Employment Schools 2 Branch Sanctuary Buildings Great Smith Street Westminster London SW1P 3BT
Contact Lens	The Registrar General Optical Council 41 Harley Street London W1N 2DJ
Dental, Dentistry	The Registrar General Dental Council 37 Wimpole Street London W1M 8DQ

36.3 Names and Business Names

District Nurse,
Health Visitor,
Midwife, Midwifery,
Nurse, Nursing

The Registrar and Chief Executive
UK Central Council for
Nursing, Midwifery and
Health Visiting
23 Portland Place
London W1N 3AF

Health Centre

Office of the Solicitor
DHSS
48 Carey Street
London WC2A 2LS

Health Service

NHS Management Executive
Department of Health
Eileen House
80–94 Newington Causeway
London SE1 6EF

Pregnancy Termination,
Abortion

Department of Health
Area 423
Wellington House
133–135 Waterloo Road
London SE1 8UG

Charity,
Charitable

England and Wales:
Charity Commission
Registration Division
St Albans House
57–60 Haymarket
London SW1Y 4QX

Companies not intending
to register as a charity;
Charity Commission
2nd Floor
20 Kings Parade
Queens Dock
Liverpool L3 4DQ

Scotland:
Inland Revenue
Claims Branch
Trinity Park House
South Trinity Road
Edinburgh EG5 3SD

Apothecary

England and Wales:
The Worshipful Society of
Apothecaries of London
Apothecaries Hall
Blackfriars Lane
London EC4V 6EJ

Scotland:
The Pharmaceutical Society of
Great Britain
Law Department
1 Lambeth High Street
London SE1 7JN

University

Privy Council Office
68 Whitehall
London SW1A 2AT

Polytechnic

Department for Education and
Science
FHE 1B
Sanctuary Buildings
Great Smith Street
Westminster
London SW1P 3BT

LIST C

Word or expression	*Appropriate body*
Anzac	Seek advice of Companies House
Architect	Architects Registration Council of the United Kingdom 73 Hallam Street London W1N 6EE
Bank, Banker, Banking, Deposit	Bank of England Supervision & Surveillance Threadneedle Street London EC2R 8AH
Building Society	Building Societies Commission 15/17 Great Marlborough Street London W1V 2LL
Credit Union	England and Wales: The Registrar of Friendly Societies 15/17 Great Marlborough Street London W1V 2LL
	Scotland: Assistant Registrar of Friendly Societies 58 Frederick Street Edinburgh EH2 1NB
Dentist, Dental Surgeon, Dental Practitioner	The Registrar General Dental Council 37 Wimpole Street London W1M 8DQ

36.3 Names and Business Names

Drug, Druggist,
Pharmaceutical,
Pharmaceutist,
Pharmacist,
Pharmacy

England and Wales:
The Director of Legal Services
The Royal Pharmaceutical Society
of Great Britain
1 Lambeth High Street
London SE1 7JN

For Scotland:
The Pharmaceutical Society
36 York Place
Edinburgh EH1 3HU

Insurance Broker,
Assurance Broker,
Re-insurance Broker,
Re-assurance Broker

Insurance Brokers
Registration Council
15 St Helens Place
London EC3A 6DS

Optician,
Ophthalmic Optician,
Dispensing Optician,
Enrolled Optician,
Registered Optician,
Optometrist

The Registrar
General Optical Council
41 Harley Street
London W1N 2DJ

Patent Office,
Patent Agent

IPCD
Hazlitt House
45 Southampton Buildings
London WC2A 1AR

Red Cross,
Geneva Cross,
Red Crescent,
Red Lion and Sun

Seek advice of Companies House

Veterinary Surgeon,
Veterinary, Vet

The Registrar
Royal College of Veterinary Surgeons
62–64 Horseferry Road
London SW1P 2AF

*Chiropodist,
*Dietician,
*Medical Laboratory Technician,
*Occupational Therapist,
*Orthoptist,
*Physiotherapist,
*Radiographer,
*Remedial Gymnast,

Department of Health
Room 12.26
HAP4 Division
Hannibal House
Elephant and Castle
London SE1 6TE

*Institute of Laryngology,
*Institute of Otology,
*Institute of Urology,
*Institute of Orthopaedics

University College
Gower Street
London WC1E 6BT

*Where preceded by the words Registered or State Registered

(Companies House Notes for Guidance CHN2, CHN11).

36.4   **How to register a company name**

Applicants are advised to check whether the name proposed is the same as one already registered by referring to the Index which can be inspected free of charge at the Companies House branches in Cardiff, Edinburgh and London (see 48.1 REGISTRAR OF COMPANIES) or the satellite offices at Leeds, Manchester, Birmingham and Glasgow. They should also consider whether it is 'too like' another name so that, although it may be accepted by the Registrar, another company complains and a direction to change the name is made under 36.5(*a*) below.

The Registrar of Companies does not consult the Trade Marks Register when considering applications for new company names. The registration of a particular name is not therefore an indication that trade mark rights do not already exist in that name. Applicants are advised also to investigate the possibility that others may already have trade mark rights in the name proposed (or parts of such name) by making a search at the Patent Office, 25 Southampton Buildings, London WC2A 1AY or, by prior arrangement, at Central Enquiry Unit, Concept House, Tredegar Park, Cardiff Road, Newport, Gwent NP9 1RH (tele: 0645 500505).

Registration of a company name should not be assumed to imply any subsequent acceptance of the same name for the purpose of the *Consumer Credit Act 1974*. Applicants who require a licence under that Act are advised to consult the licensing branch of the Office of Fair Trading, 3rd Floor, Craven House, 40 Uxbridge Road, Ealing, London W5 2BS (tele: 0171 242 2858) to ascertain whether the name is likely to be acceptable for the purposes of the Act.

If the name is not the same as one in the Index, and does not require prior approval of the Secretary of State, the incorporation documents (or, in the case of a change of name, the special resolution) should be submitted to the appropriate Registrar of Companies. If the name is acceptable and the documents correctly completed, the company name will be registered.

For all names requiring the approval of the Secretary of State (see 36.3, Lists A and B above), applicants should seek the advice of New Companies Section at Companies House in Cardiff (companies intending to have their registered office in England or Wales) or Edinburgh (companies intending to have their registered office in Scotland). Details about the requirements on the use of the name will then be sent to the applicant.

If the name includes any of the words or expressions in 36.3, List B above, applicants must request the relevant body in writing to indicate whether (and if so why) it has any objections to the proposal. A statement that such a request has been made and any response received should then be submitted to Companies Registration Office with the registration documents (or, in the case of a change of name, the special resolution). [*Sec 29(2)(3)*].

If the name includes any of the words or expressions in 36.3, List C above, applicants should initially seek the advice of the appropriate Companies Registration Office. They may be asked to seek confirmation from the appropriate body listed that the use of the word does not contravene the relevant legislation.

(Companies House Notes for Guidance CHN2).

36.5   **Direction to change name**

The Secretary of State may direct a company to change its name in the following circumstances.

(*a*)   Where a company has been registered with a name which is 'the same as' or, in his opinion, 'too like' a name appearing in the Index of names at the time of registration. See 36.2 above for *'the same as'*. The direction must be in writing and made within twelve months of the date of registration. It must be complied with in the period specified in the direction (or such longer period as is allowed by further direction in writing). [*Sec 28(2)(4)*].

A direction to change the name on the grounds that it is 'too like' a previously registered name usually arises as a result of an objection from an existing company. When such an objection is received, Companies House first compares the names visually on a side-by-side basis then phonetically to see whether they are 'like' each other. If they are not, the objection is rejected. If the names are 'like' each other, the next stage is to consider whether they are potentially 'too like' each other in that there is a risk that people could mistake one name for the other. Factors such as nature and location of the respective companies' business activities may be considered. The objection will be rejected if Companies House are not satisfied that they are potentially 'too like' (e.g. generally where there is one word different between the names). Where names are still potentially 'too like', each party will be given the opportunity to make representations which they wish to be taken into account before a final decision is reached. Such representations are invited by a questionnaire letter sent to each party. The decision will be explained and, although there is no statutory right of appeal, the losing party can make further representations. It is unlikely, however, that the decisions will be reversed unless the representations contain significant and relevant new information. If a direction is issued, the company concerned must normally change its name within a period of 12 weeks. Companies House will assist in the choice of a new name. (Companies House: The Register, Issue 17, Summer 1992; Companies House Notes for Guidance CHN2).

(*b*)   Where it appears that misleading information has been given for the purposes of the company's registration with a particular name or that undertakings or assurances given for that purpose have not been fulfilled. Such a direction can be made within five years of the date of registration. It must be complied with in the period specified in the direction (or such longer period as is allowed by further direction in writing). [*Sec 28(3)(4)*].

(*c*)   Where the name by which a company is registered is so misleading an indication of the nature of its activities as to be likely to cause harm to the public. Subject to below, the direction must be complied with within six weeks of the direction or such longer period as is allowed. The company may, however, within three weeks of the direction, apply to the court for the direction to be set aside. If the direction is confirmed by the court, it must specify the period within which the direction must be complied with. [*Sec 32(1)-(3)*].

Penalties. A company which fails to comply with any of the above directions, and any officer of it who is in default, is liable to a penalty up to the level in 40.1(*f*) PENALTIES. [*Secs 28(5), 32(4), 24 Sch*].

New certificate of incorporation. Where a company changes its name under any of the above provisions, the Registrar of Companies must enter the new name on the register in place of the old name and issue a certificate of incorporation altered to meet the circumstances of the case. The change of name has effect from the date the altered certificate is issued. [*Secs 28(6), 32(5)*].

Legal consequences. The change of name does not affect any rights or obligations of the company or render defective any legal proceedings by or against it. [*Secs 28(7), 32(6)*].

36.6   Change of name

A company may at any time change its name by special resolution. The same provisions apply on the use of certain names as in 36.2 and 36.3 above and directions to change the name under 36.5 above. [*Sec 28(1)(6)(7)*]. A signed copy of the resolution must be forwarded to the Registrar of Companies together with the requisite fee (see 26.1 FEES). The change will normally take five working days but, for a charge of £100, Companies House operates a premium service whereby the change of name certificate can be issued on the same day as delivery of the resolution. (Companies House Notes for Guidance CHN4).

36.7   Display of name outside place of business

Every company must paint or affix, and keep painted or affixed, its name on the outside of every office or place in which the business is carried on. This must be done in a conspicuous position and in letters easily legible. If not, the company and every officer in default is liable to a fine up to the level in 40.1(*f*) PENALTIES. [*Sec 348, 24 Sch*].

See also 16.15 DEALINGS WITH THIRD PARTIES for disclosure of name in correspondence, etc.

36.8   Improper use of name

It is an offence for

- *either* a person who is not a public company *or* an 'old public company' to carry on any trade, profession or business under a name which includes, as its last part, the words 'public limited company' or the Welsh equivalent 'cwmni cyfyngedig cyhoeddus' (or abbreviations thereof);

- a public company to use a name which may reasonably be expected to give the impression that it is a private company in circumstances in which the fact that it is a public company is likely to be material to any person; or

- any person to trade or carry on a business under a name of which 'limited' or 'cyfyngedig' (or any contraction or imitation of either of those words) is the last word unless that person is duly incorporated with limited liability.

A person guilty of an offence under the above or any officer of a company which is in default is liable to a fine up to the level in 40.1(*f*) PENALTIES.

See 18.1 DEFINITIONS for *'old public company'*.

[*Secs 33, 34, 24 Sch; CC(CP)A 1985, s 8*].

36.9   BUSINESS NAMES

BNA 1985 applies to any person who has a place of business, and carries on a business, in Great Britain under a name which

(*a*)   *in the case of a partnership*, does not consist of the 'surnames' of all the partners who are individuals and the corporate names of all partners who are bodies corporate, without any addition other than

  (i)   the forenames or 'initials' of the individual partners;

  (ii)   where two or more partners have the same surname, the addition of 's' at the end of that surname; and

(iii)   one indicating that the business is carried on in succession to a former owner of the business;

(*b*)   *in the case of an individual,* does not consist of his surname without any addition other than his forenames or initials or an addition within (*a*)(iii) above; and

(*c*)   *in the case of a company,* does not consist of its corporate name without any addition other than one within (*a*)(iii) above.

'Surname' in relation to a peer or person usually known by a British title different from his surname, means the title by which he is known.

'Initials' include any recognised abbreviation of a name.

[*BNA 1985, ss 1, 8*].

Although there is no requirement for owners of businesses to register their business names, certain names require written approval (see 36.10 below).

36.10 **Prohibition on the use of certain business names**

A person to whom *BNA 1985* applies (see 36.9 above) must not, without written approval of the Secretary of State, carry on business in Great Britain under a name which

●   would be likely to give the impression that the business is connected with the government or a local authority; or

●   includes words or expressions as in 36.3, List A or List B above.

This does not apply to the carrying on of a business by

●   a person who carried it on immediately before 26 February 1982 if he continues to carry it on under the name which immediately before that date was its lawful business name; or

●   a person to whom it has been transferred within the previous twelve months if he continues to carry it on under the name which immediately before the date of transfer was its lawful business name.

[*BNA 1985, ss 2(1)-(3), 3(1); SI 1981 No 1685; SI 1982 No 1653*].

See 36.13 below for failure to comply with the above provisions.

36.11 **Application for names**

For all names requiring the approval of the Secretary of State, applicants should seek the advice of Companies Registration Office in Cardiff (businesses in England or Wales) or Edinburgh (businesses in Scotland). Details about the requirements on the use of the name will then be sent to the applicant.

The application, together with any supporting information, should be submitted to the Secretary of State at the appropriate Companies Registration Office. If the name includes any word or expression within 36.3, List B above, the applicant must request (in writing) the relevant body to indicate whether (and if so why) it has any objection to the proposal. A statement that such a request has been made, and a copy of any response received, should be submitted with the application. [*BNA 1985, s 3(2)*].

Note that although the words in 36.3, List C above do not require the permission of the Secretary of State, their use may constitute a criminal offence. Owners of businesses wishing to use any of these words in a name should seek legal advice and confirmation from the body concerned that the use of the word does not contravene the legislation (although such confirmation should not be regarded as conclusive).

36.12 Display of name outside place of business

A person to whom *BNA 1985* applies (see 36.9 above) must display in a prominent position so that it may easily be read, in any premises where business is carried on and to which customers or suppliers have access, a notice containing

- in the case of a partnership, the name of each partner;

- in the case of an individual, his name;

- in the case of a company, its corporate name; and

- in relation to each person so named, an address in Great Britain at which service of any document relating in any way to the business will be effective.

[*BNA 1985, s 4(1)(b)*].

Civil remedies for breach. Any legal proceedings brought by a person to enforce a right arising out of a contract made in the course of a business in respect of which, at the time the contract was made, he was in breach of the above provisions must be dismissed if the defendant (in Scotland, the defender) shows that, because of the plaintiff's (pursuer's) breach,

- he has a claim against the plaintiff (pursuer) arising out of that contract which he has been unable to pursue; or

- he has suffered some financial loss in connection with the contract.

This does not apply if the court is satisfied that it is just and equitable to permit the proceedings to continue and is without prejudice to the right of any person to enforce such rights as he may have against another person in any proceedings brought by that person.

[*BNA 1985, s 5*].

See 36.13 below for failure to comply with the above provisions.

See also 16.18 DEALINGS WITH THIRD PARTIES for disclosure of business name in correspondence, etc.

36.13 Offences

A person who contravenes the provisions of 36.10 above or, without reasonable excuse, the provisions of 36.12 above is guilty of an offence and liable to a fine up to the level in 40.1(*f*) PENALTIES.

If an offence committed by a body corporate is proved to have been committed with the consent or connivance of, or to be attributable to any neglect on the part of,

- any director, manager, secretary or similar officer,

- any person purporting to act in such a capacity, or

- a member where the affairs of the body are managed by that member

he as well as the body corporate is guilty of the offence and liable to a similar fine.

[*BNA 1985, ss 2(4), 4(6), 7*].

37 Open-ended Investment Companies

37.1   From January 1997, it became possible to incorporate a new type of company, formally known as an investment company with variable capital but more commonly referred to as an open-ended investment company. (OEIC). Such a company is a collective investment scheme within the meaning of *FSA 1986, s 75*, the object of which is investment in a limited class of investments. Traditionally, collective investment schemes in the UK had taken the form of unit trusts.

The regulations making provision for OEICs are *The Open-Ended Investment Companies (Investment Companies with Variable Capital) Regulations 1996 (SI 1996 No 2827)*. These regulations are concerned with

- the formation and subsequent control and supervision of OEICs; and

- the corporate framework within which an OEIC operates;

Under *Reg 6* of those regulations, the Securities Investment Board (SIB) are given powers to make additional regulations on both the constitution and management of OEICs and the publication of scheme particulars. The SIB has used these powers and made *The Financial Services (Open-ended Investment Companies) Regulations 1997*.

Detailed coverage of the provisions of these two sets of regulations are beyond the scope of this book.

38   Oversea Companies

Cross-references. See 1.5 ACCOUNTING REFERENCE DATES AND PERIODS; 16.4, 16.5 DEALING WITH THIRD PARTIES for contracts in England and Wales; 16.7, 16.8 DEALING WITH THIRD PARTIES for execution of documents under the laws of England and Wales, and Scotland respectively; 31.7 INVESTIGATIONS; 36.9 *et seq.* NAMES AND BUSINESS NAMES for use of business names by an oversea company; 50 REGISTRATION OF CHARGES.

The contents of this chapter are as follows.

38.1   DEFINITION

An *'oversea company'* is a company incorporated elsewhere than in Great Britain which

- after 30 June 1985 'establishes a place of business' in Great Britain; or

- before 1 July 1985 established a place of business and continues to have an established place of business in Great Britain after that date.

[*Sec 744*].

There is no precise statutory definition of the meaning of *'establishes a place of business'*. In *A/S Dampskib 'Hercules' v Grand Trunk Pacific Railway Co [1912] 1 KB 222*, Buckley LJ said on this point: 'We have only to see whether the corporation is 'here''. . . . the best test is to ascertain whether the business is carried on here and at a defined place'. It was held that a company, whose main object was to establish and maintain a railway company in Canada and which raised capital in London to do so, had established a place of business in England.

In *South India Shipping Corporation Ltd v Export-Import Bank of Korea [1985] 2 All ER 219*, it was held that a bank, which had premises and staff in England and carried on there the preliminary work necessary for granting and obtaining loans and giving publicity to the bank's activities, had established a place of business there. In *Re Oriel [1985] 3 All ER 216*, Oliver LJ said that the meaning of the phrase 'established place of business' connotes not only the setting up of a place of business at a specific location, but also a degree of permanence as the location of the company's business. It need not necessarily be owned, or even leased, by the company but at least must be associated with it and business must be conducted from it habitually or with some degree of regularity.

38.2   REGISTRATION AND FILING REQUIREMENTS ETC. – PLACE OF BUSINESS REGISTRATION REGIME

As the general provisions of *CA 1985* apply only to companies formed and registered under the Act, special provisions apply regarding registration and filing requirements of oversea companies.

38.3 Oversea Companies

Subject to the transitional provisions in 38.15 below, the provisions in 38.3 and 38.4 below do not apply to any limited company which is incorporated outside the UK and Gibraltar and which has a *branch* in Great Britain. [*Sec 690B; SI 1992 No 3179, 2 Sch 2*]. A special branch registration regime applies to such companies (see 38.5 to 38.15 below). Where a company so incorporated has a place of business in Great Britain that is not a branch, and has no other branch in the UK, it remains subject to the provisions in 38.3 and 38.4 below.

'*Branch*' means a branch within the meaning of the 11th EC Company Law Directive (*89/666/EEC*) (see 25.3 EUROPEAN COMMUNITY LEGISLATION), and where a branch comprises places of business in more than one part of the UK, it is treated as being situated in that part of the UK where its principal place of business is situated. [*Sec 698(2); SI 1992 No 3179, 2 Sch 13(3)*]. In fact, the 11th Directive does not specifically define a branch; its meaning ultimately depends on the views of the European Court of Justice when called upon to interpret the 11th Directive. A Department of Trade and Industry Consultative Document published in July 1992 (Implementation of EC 11th Company Law Directive and Bank Branches Directive) gives useful guidance. It states that, in principle, a branch is a place of business which a company establishes in another state through which the company conducts its business such that persons resident in that state can deal with the branch instead of dealing directly with the representatives of the company in the company's home state. Places of business which perform operations ancillary or incidental to the company's business are, in general terms, not branches within the meaning of the 11th Directive. Thus, 'branch' is a narrower concept than place of business, every company with a branch has a place of business, but not every place of business is a branch, and one branch can cover many places of business where there is a unified management structure.

38.3 Documents to be delivered to the Registrar of Companies on establishing a place of business in Great Britain

When a company incorporated outside Great Britain establishes a place of business in Great Britain, it must within one month deliver the following to the appropriate Registrar of Companies for registration. See 38.52 below for the appropriate Registrar.

(*a*) A certified copy of the charter, statutes or memorandum and articles of the company or other instrument constituting or defining its constitution, together with a certified translation (see 28.2 FORMS) if the original is not in English). The copy of the instrument constituting or defining the company's constitution must be certified, in the place of incorporation of the company, to be a true copy by

    (i) an official of the government to whose custody the original is committed;

    (ii) a notary public; or

    (iii) an officer of the company on oath taken before a person authorised to administer oaths in that place or any of the British Officials mentioned in *Commissioners for Oaths Act 1889, s 6*.

(*b*) A return in the prescribed form (Form 691) with details of the following.

    (i) Directors (including any person in accordance with whose instructions the directors of the company are accustomed to act) and secretary (or any person occupying the position of secretary by whatever name called) as in 49.1(*c*)(i) and (ii) REGISTRATION AND RE-REGISTRATION except that it is only necessary to give details of other directorships if the director has no business occupation in which case details of all other current directorships must be given.

(ii)   Names and addresses of one or more persons resident in Great Britain authorised to accept on the company's behalf service of process and any notices required to be served on it.

(iii)   Documents delivered under (*a*) above.

(iv)   A statutory declaration by a director, secretary or person within (ii) above stating the date on which the company's place of business in Great Britain was established.

[*Secs 691, 698; CA 1989, 19 Sch 6; SI 1985 No 854, Reg 7(4)*].

See 38.21 below for penalties for non-compliance.

38.4   Registration of change in particulars

If any alteration is made in

(*a*)   any of the documents within 38.3(*a*) above, or

(*b*)   the directors or secretary or the particulars contained in the list of directors under 38.3(*b*)(i) above, or

(*c*)   the names and addresses of the persons authorised to accept service on behalf of the company under 38.3(*b*)(ii) above, or

(*d*)   the corporate name of the oversea company,

the company must, within the specified time, deliver to the appropriate Registrar of Companies a return in the prescribed form (Forms 692(1)(a), 692(1)(b), 692(1)(c) and 692(2) respectively) containing particulars of the alteration or change. See 38.52 below for the appropriate Registrar.

In the case of an alteration within 38.3(*b*)(ii) above the specified time is 21 days after the date of alteration. Otherwise it is 21 days from the date on which notice of the alteration could have been received in Great Britain by post (assuming despatched with due diligence).

[*Sec 692*].

See 38.21 below for penalties for non-compliance.

38.5   REGISTRATION AND FILING REQUIREMENTS ETC. – BRANCH REGISTRATION REGIME

The provisions described at 38.6 to 38.14 below apply (subject to transitional provisions described at 38.15 below) to any limited company which is incorporated outside the UK and Gibraltar and which has a 'branch' (as defined in 38.2 above) in Great Britain. [*Sec 690A; SI 1992 No 3179, 2 Sch 2*].

38.6   Duty to register and documents to be delivered

A company within 38.5 above must, within one month of having opened a branch in a part of Great Britain (or within one month of a branch having become situated in a part of Great Britain on ceasing to be situated elsewhere), deliver to the appropriate Registrar of Companies (see 38.53 below), for registration, a return in the prescribed form containing the particulars set out at 38.7 and 38.8 below. Further particulars and documents are required as set out at 38.9 and 38.10 below, subject to the exceptions noted in those paragraphs. [*21A Sch 1(1)(4); SI 1992 No 3179, 2 Sch 3*].

38.7 Oversea Companies

Sec 705A governs the duties and functions of the Registrar of Companies as regards branches of oversea companies. In particular, he must keep, for each company within 38.5 above, a register of branches registered by it under the above provisions, and must allocate a number to each such branch (to be known as the branch's registered number). [*Sec 705A; SI 1992 No 3179, Reg 3(2)*].

Further returns are required, under *Sec 703P* or *703Q* (as inserted by *SI 1992 No 3179, 2 Sch 19*) if on the date the Great Britain branch is opened, the company is subject to winding up or insolvency proceedings or if, on or before that date, a liquidator has been appointed and he continues in office at that date. [*21A Sch 1(5); SI 1992 No 3179, 2 Sch 3*].

See 38.21 below for penalties for non-compliance.

38.7 *Particulars required about the company*

The return referred to at 38.6 above must contain the following particulars about the company.

(*a*)　Its corporate name.

(*b*)　Its legal form.

(*c*)　If it is registered in the country of its incorporation, the identity of the register in which, and the number with which, it is registered.

(*d*)　A list of its directors and secretary, containing

    (i)　with respect to each director (if an individual)

        (A)　his name (meaning usually his forename and surname);

        (B)　any former name (but excluding certain former names, e.g. a married woman's maiden name);

        (C)　his usual residential address;

        (D)　his nationality;

        (E)　his business occupation (if any);

        (F)　particulars of any other directorships held by him; and

        (G)　his date of birth;

    (ii)　with respect to the secretary (or each of joint secretaries) (if an individual) the same particulars as those required by (i)(A)–(C) above with respect to directors (except that where all the partners in a firm are joint secretaries, the name and principal office of the firm may be stated instead); and

    (iii)　with respect to each director and secretary (if a corporation or Scottish firm), its corporate or firm name and registered or principal office.

(*e*)　The extent of the powers of the directors to represent the company in dealings with third parties and in legal proceedings, together with a statement as to whether they may act alone or must act jointly and, if jointly, the name of any other person concerned.

(*f*)　Whether the company is a credit or financial institution within *Sec 699A* (see 38.47 below) (or equivalent NI provision).

The following additional particulars are required if the company is not incorporated in an EC member state.

- The law under which the company is incorporated.

- In the case of a company within the 'delivery of accounts' requirements of either *21C Sch 2, 3* (see 38.49 below) or *21D Sch* (see 38.39 to 38.46 below), the period for which it is required, by the law under which it is incorporated, to prepare accounts, and the period allowed for the preparation and public disclosure of accounts for such an accounting period.

- Unless otherwise disclosed by the documents referred to at 38.10 below (where relevant)

    (i)   the address of its principal place of business in its country of incorporation;

    (ii)   its objects; and

    (iii) the amount of its issued share capital.

Where

- at the time the return referred to at 38.6 above is delivered, the company has another branch in the same part of Great Britain as the branch covered by the return;

- the company has delivered the above particulars with respect to that other branch (or has done so to the extent required under the transitional provisions described at 38.13 below); and

- the company has no outstanding obligation to make a return in relation to any alteration of those particulars (see 38.11 below),

then instead of providing the particulars again, the company may simply refer in the current return to the fact that the particulars have been filed in respect of the other branch, giving the number with which the other branch is registered.

[*21A Sch 2; SI 1992 No 3179, 2 Sch 3*].

38.8   *Particulars required about the branch*

The return referred to at 38.6 above must also contain the following particulars about the branch.

(*a*)   Its address.

(*b*)   The date on which it was opened.

(*c*)   The business carried on at it.

(*d*)   If different from the name of the company, the name in which that business is carried on.

(*e*)   A list of the names and addresses of all persons resident in Great Britain authorised to accept on the company's behalf service of process in respect of the business of the branch and of any notices required to be served on the company in respect of that business.

(*f*)   A list of the names and usual residential addresses of all persons authorised to represent the company as its permanent representatives for the branch business.

(*g*)   The extent of the authority of any person within (*f*) above, including whether that person is authorised to act alone or jointly.

(*h*)   If a person within (*f*) above is not authorised to act alone, the name of any person with whom he is authorised to act.

[*21A Sch 3; SI 1992 No 3179, 2 Sch 3*].

38.9 Oversea Companies

38.9 *Particulars in relation to registration of documents*

Unless the company is a credit or financial institution to which *Sec 699A* applies (see 38.47 below), the return referred to at 38.6 above must state whether it is intended to register documents under *21D Sch 2(2)* or, as the case may be, *21D Sch 10(1)* (duty to deliver accounts and reports – see 38.41 and 38.45 below respectively) in respect of the branch in question or in respect of some other branch in the UK. If the latter, the place of registration of the other branch and its registered number must also be stated. [*21A Sch 1(1)(c), 4; SI 1992 No 3179, 2 Sch 3*].

38.10 *Documents required*

The return referred to at 38.6 above must be accompanied by certain documents unless

(*a*)   at the time of delivery of the return, the company has another branch in the UK;

(*b*)   the return contains a statement to the effect that the documents otherwise required are included in the material registered in respect of the other branch; and

(*c*)   the return states where the other branch is registered and gives its registered number.

The documents required in respect of all companies to which the above exception does not apply are a certified copy of the company's charter, statutes or memorandum and articles (or other instrument constituting or defining the company's constitution), together with an English translation (if the document is not written in English) certified in the prescribed manner to be a correct translation.

In the case of a company which is not a credit or financial institution within *Sec 699A* (see 38.47 below) and which is required by its parent law (i.e. the law of the country in which the company is incorporated) to prepare, have audited and disclose accounts, certain accounting documents are also required (unless the above exception applies). These accounting documents (i.e. accounts, consolidated accounts (if any), directors' report (if any) and auditors' report) in relation to a financial period of the company (i.e. a period for which it is required or permitted by its parent law to prepare accounts), being the latest documents to have been publicly disclosed in accordance with the company's parent law before the earlier of the expiry of the one-month period allowed for complying with 38.6 above and the actual date of compliance. If any of the accounting documents is not written in English, an English translation, certified in the prescribed manner to be a correct translation, must also be provided.

[*21A Sch 1(2)(3), 5, 6; SI 1992 No 3179, 2 Sch 3*].

38.11 **Registration of alterations in particulars**

If, after a company has delivered a return under 38.6 above, any alteration is made in

(*a*)   its charter, statutes or memorandum and articles (or other instrument constituting or defining its constitution), or

(*b*)   any of the particulars referred to in 38.7 to 38.9 above,

the company must deliver to the appropriate Registrar of Companies (see 38.53 below), for registration, a return in the prescribed form containing the prescribed particulars of the alteration. If the alteration is one within (*a*) above, the return must be accompanied by a certified copy of the document as altered, together with, if the document is not written in English, an English translation certified in the prescribed manner to be a correct translation.

The return must be delivered within 21 days after the making of any alteration of the particulars in 38.8 above (particulars about the branch) or, as regards any other alteration, within 21 days after the date on which notice of the alteration could have been received by post in Great Britain (if despatched with due diligence).

Where a company has more than one branch in Great Britain and an alteration relates to more than one such branch, a return must be delivered in respect of each branch affected. For this purpose, an alteration in any of the particulars in 38.7 above (particulars about the company) is to be treated as relating to every branch. However, if there is more than one branch in a part of Great Britain, one return giving the branch numbers of two or more such branches counts as a return for each branch so specified. An alteration within (*a*) above is only treated as relating to a branch if the document altered is included in the material registered in respect of that branch.

[*21A Sch 7; SI 1992 No 3179, 2 Sch 3*].

Action is also needed if the return under 38.6 above included a statement under 38.10(*b*) above and that statement ceases to be true so far as concerns the documents, other than accounting documents, mentioned in 38.10. The company must then deliver for registration either the said documents or, if applicable, a return in the prescribed form containing a further statement to the effect that those documents are included in material registered in respect of another branch of the company in the UK, and stating the place of registration and registered number of that other branch. These provisions apply in respect of any such further statement as they apply in respect of the original statement. Where there is more than one branch affected, a single return under these provisions will cover more than one branch in a part of Great Britain to the extent that the relevant branch numbers are given in the return.

The above delivery requirements must be complied with within 21 days after the date on which notice of the fact that the statement in the earlier return has ceased to be true could have been received in Great Britain by post (if despatched with due diligence).

[*21A Sch 8; SI 1992 No 3179, 2 Sch 3*].

See 38.21 below for penalties for non-compliance.

38.12 CHANGE IN REGISTRATION REGIME

The provisions described at 38.13 and 38.14 below cover the situation where a company makes a transition from being within the place of business registration regime to being within the branch registration regime, or vice versa. Separate transitional provisions apply in consequence of the introduction of the branch registration regime in Great Britain on 1 January 1993, and these are covered at 38.15 below.

38.13 Change from place of business regime to branch regime

The following provisions apply where a company becomes a company to which *Sec 690A* applies (branch registration regime) (see 38.5 above), having immediately beforehand been within *Sec 691* (place of business registration regime) (see 38.3 above).

The company need not include the particulars at 38.7(*d*) above (list of directors and secretary) in its first return to be delivered under 38.6 above to the Registrar for a part of Great Britain (see 38.53 below) if, at the time of transition,

- it had an established place of business in that part;

- it had complied with 38.3(*b*)(i) above (details of directors and secretary); and

- it had no outstanding obligation to make a return under *Sec 692(1)* in respect of an alteration of the kind mentioned at 38.4(*b*) above (concerning directors and secretary).

To take advantage of this exemption, the company must state in the return under 38.6 above that the particulars have been previously filed in respect of a place of business in that part of Great Britain, giving the company's registered number.

A similar exemption applies with regard to the delivery of documents, other than accounting documents, referred to in 38.10 above, which broadly corresponds with the requirement at 38.3(*a*) above under the place of business registration regime.

[*21B Sch 1; SI 1992 No 3179, 2 Sch 5*].

Where a company

- becomes a company to which *Sec 690A* applies (see 38.5 above),

- immediately afterwards has in a part of Great Britain an established place of business but no branch, and

- immediately beforehand had an established place of business in that part of Great Britain,

then, in relation to that part of Great Britain, *Secs 691, 692* (place of business registration regime) (see 38.3 and 38.4 above) continue to apply to the company (notwithstanding *Sec 690B* – see 38.2 above) until such time as it gives notice to the Registrar for that part of Great Britain (see 38.53 below) that it is a company within *Sec 690A* (branch registration regime). [*Sec 692A(3); SI 1992 No 3179, 2 Sch 4*].

38.14 Change from branch regime to place of business regime

The following provisions apply where a company becomes a company to which *Sec 691* applies (place of business registration regime) (see 38.3 above), having immediately beforehand been within *Sec 690A* (branch registration regime) (see 38.5 above).

The company need not deliver the documents referred to at 38.3(*a*) above to the Registrar for a part of Great Britain (see 38.52 below) if, at the time of transition,

- it had a branch in that part;

- the documents, other than accounting documents, referred to in 38.10 above were included in the material registered in respect of the branch; and

- the company had no outstanding obligation to make a return to the Registrar for that part of Great Britain under *21A Sch 7* (return of alterations – see 38.11 above) as regards any alteration in the said documents.

To take advantage of this exemption, the company must state in its return under *Sec 691* (see 38.3(*b*) above) that the documents have been previously filed in respect of a branch of the company, giving the branch's registered number.

A similar exemption applies with regard to the information required by *Sec 691(1)(b)(i)* (details of directors and secretary – see 38.3(*b*)(i) above) which broadly corresponds with the requirement at 38.7(*d*) above under the branch registration scheme.

[*21B Sch 2; SI 1992 No 3179, 2 Sch 5*].

Where a company ceases to be a company to which *Sec 690A* applies (branch registration regime) (see 38.5 above) and, immediately afterwards,

- continues to have in Great Britain a place of business which it had immediately beforehand, and

● does not have a branch in Northern Ireland,

it is treated for *Sec 691* purposes (place of business registration regime) (see 38.3 above) as having established the place of business on the date when it ceased to be a company to which *Sec 690A* applies. [*Sec 692A(1); SI 1992 No 3179, 2 Sch 4*].

Where a limited company incorporated outside the UK and Gibraltar

● ceases to have a branch in Northern Ireland, and

● both immediately beforehand and immediately afterwards, has a place of business, but not a branch, in Great Britain,

it is treated for *Sec 691* purposes as having established the place of business on the date when it ceased to have a branch in Northern Ireland. [*Sec 692A(2); SI 1992 No 3179, 2 Sch 4*].

38.15 **Transitional provisions**

Branch in part of Great Britain at 1 January 1993. The following provisions apply to any limited company incorporated outside the UK and Gibraltar which, immediately after 31 December 1992, has a branch in England and Wales which it had there immediately before 1 January 1993. Identical provisions apply where the branch in question is in Scotland.

Such a branch is treated for the purposes of *21A Sch 1(1)* (duty to register – see 38.6 above) as having been opened by the company on 1 January 1993. If the company was a 'registered oversea company' in relation to England and Wales immediately before 1 January 1993, it is given six months (rather than the usual one month) from that date to comply with *21A Sch 1(1)*. For this purpose, a company was a 'registered oversea company' in relation to England and Wales if it had duly delivered documents to the Registrar for England and Wales under *Sec 691* (place of business registration regime) (see 38.3 above) and had not subsequently given him notice under *Sec 696(4)* (see 38.52 below) that it had ceased to have an established place of business there.

Until such time as such a company either complies with *21A Sch 1* in respect of a branch in England and Wales or ceases to have a branch there, *Secs 691* and *692* (see 38.3 and 38.4 above) continue to apply to the company (notwithstanding *Sec 690B* – see 38.2 above) in relation to England and Wales. However, those *sections* do not apply to any such company if it had no place of business in England and Wales immediately before 1 December 1992.

[*SI 1992 No 3179, 4 Sch 1*].

There are also provisions to ensure that documents registered by such a company under *Sec 691(1)(a)* (see 38.3(*a*) above) are treated as having been registered under *21A Sch 1* in respect of the first branch registered in England and Wales under the branch registration regime. [*SI 1992 No 3179, 4 Sch 3*].

Place of business in part of Great Britain at 1 January 1993. The following provision applies to any limited company incorporated outside the UK and Gibraltar which has an established place of business in England and Wales both immediately before 1 January 1993 and immediately after 31 December 1992 and does not have a branch there immediately after 31 December 1992. Where, immediately after 31 December 1992, such a company has a branch elsewhere in the UK, *Secs 691* and *692* (place of business registration regime) (see 38.3 and 38.4 above) continue to apply to the company in relation to England and Wales (notwithstanding *Sec 690B* – see 38.2 above) until such time as it gives the Registrar notice of the fact that it is a company to which *Sec 690A* applies (branch registration regime) (see 38.5 above). An identical provision applies where the established place of business is in Scotland. [*SI 1992 No 3179, 4 Sch 2*].

38.16 MISCELLANEOUS MATTERS

Places of business. An oversea company must conspicuously exhibit in every place where it carries on business in Great Britain

- its name;

- its country of incorporation; and

- if applicable, the fact that its members have limited liability.

[*Sec 693(1)(b)(d); SI 1992 No 3179, 2 Sch 6*].

See 38.21 below for penalties for non-compliance.

38.17 Letter paper, notices, etc.

An oversea company must state in legible characters in all bill-heads, letter paper, notices and official publications

- its name and the country of incorporation; and

- if applicable, the fact that the liability of members is limited.

[*Sec 693(1)(c)(d); SI 1992 No 3179, 2 Sch 6*].

See 38.21 below for penalties for non-compliance.

38.18 Duty to state name, etc. – branches

The following provisions apply only to companies within *Sec 690A* (branch registration regime – see 38.5 above), and apply in addition to those relating to oversea companies generally at 38.16 and 38.17 above.

In the case of each company branch registered under *21A Sch 1* (see 38.6 above), the following particulars must be stated in legible characters in all letter paper and order forms used in carrying on the business of the branch.

(*a*) As regards such branches of all companies within *Sec 690A* (see 38.5 above)

    (i) the place of registration of the branch; and

    (ii) the registered number of the branch.

(*b*) As regards such branches of every company within *Sec 690A* which is not incorporated in an EC member state and which is required by the law of the country in which it is incorporated to be registered

    (i) the identity of the registry in which the company is registered in its country of incorporation; and

    (ii) the number with which it is registered.

(*c*) As regards such branches of every company within *Sec 690A* which is not incorporated in an EC member state

    (i) the legal form of the company;

    (ii) the location of its head office; and

    (iii) if applicable, the fact that it is being wound up.

[*Sec 693(2)-(4); SI 1992 No 3179, 2 Sch 6*].

Where a company is notified by the Registrar of a change of a branch's registered number, it may continue to use the old number for three years beginning with the date of notification without contravening (*a*)(ii) above. [*Sec 705A(5); SI 1992 No 3179, Reg 3*].

38.19 Company name

See 38.4 above for notification of change of name to Registrar of Companies and 38.17 and 38.18 above for disclosure of name on letter paper, etc.

Notice may be served on an oversea company within twelve months of the 'relevant date' to the effect that

(*a*)   its name would have been prohibited under *Sec 26* if it had been formed under *CA 1985* (see 36.2 NAMES AND BUSINESS NAMES); or

(*b*)   its name is too like a name already appearing in the Index of names kept by the Registrar of Companies.

The 'relevant date' is the date on which the company complied with the provisions of 38.3 above or those of 38.6 above, or the first such date, if more than one, since it became an oversea company. However, if on a later date the company's corporate name has been changed, the 'relevant date' is the date on which the company complied with the provisions of 38.4(*b*) above or those of *21A Sch 7* (see 38.11 above) in respect of the change or, if more than one, the latest change.

The notice, which may be withdrawn within two months of service, must state the reason under (*a*) or the similar name under (*b*). The oversea company must not then, at any time after the expiration of two months from the date of notice, carry on business in Great Britain using the corporate name (although doing so does not invalidate any transaction entered into by the company). If it does, the company and every officer or agent who knowingly and wilfully authorises or permits the contravention is guilty of an offence and liable to a fine up to the level in 40.1(*c*) PENALTIES.

The company may, however, deliver to the appropriate Registrar of Companies (see 38.52 and 38.53 below) a statement in the prescribed form (Form 694(a)) specifying a name, other than its corporate name, under which it proposes to carry on business in Great Britain. This name may also be subsequently changed using Form 694(b). The new registered name is then deemed to be the company's corporate name but without affecting any rights or obligations of the company or any legal proceedings against the company under its corporate name or any previously registered name.

[*Secs 694, 697(2), 24 Sch; SI 1992 No 3179, 2 Sch 7*].

38.20 Service of documents on an oversea company

Any process or notice required to be served on an oversea company within *Sec 691* (place of business regime, see 38.3 above) is sufficiently served if addressed to any person whose name has been delivered to the Registrar of Companies under 38.3 or 38.4 above and left at, or sent by post to, his address. Where this is not possible (because no such names have been delivered or the persons named are dead, have moved or refuse to accept service) a document may be served on the company by leaving it at, or sending it by post to, any place of business established by the company in Great Britain. [*Sec 695; SI 1992 No 3179, 2 Sch 9*]. The place of business must exist at the time of the service and cannot merely be a former place of business (*Deverall v Grant Advertising Inc [1954] 3 All ER 389*).

Any process or notice required to be served on a company within *Sec 690A* (branch registration regime) (see 38.5 above) in respect of the carrying on of the business of a registered branch is sufficiently served if addressed to any person whose name has, in respect of the branch, been delivered to the Registrar as a person falling within 38.8(*e*) above and left at, or sent by post to, the address of that person which has been so delivered. Where this is not possible, the same provisions apply as under *Sec 695* (see above). Where such a company has more than one branch in Great Britain, any process or notice which does not relate to the business of any one branch is treated for these purposes as being required to be served in respect of the business of each branch. [*Sec 694A; SI 1992 No 3179, 2 Sch 8*].

38.21 Penalties

If an oversea company fails to comply with any of the provisions of 38.3, 38.4, 38.16 or 38.17 above or 38.52 below, the company and every officer or agent of the company who knowingly and wilfully authorises or permits the default is liable to a fine up to the level in 40.1(*f*) PENALTIES. [*Sec 697(1), 24 Sch*].

If an oversea company fails to comply with any of the provisions of 38.6 to 38.11 above or 38.53 below, the company and every officer or agent who knowingly and wilfully authorises or permits the default is liable on summary conviction to a maximum fine of one-fifth of level 5 on the standard scale (see 40.1 PENALTIES) and, in the case of a continuing offence, a daily default fine (see 40.1 PENALTIES) of £100. [*Sec 697(3), 24 Sch; SI 1992 No 3179, 2 Sch 12*].

38.22 Channel Islands and Isle of Man companies

Subject to the exceptions below, the provisions of *CA 1985* requiring documents to be delivered or filed with the Registrar of Companies apply to an oversea company which is within *Sec 691* (place of business regime, see 38.3 above) and which is incorporated in the Channel Islands and the Isle of Man

- as if it were formed under *CA 1985*;

- if it has an established place of business in England and Wales, as if it were registered in England and Wales;

- if it has an established place of business in Scotland, as if it were registered there;

- if it has an established place of business in both England and Wales and Scotland, as if it were registered in both England and Wales and Scotland; and

- in a similar way to documents relating to things done outside Great Britain, as if they had been done in Great Britain.

The exceptions are as follows (for which the normal rules for oversea companies apply).

- *Sec 6(1)* (resolution altering the company's objects).

- *Sec 18* (alteration of memorandum and articles by statute or statutory instrument).

- *Sec 242(1)* (directors' duty to file accounts).

- *Sec 288(2)* (notice to Registrar of Companies of change of directors or secretary).

- *Sec 380* (copies of certain resolutions and agreements to be sent to the Registrar of Companies within 15 days), so far as applicable to a resolution altering a company's memorandum or articles.

[*Sec 699; CA 1989, 10 Sch 12; SI 1992 No 3179, 2 Sch 14*].

38.23 ACCOUNTS AND REPORTS

Every oversea company, other than those within 38.24 and 38.25 below, must, in respect of each financial year of the company, prepare like accounts and directors' report, and cause to be prepared such an auditors' report, as would be required if the company were formed and registered under *CA 1985*. [*Sec 700(1)*]. The Secretary of State may, however, modify or exempt an oversea company from these requirements [*Sec 700(2)-(4)*] and this has been done by the *Oversea Companies (Accounts) (Modifications and Exemptions) Order 1990 (SI 1990 No 440)*. The effect of the order is that, for accounts purposes, oversea companies are subject to certain of the provisions of *CA 1985, Part VII* (accounts and audit) as if that part had not been amended by *CA 1989*.

This is considered more fully in 38.26 to 38.36 below. Note that if the company is listed, or shares in it are traded on the USM, it must comply with certain necessary requirements, including circulating audited financial statements to members. Such a company may not therefore be able to take advantage of the exemptions available.

38.24 Exceptions

Oversea company with UK branch. Subject to the transitional provisions in 38.42 and 38.46 below, the provisions of 38.23 above and 38.26 to 38.38 below do not apply to any limited company which is incorporated outside the UK and Gibraltar and has a branch (as defined in 38.2 above) in the UK. [*Sec 699B; SI 1992 No 3179, Reg 2(1), 2 Sch 17*].

See also 38.39 to 38.46 below.

38.25 *Oversea credit or financial institution with branch in Great Britain*

Subject to the transitional provisions in 38.50 and 38.51 below, the provisions of 38.23 above and 38.26 to 38.38 below do not apply to any credit or financial institution which

* is incorporated or otherwise formed outside the UK and Gibraltar,

* whose head office is outside the UK and Gibraltar, and

* which has a branch in Great Britain.

[*Sec 699B; SI 1992 No 3179, Reg 2(1)*].

See 38.47 to 38.51 below for the provisions applying to such institutions. See 38.47 below for the meaning of 'credit institution', 'financial institution' and, for these purposes, 'branch'.

38.26 Duty to prepare annual accounts

For every oversea company, the directors must prepare a profit and loss account (or, if not trading for profit, an income and expenditure account) for each financial year and a balance sheet as at the last day of that year. In the case of a holding company, the directors must ensure that, except where there are good reasons, the financial year of its subsidiaries coincides with the company's own financial year. [*Sec 227 as originally enacted*].

38.27 Individual accounts: form and content

The balance sheet and profit and loss account must give a true and fair view (see 3.13 ACCOUNTS: GENERAL) of the state of affairs of the company as at the end of the financial year and its profit or loss for that year.

38.27   Oversea Companies

The following information must be given as appropriate on the balance sheet, profit and loss account or in the notes. The Secretary of State may, on application or with the consent of the company's directors, modify any of the requirements in relation to the company in order to adapt them to the circumstances of the company.

(1)   **Assets and liabilities generally**. Liabilities and assets must be summarised with such particulars as may be necessary to disclose their general nature. They must be classified under headings appropriate to the company's business unless a particular class is immaterial or, in the case of a class of assets, inseparable from another.

Fixed assets, current assets, and those neither fixed nor current, must be separately identified.

If the directors are of the opinion that any current assets would not realise their balance sheet value if realised in the ordinary course of business, they must state that fact in a note.

(2)   **Fixed assets**.

(*a*)   The method or methods used to arrive at the amount of fixed assets under each heading must be stated.

(*b*)   Subject to the exceptions below, the method of arriving at the amount of any fixed asset is to be taken as the difference between its cost (or, if standing in the company's books at valuation, its valuation) and the aggregate amount provided or written off since the date of acquisition (or valuation) for depreciation or diminution in value. Such totals must be given for each heading. Where the assets are included at valuation, the year of valuation (if known) must be stated in the notes. If valued during the financial year, the names and qualifications of the valuers, and basis of valuation, must also be given.

The above does not apply to the following assets.

- Assets the replacement of which is provided either by making provision for renewals and charging the cost of replacement against that provision or by charging the cost of replacement direct to revenue. For such assets there must be stated the means by which their replacement is provided for and the aggregate amount of the provision (if any) made for renewals and not used.

- Listed or unlisted investments (see (6) and (7) below) of which the directors' valuation is shown either as a balance sheet figure or by way of note.

- Goodwill, patents or trade marks (see (4) below).

The aggregate amounts of assets acquired, and assets disposed of or destroyed, during the financial year must be stated by way of note for fixed assets under each heading.

(3)   **Preliminary expenses**. The amount of preliminary expenses (so far as not written off) must be shown in the balance sheet under a separate heading.

(4)   **Goodwill, patents, etc**. The amount of goodwill, and of any patents or trade marks, so far as not written off, must be disclosed as a single item under a separate heading provided the amount is ascertainable from the company's books or from any contract or document relating to the sale or purchase.

(5)   **Land**. In relation to any fixed asset shown in the balance sheet consisting of land there must be stated how much is ascribable to freehold land (or Scottish

equivalent) and how much to leasehold land (or Scottish equivalent) and, of the latter, how much is ascribable to '*long leases*' (i.e. 'leases' with an unexpired term at the end of the financial year of at least 50 years) and how much to '*short leases*' (i.e. any other lease). '*Lease*' includes an agreement for a lease.

(6) **Listed investments**.

(*a*) The aggregate amount of the company's 'listed investments' must be shown under a separate heading, subdivided where necessary to distinguish

- those listed on a recognised investment exchange other than an overseas investment exchange within the meaning of *FSA 1986*; and

- those not so listed.

(*b*) There must be shown by way of note

- the aggregate market value of the listed investments where it differs from the amount as stated in the balance sheet; and

- the stock exchange value of any investments of which the market value is shown as a higher figure.

'*Listed investments*' are those which have been granted a listing either on a recognised investment exchange (other than an overseas investment exchange within the meaning of *FSA 1986*) or on any stock exchange of repute outside Great Britain.

(7) **Unlisted investments**.

(*a*) The aggregate amount of the company's 'unlisted investments' must be shown under a separate heading.

(*b*) In the case of such investments in equity shares of other companies, unless the directors' estimated valuation is either included as the balance sheet figure or disclosed in a note, the following information must be stated by way of note.

- The aggregate amount of the company's income for the financial year ascribable to the investment.

- The amount of the company's share in the net aggregate pre-tax profits of the companies in which the investments are held, and the amount of that share after taxation.

- The amount of the company's share in the net aggregate undistributed profits (less losses) accumulated by those companies since the time the investments were acquired.

- The manner in which any losses incurred by those companies have been dealt with in the company's accounts.

'*Unlisted invesments*' are any investments other than listed investments (see (6) above).

(8) **Group undertakings**. Where the company is a parent company, there must be disclosed separately on the balance sheet

- the aggregate amount of assets consisting of shares in, or amounts owing from, the company's subsidiary undertakings (distinguishing shares from indebtedness); and

- the aggregate amount in indebtedness to the company's subsidiary under-takings.

38.27 Oversea Companies

Where the company is a subsidiary undertaking, the balance sheet must show the aggregate amount of

- indebtedness to undertakings of which it is a subsidiary undertaking or which are fellow subsidiary undertakings;

- indebtedness of all such undertakings to it, distinguishing in each case between indebtedness in respect of debentures and otherwise; and

- assets consisting of shares in fellow subsidiary undertakings.

(9) **Current assets**.

(*a*) *Stocks*. The manner in which stock and work in progress has been computed must be stated by way of note if the amount is material to the company's state of affairs or its profit or loss for the financial year.

(*b*) *Foreign currencies*. The basis on which foreign currencies have been converted into sterling must be stated by way of note, if material.

(*c*) *Loans to purchase own shares*. There must be stated the aggregate amount of outstanding loans

- to employees' share schemes under *Sec 153(4)(b)* or employees and their families under *Sec 153(4)(c)*, or

- by private companies under *Sec 155*

for the purpose of giving financial assistance to purchase shares in the company.

(10) **Loans**. There must be shown under separate headings

(*a*) the aggregate of bank loans and overdrafts; and

(*b*) the aggregate amount of other loans made to the company which are repayable

- otherwise than by instalments and which fall due for repayment after the end of a five-year period beginning with the day after the end of the financial year; or

- by instalments any of which fall due after the end of that period.

For loans under (*b*) above, the terms of repayment and rate of interest for each loan must be disclosed by way of note unless, because of the number of such loans, the directors are of the opinion that compliance would result in a statement of excessive length. In such a case, a general indication of the terms and interest rates is sufficient.

A loan, or an instalment of a loan, is deemed to be due for repayment on the earliest date on which the lender could require repayment if he exercised all options and rights available to him.

(11) **Taxation**. There must be stated

(*a*) the amount, if any, set aside to prevent undue fluctuations in charges to tax and, if during the financial year such a fund has been used for any other purpose, the amount used and the fact that it has been so used; and

(*b*) particulars of any special circumstances affecting liability in respect of taxation of profits, income or capital gains for the financial year in question and/or succeeding financial years.

(12)   **Secured liabilities**. Where any liability of the company is secured otherwise than by operation of the law on any asset of the company, that fact must be stated (although it is not necessary to specify the asset in question).

(13)   **Guarantees and other financial commitments**. The following information must be stated.

(*a*)   Particulars of any charge on the company's assets to secure the liabilities of any other person, including, where practicable, the amount secured.

(*b*)   The general nature of any contingent liabilities not provided for and, where practicable, the aggregate amount or estimated amount if material.

(*c*)   Where practicable, the aggregate amount or estimated amount, if material, of

- contracts for capital expenditure, so far as not provided for; and

- capital expenditure authorised by the directors which has not been contracted for.

(14)   **Distributions**. The aggregate amount of recommended dividends must be disclosed under a separate heading. In addition, there must be shown by way of note

(*a*)   the amount of any arrears of fixed cumulative dividends on the company's shares and the period for which they are in arrears (detailing each class separately if more than one); and

(*b*)   any distribution by an 'investment company' which reduces the amount of its net assets to less than the aggregate of called-up share capital and 'undistributable reserves'. See 23.1 DISTRIBUTIONS for '*investment company*' and '*undistributable reserves*'.

(15)   **Debentures**. There must be stated

(*a*)   particulars of any redeemed debentures which the company has power to reissue;

(*b*)   to the extent that they are not written off, and, if not, under separate headings

- any expenses incurred in connection with any issue of debentures;

- any sums paid by way of commission in respect of any debentures; and

- any sums allowed by way of discount in respect of any debentures; and

(*c*)   the nominal amount of any of the company's debentures which are held by a nominee of, or a trustee for, the company, together with the amount at which that are stated in the books of the company.

(16)   **Reserves and provisions**.

(*a*)   'Reserves' and 'provisions' must be classified under headings appropriate to the company's business; provided that where the amount of any class is not material, it may be included under the same heading as some other class.

(*b*)   There must be stated (if material)

- the aggregate amount respectively of reserves and provisions (other than provisions for depreciation, renewals or diminution in value of assets) under separate headings; and

- (unless shown in the profit and loss account or by way of note) the source of any increase as compared with the amount at the end of the previous financial year and the application of any decrease.

If the reserves or provisions are divided into sub-headings, this information must be given for each sub-heading.

'*Provision*' means any amount written off or retained by way of providing for depreciation, renewals or diminution in value of assets or retained by way of providing for any known liability the amount of which cannot be determined with substantial accuracy. Where, however, such amount is in excess of that which in the opinion of the directors is reasonably necessary for the purpose, the excess is to be treated as a reserve and not as a provision.

'*Reserve*' does not include any provision (other than any excess provision as above) or any sum set aside to prevent undue fluctuations in charges for taxation.

The Secretary of State may direct that a separate statement of provisions is not required if satisfied that it would not be in the public interest and would prejudice the company.

(17) **Share premium**. The amount of the share premium account must be specified on the balance sheet. See 56 SHARE PREMIUM.

(18) **Share capital**. There must be stated

(*a*) the authorised and issued share capital;

(*b*) any part of the issued share capital that consists of redeemable shares together with

- the earliest and latest dates on which the company has power to redeem those shares;

- whether the shares must be redeemed in any event or are liable to be redeemed at the option of the company or the shareholder; and

- whether any (and, if so, what) premium is payable on redemption;

(*c*) (if not stated in the profit and loss account) any share capital on which interest has been paid out of capital during the financial year; and the rate at which interest has been so paid;

(*d*) to the extent that they are not written off, and if not under separate headings

- any expenses incurred in connection with any issue of share capital;

- any sums paid by way of commission in respect of any shares; and

- the amount of the discount allowed on any issue of shares;

(*e*) the number, description and amount of any shares in the company which any person has the option to subscribe for, together with details of

- the period during which the option is exercisable; and

- the price to be paid for the shares subscribed for under the option; and

(*f*) where shares in a public company are purchased or acquired by the company (by forfeiture or surrender in lieu) or by another person on the company's behalf, details must be given of the

- number and nominal value of the shares involved;

- consideration paid, if any, and reason for the purchase;

- maximum number and nominal value of shares held during the year;

- number and nominal value of shares so acquired which are disposed of or cancelled in the year and the consideration; and

- percentage of the called-up share capital involved for each of the above items.

(19) **Separate statement of certain items of income and expenditure**. The following must be stated.

(*a*)   The amount of interest on

- bank loans and overdrafts and other loans made to the company which are repayable *either* otherwise than by instalments and fall due before the end of a five-year period beginning with the day after the end of the financial year *or* by instalments the last of which falls due for payment before the end of that period; and

- loans of any other kind made to the company.

A loan or an instalment of a loan, is deemed to be due for repayment on the earliest date on which the lender could require repayment if he exercised all options and rights available to him.

(*b*)   The amounts respectively set aside for redemption of share capital and for redemption of loans.

(*c*)   The amount of income from listed investments and unlisted investments (see (6) and (7) above).

(*d*)   The amount of rents from land (net of ground rents, rates and other outgoings including, in Scotland, feu-duty and ground annual) but only if a substantial part of the company's revenue for the financial year consists of such rents.

(*e*)   The amount, if material, charged to revenue for the hire of plant and machinery.

(20) **Depreciation**. The amount charged to revenue by way of provision for depreciation, renewals or diminution in value of fixed assets must be shown. In the case of assets for which an amount is charged to revenue by way of provision for depreciation or diminution in value

(*a*)   if an amount is also charged by way of provision for renewal, that amount must be shown separately; and

(*b*)   if the amount charged to revenue has been determined otherwise than by reference to the amount of those assets as determined for balance sheet purposes, that fact must be stated. This does not apply to provisions for diminution in investments.

If depreciation or replacement of fixed assets is provided for by some method other than a depreciation charge or provision for renewals (or is not provided for), the method by which it is provided (or that fact) must be stated by way of note.

(21) **Directors' emoluments**. Details must be disclosed of directors' emoluments, pensions of directors and past directors and compensation to directors for loss of office. See 5.34, 5.36 and 5.37 ACCOUNTS: INDIVIDUAL COMPANIES which apply ignoring

(a)   amounts paid to or receivable by a connected person or a body corporate controlled by the director; and

(b)   in relation to pensions and compensation for loss of office, the nature and estimated money value of any benefits paid otherwise than in cash.

Comparative figures for the immediately preceding financial year must also be given.

(22)   **Dividends and transfers to and from reserves**. There must be disclosed

(a)   the aggregate amount of dividends paid and proposed;

(b)   the amount, if material, set aside to, or withdrawn from, provisions other than those within (20) above. The Secretary of State may, however, direct that the company is not obliged to show such amount if it is not in the public interest and would prejudice the company.

See (16) above for 'provisions' and 'reserves'.

(23)   **Auditors' remuneration**. The amount of auditors' remuneration (if any) including expenses must be stated.

(24)   **Miscellaneous**.

(a)   The amount of any charge arising in consequence of the occurrence of an event in the preceding financial year and of any credit so arising must, if not included in a heading related to other matters, be stated under a separate heading.

(b)   Where any items in the profit and loss account are materially affected by

- transactions of a sort not usually undertaken by the company or by circumstances of an exceptional or non-recurrent nature, or

- any change in the basis of accounting,

this fact must be stated by way of note.

(25)   **Comparative figures**. Comparative figures for all items in the balance sheet and profit and loss account at the end of, or for, the immediately preceding financial year must be shown.

[Sec 258(1)(4), 9 Sch Part I as originally enacted; SI 1990 No 440].

38.28 *Group undertakings*

Where the company is a holding company (whether or not it is itself a subsidiary) the following must be disclosed separately as indicated.

(a)   The aggregate amount of assets consisting of shares in, or the amount owing from, the company's subsidiaries (distinguishing shares from indebtedness) must be shown in the balance sheet.

(b)   The aggregate amount of indebtedness to the company's subsidiaries must be shown in the balance sheet.

(c)   The number, description and amount of the shares in, and debentures of, the company held by its subsidiaries or their nominees must be shown as a note. Excluded are any shares held as personal representative or as trustee where neither the company or any subsidiary is beneficially interested under the trust.

(d)   Where group accounts are not submitted, there must be annexed to the balance sheet a statement showing

(i)   the reasons why subsidiaries are not dealt with in group accounts;

(ii)   the net aggregate amount, so far as it concerns members of the holding company and is not dealt with in the company's accounts, of the subsidiaries' profits after deducting losses (or vice versa) for the financial years of the subsidiaries ending with, or during, the financial year of the company. Comparative figures must also be given if they were then subsidiaries;

(iii) the net aggregate amount of the subsidiaries' profits after deducting losses (or vice versa) for the financial years of the subsidiaries ending with or during the financial year of the company so far as those profits are dealt with, or provision is made for those losses, in the company's accounts. Comparative figures must also be given if they were then subsidiaries;

(iv)   any qualifications contained in the audit reports of the subsidiaries (or notes to the accounts which would have properly been referred to in such a qualification if not so disclosed) which is not covered in the company's own accounts and is material to the members;

(v)   if any of the information required under (i) to (iv) above is not obtainable, a statement to that effect; and

(vi)   in relation to any subsidiaries whose financial years do not end with that of the company, the directors' reasons for this and the dates on which the subsidiaries' financial years ended last before the end of the company's financial year (or the earliest and latest of those dates).

The provisions of (ii) and (iii) above only apply to profits properly treated as revenue profits (with certain exceptions). They do not apply where the company is a wholly-owned subsidiary of another company incorporated in Great Britain provided a statement is attached to the balance sheet that, in the directors' opinion, the aggregate values of the shares in, and amounts owing, from the company's subsidiaries is not less than the aggregate amounts at which those assets are stated or included in the balance sheet.

Where a company is a subsidiary (whether or not it is itself a holding company) the balance sheet must show the aggregate amount of

- indebtedness to companies of which it is a subsidiary or a fellow subsidiary;

- indebtedness of all such companies to it, distinguishing in each case between indebtedness in respect of debentures and otherwise; and

- assets consisting of shares in fellow subsidiaries.

[*9 Sch 19, 20 as originally enacted; SI 1990 No 440*].

38.29   Group accounts of holding company

Subject to below, if an oversea company has subsidiaries at the end of its financial year, the directors must, in addition to the individual accounts, prepare a consolidated profit and loss account and balance sheet dealing with the state of affairs and profit or loss of the company and its subsidiaries. This does not apply if

(*a*)   the company is, at the end of the financial year, a wholly-owned subsidiary of another body corporate incorporated in Great Britain; or

(*b*)   the directors are of the opinion that

- it would be impracticable, disproportionately expensive or misleading;

- (provided the Secretary of State agrees) the result would be harmful or the businesses are so different that they cannot reasonably be treated as a single undertaking; or

- instead of consolidating figures for the whole group, either more than one set of consolidated accounts are prepared *or* separate accounts are prepared for each subsidiary *or* statements expanding on the information about the subsidiaries are given in the company's individual accounts *or* any combination of those forms.

[*Sec 229 as originally enacted*].

38.30 *Form and content of group accounts*

The group accounts must give a true and fair view (see 3.13 ACCOUNTS: GENERAL) of the state of affairs and profit or loss of the company and the subsidiaries dealt with by those accounts as a whole, so far as concerns members of the company.

Where the financial year of a subsidiary does not coincide with that of the holding company, the group accounts must deal with the subsidiary's state of affairs as at the end of its 'relevant financial year' and its profit or loss for that year. The '*relevant financial year*' is the financial year ending with that of the holding company or, if the subsidiary has no financial year so ending, its financial year ending last before that date.

The consolidated balance sheet and profit and loss account must combine the information contained in the separate balance sheets and profit and loss accounts of the holding company and subsidiaries dealt with by the consolidated accounts but with such adjustments as the directors of the holding company think necessary. Subject to that, the group accounts must comply, so far as practicable, with the provisions listed in 38.27 above as if the 'group' (meaning, for these purposes, all the companies included in the consolidation) were an individual company.

Where any subsidiaries of the holding company are not dealt with by the consolidated accounts

- the provisions of 38.28(*a*)–(*c*) above apply as if such subsidiaries were subsidiaries of the 'group'; and

- there must be annexed to the accounts the like statement as is required by 38.28(*d*)(i)–(iv) above but as if references to the holding company's accounts were references to the consolidated accounts.

In relation to any subsidiary (whether or not dealt with in the consolidated accounts) whose financial year did not end with that of the company, there must be annexed the like statement as is required under 38.28(*d*)(vi) above where there are no group accounts.

[*Sec 259, 9 Sch 21-26, 31 as originally enacted; SI 1990 No 440*].

38.31 **Small and medium-sized companies**

The provisions for small and medium-sized companies do *not* apply to oversea companies. [*SI 1990 No 440, Art 2(c)*].

38.32 **Directors' report**

An oversea company need not prepare a directors' report or disclose any of the information required in such a report under *7 Sch* or *10 Sch*. [*SI 1990 No 440, 1 Sch 3*].

38.33 Auditors' report

An oversea company is not required to have an auditors' report attached to its accounts. [*SI 1990 No 440, 1 Sch 4*].

38.34 Signing of the balance sheet

An oversea company's accounts must be approved by the board and signed on its behalf by two directors (if there is only one director, by that one). Every copy laid before the company in general meeting or delivered to the Registrar of Companies (see 38.38 below) must be signed. If not, or if a copy is otherwise issued, circulated or published without being signed or bearing a copy of the signature(s), the company and every officer in default is liable to a fine up to the level in 40.1(*g*) PENALTIES. [*Sec 238 as originally enacted; SI 1990 No 440, 1 Sch 4*].

38.35 Dormant companies

The provisions of *Secs 252, 253 as originally enacted* (resolution of dormant company not to appoint auditors and laying and delivery of unaudited accounts) do not apply to oversea companies. [*SI 1990 No 440, Reg 2(c)*].

38.36 Unlimited oversea companies

An unlimited oversea company which at no time during the accounting reference period

- has been, to its knowledge, the subsidiary of a limited company, or

- has had, to its knowledge, shares owned or power exercised by two or more companies which if exercised by one would have made the company its subsidiary, or

- has been a promoter of a trading stamp scheme

is not required to prepare accounts or deliver them to the Registrar of Companies. [*Secs 241(4), 700(3) as originally enacted; SI 1990 No 440, Reg 2(3)*].

38.37 Accounting reference dates

The provisions in ACCOUNTING REFERENCE DATES AND PERIODS (1) apply to oversea companies subject to the modification in 1.5.

38.38 Delivery of accounts to the Registrar of Companies

Subject to the following exceptions, the accounts and reports must be delivered to the appropriate Registrar of Companies (see 38.52 below), together with a certified translation if in a language other than English, within 13 months (or such longer period as the Secretary of State allows) after the end of the relevant accounting reference period. The exceptions are as follows.

- If the relevant accounting reference period is the company's first and is for a period of more than twelve months, the period allowed is 25 months from the company's establishing a place of business in Great Britain.

- If the relevant accounting period is shortened by notice under *Sec 225* (see 1.4 ACCOUNTING REFERENCE DATES AND PERIODS), the period allowed is 13 months after the end of the relevant accounting reference period or three months from the date of notice, whichever last expires.

[Sec 702; CA 1989, 10 Sch 13].

Penalties. Where the accounts are not filed in the period allowed or do not comply with the requirements of *CA 1985*, the company and every person who immediately before the end of that period was a director of the company is guilty of an offence and liable to a fine up to the level in 40.1(c) PENALTIES. It is a defence for a person charged with such an offence to prove that he took all reasonable steps to secure that the requirements in question were complied with but it is not a defence in relation to failure to deliver copies to the Registrar to prove that the documents were not in fact prepared as required by *CA 1985*. *[Sec 703, 24 Sch; CA 1989, 10 Sch 13].*

38.39 ACCOUNTS AND REPORTS – COMPANIES WITH BRANCHES IN GREAT BRITAIN

The provisions at 38.40 to 38.46 below apply with effect from 1 January (subject to the transitional provisions at 38.42 and 38.46 below) to any company within *Sec 699AA*, i.e. any limited company which

- is incorporated outside the UK and Gibraltar,

- has a branch in Great Britain, and

- is not a credit or financial institution within *Sec 699A* (see 38.47 below).

[Sec 699AA; SI 1992 No 3179, 2 Sch 16].

38.40 Companies required to make disclosure under parent law

The provisions at 38.41 and 38.42 below apply to any company within 38.39 above which is required by its parent law (i.e. the law of the country in which it is incorporated) to prepare, have audited and publicly disclose accounts.

38.41 *Duty to deliver accounting documents*

The following provisions apply in respect of each branch which a company within 38.40 above has in Great Britain.

The company must deliver to the Registrar of Companies, for registration in respect of the branch, copies of all the 'accounting documents' prepared in relation to a 'financial period' of the company which are disclosed in accordance with its parent law (i.e. the law of the country in which it is incorporated), where such disclosure occurs

- after the end of the period allowed for compliance with *21A Sch 1* in respect of the branch (see 38.6 above), or, if earlier,

- on or after the date on which such compliance occurs.

For these purposes, the following are '*accounting documents*' in relation to a 'financial period' of a company.

(i)   The accounts of the company for the period, including, if it has one or more subsidiaries, any consolidated accounts of the group.

(ii)   Any annual report of the directors for the period.

(iii)   The auditors' report on the accounts in (i) above.

(iv)   Any auditors' report on the report in (ii) above.

A *'financial period'* of a company means a period for which it is required or permitted by its parent law to prepare accounts.

Where the company's parent law permits it to publicly disclose accounting documents in a modified form only, the company will satisfy these provisions if it delivers copies of documents as so modified.

If any document is in a language other than English, there must be annexed to the copy delivered an English translation, certified in the prescribed manner to be a correct translation.

Documents are not required to be delivered for a particular branch if

• they are delivered in respect of another UK branch within the time limit allowed; and

• the particulars registered under *21A Sch* in respect of the branch indicate an intention that the documents are to be registered in respect of that other branch and include the required details of that other branch. See 38.9 above.

Time limit. The period allowed for delivery, in relation to any document within these provisions, is three months from the date on which the document is first publicly disclosed in accordance with the company's parent law.

Penalties. On the failure of the company to comply with these provisions within the time limit, the company and every person who was a director immediately before expiry of the time limit is guilty of an offence and liable to a fine up to the level in 40.1(*h*) PENALTIES. It is a defence for a person charged with such an offence to prove that he took all reasonable steps to secure compliance.

[*21D Sch 2-6, 24 Sch; SI 1992 No 3179, 2 Sch 18*].

38.42 *Transitional provisions*

Where, immediately before 1 January 1993, a company was subject to the requirements of 38.23 and 38.26 to 38.38 above (the general provisions) and immediately after 31 December 1992, it is within 38.40 above, then

• for a financial year beginning before 1 January 1993, it continues to be subject to the general provisions (notwithstanding 38.24 above); and

• the requirements of 38.41 above first apply with respect to accounting documents which have been prepared with reference to a period ending after the end of the company's last financial year to which the general provisions apply.

[*SI 1992 No 3179, 4 Sch 6*].

Where a company is within 38.40 above, but the above transitional provisions are not applicable, the requirements of 38.41 above first apply with respect to accounting documents which have been prepared with reference to a period commencing after 31 December 1992. [*SI 1992 No 3179, 4 Sch 8*].

38.43   Oversea Companies

38.43   Companies not required to make disclosure under parent law

The provisions at 38.44 to 38.46 below apply to any company within 38.39 above which is *not* required by its parent law (i.e. the law of the country in which it is incorporated) to prepare, have audited and publicly disclose accounts.

38.44   *Preparation of accounts and reports*

A company within 38.43 above must prepare the like accounts and directors' report, and cause to be prepared such an auditors' report, as would be required if the company were within *Sec 700* (see 38.23 above).

The provisions in 1.1 to 1.4 ACCOUNTING REFERENCE DATES AND PERIODS and the definition of 'financial year' in 2.1 ACCOUNTS: DEFINITIONS apply with the following modifications.

(*a*)   For the references to the incorporation of a company, there should be substituted references to its becoming a company within 38.43 above; and

(*b*)   The restrictions in 1.4 on the frequency with which the current accounting reference period may be extended do not apply.

[*21D Sch 8, 9; SI 1992 No 3179, 2 Sch 18*].

38.45   *Duty to deliver accounts and reports*

In respect of each financial year and in respect of each branch which it has in Great Britain at the end of that financial year, a company within 38.43 above must deliver to the Registrar of Companies copies of the accounts and reports prepared in accordance with 38.44 above. If any document comprised in those accounts or reports is in a language other than English, there must be annexed to the copy delivered an English translation, certified in the prescribed manner to be a correct translation.

Documents are not required to be delivered for a particular branch if

* they are delivered in respect of another UK branch within the time limit allowed; and

* the particulars registered under *21A Sch* in respect of the branch indicate an intention that the documents are to be registered in respect of that other branch and include the required details of that other branch. See 38.9 above.

Time limits. The period allowed for delivering accounts and reports under these provisions is 13 months after the end of the relevant accounting reference period (i.e. the accounting reference period by reference to which the financial year for the accounts in question was determined), subject to the following exceptions.

(i)   If the relevant accounting reference period is the company's first and it exceeds 12 months, the period allowed is 13 months from the first anniversary of the company's becoming a company within 38.43 above.

(ii)   If the relevant accounting reference period is treated as shortened by virtue of a notice given by the company under *Sec 225* (see 1.4 ACCOUNTING REFERENCE DATES AND PERIODS), the period allowed is that normally applicable or three months from the date of the said notice, whichever last expires.

(iii)   The Secretary of State has the power, on an application made within the period otherwise allowed, to extend that period by such further period as he specifies in a written notice to the company.

Penalties. On the failure of the company to comply with these provisions within the time limit applicable, or if the accounts and reports delivered do not comply with the statutory requirements, the company and every person who was a director immediately before expiry of the time limit is guilty of an offence and liable to a fine up to the level in 40.1(*h*) PENALTIES. It is a defence for a person charged with such an offence to prove that he took all reasonable steps to secure compliance. It is not a defence, in relation to a failure to deliver copies, to prove that the documents in question were not in fact prepared as statutorily required.

[*21D Sch 10-13, 24 Sch; SI 1992 No 3179, 2 Sch 18*].

38.46 *Transitional provisions*

Where, immediately before 1 January 1993, a company was within 38.23 above and immediately after 31 December 1992, it is within 38.43 above, then the requirements of 38.44 and 38.45 above apply in respect of financial years ending after 31 December 1992.

In the application of 38.44(*a*) and 38.45(i) above to such a company, the references to the company becoming a company within 38.43 above are to be taken as references to its establishing a place of business in Great Britain.

[*SI 1992 No 3179, 4 Sch 7*].

38.47 ACCOUNTS AND REPORTS – CREDIT AND FINANCIAL INSTITUTIONS WITH BRANCHES IN GREAT BRITAIN

The provisions at 38.48 to 38.51 below apply (subject to the transitional provisions at 38.50 and in 38.51 below) to any 'credit institution' or 'financial institution' (see below) within *Sec 699A*, i.e. any such institution

* which is incorporated or otherwise formed outside the UK and Gibraltar,

* whose head office is outside the UK and Gibraltar, and

* which has a 'branch' (see below) in Great Britain.

'Credit institution' means a credit institution as defined in *Art 1* of the EC First Council Directive on the co-ordination of laws, regulations and administrative provisions relating to the taking up and pursuit of the business of credit institutions (*77/780/EEC*), i.e. an 'undertaking' (see 2.1 ACCOUNTS: DEFINITIONS) whose business is to receive deposits or other repayable funds from the public and to grant credits for its own account.

'Financial institution' means a financial institution within the meaning of *Art 1* of the EC Council Directive on the obligations of branches, established in a member state, of credit and financial institutions having their head offices outside that member state regarding the publication of annual accounting documents (the 'Bank Branches Directive') (*89/117/EEC*) (see 25.3 EUROPEAN COMMUNITY LEGISLATION).

'Branch', in relation to a credit or financial institution, means a place of business which forms a legally dependent part of the institution and which conducts directly all or some of the operations inherent in its business.

[*Sec 699A; SI 1992 No 3179, Reg 2(1)*].

38.48 Institutions required to prepare accounts under parent law

The provisions at 38.49 and 38.50 below apply to any institution within 38.47 above which is required by its parent law (i.e. the law of the country in which it has its head office) to prepare and have audited accounts for its 'financial periods' (see 38.49 below) and whose only or principal 'branch' (see 38.47 above) within the UK is in Great Britain.

38.49 *Duty to deliver accounting documents*

Initial requirement. An institution within 38.48 above must, within one month of its becoming such an institution, deliver to the appropriate Registrar of Companies (see below), for registration, copies of the latest 'accounting documents' (see below) of the institution prepared in accordance with its parent law (i.e. the law of the country in which it has its head office) to have been 'disclosed' (see below) *before* the earlier of the end of the said one-month period allowed for compliance and the actual date of compliance. If any of the said documents is not written in English, there must also be delivered an English translation certified in the prescribed manner to be a correct translation.

Where an institution within 38.48 above had, immediately prior to becoming such an institution, a branch in Northern Ireland which was its only or principal branch within the UK, it need not deliver the said documents if they have been delivered to the Registrar for Northern Ireland pursuant to *The Companies (Northern Ireland) Order 1986 (SI 1986 No 1032)*. Instead, it may deliver a notice that it has become an institution within 38.48 above.

[21C Sch 2; SI 1992 No 3179, 1 Sch].

Subsequent requirements. An institution within 38.48 above must deliver to the appropriate Registrar of Companies (see below), for registration, copies of all the 'accounting documents' (see below) of the institution prepared in accordance with its parent law which are 'disclosed' (see below) *after* the earlier of the end of the one-month period allowed for compliance with the above initial requirement and the actual date of such compliance. The same provision applies as above as regards English translations where appropriate.

The period allowed for delivery, in relation to any such document, is three months from the date on which the document is first 'disclosed'.

[21C Sch 3; SI 1992 No 3179, 1 Sch].

Exceptions. An institution is excepted from both the initial and subsequent requirements above if, at the end of the period allowed for compliance with the relevant requirement,

- the institution is not required by its parent law to register the documents;

- the documents are made available for inspection at each branch of the institution in Great Britain; and

- copies of the documents are available on request at a cost not exceeding the cost of supplying them.

If any of the above conditions cease to be met, the institution must deliver copies of the documents to the Registrar, for registration, within seven days of the condition ceasing to be met.

[21C Sch 5; SI 1992 No 3179, 1 Sch].

General. Where the company's parent law permits it to disclose accounting documents in a modified form only, the company will satisfy the above provisions if it delivers copies of documents as so modified.

For the purposes of these provisions, a 'financial period', in relation to an institution, means a period for which it is required or permitted by its parent law to prepare accounts.

'Accounting documents' has the same meaning as in 38.41 above, substituting 'institution' for 'company' and, in the case of an institution which does not have directors, substituting for 'directors' the persons occupying equivalent offices.

References in these provisions to disclosure are normally to public disclosure, except for an institution which is not required either by its parent law or by statute having effect in Great Britain or by its own constitution to publicly disclose accounts, in which case references to disclosure are to the disclosure of the accounts to the persons for whose information they have been prepared.

[*21C Sch 4, 8; SI 1992 No 3179, 1 Sch*].

Appropriate Registrar of Companies. The documents required to be delivered under these provisions are to be delivered to

- the Registrar for England and Wales if the institution's only branch, or its principal branch within the UK, is in England and Wales; and

- the Registrar for Scotland if the institution's only branch, or its principal branch within the UK, is in Scotland.

[*21C Sch 6; SI 1992 No 3179, 1 Sch*].

Penalties. On the failure of the institution to comply with any of the above provisions (including the delivery requirement under '*Exceptions*') within the time limit applicable, the institution and every person who was a director immediately before expiry of the time limit is guilty of an offence and liable to a fine up to the level in 40.1(*h*) PENALTIES. In the case of an institution not having directors, a person occupying an equivalent office is so liable. It is a defence for a director or other person charged with such an offence to prove that he took all reasonable steps to secure compliance. [*21C Sch 7, 24 Sch; SI 1992 No 3179, 1 Sch*].

38.50 *Transitional provisions*

Where, immediately before 1 January 1993, a company was subject to the requirements of 38.23 above and immediately after 31 December 1992, it is an institution within 38.48 above, then

- for a financial year beginning before 1 January 1993, it continues to be subject to the provisions in 38.23 and 38.26 to 38.38 above (the general provisions) (notwithstanding 38.25 above); and

- the requirements of 38.49 above first apply with respect to accounting documents which have been prepared with reference to a period ending after the end of the company's last financial year to which the general provisions apply.

[*SI 1992 No 3179, 4 Sch 4*].

Where an institution is within 38.48 above, but the above transitional provisions are not applicable, the requirements of 38.49 above first apply with respect to accounting documents which have been prepared with reference to a period commencing after 31 December 1992. [*SI 1992 No 3179, 4 Sch 8*].

38.51 **Institutions not required to prepare accounts under parent law**

As regards an institution within 38.47 above which is incorporated and which is *not* required by its parent law (i.e. the law of the country in which it has its head office) to prepare, and have audited, accounts, provisions and transitional provisions almost identical to those in 38.44 to 38.46 above (substituting 'institution' for 'company') apply as regards its duty both to prepare and to deliver accounts and reports. The only differences of substance are as follows.

- The requirement to deliver accounts and reports does not apply separately in respect of each branch in Great Britain.

- There are additional provisions as to the appropriate Registrar of Companies to whom documents are to be delivered – these are similar to those in 38.49 above, substituting 'Great Britain' for 'the UK'.

- Penalties for non-compliance apply, as they would to directors, to persons occupying an equivalent office in the case of an institution which does not have directors.

Thus, under the transitional provisions, the new provisions first apply in respect of financial years ending after 31 December 1992.

[*21C Sch 9-15; SI 1992 No 3179, 1 Sch, 4 Sch 5*].

38.52 APPROPRIATE REGISTRAR OF COMPANIES

Companies within place of business registration regime. The documents which an oversea company within *Sec 691* (see 38.3 above) is required to deliver to the Registrar of Companies must be delivered to

- the Registrar for England and Wales if the company has established a place of business in England and/or Wales; and

- the Registrar for Scotland if the company has established a place of business in Scotland.

If the company has an established place of business in both parts of Great Britain, documents must be delivered to both Registrars although if it subsequently ceases to have an establishment in one part, it must give notice of that fact to the Registrar for that part and is then only obliged to deliver documents to the other Registrar.

[*Sec 696; CA 1989, 19 Sch 13; SI 1992 No 3179, 2 Sch 11, 3 Sch 17*].

See 38.21 above for penalties for non-compliance.

38.53 Companies within branch registration regime

The documents which a company within *Sec 690A* (see 38.5 above) is required to deliver to the Registrar of Companies must be delivered to

- the Registrar for England and Wales, if required to be delivered in respect of a branch in England and Wales; and

- the Registrar for Scotland, if required to be delivered in respect of a branch in Scotland.

If the company closes a branch in a part of Great Britain, or a branch ceases to be situated in that part on becoming situated elsewhere, it must give notice of that fact to the Registrar for that part and is then no longer obliged to deliver documents to that Registrar in respect of that branch.

[*Sec 695A; SI 1992 No 3179, 2 Sch 10*].

See 38.21 above for penalties for non-compliance.

39   Partnerships

Cross-references. See 32.5 LEGAL PROCEEDINGS for criminal proceedings against unincorporated bodies.

39.1   PROHIBITION OF PARTNERSHIPS WITH OVER 20 MEMBERS

No company, association or partnership consisting of more than 20 persons can be formed to carry on a business the object of which is the acquisition of gain by the company etc. or its individual members unless it is registered as a company under *CA 1985* or formed in pursuance of another Act of Parliament or of letters patent. This does not, however, prohibit the formation of a partnership for the purposes of carrying on business as

- solicitors where all the partners are solicitors of the Supreme Court (in Scotland persons enrolled or deemed enrolled as solicitors in pursuance of *Solicitors (Scotland) Act 1980*);

- accountants where the partnership is eligible for appointment as company auditors (see 12.5 AUDITORS);

- a member firm of a recognised stock exchange, including the International Stock Exchange of the United Kingdom and the Republic of Ireland Limited (the 'London Stock Exchange') where each of the partners is a member of that exchange and a member firm of the London Stock Exchange which is, upon formation, a member firm of that Exchange by virtue of succeeding to the business of another partnership which was such a member firm;

- an investment company with variable capital;

- patent agents where the name of each of the partners is entered in the register kept under *Copyright, Designs and Patents Act 1988, s 275* or registered trade mark agents where the name of each partner is entered in the register kept under *s 282* of that *Act* or patents agents and/or registered trade mark agents where the partnership satisfies the conditions in *Rule 3* of either *Patent Agents (Mixed Partnerships and Bodies Corporate) Rules 1994* or *Registered Trade Mark Agents (Mixed Partnerships and Bodies Corporate) Rules 1994*;

- surveyors, auctioneers, valuers, estate agents, land agents or estate managers and consisting of persons not less than three-quarters of whom are members of the Royal Institution of Chartered Surveyors, the Chartered Land Agents' Society, the Chartered Auctioneers' and Estate Agents' Institute or the Incorporated Society of Valuers and Auctioneers;

- actuaries where at least three-quarters of the partners are (before 15 March 1996, all of the partners were) fellows of the Institute of Actuaries or the Faculty of Actuaries;

- consulting engineers provided the majority of partners are recognised by The Engineering Council as chartered engineers;

- building designers provided at least three-quarters of the partners are registered under *Architects (Registration) Act 1931* or recognised by The Engineering Council as a chartered engineer or by the Royal Institution of Chartered Surveyors as a chartered surveyor;

- loss adjusters provided at least three-quarters of the partners are members of the Chartered Institute of Loss Adjusters;

39.2 Partnerships

- insurance brokers where each of the partners is a registered insurance broker or an enrolled body corporate (as defined in *Insurance Brokers (Registration) Act 1977*);

- town planners provided at least three-quarters of the partners are members of the Royal Town Planning Institute; or

- lawyers in a multinational partnership within the meaning of *Courts and Legal Services Act 1990, s 89(9)*.

- practitioners in relation to matters connected with the European Patent Convention signed in Munich in October 1973 where the majority of partners are members of the Institute of Professional Representatives before the European Patent Office.

- a general medical practice provided the majority of partners are registered medical practitioners in general medical practice or, if not so registered, have been awarded diplomas, certificates and other evidence of formal qualifications the natural recognition of which is provided for in *EC Council Directive 93/16/EEC* (see OJ L165, 7 July 1993, page 1).

The provisions do not in any case apply to any approved body the objects of which are, or include, the carrying on of business by way of the reinsurance of risks which may be reinsured under any agreement for the purpose mentioned in *Marine and Aviation (War Risks) Act 1952, s 1(1)(b)*.

[*Sec 716; CA 1989, 19 Sch 15; SI 1968 No 1222; SI 1970 No 835; SI 1970 No 992; SI 1970 No 1319; SI 1982 No 530; SI 1990 No 1581; SI 1990 No 1969; SI 1991 No 1997, 1 Sch 53; SI 1991 No 2729; SI 1992 No 1028; SI 1992 No 1438; SI 1992 No 1439; SI 1994 No 644; SI 1996 No 262; SI 1996 No 2827, 8 Sch 8; SI 1997 No 1937; SI 1999 No 2464*].

39.2 LIMITED PARTNERSHIPS

Definition and constitution. Under the *Limited Partnership Act 1907*, a limited partnership consists of one or more persons called general partners (who are liable for all debts and obligations of the firm) and one or more persons called limited partners (who are not so liable). A limited partner must contribute a sum or sums of money as capital or property valued at a stated amount. During the term of the limited partnership, a limited partner cannot draw out or receive back this contribution in any way. If he does, he is liable for all the debts and obligations of the firm up to the amount drawn out, etc. A limited partner cannot take part in the management of the firm and does not have the power to bind it. If he does, he becomes liable for all the debts and obligations incurred while taking part in the management as if he were a general partner. A person cannot be a general partner and a limited partner at the same time.

Registration. A limited partnership must be registered in accordance with the provisions of *Limited Partnership Act 1907*. If it fails to do so, it is deemed to be a general partnership and all limited partners are to be treated as general partners. Registration is effected by delivering a statement (Form LP5), signed by all the partners, together with a registration fee, to the Registrar of Companies at Companies House in that part of the UK in which the principal place of business of the limited partnership is situated or proposed to be situated. The information to be supplied on the application form should include

- the firm's name;

- the general nature of business;

- the address of principal place of business;

- the full name of each partner, listing general and limited partners separately;

- the term, if any, for which the partnership is entered into;

- the date of commencement;

- a statement that the partnership is limited; and

- the sum contributed by each limited partner, and how paid (in cash or otherwise).

If all these particulars are in order and the proposed business name is acceptable (see 36.9 *et seq.* NAMES AND BUSINESS NAMES), a certificate of registration will be issued by the Registrar.

Restrictions on size. A limited partnership must not consist of more than 20 persons (ten persons in the case of a partnership carrying on the business of banking) except for a partnership carrying on business

- solicitors where all the partners are solicitors of the Supreme Court (in Scotland persons enrolled or deemed enrolled as solicitors in pursuance of *Solicitors (Scotland) Act 1980*);

- accountants where the partnership is eligible for appointment as company auditors (see 12.5 AUDITORS);

- members of a recognised stock exchange where each of the partners is a member of that stock exchange;

- members firms of the International Stock Exchange of the United Kingdom and the Republic of Ireland Limited;

- insurance brokers where each of the partners is a registered insurance broker or an enrolled body corporate (as defined in *Insurance Brokers (Registration) Act 1977*); or

- as surveyors, auctioneers, valuers, estate agents, land agents or estate managers and consisting of persons not less than three-quarters of whom are members of the Royal Institute of Chartered Surveyors or the Incorporated Society of Valuers and Auctioneers and not more than one-quarter of whom are limited partners.

[*Sec 717; CA 1989, 19 Sch 16; SI 1971 No 782; SI 1990 No 1580; SI 1991 No 1997, 1 Sch 53; SI 1992 No 1027; SI 1995 No 1163*].

Alteration of registered particulars must be delivered to the Registrar of Companies within seven days in the prescribed form (Form LP6).

Changes in limited partners. Notice of any arrangement under which a general partner becomes a limited partner, or a limited partner's share in the firm is assigned to another person, must be advertised in the London/Edinburgh/Belfast Gazette. Until this is done, the arrangement has no effect.

Inspection of documents. All registration documents relating to limited partnerships can be inspected at Companies House at Cardiff, Edinburgh or Belfast (depending upon where the principal place of business is situated). Documents relating to English and Welsh partnerships can also be made available for inspection at the London Branch by giving two days' notice.

(Companies House Notes for Guidance CHN13).

39.3   **PARTNERSHIP COMPANIES**

From a date to be appointed, the Secretary of State has powers to prescribe a *Table G* containing articles of association for a *'partnership company'* i.e. a company limited by shares whose shares are intended to be held to a substantial extent by or on behalf of its employees. [*Sec 8A; CA 1989, s 128*].

39.4 QUALIFYING PARTNERSHIPS

Subject to the exemption below, the provisions in 39.5 and 39.6 below apply to the preparation and publication of the accounts of a 'qualifying partnership'.

A '*qualifying partnership*' is any partnership governed by the laws of any part of Great Britain where each of the members of the partnership is

(*a*)   a limited company (or comparable undertaking incorporated or formed outside Great Britain); or

(*b*)   an unlimited company, or a Scottish firm, each of whose members is a limited company (or comparable undertaking incorporated or formed outside Great Britain).

Where the members of a qualifying partnership include *either* an unlimited company or firm within (*b*) above *or* a member of another partnership each of whose members falls within (*a*) or (*b*) above, any reference in 39.5 to 39.7 below to the members of the qualifying partnership includes a reference to the members of that company, firm or other partnership.

[*SI 1993 No 1820, Reg 3*].

Exemption. The members of a qualifying partnership are exempt from the requirements of 39.5 and 39.6 below if the partnership is dealt with on a consolidated basis in group accounts prepared by

●   a member of the partnership established under the law of a member state, or

●   a parent undertaking of such a member which is so established.

The group accounts must be prepared and audited under the law of the member state concerned and the notes to the accounts must disclose that advantage has been taken of the exemption.

Where advantage is taken of the exemption, any member of the qualifying partnership which is a limited company must disclose, on request, the name of at least one member or parent undertaking in whose group accounts the partnership is dealt with on a consolidation basis.

[*SI 1993 No 1820, Reg 7*].

39.5 Preparation of accounts

Subject to the exemptions in 39.4 above, the members of a qualifying partnership must prepare, for each financial year of the partnership, the like annual accounts and annual report it would be required to prepare if it were a company formed and registered under *CA 1985*. To this extent, the requirements of *CA 1985, Part VII* relating to the content of accounts apply with all necessary modifications to take account of the fact that the partnership is unincorporated and with the following additional modifications.

●   *4 Sch* (form and content of company accounts, see 5.3 to 5.31 ACCOUNTS INDIVIDUAL COMPANIES) applies apart from

(i)   under 5.3, the prohibition of treating preliminary expenses and research costs as assets in the balance sheet and the requirement of the profit and loss account to show profit or loss on ordinary activities before taxation;

(ii)   under 5.8, the provisions relating to *Development costs*;

(iii)   under 5.15, the provisions relating to *Accounting standards*;

(iv)   under 5.17, the provisions relating to *Debentures*;

(v)   under 5.18, the provisions relating to *Assets included at valuation* and *Land and Buildings*;

(vi)   5.19, 5.23(*c*), 5.25 and 5.26.

- *4A Sch* (form and content of group accounts, see 4.12 to 4.22 ACCOUNTS: GROUPS OF COMPANIES) applies apart from 4.17(*c*)–(*d*) and (i) and (ii).

- *5 Sch Part I* (disclosure of information: related undertakings, see 5.46 to 5.53 ACCOUNTS: INDIVIDUAL COMPANIES) applies apart from 5.49 and 5.53(*a*).

- *5 Sch Part II* (disclosure of information: related undertakings, see 4.24 to 4.32 ACCOUNTS: GROUPS OF COMPANIES) applies apart from 4.32.

- *6 Sch* (emoluments and other benefits of directors and others, see 5.33 to 5.43 ACCOUNTS: INDIVIDUAL COMPANIES) applies apart from 5.35, 5.37 and 5.38.

- *7 Sch* (directors' report, see 20 DIRECTORS' REPORT) applies apart from 20.13.

The accounts must be prepared within ten months of the end of the financial period and must state that they have been prepared under these provisions.

Audit. The accounts so prepared must be audited and contain an auditors' report. The provisions in *CA 1989* relating to eligibility for appointment as auditors (see 12.5 to 12.9 AUDITORS) equally apply to auditors appointed for this purpose.

[*SI 1993 No 1820, Regs 4, 12, Sch*].

39.6   Filing and publication of accounts

Subject to the exemptions in 39.4 above, every limited company which is a member of a qualifying partnership must

(*a*)   where it is a member at the end of any financial year of that partnership, attach a copy of the partnership accounts to the set of its own annual accounts next delivered to the Registrar of Companies under *Sec 242* (see 3.5 ACCOUNTS: GENERAL); and

(*b*)   supply to any person on request the name of

- each member liable to deliver a copy of the latest accounts to the Registrar under (*a*) above; and

- each member incorporated in another member state liable to publish the latest accounts of the partnership under the provisions of *4th EC Directive* or *7th EC Directive*.

Where a qualifying partnership has its head office in Great Britain but the accounts are not delivered to the Registrar of Companies (because each of its members is directly or indirectly the equivalent of a limited company incorporated outside the UK), then unless the accounts are appended to the accounts of any undertaking incorporated in another member state and published under the law of the state, the members must make the latest accounts of the partnership available for inspection at the head office (during business hours and without charge). If any document comprised in the accounts is not in English, the members must annex an English translation, certified in the prescribed manner (see 28.2 FORMS) to be a correct translation. Copies of the accounts and any certified translation must also be supplied to any person on request at a price not exceeding the administrative cost of making the copy.

[*SI 1993 No 1820, Regs 5, 6*].

39.7 Penalties for non-compliance

Where

(*a*) accounts are not prepared within ten months of the end of the financial year, or

(*b*) the accounts (as delivered to the Registrar of Companies or made available for inspection) do not comply with the necessary requirements

every person who was a member of the partnership or a director of such a member at the end of that year (or, where (*b*) applies, when the accounts were delivered or made available) is guilty of an offence and liable, on summary conviction to a fine not exceeding level 5 on the standard scale (see 40.1 PENALTIES).

Where any member of a qualifying partnership fails to comply with the requirements of 39.6 above (or, being exempt from those requirements under 39.4 above, fails to disclose on request the name of a member or parent undertaking in whose group accounts the partnership is dealt with on a consolidation basis) that member and any director of that member is guilty of an offence and liable, on summary conviction, to a fine not exceeding level 5 on the standard scale (see 40.1 PENALTIES).

Defence against a penalty. It is a defence for a person charged to show that he took all reasonable steps to secure that the requirement in question would be complied with.

The provisions of 32.2, 32.4 and 32.5 LEGAL PROCEEDINGS apply to such an offence.

[*SI 1993 No 1820, Reg 8*].

39.8 Disclosure of membership of a qualifying partnership

Where, at the end of its financial year, a company is a member of a qualifying partnership, it must disclose certain information, if material, in its accounts. See 4.31 ACCOUNTS: GROUPS OF COMPANIES and 5.52 ACCOUNTS: INDIVIDUAL COMPANIES.

39.9 LIMITED LIABILITY PARTNERSHIPS

In September 1998, the Department of Trade and Industry issued a consultation document entitled Limited Liability Partnerships, accompanied by a draft Bill and draft regulations. Under the Bill, the Government proposes to introduce a new form of corporate business association, the limited liability partnership (LLP), the object of which would be to allow a business to trade with limited liability while retaining the organisational flexibility of a partnership, the partnership practice of distributing profits to members annually, and the associated partnership basis of taxation.

The consultation document stated that the draft legislation was based on three general principles drawn from company and partnership law and practice in Great Britain.

- **Limited liability.** Since creditors will only have access to the assets of the business, the LLP would be required to file financial and other information on the public record similar to that filed by limited liability companies in Great Britain.

- **Corporate personality.** The LLP will be a body corporate in its own right, and will carry on the relevant business or professional practice for its own account. Its members will have no personal liability for its acts or obligations except as provided in the draft regulations. Members may have personal liability in circumstances where, under the general law, they have been in breach of duties owed on their own account to customers or clients of the LLP.

- **Partnership flexibility.** The members of an LLP should generally be free to organise their business on any basis which they agree amongst themselves, subject to the above and to provisions which will apply in default of an agreement between the members. They will not be required to publish the details of their internal arrangements.

The draft Bill provides a framework for the new entity and the draft regulations contain provisions for setting up and dissolving an LLP, financial reporting requirements, insolvency procedures, and the rules as to which businesses will be able to be organised as LLPs.

Following the consultation exercise, the Department of Trade and Industry issued a revised draft Bill and regulations for further consultation, reflecting changes made following the initial consultation process. Among the changes is the policy change which removes the restriction on eligibility to regulated professions, so that limited liability partnerships will be available to two or more persons carrying on any trade or profession.

40 Penalties

40.1 There are a large number of offences for failure to comply with the requirements of the *Companies Acts*. These are dealt with in the appropriate part of the text. The penalties for conviction of offences under *CA 1985* are listed in *24 Sch*. The levels of penalties in order of seriousness are as follows.

		Punishment	*Daily default fine*
(a)	On indictment	7 years or a fine; or both	
	Summary	6 months or statutory maximum; or both	
(b)	On indictment	2 years or a fine; or both	
	Summary	6 months or statutory maximum; or both	
(c)	On indictment	A fine	
	Summary	Statutory maximum	One-tenth of statutory maximum
(d)	On indictment	A fine	
	Summary	Statutory maximum	
(e)	Summary	Statutory maximum	One-tenth of statutory maximum
(f)	Summary	One-fifth of statutory maximum	One-fiftieth of statutory maximum
(g)	Summary	One-fifth of statutory maximum	
(h)	On indictment	A fine	
	Summary	Statutory maximum	£100

Punishment is the maximum fine or imprisonment which can be imposed on a person convicted of the offence in the way specified, a reference to a period of years or months being to a term of imprisonment of that duration. The fine on conviction on indictment is unlimited.

Daily default fine. Where a person is convicted of an offence (and incurs a penalty as under the *Punishment* column) but continues in contravention of the relevant provision, then, on a second or subsequent summary conviction of the offence, he is liable to a default fine for each day on which the contravention is continued (instead of the penalty under the *Punishment* column).

Statutory maximum means, in England and Wales, the sum prescribed under *Magistrates' Courts Act 1980, s 32* and, in Scotland, the sum prescribed under *Criminal Procedure (Scotland) Act 1975, s 289B*. The statutory maximum is currently £5,000 (£2,000 before 1 October 1992).

[*Sec 730, 24 Sch; SI 1992 No 3179, 3 Sch 9*].

Standard scale Certain new penalties under *CA 1985* are determined by reference to the 'standard scale' (level 5 on which is equivalent to the statutory maximum).

'*Standard scale*' means the scale laid down by the *Criminal Justice Act 1982, s 37* (in Scotland the *Criminal Procedure (Scotland) Act 1975, s 289G*) and is as follows.

1 October 1992 onwards (see *CJA 1991, s 17*)

Level on the scale	Amount of fine
1	£200
2	£500
3	£1,000
4	£2,500
5	£5,000

41 Private Companies

Cross-references. See 35.3 MEMORANDUM OF ASSOCIATION for model memoranda for private companies; 49.4 to 49.7 REGISTRATION AND RE-REGISTRATION for re-registration of a private company as a public company.

41.1 A private company allows those carrying on a family business to reap the advantages of trading as a company. It also avoids the strict requirements applicable to a public company when used as a subsidiary in a group of companies.

41.2 **DEFINITION**

Private companies are defined as those companies which are not public companies. [*Sec 1(3)*]. This includes the following.

- Companies limited by shares which, when their memorandum of association is registered under *Sec 13* (see 49.2 REGISTRATION AND RE-REGISTRATION), are not specifically registered as public companies.

- Companies already registered as private companies under *Companies Acts 1948* to *1976* (i.e. before *CA 1980, s 3* affecting the registration of public and private companies came into force) and which have not re-registered as a public company.

- UNLIMITED COMPANIES (60).

- GUARANTEE COMPANIES (29) formed after 21 December 1980 or formed before that date with a share capital and which have not re-registered as public companies.

41.3 **COMPARISON WITH A PUBLIC COMPANY**

The differences between private and public companies include the following.

- **Name.** The name of a private company (except certain companies limited by guarantee) must end in 'limited' or Welsh equivalent. The name of a public company must end with 'public limited company'. See 36.1 NAMES AND BUSINESS NAMES.

- **Authorised minimum share capital** (see 58.12 SHARES AND SHARE CAPITAL) only applies to public companies.

- **Memorandum of association.** The memorandum of a public company must contain a clause stating that it is a public company (see 35.2(*b*) MEMORANDUM OF ASSOCIATION). There is no equivalent requirement for a private company.

- **Trading certificate.** A public company requires a certificate from the Registrar of Companies before it can do business or exercise any borrowing powers (see 43.3 PUBLIC AND LISTED COMPANIES).

- **Directors.** A private company needs only one director; a public company must have at least two (see 19.2 DIRECTORS). The provisions regarding age limit for directors (see 19.8 DIRECTORS) do not apply to private companies unless subsidiaries of public companies.

- **Company secretaries** of private companies need not be qualified in the terms required for public companies (see 55.2 SECRETARY).

- **Accounts.** A private company, or a group of companies all of which are private companies, may take advantage of the exemptions for small and medium-sized companies (see 7 ACCOUNTS: SMALL AND MEDIUM-SIZED COMPANIES).

A public company may, subject to certain conditions, send its members summary financial statements instead of full annual accounts (see 43.23 *et seq.* PUBLIC AND LISTED COMPANIES).

The period allowed after the end of the relevant accounting reference period for laying accounts and reports before the company in general meeting, and for delivering a copy of them to the Registrar of Companies, is seven months for a public company and ten months for a private company. See 3.8 ACCOUNTS: GENERAL.

- **Resolutions.** Private companies may act by a unanimous written resolution of its members, without a meeting or previous notice, instead of by a resolution of the company, or any class of members, in general meeting (see 51.4 RESOLUTIONS). They may also, by unanimous elective resolution, opt out of the requirements relating to

  (i)   duration of authority for certain allotments of shares under *Sec 80A* (See 9.2 ALLOTMENT OF SHARES);

  (ii)   laying of accounts and reports before general meetings under *Sec 252* (see 3.6 ACCOUNTS: GENERAL);

  (iii) annual general meetings under *Sec 366A* (see 33.3 MEETINGS);

  (iv) authorisation of short notice of a meeting under *Secs 369(4), 378(3)* (see 33.5 MEETINGS and 51.2 RESOLUTIONS); and

  (v)   annual appointment of auditors under *Sec 386* (see 12.2 AUDITORS).

- **Proxies at meetings.** A member of a private company is not entitled to appoint more than one proxy to attend a meeting on the same occasion. However, any proxy so appointed has the same right as the member to speak at the meeting (see 33.12 MEETINGS).

- **Allotment of shares.** There are a number of important differences between private and public companies in relation to allotments. See 9 ALLOTMENT OF SHARES generally but in particular 9.2 (restrictions on public offers by private companies); 9.3 (allotment where public company issue not fully subscribed); 9.8 (exclusion of pre-emption rights by private companies); 9.11 to 9.14 (payment for shares on allotment); 9.15 to 9.18 (valuation of non-cash consideration in connection with public company allotments); 9.19 to 9.21 (transfer of non-cash assets to public companies in initial period); and 9.22 (shares issued to subscribers of public companies).

- **Maintenance of capital.** A public company must call an extraordinary general meeting where its net assets are half or less of its called-up share capital (see 58.30 SHARES AND SHARE CAPITAL).

- **Forfeiture and surrender of share capital.** Special provisions apply to public companies (see 58.27 SHARES AND SHARE CAPITAL).

- **Lien on share capital.** Any lien or other charge of a public company on its own shares, except as specifically allowed, is void (see 58.29 SHARES AND SHARE CAPITAL).

- **Acquisition of own shares.** Subject to conditions, a private company may give financial assistance for the acquisition of its own shares (see 8.21 ACQUISITION OF OWN SHARES). It may also redeem or purchase its own shares out of capital (see 8.12 ACQUISITION OF OWN SHARES).

41.3 Private Companies

- **Offers for unlisted securities**. No private company may offer its shares or debentures to the public in the UK or allot them with a view to all or part being offered for sale to the public (see 9.2 ALLOTMENT OF SHARES).

- **Distributions**. A public company may only make a distribution if, after that distribution, the net assets are not less than the aggregate of called-up share capital and undistributed reserves (see 23.5 DISTRIBUTIONS).

- **Disclosure of interests in shares**. A person who is interested in 3% or more of the nominal share capital of a public company has an obligation to notify the company of that interest. The company also has powers to require particulars of interests in its shares. See 21 DISCLOSURE OF INTERESTS IN PUBLIC COMPANY SHARES.

- **Striking off**. A public company cannot apply for voluntary striking off under *Sec 652A* (see 22.2 DISSOLUTION AND STRIKING OFF).

42   Prospectuses and Public Issues

Cross-references. See 43.4 *et seq.* PUBLIC AND LISTED COMPANIES.

The contents of this chapter are as follows.

42.1   **INTRODUCTION**

This chapter deals with public issues of both listed and unlisted securities.

(*a*)   *Offers to the public of listed securities.* The law governing issues of listed securities is in *FSA 1986, Part IV.* The regulation of listing and related matters is delegated to a large extent to the London Stock Exchange ('The Stock Exchange') and the detailed regulations governing offers of listed securities (and many other matters) are found in the *Listing Rules* of The Stock Exchange (known) as the 'Yellow Book'). For this purpose, securities which are quoted on the Alternative Investment Market established by the Stock Exchange (AIM) are not treated as 'listed'. See 42.2 to 42.18 below for further details.

(*b*)   *Offers to the public of unlisted securities.* The law governing issues of unlisted securities is in *The Public Offers of Securities Regulations 1995 (SI 1995 No 1537)* which came into force on 19 June 1995 (to coincide with the first day of dealings in shares on the AIM). See 42.19 to 42.34 below for further details.

42.2 Prospectuses and Public Issues

(c) *Offers of unlisted securities other than to the public.* Such offers are in theory unregulated. However, any representation made or document employed in the offer of such securities is classed as an 'investment advertisement' under *FSA 1986, s 57* and it is an offence to make such a statement or provide such a document to any person unless it has been approved by an authorised person. See 42.41 below for further details. Certain offers are exempt from these requirements by the *Investment Advertisements (Exemptions) Order 1996 (SI 1996 No 1586, as amended)* or the *Investment Advertisements (Exemptions (No 2) Order 1995 (SI 1995 No 1536)*. Such exempt offers, the most important of which being those made exclusively to expert investors, may be made using any representations or documents which the offeror may wish.

A company seeking to raise capital, whether for expansion, an acquisition or a particular project, has various options available, e.g. borrowing money from a bank or selling assets, but the most common method when large sums of money are involved is to issue and sell shares or debentures in the company. If the shares are to be admitted to the Official List, the issue and listing will be subject to *FSA 1986, Part IV* and the *Listing Rules*. The advantage of listing is that the shares can be freely traded in an accessible market. This may well enhance the value of the shares to a potential investor and is essential in the case of a major flotation. Alternatively, the shares may be traded on an investment exchange or, in the case of a relatively small issue which is placed directly with a financial institution, not traded at all. If shares which are not to be admitted to listing are to be publicly issued, the provisions of *SI 1995 No 1537* will (or may) apply.

42.2 LISTED SECURITIES

The term *'listed securities'*, as used here, means securities which have either been admitted to the Official List of The Stock Exchange or are the subject of an application for such admission. The shares may be new shares or existing shares either already traded on another market (e.g. AIM or a foreign stock exchange) or, possibly, not traded at all. The relevant securities to which *FSA 1986, Part IV* applies are as follows.

(a) Shares and stock in the share capital of

- any body corporate (i.e. whether a domestic or oversea company), or

- any unincorporated body which is constituted under the law of a country or territory outside the UK

but which is not an open-ended investment company.

(b) Debentures, including debenture stock, loan stock, bonds, certificates of deposit and other instruments creating or acknowledging indebtedness but not

- instruments acknowledging the consideration payable under a contract for the supply of goods;

- cheques, bills of exchange, bankers' drafts etc; or

- bank-notes, bank statements, leases containing financial obligations, heritable securities or insurance policies.

Included is loan stock etc. issued by a government or local authority outside the EC.

(c) Warrants and other instruments entitling the holder to subscribe for securities within (a) above.

(d) Certificates representing securities within (a) above.

The above securities may be admitted to listing only in accordance with the provisions of *FSA 1986, Part IV* which establishes The Stock Exchange (the *'Exchange'*) as the 'competent authority' both for making listing rules for the purposes of *Part IV* and determining applications for admission to listing. Any functions of the Exchange may be exercised by its board of directors or delegated to any committee, sub-committee, officer or servant except that the listing rules may only be made by the board, a committee or sub-committee and, when such rules are not made by the board itself, cease to have effect at the end of 28 days unless confirmed by the board within that period. Any day-to-day decisions on listing matters are taken by the Listing Department.

[*FSA 1986, ss 142, 143(1), 1 Sch 1, 2, 4, 5; SI 1991 No 2000, Reg 3*].

42.3   Conditions for listing

The Exchange may make the admission of securities to listing subject to any special conditions it considers appropriate in the interests of protecting investors. Any such conditions must be explicitly informed to the applicant.

Conditions relating to applicants. An applicant for listing must comply with the following pre-conditions.

(*a*)   The applicant must be duly constituted under the law of the place where it is incorporated or otherwise established and must be operating in conformity with its memorandum and articles of association (or equivalent documents). If incorporated in the UK, it must not be a private company or an 'old public company' (see 18.1 DEFINITIONS).

(*b*)   An applicant which is a company must have published or filed audited accounts (consolidated where it has subsidiary undertakings) which

- cover at least three years, the latest of which, in the case of a new applicant, must end not more than six months (twelve months in the case of an AIM company) before the date of the listing particulars. A shorter period than three years may be acceptable if listing is desirable in the interests of the applicant or of investors and investors have available the necessary information to reach an informed judgement on the applicant and the securities to be listed;

- have been prepared in accordance with the applicant's national law, generally accepted accounting principles and international accounting standards; and

- have been independently audited in accordance with international auditing standards (without qualification or reference to a matter of fundamental uncertainty in the case of new applicants).

(*c*)   Unless the Exchange otherwise allows, an applicant which is a company must have been carrying on as its main activity (by itself or through one or more subsidiaries) an independent business which is supported by its historic revenue earning record and which gives it control over a majority of its assets. It must have been doing so for at least the period covered by the accounts under (*b*) above.

(*d*)   The board of directors and senior management of an applicant must have collectively appropriate expertise and experience for the management of the business and the company must ensure that each director is free of conflicts between duties to the company and private interests.

(*e*)   The applicant must be satisfied that the working capital available is sufficient.

(*f*)   Where an applicant is a company which has a 'controlling shareholder' it must be capable at all times of carrying on its business independently of that shareholder and any associates. All transactions and relationships between the company and the controlling shareholder must be at arm's length and on a normal commercial basis. '*Controlling shareholder*' means any person (or persons acting jointly by agreement) entitled to exercise, or control the exercise of, 30% or more of the voting rights or able to control the appointment of a majority of the board of directors.

Conditions relating to securities. Any securities for which listing is sought must comply with the following conditions.

(i) The securities must be issued in conformity with the law of the place where the issuer is incorporated or otherwise established and with its memorandum and articles (or equivalent documents). All necessary statutory or other consents must have been duly given.

(ii) The securities must be freely transferable. Partly-paid securities will normally be regarded as meeting this condition if, in the opinion of the Exchange, their transferability is not unreasonably restricted and investors have been provided with all appropriate information to enable dealings to take place on an open and proper basis.

(iii) Except for further issues of securities of a class already listed, the expected market value of the securities to be listed must be at least £700,000 in the case of shares and £200,000 in the case of debt securities (except there is no minimum on tap issues where the amount of the debt securities is not fixed). Securities of a lower value may be admitted to listing if the Exchange is satisfied that adequate marketability can be expected.

(iv) Normally, at least 25% of any class of shares for which listing is sought must, not later than the time of admission, be in the hands of the 'public' in one or more member states. '*Public*' broadly means persons other than the directors, persons connected with directors, trustees of any employees' share scheme or pension fund and persons interested in 5% or more of the shares of the relevant class.

(v) Applications must relate to all securities of any class (where some securities of that class are already listed, all further securities of that class) issued or proposed to be issued.

(vi) Normally the issue of warrants or options to subscribe for equity capital must be limited to 20% of the issued equity share capital at the time the warrants or options are issued.

(vii) Convertible securities will normally be admitted to listing only if the securities into which they are convertible are, or will become at the same time, listed.

(viii) Any fee or other remuneration or consideration to be paid or given to any director, officer or adviser of the applicant in connection with the issue or listing may be made otherwise than in cash provided the Exchange is satisfied that full disclosure of the method of payment is made in the listing particulars and the independence of the director, etc. is not compromised to the detriment of the shareholders generally.

(ix) Where application is made to list certificates representing shares, the issuer of the shares is the issuer for listing purposes and the application will be dealt with as if it were an application for the listing of shares. Certificates representing shares will only be admitted to listing if the shares represented are already, or will become at the same time, listed. The issuer of the certificates must comply with the requirements of (*a*) above; must be a suitably authorised and regulated financial institution; and must hold the shares to which the certificates relate, and all the rights and benefits thereto, on trust for the sole benefit of the certificate holders. The certificates must satisfy the conditions in (i)–(v) above, reading 'certificates' for 'shares'.

[*The Listing Rules, Chapter 3*].

Special cases. There are additional and alternative conditions for listing dealing with oversea companies, property companies, mineral companies, scientific research-based companies, investment entities, public sector issuers, issuers of specialist debt securities (including specialist certificates representing shares) and miscellaneous securities and venture capital trusts. See the *Listing Rules, Chapters 17 to 26*.

42.4 **Methods of bringing securities to listing**

Applicants with equity shares already listed may bring securities (whether or not of a class already listed) to listing by any of the following methods.

- An 'offer for subscription' or 'offer for sale'.

  An '*offer for subscription*' is an invitation to the public by, or on behalf of, an issuer to subscribe for securities of the issuer not yet in issue or allotted (and may be in the form of an invitation to tender at or above a stated minimum price).

  An '*offer for sale*' is an invitation to the public by, or on behalf of, a third party (usually a merchant bank or stockbroking firm) to purchase securities of the issuer already in issue or allotted (and may be in the form of an invitation to tender at or above a stated minimum price).

- A '*placing*' i.e. a marketing of securities already in issue but not listed or not yet in issue to specified persons or clients of the sponsor (or any securities house assisting in the placing) which does not involve an offer to the public or to existing holders of the issuer's securities generally.

- An '*intermediaries offer*' i.e. a marketing of securities already or not yet in issue, by means of an offer by, or on behalf of, the issuer to intermediaries for them to allocate to their own clients.

- A '*rights issue*' i.e. an offer to existing holders of securities to subscribe or purchase further securities in proportion to their holdings made by means of the issue of a renounceable letter or other negotiable document. See 52 RIGHTS ISSUES.

- An '*open offer*' i.e. an invitation to existing holders of securities to subscribe or purchase securities in proportion to their holdings, which is not made by means of a renounceable letter or other negotiable document.

- An '*acquisition or merger issue*' i.e. an issue of securities in consideration for the acquisition of assets, or an issue of securities on an acquisition of, or merger with, another company as consideration for the securities of that other company.

- A '*vendor consideration placing*' i.e. a marketing, by or on behalf of vendors, of securities that have been allotted as consideration for an acquisition.

- A '*bonus issue*', in lieu of dividends or otherwise, is an issue to existing holders of securities, in proportion to their holdings, of further shares credited as fully paid out of the issuer's reserves. See 13 BONUS ISSUES.

- An '*issue for cash*' i.e. an issue of securities for cash to persons who are specifically approved by shareholders in general meeting or an issue pursuant to a general disapplication of *Sec 89* (see 9.5 ALLOTMENT OF SHARES) approved by shareholders in general meeting.

42.5 Prospectuses and Public Issues

- A conversion of securities of one class into securities of another class.

- An exercise of options or warrants to subscribe securities.

- Such other method as may be accepted by the Exchange either generally or in any particular case.

Applicants without equity shares already listed may bring securities to listing by any of the following methods. In all cases, the securities in issue must be sufficiently widely held that their marketability when listed can be assumed. In cases of doubt the Exchange must be consulted at an early stage.

- An '*offer for subscription*' or an '*offer for sale*' (see above).

- A '*placing*' (see above).

- An '*intermediaries offer*' (see above).

- An '*introduction*' i.e. a method of bringing securities to listing not involving an issue of new securities or any marketing of existing securities because the securities are already widely held by the public.

- Such other method as may be accepted by the Exchange either generally or in any particular case.

[*The Listing Rules, Chapter 4*].

42.5 Listing application procedure

Applications for admission to listing are considered by the Exchange every Wednesday and Friday. In this connection,

- certain documents etc. must be lodged in final form with the Exchange no later than midday at least two business days before hearing of the application (the '*48 hour documents*');

- by no later than 9.00a.m. on the day of the consideration of the application for listing, there must be lodged with the Exchange

    (i) payment of the appropriate charge for listing and, where relevant, the first annual charge; and

    (ii) where no prospectus has been published, a letter signed by the issuer/offeror confirming that it has not and will not offer the securities to the public for the first time prior to admission; and

    (iii) a duly completed shareholder or pricing statement in the appropriate form; and

- certain documents must be lodged as soon as practicable after the hearing of the application but no later than five business days after they become available.

For full details, see the *Listing Rules, Chapter 7.1–7.8*.

Public sector issuers, and issuers of specialist and miscellaneous securities. There are additional and different requirements for listing application procedures. See *The Listing Rules, Chapters 22–24*.

42.6 Prospectuses and listing particulars

The Stock Exchange must not admit any securities to the Official List unless a proper application is made and the requirements set out in the *Listing Rules* are complied with.

As a condition of the admission to the Official List of any securities for which application for admission has been made and which are to be offered to the public in the UK for the first time before admission, the *Listing Rules* must require that a prospectus is submitted to, and approved by, The Stock Exchange and that such prospectus is published.

Where the *Listing Rules* require a document to be submitted for approval and published otherwise than on an offer to the public in the UK for the first time, the document is referred to as 'listing particulars'.

[FSA 1986, s 144(1)(2); SI 1995 No 1537, 2 Sch 2, 3].

Contravention. Where the *Listing Rules* require the publication of a prospectus, it is not lawful, before the time of publication of the prospectus, to offer the securities in question to the public in the UK. An authorised person who contravenes this provision is treated as having contravened the conduct of business rules under *FSA 1986, Part I* or, as the case may be, the rules of the recognised self-regulating organisation or recognised professional body through which his authorisation derives. This also applies to a European Institution carrying on home-regulated investment business in the UK. A person other than an authorised person who contravenes this provision is guilty of an offence and liable, on conviction on indictment, to imprisonment for up to two years or a fine or both and, on summary conviction, to imprisonment for up to three months or a fine up to level 5 on the standard scale (see 40.1 PENALTIES). *[FSA 1986, s 156B; SI 1995 No 1537, 2 Sch 2].*

Offers of securities. A person is regarded as offering securities if, as principal

- he makes an offer which, if accepted, would give rise to a contract for their issue or sale by him or by another person with whom he has made arrangements for their issue or sale; or

- he invites a person to make such an offer.

Offers of securities to the public in the UK. Subject to the exceptions below, a person offers securities to the public in the UK if, to the extent that the offer is made to persons in the UK, it is made to the public. For this purpose, an offer to any section of the public, whether selected as members or debenture holders of a company, as clients of the person making the offer, or in any other manner, is regarded as made to the public.

Exceptions. In the following circumstances, an offer of securities, to the extent that it is made to persons in the UK, is not deemed to be an offer of securities to the public in the UK.

(*a*) The offer is to

- persons whose ordinary business activities involve them in acquiring, holding, managing or disposing of investments;

- persons who it is reasonable to expect will acquire, hold, manage or dispose of investments for the purpose of their business; or

- persons in the context of their trades, professions or occupations.

(*b*) The offer is to no more than 50 people. For this purpose, the offer must be taken together with any other offer of the same securities made by the same person within the preceding twelve months, and which was deemed not to have been a public offer because it fell within the exemption of an offer to less than 50 persons. An offer to trustees or a partnership or any two or more persons jointly is treated as an offer to a single person.

(*c*) The offer is to members of a club or association where the members have a common interest with each other and the club, etc. and with what is to be done with the proceeds of the offer.

42.6 Prospectuses and Public Issues

(*d*) The offer is to a restricted circle of persons whom the offeror reasonably believes to be sufficiently knowledgeable to understand the risks involved in accepting the offer. Information supplied by the offeror is to be disregarded in determining the degree of knowledge, except for information supplied about the issuer of any securities to be acquired under the offer.

(*e*) The securities are offered in connection with a *bona fide* invitation to enter into an underwriting agreement with respect to them.

(*f*) The securities are offered to a government, local authority or public authority.

(*g*) The total consideration payable for all securities cannot exceed ECU 40,000 (or an equivalent amount). For this purpose, the offer must be taken together with any other offer of the same securities made by the same person within the preceding twelve months, and which was deemed not to have been a public offer because it fell within this exemption.

(*h*) The minimum consideration which may be paid by any person for securities acquired by him under the offer is ECU 40,000 (or an equivalent amount).

(*i*) The securities are denominated in amounts of at least ECU 40,000 (or an equivalent amount).

(*j*) The securities in question are offered in connection with a takeover offer i.e. either (i) a takeover offer within *Secs 428–430F* (see 59.19 *et seq.* TAKEOVER OFFERS); or (ii) an offer to acquire all (or substantially all) the shares, or shares of a particular class, in a body corporate incorporated outside the UK; or (iii) an offer made to all the holders of shares (or shares of a particular class) to acquire a specified proportion of those shares.

(*k*) The securities are offered in connection with a merger within the meaning of *EC Council Directive 78/855/EEC*.

(*l*) The securities are shares and are offered free of charge to any or all of the holders of shares in the issuer. The holders of shares are the persons who held the shares at the close of business on the date specified in the offer, which date must be within 60 days before the date on which the offer is first made.

(*m*) The securities are shares (or investments falling within 42.2(*c*) or (*d*) above relating to shares) in a company, are offered in exchange for shares in the same company, and the offer cannot result in any increase in the issued share capital of the company.

(*n*) The securities are issued by a body corporate and offered by the issuer (or a body corporate connected with the issuer or by relevant trustees, as defined) on terms that a contract to acquire such securities may be entered into only by the qualifying person to whom the offer was made or, if the terms of the offer permit, any qualifying person. '*Qualifying persons*' in relation to a company are its employees or former employees (or those of another member of the same group of companies) or the wife, husband, widow, widower or child (or stepchild) under the age of 18 or an employee or former employee.

(*o*) The offer relates to securities which result from the conversion of 'convertible securities' and listing particulars or a prospectus relating to the convertible securities has been published in the UK under *FSA 1986, Part IV, CA 1985, Part III* or the *POS Regulations*. '*Convertible securities*' means

    (i) securities falling within 42.2(*b*) above which can be converted into or exchanged for, or which confer rights to acquire, securities; or

(ii)   securities falling within 42.2(*c*) or (*d*) above.

(*p*)   The securities are issued by a charity, housing association, industrial or provident society or non-profit making association or body and the proceeds of the offer are used for the purposes or the issuer's objectives.

(*q*)   The securities offered are shares which are issued by, or ownership of which entitles the holder to membership of or to obtain the benefit of services provided by

- a building society incorporated under UK law;

- an industrial or provident society or credit union incorporated under UK law; or

- a similar body established in a member state.

(*r*)   The securities offered are Euro-securities and no advertisement (other than one falling within *SI 1995 No 1536, Art 8* or *SI 1996 No 1586, Art 11*) relating to the offer is issued or caused to be issued in the UK by the issuer or any credit or financial institution through which the Euro-securities can be acquired (or any body corporate which is a member of the same group as the issuer or any of those institutions).

(*s*)   The securities are of the same class, and were issued at the same time, as securities in respect of which a prospectus has been published under *FSA 1986, Part IV, CA 1985, Part III* or the *POS Regulations*.

(*t*)   The securities are investments falling within 42.2(*b*) above with a maturity of less than one year from their date of issue.

(*u*)   The securities are loan stock, bonds or other instruments creating or acknowledging indebtedness issued by or on behalf of a government, local authority or public authority.

(*v*)   The offer relates to securities which are not transferable.

(*w*)   The condition specified under one of the headings (*a*)–(*f*), (*j*)–(*p*) or (*s*) above is satisfied in relation to part (but not the whole) of the offer and, in relation to each other part of the offer, the condition specified under a different one of those headings is satisfied.

[*FSA 1986, s 142(7A), 11A Sch; SI 1995 No 1537, 2 Sch 1, 3 Sch; SI 1999 No 734, Reg 4; SI 1999 No 1146*].

In most cases whether the document is, by the *Listing Rules*, called a prospectus or listing particulars will have little practical effect. The *Listing Rules* specify the information to be included in the document and *FSA 1986, Part IV* applies to the document whether it is a prospectus or listing particulars. [*FSA 1986, s 154A; SI 1995 No 1537, 2 Sch 2*].

42.7   Contents of prospectuses and listing particulars

The requirements for inclusion in a prospectus or in listing particulars vary according to the nature and circumstances of the issuer and the type of security to be listed. The items of information which may be required to be included are set out in detail in the *Listing Rules, Chapter 6*. See, however, *Chapter 5, appendices* and *Chapters 17–26* (overseas companies, property companies, mineral companies, scientific research based companies, investment entities, public sector issuers, issuers of specialist debt securities, miscellaneous securities and venture capital trusts) for the specific requirements for a particular issue.

The information required by *Chapter 6* for the admission of shares and debt securities to listing is set out in seven categories headed as follows.

42.8   Prospectuses and Public Issues

(*a*)   The person responsible for the prospectus or listing particulars, the auditors and other advisers. This must include a declaration in the following form.

'The directors of [the issuer], whose names appear on page [ ], accept responsibility for the information contained in this document. To the best of the knowledge and belief of the directors (who have taken all reasonable care to ensure that such is the case) the information contained in this document is in accordance with the facts and does not omit anything likely to affect the import of such information.'

(*b*)   The shares/debt securities for which application is being made.

(*c*)   The issuer and its capital.

(*d*)   The group's activities.

(*e*)   The issuer's assets and liabilities, financial position and profits and losses.

(*f*)   The management.

(*g*)   The recent development and prospects of the group.

The information required by *Chapter 6* for the admission of certificates representing shares to listing is restricted to two categories.

*   General information about the issuer.

*   Information about the certificates.

42.8   *Supplementary prospectuses and listing particulars*

If, between submission of the prospectus or listing particulars to the Exchange for approval and commencement of dealings, the persons responsible for the document become aware of any significant change affecting any matter included in the document or any significant new matter the inclusion of which would have been required in the prospectus or listing particulars if it had arisen at that time, the Exchange must be informed immediately and a supplementary prospectus or listing particulars submitted. [*FSA 1986, ss 147, 154A*].

Supplementary prospectuses or listing particulars must

*   give details of the change or new matter;

*   contain the statement required under 42.7(*a*) above;

*   contain a statement that, save as disclosed, there has been no significant change and no significant new matter has arisen since publication of the previous document; and

*   contain a statement that a copy of the supplementary particulars has been delivered to the Registrar of Companies.

[*The Listing Rules, Chapter 5.16*].

42.9   *General duty of disclosure*

Apart from the listing rules under 42.3 to 42.8 above, the persons responsible for the prospectus or listing particulars have a duty to disclose in the document all such information as investors and their professional advisers reasonably require, and might reasonably expect to be included, for the purpose of making an informed judgement about

*   the assets and liabilities, financial position, profits and losses, and prospects of the issuer of the securities; and

- the rights attaching to the securities.

The information to be included is that which is within the knowledge of the persons responsible for the prospectus or listing particulars or which it would be reasonable for them to ascertain by making enquiries. In determining this, regard must be had to

- the nature of the securities and of the issuers of the securities;

- the nature of the potential investors;

- the fact that certain information may reasonably be expected to be within the knowledge of professional advisers which potential investors may reasonably be expected to consult; and

- any information available to investors or their professional advisers.

[*FSA 1986, ss 146, 154A*].

42.10 Exemptions and partial exemptions from the prospectus or listing particulars requirements

There are very few total exemptions as whatever the status of the issue and the issuer may be, once the shares have been admitted to listing they are open to trading on a market which is, indirectly, freely accessible to the public. See, however, 42.11 below. Partial exemption is available in a wide range of circumstances, some of which are considered under 42.12 below.

42.11 *Total exemptions*

Listing particulars are not normally required for issues of shares by an issuer whose shares are already listed or issues of certificate representing shares which fall into the following categories.

(*a*)   Capitalisation issues.

(*b*)   Shares resulting from the conversion of convertible debt securities or the exercise of rights under warrants.

(*c*)   Shares issued to replace shares already listed (provided that there is no increase in the nominal value of the share capital as a result).

(*d*)   Shares which would increase the shares of a class already in issue by less than 10%. A series of issues in connection with a single transaction, or a series of transactions regarded by the Exchange as a single transaction, will be regarded as a single issue.

(*e*)   Shares allotted to employees if shares of the same class are already issued.

(*f*)   Certificates representing shares issued in exchange for shares provided that certificates of the same class are already listed and that there is no increase in the nominal value of the company's share capital as a result.

In the cases above where listing particulars are not required, the following information must be notified to the CAO and must be published in printed form as if the document comprised listing particulars.

- Where (*a*) to (*c*) above apply and the issue would increase the shares of the relevant class by 10% or more, the information required by 42.7(*b*) above (with certain exceptions).

- In all other cases, the number and type of securities to be admitted and the circumstances of their issue.

42.12 Prospectuses and Public Issues

[*The Listing Rules, Chapter 5.27–5.29*].

See also 42.12(*d*), (*e*) below.

42.12 *Partial exemptions*

Partial exemptions are numerous and vary greatly in the degree of exemption afforded. The following are the main partial exemptions.

(*a*) If any information required is not applicable and no equivalent information is available, it need not be included provided the Exchange is informed in writing by the issuer, sponsor or listing agent.

(*b*) The Exchange may authorise the omission of information if it considers that

- it is of minor importance only and will not influence assessment of the assets and liabilities, financial position, profits and losses and prospects of the issuer;

- disclosure would be contrary to the public interest; or

- disclosure would be seriously detrimental to the issuer and omission would not be likely to mislead investors.

(*c*) The Exchange may, on request, allow all or part of a material contract to be withheld from public inspection.

(*d*) If the securities in question have, prior to the application, been

- the subject of a public issue,

- issued in connection with a takeover offer, or

- issued in connection with a merger involving the acquisition of another company or formation of a new company, the division of a company, the transfer of all or part of a company's assets and liabilities or as consideration for the transfer of assets other than cash,

then the Exchange may exempt the issuers from the obligation to provide listing particulars provided that, within the period of twelve months preceding the admission of the securities, a document (the 'relevant document') has been published in the UK which, in the opinion of the Exchange, contained information equivalent to that which would have been required by the listing rules.

(*e*) The Exchange may exempt issuers from the obligation to publish a prospectus or listing particulars where

- those securities have been listed in another EU member state for not less than three years before the application and the Exchange receives confirmation from the competent authority in the member state that the issuer has complied with all requirements as to information and admission to listing imposed by the relevant *EC Directives*; or

- the issuer's shares have been traded on the AIM for at least the preceding two years and, in the opinion of the Exchange, equivalent information to that required by the *EC Listing Particulars Directive* is available to investors before the date of admission.

(*f*) Where an issuer

- applies for admission to listing of securities which are to be offered to the public for the first time before admission, and

- the issuer has published a full prospectus in respect of different securities in the twelve months before the date of offer,

the prospectus in relation to the application need only contain those differences which have arisen since the full prospectus and which are likely to influence the value of the securities.

Where exemption is given under (*d*) or (*e*) above, specified information must be published in printed form in an exempt listing document instead of listing particulars.

[*FSA 1986, ss 148(1)(2), 154A; The Listing Rules, Chapter 5.17–5.25, Appendix 2*].

42.13 Registration of prospectuses and listing particulars

On or before the date on which a prospectus or listing particulars under 42.6 above or a supplementary prospectus or supplementary listing particulars under 42.8 above are published as required by 42.14 below, a copy of the document must be delivered for registration to the Registrar of Companies and a statement that a copy has been delivered must be included in the document. In default, the issuer of the securities in question and any person knowingly a party to the publication is guilty of an offence and liable to a penalty up to the level in 40.1(*d*) PENALTIES. [*FSA 1986, ss 149, 154A*].

42.14 Publication and circulation of prospectuses and listing particulars

Prospectuses and listing particulars (including supplementary ones) must not be published, advertised or circulated until they have been approved by, or authorised for issue by, the Exchange [*FSA 1986, ss 154(1), 154A*] and must not be circulated or made available publicly unless they have been published as required below. Draft prospectuses and listing particulars, clearly marked as such, may however be circulated without approval for the purpose of arranging a placing, syndication, underwriting or for marketing an intermediaries offer.

Publication of prospectuses and listing particulars. Prospectuses and listing particulars must be published by making them available to the public (free of charge in printed form and in sufficient numbers to satisfy public demand) at the issuer's registered office in the UK and the offices of any paying agent of the issuer in the UK. The copies must be available for at least 14 days from earliest of the date of any advertisement in a national daily newspaper (see below), the business day following that on which the document is sent to the shareholders or the business day on which admission to listing is expected to become effective. Copies must also be made available at the CAO.

Advertising. Unless the securities are of a class already issued, a 'formal notice' must be inserted in at least one national newspaper no later than the next business day following publication of the prospectus or listing particulars. In the case of an offer for sale or subscription, the issuer may elect instead to insert an 'offer notice', mini-prospectus (see 42.15 below) or full listing particulars.

A '*formal notice*' is an advertisement (not being a prospectus or listing particulars) stating

- the name and country of incorporation of the issuer and, if desired, a brief statement of the issuer's business;

- the amount and title of the securities to be listed;

- the name and country of incorporation of any guarantor of the principal or interest on such securities;

42.14 Prospectuses and Public Issues

- that listing particulars or a prospectus have been published and the addresses and times at which copies of the document are available to the public;

- (if applicable) in the case of a marketing by a new applicant of equity securities with a value at offer price of not more than £50 million, the proportion of the securities made available directly to the public by means of an offer for sale or subscription or the proportion marketed by way of an intermediaries offer;

- the date of the notice;

- in the case of non-equity securities and where there is a facility to issue further tranches, the total amount of the securities which could be issued under that facility; and

- the name of the sponsoring member firm or listing agent.

Such a notice requires formal approval by the Exchange before issue.

An '*offer notice*' is a document (not being a prospectus or listing particulars) which has attached to it, or which contains, an application form. The notice must also include all the information required by a formal notice and a statement to the effect that listing particulars or a prospectus have been published which alone contain full details of the issuer and the securities being offered. Such a notice requires formal approval by the Exchange before issue.

Timing. Normally, a prospectus or listing particulars must be published, and any relevant advert inserted in a national newspaper, at least two business days before the expected date of the consideration of the application for admission to listing.

Circulation to shareholders. Where listing particulars or summary particulars are produced

- in connection with a rights issue or open offer, the issuer must circulate a copy to the relevant shareholders with the relevant circular;

- in respect of securities issued in consideration for a takeover or merger, the issuer must circulate a copy to the shareholder of the offeree company with the offer document; and

- on a reverse takeover, a copy must be circulated to the issuer's shareholders with the Class 1 circular giving details of the transaction.

In all other cases where a circular to holders of securities is required, the listing particulars or supplementary particulars need not be sent with the circular unless those shareholders are being offered an opportunity to subscribe for, or acquire, the securities concerned. Where listing particulars are published but not sent, the circular must include a statement that the listing particulars are obtainable free of charge on request.

Supplementary prospectuses and listing particulars must be made available to the public at the issuer's registered office in the UK and the office of any paying agent in the UK (for a period of 14 days) and at the CAO. They must also be circulated to shareholders where a prospectus, listing particulars or summary particulars were so circulated (see above).

[*The Listing Rules, Chapter 8.1–8.11, 8.14–8.20*].

Additional and alternative publication requirements apply to investment entities, public sector issuers and issuers of specialist securities and miscellaneous securities. See the *Listing Rules, Chapters 21–24*.

Penalties. An authorised person who issues an advertisement or other information in breach of the above rules will be treated as having contravened the conduct of business rules under *FSA 1986, Part 1* or the rules of the recognised self-regulating organisation or recognised professional body through which he is authorised. [*FSA 1986, s 154(2)*]. With effect from 1 January 1993, this also applies to a European Institution carrying on home-regulated investment business in the UK. [*SI 1992 No 3218, 9 Sch 37*].

In the case of a person who is not authorised, he will be guilty of an offence and liable, on conviction on indictment, to imprisonment for up to two years or a fine or both and, on summary conviction, to a fine up to the statutory maximum (see 40.1 PENALTIES). It is a defence for a person who, on behalf of another, issues the advertisement in the ordinary course of a business other than an investment business to prove that he believed on reasonable grounds that publication had been approved. [*FSA 1986, s 154(3)(4)*].

Where the information has been approved or its issue has been authorised under the above, neither the person issuing it nor any person responsible for the listing particulars can incur any civil liability for any statements in, or omissions from, the advertisement, etc. if that information and the listing particulars, taken together, would not be likely to mislead potential purchasers of the securities. [*FSA 1986, s 154(5)*].

42.15 Mini-prospectuses

In major flotations it is not unusual to publish a 'mini-prospectus' in place of the listing particulars. A '*mini-prospectus*' is a document (not being listing particulars) which has attached to it, or which contains, an application form and includes such additional information about the issuer and the securities as the issuer decides. It must, however, include only information taken from the listing particulars and must include

- a statement that listing particulars have been published which alone contain the full details of the issuer and of the securities being offered;

- the date of the listing particulars;

- a statement that the listing particulars are obtainable on request, free of charge, until the last day for acceptance and details of how they may be obtained;

- a statement that the directors are satisfied that the mini-prospectus contains a fair summary of the key information set out in the listing particulars; and

- a statement that the issue of the mini-prospectus has been authorised by the Exchange without approval of its contents.

[*The Listing Rules, Chapter 8.12, 8.13*].

42.16 Refusal of application and notification of decision

The Exchange may refuse an application for listing

- if it considers that, by reason of any matter relating to the issuer, the admission of the securities would be detrimental to the interests of the investor; or

- in the case of securities already officially listed elsewhere in the EC, if the issuer has failed to comply with any obligations to which he is subject by virtue of that listing.

The Exchange must notify the applicant of its decision within six months of the date of application or, where further information has been requested, within six months from the date that information is furnished. If it does not do so, it is to be taken as having refused the application.

[*FSA 1986, s 144(3)-(5)*].

42.17 Prospectuses and Public Issues

42.17 Discontinuance and suspension of listing

The Exchange may, in accordance with the listing rules

- discontinue the listing of any securities if satisfied that there are special circumstances which preclude normal dealings in the securities; and

- suspend the listing of any securities.

[*FSA 1986, s 145*].

For enforcement of the listing rules generally, see 43.22 PUBLIC AND LISTED COMPANIES.

42.18 Liability for prospectuses and listing particulars

See 42.36 to 42.40 below.

42.19 UNLISTED SECURITIES

The *Public Offers of Securities Regulations 1995 (SI 1995 No 1537* (the '*POS Regulations*') came into force on 19 June 1995 and introduced revised rules for public offers of unlisted securities.

In addition to the legislative requirements, companies whose shares are admitted to trading on the Alternative Investment market ('AIM'), which opened for business on 19 June 1995 are subject to the rules of that market. The interrelationship between the *AIM Rules* and *SI 1995 No 1537* is close, so the *AIM Rules* must always be read in conjunction with those *Regulations*.

42.20 Investments to which the *POS Regulations* apply

The provisions of 42.21 to 42.30 below apply to any investment which is not admitted to official listing, nor the subject of an application for listing, and falls within one of the following categories.

(*a*)   Shares and stock in the share capital of

    (i)   any body corporate (i.e. whether a domestic or overseas company), or

    (ii)   any unincorporated body which is constituted under the law of a country or territory outside the UK

    but which is not a UK building society or an open-ended investment company.

(*b*)   Debentures, including debenture stock, loan stock, bonds, certificates of deposit and other instruments creating or acknowledging indebtedness but not

    (i)   debentures having a maturity of less than one year from their date of issue;

    (ii)   instruments acknowledging the consideration payable under a contract for the supply of goods;

    (iii)   cheques, bills of exchange, bankers' drafts, etc; or

    (iv)   bank-notes, bank statements, leases containing financial obligations, heritable securities or insurance policies.

(*c*)   Warrants and other instruments entitling the holder to subscribe for or acquire investments falling within (*a*) or (*b*) above.

(*d*)   Certificates representing securities of a kind within (*a*)–(*c*) above.

[*FSA 1986, 1 Sch 1, 2, 4, 5; SI 1995 No 1537, Reg 3*].

42.21 **Offers**

Subject to the exemptions in 42.22 below, when securities are offered to the public in the UK for the first time, the offeror must publish a prospectus by making it available to the public, free of charge, at an address in the UK, from the time he first offers the securities until the end of the period during which the offer remains open.

For this purpose

(*a*)   a person is regarded as offering securities if, as principal

- he makes an offer which, if accepted, would give rise to a contract for the issue or sale of the securities by him or by another person with whom he has made arrangements for the issue or sale of the securities; or

- he invites a person to make such an offer; and

(*b*)   a person offers securities to the public in the UK if, to the extent that the offer is made to persons in the UK, it is made to the public. An offer to any section of the public, whether selected

- as members or debenture holders of a company,

- as clients of the person making the offer, or

- in any other manner

is regarded as made to the public.

[*SI 1995 No 1537, Regs 4(1), 5, 6*].

42.22 **Exemptions**

In the following circumstances, an offer of securities, to the extent that it is made to persons in the UK, is not deemed to be an offer of securities to the public in the UK. As a result, there is no requirement for a prospectus complying with the *POS Regulations*.

(*a*)   The offer is to

- persons whose ordinary business activities involve them in acquiring, holding, managing or disposing of investments;

- persons who it is reasonable to expect will acquire, hold, manage or dispose of investments for the purpose of their business; or

- persons in the context of their trades, professions or occupations.

(*b*)   The offer is to no more than 50 people. For this purpose, the offer must be taken together with any other offer of securities of the same class made by the same person within the preceding twelve months, and which was deemed not to have been a public offer because it fell within the exemption of an offer to less than 50 persons. An offer to trustees or a partnership or any two or more persons jointly is treated as an offer to a single person.

(*c*)   The offer is to members of a club or association where the members have a common interest with each other and the club, etc. and with what is to be done with the proceeds of the offer.

(*d*)   The offer is to a restricted circle of persons whom the offeror reasonably believes to be sufficiently knowledgeable to understand the risks involved in accepting the offer. Information supplied by the offeror is to be disregarded in determining the degree of knowledge, except for information supplied about the issuer of any securities to be acquired under the offer.

42.22 Prospectuses and Public Issues

(*e*)   The securities are offered in connection with a *bona fide* invitation to enter into an underwriting agreement with respect to them.

(*f*)   The offer is of securities in a private company and is made by that company to

- members or employees of the company;

- their families (i.e. husbands, wives, widows, widowers, children (including stepchildren) and their descendants;

- trustees of any trust the principal beneficiary of which is a member or employee of the company (or their family or descendants); or

- holders of company's debentures, etc. within 42.20(*b*) above (but ignoring 42.20(*b*)(i)).

(*ff*)   The securities are in a private company and are offered to holders of other securities in that company (whether or not of the same class) under a requirement imposed by the articles of association or in an agreement between all the holders of securities, or all the holders of one or more classes of security, of that company.

(*g*)   The securities are offered to a government, local authority or public authority.

(*h*)   The total consideration payable for all securities cannot exceed ECU 40,000 (or an equivalent amount). For this purpose, the offer must be taken together with any other offer of securities of the same class made by the same person within the preceding twelve months, and which was deemed not to have been a public offer because it fell within this exemption.

(*i*)   The minimum consideration which may be paid by any person for securities acquired by him under the offer is ECU 40,000 (or an equivalent amount).

(*j*)   The securities are denominated in amounts of at least ECU 40,000 (or an equivalent amount).

(*k*)   The securities in question are offered in connection with a takeover offer i.e. either (i) a takeover offer within *Secs 428–430F* (see 59.19 *et seq.* TAKEOVER OFFERS); or (ii) an offer to acquire all (or substantially all) the shares, or shares of a particular class, in a body corporate incorporated outside the UK; or (iii) an offer made to all the holders of shares (or shares of a particular class) to acquire a specified proportion of those shares.

(*l*)   The securities are offered in connection with a merger within the meaning of *EC Council Directive 78/855/EEC.*

(*m*)   The securities are shares and are offered free of charge to any or all of the holders of shares in the issuer. The holders of shares are the persons who held the shares at the close of business on the date specified in the offer, which date must be within 60 days before the date on which the offer is first made.

(*n*)   The securities are shares (or investments falling within 42.20(*c*) or (*d*) above relating to shares) in a company, are offered in exchange for shares in the same company, and the offer cannot result in any increase in the issued share capital of the company.

(*o*)   The securities are issued by a body corporate and offered by the issuer (or a body corporate connected with the issuer or by relevant trustees, as defined) on terms that a contract to acquire such securities may be entered into only by the qualifying person to whom the offer was made or, if the terms of the offer permit, any qualifying person. '*Qualifying persons*' in relation to a company are its employees or former employees (or those of another member of the same group of companies) or the wife, husband, widow, widower or child (or stepchild) under the age of 18 or an employee or former employee.

(*p*) The offer relates to securities which result from the conversion of 'convertible securities' and listing particulars or a prospectus relating to the convertible securities has been published in the UK under *FSA 1986, Part IV, CA 1985, Part III* or the *POS Regulations*. '*Convertible securities*' means

  • securities falling within 42.20(*b*) above which can be converted into or exchanged for, or which confer rights to acquire, securities; or

  • securities falling within 42.20(*c*) or (*d*) above.

(*q*) The securities are issued by a charity, housing association, industrial or provident society or non-profit making association or body and the proceeds of the offer are used for the purposes or the issuer's objectives.

(*r*) The securities offered are shares, ownership of which entitles the holder

  • to obtain the benefit of services provided by a building society, industrial or provident society or a similar body established in a member state; or

  • to membership of such a body.

(*s*) The securities offered are Euro-securities and no advertisement (other than one falling within *SI 1995 No 1536, Art 8* or *SI 1996 No 1586, Art 11*) relating to the offer is issued or caused to be issued in the UK by the issuer or any credit or financial institution through which the Euro-securities can be acquired (or any body corporate which is a member of the same group as the issuer or any of those institutions).

(*t*) The securities are of the same class, and were issued at the same time, as securities in respect of which a prospectus has been published under *FSA 1986, Part IV, CA 1985, Part III* or the *POS Regulations*.

(*u*) The offer relates to securities which are not transferable.

(*v*) The condition specified under one of the headings (*a*)–(*f*), (*g*), (*k*)–(*q*) or (*t*) above is satisfied in relation to part (but not the whole) of the offer and, in relation to each other part of the offer, the condition specified under a different one of those headings is satisfied.

[*SI 1995 No 1537, Regs 2, 7; SI 1999 No 734, Reg 2; SI 1999 No 1146*].

42.23 Registration of prospectus

The offeror (see 42.21 above) must, before the prospectus is published, deliver a copy of it to the appropriate Registrar of Companies for registration. [*SI 1995, No 1537, Reg 4(2)*]. As the prospectus must be published from the time of the offer (see 42.21 above), it follows that it must be registered before the offer is made.

The Registrar of Companies with whom the prospectus must be registered depends upon where the company issuing the securities is incorporated. If the company is incorporated in Great Britain and has its registered office in England and Wales it means the Registrar of Companies in England and Wales; if its registered office is in Scotland, it means the Registrar of Companies in Scotland. If the company is incorporated in Northern Ireland, the prospectus must be registered with the Registrar of Companies in Northern Ireland. In any other case, the prospectus may be registered with any of those Registrars. [*SI 1995 No 1537, Reg 2*].

42.24 Form and content of prospectus

The information in a prospectus must be presented in as easily analysable and comprehensible a form as possible. [*SI 1995 No 1537, Reg 8(3)*].

42.25 Prospectuses and Public Issues

Exemptions from providing full information

A prospectus need not contain all the information required under 42.26 below in the following circumstances.

(*a*)   Where the required information is inappropriate to

- the issuer's sphere of activities or the legal form or the issuer or offeror, or

- the securities to which the issue relates

the prospectus should contain information equivalent to the required information. If there is no such equivalent information, the requirement does not apply. [*SI 1995 No 1537, Reg 8(2); SI 1999 No 734, Reg 2*].

(*b*)   Where shares within 42.20(*a*) above are offered on a pre-emptive basis to some or all of the existing holders (i.e. a rights or similar issue) and the shares will be admitted to dealing on an approved exchange, the Treasury may designate a person to authorise the omission of information within 42.26(*e*)–(*g*) below provided that up-to-date equivalent information is available as a result of the requirements of the approved exchange. [*SI 1995 No 1537, Reg 8(4)(4A); SI 1999 No 734, Reg 2*]. The Stock Exchange has been designated as the relevant person and both the AIM and USM have been given the status of approved exchanges for this purpose. The Stock Exchange requires written confirmation from the nominated adviser or sponsor that the relevant information is available.

(*c*)   Where shares within 42.20(*a*) above have been admitted to dealing on an approved exchange, a person designated by the Treasury may authorise the making of an offer without a prospectus provided

- the number, estimated market value, nominal value or accounting par value of the securities offered is less than 10% of the number or corresponding value of securities of the same class already admitted to dealing; and

- up-to-date information equivalent to that otherwise required is available as a result of the requirements of the approved exchange.

[*SI 1995 No 1537, Reg 8(5)*].

The Stock Exchange has been designated as the relevant person and both the AIM and the USM have been given the status of approved exchanges for this purpose. The Stock Exchange requires written confirmation from the nominated adviser or sponsor that the relevant information is available.

(*d*)   Where an offer is made to the public in the UK and, within the preceding twelve months, a full prospectus has been published relating to a different class of securities or an earlier issue of the same securities, the offeror may alternatively publish a limited prospectus which contains only the differences which have arisen since the earlier prospectus and which are likely to influence the value of the securities. The limited prospectus must either be accompanied by the earlier full prospectus (and any supplementary prospectus) or must contain a reference to it (or them). [*SI 1995 No 1537, Reg 8(6)*].

(*e*)   The Treasury or the Secretary of State may authorise the omission from a prospectus or supplementary prospectus of information otherwise required if disclosure would be contrary to the public interest. [*SI 1995 No 1537, Reg 11(1)*].

(*f*)   An offeror may omit information from a prospectus or supplementary prospectus information that would otherwise be required with regard to an *'issuer'* (i.e. the person by whom the securities have been or are to be issued) where

- the offeror is not the issuer nor acting in pursuance of an agreement with the issuer;

- the information is not available to the offeror because he is not the issuer; and

- the offeror is unable, despite reasonable efforts, to obtain the information.

[*SI 1995 No 1537, Reg 11(2)*].

(*g*)   The Stock Exchange may authorise omission from a prospectus or supplementary prospectus of information otherwise required if

- it is of minor importance and not likely to influence the assessment of the issuer's assets and liabilities, financial position, profits and losses and prospects; or

- disclosure of the information would be seriously detrimental to the issuer and its omission would not be likely to mislead investors with regard to facts and circumstances necessary for an informed assessment of the securities.

[*SI 1995 No 1537, Reg 11(3)*].

42.26 *Information to be included in the prospectus*

Subject to the exemptions in 42.25 above, information must be included in the prospectus under the following categories.

(*a*)   General requirements.

(*b*)   The persons responsible for the prospectus and advisers.

(*c*)   The securities to which the prospectus relates and the offer.

(*d*)   General information about the issuer and its capital.

(*e*)   The issuer's principal activities.

(*f*)   The issuer's assets and liabilities, financial position and profits and losses.

(*g*)   The issuer's administration, management and supervision.

(*h*)   Recent developments in the issuer's business and prospects.

(*i*)   Convertible securities and guarantees debentures.

[*SI 1995 No 1537, Reg 8(1), 1 Sch; SI 1999 No 734, Reg 2*].

Additionally, any information required by the *AIM Rules* or *USM Rules* must also be included.

42.27 *General duty of disclosure*

In addition to the information required to be in a prospectus under 42.26 above, a prospectus must contain all such information as investors would reasonably require, and might reasonably expect to be included, for the purpose of making an informed assessment of

- the assets and liabilities, financial position, profits and losses, and prospects of the issuer of the securities; and

- the rights attaching to those securities.

The information to be included is that which is within the knowledge of any person responsible for the prospectus or which it would be reasonable for him to obtain by making enquiries. In determining this, regard must be had to the nature of the securities.

[*SI 1995 No 1537, Reg 9*].

42.28 Supplementary prospectus

Where a prospectus has been registered under these provisions and, at any time while an agreement in respect of those securities can be entered into under the offer

- there is a significant change affecting any matter which had to be contained in the prospectus under 42.26 or 42.27 above,

- a significant new matter arises which would have had to be included if known at the time, or

- there is a significant inaccuracy in the prospectus,

the offeror must deliver to the Registrar of Companies and publish a supplementary prospectus containing the appropriate information. The provisions of 42.21 and 42.23 above as regards publishing and registering of a prospectus also apply to a supplementary prospectus except that the obligation to publish begins with the time the supplementary prospectus is delivered for registration.

[*SI 1995 No 1537, Reg 10*].

42.29 Advertisements, etc. in connection with offer of securities

An advertisement, notice, poster or document (other than a prospectus) announcing a public offer of securities for which a prospectus is or will be required can only be issued if the advertisement, etc. states that a prospectus is or will be published and gives the address in the UK from which it can be obtained or will be obtainable. [*SI 1995 No 1537, Reg 12*].

42.30 Contraventions of the *POS Regulations*

An authorised person who

(*a*) contravenes the provisions of 42.21, 42.23 or 42.29 above, or

(*b*) assists another person to contravene any of those provisions

is treated as having contravened the conduct of business rules under *FSA 1986, Part I* or, as the case may be, the rules of the recognised self-regulating organisation or recognised professional body through which his authorisation derives. This also applies to a European Institution carrying on home-regulated investment business in the UK.

A person other than an authorised person acting within (*a*) or (*b*) above is guilty of an offence and liable, on conviction on indictment, to imprisonment for up to two years or a fine or both and, on summary conviction, to imprisonment for up to three months or a fine up to level 5 on the standard scale (see 40.1 PENALTIES).

[*SI 1995 No 1537, Reg 16*].

42.31 Acceptance of applications and allotment of shares

A prospectus will usually invite the public to apply for shares by returning an application form. The prospectus will state the time by which the application form must be received and to whom it should be sent. Usually the application must be accompanied by a cheque. The prospectus will contain detailed terms and conditions on the basis of which applications will be made. For example, the issuer or vendor will reserve the right to reject any application and, if appropriate, aggregate or prohibit multiple applications.

Acceptance of applications is often effected by posting renounceable letters of allotment or acceptance rather than definitive certificates. This allows the registrars more time to prepare definitive certificates and, in the case of an offer for sale, it provides a convenient mechanism whereby the price can be made payable by instalments.

42.32 *Application for, and allotment of, shares and debentures*

No allotment of shares or debentures must be made in respect of a prospectus issued generally until the beginning of the third working day after the prospectus is first issued or until such later time as is specified in the prospectus ('*the time of opening of the subscription lists*'). A prospectus is '*first issued*' on the day it is first issued in any manner unless, before the third day after that day, it is issued as a newspaper advertisement in which case that later date is the day of first issue.

In contravention of the above, the company and every officer in default is liable to a fine up to the level in 40.1(*d*) PENALTIES. The commission of such an offence does not however affect the validity of any allotment.

[*Sec 82(1)-(5), 24 Sch*].

The above provisions also apply to a prospectus offering shares or debentures for sale but substituting 'sale' for 'allotment'. The penalty provisions apply to any person by or through whom the offer is made and who knowingly and wilfully authorises or permits the contravention. [*Sec 82(6)*].

An application made pursuant to a prospectus issued generally is not normally revocable until after the expiration of the third working day after the time of the opening of the subscription lists. (Applications, which in contractual terms are offers, should therefore be accepted before the end of that third day.) Revocation may take place earlier if, before that time, a person responsible for the prospectus or any part of it gives public notice so as to limit or exclude his liability. [*Sec 82(7)*].

42.33 *No allotment without minimum subscription*

On the first occasion of the allotment of shares to the public for subscription by a company, no allotment must be made unless

(*a*)   the 'minimum subscription' has been raised; and

(*b*)   the sum payable on application has been paid to, or received by, the company.

A cheque received in good faith which the directors have no reason to believe will not be paid is deemed to be paid and received for the purpose of (*b*) above.

'Minimum subscription' is the amount stated in the prospectus and reckoned exclusively of any amount payable otherwise than in cash.

The above conditions must be complied with within 40 days of the first issue of the prospectus (see 42.32 above). If not, all money received from applicants must be repaid and, where not repaid within 48 days, the directors are jointly and severally liable to repay it with interest at 5% per annum from the 48th day. A director is not so liable if he proves that the default in repayment was not due to any misconduct or negligence on his part.

Any condition requiring or binding an applicant to waive compliance with any of the above requirements is void.

[*Sec 83*].

42.34   *Allotment of shares, etc. to be dealt in on a stock exchange*

Before 10 May 1999, where any prospectus stated that application had been or would be made for permission for the shares or debentures offered to be listed on any stock exchange, any allotment (or, in the case of an offer for sale, sale) was void if

• permission had not been applied for before the third working day after the first issue of the prospectus (see 42.32 above); or

• permission had been refused within three weeks from the date of closing of the subscription lists or such longer period (not exceeding six weeks) as the stock exchange allowed.

The company (or, in the case of an offer for sale, the offeror) then had to repay forthwith all money received from the applicants and, where not repaid within eight working days of that time, the directors were jointly and severally liable (or the offeror was liable) to repay it with interest at 5% per annum from the eighth day. A director was not so liable if he proved that the default in repayment was not due to any misconduct or negligence on his part.

All money received from applicants had to be kept in a separate bank account as long as the company (or offeror) could become liable to repay it. In default, the company and every officer in default (or, in the case of an offer for sale, any person by or through whom the offer was made and who knowingly and wilfully authorised or permitted the default) was liable to a fine up to the level in 40.1(*d*) PENALTIES.

Any condition requiring or binding the applicant to waive compliance with any of the above requirements was void.

The provisions applied to shares, etc. agreed to be taken up by a person underwriting the offer as if he had applied for them in pursuance of the prospectus.

[*Secs 86, 87, 24 Sch; SI 1999 No 727*].

42.35   **MUTUAL RECOGNITION OF PROSPECTUSES AND LISTING PARTICULARS**

Listed securities. In general, where a prospectus or listing particulars have been approved by a competent authority in another member state, *FSA 1986, Part IV* applies to that document but nothing in those provisions is to be taken as requiring the approval of The Stock Exchange of the document.

Unlisted securities. In general, where a prospectus has been approved in another member state, that prospectus is deemed to comply with the requirements of a prospectus for unlisted securities provided that

(*a*)   the offer of securities to which the prospectus relates is made in the UK simultaneously with the making of an offer in the member state where the prospectus was approved or within three months after the making of that offer;

(*b*)   if not included in the prospectus as approved in the other member state, there must also be added and disclosed

  •   the names and addresses of the paying agents for the securities in the UK (if any); and

  •   a statement of how notice of meetings and other notices from the issuer of the securities will be given to UK resident holders of the securities; and

(*c*)   where any exemption from disclosure requirements has been granted in the other member state, that exemption must correspond to a similar exemption in the UK and the circumstances that justify the exemption must also exist in the UK.

[*SI 1995 No 1537, 4 Sch; SI 1999 No 734, Reg 2*].

42.36 LIABILITIES FOR PROSPECTUSES AND LISTING PARTICULARS

Specific remedies for persons suffering loss through false or misleading information in a prospectus or listing particulars are provided for in *FSA 1986, Part IV* and the *POS Regulations* (*SI 1995 No 1537*). See 42.37 to 42.39 below. Apart from those specific remedies, a person suffering loss by virtue of any untrue or misleading statement or omission may have remedies in contract or tort. See 42.40 below.

42.37 Liability under *FSA 1986* and the *POS Regulations*

The provisions under *FSA 1986, ss 150–152* are similar to those in *SI 1995 No 1537, Regs 13–15* and are considered together in 42.38 and 42.39 below.

In addition, a person who knowingly or recklessly makes a misleading, false or deceptive statement, promise or forecast for the purpose of inducing another person to enter into an investment agreement is guilty of an offence and, on conviction, liable to a penalty up to the level in 40.1(*a*) PENALTIES. [*FSA 1986, s 47(1)*].

42.38 *Compensation for misrepresentation and omissions*

A remedy is available to an investor who acquires securities or an interest in securities and suffers loss by reason of false or misleading information in the prospectus or listing particulars. This remedy is in addition to any other statutory or common law remedy available to the injured party. Subject to 42.39 below, there are two heads of liability.

(*a*)   'Persons responsible' for any prospectus or listing particulars (or supplementary prospectus or listing particulars) are liable to compensate anyone who has acquired any of the securities in question, and suffered loss in respect of them, as a result of any untrue or misleading statement in the document in question or the omission of any matter required to be included. For these purposes, where the appropriate rules require a statement either as to the existence of a matter or, if there is none, a negative statement, the omission of the information is treated as a statement that there is no such matter.

(*b*)   Any person who fails to issue a supplementary prospectus or supplementary listing particulars when they are required or otherwise fails to comply with the rules relating thereto, is liable to pay compensation to anyone who has acquired the securities and suffered loss as a result of the failure.

[*FSA 1986, s 150; SI 1995 No 1537, Reg 14*].

The following are '*persons responsible*'.

(i) The issuer of the securities (for unlisted securities, only where the issuer has made or authorised the offer). A person is not responsible where he is not the issuer but is making the offer in association with the issuer *and* the prospectus or supplementary prospectus was drawn up primarily by the issuer (or one or more persons acting on his behalf).

(ii) The directors of the issuing company at the time when the document is submitted to The Stock Exchange (in the case of unlisted securities, when the prospectus is published). This does not apply

- if the document is published without the director's knowledge or consent and, on learning of its publication, the director gives reasonable public notice that the document was so published; or

- in the case of unlisted securities, unless the issuer has made or authorised the offer.

(iii) Where the issuer is a body corporate, each person who has authorised himself to be named in, and is named in, the document as a director or as having agreed to become a director either immediately or at a future time (but for unlisted securities only where the issuer has made or authorised the offer).

(iv) Each person who accepts, and is stated in the document as accepting, responsibility for the document or any part of it (but in the latter case only for that part and only if it is substantially included in the form and context to which he has agreed).

(v) (For unlisted securities), the offeror of the securities where he is not the issuer. This does not apply if the issuer is responsible for the prospectus/supplementary prospectus which was drawn up by him (or by one or more persons acting on his behalf) and the offeror is making the offer in association with the issuer.

(vi) (For unlisted securities), where the offeror is a company, but is not the issuer and is not making the offer in association with the issuer, each person who is a director of that company at the time when the prospectus or supplementary prospectus is published.

(vii) Any other person not falling within (i)–(vi) above who has authorised the document or any part of it (but in the latter case only for that part and only if it is substantially included in the form and context to which he has agreed).

The above is not, however, to be construed as making a person responsible for any document by reason only of giving advice as to its contents in a professional capacity.

For listed securities, where the document relates to securities which are to be issued in connection with the acquisition of the whole undertaking of another person or all the shares of a company, if that other person or the directors of that company are responsible under (iv) above for any particulars relating to the undertaking or company, no person is responsible for those particulars under (i)–(iii) above. (Similar provisions are not required for unlisted securities as takeovers are deemed not to be offers to the public).

There are also special provisions for listed securities as to who is a responsible person in relation to international securities.

[*FSA 1986, ss 152(1)–(8), 154A(2); SI 1995 No 1537, Reg 13(1)-(4); SI 1999 No 734, Regs 2, 3*].

Where the issuer of any shares is liable to pay compensation under the above provisions for loss suffered on those shares by a subscriber, that compensation cannot be taken into account in determining the amount paid on subscription for those shares or the amount paid or deemed to be paid up on them. [*FSA 1986, s 152(9); SI 1995 No 1537, Reg 13(5)*].

42.39 *Exemption from liability*

A person does not incur liability under 42.38(*a*) above in the following circumstances.

(*a*)   If he satisfies the court that, having made reasonable enquiries, he reasonably believed at the time of the submission of the document (for unlisted securities at the time it was delivered for registration) that the statement complained of was true or that the matter omitted was properly omitted. He must also show that

- he continued in that belief until the securities were acquired; or

- they were acquired before it was reasonably practicable to bring a correction to the attention of potential investors; or

- he had, before the securities were acquired, taken all reasonable steps to bring a correction to the attention of potential investors; or

- (in the case of listed securities) he continued in that belief until after the commencement of dealings in the securities following their admission to the official list and that the securities were acquired after such a lapse of time that he ought to be excused; or

- (in the case of unlisted securities) the securities were acquired after such a lapse of time that he ought to be excused and he continued in that belief until after the commencement of dealings in the securities on an approved exchange (if appropriate).

(*b*)   If the statement was made by another person as an 'expert' and was included (and was stated to be included) with the consent of the expert, provided he satisfies the court that, when the document was submitted for approval (for unlisted securities, when the document was delivered for registration), he believed on reasonable grounds that the expert was competent to make the statement and had consented to its inclusion. He must in addition satisfy the court that

- he continued in that belief until the securities were acquired; or

- they were acquired before it was reasonably practicable to bring the fact that the expert was not competent or had not consented to the attention of potential investors; or

- he had, before the securities were acquired, taken all reasonable steps to bring those facts to the attention of potential investors; or

- (in the case of listed securities) he continued in that belief until after the commencement of dealings in the securities following their admission to listing and the securities were acquired after such a lapse of time that he ought to be excused; or

- (in the case of unlisted securities) the securities were acquired after such a lapse of time that he ought to be excused and he continued in that belief until after the commencement of dealing in the securities on an approved exchange (if appropriate).

(*c*)   If he satisfies the court that

- before the securities were acquired, there had been published, in a manner calculated to bring it to the attention of potential investors, a correction or the fact that the expert was not competent or had not consented; or

- he has taken all reasonable steps to secure such publication and reasonably believed that publication had taken place before the securities were acquired.

(d)   If the statement was made by an official person or contained in a public official document and if he satisfies the court that it is accurately and fairly reproduced.

(e)   If the person suffering the loss acquired the securities with knowledge of the defect in the particulars, etc.

[*FSA 1986, s 151(1)-(5); SI 1995 No 1537, Reg 15(1)-(5)*].

A person does not incur liability under 42.38(*b*) if he satisfies the court that he reasonably believed that the change or new matter did not call for supplementary listing particulars or a supplementary prospectus or if the person suffering the loss acquired the securities with knowledge of the defect in the particulars, etc. [*FSA 1986, s 151(5)(6); SI 1995 No 1537, Reg 15(5)(6)*].

'*Expert*' includes any engineer, valuer, accountant or other person whose profession, qualifications or experience give authority to a statement made by him. [*FSA 1986, s 151(7); SI 1995 No 1537, Reg 15(7)*].

42.40 Common law remedies

Negligent misstatement. The principles enunciated in *obiter dicta* in *Hedley Byrne & Co Ltd v Heller & Partners Ltd [1964] AC 465* established a remedy for loss suffered as a result of a negligent misstatement, provided that the person making the statement owed a duty of care to the person suffering loss in reliance on it. Such a duty of care arises when there is a special relationship between the parties. It has been held that such a relationship exists between the persons putting their names behind a prospectus and persons who subscribe or purchase shares in reliance on that prospectus (*Al-Nakib Investments (Jersey) Ltd and another v Longcroft and others [1990] 1 WLR 1390*) although that case still stands as authority for the proposition that any duty of care which is owed in relation to a prospectus is owed only to the initial subscribers and not to subsequent purchasers.

Contract and the Misrepresentation Act 1967. Actions for damages for breach of contract will only be available against persons who have privity of contract with the claimant. Thus only the actual vendor of the shares to the claimant would be liable in contract. However, an incorrect statement in a prospectus will not give rise to a breach of contract unless the statement became a term of the contract. The courts are not usually prepared to regard statements in prospectuses as other than mere representations which induce a subscriber to apply for shares to be allotted to him.

If the prospectus contains an untrue or misleading statement, or there is an omission which renders a statement in the prospectus misleading, the injured party may have a remedy under the *Misrepresentation Act 1967* (not applicable to Scotland – but see *Law Reform (Miscellaneous Provisions) (Scotland) Act 1985, s 10*). The remedies provided are rescission of the contract and/or damages. The remedy of rescission will be lost if the subscriber or purchaser affirms the contract by failing to act within a reasonable time of discovering the truth. Furthermore, the right of rescission only extends to the original purchaser or subscriber and not to a subsequent purchaser. As in the case of an action founded on breach of contract, a claim under *Misrepresentation Act 1967* lies only against another party to the contract, i.e. the issuer in an offer for subscription or the vendor in an offer for sale. It is a defence to a claim for damages, but not rescission, for the defendant to prove that he believed on reasonable grounds, up to the time the contract was made, that the statement complained of was true.

42.41 INVESTMENT ADVERTISING

It is possible that securities are offered in the UK which are not listed securities but in circumstances where the *POS Regulations* do not apply (see 42.22 above). In this situation, the provisions prohibiting the publication of investment advertisements in *FSA 1986, s 57* outlined below must be complied with.

Subject to certain exceptions, no person other than an authorised person can issue or cause to be issued an 'investment advertisement' in the UK unless its contents have been approved by an authorised person.

'Investment advertisement' means any advertisement inviting persons to enter or offer to enter into an investment agreement or to exercise any rights conferred by an investment to acquire, dispose of, underwrite or convert an investment or containing information calculated to lead directly or indirectly to persons doing so.

'Advertisement' includes every form of advertising, whether in a publication, by the display of notices, signs, labels or showcards, by means of circulars, catalogue, price lists or other documents, by an exhibition of pictures or photographic or cinematographic films, by way of sound broadcasting or television, by the distribution of recordings, or in any other manner.

Effects of contravention

(*a*)   Any person who contravenes the above provisions is guilty of an offence and, on conviction, liable to a penalty up to the level in 40.1(*b*) PENALTIES. However, a person who in the ordinary course of business (other than investment business) issues an advertisement to the order of another person is not guilty of an offence if he proves that he believed on reasonable grounds that

- the person to whose order the advertisement was issued was an authorised person;

- the contents of the advertisement were approved by an authorised person; or

- the advertisement fell within the class of permitted exceptions.

(*b*)   Where a person issues an advertisement in contravention of the provisions

- the issuer cannot enforce any agreement to which the advertisement related and which was entered into after the issue of the advertisement,

- the issuer cannot enforce any obligation to which the other party is subject as a result of exercising, after the issue of the advertisement, of any rights to which the advertisement related, and

- the other party is entitled to recover any money or property paid or transferred, together with compensation for any loss sustained as a result.

This does not apply if the court is satisfied that the other party was not influenced to a material extent by the advertisement in making his decision or the advertisement was not misleading as to the nature of the investment, the terms of the agreement or the consequences of exercising the rights (as the case may be) and fairly stated any risks involved in those matters.

[*FSA 1986, ss 57, 58, 207(2); SI 1995 No 1537, 2 Sch 5, 6*].

43   Public and Listed Companies

The contents of this chapter are as follows.

43.1   PUBLIC COMPANIES

A public company is a company limited by shares, or limited by guarantee and having a share capital. It must comply with the following requirements.

- Its memorandum of association must state that it is a public company [*Sec 1(3)*] and must be in the form specified in Table F in *SI 1985 No 805* [*Sec 3*].

- It must have complied with the provisions of *CA 1985* (or the former *Companies Acts*) as to registration or re-registration of a company as a public company. See 49 REGISTRATION AND RE-REGISTRATION.

- Its name must end with 'public limited company' or 'plc' (or the Welsh equivalents) [*Secs 25, 27*].

- It must have an authorised share capital of at least the 'authorised minimum' (currently £50,000). See 58.12 SHARES AND SHARE CAPITAL.

- Before it commences business, it must have completed a statutory declaration and obtained a certificate from the Registrar of Companies. See 43.3 below. Note that one requirement for this is that the nominal value of the company's allotted share capital must be at least £50,000. [*Sec 117(3)(a)*]. Each share allotted must be paid up to at least one quarter of its nominal value together with the whole of any premium. [*Sec 101(1)*].

  Example

  The authorised share capital of A plc is 1 million ordinary shares of 50p each. It proposes to issue shares for £1.50 each.

  The company must allot at least 100,000 of the 50p shares (so that the nominal value is at least £50,000). On allotment, shareholders must pay a minimum of 112.5p per share (100p premium + ($\frac{1}{4}$ × 50p)).

- It must have at least two directors [*Sec 282*] and the company secretary must be qualified to act as such (see 55.2 SECRETARY).

43.2   Comparison with a private company

See 41.3 PRIVATE COMPANIES.

43.3   Certificate to commence business

A company registered as a public company on its original incorporation must not do business or exercise any borrowing powers unless

(*a*)   the Registrar of Companies has issued it with a certificate under the following provisions; or

(*b*)   the company is re-registered as a private company (see 49.11 to 49.13 REGISTRATION AND RE-REGISTRATION).

544

The company must apply for a certificate to the Registrar in the prescribed form (Form 117) and deliver a statutory declaration signed by a director or secretary

- stating that the nominal value of the allotted share capital is not less than the authorised minimum (see 58.12 SHARES AND SHARE CAPITAL);

- specifying the amount paid up, at the time of the application, on the allotted share capital;

- specifying the amount, or estimated amount, of the company's preliminary expenses and the persons by whom any of those expenses have been paid or are payable; and

- specifying the amount or benefit paid or given, or intended to be paid or given, to any promoter of the company, and the consideration for the payment or benefit.

For the purposes of (*a*) above, a share allotted under an employees' share scheme must not be taken into account in determining the nominal value of the allotted share capital unless at least one-quarter of the nominal value, and the whole of any premium, has been paid up.

On receipt of the application, if the Registrar is satisfied that (*a*) above is true, he must issue the company with a certificate. For these purposes, the Registrar may accept a statutory declaration as sufficient evidence of the matters stated in it. Once issued, the certificate is conclusive evidence that the company is entitled to do business and exercise any borrowing powers.

Penalties. If a company does business or exercises borrowing powers without the required certificate, the company and any officer of it who is in default is liable to a fine up to the level in 40.1(*d*) PENALTIES.

Failure to comply with the provisions does not affect the validity of any transaction entered into by the company but if it then fails to comply within 21 days of being called upon to do so, the directors are jointly and severally liable to indemnify the other party to the transaction in respect of any loss or damage suffered by reason of the company's failure.

[*Sec 117, 24 Sch*].

43.4   LISTED COMPANIES – THE LISTING RULES

A company, any part of whose shares or debt securities has been admitted to listing (a '*listed company*') must, in addition to complying with the provisions of the *Companies Acts*, also comply with the requirements of The Listing Rules. These rules, which are made by The International Stock Exchange of the United Kingdom and the Republic of Ireland Limited (the '*Exchange*') govern

- admission to listing;

- the continuing obligations of issuers and the enforcement of those obligations; and

- suspension and cancellation of listing.

In applying the listing rules, the Exchange has regard to the following objectives and principles.

- To seek a balance between providing issuers with ready access to the market for their securities and protecting investors.

- Securities will be admitted to listing only if the Exchange is satisfied that the applicant is suitable and that it is appropriate for those securities to be publicly held and traded.

43.5 Public and Listed Companies

- Securities should be brought to the market in a way appropriate to their nature and number and which will facilitate an open and efficient market for trading in those securities.

- An issuer must make full and timely disclosure about itself and its listed securities, at the time of listing and subsequently.

- The listing rules, and in particular the continuing obligations, should promote investor confidence in standards of disclosure, in the conduct of companies' affairs and in the market as a whole.

- Holders of equity shares should be given adequate opportunity to consider in advance and vote upon major changes in the company's business operations and matters of importance concerning the company's management and constitution.

(The Listing Rules, Introduction).

The Listing Rules are divided into 26 chapters (with supporting schedules) as follows.

1   Compliance with and enforcement of the listing rules. See 43.22 below.
2   Sponsors and listing agents.
3   Conditions for listing. See 42.3 PROSPECTUSES AND PUBLIC ISSUES.
4   Methods of bringing securities to listing. See 42.4 PROSPECTUSES AND PUBLIC ISSUES.
5   Listing particulars. See 42.6 to 42.12 PROSPECTUSES AND PUBLIC ISSUES.
6   Contents of listing particulars. See 42.6 PROSPECTUSES AND PUBLIC ISSUES.
7   Listing application procedures. See 42.5 PROSPECTUSES AND PUBLIC ISSUES.
8   Publication and circulation of listing particulars. See 42.14 and 42.15 PROSPECTUSES AND PUBLIC ISSUES.
9   Continuing obligation. See 43.5 to 43.11 below.
10   Transactions. See 43.12 below.
11   Transactions with related parties. See 43.13 below.
12   Financial information. See 43.14 to 43.17 below.
13   Documents not requiring prior approval. Generally, if a document complies with the requirement of this chapter of the Listing Rules, the company need not submit a draft of it to the Exchange. See 43.18 below for the necessary requirements of the articles of association.
14   Circulars. See 43.19 below.
15   Purchase of own securities. See 43.20 below.
16   Directors. See 43.21 below.
17   Oversea companies.
18   Property companies.
19   Mineral companies.
20   Scientific research based companies.
21   Investment entities.
22   Public sector issuers.
23   Specialist debt securities (including eurobonds).
24   Miscellaneous securities.
25   Companies undertaking major capital projects.
26   Venture capital trusts.

Where there is no cross reference to the text against any of the above chapters, the provisions are specialist requirements and not covered in this book.

43.5   Continuing obligations

Once its securities have been admitted to listing, there are still continuing obligations which a listed company must observe. Observance of these continuing obligations is essential to the maintenance of an orderly market in securities and to ensure that all users of the market have simultaneous access to the same information. If a company fails to comply with any continuing obligation, the Exchange may take any of the steps under 43.22 below.

Information required to be notified must be delivered to the Company Announcements Office ('CAO') following the Regulatory News Service Guidelines published by the Exchange. If the CAO is not open for business at the relevant time, a company must ensure that there is adequate coverage of the information by also distributing it to not less than two national daily newspapers in the UK and to two newswire services operating in the UK.

(*The Listing Rules, Chapter 9, Introduction, 9.15*).

The continuing obligations are considered in 43.6 to 43.21 below.

43.6 *General obligation to disclose*

Unless prejudicial to its legitimate interests, a company must notify the CAO without delay of

- any major new developments in its sphere of activities (which are not public knowledge) and which may lead to substantial movement in the price of its listed securities or, in the case of a company with listed debt securities, affect its ability to meet its commitments; and

- all relevant information concerning a change in the company's financial condition or in the performance of its business or in the company's expectation of its performance, knowledge of which may lead to a substantial movement in the price of its listed securities.

These requirements are in addition to any specific requirements regarding notification in the listing rules. A company need not notify to the CAO information about impending developments or matters in the course of negotiation.

Information required to be passed to the CAO must not first be passed to a third party (with certain exceptions). Where it is proposed to announce at a meeting of the holders of the company's listed securities any information which might lead to substantial movement in their price, that information must be notified to the CAO so that the announcement at the meeting is made no earlier than the time at which the information is published to the market.

Where its securities are also listed on another stock exchange, a company must ensure that equivalent information is made available to each exchange at the same time.

(*The Listing Rules, Chapter 9.1 – 9.9*).

See also the booklet *Guidance on the dissemination of price sensitive information* issued by the London Stock Exchange.

43.7 *Notification relating to share capital*

A company must notify the CAO without delay of the following information relating to its capital.

(*a*)   Any proposed change in the capital structure including listed debt securities.

(*b*)   Where a company has listed debt securities, any new issues of debt securities and, in particular, any guarantee or security in respect thereof.

(c) Any changes in the rights attached to any class of listed securities or to any securities into which listed debt securities are convertible.

(d) Any drawing or redemption of listed securities. Prior to any drawing, the amount and date of the drawing and the date of entitlement (if registered) must be notified. After any drawing has been made, details of the amount of the security outstanding must also be notified.

(e) The basis of allotment of listed securities offered generally to the public for cash and of open offers to shareholders.

(f) Any extension of time granted for the currency of temporary documents of title.

(g) The effect, if any, of any issue of further securities or the terms of the exercise of rights under options, warrants and convertible securities (companies with listed equities only).

(h) The results of any new issue of listed securities (other than specialist securities) or of the public offering of existing securities.

(*The Listing Rules, Chapter 9.10, 9.46, 9.47*).

43.8 *Notification of major interests in shares*

A company with listed equity securities must notify the CAO without delay (by the end of the business day following receipt of the information) of any information notified to it under *Secs 198-208* (including date of disclosure and date the transaction was effected, if known) or any information obtained by it under *Sec 212* which should have been so disclosed. See 21 DISCLOSURE OF INTERESTS IN PUBLIC COMPANY SHARES. (*The Listing Rules, Chapter 9.11 – 9.14, 9.46, 9.47*).

43.9 *Rights as between holders of securities*

(a) *Equality of treatment.* A company having listed shares/debt securities must ensure equality of treatment for all holders of such shares/debt securities.

(b) *Pre-emption rights.* Unless shareholders otherwise permit, a company with listed equity securities proposing to issue equity securities for cash must first offer them *pro rata* to existing holders and only then, if not taken up, to other persons or the existing holders otherwise than *pro rata*.

(c) *Issues by major subsidiaries.* Unless shareholders agree otherwise, a company must obtain the consent of shareholders before any major subsidiary of the company issues equity securities for cash so as to dilute the interest of the company in that subsidiary.

(*The Listing Rules, Chapter 9.16 – 9.23, 9.46, 9.47*).

43.10 *Communication with shareholders*

(a) *Information to shareholders.* A company must ensure that, at least in each member state where the securities are listed, the necessary facilities and information are available to enable the holders to exercise their rights. In particular it must notify them of meetings they are entitled to attend, enable them to exercise their right to vote and publish or distribute details of dividends, new issues and redemption or repayment of securities.

(b) *Registrar/paying agent.* The company must appoint a registrar and, where appropriate, a paying agent in the UK unless the company performs these functions itself.

(c)   *Proxy forms.* The company must send, with the notice convening a meeting, a proxy form, with provision for two-way voting, for all resolutions to be proposed.

(d)   *Other classes of security.* If a circular is issued to the holders of any class of security, the company must also issue a copy or summary to the holders of all other listed securities unless the contents are irrelevant to them.

(e)   *Holders of bearer securities.* If there is need to communicate with the holders of listed bearer securities, the company must publish an advertisement in at least one national daily newspaper referring to the communication and giving the address from which copies can be obtained.

(f)   *Mail.* Airmail (or an equivalent service which is no slower) must be used when communicating with overseas holders of listed securities in non-member states. First class mail (or an equivalent service which is no slower) must be used when sending documents of title to holders of listed securities in the UK and other member states.

(g)   *Copies to the CAO.* A company must send to the CAO

- six copies of all circulars, notices, reports, announcements and other documents at the same time as they are issued; and

- six copies of all resolutions passed by the company (other than routine business at an AGM) without delay after the relevant general meeting.

(*The Listing Rules, Chapter 9.24 – 9.32, 13.28, 13.29*).

43.11 *Miscellaneous obligations*

(a)   *Further issues.* Where further securities are allotted of a class already listed, application for listing of the further securities must be made within one month of allotment.

(b)   *Board decisions.* Decisions by the board on dividends, profits and other matters requiring announcement must be notified to the CAO without delay and not later than 8.30 a.m. on the following business day.

(c)   *Annual listing fee.* A company must pay the annual fee for listing as soon as it becomes due.

(d)   *Shares in public hands.* A company with listed equity securities or listed debt securities must inform the Exchange in writing without delay if it becomes aware that the proportion of any class of listed securities held by the public falls below 25% or such lower percentage as the Exchange may have agreed.

(e)   *Restrictions on dealing.* No dealing in any securities may be effected by or on behalf of the company or any group member at a time when, under the provisions of the Model Code, a director would be prohibited from dealing in its securities (apart from dealings in the normal course of business by a securities dealing business or by the company or any group member on behalf of third parties).

(f)   *Controlling shareholder.* A company with a controlling shareholder must be capable at all times of carrying on its business independently of that shareholder (any of its associates) and all transactions between the company and any controlling shareholder (or associate) must be at arm's length on a normal commercial basis.

(g)   *Change of name.* A company which changes its name must notify the CAO without delay and, where appropriate, send it a copy of any revised certificate of incorporation.

(*The Listing Rules, Chapter 9.33 – 9.40, 9.46, 9.47*).

43.12   Public and Listed Companies

43.12 *Substantial transactions*

There are special rules for disclosure of details of certain transactions, principally acquisitions and disposals, by companies with listed equity securities. A transaction is classified (by assessing its size relative to that of the company proposing to make it) as Class 3 (where all the 'percentage ratios' are less than 5%), Class 2 (where any percentage ratio is 5% or more but each is less than 25%), Class 1 (where any percentage ratio is 25% or more) and Reverse takeover (an acquisition of a business, unlisted company or assets where any percentage ratio is 100% or more or which would result in a fundamental change in the business or in a change in the board or voting control of the listed company).

The '*percentage ratios*' are

(i) *assets ratio* i.e. the gross assets the subject of the transaction divided by the gross assets of the listed company;

(ii) *profits ratio* i.e. the profits attributable to the assets the subject of the transaction divided by the profits of the listed company;

(iii) *turnover ratio* i.e. the turnover attributable to the assets the subject of the transaction divided by the turnover of the listed company;

(iv) *consideration to market capitalisation ratio* i.e. the consideration divided by the aggregate market value of all the ordinary shares of the listed company; and

(v) *gross capital ratio* i.e. the gross capital of the company or business being acquired divided by the gross capital of the listed company.

The requirements for various classifications of transaction are as follows.

(*a*)   In the case of a Class 3 transaction which is an acquisition in respect of which the consideration includes the issue of securities for which listing will be sought, the company must notify the CAO of the terms of the acquisition.

(*b*)   In the case of any other Class 3 transaction, if the company releases any details to the public they must also be notified to the CAO.

(*c*)   In the case of a Class 2 transaction, the company must notify the CAO without delay after the terms of the transaction are agreed. Notification must include

(i) particulars of the transaction;

(ii) a description of the business carried on by, or using, the net assets the subject of the transaction;

(iii) the consideration and how it is being satisfied;

(iv) the value of the net assets the subject of the transaction;

(v) the profit attributable to those assets;

(vi) the effect of the transaction on the listed company;

(vii) details of any service contracts of proposed directors of the listed company;

(viii) in the case of a disposal, the application of the sales proceeds; and

(ix) in the case of a disposal where securities are to form part of the consideration, a statement whether such securities are to be sold or retained.

The Exchange must also be advised (and a supplementary notification made to the CAO) if, at any time after that notification has been made, the company becomes

550

aware that there has been a significant change in any matter contained in the earlier notification or there is any significant new matter which requires notification.

(*d*)   In the case of a Class 1 transaction, in addition to the Class 2 requirements (see (*c*) above), an explanatory circular (containing detailed information asspecified in *The Listing Particulars*) must be sent to the shareholders and the company must obtain prior approval of its shareholders in general meeting. Any agreement effecting the transaction must be conditional upon such approval being granted.

(*e*)   Upon the announcement of a reverse takeover, the Exchange will suspend listing of the company's securities. The company must prepare a Class 1 circular (see (*d*) above), obtain prior approval of the shareholders and, if the company wishes to be listed following completion of the transaction, prepare listing particulars as though the company were a new applicant. The listing will be restored on publication of the circular and listing particulars.

(*The Listing Rules, Chapters 9.45, 10.1 – 10.44*).

43.13 *Transactions with related parties*

Where any transaction is proposed between a company with listed equity securities (or any of its subsidiaries) and a 'related party', subject to the exceptions below, the company must

●   make any announcement, via the CAO, containing the details required under 43.12(*c*)(i)–(ix) above, together with the name of the related party and the nature and extent of his interest in the transaction;

●   send a circular (containing detailed information as specified in *The Listing Particulars*) to the shareholders;

●   obtain approval of the shareholders in general meeting either prior to the transaction or, if expressed to be conditional on such approval, prior to the completion of the transaction; and

●   ensure that the related party does not vote on the relevant resolution.

'*Related party*' is broadly defined to cover any person who is (or has been in the previous year) *either* a shareholder who controls 10% or more of the voting rights of the company *or* a director or shadow director of the company or any group company *or* any associate (as defined) of any such person or company.

The rules do not apply to a transaction with a related party if

●   the company does not have any equity securities listed;

●   the company is an oversea company with a secondary listing on the Exchange;

●   the transaction is an issue of new securities *either* for cash to all shareholders on the same terms *or* pursuant to the exercise or conversion of subscription rights attaching to listed securities or previously approved by the company in general meeting;

●   in accordance with the terms of an employees' share scheme or a long-term incentive scheme, either

    (i)   the transaction involves the receipt of any asset (including cash or securities of the company or any of its subsidiaries) by a director of the company, its parent or any of its subsidiaries; or

    (ii)   the transaction is the grant of an option or other right to such a director to acquire any asset (including cash or new or existing securities of the company or any of its subsidiaries).

43.14   Public and Listed Companies

- the transaction is a grant of credit to a related party (or, on an unsecured basis, by the related party) under normal commercial terms or terms offered generally to employees;

- the transaction is the grant of an indemnity, etc. to a director not prohibited by *Sec 310* (see 19.38 DIRECTORS);

- the transaction is a commercial underwriting by a related party of an issue of securities by the company; or

- the terms of the investment or provisions of the finance by the company are, in the opinion of an independent adviser acceptable to the Exchange, no less favourable than those applicable to the investment or provisions of finance by the related party.

- it is a small transaction i.e. one where each of the percentage ratios referred to in 43.12 above is 0.25% or less. (There is partial exemption where each of those ratios is less than 5% but one or more exceeds 0.25%.)

(*The Listing Rules, Chapters 9.45, 11*).

43.14 *Preliminary statement of annual results and dividends*

A company must notify the CAO, without delay after board approval, of the following matters relating to its preliminary statement of annual results and dividends.

(*a*)   If it has listed equity securities or listed fixed income shares, any preliminary statement of annual results. The statement must have been agreed with the auditors and show figures consistent with the presentation to be adopted in the annual accounts, including at least the items required for a half-yearly report (see 43.17 below). If the auditors' report is likely to be qualified, the nature of the qualification must be disclosed.

(*b*)   Any decision to pay a dividend or other distribution on listed equity securities or withhold any dividend or interest payment on listed securities.

Details must be given of

- the exact net amount payable per share;

- the payment date;

- the records date (if applicable); and

- any foreign income dividend election, together with any income tax treated as paid at the lower rate and not repayable.

(*The Listing Rules, Chapters 9.46, 12.40*)

43.15 *Annual report and accounts*

A company must issue an annual report and accounts, within six months of the end of the financial period to which they relate, containing the following information.

(*a*)   *Commentary on forecasts.* An explanation where the results differ by more than 10% from any published forecast or estimate made by the company.

(*b*)   *Interest capitalised.* The amount of interest capitalised by the group in the financial year, with an indication of the amount and treatment of any related tax relief.

(*c*)   *Waiver of emoluments.* If it has listed equity securities, particulars of any arrangement under which a director has waived, or agreed to waive, emoluments.

(d)   *Waiver of dividends.* If it has listed equity securities, particulars of any arrangement under which a shareholder has waived, or agreed to waive, dividends.

(e)   *Directors' interests in shares.* For UK companies, details, at the end of the period under review, of the interest of each director of the company appearing in the register of directors' interests maintained under *Sec 325* (see 47.7 REGISTERS), distinguishing between beneficial and non-beneficial interests. Any changes between the end of the period and a date not more than one month before the date of notice of the AGM should be included by way of note (or, if there have been no changes, disclosure of that fact).

(f)   *Major interests in shares.* For UK companies, details, as at a date not more than one month prior to the date of notice of the AGM, of any holding of 3% or more held by any person, other than a director, appearing in the register maintained under *Sec 211* (see 47.8 REGISTERS) (or if there is no such interest, that fact).

(g)   *Purchase of own shares.* For UK companies, details of any shareholders' authority for the purchase by the company of its own shares still valid at the end of the period under review and, in certain cases, details of the sellers of such shares purchased in the period.

(h)   *Allotments for cash.* Where there has been an issue of equity securities for cash in the year under review which was not a rights issue and was not specifically authorised by the shareholders

- the names of the allottees (if less than six) or otherwise a brief generic description of them; and

- the market price of the securities on the date the terms of the issue were fixed.

(i)   *Parent undertaking participation in a placing.* Where a company has listed shares in issue and is a subsidiary of another company, details of the participation by the parent company in any placing made during the period under review.

(j)   *Interests in contracts.* Particulars of any 'contract of significance' existing during the period under review in which a director is or was materially interested.

A '*contract of significance*' is one which represents, depending on the nature of the contract, 1% or more of the group's share capital and reserves, annual purchases, sales, payments or receipts.

(k)   *Contracts of significance.* Particulars of any contract of significance (see (j) above) during the period under review between the company, or one of its subsidiaries, and a '*controlling shareholder*' i.e. a person entitled to exercise or control 30% or more of the voting power at general meetings or control the composition of a majority of the board.

(l)   Particulars of any contract for the provision of services to the company or any subsidiary by a controlling shareholder (see (k) above) during the period under review.

(m)   *Small related-party contracts.* If it has listed equity securities, details of transactions with related parties (see 43.13 above) where each of the percentage ratios in 43.12 above is less than 5% but one or more is in excess of 0.25%.

(n)   *Long-term incentive schemes.* Details of any long-term incentive scheme in which the only participant is a director (or contemplated director) of the company and where the arrangement is established specifically to facilitate, in unusual circumstances, the recruitment or retention of the relevant individual. (This information need only be disclosed in the first annual report following the date on which the relevant individual becomes eligible to participate.)

(*o*) *Going concern.* For UK companies, a statement by the directors that the business is a going concern (with supporting assumptions and qualifications if necessary). Such statement must be reviewed by the auditors.

(*p*) *Application of the Combined Code.* For UK companies, a narrative statement of how it has applied the principles set out in Section 1 of the Combined Code, providing explanations which enable the shareholders to evaluate how the principles have been applied. See the Appendix at the end of this chapter for the provisions of Section 1 of the Combined Code.

(*q*) *Statement on compliance with the Combined Code.* For UK companies, a statement as to whether or not the company has complied throughout the accounting period with the provisions set out in Section 1 of the combined Code. A company which has not complied with those provisions (or only some of them) or has complied with them for only part of the accounting period, must specify the Code provisions it has not complied with and (where relevant) for what part of such period such non-compliance has continued, and give reasons for any non-compliance. See the Appendix at the end of this chapter for the provisions of Section 1 of the Combined Code.

(*r*) *Directors' remuneration.* For UK companies, a report to the shareholders containing the following details.

   (i) A statement of the company's policy on executive directors' remuneration.

   (ii) For each director by name,

   - the amount of each element in the remuneration package for the period under review, including (but not restricted to) basic salary and fees, estimated money value of benefits in kind, annual bonuses, deferred bonuses, compensation for loss of office and payments for breach of contract or other termination payments; and

   - the total remuneration for the period under review and the corresponding prior period.

   Any significant payments in the period to former directors must also be shown.

   All the information should, unless inappropriate, be in tabular form and be accompanied by explanatory notes.

   (iii) For each director by name, information on share options (including SAYE options), in tabular form and accompanied by explanatory notes.

   (iv) For each director by name, details of any long-term incentive schemes (other than share options within (iii) above) including

   - interests at the start of the period;

   - entitlements and awards granted and commitments made during the period (showing which crystallise either in the same year or subsequent years);

   - the money value and number of shares, cash payments or other benefits received under such schemes during the period; and

   - interests at the end of the period.

(v)   Explanation and justification of any element of remuneration other than basic salary, which is pensionable.

(vi)   Details of any directors' service contract with a notice period in excess of one year or with provisions for pre-determined compensation on termination which exceeds one year's salary and benefits in kind, giving the reasons for such notice period.

(vii)   The unexpired term of any directors' service contract of a director proposed for election or re-election at the forthcoming annual general meeting and, if any director proposed for election or re-election does not have a directors' service contract, a statement to that effect.

(viii)   A statements of the company's policy on the granting of options or awards under its employees' share schemes and other long-term incentive schemes, explaining and justifying any departure from that policy in the period under review and any change in the policy from the preceding year.

(ix)   For pension schemes which are not money purchase schemes,

- details of the amount of the increase during the period under review (excluding inflation) and of the accumulated total amount at the end of the period in respect of the accrued benefit to which each director would be entitled on leaving service (or is entitled having left service during the period); and

- the transfer value (less director's contributions) of the relevant increase in accrued benefits, calculated in accordance with actuarial guidelines, as at the end of the period. Alternatively, so much of the following information must be given as is necessary to make a reasonable assessment of the transfer value in respect of each director, viz. current age; normal retirement age; the amount of any contributions payable by the director under the terms of the scheme during the period under review; details of spouse's and dependants' benefits; early retirement rights and options; expectations of pension increases after retirement (whether guaranteed or discretionary); discretionary benefits for which allowance is made in transfer values on leaving any other information which will significantly affect the value of the benefits.

Voluntary contributions and benefits should not be disclosed.

(x)   For pension schemes which are money purchase schemes, details of the contribution or allowance payable or made by the company in respect of each director during the period under review.

The scope of the auditors' report must cover the disclosures in (ii)(iii)(iv)(ix)(x) above. If, in their opinion, the company has not complied with any of these requirements the auditors must so state in their report and, in such a case, must include (so far as they are reasonably able to do so) a statement giving the required particulars. (*Listing Rules, Chapter 12.43A*).

(*The Listing Rules, Chapters 9.46, 9.47, 12.41 – 12.44*).

43.16 *Summary financial statements*

Where a company issues a summary financial statement (see 43.23 below) the statement should also disclose earnings per share in addition to the other required contents. (*The Listing Rules, Chapter 12.45*).

43.17   Public and Listed Companies

43.17 Half-yearly report

Companies with listed equity securities or listed fixed income shares must prepare a half-yearly report, on a group basis where relevant, on its activities and profit or loss for the first six months of each financial year. It must be published as soon as possible and in any event within four months of the end of the period to which it relates. A company must publish the half-yearly report by notifying it to the CAO without delay after board approval and where the company's shares are listed in another member state, simultaneously to the competent authority of each other member state in which the company's shares are listed, not later than the time the report is first published in the member state. In addition, the company must either send the half-yearly report to the holders of its listed securities or insert it, as a paid advertisement, in at least one national newspaper.

Accounting policies and presentation applied to interim figures must be consistent with those applied in the latest published annual accounts unless the Exchange agrees otherwise or they are to be changed in the subsequent annual accounts (in which case the change and reasons for change must be disclosed).

The half yearly report must contain the following information in respect of the group's activities and profit or loss during the relevant period.

(*a*)   The following figures presented in tabular form (appropriate adjustments may be made if any of the items are unsuited to the company's activities).

- Net turnover.

- Profit or loss before taxation and extraordinary items.

- Taxation on profits (showing UK and, if material, overseas and share of associated undertakings' taxation separately).

- Minority interests.

- Profit or loss attributable to shareholders, before extraordinary items.

- Extraordinary items (net of taxation).

- Profit or loss attributable to shareholders.

- Rates and amounts of dividends paid and proposed.

- Earnings per share.

- Comparative figures for each of the above for the corresponding period in the preceding financial year.

Where the figures have been audited, the auditors' report must be set out in the report. Where the figures have not been audited, a statement to that effect must be included.

(*b*)   An explanatory statement including any significant information enabling investors to make an informed assessment of the trend of the group's activities and profit or loss.

(*c*)   An indication of any special factor which has influenced those activities and the profit or loss during the period in question.

(*d*)   Enough information to enable a comparison to be made with the corresponding figures of the preceding financial year.

(*e*)   So far as possible, a reference to the group's prospects in the current financial year.

Change of accounting reference date. If a company with listed securities changes its accounting reference date (see 1.3 ACCOUNTING REFERENCE DATES AND PERIODS) it must notify the CAO without delay of the new date. If the effect of this change is to extend the accounting period to one of more than 14 months, the company must prepare and publish a second interim report as above for either

- the period up to the old accounting reference date; or

- the period up to a date not more than six months before the new accounting reference date.

(*The Listing Rules, Chapters 9.46, 12.46–12.60*).

43.18 *Articles of association*

If the articles of association of a company (or any amendments to them) comply with the requirements listed below (and have no unusual features), they do not need to be approved by the Exchange although two copies must still be lodged with the Exchange (marked for the attention of the Listing Department), together with a letter of compliance from the company's legal advisers.

(*a*)   *Capital structure.* Where there is more than one class of share, the name of each class must be stated and how the various classes rank for dividends and return of capital.

(*b*)   *Non-voting and restricted voting shares.* Where the capital of the company includes non-voting shares, the words 'non-voting' must appear in the designation of such shares. Where it includes shares with different voting rights, the designation of every class of shares, other than those with the most favourable voting rights, must include the words 'restricted voting' or 'limited voting'.

(*c*)   *Preference shares.* Where these are listed, they must carry voting rights in at least the following circumstances.

(i)   When dividends on such shares are more than six months in arrears.

(ii)   On any winding up resolution.

(*d*)   *Transfer and registration.* Transfers, and other documents or instructions relating to or affecting the title to any shares, must be registered without payment of any fee.

(*e*)   *Restriction of transfer.* Fully-paid shares must be free from all liens and any restriction on the right of transfer (except any restriction imposed on a shareholder in default under *Sec 212*, see 21.7 DISCLOSURE OF INTERESTS IN PUBLIC COMPANY SHARES). Partly-paid shares which are listed may be subject to restrictions unless they prevent dealings in the shares on an open and proper basis.

(*f*)   *Joint shareholders.* Any restriction in the articles to limit the number of share-holders in a joint account must not prevent the registration of up to four persons.

(*g*)   *Register.* The closing of the register must be discretionary.

(*h*)   *Definitive certificates.* New certificates replacing old ones lost, worn out or destroyed must be issued without charge (other than exceptional out of pocket expenses) although an indemnity may be required before issue. Balancing certificates must also be issued free of charge.

(*i*)   *Bearer warrants.* Where a power is taken to issue share warrants to bearer, a new share warrant must not be issued to replace one that has been lost unless the company is satisfied beyond reasonable doubt that the original has been destroyed.

(*j*)   *Proxies.* A corporate shareholder in the company must be able to execute a form of proxy under the hand of a duly authorised officer.

(*k*)   *Sanctions.* Where the articles permit sanctions to be imposed on a shareholder in default of a notice under *Sec 212* (see 21.7 DISCLOSURE OF INTERESTS IN PUBLIC COMPANY SHARES) sanctions must not take effect within 14 days after service of the notice. For shareholders holding less than 0.25% of the relevant class, the only sanction is a prohibition against attending meetings and voting. For other shareholders, the articles may also provide for the withholding of dividends on the shares concerned and placing of restrictions on their transfer other than on sale to a *bona fide* unconnected third party. Any sanctions imposed must cease to apply within seven days of receipt of notice that the shares have been sold as indicated or the notice under *Sec 212* has been complied with.

(*l*)   *Untraceable members.* Where power is taken to cease sending dividend warrants by post if such warrants have been returned undelivered or left uncashed, the power must not be exercised until either warrants have been so returned or left uncashed on two consecutive occasions or reasonable enquiries after one such occasion have failed to establish a new address.

Where power is taken to sell shares of a member who is untraceable, it must not be exercised unless

- during a period of twelve years at least three dividends on the shares have become payable and no dividends during that period has been claimed; and

- on expiry of the twelve years, the company gives notice (by advertisement in a national newspaper and a newspaper circulating in the area of the last known address of the member) of its intention to sell the shares and has notified the Exchange of such intention.

(*m*)   *Dividends.* Any amount paid up in advance of calls on any shares may entitle the holder to interest but must not entitle him to participate in respect of that amount in any dividend.

Any power to forfeit unclaimed dividends cannot be exercised within twelve years of the date the dividend to be forfeited was declared or became due for payment.

(*n*)   *Notices.* Where power is taken to give notice by advertisement, such advertisement must be inserted in at least one national paper.

Where the articles provide that notices will only be given to those members whose registered addresses are within the UK, any member whose registered address is outside the UK must be entitled to name an address within the UK which will be considered his address for the purpose of notices.

(*o*)   *Directors.* With certain exceptions, the articles must prohibit a director from voting on any contract, etc. in which he has an interest which to his knowledge is a material interest other than by virtue of his interest in the company's securities.

(*p*)   *Casual vacancies.* Any person appointed by the directors to fill a casual vacancy on, or as an addition to, the board, must retire from office at the next AGM and will then be eligible to stand for election.

(*q*)   *Election of directors.* Where any person, other than a director retiring at the meeting or a person recommended by the directors, is to be proposed for re-election or election as a director, notice must be given to the company of the intention to propose him and of his willingness to serve as a director. The period of notice must be specified in the articles and must be not less than seven days and not more than 42 days.

Amendments. Any circular to shareholders in connection with proposed amendments to the articles must, in addition to complying with the general requirements for all circulars under 43.19 below, include

- an explanation of the effect of the proposed amendments; and

- either the full terms of the proposed amendments or a statement that those terms will be available for inspection both at a named place until the close of the relevant general meeting and at the place of the general meeting for at least 15 minutes before and during that meeting.

(*The Listing Rules, Chapter 13.1 – 13.9, Appendix 1*).

43.19 *Circulars*

Any circular sent out by a company to the holder of its listed securities must provide a clear and adequate explanation of its subject matter. If voting or other action is required, it must contain all information necessary to allow shareholders to make properly informed decisions and must contain a heading drawing attention to the importance of the document and the possible need to consult independent advisers.

Formal approval. Subject to certain exceptions, no circular may be circulated or made available publicly until formal approval of the Exchange has been received for the final form. To obtain approval, three copies of the circular and certain other documents must be submitted (marked for the attention of the Listing Department) at least 10 days prior to intended publication.

Lodging of copies. Six copies of any circular in its final form (whether or not it is required to be submitted for approval) must be lodged with the CAO at the same time as it is despatched to shareholders.

Exceptions. A circular of any of the following types need not be submitted for approval before publication if it complies with general requirements for all circulars and the specific requirements for that type (as detailed in the *Listing Rules*), and has no unusual features.

- Proposed change of name.

- Authority to allot shares.

- Disapplication of pre-emption rights.

- Increase in authorised share capital.

- Reduction of capital.

- Capitalisation issue.

- Scrip dividend alternative.

- Scrip dividend mandate scheme.

- Purchase of own securities.

- Notices of meetings.

- Resolutions proposing to approve the adoption or amendment of the memorandum or articles of association, trust deeds, employees' share schemes, long-term incentive schemes and discounted option arrangements.

43.20 Public and Listed Companies

- Early redemption of securities.

- Reminders of conversion rights.

(*The Listing Rules, Chapter 14*).

43.20 *Purchase of own securities*

The following rules apply to a company wishing to purchase its own listed securities, whether as a market or off-market purchase. The rules do not apply to transactions entered into

- in the ordinary course of business by securities dealing businesses; or

- on behalf of third parties either by the company or any other member of its group.

General. A company must not purchase its own securities at a time when, under the provisions of the Model Code, a director of the company would be prohibited from dealing in its securities.

Where a purchase by a company of its own securities is to be made from a related party, the provisions of 43.13 above must also be complied with unless

- a tender or partial offer is made to all holders on the same terms; or

- in the case of a market purchase authorised under a general authority granted by shareholders, it is made without prior understanding, arrangement or agreement between the company and any related party.

Equity shares. Any decision by the board to submit to shareholder a proposal for the company to be authorised to purchase its own equity shares (other than a renewal of an existing authority) must be notified to the CAO without delay. Notification must indicate whether the proposal relates to specific purchases (in which case details must be given) or a general authorisation to make purchases. The outcome of the shareholders' meeting must also be notified and six copies of the relevant resolutions lodged with them.

A circular seeking shareholders' authority must contain specified information (as detailed in the Listing Rules) but need not be submitted to the Exchange unless it relates to a purchase from a related party (see above) or where the exercise in full of the authority sought would result in the purchase of 15% or more of the issued equity shares.

Purchases of less than 15% of any class of its equity shares under a general authority granted by shareholders cannot be made through the market unless

- a tender or partial offer is made to all holders of the class of securities on the same terms; or

- the price to be paid is not more than 5% above the average of the market values of those shares for the five business days before the purchase is made.

Purchases of more than 15% of any class of equity under a general authority granted by shareholders must be made by way of either a tender or partial offer to all holders of that class on the same terms.

Purchases must normally be notified to the CAO no later than 8.30a.m. on the next business day. Notification must include date, number of shares and price (or highest and lowest prices where relevant).

Where there are in issue listed convertible securities which are convertible into the equity shares in question, a separate meeting of the holders of those convertible securities must also be held.

Securities other than equity securities. Unless the transaction would be in accordance with the terms of issue, where a company intends to make a proposal, open to all holders, to purchase any of its listed securities other than equity securities, it must notify the CAO. While the proposal is being actively considered, the company must ensure that no dealings in the relevant securities are carried out by or on behalf of the company (or another group member) until the proposal has either been notified to the CAO or abandoned.

Any purchases, early redemptions or cancellations must be notified to the CAO when an aggregate of 10% of the initial nominal amount has been purchased, redeemed or cancelled and for each 5% in aggregate acquired thereafter. This must be done no later than 8.30a.m. on the next business day. Notification must include the nominal amount acquired, redeemed or cancelled since the last notification, the nominal amount remaining outstanding and whether or not securities acquired are to be cancelled.

In the case of securities convertible into, exchangeable for, or carrying a right to subscribe for equity securities, then unless a tender or partial offer is made to all holders of the class on the same terms, purchases must not normally be made at a price more than 5% above the average of the market values for the securities for the five business days immediately before the date of purchase.

(*The Listing Rules, Chapter 15*).

43.21 *Directors*

In addition to the requirements for transactions between a company and any of its director under 43.13 above, the following obligations are imposed relating to directors.

(*a*)   A listed company must submit to the Exchange a director's declaration as to business activities in respect of every new director within 14 days of appointment. A new declaration must be submitted within 14 days for any director if there are subsequent changes in the details in a declaration (unless a declaration in respect of that director has been made by another listed company). In any case, a new declaration must be submitted for every director within 30 days of the third aniversary of the date when a declaration was last lodged.

(*b*)   Any changes in the directors, and any important change in the functions or executive responsibilities of a director, must be notified to the CAO without delay (by the end of the business day following the change).

(*c*)   In the case of companies with listed equity securities, copies of all directors' service contracts must be available for inspection

   • at the registered office (or, in the case of an oversea company, the offices of the paying agent) during normal business hours on each business day;

   • at the place of the meeting for at least 15 minutes before and during the meeting.

   The service contracts (or memorandum attached) must disclose the name of the employing company; the date of the contract, the unexpired term and details of any notice periods; full particulars of remuneration and benefits; any commission or profit sharing arrangements; any provision for compensation on early termination of the contract; and details of any other arrangements which are necessary to enable investors to estimate the company's liability upon early termination of the contract.

(*d*)   A company with listed equity securities must notify the CAO without delay (by the end of the business day following the change) of

   • any information relating to interests in securities which is disclosed to the company under *Sec 324* or *328* (shareholding of directors, spouses and

43.22 Public and Listed Companies

children, see 19.76 *et seq* DIRECTORS) or entered in the register of directors' interests (see 47.7 REGISTERS);

- information relating to any interest of a person connected with a director (see 19.94 DIRECTORS) which would have to be disclosed under the above if the connected person were a director; and

- the granting to, or acceptance by, a director or person connected with him of any option or other right or obligation to acquire or dispose of listed securities in the company or any dealings in such options.

The Exchange has issued a special form for notification of such interests.

(*e*)   A company must adopt by board resolution, and ensure compliance with, a code of dealing in the company's listed securities no less exacting than those of the Model Code issued by the Exchange (see 30.7 INSIDER DEALING).

(*The Listing Rules, Chapters 9.46, 9.47, 16*).

43.22 *Enforcement of listing rules*

Companies must provide the Exchange without delay with all the information and explanations that it requires to

(*a*)   decide whether to grant listing;

(*b*)   protect investors or ensure the smooth operation of the market; and

(*c*)   verify whether the listing rules are being complied with.

The Exchange may, at any time, require the company to publish such information as it considers appropriate for the purposes of (*b*) above and, if it fails to do so, publish the information itself.

If the Exchange considers that the listing rules have been contravened, it may do one or more of the following.

- Censure the company (and publish such censure).

- Suspend or cancel the listing of the company's securities or any class thereof.

- If it considers that the contravention is due to the failure of one or more of the directors

    (i)   censure the relevant directors (and publish such censure);

    (ii)   in the case of wilful or persistent failure, state publicly that in its opinion the director should not remain in office; and

    (iii)   if, despite (ii) above, the director remains in office, suspend or cancel the listing of the company's securities (or any class of them).

(*The Listing Rules, Chapter 1*).

43.23 SUMMARY FINANCIAL STATEMENTS

A *public company*, any class of whose shares or debentures are 'listed' need not, subject to satisfying the conditions in 43.24 below, send copies of the full accounts and reports to 'entitled persons' but may instead send them a summary financial statement (SFS) derived from those accounts, the form and content of which is detailed in 43.28 to 43.35 below. Copies of the full accounts must, however, be sent to any entitled person who wishes to receive them. See 43.25 below for the manner in which it is to be ascertained whether an entitled person (or potential entitled person) wishes to receive the full accounts.

'*Listed*' means admitted to the Official List of The International Stock Exchange of the United Kingdom and the Republic of Ireland Limited.

'*Entitled persons*' means such of the persons specified in *Sec 238(1)* to whom copies of the annual accounts and reports must normally be sent (see 3.3 ACCOUNTS: GENERAL).

[*Sec 251(1)-(3); CA 1989, s 15; SI 1992 No 3003, Regs 1, 3*].

The current detailed provisions are contained in *The Companies (Summary Financial Statement) Regulations 1995 (SI 1995 No 2092)* which have effect after 31 August 1995.

The provisions of 3.5 ACCOUNTS: GENERAL (requirements in connection with publication of accounts) do not apply in relation to the provision to entitled persons of a SFS. [*Sec 251(7); CA 1989, s 15; SI 1992 No 3003, Regs 1, 3*].

Penalties. If default is made in complying with any of the provisions relating to a SFS, the company and every officer of it who is in default is guilty of an offence and liable to a fine up to the level in 40.1(*g*) PENALTIES. [*Sec 251(6), 24 Sch; CA 1989, s 15*].

43.24 **Conditions for sending out summary financial statement**

A listed public company may not send a SFS to an entitled person, in place of its full accounts and reports,

- if it is prohibited from doing so by any provision in its memorandum or articles of association, or, where applicable, any instrument governing debentures, which requires copies of the full accounts and reports to be sent to entitled persons or which forbids the sending of a SFS;

- unless it has ascertained, in accordance with 43.25 below, that the entitled person does not wish to receive copies of the full accounts and reports;

- unless the period allowed for laying and delivering full accounts and reports (see 3.8 ACCOUNTS: GENERAL) for the financial year in question has not expired; and

- unless the SFS has been approved by the board and the original statement signed on behalf of the board by a director of the company.

[*SI 1995 No 2092, Regs 3, 4(1)(4)*].

43.25 *Ascertainment of entitled person's wishes*

Whether or not an entitled person wishes to receive copies of the full accounts and reports for a financial year is to be ascertained

(*a*)   from any 'relevant notification' in writing he has given the company (either as an entitled person or 'potential entitled person') as to his wishes; or

(*b*)   in the absence of such express notification, from any failure to respond to an opportunity given to him (either as an entitled person or 'potential entitled person') to elect to receive full accounts and reports either (i) in response to a notice sent by the company (see 43.26 below) or (ii) as part of a 'relevant consultation' of his wishes (see 43.27 below).

A notification is a '*relevant notification*' in relation to a financial year for the purposes of (*a*) above if it relates to that year (whether or not it is given at the company's invitation) and is received by the company not later than 28 days before the first date on which copies of the full accounts and reports for that year are sent to entitled persons under the provisions in 3.3 ACCOUNTS: GENERAL.

43.26 Public and Listed Companies

A *'potential entitled person'* is a person who is entitled, either conditionally or unconditionally, to become, but has not yet become, an entitled person in relation to the company.

[*SI 1995 No 2092, Reg 4(2)(3)(5)*].

43.26 *Consultation by notice*

A listed public company may give to an entitled person or potential entitled person (see 43.25 above), by post or any other manner authorised by the articles of association, a notice, which must

- state that in future, so long as he is an entitled person, he will be sent a SFS instead of full accounts, unless he notifies the company in writing that he wishes to receive full accounts;

- state that the SFS will contain a summary of the company's or group's profit and loss account, balance sheet and directors' report;

- be accompanied by a postage-paid printed card or form so worded as to enable an entitled person or potential entitled person, by marking a box and returning the card or form, to notify the company that he wishes to receive full accounts for the next financial year for which he is so entitled and for all subsequent financial years (except that the company need not pay the postage in the case of persons whose address is outside an EEA State);

- state that the aforementioned card or form must be returned by a specified date, being a date not less than 21 days after service of the notice nor less than 28 days before the first date on which copies of the full accounts for the next financial year are sent to entitled persons under the provisions in 3.3 ACCOUNTS: GENERAL;

- include a statement in a prominent position to the effect that a SFS will not contain sufficient information to allow as full an understanding of the company's or group's results and state of affairs as would be provided by the full annual accounts and that members and debenture holders have the right to obtain a free copy of the last full accounts; and

- state that the SFS will contain a statement by the auditors as to whether it is consistent with the full accounts, whether it complies with the statutory requirements with regard to summary financial statements and whether the auditors' report on the accounts was qualified.

[*SI 1995 No 2092, Reg 5*].

43.27 *Relevant consultation*

As a means of ascertaining the wishes (see 43.25 above) of an entitled person, a listed public company may conduct a *'relevant consulation'*, i.e. a notice given to such a person (including a potential entitled person, see 43.25 above), by post or any other manner authorised by the articles of association, which

- states that in future, so long as he is an entitled person, he will be sent a SFS instead of full accounts, unless he notifies the company in writing that he wishes to receive full accounts;

- accompanies both a copy of the full accounts and reports and a SFS for the same financial year which is identified in the notice as an example of the document which the entitled person will receive for the future, so long as he is an entitled person, unless he notifies the company to the contrary; and

● be accompanied by a postage-paid printed card or form so worded as to enable an entitled person or potential entitled person, by marking a box and returning the card or form, to notify the company that he wishes to receive full accounts for the next financial year for which he is so entitled and for all subsequent financial years. The company need not pay the postage in the case of persons whose address is outside an EEA State.

[*SI 1995 No 2092, Reg 6*].

43.28 **Form and content of summary financial statements**

This depends on the type of accounts being prepared (individual company or group) and the nature of the company or group (i.e. general, insurance or banking).

In all cases the SFS must state

(*a*)   the name of the person who signed it on behalf of the board;

(*b*)   that it is only a summary of information in the company's annual accounts and directors' report;

(*c*)   the opinion of the auditors as to whether the SFS is consistent with the full accounts and directors' report and complies with the statutory requirements (see *Example 4* under 12.29 AUDITORS for a suggested form of the report);

(*d*)   whether the auditors' report on the annual accounts was unqualified or qualified, and if the latter set out the report in full together with any further material needed to understand the qualification; and

(*e*)   whether the auditors' report on the annual accounts contained a statement under 12.23(i) or (ii) AUDITORS and if so, set out the statement in full.

The SFS must also include a statement in a prominent position to the effect that it does not contain sufficient information to allow as full an understanding of the results of the company (or, where appropriate, the group) and state of affairs of the company (together, where appropriate, with that of the group) as would be provided by the full annual accounts and reports, and that members and debenture holders requiring more detailed information have the right to obtain, free of charge, a copy of the company's last full accounts and reports. The SFS must additionally contain a clear, conspicuous statement of how such a copy can be obtained and of how members and debenture holders may elect in writing to receive full accounts and reports instead of a SFS for all future financial years.

[*Sec 251(4); SI 1995 No 2092, Reg 7*].

In all cases the SFS must

(i)   contain the information detailed in 43.29 to 43.35 below in such order and under such headings as the directors consider appropriate, together with any other information necessary to ensure that the SFS is consistent with the full accounts and reports for the financial year in question;

(ii)   in respect of every profit and loss account and balance sheet item, show the corresponding amount for the immediately preceding financial year as disclosed in the SFS for that year (or the amount which would have been shown had such a statement been prepared), after any adjustments necessary to ensure that the amount is comparable; and

(iii)   disclose earnings per share (*The Listing Rules, Chapter 12.45*).

Nothing in (i) above prevents a company from including in the SFS any additional information derived from the full accounts and directors' report.

[*SI 1995 No 2092, Regs 8-10, 1 Sch 1, 7, 2 Sch 1, 7, 3 Sch 1, 2, 8*].

43.29 *Summary directors' report*

For all companies, the SFS must contain the whole of, or a summary of, that portion of the directors' report for the year which sets out

(*a*)   the review of developments (see 20.2 DIRECTORS' REPORT);

(*b*)   the recommended dividend, if not shown in the summary profit and loss account; and

(*c*)   important post-balance sheet events and likely future developments in the business (see 20.13(*a*)(*b*) DIRECTORS' REPORT);

and must also contain the list of directors' names (see 20.4 DIRECTORS' REPORT).

Item (*b*) above was not required under the old provisions.

[*SI 1995 No 2092, 1 Sch 2, 2 Sch 2, 3 Sch 3*].

43.30 *Summary profit and loss account (other than banking and insurance companies and groups)*

Individual accounts. The following items, or combinations of items, must be shown, in so far as they can be derived from the full profit and loss account, in the order set out and in each case under an appropriate heading.

(*a*)   Turnover.

(*b*)   The combination of income from shares in 'group undertakings' and income from 'participating interests'.

(*c*)   The net figure resulting from the combination of other interest receivable (and similar income) and interest payable (and similar charges).

(*d*)   The profit or loss on ordinary activities before taxation.

(*e*)   Tax on profit or loss on ordinary activities.

(*f*)   Profit or loss on ordinary activities after tax.

(*g*)   The net figure resulting from the combination of extraordinary income and charges after tax.

(*h*)   Profit or loss for the financial year.

(*i*)   The aggregate amount of dividends paid and, if not disclosed in the summary directors' report (not applicable under the old provisions), proposed.

At the end of the summary profit and loss account, the aggregate amount of directors' emoluments under *6 Sch 1* (see 5.34 ACCOUNTS: INDIVIDUAL COMPANIES) must be shown.

Group accounts. The summary consolidated profit and loss account must be drawn up as for individual accounts above except that

(i)   instead of (*b*), there must be shown income from interests in associated under-takings;

(ii)   between (*f*) and (*g*) above, minority interests must additionally be shown under an appropriate heading; and

(iii)   the figure required by (*g*) above must be shown after the deduction or the addition of minority interests therein.

[*SI 1995 No 2092, 1 Sch 3, 4*].

43.31 Summary profit and loss account (insurance companies and groups)

Individual accounts. The following items, or combinations of items, must be shown, in so far as they can be derived from the full profit and loss account, in the order set out and in each case under an appropriate heading.

(*a*)   Gross premiums written – general business.

(*b*)   Gross premiums written – long term business.

(*c*)   Balance on the technical account for general business.

(*d*)   Balance on the technical account for long term business.

(*e*)   The net figure resulting from the combination of the following items on non-technical account: investment income, unrealised gains on investments, allocated investment return transferred from long term business account, investment expenses and charges, unrealised losses on investments, allocated investment return transferred to general business account, other income and other charges (including value adjustments).

(*f*)   Profit or loss on ordinary activities before tax.

(*g*)   Tax on profit or loss on ordinary activities.

(*h*)   Profit or loss on ordinary activities after tax.

(*i*)   Extraordinary profit or loss after tax (the net figure resulting from the combination of extraordinary profit or loss and tax thereon).

(*j*)   Other taxes.

(*k*)   Profit or loss for the financial year.

(*l*)   The aggregate amount of dividends paid and, if not disclosed in the summary directors' report, proposed.

At the end of the summary profit and loss account, the aggregate amount of directors' emoluments under *6 Sch 1* (see 5.34 ACCOUNTS: INDIVIDUAL COMPANIES) must be shown.

Group accounts. The summary consolidated profit and loss account must be drawn up as for individual accounts above except that

(i)   between (*e*) and (*f*) above, there must additionally be shown under an appropriate heading income from interests in associated undertakings;

(ii)   between (*h*) and (*i*) above, minority interests must additionally be shown under an appropriate heading; and

(iii)   the figures required at (*i*) and (*j*) above must each be shown after the deduction or addition of minority interests therein.

[*SI 1995 No 2092, 3 Sch 4, 5*].

43.32 **Summary profit and loss account (banking companies and groups)**

Individual accounts. The following items, or combinations of items, must be shown, in so far as they can be derived from the full profit and loss account, in the order set out and in each case under an appropriate heading.

(*a*)   The net figure resulting from the combination of interest receivable and payable.

(*b*)   The net figure resulting from the combination of dividend income, fees and commissions receivable and payable, dealing profits or losses and other operating income.

(*c*)   The net figure resulting from the combination of administrative expenses, depreciation and amortisation, other operating charges, amounts written off, and adjustments to amounts written off, fixed asset investments.

(*d*)   The net figure resulting from the combination of provisions and adjustments to provisions.

(*e*)   Profit or loss on ordinary activities before tax.

(*f*)   Tax on profit or loss on ordinary activities.

(*g*)   Profit or loss on ordinary activities after tax.

(*h*)   Extraordinary profit or loss after tax.

(*i*)   Other taxes not shown under the preceding items.

(*j*)   Profit or loss for the financial year.

(*k*)   The aggregate amount of dividends paid and, if not disclosed in the summary directors' report (not applicable under the old provisions), proposed.

At the end of the summary profit and loss account, the aggregate amount of directors' emoluments under *6 Sch 1* (see 5.34 ACCOUNTS: INDIVIDUAL COMPANIES) must be shown.

Group accounts. The summary consolidated profit and loss account must be drawn up as for individual accounts above except that

(i)   between (*d*) and (*e*) above, there must be shown income from associated undertakings;

(ii)   between (*g*) and (*h*) above, minority interests must additionally be shown under an appropriate heading; and

(iii)   the figures required by (*h*) and (*i*) above must be shown after the deduction or the addition of minority interests therein.

[*SI 1995 No 2092, 2 Sch 3, 4*].

43.33   *Summary balance sheet (other than banking and insurance companies and groups)*

Individual accounts. In so far as it can be derived from the full balance sheet, the summary balance sheet must show, under an appropriate heading, a single item for each of the headings to which letters are assigned in the balance sheet format set out in 5.4 ACCOUNTS: INDIVIDUAL COMPANIES which has been used for the full balance sheet (where necessary by a combination of the items to which Roman and Arabic numbers are assigned). The same order must be followed. However

•   where an alternative position is permitted for any item in either format, the summary balance sheet must use the position used by the full balance sheet; and

•   in the case of Format 2, heading C under 'Liabilities' two figures must be shown, for amounts falling due within one year and after one year respectively.

Group accounts. Similar figures must be disclosed as for individual companies above with the addition of an item for minority interests as required under 4.18 ACCOUNTS: GROUPS OF COMPANIES.

[*SI 1995 No 2092, 1 Sch 5, 6*].

43.34 *Summary balance sheet (insurance companies and groups)*

Individual accounts. The following items, or combinations of items, must be shown, in so far as they can be derived from the full balance sheet, in the order set out and in each case under an appropriate heading.

(*a*)   The aggregate of investments and assets held to cover linked liabilities.

(*b*)   Reinsurers' share of technical provisions.

(*c*)   The aggregate of called up share capital not paid, intangible assets, debtors arising out of direct insurance and reinsurance operations and other debtors, other assets, and prepayments and accrued income.

(*d*)   Total assets.

(*e*)   Capital and reserves.

(*f*)   Subordinated liabilities.

(*g*)   Fund for future appropriations.

(*h*)   Gross technical provisions (the aggregate of equalisation provision and the gross amounts of provision for unearned premiums, long term business provision, claims outstanding, provision for bonuses and rebates, other technical provisions and technical provisions for linked liabilities).

(*i*)   Technical provisions – reinsurance amounts (the aggregate of the reinsurance amounts of provisions for unearned premiums, long term business provision, claims outstanding, provision for bonuses and rebates, other technical provisions and technical provisions for linked liabilities).

(*j*)   The aggregate of provisions for other risks and charges, deposits received from reinsurers, creditors, and accruals and deferred income.

(*k*)   Total liabilities.

Group accounts. The summary consolidated balance sheet must be drawn up as for individual accounts above except that between (*d*) and (*e*) above, minority interests must additionally be shown under an appropriate heading.

[*SI 1995 No 2092, 3 Sch 6, 7*].

43.35 *Summary balance sheet (banking companies and groups)*

Individual accounts. The following items, or combinations of items, must be shown, in so far as they can be derived from the full balance sheet, in the order set out and under appropriate headings.

(*a*)   Cash and balances at central (or post office) banks, treasury bills and other eligible bills.

(*b*)   Loans and advances to banks.

(*c*)   Loans and advances to customers.

(*d*)   The aggregate of debt securities (and other fixed income securities), equity shares (and other variable-yield securities), participating interests and shares in group undertakings.

(*e*) The aggregate of intangible and tangible fixed assets.

(*f*) The aggregate of called up capital not paid, own shares, other assets and prepayments and accrued income.

(*g*) Total assets.

(*h*) Deposits by banks.

(*i*) Customer accounts.

(*j*) Debt securities in issue.

(*k*) The aggregate of other liabilities, accruals and deferred income and provisions for liabilities and charges.

(*l*) Subordinated liabilities.

(*m*) The aggregate of called up share capital, share premium account, reserves, revaluation reserve and profit and loss account.

(*n*) Total liabilities.

(*o*) Contingent liabilities.

(*p*) Commitments.

Group accounts. The summary consolidated balance sheet must be drawn up as for individual accounts above except that between (*l*) and (*m*) above or after (*m*) above (whichever is the position adopted for the full accounts), minority interests must additionally be shown under an appropriate heading.

[*SI 1995 No 2092, 2 Sch 5, 6*].

43.36 Revision of defective accounts and reports: voluntary revision

Where the directors have prepared revised accounts or a revised directors' report under *Sec 245* (see 3.9 ACCOUNTS: GENERAL) and a SFS based on the original annual accounts or directors' report has been sent out to any person under *Sec 251*, the provisions described below apply.

Where the original SFS would, if it had been based on the revised accounts or report, fail to comply with *Sec 251* or *SI 1995 No 2092*, a revised SFS must be prepared and sent out to any person who received the original SFS and any person to whom the company would be entitled, as at the date of preparation of the revised SFS, to send a SFS for the current financial year. *Sec 251(1)-(4)(7)* apply with the appropriate modifications to a revised SFS. A revised SFS must contain a short statement of the revisions made and their effect.

Where the original SFS would, if it had been based on the revised accounts or report, comply with *Sec 251* etc., then instead of a revised SFS, a note must be sent to the above-mentioned persons, stating that the annual accounts of the company for the relevant financial year (specifying it) or (as the case may be) the directors' report for that year have or has been revised in a respect which has no bearing on the SFS for that year. If the auditors' report on the revised accounts or directors' report (see 12.22 AUDITORS) is qualified, a copy of that report must be attached to the note sent out.

The revised SFS or note must be sent out within 28 days after the date of revision of the accounts or report.

Where, between the sending out of the original SFS and the revision of the accounts or directors' report, there are amendments to *Sec 251* or the regulations made under that section, references above to that section or those regulations are to the provisions in force at the date of the sending out of the original SFS.

The penalty provisions of *Sec 251(6)* referred to at 43.23 above also apply with respect to the above provisions, but as if the reference to 'the company and every officer of it who is in default' were a reference to each of the directors who approved the revised accounts or revised directors' report.

[*SI 1992 No 3075, Reg 10(3); SI 1995 No 2092, Reg 12*].

Appendix: The Combined Code, Section 1 (Companies)

A.   DIRECTORS

A.1   The Board

Principle. Every listed company should be headed by an effective board which should lead and control the company.

Code provisions

A.1.1   The board should meet regularly.

A.1.2   The board should have a formal schedule of matters specifically reserved to it for decision.

A.1.3   There should be a procedure agreed by the board for directors in the furtherance of their duties to take independent professional advice if necessary, at the company's expense.

A.1.4   All directors should have access to the advice and services of the company secretary, who is responsible to the board for ensuring that board procedures are followed and that applicable rules and regulations are complied with. Any question of the removal of the company secretary should be a matter for the board as a whole.

A.1.5   All directors should bring an independent judgement to bear on issues of strategy, performance, resources, including key appointments, and standards of conduct.

A.1.6   Every director should receive appropriate training on the first occasion that he or she is appointed to the board of a listed company, and subsequently as necessary.

A.2   Chairman and chief executive officer (CEO)

Principle. There are two key tasks at the top of every public company – the running of the board and the executive responsibility for the running of the company's business. There should be a clear division of responsibilities at the head of the company which will ensure a balance of power and authority, such that no one individual has unfettered powers of decision.

Code provision

A.2.1   A decision to combine the posts of chairman and CEO in one person should be publicly justified. Whether the posts are held by different people or by the same person, there should be a strong and independent non-executive element on the board, with a recognised senior member other than the chairman to whom concerns can be conveyed. The chairman, CEO and senior independent director should be identified in the annual report.

A.3   Board balance

Principle. The board should include a balance of executive and non-executive directors (including independent non-executives) such that no individual or small group of individuals can dominate the board's decision taking.

Code provisions

A.3.1   The board should include non-executive directors of sufficient calibre and number for their views to carry significant weight in the board's decisions. Non-executive directors should comprise not less than one third of the board.

A.3.2   The majority of non-executive directors should be independent of management and free from any business or other relationship which could materially interfere with the exercise of their independent judgement. Non-executive directors considered by the board to be independent in this sense should be identified in the annual report.

A.4   **Supply of information**

Principle. The board should be supplied in a timely manner with information in a form and of a quality appropriate to enable it to discharge its duties.

Code provision

A.4.1   Management has an obligation to provide the board with appropriate and timely information, but information volunteered by management is unlikely to be enough in all circumstances and directors should make further enquiries where necessary. The chairman should ensure that all directors are properly briefed on issues arising at board meetings.

A.5   **Appointments to the board**

Principle. There should be a formal and transparent procedure for the appointment of new directors to the board.

Code provision

A.5.1   Unless the board is small, a nomination committee should be established to make recommendations to the board on all new board appointments. A majority of the members of the committee should be non-executive directors, and the chairman should be either the chairman of the board or a non-executive director. The chairman and members of the nomination committee should be identified in the annual report.

A.6   **Re-election**

Principle. All directors should be required to submit themselves for re-election at regular intervals and at least every three years.

Code provisions

A.6.1   Non-executive directors should be appointed for specified terms subject to re-election and to *CA 1985* provisions relating to the removal of a director, and re-appointment should not be automatic.

A.6.2   All directors should be subject to election by shareholders at the first opportunity after their appointment, and to re-election thereafter at intervals of not more than three years. The names of the directors submitted for election or re-election should be accompanied by sufficient biographical details to enable shareholders to take an informed decision on their election.

43. App   Public and Listed Companies

B   DIRECTORS' REMUNERATION

B.1   The level and make-up of remuneration

Principle. Levels of remuneration should be sufficient to attract and retain the directors needed to run the company successfully, but companies should avoid paying more than is necessary for this purpose. A proportion of executive directors' remuneration should be structured so as to link rewards to corporate and individual performance.

Code provisions

Remuneration policy

B.1.1   The remuneration committee should provide the packages needed to attract, retain and motivate executive directors of the quality required but should avoid paying more than is necessary for this purpose.

B.1.2   Remuneration committees should judge where to position their company relative to other companies. They should be aware of what comparable companies are paying and should take account of relative performance. But they should use such comparisons with caution, in view of the risk that they can result in an upward ratchet of remuneration levels with no corresponding improvement in performance.

B.1.3   Remuneration committees should be sensitive to the wider scene, including pay and employment conditions elsewhere in the group, especially when determining annual salary increases.

B.1.4   The performance-related element of remuneration should form a significant part of the total remuneration package of executive directors and should be designed to align their interests with those of shareholders and to give these directors keen incentives to perform at the highest levels.

B.1.5   Executive share options should not be offered at a discount save as permitted by *Listing Rules, Chapter 13.30, 13.31.*

B.1.6   In designing schemes of performance-related remuneration, remuneration committees should consider whether directors should be eligible for annual bonuses and benefits under long-term incentive schemes, and the pension consequences and associated costs to the company of basic salary increases and other changes in remuneration, particularly for directors close to retirement. In general, neither annual bonuses nor benefits in kind should be pensionable.

Service contracts and compensation

B.1.7   There is a strong case for setting notice or contract periods at, or reducing them to, one year or less. Boards should set this as an objective; but they should recognise that it may not be possible to achieve it immediately.

B.1.8   If it is necessary to offer longer notice or contract periods to new directors recruited from outside, such periods should reduce after the initial period.

B.1.9   Remuneration committees should consider what compensation commitments (including pension contributions) their directors' contracts of service, if any, would entail in the event of early termination. They should in particular consider the advantages of providing explicitly in the initial contract for such compensation commitments except in the case of removal for misconduct.

B.1.10   Where the initial contract period does not explicitly provide for compensation commitments, remuneration committees should, within legal constraints, tailor their approach in individual early termination cases to the wide variety of circumstances. The board aim should be to avoid rewarding poor performance while dealing fairly with cases where departure is not due to poor performance and to take a robust line on reducing compensation to reflect departing directors' obligations to mitigate loss.

B.2   **Procedure**

Principle. Companies should establish a formal and transparent procedure for developing policy on executive remuneration and for fixing the remuneration packages of individual directors. No director should be involved in deciding his or her own remuneration.

Code provisions

B.2.1   To avoid potential conflicts of interest, boards of directors should set up remuneration committees of independent non-executive directors to make recommendations to the board, within agreed terms of reference, on the company's framework of executive remuneration and its cost; and to determine on their behalf specific remuneration packages for each of the executive directors, including pension rights and any compensation payments.

B.2.2   Remuneration committees should consists exclusively of non-executive directors who are independent of management and free from any business or other relationship which could materially interfere with the exercise of their independent judgement.

B.2.3   The members of the remuneration committee should be listed each year in the board's remuneration report to shareholders (see B.3.1 below).

B.2.4   The board itself or, where required by the Articles of Association, the shareholders should determine the remuneration of non-executive directors, including members of the remuneration committee, within the limits set in the Articles of Association. Where permitted by the Articles, the board may however delegate this responsibility to a small sub-committee, which might include the CEO.

B.2.5   Remuneration committees should consult the chairman and/or CEO about their proposals relating to the remuneration of other executive directors and have access to professional advice inside and outside the company.

B.2.6   The chairman of the board should ensure that the company maintains contact as required with its principal shareholders about remuneration in the same way as for other matters.

B.3   **Disclosure**

Principle. The company's annual report should contain a statement of remuneration policy and details of the remuneration of each director.

Code provisions

B.3.1   The board should report to the shareholders each year on remuneration. The report should form part of, or be annexed to, the company's annual report and accounts. It should be the main vehicle through which the company reports to shareholders on directors' remuneration.

B.3.2   The report should set out the company's policy on executive directors' remuneration. It should draw attention to factors specific to the company.

B.3.3   In preparing the remuneration report, the board should include full details of all elements in the remuneration package of each individual director by name (basic salary, bonuses, benefits, etc.) and pension entitlements earned during the year. If annual bonuses or benefits in kind are pensionable, the report should explain and justify. Any service contracts which provide for, or imply, notice periods in excess of one year (and any provisions for predetermined compensation or termination which exceed one year's salary and benefits) should be disclosed and the reason for longer notice periods explained. See 43.15(*r*) above for fuller details of the requirements of the remuneration report as required under the *Listing Rules*.

B.3.4   Shareholders should be invited specifically to approve all new long-term incentive schemes (other than arrangements offered on similar terms to substantially all employees or an arrangement established specifically to facilitate, in unusual circumstances, the recruitment or retention of one particular director).

B.3.5   The board's annual remuneration report to shareholders need not be a standard item of agenda for AGMs. But the board should consider each year whether the circumstances are such that the AGM should be invited to approve the policy set out in the report and should minute their conclusions.

C   RELATIONS WITH SHAREHOLDERS

C.1   Dialogue with institutional shareholders

Principle. Companies should be ready, where practicable, to enter into dialogue with institutional shareholders based on the mutual understanding of objectives.

C.2   Constructive use of the AGM

Principle. Boards should use the AGM to communicate with private investors and encourage their participation.

Code provisions

C.2.1   Companies should count all proxy votes and, except where a poll is called, should indicate the level of proxies lodged for each resolution, and the balance for and against the resolution, after it has been dealt with on a show of hands.

C.2.2   Companies should propose a separate resolution at the AGM on each substantially separate issue, and should in particular propose a resolution at the AGM relating to the report and accounts.

C.2.3   The chairman of the board should arrange for the chairman of the audit, remuneration and nomination committees to be available to answer questions at the AGM.

C.2.4   Companies should arrange for the Notice of the AGM and related papers to be sent to shareholders at least 20 working days before the meeting.

D   ACCOUNTABILITY AND AUDIT

D.1   Financial reporting

Principle. The board should present a balanced and understandable assessment of the company's position and prospects.

Code provisions

D.1.1   The directors should explain their responsibilities for preparing the accounts, and there should be a statement by the auditors about their reporting responsibilities.

D.1.2   The board's responsibility to present a balanced and understandable assessment extends to interim and other price-sensitive public reports and reports to regulators as well as to information required to be presented by statutory requirements.

D.1.3   The directors should report that the business is a going concern, with supporting assumptions or qualifications as necessary.

D.2   **Internal control**

Principle. The board should maintain a sound system of internal control to safeguard shareholders' investment and the company's assets.

Code provisions

D.2.1   The directors should, at least annually, conduct a review of the effectiveness of the group's internal control and should report to shareholders that they have done so. The review should cover all controls, including financial, operational and compliance controls and risk management.

D.2.2   Companies which do not have an internal audit function should from time to time review the need for one.

D.3   **Audit committee and auditors**

Principle. The board should establish formal and transparent arrangements for considering how they should apply the financial reporting and internal control principles and for maintaining an appropriate relationship with the company's auditors.

Code provisions

D.3.1   The board should establish an audit committee of at least three directors, all non-executive, with written terms of reference which deal clearly with its authority and duties. The members of the committee, a majority of whom should be independent non-executive directors, should be named in the report and accounts.

D.3.2   The duties of the audit committee should include keeping under review the scope and results of the audit and its cost effectiveness and the independence and objectivity of the auditors. Where the auditors also supply a substantial volume of non-audit services to the company, the committee should keep the nature and extent of such services under review, seeking to balance the maintenance of objectivity and value for money.

Committee on Corporate Governance, The Combined Code – Reproduced with the permission of Gee Publishing Ltd.

44 Reconstructions and Mergers

Cross-references. See 58.16 SHARES AND SHARE CAPITAL for reduction of share capital; 59.2 – 59.17 TAKEOVER OFFERS for the provisions of the City Code on takeovers and mergers; 59.18 TAKEOVER OFFERS for the provisions of the Listing Rules relating to takeovers and mergers.

The contents of this chapter are as follows

44.1 COMPROMISE WITH CREDITORS AND/OR MEMBERS

Where a compromise or 'arrangement' is proposed between a company and either

- its creditors, or any class of them, or

- its members, or any class of them,

a court having jurisdiction to wind up the company may, on the application of any creditor or member of the company (or, where appropriate, of the liquidator or administrator), order a meeting of those with whom the compromise or arrangement with the company is proposed. The meeting is summoned as directed by the court. An order pronounced in Scotland by the judge acting as vacation judge is not subject to review, reduction, suspension or stay of execution.

At such a summoned meeting, if a majority representing three-quarters in value of those present and voting (in person or by proxy) agree to any compromise or arrangement, it will (if sanctioned by the court) be binding on all the creditors or members (or class) concerned and on the company (or, where the company is being wound up, on the liquidator and contributories of the company).

The court's order does not take effect until an office copy (in Scotland a certified copy interlocutor) has been delivered to the Registrar of Companies for registration. A copy of the order must be annexed to every copy of the company's memorandum of association (or other instrument constituting the company or defining its constitution) issued after the order has been made. In default the company and every officer in default is liable to a fine up to the level in 40.1(g) PENALTIES.

'Arrangement' includes a reorganisation of the company's share capital by consolidation of different classes and/or by division of shares into different classes.

[*Secs 425, 743A, 24 Sch; IA 1985, s 109, 6 Sch 11; CA 1989, 19 Sch 19*].

A 'class' must be confined to those persons whose rights are not so dissimilar as to make it impossible for them to consult together with a view to their common interest (*Sovereign Life Assurance Co v Dodd [1892] 2 QB 573*). See, for example, *Re Hellenic & General Trust Ltd [1975] 3 All ER 382* where 53% of the ordinary shares were held by a company interested in the proposed arrangement. It was held that the remaining 47% of shareholders formed a separate class of whom the necessary three-quarters majority approval was required.

In deciding whether to sanction the compromise etc., the court must ensure not only that the statutory provisions are complied with but also that the majority has acted bona fide. It must see that the minority is not being overridden by a majority with adverse interests and that the scheme overall is reasonable. A scheme cannot be reasonable where a party gets nothing and gives up everything (*Re Alabama, New Orleans, Texas and Pacific Junction Rly Co [1891] 1 Ch 213*). See also *Re National Farmers' Union Development Trust Ltd [1973] 1 All ER 135.*

44.2   Information to be circulated

Every notice summoning such a meeting under 44.1 above must be accompanied by a statement explaining the effect of the proposed compromise or arrangement. In particular, it must state any material interests of the company's directors (in whatever capacity), or, where the rights of debenture-holders are affected, of the trustees of any deed for securing the issue of the debentures, and the effect of the proposed compromise or arrangement on those interests in so far as it differs from the effect on like interests of other persons. Where the notice is given by advertisement, it must either include such a statement or indicate how those entitled to attend may obtain copies (which must be supplied free of charge). [*Sec 426(1)-(5)*]. It is essential that the explanatory circulars sent out by the company are perfectly fair and, as far as possible, give all the information reasonably necessary to enable the recipients to determine how to vote (*Re Dorman Long & Co Ltd [1934] Ch 635*).

If the company defaults in complying with any of the above requirements, the company and every officer in default (which for this purpose may include a liquidator, administrator or trustees for debenture-holders) is liable to a fine up to the level in 40.1(*d*) PENALTIES. No fine is imposed on a person whose default was due to the refusal of a director or trustee for debenture-holders to supply the necessary particulars of his interests.

Directors and trustees for debenture-holders are required to give the company notice of matters relating to themselves which are necessary for compliance with these requirements. In default such a person is liable to a fine up to the level in 40.1(*g*) PENALTIES. [*Sec 426(6)(7), 24 Sch; IA 1985, s 109, 6 Sch 12*].

44.3   Company reconstruction or amalgamation

Where the proposed compromise or arrangement is for the purposes of, or connected with, a scheme of reconstruction or amalgamation under which the whole or a part of the undertaking or 'property' of one company is to be transferred to another, the court may provide, either by the sanctioning order or by any subsequent order, for all or any of

- the transfer of the whole or a part of its undertaking, and of its property or 'liabilities', from any transferor company to the transferee company,

- the allotting or appropriation of transferee company shares, debentures, policies, etc. under the compromise or arrangement,

- the continuation by or against the transferee company of any legal proceedings pending by or against any transferor company,

- the dissolution, without winding up, of any transferor company, and

- the provision to be made for dissenters,

and any other necessary incidental, consequential and supplemental matters.

'Property' for these purposes includes property, rights and powers of every description, and *'liabilities'* includes duties.

If the order provides for the transfer of property or liabilities, that property is thereby transferred to and vests in the transferee company, and those liabilities are transferred and

44.4 Reconstructions and Mergers

become liabilities of that company. Property vests free of any charge ceasing to have effect by virtue of the compromise or arrangement, if the order so directs.

Every company in relation to which such an order is made must cause an office copy (in Scotland a certified copy interlocutor) to be delivered to the Registrar of Companies for registration within seven days of its making. In default the company and every officer in default is liable to a fine up to the level in 40.1(*f*) PENALTIES.

[*Secs 427, 743A, 24 Sch; CA 1989, 19 Sch 19*].

44.4 Mergers and divisions of public companies

Where a compromise or arrangement as under 44.1 above involving a public company is proposed for the purposes of, or in connection with, a scheme of reconstruction or amalgamation, the provisions in *15B Sch* (see below) apply where

- the circumstances are as specified in any of Cases 1, 2 or 3 below, and

- the consideration for any transfer envisaged in the Case in question is to be shares in the transferee company or companies, receivable by members of the transferor company or companies, with or without a cash payment,

provided that the public company in respect of which the compromise or arrangement is proposed is not being wound up, and that the application to the court for a sanctioning order was not made before 1 January 1988.

The Cases referred to above are as follows.

Case 1

Where under the scheme the undertaking, 'property' and 'liabilities' of the company in respect of which the compromise or arrangement in question is proposed are to be transferred to another public company, other than one formed for the purpose of, or in connection with, the scheme.

Case 2

Where under the scheme the undertaking, property and liabilities of each of two or more public companies concerned in the scheme, including the company in respect of which the compromise or arrangement in question is proposed, are to be transferred to a company (whether or not a public company) formed for the purpose of, or in connection with, the scheme.

Case 3

Where under the scheme the undertaking, property and liabilities of the company in respect of which the compromise or arrangement in question is proposed are to be divided among and transferred to two or more companies each of which is either

- a public company; or

- a company (whether or not a public company) formed for the purposes of, or in connection with, the scheme.

'Property' and *'liabilities'* for these purposes have the extended meanings specified in 44.3 above.

Before sanctioning any compromise or arrangement, the court may, on the application of any transferee company under the relevant Case (other than one formed for the purpose of or in connection with the scheme) or of any member, creditor or (where appropriate) administrator of it, order a meeting of the members or creditors of the company, or of any class of them, to be summoned as directed by the court.

Northern Ireland. These provisions also extend to NI to the extent that the transferee company, or any of the transferee companies, is a company within the meaning of *Companies (NI) Order 1986, Art 3* (and thus not otherwise a 'company' within these provisions).

[*Sec 427A; CA 1989, s 114; SI 1987 No 1991*].

The provisions of *15B Sch* as inserted by *SI 1987 No 1991* impose detailed requirements before the court will sanction any compromise or arrangement as above. These relate to the following.

- A requirement, subject to exceptions, for a three-quarters majority in favour in meetings of each class of members of every transferee company involved, other than ones formed for the purposes of or in connection with the scheme. [*15B Sch 1*].

- The drawing up and publication of the proposed terms of the scheme. [*15B Sch 2*].

- The drawing up and contents of the directors' reports. [*15B Sch 3, 4*].

- The drawing up and contents of the experts' reports. [*15B Sch 3, 5*].

- The documents and information to be made available to members. [*15B Sch 3, 6; CA 1989, 10 Sch 22*].

- The allotment of shares to a transferor company (or its nominee) in respect of its own shares held by it or by its nominee. [*15B Sch 7*].

- Securities (other than shares) to which special rights are attached. [*15B Sch 8*].

- Determination of the date the scheme is to come into operation. [*15B Sch 9*].

- In relation to Case 1 and Case 3 schemes, amendments to the above requirements in certain circumstances where shares etc. in transferor companies are held by or on behalf of transferee companies. [*15B Sch 12-14*].

- In relation to Case 3 schemes, the liability of transferee companies for the default of another. [*15B Sch 15*].

44.5 VOLUNTARY WINDING UP – ACCEPTANCE OF SHARES, ETC. AS CONSIDERATION FOR SALE OF PROPERTY

The liquidator of a company being, or proposed to be, voluntarily wound up may, in compensation (in whole or part) for the transfer or sale of the whole or part of its business or property to another company, receive shares, policies, etc. in that company for distribution among its members, or enter into any other arrangement whereby members may instead (or in addition) participate in profits of, or receive any other benefit from, that company. Such a sale or arrangement is binding on the members, and requires the sanction

- in the case of a members' voluntary winding up, of a special resolution of the company, conferring on the liquidator either a general authority or authority in respect of a particular arrangement; and

- in the case of a creditors' voluntary winding up, of the court or the liquidation committee.

44.6 Reconstructions and Mergers

A special resolution is not invalid for these purposes by reason of being passed before or at the same time as a resolution for voluntary winding up or for appointing liquidators, but if within a year an order for winding up is made by the court, the special resolution is valid only if sanctioned by the court. [*IA 1986, s 110*].

Where there is an arrangement under the above provisions, there is no power given to the company in general meeting to alter the rights of the contributories *inter se*, and they must share according to their rights and interests on winding up (*Griffith v Paget (1877) 5 ChD 894*).

If a member who did not vote in favour of the special resolution expresses dissent in writing to the liquidator within seven days of its being passed, he may require the liquidator either to abstain from carrying the resolution into effect or to purchase his interest. The right of a member to dissent cannot be overridden by the company's memorandum (*Bisgood v Henderson's Transvaal Estates Ltd [1908] 1 Ch 743*). If the liquidator elects to purchase the interest, he must raise the purchase money in such manner as may be determined by special resolution and it must be paid before the company is dissolved. The price at which he must purchase the interest, if not agreed, is to be determined by arbitration. [*IA 1986, s 111*].

44.6 COMPANY INSOLVENCY: VOLUNTARY ARRANGEMENTS

Under *IA 1986, ss 1-7* and *The Insolvency Rules 1986 (SI 1986 No 1925)*, a proposal may be made to a company and its creditors for a voluntary arrangement consisting of either a composition in satisfaction of its debts or a scheme of arrangement of its affairs. The proposal must provide for a nominee (qualified to act as an insolvency practitioner in relation to the company) to supervise implementation of the voluntary arrangement, as trustee or otherwise. Such a proposal may be made by the administrator where an administration order is in force in relation to the company, by the liquidator where the company is being wound up, or otherwise by the directors of the company. [*IA 1986, s 1*]. The requirements as to the contents of the proposal are set out in *SI 1986 No 1925, Rules 1.3, 1.10, 1.12*.

Where the nominee is *not* the liquidator or administrator, he must, within 28 days (longer if the court allows) of being given notice of the proposal, report to the court whether, in his opinion, meetings of the company and of its creditors should be summoned to consider the proposal, and if so the proposed time and place of such meetings. If the nominee fails to make such a report, the person intending to make the proposal may apply to the court for his replacement. The person intending to make the proposal must submit to the nominee a document setting out the terms of the proposed voluntary arrangement and a statement of the company's affairs containing prescribed information, in particular in relation to the company's creditors, its liabilities and its assets (see *SI 1986 No 1925, Rules 1.4, 1.5*). If the nominee has reported that meetings should be summoned to consider the proposal, then, unless the court directs otherwise, those meetings must be summoned at the proposed times and places. [*IA 1986, ss 2, 3(1); SI 1986 No 1925, Rules 1.7-1.9, 1.11*].

Where the nominee *is* the liquidator or administrator, he must summon meetings of the company and of its creditors to consider the proposal at a time and place he thinks fit. [*IA 1986, s 3(2)*].

The persons to be summoned to a creditors' meeting must include every one of the company's creditors of whose claim and address the person summoning the meeting is aware. [*IA 1986, s 3(3)*].

44.7   Consideration and implementation of proposal

The meetings summoned under 44.6 above are conducted in accordance with *The Insolvency Rules 1986 (SI 1986 No 1925, Rules 1.13-1.21)*, and must decide whether to approve the proposed voluntary arrangement. Modifications may be made to the proposal, including a change in the person proposed to supervise its implementation, but not so as to cause the proposal to cease to be within 44.1 above. The meeting may not approve a proposal or modification which diminishes the rights of a secured or preferential creditor unless the creditor concurs. On conclusion of each of the meetings, the chairman must report the result to the court and immediately thereafter give notice of the result to all those to whom notice of the meeting was sent (see *SI 1986 No 1925, rule 1.24*). [*IA 1986, s 4*].

Where each of the meetings approves the proposal, either unmodified or with the same modifications, the voluntary arrangement so approved takes effect as if made by the company at the creditors' meeting, and binds all those who had notice of, and were entitled to vote at, that meeting, as if they were parties to the voluntary arrangement. An approval is not invalidated by any irregularity at or in relation to a meeting unless the decision is successfully challenged on application to the court (see 44.8 below).

If the company is being wound up or an administration order is in force, the court may by order do either or both of the following.

(*a*)   Stay or sist all proceedings in the winding up or discharge the administration order.

(*b*)   Give appropriate directions regarding the winding up or administration to facilitate the implementation of the voluntary arrangement.

An order under (*a*) may not be made within 28 days of the reports of the results of each of the meetings required as above being made to the court, or if a challenge to the decisions made at those meetings (see 44.8 below) has been or could still be made.

[*IA 1986, ss 5, 6(7)*].

44.8   Challenge of decisions

An application may be made to the court on the grounds that either or both of the following apply.

(*a*)   The voluntary arrangement approved at the meetings under 44.7 above unfairly prejudices the interests of a creditor, member or contributory of the company.

(*b*)   There has been some material irregularity at or in relation to either of the meetings.

The application may be made by any person entitled to vote at either meeting, by the nominee appointed to supervise implementation of the arrangement (or his replacement, see 44.7 above), or (where relevant) by the administrator or liquidator of the company, and must be made within 28 days of the reports of the results of each of the meetings being made to the court.

If the court is satisfied as to either (*a*) or (*b*) above it may do either or both of the following.

•   Revoke or suspend the approvals given by the meetings or that given by the meeting at or in relation to which the irregularity occurred.

•   Direct that either further meetings be summoned to consider any revised proposal by the original proposer, or, where there was a material irregularity at the original

44.9 Reconstructions and Mergers

company or creditors' meeting, a further such meeting be summoned to reconsider the original proposal.

Where a direction is given under (*b*) above for the summoning of a meeting to consider a revised proposal, and the court is subsequently satisfied that the original proposer does not intend to submit such a revised proposal, the court must revoke the direction and revoke or suspend any approval given at the previous meetings. The court may give such supplemental directions as it thinks fit, in particular in relation to things done since the meeting under any voluntary arrangement approved by the meeting, where, on an application under these provisions, it has given a direction that further meeting(s) be summoned under (*b*) above or has revoked or suspended an approval.

[*IA 1986, s 6; SI 1986 No 1925, rule 1.25*].

44.9 Implementation of proposal

Where a voluntary arrangement has been approved and taken effect under 44.7 above, the nominee appointed to supervise implementation of the arrangement (or his replacement) becomes the supervisor of the arrangement. Any person dissatisfied with any act, omission or decision of the supervisor may apply to the court, which may make such orders or give such directions as it thinks fit. The supervisor may himself apply to the court for directions, and is one of the persons who may apply to the court for the company to be wound up or for an administration order to be made in relation to it. The court may, where appropriate, appoint a supervisor in substitution for the existing supervisor or to fill a vacancy, either to increase the number of persons exercising the functions of supervisor or (where there is more than one such person) to replace existing such persons. [*IA 1986, s 7; SI 1986 No 1925, rules 1.22, 1.23, 1.26-1.29*].

44.10 MERGER REFERENCES

The provisions of *sections 64* to *75K* of, and *Part I* of *Schedule 8* to, the *Fair Trading Act 1973* (*FTA 1973*), described below at 44.11 to 44.18, apply to all merger references other than newspaper merger references made under *FTA 1973, s 59*, to which *FTA 1973, ss 57-62, 8 Sch* apply. [*FTA 1973, s 63(1); CA 1989, 20 Sch 3*]. The provisions also extend to NI.

The Director General of Fair Trading (*'the Director'*) is required to keep himself informed of actual and prospective arrangements or transactions which may need to be considered for a reference to the Competition Commission (*'the Commission'*), and to make recommendations for appropriate action to the Secretary of State. The Director must take into consideration any representations made to him by interested persons or bodies representing such persons. [*FTA 1973, s 76; CA 1989, 20 Sch 11*].

44.11 Merger situations qualifying for investigation

A merger reference may be made by the Secretary of State to the Commission where he considers that two or more 'enterprises' have ceased to be distinct enterprises, and that either of the following conditions have been satisfied.

(*a*)   Following the merger (whether as a result of it or otherwise) at least one-quarter of supplies of goods or services of any description in the UK (or in 'a substantial part of the UK') are supplies either

- by or to (or for) the same person, or

- by or to (or for) the enterprises concerned in the merger.

[*FTA 1973, s 64(2)(3); CA 1989, 20 Sch 6*].

For a consideration of the meaning of the phrase *'a substantial part of the UK'*, see *R v Monopolies and Mergers Commission, ex p South Yorkshire Transport Ltd [1993] 1 All.*

Where there are materially different forms of supply of goods or services, they may be considered separately, together or in groups. The Secretary of State or the Commission, as the case may be, has powers to determine what constitutes a material difference in forms of supply, as it has in deciding criteria by which the one-quarter limit is to be determined and whether goods or services are to be treated as being of a separate description. [*FTA 1973, s 68*].

(b)   The value of the assets taken over exceeds £70 million (£30 million in relation to any merger reference made before 9 February 1994). This figure may be amended by statutory instrument (but not to less than £5 million). [*FTA 1973, s 64(1)(7); SI 1994 No 72*]. The value of assets taken over is broadly the total book value of all assets employed in or appropriated to enterprises ceasing to be distinct enterprises, other than those which remain under the same ownership and control (or, if no enterprise so remains, other than the enterprise having the highest asset value), less relevant provisions for depreciation, renewals or diminution in value. [*FTA 1973, s 67; CA 1989, 20 Sch 5*].

At least one of the 'enterprises' must have been carried on in the UK or by or under the control of a UK-incorporated body corporate, and the enterprises must have ceased to be distinct enterprises within the four months (before 19 March 1996, six months) preceding the making of the merger reference. If they ceased to be distinct enterprises without prior notice of material facts about the relevant arrangements or transactions having been given to the Secretary of State or to the Director or made public, the merger reference may be made within four months (before 19 March 1996, six months) of those facts being so notified or made public. [*FTA 1973, s 64(1)(4)(9); SI 1984 No 932; SI 1996 No 345*]. A merger reference may also be made at any time when, because of the EC merger control regulation under 44.19 below, it could not have been made earlier than six months before the date on which it is made. [*SI 1990 No 1563*].

'Enterprise' for these purposes means the activities, or any part of the activities, of a business. [*FTA 1973, s 63(2)*].

The circumstances in which any two enterprises may cease to be distinct enterprises require generally either that they are brought under common ownership or control, or that one of them ceases to be carried on at all in consequence of arrangements or transactions entered into to prevent competition between the enterprises. [*FTA 1973, ss 65, 77*]. The enterprises cease to be distinct when the parties to the arrangements or transactions become bound to the extent necessary to achieve that result, options and conditional rights being taken into account only when the option is exercised or the condition(s) fulfilled. The Secretary of State or the Commission may treat successive linked events under the arrangements or transactions over a two-year period as having occurred on the date of the last of the events. [*FTA 1973, s 66; CA 1989, 20 Sch 4*]. Similarly, in relation to merger references made after 15 November 1989, certain transactions over a two-year period leading to a change of control over an enterprise may be treated as having occurred on the date of the last of the transactions. [*FTA 1973, s 66A; CA 1989, s 150*].

In order to avoid uncertainty, the Secretary of State must determine as soon as is reasonably practicable whether or not to make a merger reference. If he decides to do so, he must arrange for its publication in a manner he considers best suited to bringing it to the attention of affected persons. [*FTA 1973, s 64(5)(6)*].

'Business', *'goods'* and *'supply'* are given extended meanings for these purposes, and 'the supply of services' does not include the rendering of any services under a contract of

44.12   Reconstructions and Mergers

employment. Electricity supply is a supply of services rather than goods. [*FTA 1973, s 137(2)-(4)*].

44.12 Requirements of the merger reference

On a merger reference, the Commission are required to investigate and report on

(*a*)   whether the conditions described in 44.11 above for a merger reference have been met; and

(*b*)   if so, whether the creation of that merger situation operates, or may be expected to operate, against the public interest.

As regards (*a*) above, the reference may require the Commission to exclude either 44.11(*a*) or 44.11(*b*) above from its considerations, or to exclude one if the other is satisfied, and in investigating 44.11(*a*), they may be required to confine their considerations to supplies in a specified part of the UK. If (*a*) above is answered positively, the reference may require the Commission to limit their considerations thereafter to specified elements in or consequences of the creation of the merger situation. [*FTA 1973, s 69*].

The reference must specify a period, not exceeding six months from the date of the reference, within which the report by the Commission must be made, and no further action may be taken under *FTA 1973* unless the report is made within that period. The Secretary of State may, following representations by the Commission, extend the period for up to three months if there are special reasons why the report cannot be made within the original period. [*FTA 1973, s 70*].

44.13 Variations of merger references

The Secretary of State may at any time vary a merger reference, but see 44.12 above for the restricted power in relation to extension of the period specified in the reference within which a report must be made. [*FTA 1973, s 71; CA 1989, 20 Sch 7*].

44.14 Report of Commission on merger reference

The Commission's report must include definite conclusions on the questions comprised in the reference, with supporting reasons and a general survey to facilitate a proper understanding of the questions and of their conclusions. Where there is a finding that a merger situation meeting the conditions in 44.11 above operates or may be expected to operate against the public interest, the report must specify the particular adverse effects resulting from the merger situation, and must also consider and, if they think fit, recommend appropriate remedial or preventive action. [*FTA 1973, s 72*].

Following the laying before Parliament of a report which has found a merger situation within 44.11 above and has specified particular adverse effects as above, the Secretary of State may, by statutory instrument, exercise any of a broad range of remedial or preventive powers, taking into account any recommendations made by the Commission and any advice given by the Director. The powers available to the Secretary of State are specified in *FTA 1973, 8 Sch*. [*FTA 1973, ss 73, 77*].

44.15 Interim orders

The Secretary of State may prevent any action which might prejudice a merger reference, or impede the measures warranted by the report on the reference, by order made by statutory instrument

●   prohibiting or restricting such actions; or

- imposing obligations on any person concerned as to the carrying on of any activities or the safeguarding of any assets; or

- providing for the carrying on of any activities or the safeguarding of any assets in any manner; or

- prohibiting or restricting the acquisition by any person of the whole or part of the undertaking or assets of another person's business, or the doing of anything which will lead to bodies corporate becoming *'interconnected'* (i.e. one becoming the subsidiary of the other, or both becoming subsidiaries of a third body corporate) or ceasing to be distinct enterprises, or imposing prohibitions or restrictions on persons concerned in such acquisitions or actions; or

- requiring any person to furnish specified information.

Such orders may not be made, and if made cease to have effect, after the earliest of the following events has occurred, namely

- the time by which the report on the reference must be made (see 44.12 above) has expired without the report being made; and

- 40 days have passed following the laying before Parliament of the report on the reference.

[*FTA 1973, ss 74, 137(5); CA 1989, 20 Sch 8*].

44.16 References in anticipation of merger

The provisions described at 44.11 to 44.15 above apply with appropriate modification in relation to a merger reference made by the Secretary of State where it appears to him that arrangements may be in contemplation or in progress which, if carried into effect, would fall within 44.11 above. Following such a reference, restrictions are imposed on the acquisition of interests in companies carrying on or controlling enterprises concerned in the reference. If it appears to the Commission during its investigations that the proposed arrangements have been abandoned, it must (if the Secretary of State consents) lay the reference aside and furnish to the Secretary of State such information as he requires as to the results of its investigations to that time. [*FTA 1973, s 75; CA 1989, s 149, 20 Sch 9*].

44.17 Prior notice of proposed merger

A notice may be given to the Director (in a form prescribed by him), by any person ('the proposer') carrying on an enterprise, of proposed arrangements which might result in a merger situation within 44.11 above. The notice must state that the existence of the proposal has been made public.

The Director must, on receipt of such notice and payment of any applicable fee (see below), bring the existence of the proposal, the giving of the notice and the date on which the period for considering the notice expires to the attention of those he considers would be affected if the arrangements were carried into effect. The period for considering the notice is 20 working days, beginning with the first working day after receipt of the notice and payment of any applicable fee (see *CA 1989, s 152* and *SI 1990 No 1660*). The period may be extended by fifteen working days by the Director giving notice (which the Secretary of State may require him to do) to the proposer. He may also give notice to the proposer requiring the provision of specified information within a specified time, or stating that the Secretary of State is seeking undertakings as an alternative to a merger reference (see 44.18 below). Any notice to the proposer must be given before expiry of the period for considering the notice (see above) or posted so as, in the ordinary course of post, to be delivered before that time.

The Director may, at any time before the period for considering the notice expires, reject the notice if

- he suspects that he has been given materially false or misleading information or that it is not proposed to carry the proposals into effect;

- any information prescribed by the Director is not given in the merger notice or in response, within the specified time, to a notice requiring such information; or

- it appears to him that the arrangement may result in a concentration with Community dimensions within 44.19 below.

If the period for considering the notice expires without either a reference being made to the Commission (see 44.11 above), or the notice being rejected as above, or any of the enterprises concerned having ceased to be distinct enterprises (see 44.11 above), no reference may subsequently be made with respect to the arrangements concerned or any consequent merger situation, unless

- the Director has given notice that the Secretary of State is seeking undertakings as an alternative to a merger reference (see above), and ten working days have elapsed since notice was received in response from the recipient that he does not intend to give such undertakings; or

- material information has not been disclosed at least five working days before the end of the period for considering the notice; or

- any of the enterprises concerned is merged with another before being merged in accordance with the arrangements in the notice; or

- six months have elapsed since the end of the period for considering the notice without the proposed arrangements coming into effect; or

- any materially false or misleading information has been given in respect of the notified arrangements; or

- the merger notice is withdrawn.

In certain circumstances where transactions may be treated as occurring simultaneously on a particular date (see 44.11 above), and a reference is not prevented in relation to the last such transaction, a merger reference may be made with respect to transactions which actually occurred in the six months before the date of the earliest transaction with respect to which a reference may be made (whether under this provision or otherwise).

The necessary regulatory powers are given to the Secretary of State, including powers to amend certain of the statutory provisions in any particular case. *The Merger (Prenotification) Regulations 1990 (SI 1990 No 501)* provide detailed rules as to the manner in which the various notices are to be given and fees paid, and as to various other administrative procedures.

[*FTA 1973, ss 75A–75F; CA 1989, s 146; SI 1990 No 501, Regs 2, 3; SI 1990 No 1563; 1994 No 1934*].

44.18 Undertakings as alternative to merger reference

Where the Director has advised the Secretary of State of the particular effects, adverse to the public interest, which might result from the merger situation, and has recommended that a merger reference be made, the Secretary of State may alternatively seek and accept undertakings from the parties concerned which he considers appropriate to remedy or prevent those adverse effects.

If one or more undertakings has been accepted by the Secretary of State, no reference may be made with respect to the merger situation concerned, unless material facts about the arrangements or transactions involved were not notified to the Secretary of State or the Director or made public before the undertakings were accepted. [*FTA 1973, s 75G; CA 1989, s 147; Deregulation and Contracting Out Act 1994, s 9*].

There are provisions for publication by the Secretary of State of the advice received from the Director, the undertakings accepted, and any release or variation of an undertaking. Matters whose publication might seriously and prejudicially affect the interests of a private individual or a particular body of persons and would not be in the public interest, and any other matters whose publication would be against the public interest, may be excluded from publication, but absolute privilege attaches to any advice given by the Director to the Secretary of State. [*FTA 1973, s 75H; CA 1989, s 147*]. The Director must monitor the carrying out of undertakings and consider whether they should be released, varied or superseded, and advise the Secretary of State accordingly. [*FTA 1973, s 75J; CA 1989, s 147*]. Where the Secretary of State considers that an undertaking is not being or will not be fulfilled, remedial and preventive powers are available to him, in consultation with the Director. [*FTA 1973, s 75K; CA 1989, s 147; Deregulation and Contracting Out Act 1994, s 9*].

44.19 EC MERGER CONTROL REGULATIONS

The *EC Council Regulation* of 21 December 1989 [*89/4064/EEC*] (as amended with effect from 1 March 1988 by *Council Regulation 1310/97*) is designed to deal specifically with cross-border mergers. The Regulation came into force on 21 September 1990 and has direct effect in the UK in relation to 'concentrations' with a 'community dimension'. Any concentration having a community dimension is dealt with by the European Commission (see below) unless remitted to a member state. [*Art 9*]. Conversely, a concentration falling short of having a Community dimension will be dealt with by the member state applying its own national law (see 44.10 to 44.18 above for UK provisions) although a member state can choose to refer the matter to the Commission. Where, therefore, it is common ground that a concentration falls short of having a community dimension, the Secretary of State is not under a duty to apply the EC provisions in reaching a decision on a proposed merger (*R v Secretary of State for Trade and Industry, ex parte Airlines of Britain Holdings plc [1993] BCC 89*).

A *'concentration'* arises where two or more previously independent undertakings merge or where one or more undertakings acquire direct or indirect control over the whole or part of one or more other undertakings. [*Art 3*].

A concentration has a *'Community dimension'* if

• the undertakings involved have an aggregate world-wide turnover exceeding 5 billion ECUs, and

• at least two of the undertakings have a turnover within the EC of 250 million ECUs

but not if two-thirds of the aggregate turnover within the EC of each of the undertakings is derived in the same member state. [*Art 1*].

In determining whether a concentration is incompatible with EC policy, the Commission will consider the need to maintain and develop effective competition within the EC and the market position and economic and financial power of the undertakings involved. To be incompatible with EC policy, the proposed concentration would have to create or strengthen a dominant position which would significantly impede competition in the EC or a substantial part of it. [*Art 2*].

44.19 Reconstructions and Mergers

Concentrations with a Community dimension must be notified to the Commission within one week of the making of the agreement, announcement of the public bid or acquisition of the controlling interest, whichever occurs first. [Art 4]. A concentration must not be put into effect either before notification or until the commission has declared it compatible with EC policy or the time limit for the Commission to decide on this has expired. [Art 7]. On receipt of the notification, the Commission must consider it immediately and decide whether the concentration has a Community dimension and raises serious doubts as to the compatibility with EC policy. [Art 6]. This decision must normally be made within one month [Art 10] and notified to the undertakings involved and the competent authorities of the member states. [Art 6]. If it fails to make a decision in that time, the concentration will automatically be deemed to be compatible with EC policy. [Art 10].

Where the Commission decides that the concentration does raise serious doubts, it must start proceedings and declare within four months whether the concentration is compatible or incompatible with EC policy. [Art 10]. It has wide powers to request information [Art 11] and make investigations [Art 13] and may impose fines for failure to comply with obligations or to co-operate. [Art 14]. Failure to make such a declaration within the time limit means that the concentration is deemed to be compatible. [Art 10]. If the Commission determines that the concentration is incompatible, it must either not be proceeded with or, where it has already been implemented, be divested. [Art 8].

45 Records

Cross-references. See 8.9 ACQUISITION OF OWN SHARES for contracts for purchase of own shares; 8.15 ACQUISITION OF OWN SHARES for statutory declaration and auditors' report following resolution to purchase or redeem shares out of capital; 19.55 *et seq.* DIRECTORS for directors' service contracts; 33.15 MEETINGS for minutes of meetings; 47 REGISTERS.

45.1 DUTY TO KEEP ACCOUNTING RECORDS

Every company must keep 'accounting records' sufficient to show and explain the company's transactions and to

- 'disclose' with reasonable accuracy, 'at any time', the 'financial position' of the company at that time; and

- enable the directors to ensure that any balance sheet and profit and loss account prepared complies with the requirements of *CA 1985*.

The accounting records must contain 'day-to-day' entries of the amounts and nature of all money received and expended by the company and a 'record of its assets and liabilities'. If the company's business involves dealing in goods, the accounting records must also contain

(i) 'statements of stock' held at the end of each financial year;

(ii) all stock-taking statements from which (i) above has been or is to be prepared; and

(iii) (except in the case of goods sold by ordinary retail sale) 'statements of all goods sold and purchased', showing sufficient detail of the goods, buyers and sellers to enable all these to be identified.

A parent company with a subsidiary undertaking to which the above does not apply must take reasonable steps to ensure that the undertaking keeps accounting records which will enable the directors of the parent company to prepare a balance sheet and profit and loss account which complies with the requirements of *CA 1985*.

[*Sec 221(1)-(4); CA 1989, s 2*].

Penalties. If a company fails to comply with the above provisions, every officer of the company in default is guilty of an offence unless he shows that he acted honestly and that under the circumstances the default was excusable. A person found guilty is liable to a fine up to the level in 40.1(*b*) PENALTIES. [*Sec 221(5)(6), 24 Sch; CA 1989, s 2*].

Interpretation of the above provisions. *Sec 221* is derived from *CA 1976, s 12*. Counsel's opinion was taken on certain points of difficulty with the earlier provisions and was published in 'True and Fair' Issue No 6, Winter 1977/78. The following summary of that opinion applies equally to *Sec 221*.

'Accounting records'. These need not be in book form e.g. a loose-leaf binder or computer tape is acceptable. Books of prime entry may take the form of a secure clip of invoices with an add-list attached. The information must, however, be organised and labelled. A carrier bag full of invoices is not sufficient.

'Disclose'. The records maintained must disclose the basic information from which the financial position can be ascertained. This does not mean that the financial position needs to be displayed after each transaction has been recorded but that information is available from which a financial statement can be prepared.

'At any time'. The information need not be recorded instantaneously but must be in a form sufficient to enable a statement of the financial position to be drawn up at any selected date.

45.2   Records

'Financial position'. CA 1985 recognises that it is not practical to draw up financial statements giving a 'true and fair view' at any time during the year. However, it does require that the directors should have available to them 'at any time' an adequate statement of the company's financial position, even though this is drawn up to a less rigorous standard than the 'true and fair view' concept. *Sec 221* seems to indicate that directors should be in a position to prepare a statement showing cash and other tangible assets, liabilities and pre-tax results at any given date. Although a company would need to establish its stock figure to do this, this does not necessarily require physical stocktake or maintenance of continuous stock records. The company may also estimate its results and stock level by applying gross profit margins to sales or keeping detailed records of costs of sales.

'Day-to-day'. Clearly, transactions cannot be recorded instantaneously. What is necessary is that, when the entries are made, each transaction is shown separately and is identified by its date and explanation of the matter to which it relates. In the case of retail shops, a record of the day's total cash takings will suffice.

'Record of assets and liabilities'. Records must contain details of all the company's assets and liabilities such as debtors, creditors and plant. There is no specific requirement that this is kept up-to-date on a daily basis but the records must show the assets and liabilities of the company at any particular time. The records must, therefore, be updated at frequent intervals and must contain details of dates of acquisitions and disposals of assets and the dates on which liabilities are incurred and discharged. Stocks are specifically excluded from this requirement.

'Statements of stock'. This is taken to mean a summary supporting the amount included in the accounts in respect of stock. Stocktaking records that support the year-end stock summary must also be retained. *CA 1985* therefore imposes an obligation to retain documentation supporting year-end stock valuations but allows considerable flexibility in meeting the requirements to disclose the financial position 'at any time'.

'Statements of all goods sold and purchased'. The intention of *CA 1985* appears to be to ensure that the substance of transactions is properly recorded. With products where the individual item identity of the product is irrelevant to the seller and purchaser, product type identity will normally be sufficient. In practical terms the identity of the buyer and seller will normally be available from the purchases and sales ledgers.

Lien over accounting records. As *Sec 221* above imposes mandatory duties on a company in connection with the keeping of accounting records and criminal penalties for breach of those duties, an accountant (or solicitor) cannot claim a lien over books and documents for unpaid fees. See *DTC (CNC) Ltd v Gary Sargeant & Co (a firm) [1996] 1 WLR 797, [1996] 1 BCLC 529* where an accountant asserted a lien over sales and purchase invoices, cheque books, paying-in books and bank statements. A document created as an accounting record under *Sec 221* does not cease to be such because the information contained in it has been collated or transposed into some other document.

45.2   Location and inspection of accounting records

The accounting records must be kept at the company's registered office or such other place as the directors think fit and must at all times be open to inspection by the company's officers.

If the accounting records are kept outside Great Britain, accounts and returns which

- disclose with reasonable accuracy the financial position of the business at intervals of not more than six months, and

- enable the directors to ensure that the company's balance sheet and profit and loss account comply with the requirements of *CA 1985*

must be sent to, and kept in, a place in Great Britain, and must at all times be open to inspection by the company's officers.

[*Sec 222(1)-(3); CA 1989, s 2*].

If the records are on computer, a reproduction of the relevant recording must be provided in legible form. [*Sec 723(3)*].

Penalties. If a company fails to comply with the above provisions, similar penalties apply as in 45.1 above. [*Sec 222(4), 24 Sch; CA 1989, s 2*].

See also 45.6 and 45.7 below.

45.3   Preservation of accounting records

The accounting records required under 45.1 above must be preserved for three years from the date made in the case of a private company and six years in the case of a public company. [*Sec 222(5); CA 1989, s 2*]. Note, however, that records may be required to be preserved longer for other purposes. Customs and Excise require VAT records to be preserved for six years or such lesser period as they allow and the Inland Revenue may raise assessments for up to six years after the chargeable accounting period (20 years in the case of fraud or negligent conduct).

Penalties. An officer of the company is guilty of an offence if he fails to take all reasonable steps for securing compliance with these provisions or intentionally causes any default by the company. If found guilty, he is liable to a fine up to the level in 40.1(*b*) PENALTIES. [*Sec 222(6), 24 Sch; CA 1989, s 2*].

45.4   Criminal destruction etc. of accounting records

Where a person dishonestly, with a view to gain for himself or another or intent to cause loss to another,

- destroys, defaces, conceals or falsifies any account or any other record or document made or required for any accounting purpose, or

- makes use of any such account etc. which he knows to be materially misleading, false or deceptive

he is, on conviction, liable to imprisonment for a term not exceeding seven years. [*Theft Act 1968, s 17*].

45.5   FORM OF RECORDS GENERALLY

Any accounting records, minute book or index required to be kept by a company may be kept by either making entries in bound books or by any other means. In the latter case, adequate precautions must be taken to safeguard against falsification and facilitating its discovery otherwise the company and every officer in default is liable to a fine up to the level in 40.1(*f*) PENALTIES. [*Sec 722, 24 Sch*].

Computers etc. The records may be kept on computer or otherwise than in legible form provided the recording is capable of being reproduced in legible form. Where a record is kept on a computer, etc. any duty imposed by *CA 1985* to allow inspection of, or furnish a copy of, the record is to be treated as applying to a reproduction in legible form. [*Sec 723(1)(3)*].

45.6   PRODUCTION AND INSPECTION OF BOOKS WHERE OFFENCE SUSPECTED

Where there is a reasonable cause to believe that any person has, while an officer of a company, committed an offence in connection with the management of the company's affairs and that evidence of this is to be found in any 'books or papers' of, or under the control of, the company, the Director of Public Prosecutions, the Secretary of State or a chief officer of police (in Scotland, the Lord Advocate) may obtain a court order

- authorising any person to inspect the books and papers in question in order to investigate the offence; and

- (except in the case of a banking company) requiring an officer to produce the books etc. named in the order at a place so named.

There is no appeal against such an order.

'Books or papers' include accounts, deeds, writings and documents.

[*Secs 721, 744*].

45.7 INSPECTION OF RECORDS BY SHAREHOLDERS

A shareholder has no right to inspect the accounting records or other books and documents of the company unless given that right by the articles. *Table A, Art 109* provides that no member has any right of inspection except as conferred by statute or authorised by the directors or by ordinary resolution of the company. See *McCusker v McRae, 1966 SC 253* and *Conway v Petronius Clothing Co Ltd [1978] 1 All ER 185*.

45.8 PRESERVATION OF RECORDS

CA 1985 does not specify any period for preservation of a company's records other than the requirement to keep

- accounting records as under 45.3 above;

- contracts for purchase of own shares for ten years (see 8.9 ACQUISITION OF OWN SHARES);

- the register of interests in public company shares for six years after the company ceases to be a public company (see 47.8 REGISTERS);

- reports on investigations into share holding on requisition by members for six years (see 21.8 DISCLOSURE OF INTERESTS IN PUBLIC COMPANY SHARES);

- entries in the register of members relating to former members for 20 years from ceasing to be a member (see 47.4 REGISTERS); and

- minutes of all general meetings from 1 November 1929 onwards (see 33.15 MEETINGS).

Apart from the above, it is recommended practice to keep

- memorandum of association, articles of association, certificate of incorporation, statutory registers and copies of published accounts for the life of the company;

- invoices, receipts, returned cheques, paying-in books, bank statements, etc. for six years;

- title deeds and related correspondence for twelve years after disposal; and

- contracts and agreements for six years after expiry (twelve years if under seal).

46   Registered Office

Cross-references. See 16.17 DEALINGS WITH THIRD PARTIES for disclosure in business letters, etc; 35.2 MEMORANDUM OF ASSOCIATION for statement of situation of registered office.

46.1   A company must at all times have a registered office to which all communications and notices may be addressed. On incorporation, the address is that specified in the statement sent to the Registrar of Companies under *Sec 10* (see 49.1 REGISTRATION AND RE-REGISTRATION). [*Sec 287(1)(2); CA 1989, s 136*].

46.2   **CHANGE OF ADDRESS**

A company may change the situation of its registered office by giving notice in the prescribed form (Form 287).

The change takes effect when the notice is registered but for the next 14 days any document can still be validly served at the previous registered office. At any time after giving notice, the company may act on the change in respect of its duty to

(*a*)   keep, or make available for inspection, any registers, indexes or other documents at the registered office, and

(*b*)   mention the address in any document

but it must so act after 14 days from giving notice.

[*Sec 287(3)-(5); CA 1989, s 136; SI 1990 No 1766*].

46.3   **Offences**

In proceedings for an offence for failing to comply with a duty within 46.2(*a*) or (*b*) above it is for the person charged to show that no offence was committed. For these purposes, where a company unavoidably ceases to perform at its registered office any duty within 46.2(*a*) above in circumstances in which it was not practical to give prior notice to the Registrar of Companies of a change in the situation of its registered office, then it is not treated as having failed to comply with that duty provided

●   it resumes performance of that duty elsewhere as soon as practicable; and

●   it gives proper notice to the Registrar of the change in the situation of its registered office within 14 days of doing so.

[*Sec 287(6)(7); CA 1989, s 136*].

47 Registers

47.1 *CA 1985* contains provisions relating to the keeping of registers by companies of

- directors and secretaries (see 47.3 below);
- members (see 47.4 to 47.6 below);
- directors' interests (see 47.7 below);
- certain interests in shares (see 47.8 to 47.10 below);
- charges (see 47.11 below); and
- debenture-holders (see 47.12 below).

In addition, under *CA 1989, ss 35, 36,* the recognised supervisory bodies which maintain and enforce rules as to the eligibility of persons for appointment as company auditors must keep a register of firms and individuals so eligible. See 47.13 below.

47.2 FORM IN WHICH REGISTER KEPT

Any register or index to be kept by a company may be kept by either making entries in a bound book or by any other means. In the latter case, adequate precautions must be taken to safeguard against falsification and to facilitate its discovery; otherwise the company and every officer in default is liable to a fine up to the level in 40.1(*f*) PENALTIES. [*Sec 722, 24 Sch*].

Computers, etc. The records may be kept on a computer or otherwise than in legible form provided the recording is capable of being reproduced in legible form. Where a register is kept on a computer etc. any duty imposed by *CA 1985* to allow inspection of, or furnish a copy of, the register is to be treated as applying to a reproduction in legible form. [*Sec 723(1)(3)*].

47.3 REGISTER OF DIRECTORS AND SECRETARIES

Every company must keep a register of directors and secretaries open to inspection to any member free of charge and to any other person on payment of a maximum fee (see 26.2 FEES), for not less than two hours during the period 9a.m. to 5p.m. every Monday to Friday (other than public and bank holidays). A person inspecting the register must be permitted to copy any information made available by taking notes or making a transcript but the company is not obliged to provide any additional facilities other than those to facilitate inspection. If inspection is refused, the company and every officer in default is liable to a penalty up to the level in 40.1(*e*) PENALTIES and the court may, by order, compel an immediate inspection. [*Sec 288(1)(3)-(5); CA 1989, s 143; SI 1991 No 1998*].

Directors. The register must contain the following particulars about each director or '*shadow director*' (i.e. any person in accordance with whose directions and instructions the directors of the company are accustomed to act).

(*a*)   *In the case of an individual*

    (i)   his present 'name';

    (ii)   any 'former name';

    (iii)   his usual residential address;

    (iv)   his nationality;

    (v)   his business occupation (if any);

    (vi)   particulars of other directorships held in the last five years (excluding any which is and has been, or was, during those five years held in a 'dormant' company, or a company 'grouped' with the company delivering the statement, throughout the directorship); and

    (vii)   date of birth.

(*b*)   *In the case of a corporation* (or Scottish firm), its corporate (or firm) name and registered or principal office.

'Name' means Christian name (or other forename) and surname. A peer, or individual known by a title, may alternatively or additionally state his title.

'Former name' does not include the name of a peer etc. before adopting his title; a former name changed or disused before the age of 18 or for 20 years or more; and a married woman's name before her marriage.

A company is *'dormant'* during a period in which no accounting transaction occurs which is required to be entered in the company's accounting records.

A company is treated as *'grouped'* with another company at any time if that other company is, or was, a wholly-owned subsidiary of it (or vice versa) or if both are, or were, wholly-owned subsidiaries of a third company.

[*Secs 288(6), 289, 741(2); CA 1989, 10 Sch 9, 19 Sch 2*].

Secretaries. The register must contain particulars about the secretary or, where there are joint secretaries, about each of them, as in (*a*)(i)-(iii) and (*b*) above. Where all partners in a firm are joint secretaries, the name and principal office of the firm may be stated instead. [*Sec 290; CA 1989, 19 Sch 3*].

Location of register. The register must be kept at (or if in non-legible form be available for inspection at) the registered office. [*Sec 288(1); SI 1985 No 724, Reg 2*].

47.4 **REGISTER OF MEMBERS**

Every company must keep a register of its members containing the following information.

- The names and addresses of the members.
- The date on which each person was registered as a member.
- The date at which any person ceased to be a member.
- In the case of a company having a share capital

    (i)   the shares held by each member, distinguishing each share by its number and class where applicable, and

    (ii)   the amount paid (or agreed to be considered as paid) on the shares,

    or, where the company has converted any of its shares into stock and given notice of the conversion to the Registrar of Companies, the amount and class of stock held by each member.

- In the case of a company which does not have a share capital but has more than one class of members, the class to which each member belongs.

[*Sec 352(1)-(4)*].

An entry relating to a former member may be removed after 20 years from the date on which he ceased to be a member. [*Sec 352(6)*].

Liability incurred by a company from the making or deleting of an entry in its register of members (or the failure to do so) is not enforceable more than 20 years after the date of the error or failure. [*Sec 352(7)*].

Index. A company with more than 50 members must also keep an index of the names of its members unless the register itself is in such a form as to constitute an index. It must enable the account of any member in the register to be readily found. Any necessary alteration to the index must be made within 14 days of an alteration to the register. [*Sec 354(1)(2)*].

Penalties. If a company fails to comply with any of the above provisions relating to the register or any index, the company and every officer in default is liable to a fine up to the level in 40.1(*f*) PENALTIES. [*Secs 352(5), 354(4), 24 Sch*].

Companies with only one member. If, after 14 July 1992, the number of members of a private company limited by shares or guarantee falls to one (or increases from one to two or more), a statement that the company has (or has ceased to have) one member and the date of occurrence must at that time be entered in the register of members with the name and address of the sole member. In default, the company and every officer in default is liable, on summary conviction, to a fine of up to level 2 on the standard scale and for continued contravention, a daily default fine of one-tenth of level 2 on the standard scale (see 40.1 PENALTIES). [*Sec 352A, 24 Sch; SI 1992 No 1699*].

Share warrants. On the issue of a share warrant, the company must strike out of the register the name of the member then entered as holding the shares and enter instead the fact and date of the issue of the warrant and a statement of the shares included in the warrant (distinguishing each share by its number if it has one). On surrender of the warrant, the date of surrender must be entered and, subject to the company's articles, the bearer is entitled to have his name entered as a member in the register. The company is responsible for any loss incurred by any person as a result of the name of a bearer of a share warrant being entered in the register without it being surrendered or cancelled. [*Sec 355(1)-(4)*].

Shares held by trusts. No notice of any trust (expressed, implied or constructive) must be entered on the register in the case of companies registered in England and Wales. [*Sec 360*]. The company is not therefore required to enquire as to whether the transfer is within the powers of the trustees.

Power to close register. A company may close the register for any time or times not exceeding 30 days in each year provided that it advertises the fact by advertising in a newspaper circulating in the district in which the registered office is situated. [*Sec 358*].

Power of court to rectify register. If any person's name is, without sufficient cause, entered in or omitted from the register of members or there is default or delay in showing that a person has ceased to be a member, that person, or the company or any member of the company, can apply to the court for rectification of the register. The court may decide any question relating to the title of a person who is a party to the application to have his name entered in or removed from the register. It may order payment by the company of damages sustained by any aggrieved party. Where the company is required to send a list of its members to the Registrar of Companies, the court must, when making an order of rectification, direct such notice to be given to the Registrar. [*Sec 359*]. See also *Re Sussex Brick Co [1904] 1 Ch 598*.

Register as evidence. The register of members is *prima facie* (but not conclusive) evidence of any matters which are directed or authorised by *CA 1985* to be inserted in it. [*Sec 361*].

Changes in particulars. It is the responsibility of members to keep the company informed of any changes in address or name. Any change of address should be signed by the member. In practice, companies frequently send out a standard form for the member to sign and return. On a change of name, more formal documentary proof is required if fraud is to be avoided e.g. production of the marriage certificate. On the change of name of a corporate member, a copy of the new certificate of incorporation should be produced. All such amendments have to be approved by the directors.

47.5   **Location and inspection**

If in legible form, the register of members must be kept at the registered office except that

(*a*)   if the work of making it up is done at another office, it may be kept there, and

(*b*)   if the company arranges for an agent to make up the register on its behalf, it may be kept at the office of that agent where the work is done

subject to the overriding provision that it must be kept in England or Wales for a company registered in England and Wales, and in Scotland for a company registered there. Where the register is in non-legible form, for references to 'kept' there should be substituted 'available for inspection'. [*Sec 353(1); SI 1985 No 724, Reg 2*].

Location of index. The index must be kept at the same place as the register of members or, if that register is in non-legible form, the place where it is available for inspection. [*Sec 354(3); SI 1985 No 724, Reg 2*].

Notice to Registrar of Companies where register in legible form. A company must give notice in the prescribed form (Form 353 or Form 363s) of the place where the register is *kept*, and of any changes in that place, unless the register has at all times (or, in the case of a register in existence on 1 July 1985, at all times since that date) been kept at the registered office.

Notice to Registrar of Companies where register in non-legible form. A company must give notice in the prescribed form (Form 353a) of the place for *inspection* of the register, and of any changes in that place, except where the register is changed from legible to non-legible form and the place for inspection in non-legible form is the same as the place it was kept in legible form or where it has at all times been in non-legible form and available for inspection at the registered office.

If either of these provisions is not complied with within 14 days, the company and every officer in default is liable to a fine up to the level in 40.1(*f*) PENALTIES.

[*Secs 353(2)-(4), 354(3), 24 Sch; SI 1985 No 724, Reg 3; SI 1991 No 879*].

Inspection of register and index. Except when the register is closed (see 47.4 above), the register and index must be open to inspection by any member free of charge, and by any other person on payment of a maximum fee (see 26.2 FEES), for not less than two hours during the period 9a.m. to 5p.m. every Monday to Friday (other than public and bank holidays). A person inspecting the register must be permitted to copy any information made available by taking notes or making a transcript but the company is not obliged to provide any additional facilities other than those to facilitate inspection. Copies of the register, or any part, must be sent to any person on request within ten days on payment of a maximum fee (see 26.2 FEES). A company is not obliged to group entries in the register or index for inspection, or extract entries when sending out copies, by geographical location, nationality, size of holding, or gender or nature of the holder. If inspection is refused or the required copy not sent in the proper time, the company and every officer in default is liable to a fine up to the level in 40.1(*g*) PENALTIES for each offence. In addition, the court may by order compel an immediate inspection or direct that the copies be sent. [*Sec 356; CA 1989, s 143; SI 1991 No 1998*].

Non-compliance by agents. Where the register of members is kept at the office of an agent under (*b*) above, that agent is liable to the same penalties as if he were an officer of the company where, through his default, the company fails to comply with the above provisions regarding *Location of index, Notice to Registrar of Companies* or *Inspection of register*. The power of the court to compel an immediate inspection is also similarly extended. [*Sec 357; SI 1985 No 724, Reg 6(2)*].

47.6 Overseas branch registers

A company whose objects comprise the transaction of business in any of the countries or territories listed below may keep there a branch register of members resident in that country or territory. Such a register is known as an *'overseas branch register'* and a reference in any Act or the articles of a company to a dominion register or colonial register are to be read as referring to an overseas branch register.

The countries and territories referred to above are Northern Ireland, any part of the dominions outside the UK, Channel Islands or Isle of Man, together with

Bangladesh	Lesotho	Sierra Leone
Cyprus	Malawi	Singapore
Dominica	Malaysia	South Africa
The Gambia	Malta	Sri Lanka
Ghana	Nigeria	Swaziland
Guyana	Pakistan	Trinidad and Tobago
India	Republic of Ireland	Uganda
Kenya	Seychelles	Zimbabwe
Kiribati		

With effect from 1 July 1997, the Hong Kong Special Administrative Region of the People's Republic of China is also included.

[*Sec 362(1)(2); 14 Sch Part I; SI 1997 No 1313*].

An overseas branch register is deemed to be part of the company's register of members (the *'principal register'*) and must be kept in the same manner (see 47.4 above) except that before closing the register, the advertisement must be inserted in a newspaper circulating in the district where the overseas register is kept. Any competent court in the oversea country or territory has the same powers as a court in Great Britain but only in those countries where, on 30 June 1985, such provisions had effect as part of the local law.

The company must transmit a copy of every entry in the overseas branch register to its registered office as soon as possible and keep a duplicate of that register, entered up from time to time, with the principal register. In default the company and every officer in default is liable to a fine up to the level in 40.1(*f*) PENALTIES. Where the principal register is kept by an agent, he is liable to the same penalty if responsible for the default.

Shares registered in the overseas branch register must be distinguished from those in the principal register and no transaction involving shares so registered must be registered in any other register (other than the duplicate referred to above).

If the company discontinues an overseas branch register, all entries in it must be transferred to another such register kept in the same country or territory, or to the principal register.

[14 Sch Part II, paras 2-5].

Location of register. An overseas branch register may be kept (or, if it is in non-legible form, be available for inspection) anywhere in the relevant country or territory. *Where the register is in legible form*, the company must give notice to the Registrar of Companies in the prescribed form (Form 362) of the situation of the office where the register is *kept*, any changes in that place, and any discontinuance to keep such a register. *Where the register is in non-legible form*, the company must give notice to the Registrar of Companies in the prescribed form (Form 362a) of the place for *inspection* of the register, and of any changes in that place, except where the register is changed from legible to non-legible form and the place for inspection in non-legible form is the same as the place where it was kept in legible form. If either of these provisions is not complied with within 14 days, the company and every officer in default is liable to a fine up to the level in 40.1(*f*) PENALTIES. *[14 Sch Part II, para 1; SI 1985 No 724, Reg 3].*

47.7 REGISTER OF DIRECTORS' INTERESTS

Directors and *'shadow directors'* (i.e. persons in accordance with whose instructions the directors are accustomed to act) have a duty to disclose details of shareholdings in their own company (see 19.76 DIRECTORS) and every company must keep a special register for this purpose. *[Sec 325(1)(6)].*

A company must enter the following particulars in the register against a director's name in chronological order.

(*a*)   Any information received from the director and the date of entry.

(*b*)   Whenever it grants to a director a right to subscribe for shares in, or debentures of, the company

- the date on which the right is granted;

- the period during which, or the time at which, it is exercisable;

- the consideration for the grant (or, if there is none, that fact); and

- the description of the shares or debentures involved, the number and amount of them, and the price to be paid for them (or the consideration if not in money).

(*c*)   Whenever a right under (*b*) above is exercised

- that fact (identifying the right);

- the number or amount of shares or debentures in respect of which it is exercised;

- if they were registered in his name, that fact; and

- if they were not so registered, the person's name in whom they were registered or, if more than one, their names and the number or amount of the shares or debentures registered in the name of each of them.

The information under (*a*) to (*c*) above must be entered within three working days. A director can also require that the nature and extent of an interest is also entered.

[Secs 325(2)-(5), 741, 13 Sch 21-23].

47.8 Registers

Location and inspection. The register must be kept at the company's registered office or, if the register of members is not kept there (see 47.5 above), at the registered office or where the register of members is kept. Where the *register of members* is maintained in non-legible form, for references to 'kept' there should be substituted 'available for inspection'. It must be open to inspection by members of the company free of charge, and by any other person on payment of a maximum fee (see 26.2 FEES), for not less than two hours during the period 9a.m. to 5p.m. every Monday to Friday (other than public and bank holidays). A person inspecting the register must be permitted to copy any information made available by taking notes or making a transcript but the company is not obliged to provide any additional facilities other than those to facilitate inspection. Any person can require a copy of the register or any part of it on payment of a maximum fee (see 26.2 FEES) and the company must send it to him within ten days of request. In addition to the penalties below for non-compliance, the court may by order compel an immediate inspection or direct that the copies be sent. [*Sec 326(6), 13 Sch 25, 26; CA 1989, s 143; SI 1985 No 724, Reg 2; SI 1991 No 1998*].

Notice to Registrar of Companies where register in legible form. A company must within 14 days give notice in the prescribed form (Form 325) of the place where the register is *kept*, and of any changes in that place, unless the register has at all times been kept at the registered office.

Notice to Registrar of Companies where register in non-legible form. A company must within 14 days give notice in the prescribed form (Form 325a) of the place for *inspection* of the register, and of any changes in that place, except where either the register is changed from legible to non-legible form and the place for inspection in non-legible form is the same as the place it was kept in legible form or it has at all times been in non-legible form and available for inspection at the registered office.

[*13 Sch 27; SI 1985 No 724, Reg 3*].

Index. A company must also keep an index of the names in the register unless the register itself is in such a form as to constitute an index. It must enable the information on any director in the register to be readily found. Any necessary alteration to the index must be made within 14 days of a name being entered on the register. The index must be kept (or, if the register is in non-legible form, be available for inspection) at the same place as the register. [*13 Sch 28; SI 1985 No 724, Reg 2*].

Penalties. If default is made in complying with any of the above requirements, the company and every officer in default is liable to a fine up to the level in 40.1(*f*) PENALTIES. [*Sec 326(1)-(5)*].

Annual general meetings. The register (or a reproduction if kept in non-legible form) must be produced at the start of the AGM and remain open and available for inspection throughout to any person attending. If not, the company and every officer in default is liable to a fine up to the level in 40.1(*g*) PENALTIES. [*13 Sch 29; SI 1985 No 724, Reg 6(4)*].

47.8 REGISTER OF INTERESTS IN SHARES IN A PUBLIC COMPANY

Any person who has an interest of 3% or more of the nominal share capital of a public company is required to notify the company of that interest. See 21.1 to 21.5 DISCLOSURE OF INTERESTS IN PUBLIC COMPANY SHARES for full details of the obligation to disclose and what interests must be disclosed. Every public company must keep a register for these purposes and enter in it, against the person's name in chronological order, the information notified and the date of inscription. [*Sec 211(1)(5)*].

Without prejudice to the above, where a company receives notification that any person has ceased to be party to an agreement to acquire interests in the company under *Sec 204* (see 21.4 DISCLOSURE OF INTERESTS IN PUBLIC COMPANY SHARES), it must, if so satisfied, record that information against the person's name in every place where it appears in the register as a party to that agreement (including any entry relating to him made against another person's name). If the information is not recorded, the person may apply to the court which may, if it thinks fit, make an order for its insertion. [*Secs 211(2), 217(4)(5)*].

Entries in the register must be made within three working days of notification. [*Secs 211(3), 220*].

Index. A company must also keep an index of the names in the register unless the register itself is in such a form as to constitute an index. It must enable the information on each name in the register to be readily found. Any necessary alteration to the index must be made within ten working days of a name being entered on the register. [*Secs 211(6), 220*].

Location and inspection. The register and the index must be kept at the same place as the register of directors' interests (see 47.7 above) or, where that register is in non-legible form, must be available for inspection at the same place as that register. They must be open to inspection by any person without charge (unless containing information disclosure of which would be harmful to the company's business under *Sec 231(3)*, see 4.23 ACCOUNTS: GROUPS OF COMPANIES) for not less than two hours during the period 9a.m. to 5p.m. every Monday to Friday (other than public and bank holidays). A person inspecting the register must be permitted to copy any information made available by taking notes or making a transcript but the company is not obliged to provide any additional facilities other than those to facilitate inspection. Any person can require a copy of the register or any part of it on payment of a maximum fee (see 26.2 FEES) and the company must send it to him within ten days of request. If this is not done, in addition to the penalties below, the court may by order compel an immediate inspection or direct that the copies be sent. [*Secs 211(8)(9), 219; CA 1989, s 143, 10 Sch 3; SI 1985 No 724, Reg 2; SI 1991 No 1998*].

Ceasing to be a public company. If a company ceases to be a public company, it must continue to keep the register and any index for six years. [*Sec 211(7)*].

Penalties. If there is default in complying with any of the above provisions, the company and every officer in default is liable to a fine up to the level in 40.1(*f*) PENALTIES. [*Sec 211(10), 24 Sch*].

47.9   Information requirements imposed by the company

Where a public company has reasonable cause to believe that a person is, or at any time in the preceding three years has been, interested in the company's shares, it can impose on him a requirement to confirm or otherwise deny the fact and, if the former, give further information. See 21.7 DISCLOSURE OF INTERESTS IN PUBLIC COMPANY SHARES for full details.

Whenever a company receives information under those provisions relating to the *present* interests held in the share capital, it must enter against the name of the registered holder of those shares, in a separate part of the register of interests in shares and in chronological order

- the fact that the requirement was imposed and the date of imposition; and

- any information received.

Entries in the register must be made within three working days of notification.

47.10 Registers

The provisions in 47.8 above relating to *Index, Location and inspection, Ceasing to be a public company* and *Penalties* also apply.

[*Sec 213*].

47.10 Removal of entries from the register

Entries in a company's register of interests in shares may only be removed in the following circumstances. [*Sec 218(1)*].

- A company may remove an entry from the register if more than six years have elapsed since the date of its entry and either

    (i)   the entry recorded the fact that the person had ceased to have a notifiable interest; or

    (ii) it has been superseded by a later entry under 47.8 above in the same person's name.

    In the case of (i) above, the company may also remove the person's name from the register. In either case the company must make any necessary adjustment to any index within 14 working days.

    [*Sec 217(1)(6)*].

- Where any person gives the name and address of a second person as being interested in the shares of the company and the company enters those details in the register, it must, within 15 days of the receipt of the information, notify that second person of that fact. The notification must give details of the entry and inform him of his right to apply to have the entry removed. If satisfied on a written application that the entry is incorrect, the company must remove it from the register. If the application is refused, the applicant may apply to the court which may, if it thinks fit, make an order for its removal. Where an entry is removed, the company must make any necessary adjustment to any index within 14 working days. [*Sec 217(2)(3)(5)(6)*].

Any entry deleted in contravention of the above provisions must be restored as soon as is reasonably practicable. [*Sec 218(2)*].

Penalties. If default is made in complying with any of the above mandatory provisions, the company and every officer in default is liable to a fine up to the level in 40.1(*f*) PENALTIES. [*Secs 217(7), 218(3), 24 Sch*].

47.11 REGISTER OF CHARGES AND COPIES OF INSTRUMENTS CREATING CHARGES

Every company must keep at its registered office

(*a*)   a register of all charges specifically affecting property of the company and all floating charges on the company's undertaking or any of its property; and

(*b*)   copies of every instrument creating a charge requiring registration with the Registrar of Companies (although in the case of a series of uniform debentures a copy of one debenture in the series is sufficient).

The entry in the register under (*a*) above must give

- a short description of the property charged;

- the amount of the charge; and

- except in the case of securities to bearer, the names of the persons entitled to it.

If an officer of the company knowingly and wilfully authorises or permits the omission of an entry required to be made in the register, he is liable to a fine up to the level in 40.1(*d*) PENALTIES.

[*Secs 406, 407, 421, 422*].

Inspection and copies. The register and copies must be open for inspection by any creditor or member free of charge and by any other person on payment of the prescribed fee. If inspection is refused, every officer in default is liable to a fine up to the level in 40.1(*f*) PENALTIES. In addition, the court may by order compel an immediate inspection. [*Secs 408, 423, 24 Sch*].

Oversea companies. The above provisions also apply to charges over property situated in Great Britain of registered OVERSEA COMPANIES (38), except that in relation to such companies, references to a registered office must be construed as references to a principal place of business in Great Britain. [*Secs 409, 424*].

47.12 **REGISTER OF DEBENTURE-HOLDERS**

A company is not obliged to maintain a register of debenture-holders but, where it does, the following provisions apply.

Location.

(*a*)   A company registered in England and Wales must not keep in Scotland

   (i)   any register of debenture-holders; or

   (ii)   any duplicate of such register or duplicate of part of any such register which is kept outside Great Britain.

(*b*)   A company registered in Scotland must not keep in England and Wales any such register or duplicate as mentioned in (*a*) above.

(*c*)   None of the registers in (*a*)(i) or (ii) above must be kept in England and Wales (in the case of a company registered in England and Wales) or in Scotland (in the case of a company registered in Scotland) elsewhere than

   (i)   at the company's registered office;

   (ii)   at any office of the company at which the work of making it up is done; or

   (iii)   if the company arranges for some other person to make up the register or duplicate on its behalf, at the office of that other person at which the work is done.

(*d*)   Where both a register and a duplicate is kept, they must be kept at the same place.

Where the register is kept in non-legible form, for references above to 'keep' there should be substituted 'allow inspection' and for references to 'kept' there should be substituted 'available for inspection'.

[*Sec 190(1)-(4); SI 1985 No 724, Reg 4*].

47.13 Registers

Notice to Registrar of Companies where register in legible form. A company which keeps any such register or duplicate in England and Wales or Scotland must send notice in the prescribed form (Form 190 or Form 363s) to the Registrar of Companies of the place where it is *kept*, and of any changes in that place, unless at all times since it came into existence it has been kept at the company's registered office.

Notice to Registrar of Companies where register in non-legible form. Where the place for *inspection* of any such register or duplicate is in England and Wales or Scotland, a company must send notice in the prescribed form (Form 190a) of the place for inspection of such register, and of any changes in that place, except where either the register is changed from legible to non-legible form and the place for inspection in non-legible form is the same as the place it was kept in legible form or where it has at all times been in non-legible form and available for inspection at the registered office.

[*Sec 190(5)(6); SI 1985 No 724, Regs 4, 5; SI 1991 No 879*].

Inspection. Unless duly closed (see below) every register of debenture-holders must be open for inspection to debenture-holders and members free of charge, and to any other person on payment of a maximum fee (see 26.2 FEES), for not less than two hours during the period 9a.m. to 5p.m. every Monday to Friday (other than public and bank holidays). A person inspecting the register must be permitted to copy any information made available by taking notes or making a transcript but the company is not obliged to provide any additional facilities other than those to facilitate inspection. Copies of any entry in the register must be sent on request to any person on payment of a maximum fee. A copy of any trust deed must also be sent on request to any debenture-holder on payment of a maximum fee. See 26.2 FEES. A company is not obliged to group entries in the register or index for inspection, or extract entries when sending out copies, by geographical location, nationality, size of holding, or gender or nature of the holder. If inspection is refused or the required copy not sent, the company and every officer in default is liable to a fine up to the level in 40.1(*g*) PENALTIES for each offence. In addition, the court may by order compel an immediate inspection or direct that copies be sent. [*Sec 191(1)-(5), 24 Sch; CA 1989, s 143; SI 1991 No 1998*].

Closure of register. A register is deemed duly closed if closed in accordance with the articles or debentures during any period not exceeding 30 days in any year. [*Sec 191(6)*].

Liability of the company. Liability incurred by a company from the making or deleting of an entry in the register (or failure to do so) is not enforceable more than 20 years after the date of the error or failure. [*Sec 191(7)*].

47.13 REGISTER OF AUDITORS

Joint register. The recognised supervisory bodies which maintain and enforce rules as to the eligibility of persons for appointment as company auditors (see 12.5 AUDITORS) must keep a joint register of

(*a*) individuals and firms eligible for appointment as company auditors; and

(*b*) individuals holding an appropriate qualification (see 12.5 AUDITORS) who are responsible for company audit work on behalf of such firms.

Each entry must give the name and address of the person concerned and, in the case of (*a*) above the name of the relevant supervisory body.

The register must be kept at the principal office in the UK of any one of the supervisory bodies and must be kept in such a way that it can be inspected either alphabetically or by reference to recognised supervisory bodies.

Information about firms. Each recognised supervisory body must also keep, in relation to each firm eligible for appointment as auditors under its own rules, information as to the name and address of each partner in the firm or, where the firm is a body corporate, the name and address of each person who is a director of it or holds shares in it. The record must also show which of those persons is responsible for company audit work on behalf of the firm. It must be kept at the principal office in the UK of the supervisory body and must be kept in such a way that it can be inspected either alphabetically or by reference to firm.

Inspection and copies. Both the joint register and the information required to be kept by each supervisory body must be open for inspection by the public during a period of at least two hours every day between 9 a.m. and 5 p.m. in any business day. A maximum fee of £2.50 per hour (or part thereof) can be charged for inspection. Copies, certified to be true copies, must be made available for a fee not exceeding 5p per copy.

[*CA 1989, ss 35, 36; SI 1991 No 1566*].

48   Registrar of Companies

48.1   There must be offices for the purposes of registration of companies in England and Wales and in Scotland in such places as the Secretary of State thinks fit. [*Sec 704*]. There are Companies House branches at the following addresses.

Cardiff
Crown Way
Cardiff CF14 3UZ

Main switchboard	01222 388588
Call Centre and telesales	01222 380801
Fax	01222 380517

Stationery Section
PO Box 450
Companies House
Crown Way
Cardiff CF14 3YA
Fax requests (Fax No)   01222 380566

London
21 Bloomsbury St
London WC1B 3XD

Information and telesales	01222 380801
Fax	01222 380900

Manchester
75 Mosley Street
Manchester M2 2HR

Telephone	0161 236 7500
Fax	0161 237 5258

Birmingham
Birmingham Central
Library
Chamberlain Square
Birmingham B3 3HQ

Telephone	0121 233 9047
Fax	0121 233 9052

Leeds
25 Queen Street
Leeds LS1 2TW

Telephone	0113 233 8338
Fax	0113 233 8335

Edinburgh
37 Castle Terrace
Edinburgh EH1 2EB

Telephone	0131 535 5800
Fax	0131 535 5820

Glasgow
7 West George Street
Glasgow G2 1BQ

Telephone	0141 221 5513
Fax	0141 225 2870

48.2 **FUNCTIONS OF THE REGISTRAR OF COMPANIES**

The functions of the Registrar of Companies include the following.

(a)   The allocation of a number to every company (the company's registered number). [*Sec 705; CA 1989, 19 Sch 14; SI 1992 No 3179, 3 Sch 5*].

(b)   The keeping of a register of branches of oversea companies. [*Sec 705A; SI 1992 No 3179, Reg 3*].

(c)   The receipt of documentation for filing in legible (i.e. capable of being read with the naked eye) or other than legible form and verification that the document complies with the necessary requirements. Where the document does not comply, the Registrar may serve notice indicating the failure and if it is not corrected within 14 days, the original document is deemed not to have been delivered. [*Secs 706, 707, 715A; CA 1989, ss 125, 127; SI 1992 No 3179, 3 Sch 6*].

(d)   The recording and keeping of company records delivered to him in such form as he thinks fit provided it is possible to inspect them and produce a copy in legible form. Originals of all documents must be kept for ten years after which they may be destroyed. Apart from Scotland, where a company has been dissolved the Registrar may transfer records to the Public Records Office at any time after two years from the date of dissolution. [*Sec 707A; CA 1989, s 126*].

In practice, Companies House maintains a file for each live company and copies the entire contents on to microfilm except for

- annual returns and accounts more than three years old at the time of initial filming; and

- changes in directors, secretaries and registered office more than seven years old at that time (although the latest is filmed however old).

The filmed documents are presented on microfilmed sheets containing 60 frames (microfilmed pages) divided into general documents relating to the structure of the company; annual returns and accounts; details of mortgages and charges and appointments of receivers and liquidators; and a register of mortgages and charges. Certain long shareholders lists are not microfilmed and separate arrangements are available for inspection.

(e)   The charging and collection of fees for the receipt of certain documentation and the inspection of documents. See 26.1 FEES. [*Sec 708; CA 1989, s 127*].

(f)   Allowing any person to inspect the records kept by him and making copies, or certifying copies, of any such records. A certified copy is in all legal proceedings admissible in evidence as of equal validity with the original document. [*Sec 709; CA 1989, s 126; Civil Evidence Act 1995, 1 Sch 10*].

(g)   Supplying signed or authenticated certificates of incorporation of a company to any person. [*Sec 710; CA 1989, s 126*].

(h)   The provision and authentication of documents in non-legible form. [*Sec 710A; CA 1989, s 126*].

48.3 Registrar of Companies

(*i*)   Arranging for the publication in the *Gazette* of notice of the issue or receipt by him of certain documents as listed in *Sec 711*.

(*j*)   Enforcing a company's duty to deliver any document to the Registrar. Where a company has defaulted in delivering any document, the Registrar may give notice to the company requiring it to make good the default within 14 days and, if it fails to do so, may apply to the court for an order directing the company and any officer of it to make good the default within such time as is specified in the order. [*Sec 713; CA 1989, s 127*].

(*k*)   Keeping an index of company and corporate names. [*Sec 714; SI 1992 No 3179, 3 Sch 8*].

Contracting out of functions. The Registrar of Companies may authorise another person (or that person's employees) to exercise certain of his functions. These include any function of receiving any return, account or other document required to be filed with, delivered or sent to the Registrar; any functions relating to the incorporation, change of name or re-registration and change of status of companies; and, with certain exceptions, functions within (*a*)–(*c*) and (*f*)–(*g*) above. [*SI 1995 No 1013*].

48.3   **NOTES FOR GUIDANCE**

The following notes for guidance are available, free of charge, on written request to the Stationery Section, PO Box 450, Companies House, Crown Way, Cardiff CF4 3YA.

CHN1	New companies
CHN2	Choosing a company name
CHN3	Sensitive words and expressions
CHN4	Change of name
CHN5	Public limited companies
CHN6	European Economic Interest Groupings
CHN7	Publication of company name and particulars to be shown on company stationery
CHN8	Exemption from using the word 'limited' in a company name
CHN9	The new company looking forward
CHN10	Single member companies
CHN11	Business names and business ownership
CHN12	The registration of newspapers
CHN13	Limited partnerships
CHN14	Flat management and similar companies
CHN15	Directors and Companies House
CHN16	Company secretaries' duties and responsibilities
CHN17	Auditors
CHN18	Document quality
CHN19	Disclosure requirements
CHN20	Accounting reference dates
CHN21	Dormant company accounts
CHN22	Late filing penalties
CHN23	Company charges and mortgages
CHN23(S)	Company charges (Scotland)
CHN24	Resolutions
CHN25	Oversea companies
CHN27	Striking off, dissolution and restoration
CHN27(S)	Striking off, dissolution and restoration (Scotland)
CHN28	Liquidation and insolvency
CHN28(S)	Liquidation and insolvency (Scotland)

CHN29   Microfiche records
CHN30   Share capital
CHN31   Use of Welsh
CHN32   Products and services

48.4   QUALITY OF DOCUMENTS FILED WITH THE REGISTRAR OF COMPANIES

Documents delivered to the Registrar of Companies are photographed to produce a microfilm record for each company. The original documents are stored away and the master copy of the microfilm is used as a working record of the company. Documents delivered to the Registrar must, therefore, comply with requirements set out below as specified by the Registrar. If they do not, the Registrar can reject them (see 48.2(*b*) above).

Specification of documents (including own-produced forms, annual accounts, etc.).

• Documents should be A4 size on paper which is white or otherwise of a background density not greater than 0.3. The paper should be between 80gsm and 100gsm.

• The paper must have a matt finish.

• Each page must have a margin all round not less than 10mm wide. If the document is bound, the bound edge must have a margin of not less than 20mm.

• Letters and numbers must be clear, legible and of uniform density. They must be not less than 1.8mm high with a line width of not less than 0.25mm. They must be black or otherwise providing reflected line density of not less than 1.0.

Colour-printed glossy accounts should not be sent. Where these are sent to shareholders, a typed version or the printer's proof in black on white is acceptable (provided it has the necessary signatures on it).

Members' lists. Provided the print quality is good, these can be derived from computer prints on paper up to 14.5" × 12". Lists printed on green lined computer paper are however particularly difficult to copy. Computer-generated microfiche (comfiche) on a black master is acceptable as an alternative to paper copy provided it is capable of being duplicated on the Registrar's machines. For further guidance, contact 01222 380306.

It may also be possible to accept magnetic tape for very large listings. For further guidance, contact 01222 380242.

Completion of forms. Forms should be completed in black ink or black type using bold lettering. Carbon copies or the use of dot matrix computer printers are not acceptable.

(Companies House Notes for Guidance CHN18).

49   Registration and Re-Registration

Cross-references. See 38.2 OVERSEA COMPANIES for registration of oversea companies.

49.1   REGISTRATION

Documents to be sent to the Registrar of Companies. The following documents must be sent to the Registrar of Companies for England and Wales (for Scotland if the registered office is to be situated in Scotland) before a company can be formed. A standard registration fee is also payable. See 26.1 FEES.

(*a*)   The MEMORANDUM OF ASSOCIATION (35). If the memorandum states that the company is to be registered as a public company, the amount of share capital with which it proposes to be registered must not be less than the authorised minimum (see 58.12 SHARES AND SHARE CAPITAL). [*Sec 11*].

(*b*)   The ARTICLES OF ASSOCIATION (11), if any.

(*c*)   A statement in the prescribed form (Form 10) with details of the following.

    (i)   The first director or directors of the company. In the case of an individual particulars must be given of his present 'name'; any 'former name'; usual residential address; nationality; business occupation (if any); other director-ships held in the last five years (excluding any directorship which is and has been, or was, during those five years held in a 'dormant' company, or a company 'grouped' with the company delivering the statement, throughout the directorship); and date of birth. In the case of a corporation (or Scottish firm) particulars must be given of its corporate (or firm) name and registered or principal office.

    A company is '*dormant*' during a period in which no accounting transaction occurs which is required to be entered in the company's accounting records.

    A company is treated as '*grouped*' with another company at any time if that other company is, or was, a wholly-owned subsidiary of it (or vice versa) or if both are, or were, wholly-owned subsidiaries of a third company.

    (ii)   The first secretary or joint secretaries of the company. In the case of an individual particulars must be given of his present name; any former name; and usual residential address. In the case of a corporation (or Scottish firm) particulars must be given of its corporate (or firm) name and registered or principal office. Where all the partners in a firm are joint secretaries, the name and principal office of the firm may be stated instead.

    (iii)   The intended situation of the registered office on incorporation.

    '*Name*' means Christian name (or other forename) and surname. A peer, or individual known by a title, may alternatively or additionally state his title.

    '*Former name*' does not include the name of a peer etc. before adopting his title; a former name changed or disused before the age of 18 or for 20 years or more; and a married woman's name before her marriage.

The statement in (*c*) above must be signed by, or on behalf of, the subscribers and must contain a consent signed by each of the persons named as a director, secretary or one of the joint secretaries to act in the relevant capacity. If a memorandum is delivered by a person acting as agent for the subscribers, the statement must also specify that fact and the person's name and address.

An appointment of a person as director or secretary by the articles delivered is void unless he is also named in the statement.

[*Sec 10, 1 Sch; CA 1989, 10 Sch 17, 19 Sch 7*].

Statutory declaration. A statutory declaration in the prescribed form (Form 12) that all the requirements in respect of registration and matters precedent and incidental have been complied with must be delivered to the Registrar of Companies by either a solicitor engaged in the formation of the company or a person named as director or secretary in the statement under (*c*) above. The Registrar must not register the company's memorandum unless satisfied that all the requirements have been complied with but he may accept the statutory declaration as sufficient evidence of compliance. [*Sec 12*].

The Registrar may refuse to register a company if its objects are illegal (*R v Registrar of Companies, ex p More [1931] 2 KB 197*) but not if they are lawful (*R v Registrar of Companies, ex p Bowen [1914] 3 KB 1161*).

49.2   Effect of registration

On registration of the company's memorandum, the Registrar of Companies must give a signed or authenticated certificate that the company has been incorporated. If appropriate, the certificate must also state that the company is limited or is a public company. The certificate is conclusive evidence that the requirements of registration have been complied with and that the company is registered and, if appropriate, a public company.

From the date of incorporation in the certificate, the subscribers, and any subsequent shareholders, are a body corporate under the name contained in the memorandum which can exercise all the functions of an incorporated company. A public company, however, cannot do business or borrow money until it receives a certificate from the Registrar under *Sec 117* (see 43.3 PUBLIC AND LISTED COMPANIES).

The directors and secretary or secretaries named in the statement under 49.1(*c*) above are deemed to have been appointed the first directors etc.

[*Sec 13*].

49.3   RE-REGISTRATION

A registered company may apply for re-registration as a means of altering its status. The following possibilities are allowed for under *CA 1985*.

- A private company becoming a public company (see 49.4 to 49.7 below).

- An unlimited company becoming a public company (see 49.8 below).

- A limited company becoming an unlimited company (see 49.9 below).

- An unlimited company becoming a limited company (see 49.10 below).

- A public company becoming a private company (see 49.11 to 49.13 below).

- An 'old public company' becoming a public company (see 49.14 below).

- An 'old public company' becoming a private company (see 49.15 below).

49.4   A private company becoming a public company

A private company (other than a company not having a share capital) may be re-registered as a public company if

(*a*)   a special resolution is passed to that effect which also

49.4 Registration and Re-Registration

  (i) alters the company's memorandum so that it states that the company is to be a public company;

  (ii) makes any other alterations necessary to the memorandum so that, in substance and form, it is brought into conformity with a public company's memorandum (see *SI 1985 No 805, Table F*);

  (iii) make any necessary alterations in the company's articles; and

  (iv) if required, changes the company's name by deleting 'company' or 'and company' (or their Welsh equivalents) or any abbreviation of them;

(*b*) where shares have been recently allotted otherwise than in cash, the conditions in 49.5 below are satisfied;

(*c*) the requirements under 49.6 below with regard to share capital are satisfied; and

(*d*) an application for re-registration in the prescribed form (Form 43(3)), signed by a director or secretary, is delivered to the Registrar of Companies together with

  (i) a copy of the special resolution;

  (ii) a printed copy of the memorandum and articles of association;

  (iii) a copy of a written statement by the company's auditors that in their opinion the 'relevant balance sheet' shows that at the balance sheet date the amount of the company's 'net assets' was not less than the aggregate of its called-up share capital and 'undistributed reserves'. See *Example 2* under 12.30 AUDITORS for a suggested form of the report;

  (iv) a copy of the relevant balance sheet together with a copy of a report by the company's auditors in relation to the balance sheet which has either no qualification or a qualification stated as being not material for the purposes of giving their opinion under (iii) above;

  (v) where 49.5 below applies, a copy of the valuation report required; and

  (vi) a statutory declaration in the prescribed form (Form 43(3)(e)) by a director or secretary that conditions (*a*) to (*c*) above have been satisfied and that, between the balance sheet date and the application for re-registration, there has been no change in the company's financial position that has resulted in the amount of its net assets becoming less than the aggregate of its called-up share capital and undistributable reserves.

'Relevant balance sheet' means a balance sheet prepared as at a date not more than seven months before the company's application.

'Net assets' means the aggregate of the company's assets less the aggregate of its liabilities (including any amount retained as reasonably necessary to provide for any liability or loss likely to be incurred).

See 23.1 DISTRIBUTIONS for *'undistributable reserves'*.

Note. The special resolution must be delivered to the Registrar of Companies for filing within 15 days of passing. [*Sec 380*]. There is no time limit as such for filing the other documents.

[*Secs 43, 46, 264(2)(3), 4 Sch 89; CA 1989, 10 Sch 1*].

Example of a special resolution for the re-registration of a private company as a public company

'That pursuant to the provisions of section 43 of the Companies Act 1985 the company be and hereby is re-registered as a public company and that the memorandum of association of the company be altered as follows.

(*a*)   By deleting existing clause 1 and substituting therefor the following clauses to be numbered 1 and 2:

    1.   The name of the company is [insert name] public limited company.

    2.   The company is to be a public company.

(*b*)   By renumbering the existing clauses 2, 3, 4 and 5 as clauses 3, 4, 5 and 6 respectively.'

49.5   *Valuation of consideration for shares recently allotted*

Where the company has, between the date of the relevant balance sheet (see 49.4 above) and the passing of the special resolution, allotted shares as fully or partly paid up (as to their nominal value or any premium on them) otherwise than in cash, the Registrar of Companies cannot consider an application under 49.4 above unless beforehand

- the consideration for the allotment has been valued in accordance with 9.16 and 9.17 ALLOTMENT OF SHARES; and

- a report with respect to the valuation of the consideration has been made to the company in the six months immediately before the allotment of the shares.

The above provisions do not apply

- to the extent that the amount standing to the credit of the company's reserves or profit and loss account balance are applied in paying up the shares allotted or any premium on them;

- if the allotment is in connection with an arrangement under which the consideration is the transfer to the company, or cancellation, of shares in another company. The arrangement must be open to all the shareholders (or all the shareholders of the particular class concerned) of the other company, disregarding any held by, or as nominee of, the allotting company, its holding company or subsidiary, or a fellow subsidiary; and

- if the allotment is in connection with a proposed merger.

[*Sec 44*].

49.6   *Additional requirements relating to share capital*

Subject to the disregarded shares below, for a private company to be re-registered under 49.4 above, the following conditions must be satisfied at the time of passing the special resolution.

(*a*)   The nominal value of the company's allotted share capital must be at least the authorised minimum (currently £50,000). See 58.12 SHARES AND SHARE CAPITAL.

(*b*)   Each of the company's allotted shares must be paid up at least as to one-quarter of its nominal value and the whole of any premium.

(*c*)   If any shares or premium have been fully or partly paid up by an undertaking given by any person that he or another should do work or perform services, that undertaking must have been performed or discharged.

(*d*)   If any shares have been allotted as fully or partly paid up, as to nominal value or premium, otherwise than in cash, and the consideration for the allotment consists of or includes an undertaking to the company not falling within (*c*) above, then either

- the undertaking must have been performed or discharged; or

- there must be a contract between the company and some other person under which the undertaking is to be performed within five years of the passing of the resolution.

See 9.13 and 9.14 ALLOTMENT OF SHARES for similar restrictions to (*b*) to (*d*) above when shares are allotted in public companies.

Disregarded shares. For the purpose of determining whether (*b*), (*c*) and (*d*) above have been complied with the following shares may, however, be disregarded.

(i)   Any shares allotted before 22 June 1982 unless the aggregate nominal value of all the shares to be disregarded (including any under (ii) below) is more than one-tenth of the nominal value of the company's allotted share capital (*excluding any* shares disregarded under (ii) below).

(ii)   Any shares allotted under an 'employees' share scheme' and by reason of which, but for this provision, the company would be prevented under (*b*) above from being re-registered as a public company.

Any shares so disregarded are treated as not forming part of the allotted share capital for the purposes of (*a*) above.

[*Secs 45, 118*].

49.7   *Certificate of re-registration*

Where the Registrar of Companies is satisfied that the company should be re-registered under 49.4 above, he must retain the application and other documents delivered and issue the company with a certificate of incorporation stating that the company is a public company. He must not issue the certificate if the court has made an order confirming a reduction in the company's capital bringing the nominal value of the allotted share capital below the authorised minimum (currently £50,000).

On issue of the certificate, the company becomes a public company (the certificate being conclusive evidence of this fact) and any alterations in the memorandum or articles set out in the resolution take effect.

[*Sec 47*].

49.8   An unlimited company becoming a public company

Similar provisions as in 49.4 to 49.7 above apply to an unlimited company becoming a public company except that the special resolution under 49.4(*a*) above must also

- state that the liability of members is to be limited by shares;

- state what the company's share capital is to be; and

- make any other alterations necessary to the memorandum so that, in substance and form, it is brought into conformity with a company limited by shares (see *SI 1985 No 805, Table F*).

The certificate of incorporation under 49.7 above must also state that the company has been incorporated as a company limited by shares.

On the issue of the certificate of incorporation, the company becomes a public company limited by shares, the certificate being conclusive evidence of that fact.

[*Sec 48*].

Reserve capital. The resolution for re-registration may also

- increase the nominal amount of the company's share capital by increasing the nominal amount of each share (although no part of the increased capital is to be capable of being called up except on winding up); and/or

- provide that a specified portion of the company's uncalled share capital is not to be capable of being called up except on winding up.

[*Sec 124*].

49.9   A limited company becoming an unlimited company

A limited company (other than a public company *or* one limited by virtue of re-registration under *CA 1967, ss 44* or *51 or* a company previously re-registered as an unlimited company) may be re-registered as an unlimited company if the following documents are delivered to the Registrar of Companies.

- An application for re-registration in the prescribed form (Form 49(1)), signed by a director or secretary

  (i)   setting out such alterations as are required in the company's memorandum and articles (if any) including, if the company has a share capital, those alterations necessary so that, in substance and form, they are brought into conformity with an unlimited company having a share capital (see *SI 1985 No 805, Table E*); and

  (ii)   if articles have not been previously registered, requesting and having annexed to it, appropriate printed articles.

- The prescribed form of assent to the company being registered as unlimited (Form 49(8)(a)) subscribed by, or on behalf of, all the members of the company, together with a statutory declaration by the directors to this effect (Form 49(8)(b)).

- A printed copy of the memorandum as altered.

- If articles have been registered, a printed copy as altered.

[*Sec 49*].

Certificate of registration. The Registrar of Companies must retain the application and other documents delivered and issue the company with a certificate of incorporation stating that it is an unlimited company (with or without share capital as the case may be). On issue of the certificate the company becomes an unlimited company (the certificate being conclusive evidence of this fact) and any alteration in the memorandum or articles takes effect as if duly made by resolution of the company. [*Sec 50*].

49.10   An unlimited company becoming a limited company

An unlimited company (other than one unlimited by virtue of re-registration under *CA 1967, ss 43* or *49*) may be re-registered as a limited company (but not as a public company, for which see 49.4 above) if the following conditions are satisfied.

(*a*)   A special resolution is passed to that effect

- stating whether the company is to be limited by shares or guarantee;

- if applicable, stating what the share capital is to be; and

- providing for the making of such alterations as are necessary to the memorandum and articles so that, in substance and form, they are brought into conformity with those for a company limited by shares or, as the case may be, guarantee.

(b) There is delivered to the Registrar of Companies

- an application for re-registration in the prescribed form (Form 51), signed by a director or secretary; and

- printed copies of the memorandum and articles as altered.

The special resolution must be forwarded to the Registrar of Companies with 15 days of passing [*Sec 380*] and the documents under (b) must be lodged not earlier than the date of lodging the special resolution.

[*Sec 51*].

Certification of re-registration. The Registrar of Companies must retain the application and other documents delivered and issue the company with a certificate of incorporation stating that it is a limited company (limited by shares or guarantee as the case may be). On the issue of the certificate, the company becomes a limited company (the certificate being conclusive evidence of this fact) and any alterations to the memorandum or articles take effect. [*Sec 52*].

Reserve capital. The same provisions apply as under 49.8 above.

49.11 A public company becoming a private company

A public company may be re-registered as a private company limited by shares or guarantee provided

(a) a special resolution is passed to that effect (and is not cancelled by the court under 49.12 below) which also

- alters the company's memorandum so that it no longer states that the company is to be a public company; and

- makes any other alterations necessary to the memorandum and articles as are required under the circumstances;

(b) an application for re-registration in the prescribed form (Form 53), signed by a director or secretary, is delivered to the Registrar of Companies together with a printed copy of the memorandum and articles as altered; and

(c) either

- 28 days has expired from the passing of the resolution and no application has been made under 49.12 below; or

- an application has been made under 49.12 below but it has been withdrawn or the court has confirmed the resolution and a copy of the court order has been delivered to the Registrar.

[*Sec 53*].

Example of special resolution for the re-registration of a public company as a private company

'That the company make an application to the Registrar of Companies pursuant to section 53 of the Companies Act 1985 to be re-registered as a private company and that the memorandum of association be thereupon altered as follows:

(a)   by deleting the existing clauses 1 and 2 and substituting therefor the following clause to be numbered 1:

1.   The name of the company is [insert name] Limited.

(b)   by renumbering the existing clauses 3, 4, 5 and 6 as clauses 2, 3, 4 and 5 respectively.'

49.12 *Application to the court*

Where a resolution has been passed under 49.11 above, application may be made to the court for cancellation of the resolution by

- the holders of at least 5% in nominal value of the company's issued share capital or any class thereof,

- if the company is not limited by shares, at least 5% of its members, or

- at least 50 of the members

but not by a person who has consented to or voted in favour of the resolution. [*Sec 54(1)(2)*].

The application must be made within 28 days of the passing of the resolution and may be made on behalf of the persons entitled to make the application by one or more of their number as they appoint in writing.

If application is made, the company must give notice in the prescribed form (Form 54) to the Registrar of Companies. If it fails to do so, the company and every officer in default is liable to a fine up to the level in 40.1(*f*) PENALTIES.

The court on the hearing may, as it thinks fit,

- make an order on any terms;

- adjourn the proceedings so that an arrangement is made for the satisfactory purchase of the interests of dissentient members;

- provide for the purchase by the company of the shares of any of its members and the reduction of the company's capital; and

- make such alteration in the company's memorandum or articles as are required.

Within 15 days of the making of the order (or such longer period as the court allows) the company must send an office copy of the order to the Registrar of Companies. If not, the company and every officer in default is liable to a fine up to the level in 40.1(*f*) PENALTIES.

If the court order requires the company not to make any, or any specified, alterations to its memorandum or articles, the company may not then do so without leave of the court.

[*Sec 54(3)-(10), 24 Sch*].

49.13 *Certificate of re-registration*

Where the Registrar of Companies is satisfied that the company should be re-registered under 49.11 above, he must retain the application and other documents delivered and issue the company with a certificate of incorporation stating that the company is a private company. On issue of the certificate, the company becomes a private company (the certificate being conclusive evidence of this fact) and any alterations in the memorandum and articles set out in the resolution take effect. [*Sec 55*].

49.14   Registration and Re-Registration

49.14 An 'old public company' becoming a public company

An *'old public company'* (see 18.1 DEFINITIONS) may be re-registered as a public company if

(a)   a special resolution is passed to that effect which also

- alters the company's memorandum so that it states that the company is to be a public company; and

- makes any alterations necessary to the memorandum so that, in substance and form, it is brought into conformity with a public company's memorandum (see *SI 1985 No 805, Table F*);

(b)   at the time concerned, the conditions in 49.6(*a*)-(*d*) above were satisfied (ignoring the provisions relating to *Disregarded shares*); and

(c)   an application for re-registration in the prescribed form (Form R7), signed by a director or secretary, is delivered to the Registrar of Companies, together with

- a copy of the special resolution;

- a printed copy of the memorandum as altered; and

- a statutory declaration in the prescribed form (Form R8) by a director or secretary that (*a*) and (*b*) above have been satisfied.

Note. The special resolution must be delivered to the Registrar of Companies for filing within 15 days of passing [*Sec 380*] but there is no time limit as such for filing the other documents.

Certificate of re-registration. The provisions of 49.7 above also apply.

[*CC(CP)A 1985, ss 2, 3*].

49.15 An 'old public company' becoming a private company

An *'old public company'* (see 18.1 DEFINITIONS) may pass a special resolution *not* to be re-registered under 49.14 above as a public company. The provisions of 49.12 above apply to such a resolution as they apply to a special resolution by a public company to be re-registered as a private company. The prescribed form is Form R7a.

The Registrar of Companies must issue a certificate stating that the company is a private company if

(a)   a special resolution not to be re-registered as a public company has been passed and either

- 28 days has expired from the passing of the resolution and no application has been made under 49.12 above; or

- such an application has been made but it has been withdrawn or the court proceedings are concluded without an order for the cancellation of the resolution; or

(b)   an old public company delivers a statutory declaration in the prescribed form (Form R9), signed by a director or secretary, that the company does not at that time satisfy the conditions in 49.6 (*a*)-(*d*) above for the company to be re-registered as public.

[*CC(CP)A 1985, s 4*].

Penalties for failure to obtain a new classification. If at any time, an old public company has not

- delivered a statutory declaration under (*b*) above, or

- applied to be re-registered under 49.14 above (and the application has not been refused or withdrawn), or

- passed a special resolution as above *not* to be re-registered (and the resolution has not been revoked or cancelled by the court under 49.12 above)

the company and every officer in default is guilty of an offence and liable to a fine up to the level in 40.1(*f*) PENALTIES. [*CC(CP)A 1985, s 5*].

50   Registration of Charges

Cross-references. See 47.11 REGISTERS.

50.1   INTRODUCTION

There are statutory provisions requiring the registration with the Registrar of Companies of certain charges on a company's property. See 50.2 to 50.9 below for the provisions in respect of companies registered in England and Wales and 50.10 to 50.17 below in respect of companies registered in Scotland.

Future changes. *CA 1989, Part IV (Secs 92–107)* introduced a new regime governing the registration of charges. These provisions, however, have never been brought into force and the Department of Trade issued a consultative document in 1994 with various options for the reform of the provisions in *CA 1985, Part XII.* After considering the responses, the then Government indicated that the most likely outcome would be the retention of the 'core' provisions in *CA 1985* but with improvements incorporated. It is unlikely that any new registration provisions will be brought into force in the near future and the detailed provisions as outlined in 50.1 to 50.7 below are based on the CA 1985 provisions.

50.2   ENGLAND AND WALES

A charge (which includes a mortgage) created by a company registered in England and Wales and falling within 50.3 below is, so far as any security on the company's property or undertaking is conferred by the charge, void against the liquidator or administrator or any creditor of the company unless

- particulars of the charge (on Form 395), and

- the instrument (if any) by which the charge is created or evidenced

are delivered to the Registrar of Companies within 21 days of the charge's creation. When a charge becomes void in this way, the money secured by it immediately becomes payable. [*Secs 395, 396(4) 1A 1985, s 109, 6 Sch 10*]. The charge is void even if the liquidator or creditor has notice of the unregistered charge (*Re Monolithic Building Co [1915] 1 Ch 643*).

50.3   Charges requiring registration

The following charges require registration.

- A charge for the purpose of securing any issue of debentures.

- A charge on uncalled share capital of the company.

- A charge created or evidenced by an instrument which, if executed by an individual, would require registration as a bill of sale.

- A charge on land (wherever situated) or any interest in it, but not including a charge for any rent or other periodical sum issuing out of the land.

- A charge on book debts of the company. Where a negotiable instrument has been given to secure the payment of any book debts of the company, the deposit of the instrument to secure an advance to the company is not to be treated as a charge on those book debts.

- A floating charge on the company's undertaking or property.

- A charge on calls made but not paid.

- A charge on a ship or aircraft, or any share in a ship.

- A charge on goodwill, on a patent or a licence under a patent, on a trade mark or on a copyright or a licence under a copyright.

[*Sec 396*].

50.4   **Registration of charges associated with debentures**

Where a company issues a series of debentures containing or giving a charge which benefits the debenture-holders of the series *pari passu*, it is sufficient for the purposes of 50.2 above if the following are delivered to the Registrar of Companies within 21 days of the execution of the deed containing the charge (or, if there is no such deed, within 21 days of the execution of any debenture of the series).

(*a*)   Particulars in the prescribed form (Form 397) of

- the total amount secured by the whole series;
- the dates of the resolutions authorising the issue of the series and the date of the covering deed (if any) by which the security is created or defined;
- a general description of the property charged; and
- the names of the trustees for the debenture-holders (if any).

(*b*)   The deed containing the charge or, if there is no deed, one of the debentures of the series.

Additionally, particulars must also be sent for registration of

(i)   the date and amount of each issue of debentures in a series (on Form 397a); and

(ii)   the amount or rate per cent of any commission, allowance or discount which has been paid directly or indirectly by a company to a person subscribing for, or procuring subscriptions for, debentures of the company. The deposit of debentures as security for a debt of the company is not to be treated as the issue of debentures at a discount for these purposes.

Failure to register particulars under (i) or (ii) above does not, however, affect the validity of any of those debentures.

[*Sec 397*].

50.5   **Verification of charges on property outside England and Wales**

Charges created outside the UK on property situated outside the UK. The delivery to the Registrar of Companies of a copy of the instrument creating or evidencing the charge, verified by the company creating the charge, has the same effect for the purposes of 50.2 and 50.4 above as the delivery and receipt of the instrument itself. In such a case, 21 days after the date on which the instrument could have been received in the UK (assuming posted and despatched with due diligence) is substituted for the 21-day period there referred to. [*Sec 398(1)(2)*].

Charges created in the UK on property situated outside the UK. The instrument creating the charge may be sent for registration under 50.2 above even though further proceedings may be necessary to make the charge valid under the law of the country where the property is situated. [*Sec 398(3)*].

Property situated in Scotland or Northern Ireland. Where registration in the country in which the property is situated is necessary to make the charge valid according to the law of that country, the delivery to the Registrar of Companies in England and Wales of

- a copy of the instrument creating or evidencing the charge certified by the company creating it, and

50.6 Registration of Charges

- a certificate in the prescribed form (Form 398) stating that the charge was presented for registration in Scotland or Northern Ireland (as the case may be) on the date it was so presented

has the same effect for the purposes of 50.2 and 50.4 above as the delivery of the instrument itself. [*Sec 398(4)*].

50.6 Duties of companies

Charges created by the company. A company must send to the Registrar of Companies all particulars required under 50.2 to 50.5 above. Alternatively, particulars may be delivered for registration by any other person interested in the charge, in which case that person is entitled to recover from the company any fees paid to the Registrar in connection with the registration. If the company fails to comply with these provisions then, unless the particulars have been delivered by another person, the company and every officer in default is liable to a fine up to the level in 40.1(*c*) PENALTIES. [*Sec 399*].

Charges existing on property acquired. A company which acquires property already subject to a charge which would, if created by the company, require registration under the provisions in 50.2 to 50.5 above, must deliver

- particulars of the charge (on Form 400), and

- a certified copy of the instrument (if any) by which the charge was created or evidenced

to the Registrar of Companies within 21 days after the date on which the acquisition is completed (where the property is situated and the charge created outside Great Britain, 21 days after the date on which a copy of the instrument could have been received in the UK if posted and despatched with due diligence). In default the company and every officer in default is liable to a fine up to the level in 40.1(*c*) PENALTIES. [*Sec 400*].

Endorsement of certificate on debentures. Where debentures are secured by a registered charge, a company must cause a copy of every certificate of registration of that charge issued by the Registrar of Companies (see 50.7 below) to be endorsed on every debenture or certificate of debenture stock issued by it after the charge is created. A person who knowingly and wilfully authorises or permits the delivery of a debenture or certificate of debenture stock in default of this provision is liable (without prejudice to any other liability) to a fine up to the level in 40.1(*d*) PENALTIES. [*Sec 402*].

Relief by court. Where there has been

- an omission to register a charge in time, or

- an omission or misstatement of any particulars in respect of a charge or in a memorandum of satisfaction

the court may, on the application of the company or an interested party, order the time for registration to be extended or, as the case may be, the omission or misstatement to be rectified where it is satisfied that the error

- was accidental,

- was due to inadvertence or some other sufficient cause, or

- does not prejudice the position of creditors or shareholders

or that it is just and equitable to grant relief on other grounds. [*Sec 404*].

50.7 Duties of the Registrar of Companies

For every company, the Registrar of Companies must keep and make available for inspection a register of all charges requiring registration showing (*a*)   in the case of a charge to the benefit of which the holders of a series of debentures are entitled, the particulars specified in 50.4(*a*) above; and

(*b*)   in the case of any other charge

- the date of creation (if created by the company) or the date of acquisition of the property (if the charge was existing on property acquired by the company);

- the amount secured by the charge;

- short particulars of the property charged; and

- the persons entitled to the charge.

The Registrar must give a signed or authenticated certificate of registration of any charge so registered, stating the amount secured by the charge. Such a certificate is conclusive evidence that the registration requirements have been complied with. See *Exeter Trust Ltd v Screenways Ltd [1991] BCLC 888.*

[*Sec 401*].

On receipt of a statutory declaration in the prescribed form verifying that, with respect to a registered charge,

- the debt for which the charge has been given has been paid or satisfied in whole or in part (Form 403a), or

- part of the property or undertaking charged has been released from the charge or has ceased to form part of the company's property or undertaking (Form 403b)

the Registrar may enter a memorandum of satisfaction of that fact on the register. Where the Registrar enters a memorandum of satisfaction in whole, he must, if required, supply a copy of it to the company.

[*Sec 403*].

50.8   **Appointment of receiver, etc.**

Where a person

- obtains an order for the appointment of a receiver or manager of a company's property, or

- appoints such a person under powers contained in an instrument

he must, within seven days of the order or appointment, give notice of the fact to the Registrar of Companies in the prescribed form (Form 405(1)). The Registrar must then enter that fact on the register of charges.

Where a receiver or manager appointed under powers contained in an instrument ceases so to act, he must give notice to that effect to the Registrar who must enter the fact on the register of charges.

If a person defaults in complying with any of the above provisions, he is liable to a fine up to the level in 40.1(*c*) PENALTIES.

[*Sec 405*].

50.9   **Oversea companies**

The provisions in 50.2 to 50.8 above apply to charges on property in England and Wales which are created, and to charges on such property which is acquired, by a company

50.10   Registration of Charges

incorporated outside Great Britain which has an established place of business in England and Wales. [*Sec 409(1)*]. See 38.1 OVERSEA COMPANIES for what constitutes establishing a place of business.

50.10 SCOTLAND

A charge created by a company registered in Scotland and falling within 50.11 below is, so far as any security on the company's property or any part of it is conferred by the charge, void against the liquidator or administrator or any creditor of the company unless

- particulars of the charge (on Form 410 (Scot)), and

- a certified copy of the instrument (if any) by which the charge is created or evidenced

are delivered to the Registrar of Companies within 21 days of the 'date of creation of the charge'. When a charge becomes void in this way, the money secured by it immediately becomes payable. [*Sec 410(2)(3)*]. The charge is void even if the liquidator or creditor has notice of the unregistered charge (*Re Monolithic Building Co [1915] 1 Ch 643*).

The *'date of creation of the charge'* is

- in the case of a floating charge, when the instrument creating it is executed by the company; and

- in any other case, when the right of the person entitled to the benefit of the charge is constituted as a real right.

[*Sec 410(5)*].

50.11 Charges requiring registration

The following charges require registration.

(*a*)   A charge on land wherever situated, or any interest in such land (not including a charge for any rent, ground annual or other periodical sum payable in respect of the land but including a charge created by a heritable security within the meaning of *Conveyancing and Feudal Reform (Scotland) Act 1970, s 9(8)*).

(*b*)   A security over the uncalled share capital of the company.

(*c*)   A security over incorporeal moveable property comprising

    (i) book debts of the company;

    (ii) calls made but not paid;

    (iii) goodwill;

    (iv) a patent or a licence under a patent;

    (v) a trade mark; or

    (vi) a copyright or a licence under a copyright;

(*d*)   A security over a ship or aircraft or any share in a ship.

(*e*)   A floating charge.

For the purposes of (c)(i) above, where a negotiable instrument has been given to secure the payment of any book debts of the company, the deposit of the instrument to secure an advance to the company is not to be treated as a charge on those book debts.

[*Secs 410(4), 412*].

50.12 Charges associated with debentures

Where a company issues a series of debentures containing or giving a charge which benefits the debenture-holders of the series *pari passu*, it is sufficient for the purposes of 50.11 above if the following are delivered to the Registrar of Companies within 21 days of the execution of the deed containing the charge (or, if there is no such deed, within 21 days of the execution of any debenture of the series).

(*a*)   Particulars in the prescribed form (Form 413(Scot)) of

- the total amount secured by the whole series;
- the dates of the resolutions authorising the issue of the series and the date of the covering deed (if any) by which the security is created or defined;
- a general description of the property charged;
- the names of the trustees for the debenture-holders (if any); and
- in the case of a floating charge, details of any provision of the charge and any instrument relating to it which *either* prohibit, restrict or regulate the company's power to grant further securities ranking in priority to, or *pari passu* with, the floating charge *or* regulate the order of ranking of the floating charge in relation to subsisting securities.

(*b*)   The deed containing the charge or, if there is no deed, one of the debentures of the series.

Additionally, particulars must also be sent for registration of

(i)   the date and amount of each issue of debentures in a series (on Form 413a(Scot)); and

(ii)   the amount or rate per cent of any commission, allowance or discount which has been paid directly or indirectly by a company to a person subscribing for, or procuring subscriptions for, debenture of the company. The deposit of debentures as security for a debt of the company is not to be treated as the issue of debentures at a discount for these purposes.

Failure to register particulars under (i) or (ii) above does not, however, affect the validity of any of those debentures.

[*Sec 413*].

50.13 Charges on property outside the UK

Charges created outside the UK on property situated outside the UK. In such a case, 21 days after the date on which the copy of the instrument creating the charge could have been received in the UK (assuming posted and despatched with due diligence) is substituted for the 21-day period in 50.10 above within which the particulars and copy must be delivered to the Registrar of Companies. [*Sec 411(1)*].

Charges created in the UK on property situated outside the UK. The copy of the instrument creating the charge may be sent for registration under 50.10 above even though further proceedings may be necessary to make the charge valid under the law of the country where the property is situated. [*Sec 411(2)*].

50.14 Registration of Charges

50.14 Duties of companies

Charges created by the company. A company must send to the Registrar of Companies all particulars required under 50.10 to 50.13 above. Alternatively, particulars may be delivered for registration by any other person interested in the charge, in which case that person is entitled to recover from the company any fees paid to the Registrar in connection with the registration. If the company fails to comply with these provisions then, unless the particulars have been delivered by another person, the company and every officer in default is liable to a fine up to the level in 40.1(*c*) PENALTIES. [*See 415*].

Charges existing on property acquired. A company which acquires property already subject to a charge which would, if created by the company, require registration under the provisions in 50.10 to 50.13 above, must deliver

- particulars of the charge (on Form 416(Scot)), and

- a certified copy of the instrument (if any) by which the charge was created or evidenced

to the Registrar of Companies within 21 days after the date on which the transaction was settled (where the property is situated and the charge created outside Great Britain, 21 days after the date on which a copy of the instrument could have been received in the UK if posted and despatched with due diligence). In default the company and every officer in default is liable to a fine up to the level in 40.1(*c*) PENALTIES. [*See 416*].

Relief by court. Where there has been

- an omission to register a charge in time, or

- an omission or misstatement of any particulars in respect of a charge or in a memorandum of satisfaction

the court may, on the application of the company or an interested party, order the time for registration to be extended or, as the case may be, the omission or misstatement to be rectified where it is satisfied that the error

- was accidental,

- was due to inadvertence or some other sufficient cause, or

- does not prejudice the position of creditors or shareholders

or that it is just and equitable to grant relief on other grounds. [*See 420*].

50.15 Duties of the Registrar of Companies

For every company, the Registrar of Companies must keep and make available for inspection a register of all charges requiring registration showing

(*a*)   in the case of a charge to the benefit of which the holders of a series of debentures are entitled, the particulars specified in 50.12(*a*) above; and

(*b*)   in the case of any other charge

- the date of creation (if created by the company) or the date of acquisition of the property (if the charge was existing on property acquired by the company);

- the amount secured by the charge;

- short particulars of the property charged;

- the persons entitled to the charge; and

- in the case of a floating charge, details of any provision of the charge and any instrument relating to it which *either* prohibit, restrict or regulate the company's power to grant further securities ranking in priority to, or *pari passu* with, the floating charge *or* regulate the order of ranking of the floating charge in relation to subsisting securities.

The Registrar must give a signed or authenticated certificate of registration of any charge so registered, stating the name of the company, the person first mentioned in the charge among those entitled to the benefit of the charge (or, in the case of a series of debentures, the name of the holder of the first such debenture to be issued) and the amount secured by the charge. Such a certificate is conclusive evidence that the registration requirements have been complied with.

[*Secs 417, 418*].

On receipt of a statutory declaration in the prescribed form verifying that, with respect to a registered charge,

- the debt for which the charge has been given has been paid or satisfied in whole or in part (Form 419a(Scot)), or

- part of the property charged has been released from the charge or has ceased to form part of the company's property (Form 419b(Scot))

the Registrar may enter a memorandum of satisfaction regarding that fact on the register. Where the Registrar enters a memorandum of satisfaction in whole, he must, if required, supply a copy of it to the company. Where the particulars submitted to the Registrar relate to a floating charge, the Registrar must not issue a memorandum unless *either* the creditor entitled to the benefit of the floating charge (or a person authorised to do so on his behalf) certifies the particulars submitted as correct *or* the court, on being satisfied that such certification cannot be obtained, directs him accordingly.

[*Sec 419*].

50.16 Charges by way of ex facie absolute disposition, etc.

In the case of a charge created by way of

- an *ex facie* absolute disposition or assignation qualified by a back letter or other agreement, or

- a standard security qualified by an agreement

compliance with 50.10 above does not of itself render the charge unavailable as security for indebtedness incurred after the date of compliance.

Where the amount secured by a charge so created is purported to be increased by a further back letter or agreement, a further charge is held to have been created by the *ex facie* absolute disposition or assignation or (as the case may be) by the standard security, as qualified by the further back letter or agreement. The provisions in 50.10 to 50.15 above apply to the further charge as if references to the charge were to the further charge and references to the date of creation of the charge were references to the date on which the further back letter or agreement was executed.

[*Sec 414*].

50.17 Oversea companies

The provisions in 50.10 to 50.16 above apply to charges on property in Scotland which are created, and to charges on such property which is acquired, by a company incorporated outside Great Britain which has a place of business in Scotland. [*Sec 424(2)*].

51 Resolutions

51.1 TYPES OF RESOLUTION

A resolution is an expression of intention or an agreement or decision by the members of a company. There are several types of resolution.

- **Ordinary resolutions.** An ordinary resolution is not defined by *CA 1985* but is the resolution used for all matters not requiring another type of resolution under *CA 1985* or the company's articles of association. It is passed by a simple majority at a general meeting.

- **Extraordinary resolutions** and **special resolutions**. Extraordinary resolutions are required for certain matters relating to winding up and the modification of class rights whereas special resolutions are required for important matters such as alterations to the memorandum and articles of association and change of name. See 51.2 below.

- **Elective resolutions** may only be used by private companies and for certain specific purposes. See 51.3 below.

- **Written resolutions** can also only be used by private companies and as a substitute for a resolution of the company in general meeting or a meeting of any class of members. See 51.4 below.

- **Class resolutions** are only used when a company wishes to pass a resolution which affects the members of one class of share. See 14 CLASS RIGHTS.

- **Directors' resolutions** are agreed by the board of directors and are normally concerned only with the day-to-day running of the company. Certain resolutions of directors do, however, have to be lodged with the Registrar of Companies. See 51.9 below.

See also 51.6 below for cases where the unanimous but informal agreement of members has been held to bind the company as an informal resolution.

51.2 Extraordinary and special resolutions

An **extraordinary resolution** is one which has been passed by a majority of not less than three-fourths of members entitled to vote who do so in person or, where proxies are allowed, by proxy, at a general meeting of which notice specifying the intention to propose the resolution as an extraordinary resolution has been duly given. [*Sec 378(1)*].

A **special resolution** is one which has been passed by such majority as is required for an extraordinary resolution at a general meeting of which not less than 21 days' notice, specifying the intention to propose the resolution has been given. [*Sec 378(2)*].

A special resolution may, however, be proposed and passed at a meeting of which less than 21 days' notice has been given if this is agreed to by a majority in number of the members having the right to attend and vote at the meeting who together

- hold at least 95% in nominal value of the relevant shares; or

- where the company has no share capital, represent at least 95% of the total voting rights at that meeting of all the members.

The members must also agree to the specific resolution being passed on short notice (*Pearce Duff & Co Ltd [1960] 3 All ER 222*).

A private company may, by elective resolution, substitute a lesser percentage for 95% (but not less than 90%). See 51.3 below.

[Sec 378(3)].

Passing of extraordinary or special resolutions. The extraordinary or special resolution must be set out in the notice of the meeting and only that resolution may be passed. No amendments of any substance must be made (*Re Moorgate Mercantile Holdings Ltd [1980] 1 All ER 40*).

At a meeting at which such a resolution is submitted to be passed, a declaration by the chairman that the resolution is carried is, unless a poll is demanded, conclusive evidence of that fact. Where a poll is held, reference is to be had to the number of votes cast for and against the resolution. For procedure at meetings generally, see 33 MEETINGS.

[Sec 378(4)(5)].

51.3   Elective resolutions of private companies

Despite any contrary provision in the articles, a private company may make a resolution in general meeting for any of the following purposes.

- *Sec 80A* (election as to duration of authority to allot shares, see 9.2 ALLOTMENT OF SHARES).

- *Sec 252* (election to dispense with laying of accounts and reports before general meeting, see 3.6 ACCOUNTS: GENERAL).

- *Sec 366A* (election to dispense with holding of annual general meeting, see 33.3 MEETINGS).

- *Secs 369(4)* and *378(3)* (election as to majority required to authorise short notice of meeting, see 33.5 MEETINGS and 51.2 above respectively).

- *Sec 386* (election to dispense with annual appointment of auditors, see 12.2 AUDITORS).

Such a resolution is referred to as an *'elective resolution'* and is not effective unless

- subject to below, at least 21 days' notice in writing is given of the meeting, stating that the elective resolution is to be proposed and stating the terms of the resolution; and

- the resolution is agreed to at the meeting, in person or in proxy, by all members entitled to attend and vote at the meeting.

Less than 21 days' notice may be given provided all members entitled to attend and vote at the meeting agree to the shorter notice.

Cessation of resolution. An elective resolution ceases to have effect if revoked by the passing of an ordinary resolution to that effect or if the company is re-registered as a public company.

[Sec 379A; CA 1989, s 116; SI 1996 No 1471].

51.4   Written resolutions of private companies

The following procedure may be used notwithstanding any provision in the company's memorandum or articles although it does not prejudice any power conferred by any such provision (see below under the heading *Articles*).

51.5   Resolutions

General. Subject to the exceptions below, anything which a private company can do by resolution (whether ordinary, special, extraordinary or elective) of

- the company in general meeting, or

- a meeting of any class of members

can be done (without a meeting and without previous notice being required) by a resolution in writing. The resolution must be signed by, or on behalf of, all members who, at the 'date of the resolution' would be entitled to attend and vote at such meetings. All signatures need not be on the same document provided each copy accurately states the terms of the resolution.

The '*date of the resolution*' means when it is signed by, or on behalf of, the last member to sign.

The date of passing of a resolution is the date of the resolution.

Exceptions. The above provisions do not apply to a resolution under *Sec 303* (removal of a director before the expiration of his period of office, see 19.11 DIRECTORS) or *Sec 391* (removal of an auditor before the expiration of his term of office, see 12.11 AUDITORS).

Rights of auditors. Where a director or secretary of a company knows that a written resolution under the above procedure is proposed, and knows its terms, he must ensure that a copy of the resolution (or details of its contents) is sent to any auditors at or before the time the resolution is supplied to a member for signature. The validity of the resolution is not, however, affected by this requirement.

In the event of default, the director or secretary concerned is liable to a fine of up to Level 3 on the standard scale (see 40.1 PENALTIES). In any such criminal proceedings, it is defence for the accused to prove that

- the circumstances were such that it was not practicable for him to comply; or

- he believed on reasonable grounds that a copy of the resolution had been sent to the auditors or they had otherwise been informed.

[*Secs 381A-381C, 15A Sch I, 24 Sch; CA 1989, ss 113, 114; SI 1996 No 1471*].

Articles. A company's articles commonly provide similar powers for a resolution to be passed by unanimous assent of members without a meeting. *SI 1985 No 805, Table A, Art 53* provides that a 'resolution in writing executed by or on behalf of each member who would have been entitled to vote upon it if it had been proposed at a general meeting at which he was present shall be as effectual as if it had been passed at a general meeting duly convened and held and may consist of several instruments in the like form each executed by or on behalf of one or more members'. Where this procedure is adopted, there is no requirement to notify the auditors of the resolution. Given, however, the potential penalties for failure to notify the auditors when the statutory procedure outlined above is adopted, it would be sensible to indicate in any resolution that it is the articles that are being relied upon (and not *Sec 381A*).

51.5   *Recording of written resolution*

Where a resolution is agreed to under the provisions in 51.4 above, the company must ensure that a record of the resolution (and of all the signatures) is entered in a book in the same way as minutes of proceedings of a general meeting of the company (see 33.15 MEETINGS). Any such record, purporting to be signed by a director or the company secretary, is evidence of agreement to the resolution and, until the contrary is proved, the necessary conditions are deemed to have been complied with.

If the company fails to comply with the above provisions, the company and every officer in default is liable to a fine up to the level in 40.1(*f*) PENALTIES.

See 33.15 MEETINGS under the heading *Inspection of minute book* which provisions apply to the right of inspection of the record of any resolution.

[*Sec 382A; CA 1989, s 113*].

51.6   Informal resolutions

Unless *CA 1985* provides otherwise (see, for example, *Sec 121(4)* where the power to alter share capital must be exercised by the company in general meeting) a number of decided cases have held that a company is bound in a matter *intra vires* by the unanimous but informal agreement of its members. See, for example, *Re Express Engineering Works Ltd [1920] 1 Ch 466.* This applies even if there is no actual meeting but only informal discussions (*Parker & Cooper Ltd v Reading [1926] Ch 975*). The agreement must, however, be unanimous; it is not sufficient that a majority sufficient to pass the appropriate resolution agrees to the proposal (*EBM Co Ltd v Dominion Bank [1937] 3 All ER 555*). See also *Re Duomatic Ltd [1969] 2 Ch 365* where it was held that where all shareholders who have a right to attend and *vote* at a general meeting of the company assent to some matter which a general meeting could carry into effect, that assent is as binding as a resolution in general meeting would be. However, in that particular case the Act (now *Sec 312*) also required disclosure of the proposed transaction to all members (including non-voting members) which was not done.

51.7   CIRCULATION OF MEMBERS' RESOLUTIONS

Members have a right, in the circumstances below, to requisition the company to circulate notice of a proposed resolution. Where they cannot rely on these provisions, members must themselves give notice to all other members of any proposed resolutions.

On written request by the 'specified number of members', a company must give notice of any resolution which may be properly moved, and is intended to be moved, at the next annual general meeting to all members entitled to notice of that meeting. It must also, where requested, circulate a statement of not more than 1,000 words on the proposed resolution, or business to be dealt with at the annual general meeting, to members entitled to have notice of any general meeting. The expense must be borne by the requisitioning members unless the company resolves otherwise. [*Sec 376(1)*].

The *'specified number of members'* is either

- any number representing not less than one-twentieth of the total voting rights of all members having the right to vote at the meeting at the date of requisition; or

- not less than 100 members holding shares on which an average of £100 per member has been paid up.

[*Sec 376(2)*].

The company is not bound by these provisions unless

(*a*)   a copy or copies of the requisition signed by all the requisitionists is deposited at the company's registered office

  - in the case of a requisition requiring notice of a resolution, at least six weeks before the meeting (except that if, after the date the copy is deposited, an annual general meeting is called for a date six weeks or less after the date of deposit, the copy is deemed properly deposited); and

  - in any other case at least one week before the meeting; and (*b*)   a sum reasonable to pay the company's expenses is deposited or tendered with the requisition.

[*Sec 377(1)(2)*].

The company is also not bound to circulate a statement if, on application to a court by the company or an aggrieved party, the court is satisfied that the rights conferred by these provisions are being abused to secure needless publicity for defamatory matter. The court may, in such a case, order the costs of the application to be paid by the requisitionists, even though they are not parties to the application. [*Sec 377(3)*].

Where the company is required to comply with these provisions, notice of the resolution must be given, and any statement circulated, to members entitled to notice of the meeting by serving a copy in any manner permitted for service of notice of the meeting. Notice of the general effect of the resolution must similarly be given to any other member. In either case this should be done at the same time as notice of the meeting or as soon as practicable thereafter. [*Sec 376(3)-(5)*].

Where notice has been given, the resolution is business which may be dealt with at an annual general meeting. This is so despite the fact that, accidentally, notice is not given to one or more members, even if the articles say otherwise. [*Sec 376(6)*].

Penalties. In the event of default in complying with the above provisions, every officer who is in default is liable to a fine up to the limit in 40.1(*d*) PENALTIES. [*Sec 376(7), 24 Sch*].

51.8   Resolutions requiring special notice

Certain resolutions require special notice. In these cases, the resolution is not effective unless notice of the intention to move it has been given to the company at least 28 days before the meeting (except that, if after the date of notice, a meeting is called for a date 28 days or less after the date of notice, the notice is deemed properly given).

The company must give its members notice of any such resolutions at the same time that it gives them notice of the meeting. If that is not practicable, it must give them notice, at least 21 days before the meeting, either by advertisement in an appropriate newspaper or in any other way allowed by the company's articles.

[*Sec 379*].

51.9   REGISTRATION OF RESOLUTION

A copy of all the following resolutions must be lodged with the Registrar of Companies for filing within 15 days of it being passed. They must either be printed or in a form approved by the Registrar.

- A special or extraordinary resolution (see 51.2 above).

- An elective resolution or a resolution revoking such a resolution (see 51.3 above).

- A resolution or agreement which, had it not been unanimously agreed to by the members, would not have been effective unless passed as a special or extraordinary resolution.

- A resolution or agreement which, had it not been unanimously agreed to by the members of a certain class, would not have been effective unless passed by some particular majority or otherwise in a particular manner, and all resolutions which bind all members of any class though not agreed to by all those members.

- A resolution of the directors to change the company's name following a direction of the Secretary of State under *Sec 31(2)* (see 29.4 GUARANTEE COMPANIES).

- A resolution to give, vary, revoke or renew the directors' authority in connection with allotment of shares (see 9.2 ALLOTMENT OF SHARES).

- A resolution of the directors under *Sec 147(2)* altering the company's memorandum on ceasing to be a public company following the acquisition of its own shares (see 58.27 SHARES AND SHARE CAPITAL).

- A resolution conferring, varying, revoking or renewing authority under *Sec 166* regarding market purchase of own shares (see 8.6 ACQUISITION OF OWN SHARES).

- A resolution for voluntary winding up.

- A resolution of the directors of an old public company to re-register as a public company (see 49.14 REGISTRATION AND RE-REGISTRATION).

If the company fails to comply with these provisions, the company and every officer (including any liquidator) in default is liable to a fine up to the level in 40.1(*f*) PENALTIES.

[*Sec 380(1)(4)-(6)*].

Form of resolution for submission to the Registrar of Companies.

Number of company [   ]

THE COMPANIES ACT 1985
COMPANY LIMITED BY SHARES
ORDINARY/SPECIAL/EXTRAORDINARY/ELECTIVE[1]
RESOLUTION
OF

[   ] LIMITED/PUBLIC COMPANY LIMITED[1]

Passed [insert date]

At an [extraordinary][1] general meeting of the above company, duly convened and held at [insert address] on [insert date] at [insert time] the following resolution was passed as an ordinary/special/extraordinary/elective[1] resolution.

RESOLUTION
[Insert text of resolution]

. . . .
Chairman

[1] Delete as appropriate.

Copies to members. Where articles have been registered, a copy of each of the above resolutions must be embodied in or annexed to each copy of the company's articles issued after the passing of the resolution. Where articles have not been registered, a printed copy of every such resolution must be sent to any member on request on payment of 5 pence or such lesser sum as the company directs. If the company fails to comply with these provisions, the company and every officer (including any liquidator) in default is liable to a fine up to the level in 40.1(*f*) PENALTIES for each occasion on which copies are issued or, as the case may be, requested. [*Sec 380(2)(3)(6)(7)*].

51.10   Resolutions

Listed companies must also send copies of all resolutions passed (other than routine business at AGM) to The Stock Exchange (see 43.10(*g*) PUBLIC AND LISTED COMPANIES).

51.10 RESOLUTIONS PASSED AT ADJOURNED MEETINGS

A resolution passed at an adjourned meeting is treated as having been passed on the date on which it was in fact passed and not any earlier date. This applies to resolutions passed at an adjourned meeting of the company, of the holders of any class of shares or of the directors. [*See 381*].

51.11 RECORDING OF DECISIONS BY A SOLE MEMBER NOT TAKEN BY WRITTEN RESOLUTION

Where a private company limited by shares or guarantee has only one member and he takes any decision which may be taken by the company in general meeting, he must (unless that decision is taken by way of a written resolution) provide the company with a written record of that decision.

In default, the member is liable, on summary conviction to a fine of up to level 2 on the standard scale (see 40.1 PENALTIES).

Failure to comply with the above provisions does not affect the validity of the decision.

[*Sec 382B, 24 Sch; SI 1992 No 1699*].

52   Rights Issues

52.1   In order to raise new capital, a company may make a rights issue to existing members or debenture-holders by which they are given the right to subscribe for new securities in a fixed proportion to their existing holdings. The price at which the new securities are offered is normally below the market price. It should be noted that under *Secs 89-96* there are pre-emption provisions restricting the allotment of shares to persons other than existing members of the company (see 9.5 to 9.10 ALLOTMENT OF SHARES).

52.2   **PROCEDURE FOR MAKING RIGHTS ISSUES**

The directors must

- ensure that the company has authority under *Sec 80* to issue the securities (see 9.2 ALLOTMENT OF SHARES); and

- confirm they have the required authorised capital to make the issue.

If necessary, a general meeting of the company should be called to increase the authorised share capital or to authorise the directors to issue shares.

In the case of a private company, the procedure is relatively straightforward, an issue being made to existing members in accordance with the articles of association and the securities normally being paid for in cash at that time.

Listed companies. There are additional requirements for listed companies in *FSA 1986, ss 142-157* (see 42.2 to 42.18 PROSPECTUSES AND PUBLIC ISSUES). Such companies also have continuing obligations to The Stock Exchange. See 43.5 *et seq.* PUBLIC AND LISTED COMPANIES and in particular 43.7(*c*) and 43.9(*b*).

A rights offer is made by a renounceable letter (or other negotiable document) which may be traded (as 'nil paid' rights) for a period before payment for the securities is due. The offer must remain open for acceptance for at least 21 days.

A rights issue circular must contain a table of market values of the security in question for the first dealing day in each of the six months before the date of the circular, for the last dealing day before the announcement of the rights and (if different) the latest practicable date prior to despatch of the circular.

If the existing holders do not take up their rights to subscribe in a rights issue

- the securities to which the offer relates must be offered for subscription or purchase in terms that any premium obtained over the subscription price (net of expenses) is to be for the account of such holders, save that if the proceeds for an existing holder do not exceed £3, the proceeds may be retained for the company's benefit;

- the securities may be allotted or sold to underwriters, if on the expiry of the subscription period no premium (net of expenses) has been obtained; and

- no excess applications are permitted without the prior permission of the Exchange. A director of the issuing company will not normally be allowed to subscribe for or purchase excess securities unless they are first offered to other existing holders on the same terms.

The Company Announcement Office must be notified, without delay, of the issue price and principal terms of the issue; the results of the issue; details of the sale (including date and price per share) if any rights not taken up are sold; and the number and amount of any securities issued pursuant to any excess applications.

(*The Listing Rules, Chapter 4.16-4.21*).

53 Scotland

Cross-references. See 5.18 ACCOUNTS: INDIVIDUAL COMPANIES for Scots tenure; 17.13 DEBENTURES AND OTHER BORROWING for debentures to bearer; 32.2 LEGAL PROCEEDINGS for summary proceedings in Scotland; 32.6 LEGAL PROCEEDINGS for service of documents on a company registered in Scotland carrying on a business in England and Wales; 48.1 REGISTRAR OF COMPANIES for Companies Registration Office in Scotland; 57.14 SHARE TRANSFERS ETC. for offences in connection with share warrants.

53.1 The *Companies Acts* apply in Scotland as they do in England and Wales but subject to certain variations and modifications to allow for the different legal system applying there. Apart from the cross-references above, the main provisions which specifically refer to Scotland are as follows.

- REGISTRATION OF CHARGES (50).

- Floating charges (see 53.2 to 53.5 below).

- Charitable companies (see 53.6 and 53.7 below).

- Execution of documents (see 16.8 DEALINGS WITH THIRD PARTIES).

- References in *CA 1985* to an office copy of a court order are to be construed, as respects Scotland, as references to a certified copy interlocutor.

[*Sec 743A; CA 1989, 19 Sch 19*].

53.2 FLOATING CHARGES

Under the law of Scotland, an incorporated company (whether within the meaning of *CA 1985* or not) may, for the purpose of securing any debt or other obligation incurred or binding upon the company or any other person, create in favour of the creditor a floating charge over all or any part of its property (including uncalled capital) or undertaking.

Subject to the provisions of *CA 1985*, a floating charge in relation to any heritable property in Scotland has effect in accordance with these provisions and *IA 1986, Part III* notwithstanding that the instrument creating it is not recorded in the Register of Sasines or, as appropriate, registered in accordance with the *Land Registration (Scotland) Act 1979*.

[*Sec 462; IA 1986, 13 Sch Part I; CA 1989, 17 Sch 8; Law Reform (Miscellaneous Provisions) Scotland Act 1990, 8 Sch 33*].

Any floating charge which purported to subsist as a floating charge before 17 November 1972 and which, if created on or after that date, would have been validly created under *Companies (Floating Charges and Receivers)(Scotland) Act 1972* is deemed to have subsisted as a valid floating charge from the day of its creation. [*Sec 465(1)*].

53.3 Effect of floating charge on winding up

Where a company goes into liquidation, a floating charge created by the company attaches to the relevant property or undertaking but subject to the rights of any person who

- has executed diligence on the property (or part); or

- holds a fixed security or another floating charge over the property (or part) ranking in priority to that floating charge.

Subject to the above, the provisions of *IA 1986, Part IV* (except *section 185*) apply in relation to the floating charge as if it were a fixed security over the property to which it has attached in respect of

- the principal amount of the debt or obligation; and

- any interest which accrues thereon until payment of the sum due under the charge.

[*Secs 463, 486; IA 1986, 12 Sch, 13 Sch Part I; CA 1989, s 140(1)*].

53.4   Priority of floating charge

The order of ranking of floating charges and fixed securities is as follows.

(*a*)   Where all or part of a company's property is subject to a floating charge *and* a fixed security arising by operation of the law, the fixed security has priority.

(*b*)   Subject to (*a*) above the instrument creating a floating charge over all or any part of the company's property may

    (i)   determine the order of ranking by prohibiting or restricting the creation, after the date of the instrument, of a fixed security or other floating charge having priority over it or ranking *pari passu* with it (and, with effect from 3 July 1995, such a provision is effective to confer priority); or

    (ii)   determine the order in which the floating charge is to rank over the same property (or part) with any other subsisting or future floating charges or fixed securities. The consent is required of the holders of any subsisting floating charge or fixed security which would be adversely affected.

(*c*)   Subject to (*a*) and (*b*) above

    (i)   a fixed security, the right to which has been constituted as a real right before a floating charge has attached to all or any part of the company's property, has priority over a floating charge;

    (ii)   floating charges rank with one another according to the time of registration (see 50 REGISTRATION OF CHARGES); and

    (iii)   floating charges received by the Registrar of Companies for registration by the same postal delivery rank equally with one another.

Where the holder of a floating charge within (ii) or (iii) above has received notice in writing of the subsequent registration of another floating charge over the same property (or part), the preference in ranking of the first-mentioned floating charge is restricted to security for

- the holder's present advances;

- any further advances he is required to make under the instrument creating the floating charge or any ancillary document;

- interest due or becoming due on all such advances;

- expenses, etc. reasonably incurred; and

- in the case of a floating charge to secure a contingent liability (other than a liability arising under any further advances made from time to time), the maximum sum to which that contingent liability is capable of amounting whether or not it is contractually limited.

[*Secs 464, 486; IA 1986, 13 Sch Part I; CA 1989, s 140; SI 1995 No 1352*].

For the above purposes, any provision relating to ranking of charges contained in an instrument creating a floating charge (or any ancillary document) executed prior to 17 November 1972 and which, if made on or after that date would have been a valid provision under *Companies (Floating Charges and Receivers) (Scotland) Act 1972* is deemed to have been a valid provision from the date of its making. [*Sec 465(2)*].

53.5 Alteration of a floating charge

The instrument creating a floating charge (or any ancillary document) may be altered by the execution of an instrument of alteration by the company, the holder of the charge and the holder of any other charge (including a fixed security) which would be adversely affected by the alteration.

Without prejudice to any enactment or rule of law regarding the execution of documents, such an instrument of alteration is validly executed if it is executed

(*a*) where trustees for debenture-holders are acting in accordance with a trust deed, by those trustees; or

(*b*) where, in the case of a series of debentures, no such trustees are acting, by or on behalf of

- a majority in nominal value of those present (or represented by proxy) and voting at a meeting of debenture-holders at which holders of at least one-third in nominal value of the outstanding debentures of the series are present (or so represented); or

- where no such meeting is held, the holders of at least one-half in nominal value of the outstanding debentures of the series.

The provisions of 53.4 above apply to the instrument of alteration as they apply to the instrument creating a floating charge.

[*Secs 466, 486; CA 1989, s 140, 17 Sch 9*].

The provisions of *Sec 410(2)(3)* and *Sec 420* (see 50.10 and 50.14 REGISTRATION OF CHARGES respectively) apply to an instrument of alteration which

- prohibits or restricts the creation of any fixed security or any other floating charge having priority over, or ranking *pari passu* with, the floating charge, or

- varies, or otherwise regulates, the ranking of the floating charge in relation to fixed securities or to other floating charges, or

- releases property from a floating charge, or

- increases the amount secured by a floating charge

as if for references to 'a charge' and 'the creation of a charge' there were substituted references to 'an alteration to a floating charge' and 'the execution of an alteration to a floating charge'.

[*Sec 466(4)(5)*].

53.6 CHARITABLE COMPANIES

In Scotland, where a charity is a company or other body corporate having power to alter the instruments establishing or regulating it, no exercise of that power which has the effect of the body ceasing to be a charity is valid so as to affect the application of

(*a*) any property acquired by virtue of any transfer, contract or obligation previously effected otherwise than for full consideration in money or money's worth;

(*b*) any property representing property acquired under (*a*);

(*c*)   any property representing income which has accrued before the alteration is made; or

(*d*)   the income from any property in (*a*) to (*c*) above.

[*CA 1989, s 112(1)(2)*].

See also 16.3 DEALINGS WITH THIRD PARTIES for the restriction on the provisions of *Sec 35* (company's capacity not limited by its memorandum) and *Sec 35A* (power of directors to bind the company) in relation to such a charitable company.

53.7   **Name of company not including 'charity' etc.**

Where a company is a charity and its name does not include the word 'charity' or 'charitable', the fact that the company is a charity must be stated in English in legible characters in all

(*a*)   business letters;

(*b*)   notices and other official publications;

(*c*)   bills of exchange, promissory notes, endorsements, cheques and orders for money or goods purporting to be signed by or on behalf of the company;

(*d*)   documents for the creation, transfer, variation or extinction of an interest in land purporting to be executed by the company; and

(*e*)   bills of parcels, invoices, receipts and letters of credit.

If a company fails to comply with these provisions it is liable to a fine up to the level in 40.1(*g*) PENALTIES. An officer or a person acting on behalf of the company is liable to a similar fine if he

(i)   issues, or authorises the issue of, any document within (*a*), (*b*) or (*e*) above, or

(ii)   signs, or authorises the signing of, any document within (*c*) above

and, in breach of (ii) above is additionally personally liable to the holder of the bill of exchange etc. unless it is duly paid by the company.

[*CA 1989, s 112(6)-(8)*].

54 Seals

54.1 COMMON SEAL

A company which has a common seal must have its name engraved on it in legible characters otherwise it is liable to a fine up to the level in 40.1(g) PENALTIES. Any officer of the company, or person acting on its behalf, who uses, or authorises the use of, any seal purporting to be a company seal and on which the company's name is not engraved is liable to a similar penalty. [*Sec 350; CA 1989, 17 Sch 7*].

54.2 OFFICIAL SEAL FOR USE ABROAD

A company which has a common seal and which carries on business abroad may, if authorised by the articles, have an official seal for use in any territory, district or place outside the UK. It must be a facsimile of the common seal with the addition on its face of the name of every territory etc. where it is to be used. In England and Wales, when duly affixed to a document, it has the same effect as the company's common seal.

A company which has such a seal may, by writing under its common seal (or, in Scotland, by writing subscribed in accordance with the *Requirements of Writing (Scotland) Act 1995*), authorise any appointed agent in that territory etc. to affix the official seal to any deed or other document which the company is party to there. As between the company and a person dealing with such an agent, the agent's authority continues during the period mentioned in the instrument conferring the authority or, if no period is mentioned, until notice of the revocation or determination of the agent's authority has been given to the person dealing with him.

The person affixing the official seal on a deed or other instrument must certify in writing on the deed or instrument the date on which, and the place at which, it is affixed.

[*Sec 39; CA 1989, 17 Sch 2; Law Reform (Miscellaneous Provisions) Scotland Act 1990, 8 Sch 33; Requirements of Writing (Scotland) Act 1995, 4 Sch 53*].

54.3 OFFICIAL SEAL FOR SHARE CERTIFICATES ETC.

A company which has a common seal may have an official seal for sealing securities issued by the company and for sealing documents creating or evidencing securities so issued. It must be a facsimile of its common seal with the addition on its face of the word 'Securities'. When duly affixed to a document, it has the same effect as the company's common seal. [*Sec 40; CA 1989, 17 Sch 3*].

Where a company incorporated before 12 February 1979 has such a seal, it may so use it despite anything in any instrument constituting or regulating the company or in any instrument made before that date which relates to any securities issued by the company. Any provision of any such instrument which requires the securities etc. to be signed does not apply if they are sealed with the seal. [*CC(CP)A 1985, s 11*].

The foregoing provisions are without prejudice to the right of a company to subscribe such securities and documents in accordance with the *Requirements of Writing (Scotland) Act 1995*. [*Requirement of Writing (Scotland) Act 1995, 4 Sch 55, 57*].

54.4 AUTHORITY TO USE SEAL

Where *Table A, Art 101* in *SI 1985 No 805* has been adopted, a seal can only be used on the authority of the directors or a committee of directors authorised by the directors. The directors may determine who is to sign any instrument to which the seal is affixed; in default it must be signed by a director and by the secretary or another director.

55   Secretary

55.1   GENERAL

Every company must have a secretary. [*Sec 283(1)*]. The secretary cannot be

- the sole director of the company; or

- a corporation the sole director of which is the sole director of the company.

[*Sec 283(2)(4)(a)*].

Note also that the company secretary, or a person who is his partner or employee, cannot be the auditor of the company. [*CA 1989, s 27*]. From this it follows that the existing auditor (or a partner or employee of such a person) cannot be appointed company secretary.

If the office of secretary is vacant or if there is no secretary capable of acting, anything required to be done by or to the secretary may be done by or to any assistant or deputy secretary, or failing that by or to any officer of the company authorised by the directors. [*Sec 283(3)*].

Acts done in a dual capacity. A provision requiring or authorising a thing to be done by or to a director *and* the secretary is not satisfied by its being done by or to the same person in the dual capacity as director and as, or in place of, the secretary. [*Sec 284*].

55.2   QUALIFICATIONS FOR SECRETARIES OF PUBLIC COMPANY

The directors of a public company must take reasonable steps to secure that the secretary (or each joint secretary) is a person who appears to them to have the requisite knowledge and experience to discharge his functions as secretary and who

(*a*)   on 22 December 1980 was secretary, or assistant or deputy secretary, of the company; or

(*b*)   for at least three of the five years preceding his appointment as secretary held a similar appointment at another non-private company; or

(*c*)   is a member of

- the Institute of Chartered Accountants in England and Wales;

- the Institute of Chartered Accountants of Scotland;

- the Chartered Association of Certified Accountants;

- the Institute of Chartered Accountants in Ireland;

- the Institute of Chartered Secretaries and Administrators;

- the Institute of Cost and Management Accountants (now the Chartered Institute of Management Accountants); or

- the Chartered Institute of Public Finance and Accountancy;

(*d*)   is a barrister, advocate or solicitor called or admitted in any part of the UK; or

(*e*)   is a person who appears to the directors to be capable of discharging the functions of secretary because of some other position held or membership.

[*Sec 286*].

55.3 APPOINTMENT AND REMOVAL

Particulars of the first secretary (or joint secretaries) of a company must be given in the prescribed form (Form 10) which accompanies the memorandum of association on registration (see 49.1(*c*) REGISTRATION AND RE-REGISTRATION). On registration, the person or persons so named are deemed to be appointed. [*Sec 13(5)*].

Appointment of subsequent secretaries is regulated by the articles. Where *Table A, Art 99* in *SI 1985 No 805* is adopted, a secretary is appointed by the directors for such term, at such remuneration, and upon such conditions as they think fit; and any secretary so appointed may be removed by them. There is a similar provision in *CA 1948, Table A, Art 110*.

Examples of board resolutions

'It was resolved that . . . be and hereby is appointed secretary of the company in the place of . . . who resigned on . . . '

'It was resolved that . . . be and hereby is removed as secretary of the company with immediate effect.'

Details of the first secretary and all subsequent changes must be recorded in the register of directors and secretaries. See 47.3 REGISTERS.

55.4 Notification of changes to Companies House

The appointment of a new secretary must be notified to the Registrar of Companies on the prescribed form (Form 288) within 14 days. A consent to act, signed by the new secretary, must be on the form.

In default, the company and every officer in default is liable to a fine up to the level in 40.1(*e*) PENALTIES. [*Sec 288(2)(4), 24 Sch; SI 1990 No 1766*].

55.5 LIABILITY OF SECRETARY

An '*officer*' in relation to a company includes a director, manager or secretary. [*Sec 744*]. A secretary is, therefore, potentially liable for any of the penalties and fines imposed under *CA 1985* for default by officers. Penalties are dealt with in the appropriate part of the text but see also 32.4 LEGAL PROCEEDINGS for liability of secretary where a body corporate is guilty of certain offences; 19.41 to 19.45 and 19.48 DIRECTORS for liabilities which also apply to the secretary; 19.50 DIRECTORS for provisions indemnifying officers from liability; and 32.7 LEGAL PROCEEDINGS for the power of a court to grant relief to an officer who has acted honestly and reasonably.

The secretary will not, however, normally be liable for breach of trust or misfeasance by the directors, even if this is committed with his knowledge (*Joint Stock Discount Co v Brown (1869) LR 8 Eq 376*).

55.6 POWERS OF SECRETARY

A company secretary has been held to be a mere servant whose position is to do what he is told and that he has no authority to represent anything at all (*Barnett, Hoares & Co v South London Tramways Co (1887) 18 QBD 815*). But a modern company secretary is a much more important person. He is an officer of the company with extensive duties and responsibilities. He regularly makes representations on behalf of the board and enters into contracts on its behalf which come within the day-to-day running of the company's business. Signing contracts connected with the administrative side of the company's affairs therefore comes within his ostensible authority (*Panorama Developments (Guildford) Ltd v Fidelis Furnishing Fabrics Ltd [1971] 2 QB 711*).

55.7   DUTIES OF SECRETARY

CA 1985 does not impose any specific duties on a company secretary but the common functions which are usually undertaken by the secretary include

- keeping the company's register up-to-date (see 47 REGISTERS);

- ensuring all the statutory forms etc. which must be filed at Companies House are prepared and delivered within the appropriate time limit;

- giving notice of general meetings to members;

- distributing the accounts to members and supplying a copy of the accounts to any member on demand;

- issuing share and debenture certificates;

- preparation and keeping of minutes for board meetings and general meetings;

- paying dividends;

- keeping the memorandum and articles of association up-to-date; and

- the custody and use of any common seal.

56 Share Premium

56.1 TRANSFERS TO, AND APPLICATIONS OF, SHARE PREMIUM ACCOUNT

A company issues shares at a premium if the consideration which it receives for them exceeds in value the nominal amount of the shares issued.

Subject to 56.2 to 56.5 below, where a company issues shares at a premium, for cash or otherwise, a sum equal to the aggregate amount or value of the premiums on those shares must be transferred to an account called the 'share premium account'. See *Henry Head & Co Ltd v Ropner Holdings Ltd [1952] Ch 124* for a consideration of the words 'or otherwise' and also Viscount Simon's opinion in *Gold Coast Selection Trust Ltd v Humphrey [1948] AC 459* where an asset is difficult to value.

The share premium account may be applied by the company in

- paying up unissued shares to be allotted to members as fully paid bonus shares;
- writing off preliminary expenses;
- writing off the expenses of, or the commission paid or discount allowed on, any issue of shares or debentures; or
- providing for the premium payable on redemption of debentures.

Subject to this, the provisions of *CA 1985* relating to the reduction of a company's share capital apply as if the share premium account was part of its paid up share capital. The fact that the share premiums credited to the account arise under the same transaction as that of the reduction does not prevent the court from approving it. See *Re Ratners Group plc [1988] 4 BCC 293*; *Re European Home Products [1988] BCLC 690*; *Re Thorn EMI [1989] BCLC 612*. See also 58.17 SHARES AND SHARE CAPITAL for the reduction of share capital.

[*Sec 130*].

Regulations may be made by statutory instrument for

- relieving companies from the above requirements in relation to premiums other than cash premiums; or
- restricting or modifying any relief from those requirements as provided by 56.2 to 56.5 below.

[*Sec 134*].

56.2 RELIEF IN CERTAIN MERGER SITUATIONS

The provisions of 56.1 above do not apply to the premiums on any equity shares allotted after 3 February 1981 in pursuance of an 'arrangement' in consideration for

- the issue or transfer to the issuing company of equity shares in the other company, or
- the cancellation of any such shares not held by the issuing company

where the issuing company has secured at least a 90% equity holding in the other company (whether under the arrangement or not) and the issue does not fall within 56.3 below.

Where the equity share capital of the company being acquired is divided into different classes the requirements must be satisfied in relation to each of those classes.

Shares held by a company which is

- the issuing company's holding or subsidiary company, or

- a subsidiary of the issuing company's holding company, or

- the nominee of such a company

are regarded as held by the issuing company.

Relief is also available where the issuing company is obtaining the issue, transfer or cancellation of non-equity shares in addition to the equity shares.

See 18.1 DEFINITIONS for shares comprised in a company's equity share capital.

'Arrangement' means any agreement, scheme or arrangement (including an arrangement sanctioned under *Sec 425* (company compromise with members and creditors, see 44.1 RECONSTRUCTIONS AND MERGERS) or *IA 1986, s 110* (liquidator accepting shares etc. as consideration for sale of company property)).

[*Sec 131; IA 1986, 13 Sch Part I; CA 1989, 19 Sch 1*].

The amount which would otherwise be included in the share premium account may also be disregarded in determining the amount at which any shares, or other consideration provided for the shares issued, is to be included in the company's balance sheet. [*Sec 133(1)*].

See also 56.6 below.

56.3   RELIEF IN RESPECT OF GROUP RECONSTRUCTIONS

Where the issuing company

- is a wholly-owned subsidiary of another company (the 'holding company'), and

- after 20 December 1984 issues shares at a premium to the holding company, or to another wholly-owned subsidiary of the holding company, in consideration for the transfer to the issuing company of non-cash assets, which are assets of any company (the 'transferor company') which is a member of the group of companies made up of the holding company and all its wholly-owned subsidiaries

it is not required by the provisions in 56.1 above to transfer an amount in excess of the 'minimum premium value' to the share premium account.

'Minimum premium value' is given by the formula

$(A - L) - N$

where

A =   the base value of the assets transferred, i.e. the lesser of

- the cost of those assets to the transferor company; and

- the amount at which those assets are stated in the transferor company's accounting records immediately before the transfer.

L =   the base value of the liabilities of the transferor company assumed by the issuing company, i.e. the amount at which they are stated in the transferor company's accounting records immediately before the transfer.

N =   the aggregate nominal value of the shares issued.

[*Sec 132(1)-(6)(8)*].

56.4 Share Premium

The amount which would otherwise be included in the share premium account may also be disregarded in determining the amount at which any shares acquired is to be included in the company's balance sheet. [*Sec 133(1)*].

See also 56.6 below.

56.4 Shares issued after 3 February 1981 and before 21 December 1984

Similar provisions as in 56.3 above applied under *CA 1981, s 38* (see now *25 Sch*) except that relief was restricted to shares issued in consideration for the transfer of shares in another subsidiary (whether wholly-owned or not) of the holding company (rather than the transfer of any non-cash assets of the group member). In calculating the minimum premium value, therefore, 'shares' should be substituted for 'assets' in A and L is ignored. [*Sec 132(7), 25 Sch*]. For these purposes 'subsidiary' has the meaning given by *Sec 736* as originally enacted (see 18.1 DEFINITIONS). [*CA 1989, 18 Sch 38*].

See also 56.6 below.

56.5 Shares issued before 4 February 1981

Where a company issued shares at a premium before 4 February 1981 and

- the shares were allotted as part of an 'arrangement' (see 56.2 above), and

- the consideration for the shares allotted was provided by the issue or transfer to the issuing company of shares in another company or by the cancellation of any shares in that other company not held by the issuing company, and

- the other company was at the time of the arrangement, or as a result of it, a subsidiary of the issuing company or its holding company

any part of the premiums on the shares so issued which was not transferred to a share premium account (under *CA 1948, s 56*) is to be treated as if that section had never applied to those premiums and may be disregarded in determining

- the sum to be included in the company's share premium account; and

- the amount at which any shares acquired are to be included in the company's balance sheet.

[*Sec 133(1); CC(CP)A 1985, s 12*].

See also 56.6 below.

56.6 SUPPLEMENTARY PROVISIONS

For the purposes of 56.2 to 56.5 above

- references to

    (i) the acquisition by a company of shares in another company, and

    (ii) the issue or allotment of shares to, or the transfer of shares to or by, a company

    include (respectively) the acquisition of any of those shares by, and the issue, allotment or transfer of any of those shares to or by, nominees of that company;

- references to the transfer of shares in a company include the transfer of a right to be included in the company's register of members in respect of those shares; and

- 'company', except in references to the issuing company, includes any body corporate.

[*Sec 133(2)-(4)*].

57   Share Transfers Etc.

Cross-references. See 9 ALLOTMENT OF SHARES; 43.11(*f*) PUBLIC AND LISTED COMPANIES for requirements of listed companies under the *Listing Rules*; 58 SHARES AND SHARE CAPITAL.

The contents of this chapter are as follows.

57.1   INTRODUCTION

A company's shares are personal estate (or, in Scotland, moveable property) and can be transferred in the manner provided by the company's articles, but subject to the *Stock Transfer Act 1963* (see 57.3 below). [*Sec 182(1)*].

This chapter deals with both the transfer of shares and their transmission by operation of law (see 57.15 below).

57.2   PROCEDURE ON TRANSFER

The procedure for transferring shares is outlined in 57.3 to 57.7 below. Special provisions apply in relation to Stock Exchange transactions. These are outlined in 57.16 below.

57.3   Stock Transfer Act 1963

STA 1963 provides a simplified procedure for the transfer of fully paid-up 'registered securities' of any description, being

(*a*)   securities issued by any company within the meaning of *CA 1985* except a company limited by guarantee or an unlimited company;

(*b*)   securities issued by any other body incorporated in Great Britain by or under any enactment or by Royal Charter, except a building society or industrial and provident society;

(*c*)   UK Government securities, except stock or bonds in the National Savings Stock Register and national savings certificates;

(*d*)   local authority securities; and

(*e*)   units of an authorised unit trust scheme or a recognised scheme within the meaning of *FSA 1986*.

[*STA 1963, s 1(4)*].

'*Registered securities*' means transferable securities the holders of which are entered in a register, whether or not maintained in Great Britain.

'*Securities*' means shares, stock, debentures, debenture stock, loan stock, bonds, units of a collective investment scheme within the meaning of *FSA 1986*, and other securities of any description.

[*STA 1963, s 4(1)*].

Registered securities within (*a*) to (*d*) above may be transferred by means of an instrument in the form set out in *STA 1963, 1 Sch* (a stock transfer), executed by the transferor only and specifying

- the full name and address of the transferee;

- the consideration;

- the description and number or amount of the securities; and

- the transferor.

The form need not be attested. [*STA 1963, s 1(1)(2)*].

Nothing in the above provisions affects the validity of what would otherwise be a valid instrument of transfer. [*STA 1963, s 1(3)*]. Where, for example, *Table A, Art 23* of *SI 1985 No 805* has been adopted, the instrument of transfer of a share may be in any usual form or any other form approved by the directors, and is to be executed by or on behalf of the transferor and, if the share is not fully paid, by or on behalf of the transferee.

Note that *STA 1963* does not apply to transfers of partly paid shares. Where such shares are being transferred, the instrument of transfer will require execution by the transferee and attestation. This is because the liability to pay up the sum outstanding on the shares is being transferred from the transferor to the transferee.

For the provisions of *STA 1963* applicable to Stock Exchange transfers, see 57.16 below.

57.4 Effecting the transfer – disposal of entire holding to one transferee

In such circumstances, the transferor executes a 'proper instrument of transfer' (normally a stock transfer form – see 57.3 above) in favour of the transferee, which he hands to the transferee, together with the share certificate(s), in exchange for the agreed consideration. The transferee then pays the necessary stamp duty on the transfer (currently one half of one per cent calculated on the consideration) and delivers the transfer duly stamped, together with the share certificate(s), to the company for registration. If the company's directors approve the transfer (see 57.7 below), the transferee's name will be entered in the register of members, the previous share certificate will be cancelled, and a new certificate issued to the transferee.

57.5 Effecting the transfer – other transfers

A different procedure to that outlined in 57.4 above must be adopted where the transferor is selling only part of his holding to a particular transferee (because he is either retaining the remainder or selling it to a different transferee).

Where part only of the holding is being sold to one transferee, the transferor executes the form of transfer and hands it, together with the share certificate, to the company rather than the transferee. The form of transfer is then certificated by the company secretary, i.e. it is endorsed with the words 'certificate lodged' or similar words. [*Sec 184(3)(a)*]. The company secretary returns the certificated transfer to the transferor, but retains the share certificate. The transferor then hands the certified transfer form to the transferee, in exchange for the agreed consideration. The transferee pays the necessary stamp duty on the transfer (currently one half of one per cent calculated on the consideration) and delivers the stamped transfer to the company for registration. If the company's directors approve the transfer (see 57.7 below), new share certificates are issued to the transferor (for the balance retained) and transferee (for the shares acquired) and the transferee's name is also entered in the register of members.

Where shares are being sold to more than one transferee, a similar procedure applies but the transferor executes a separate form of transfer for each transferee.

57.6 Share Transfers Etc.

57.6 *Certification by the company*

The certification by a company of an instrument of transfer in relation to any of its shares or debentures is to be taken as a representation by the company, to any person acting on the faith of the certification, that documents have been produced to the company showing a *prima facie* title to the shares or debentures in the transferor. However, the certification is not to be taken as a representation that the transferor has any title. [*Sec 184(1)*].

A certification of an instrument of transfer is deemed to be made by a company if

(*a*)   the person issuing it is authorised to issue such a document on the company's behalf; and

(*b*)   the certification is signed by a person authorised to certificate transfers on the company's behalf, or by an officer or servant of the company or of a body corporate so authorised. A certification is deemed signed by a person if

    (i)   it purports to be authenticated by his signature or initials (whether hand-written or not); and

    (ii)   it is not shown that the signature etc. was placed there by a person other than himself or someone authorised to use his signature etc. for the purpose of certificating transfers on the company's behalf.

[*Sec 184(3)(b)(c)*].

A company is under the same liability to a person who acts on the faith of a false certification made negligently by the company as if the certification had been made fraudulently. [*Sec 184(2)*].

Where a company erroneously returned a share certificate to the transferor together with the certificated transfer, and the transferor purported to execute a second 'transfer' in favour of a third party, it was held that the company's duty in relation to the share certificate was owed only to the original transferees, and not to the third party (*Longman v Bath Electric Tramways [1905] 1 Ch 646*).

57.7   Registration of transfer

A company must not register a transfer of its shares or debentures unless a 'proper instrument of transfer' has been delivered to it, or the transfer is an exempt transfer within *STA 1982* (see 57.16 below). This applies notwithstanding anything in the company's articles. [*Sec 183(1)*]. This does not, however, prejudice any power of the company to register as a shareholder or debenture-holder a person to whom the right to any shares or debentures has been transferred by operation of the law. [*Sec 183(2)*]. See 57.15 below. A conventional stock transfer form is a '*proper instrument of transfer*' even if it does not state the consideration money and is not stamped. The defects in the form are mere irregularities and the registration of the transfer is not invalid (*Nisbet v Shepherd [1994] BCC 91*).

If a company refuses to register a transfer of shares or debentures, the company must, within two months after the date on which the transfer was lodged with it, send notice of refusal to the transferee. In default, the company and every officer in default is liable to a fine up to the level in 40.1(*f*) PENALTIES. [*Sec 183(5)(6), 24 Sch*]. In addition, failure to notify within the time limit means that the power of refusal is lost and the court may grant an application for rectification of the register under *Sec 359*, see 47.4 REGISTERS (*Re Inverdeck Ltd, [1998] BCC 256*).

The following provisions apply where a company has adopted the relevant article in *SI 1985 No 805, Table A*.

- The registration of transfers of shares, or of any class of shares, may be suspended at such times and for such periods, not exceeding 30 days in any year, as the directors may determine. [*Art 26*].

- No fee is to be charged for the registration of any instrument of transfer or other document relating to or affecting the title to any share. [*Art 27*]. (Listed companies must include such a provision, see 43.18(*d*) PUBLIC AND LISTED COMPANIES.)

- The company is entitled to retain any instrument of transfer which is registered, but any such instrument which the directors refuse to register is, when notice of the refusal is given, to be returned to the person lodging it. [*Art 28*].

A company's articles may contain other provisions restricting the right of its members to transfer their shares (see 57.9 below).

Note that on the application of the transferor of any share or interest in a company, the company must enter the transferee's name in the register of members in the same manner, and subject to the same conditions, as if the application for entry were made by the transferee.

[*Sec 183(4)*].

57.8 RESTRICTIONS ON TRANSFER

A public company which wishes to have its shares quoted on The Stock Exchange cannot impose restrictions on the transfer of its shares (other than in exceptional circumstances), since to do so would adversely affect their marketability. See 43.18(*e*) PUBLIC AND LISTED COMPANIES. By contrast, the articles of a private company frequently contain such restrictions. Where restrictions are imposed, they are normally either refusal powers (see 57.9 below) or pre-emption provisions (see 57.10 below).

57.9 Refusal powers

The articles may empower the directors to refuse to register a transfer, either at their complete discretion or on specified grounds. Such a power, as with any other power conferred on the directors, must be exercised in good faith for the benefit of the company (*Re Smith and Fawcett Ltd [1942] Ch 304*) and not for some personal motive of the directors (see *Tett v Phoenix Property and Investment Co Limited [1984] BCLC 599*). Furthermore, the power must be exercised by the making of a positive decision at a board meeting (see *Moodie v WL Shephard (Bookbinders) [1949] 2 All ER 1044*), failing which the transfer must be registered (*Re Hackney Pavilion Ltd [1924] 1 Ch 276*).

Where *SI 1985 No 805, Table A, Arts 24, 25* have been adopted, the directors

(*a*) may refuse to register the transfer of a share

- to a person of whom they do not approve where the share is not fully paid; or

- on which the company has a lien;

(*b*) may also refuse to register a transfer unless

- it is lodged at the company's registered office (or such other place as they appoint) and is accompanied by the appropriate share certificate and such other evidence as they may reasonably require to show the transferor's right to make the transfer;

- it is in respect of only one class of shares; and

- it is in favour of not more than four transferees; and

(*c*) if they do refuse to register a transfer, must notify the transferee of that fact within two months of the date on which the transfer was lodged.

Similar provisions apply under *CA 1948, Table A, Arts 24-26*.

The remedy for the refusal to register a transfer is for the person aggrieved to apply to the court for rectification of the register of members under *Sec 359*. See 47.4 REGISTERS.

57.10 Pre-emption provisions

The articles may contain pre-emption provisions, i.e. provisions requiring any member who wishes to sell his shares to offer them first to existing members, normally at a fair price to be determined by the articles. The effect of such a provision will depend on its precise wording, and there have been numerous decided cases on the subject. See, for example, *Lyle & Scott Ltd v Scott's Trustees and British Investment Trust Ltd [1959] AC 763*.

57.11 ISSUE OF CERTIFICATES

Subject to the exceptions below, every company must within two months after

- the allotment of any of its shares, debentures or debenture stock, or

- the date on which the 'transfer' of any such shares, debentures or debenture stock is lodged with it,

complete and have ready for delivery the certificates of all shares etc. allotted or transferred, unless the conditions of issue provide otherwise. [*Sec 185(1)*]. For this purpose, *'transfer'* means a duly stamped and otherwise valid transfer, or an exempt transfer within *STA 1982* (see 57.16 below), and does not include a transfer which the company is for any reason entitled to refuse to register and does not register. [*Sec 185(2)*].

The above does not apply

- where the conditions of issue provide otherwise;

- to a transfer where, by virtue of regulations made under *STA 1982*, the transferee is not entitled to a certificate or other evidence of title in relation to the securities transferred; or

- to transfers made in order to facilitate the system for stock exchange transfers (see 57.16 below).

[*Sec 185(3)(4); FSA 1986, s 194(5)*].

A company, and every officer of it, who is in default in complying with the above provisions is liable to a fine up to the level in 40.1(*f*) PENALTIES. If a company, on which notice has been served requiring it to make good any such default, fails to do so within ten days after service of the notice, the person entitled to have the certificates or debentures delivered to him may apply to the court. On such an application, the court may make an order directing the company and any officer of it to make good the default within a specified time. The order may provide that all costs of, and incidental to, the application shall be borne by the company or by an officer of it responsible for the default. [*Sec 185(5)-(7)*].

57.12 Contents and replacement of share certificates

A company's articles frequently include provisions with respect to the contents, and replacement, of share certificates. In the case of a company which has adopted *Table A* in *SI 1985 No 805*, the following provisions apply.

- Every member, on becoming a shareholder, is entitled, without payment, to one certificate for all the shares of each class held by him (and, on transferring a part of his holding of shares of any class, to a certificate for the balance of such holding). Alternatively, he is entitled to several certificates, each for one or more of his shares, upon payment for every certificate, after the first, of such reasonable sum as the directors may determine. [*Art 6*].

- Every certificate must be sealed and specify the number, class and distinguishing numbers (if any) of the shares to which it relates and the amounts or respective amounts paid up thereon. The company is not bound to issue more than one certificate for jointly-held shares and delivery of a certificate to one joint holder is a sufficient delivery to all the holders. [*Art 6*]. (See 43.18(*h*) PUBLIC AND LISTED COMPANIES for the replacement of certificates by listed companies.)

- If a share certificate is defaced, worn-out, lost or destroyed, it may be renewed on such terms (if any) as to evidence and indemnity, and payment of the company's reasonable expenses in investigating evidence, as the directors determine (but otherwise free of charge), and (in the case of defacement or wearing-out) on delivery up of the old certificate. [*Art 7*].

Example of indemnity for lost certificate

'I, [insert name of member], do hereby request that the company (or its Registrars) issue to me a duplicate certificate No [insert certificate number] for [insert number of shares] shares in the capital of the company, the certificate having been mislaid, destroyed or lost, and in consideration of the company doing so, I hereby indemnify the said company against all claims and demands, moneys, losses, damages, costs and expenses which may be brought against or be paid, incurred, or sustained by the said company by reason or in consequence of the issuing to me of the said duplicate certificate, or otherwise howsoever in relation thereto. I further undertake and agree, if the said certificate shall hereafter be found, forthwith to deliver up the same or cause the same to be delivered up to the company, its Registrars or their successors and assigns without cost, fee or reward.

Dated this   day of   19

[Signature of member]'

Listed companies. See the *Listing Rules, Chapter 13.20 – 13.27* for specifications and contents of certificates for registered and bearer securities of listed companies.

57.13 **Effect of certificate**

A certificate, under the common seal of the company specifying any shares held by a member is

- in England and Wales *prima facie* evidence, and

- in Scotland, sufficient evidence unless the contrary is shown

of his title to the shares.

Without prejudice to the above, in Scotland, a certificate specifying any shares held by a member and subscribed by the company in accordance with the *Requirements of Writing (Scotland) Act 1995* is, unless the contrary is shown, sufficient evidence of his title to the shares.

[*Sec 186; CA 1989, 17 Sch 5; Law Reform (Miscellaneous Provisions) Scotland Act 1990, 8 Sch 33; Requirements of Writing (Scotland) Act 1995, 4 Sch 55*].

57.14　Share Transfers Etc.

Share certificates are issued for the benefit of the company in general; they are a declaration by the company to all the world that the person in whose name the certificate is made out, and to whom it is given, is a shareholder in the company. The company is therefore estopped from denying the accuracy of a vendor's certificate and the purchaser is entitled to damages (*Re Bahia and San Francisco Railway Co (1868) LR 3 QB 584*).

Where a company issues an incorrect certificate, the company may also be estopped from denying the correctness of the certificate against the person to whom it is issued, in the absence of fraud or forgery, where he enters into a contract to sell the shares (*Dixon v Kennaway and Co Ltd [1900] 1 Ch 833*). See also *Bloomenthal v Ford [1897] AC 156*.

57.14　SHARE WARRANTS

A company limited by shares may, if authorised by its articles, issue with respect to any fully paid-up shares a warrant (known as a 'share warrant') stating that the bearer of the warrant is entitled to the shares specified in it. A share warrant issued under the company's common seal (or, in the case of a company registered in Scotland, subscribed in accordance with the *Requirements of Writing (Scotland) Act 1995*) entitles the bearer to the shares specified in it, and the shares may be transferred by delivery of the warrant.

The company may also provide (by coupons or otherwise) for the payment of future dividends on the shares included in the warrant.

[*Sec 188; CA 1989, 17 Sch 6; Law Reform (Miscellaneous Provisions) Scotland Act 1990, 8 Sch 33; Requirements of Writing (Scotland) Act 1995, 4 Sch 56*].

See 47.4 REGISTERS regarding entries in a company's register of members in relation to share warrants.

See 43.11(*f*) PUBLIC AND LISTED COMPANIES for requirements of listed companies in relation to share warrants.

Offences in connection with share warrants in Scotland. If in Scotland a person

- with intent to defraud, forges or alters a share warrant or coupon or, by means of such action, tries to obtain shares or dividends, or

- without lawful authority or excuse (proof of which lies on him), engraves or makes a share warrant or coupon on a plate or uses such a plate to print a share warrant or coupon or has any such plate in his possession

he is on conviction liable to punishment up to the level in 40.1(*a*) PENALTIES. [*Sec 189, 24 Sch*].

57.15　TRANSMISSION OF SHARES

Transmission occurs most commonly on the death or bankruptcy of a shareholder.

Following the death of a shareholder, the legal title to his shares vests in his personal representatives or, where the shares were held jointly, in the surviving holder(s). A company must accept the production to it of the grant of probate of the will, or letters of administration to the estate (or, in Scotland, confirmation as executor), as sufficient evidence of the grant, notwithstanding anything in the company's articles. [*Sec 187*].

A transfer of the share or other interest of a deceased member of a company made by his personal representative, although the personal representative is not himself a member, is as valid as if he had been such a member at the time of execution of the instrument of transfer. [*Sec 183(3)*]. If the personal representatives do have the shares transferred into their own names and become registered as members, they are personally liable for calls on outstanding shares (with a right of indemnity against the deceased's estate); otherwise they will only be liable for outstanding calls to the extent of the deceased's assets in their hands (*Duff's Executors' Case (1886) 32 ChD 301*). A trustee in bankruptcy may similarly transfer the bankrupt's shares without first becoming registered as a member. [*IA 1986, s 324, 5 Sch*].

Where a company has adopted *Table A* in *SI 1985 No 805* as its articles, the following provisions apply with respect to the transmission of its shares.

(*a*) If a member dies, the only persons a company can recognise as having any title to his interest are

- where he was a joint holder, the survivor or survivors; and

- where he was a sole holder or the only survivor of joint holders, his personal representatives.

However, this provision does not release the estate of a deceased member from any liability in respect of any share which had been held jointly by him. [*Art 29*].

(*b*) A person becoming entitled to a share in consequence of the death or bankruptcy of a member ('*the entitled person*') may, upon such evidence being produced as the directors may properly require, elect either to become the holder of the share or to have some person nominated by him registered as the transferee. The directors have the same right to decline registration as they would have had in the case of a transfer of the share by the member before his death.

If the entitled person elects to become the holder, he must give notice to the company to that effect. If he elects to have another person registered, he must execute an instrument of transfer of the share to that person. All the articles in *Table A* relating to the transfer of shares (see 57.7 above) then apply to the notice or instrument of transfer as if it were an instrument of transfer executed by the member and the death or bankruptcy of the member had not occurred. [*Art 30*].

(*c*) The entitled person has the rights to which he would be entitled as the holder of the share, except that he will not, before being registered as the holder of the share, be entitled in respect of it to attend or vote at any meeting of the company or any separate class meeting. [*Art 31*].

Similar provisions apply where *CA 1948, Table A, Arts 29-32* apply to the company, with the addition that, under (*c*) above, the directors may give notice to the entitled person to elect either to be registered himself or to transfer the share and, if the notice is not complied with within 90 days, the directors may thereafter withhold dividends, bonuses and any other moneys payable in respect of the share until the requirements of the notice have been complied with.

57.16 STOCK EXCHANGE TRANSFERS

A more complex system of transfers is required for dealings effected on The Stock Exchange to provide an effective centralised method for the settlement of bargains.

The *Uncertified Securities Regulations 1995 (SI 1995 No 3272)* came into force on 19 December 1995 and were made pursuant to *CA 1985, s 207*. They contain the concept of a '*relevant system*' which is defined as a computer-based system and procedures which enable title to units of security to be evidenced and transferred without a written instrument. The Treasury has powers (which it has delegated to the Securities and

Investments Board) to approve a person who wishes to be the 'Operator' of a relevant system. [*Regs 4-13, 1 Sch*].

The only current Operator is CRESTCo which has been approved as Operator of a relevant system in respect of CREST. (Other Operators may be approved if meeting certain criteria.) Under CREST, CRESTCo is responsible for establishing and running the central computer system and for specifying the technical requirements which must be met by networks through which messages are sent to and from the central computer system.

CREST enables 'participating securities' to be held without the need for a share certificate to be issued and to be transferred without the need for an executed stock transfer form to be submitted to the company. It is a voluntary system in two ways. First, an issuer may choose whether or not a particular class of securities issued by it is to be eligible for transfer through CREST. (There is no requirement that listed securities should be eligible for CREST although in practice most securities listed on the London Stock Exchange or dealt in on the Alternative Investment Market have joined CREST). Secondly, even if a particular security is admitted to CREST, a shareholder may choose whether to hold the security in certificated or uncertificated form.

The CREST central computer system maintains records called 'stock accounts'. A stock account is maintained for each separate 'participating security' held by each 'system-member'. The account relates to the entries on the register maintained by the 'participating issuer'. When the central computer system receives an instruction from a system-member transferor and a system-member transferee in relation to a transfer, it checks that the transferor is able to transfer the relevant number of securities and that the transferee has a payment bank which is willing to make the payment for the transfer. The computer system then itself generates an 'operator instruction' to the company instructing it to register the transfer which it is required to do within two hours. All messages are sent to and from the central computer system and the participants in the system (e.g. companies and their shareholders) do not communicate directly with each other. At no point does CRESTCo act as a principal either in holding securities itself or as obligor under the payment arrangements.

A '*participating security*' is a security title to units of which is permitted by an Operator to be transferred by means of a relevant system. [*Reg 3(1)*]. The Regulations allow most securities issued by companies incorporated in the UK under the Companies Acts (or equivalent legislation in Northern Ireland) to be eligible for CREST (including debenture and loan stocks, preference shares and subscription warrants). In order for a security to be admitted to CREST, an issuer must comply with the CREST procedures for admission of securities. Securities are admitted by class and thus, for example, the ordinary shares of a particular company may be a participating security whilst its preference shares exist only in certificated form.

A company's articles of association normally contain provisions concerning the transfer of shares in the company. If the articles are in all respects consistent with

(i)   holding shares of a class in uncertificated form,

(ii)   transfer of title to shares of the class by means of a relevant system, and

(iii)   the Regulations,

that class of shares may become a participating security. To the extent that a company's articles are inconsistent with (i)–(iii) above, the directors may pass a resolution that title to shares of that class may be transferred by means of a relevant system. Notice must be given to each member of the company either of the intention to pass such a resolution or that such a resolution has been passed. In the latter case, notice must be given within 60 days of the passing of the resolution. [*Regs 14-18*]. In the case of convertible and redeemable shares, other changes to the articles may be necessary to disapply the provisions relating to the *means* by which convertible shares are converted or redeemable shares are redeemed. For example, articles may require amendment so that a system message can constitute a conversion notice.

A '*participating issuer*' is a person who has issued a security which is a participating security. Except where an issuer acts as its own registrar, CREST is unlikely to have any significant impact on the issuer. The company's registrar needs to participate in CREST and be in a position to send and receive messages (or have them sent and received on their behalf).

A '*system-member*' is a person who has been permitted by CRESTCo to transfer through CREST title to uncertificated units of a participating security held by him. [*Reg 3(1)*]. The system-member is the person whose name appears on the register of securities maintained by the participating issuer. The only requirements imposed by CRESTCo on a person wishing to be a system-member are that

- a settlement bank has agreed to provide settlement bank facilities; and

- the system-member has the ability to send and receive messages through the system (either himself or through a 'sponsor').

A '*sponsored member*' is a system-member who has appointed a sponsor to send and receive messages on his behalf. Individuals are unlikely to have the necessary computer network to enable them to send and receive messages directly. The concept of a sponsored member enables a person to hold shares in uncertificated form, and therefore to be a registered shareholder, by appointing another person (e.g. a broker or bank) to send and receive electronic messages relating to those shares.

A '*system-participant*' or '*user*' is a person permitted by the Operator to send and receive messages. In practical terms this is the person with the computer and network connection. A '*sponsoring system-participant*' is a person who has been permitted to send and receive instructions on behalf of other persons. Thus a system member may, but need not be, a system-participant. A company which does not maintain its own register is not a system-participant – its registrar will be a system-participant and will be a sponsoring system-participant for the issuer.

Changes of form. There are special provisions to enable a unit of a security to be changed from certificated to uncertificated form and vice versa (whether at the time of a transfer of title or without there being a change of holder).

Registers of members. A company any of whose securities can be transferred through CREST must subdivide its register of those securities to show how many securities each person holds in uncertified form and certified form respectively. [*Reg 19*]. For these purposes, any overseas branch register (see 47.6 REGISTERS) maintained by a company is not regarded as forming part of the company's register of members. It is not therefore possible to hold shares in uncertificated form on an overseas branch register. A person who is recorded on such a register who wishes to hold shares in uncertificated form must first have his entry transferred to the principal register and then take the necessary steps to convert his holding from certificated to uncertificated form.

Rectification of a register. A participating issuer can only rectify a register of securities in relation to uncertificated units with the consent of the Operator or by order of the court. [*Reg 21*].

57.16 Share Transfers Etc.

Registration of transfers. A participating issuer

(*a*)   must register a transfer of title to uncertificated units in accordance with an operator instruction unless the transfer is prohibited by court order or the issuer has actual notice that the transfer is void by or under an enactment; and

(*b*)   must not register a transfer of title to uncertificated units unless required to do so

- by an operator instruction;
- by court order;
- by or under any enactment; or
- on compulsory purchase following a takeover.

An issuer who registers a transfer other than under (*b*) above is in breach of statutory duty and may incur liability in damages to anyone who suffers loss as a result of the default.

An issuer may refuse to register a transfer if, *inter alia*, the instruction requires a transfer of units to an entity which is not a natural or legal person or to a minor.

[*Regs 23, 37*].

58   Shares and Share Capital

Cross-references. See 8 ACQUISITION OF OWN SHARES; 9 ALLOTMENT OF SHARES; 13 BONUS ISSUES; 14 CLASS RIGHTS; 17 DEBENTURES AND OTHER BORROWING; 21 DISCLOSURE OF INTERESTS IN PUBLIC COMPANY SHARES; 23 DISTRIBUTIONS; 30 INSIDER DEALING; 42 PROSPECTUSES AND PUBLIC ISSUES; 43.7 PUBLIC AND LISTED COMPANIES for notification obligations of listed companies under the Listing Rules; 44 RECONSTRUCTIONS AND MERGERS; 52 RIGHTS ISSUES; 56 SHARE PREMIUM; 57 SHARE TRANSFERS ETC; 59 TAKEOVER OFFERS.

The contents of this chapter are as follows.

58.1   SHARES

'Share' is defined as a share in the share capital of a company, and includes stock (see 58.13 below) except where a distinction between shares and stock is express or implied. [*Sec 744*]. Shares are personal estate (or, in Scotland, moveable property) and are not real estate or heritage. [*Sec 182(1)(a)*]. See also the judicial definitions in *Borland's Trustee v Steel Brothers & Co Ltd [1901] 1 Ch 279* and *CIR v Crossman [1937] AC 26 and 66.*

The assets of a company are owned by the company itself and the ownership of shares does not entitle the holder to any property rights to the company's assets; he is merely entitled to a *share* in the company and *not* to an interest in every asset the company owns. Shares may be of different classes (see 58.2 to 58.7 below) and the rights and obligations of the holders of each class are normally set out in the memorandum and articles of association.

Each share in a limited company must have a nominal value [*Sec 2(5)*] (no-par value shares are not permitted) although this need not be paid at the time of issue. Shares may therefore be nil paid, partly paid or fully paid but where they are not fully paid the shareholder has a liability to pay up the nominal amount of his shares in the event of a call (see 58.8 below) or the winding up of the company. See, however, 9.13 ALLOTMENT OF SHARES for the minimum amount to be paid on shares allotted by a public company.

Each share in a company having a share capital must be distinguished by an appropriate number unless all the issued shares (or all the issued shares of a particular class) are fully paid-up and rank *parri passu* for all purposes in which case no number is required as long as those conditions apply. [*Sec 182(2)*].

58.2   Classification of shares

Where there are no different or separate rights attaching to a particular class of shares in a company then all shares rank equally (*Birch v Cropper (1889) 14 App Cas 525*). A company may, however, subject to the provisions of *CA 1985* and the memorandum and articles and without prejudice to any rights attaching to existing shares, issue any shares with such rights and restrictions as the company determines by ordinary resolution. See, for example, *SI 1985 No 805, Table A, Art 2* and *CA 1948, Table A, Art 2*. Different classes of shares are most commonly distinguished by different rights and restrictions relating to dividends, voting, return of capital in a winding up and transferability of shares. The more common classifications of shares are given in 58.3 to 58.7 below.

58.3   Shares and Share Capital

58.3   *Ordinary shares*

Ordinary shares, sometimes referred to as 'equity' or 'risk' capital, are the basic shares of a company and confer the remaining rights of the company on their holders i.e. after all other classes of shares have been satisfied. Generally, the ordinary shares carry voting rights and rights to dividends, and give a right to participate on a winding up in any excess assets. Some company's do, however, issue ordinary shares (sometimes referred to as 'A' ordinary shares) which do not carry voting rights.

58.4   *Preference shares*

Preference shares are not defined. Generally, preference shareholders are entitled to a dividend and to other rights, whether to income or capital, in preference to ordinary shareholders. Any rights expressed as attaching to the shares on their creation are, *prima facie*, a definition of the whole of their rights (see *Scottish Insurance Corporation v Wilsons & Clyde Coal [1949] AC 462*) and negative any other rights to which, but for the specified rights, they would have been entitled (*Re National Telephone Co [1914] 1 Ch 755*). Preference shares include the following.

- *Cumulative* preference shares where the right to a dividend, if profits are insufficient in any year, accumulates until profits become sufficient. Unless otherwise stated the right to receive a preference dividend is cumulative (*Webb v Earle (1875) LR 20 Eq 556*). Even where dividends are cumulative, there is no absolute right to the dividend unless and until the dividend is declared out of available profits (compare interest on debentures). See *Buenos Ayres Great Southern Railway Co Ltd v Preston [1947] Ch 384.*

- *Non-cumulative* preference shares where there is no right to the accumulation of unpaid dividends because this has been rebutted by the terms of issue (see, for example, *Staples v Eastman Photographic Materials Co [1896] 2 Ch 303* where dividends were to be paid 'out of the net profits each year').

- *Participating* preference shares where there is a right to a dividend and/or return of capital on winding up in preference to the ordinary shares, together with a right to participate in a further distribution of income or capital as the case may be if there remains a surplus after a dividend and/or return of capital to the ordinary shareholders. The right to participate in surplus profits must be expressly stated (*Will v United Lankat Plantations Co [1914] AC 11*) as must the rights to participate in capital (*Scottish Insurance Corporation v Wilsons & Clyde Coal Co Ltd supra; Re Isle of Thanet Electricity Supply Co [1950] Ch 161*).

- *Redeemable* preference shares which a company may redeem at a fixed time or at its option. See 8.2 ACQUISITION OF OWN SHARES which applies to the redemption of any class of shares (not just preference shares).

For voting rights of listed preference shares under the Listing Rules, see 43.18(*c*) PUBLIC AND LISTED COMPANIES.

58.5   *Founders', management and deferred shares*

Such shares are normally subscribed for by the promoters and are usually deferred in priority to the ordinary shares i.e. the rights of the holders to receive a dividend is deferred until a dividend at a specific rate has been paid out on other shares.

58.6   *Redeemable shares*

A company limited by shares, or limited by guarantee and having a share capital, may issue redeemable shares. See 8.2 ACQUISITION OF OWN SHARES.

58.7   *Employees' or workers' shares*

In recent years many companies have issued shares to their employees under one of the many employee share schemes (see 18.1 DEFINITIONS). As well as encouraging employee involvement in the company, they offer considerable tax incentives. In the early years of ownership there are normally restrictions on transfers. See 9.5 ALLOTMENT OF SHARES for the disapplication of the pre-emption rules to shares allotted to such schemes.

58.8   PAYMENT FOR SHARES

A shareholder is liable to pay up the nominal value of each of his shares and the amount owing to the company is a debt which can be 'called up'. The company may not require him to pay the full amount when he first takes up the shares (but see 9.13 ALLOTMENT OF SHARES for the minimum value which must be paid up on allotment of public company shares).

Generally, a company will call up the amount it is owed on its shares rateably for all shareholders. However, if authorised by its articles (see, for example, *SI 1985 No 805, Table A, Art 17* and *CA 1948, Table A, Art 20*), a company may make arrangements on the issue of shares for a difference between the shareholders in the amounts and times of payment of calls on their shares. [*Sec 119(a)*].

A company may also, if authorised by the articles, accept from any member the whole or any part of the amount remaining unpaid on his shares even if not called up. Where more is paid up on some shares than others, it may also pay dividends in proportion to the amount paid up. [*Sec 119(b)(c)*].

58.9   Calls

SI 1985 No 805, Table A includes the following provisions in relation to calls (which may or may not be included in a company's articles).

(*a*)   Subject to the terms of the allotment, the directors may make calls upon the members in respect of unpaid moneys on their shares (whether in respect of nominal value or premium) giving at least 14 days' notice of when and where payment is to be made. Calls may be payable by instalments and may be revoked or postponed in whole or part before receipt of any sum due. [*Art 12*].

(*b*)   A person on whom a call is made remains liable for calls made on him even if subsequently transferring the shares. [*Art 12*].

(*c*)   A call is deemed to be made at the time when the resolution of directors authorising the call was passed. [*Art 13*].

(*d*)   Joint holders of a share are jointly and severally liable to pay calls. [*Art 14*].

(*e*)   If a call is not paid by the due date, the person from whom it is due must pay interest on the unpaid amount from that date until the date of payment at the rate fixed by the terms of the allotment or call. The directors may, however, waive payment of interest in whole or part. [*Art 15*].

(*f*)   An amount payable on a share on allotment or at any fixed date (whether in respect of nominal value or premium) is deemed to be a call and if not paid the provisions of the articles apply as if the amount had become due and payable by virtue of a call. [*Art 16*].

Similar provisions apply where a company has adopted *CA 1948, Table A, Arts 15 to 19* except that a call made otherwise than under the terms of the allotment cannot exceed one-quarter of the nominal value of the share and cannot be payable less than one month after any previous call. Also the rate of interest chargeable under (*e*) above cannot exceed 5% p.a.

58.10 Lien on shares for unpaid calls

SI 1985 No 805, Table A includes the following provisions (which may or may not be included in the company's articles) in relation to a company's lien on shares for outstanding calls, etc.

(*a*)   A company has a first and paramount lien on every share which is not fully paid for all moneys (whether presently payable or not) payable at a fixed time or called in respect of that share. The directors may, however, declare that any share is wholly or partly exempt from this provision. The lien also extends to any amount payable in respect of the share (e.g. dividends). [*Art 8*]. Where a shareholder has lodged his share certificate with a bank as security for a loan and the bank has given notice of this to the company, the company cannot, in respect of moneys due to it from the shareholder after notice of the bank's security, claim priority over advances made by the bank after such notice (*The Bradford Banking Co Ltd v Briggs, Son and Co (1886) 12 App Cas 29*).

(*b*)   The company may sell any share on which the company has a lien if a sum in respect of which the lien exists is presently payable and is not paid within 14 days of notice being given to

- the holder of the share; or

- the person entitled to it in consequence of the death or bankruptcy of the holder.

The notice must demand payment and state that if the notice is not complied with the shares may be sold. [*Art 9*].

(*c*)   The share may be sold in such manner as the directors determine and they may authorise some person to execute an instrument of transfer of the shares sold to, or in accordance with the directions of, the purchaser. The title of the transferee is not affected by any irregularity in, or invalidity of, the share disposal. [*Arts 9, 10*].

(*d*)   The net proceeds of sale, after costs, must be applied in payment of so much of the sum for which the lien exists as is presently payable. Any residue must, on surrender of the share certificate for cancellation and subject to a like lien for any moneys not presently payable as existed upon the shares before the sale, be paid to the person entitled to the shares at the date of sale. [*Art 11*].

Similar provisions apply where a company has adopted *CA 1948, Table A, Arts 11 to 14* except that there is no provision for costs under (*d*) above.

58.11 Forfeiture for non-payment of calls

If the articles of a company provide, the company may forfeit shares for failure to pay calls. It may also accept a surrender in lieu of forfeiture. [*Sec 143(3)(d)*].

SI 1985 No 805, Table A includes the following provisions (which may or may not be included in a company's articles) in relation to forfeiture of shares in default of payment of a call or instalment.

(*a*)   If a call is unpaid after it becomes due and payable (see 58.9 above) the directors may give the shareholder not less than 14 days' notice requiring payment at a named place of the amount unpaid (including any unpaid interest) and stating that, in the event of non-payment, the shares are liable to be forfeited. [*Art 18*].

(*b*)   In the event of non-compliance with the notice, the shares may be forfeited by a resolution of the directors at any time before the payment required is made. Forfeiture includes all dividends and other moneys payable on the forfeited shares and not paid before forfeiture. [*Art 19*].

(*c*)   A person whose shares are forfeited ceases to be a member of the company in respect of the forfeited shares and must surrender the share certificate for cancellation. He remains liable to make payment to the company of all moneys due at the date of forfeiture, together with interest. The directors may, however, waive payment wholly or in part or enforce payment without any allowance for the value of the shares at the time of forfeiture or for any consideration received on their disposal. [*Art 21*]. See also *Ladies' Dress Association Ltd v Pulbrook [1900] 2 QB 376* and *Re Bolton [1930] 2 Ch 48*.

(*d*)   Subject to *CA 1985*, the shares forfeited can be sold, re-allotted or otherwise disposed of by the directors as they think fit (to the person from whom they were forfeited or any other person). The forfeiture can also be cancelled at any time before such sale, etc. Where the forfeited shares are to be transferred to another person, the directors may authorise some person to execute the instrument of transfer. [*Art 20*].

(*e*)   A statutory declaration by a director or secretary that a share has been forfeited is conclusive evidence of the facts stated in it as against all persons claiming to be entitled to the share. Subject to the execution of an instrument of transfer (if necessary) the declaration constitutes a good title to the share and the purchaser's title is not affected by any irregularity in, or invalidity of, the forfeiture or share disposal. [*Art 22*].

Similar provisions apply where a company has adopted *CA 1948, Table A, Arts 33* to *39* except that under (*c*) above the directors have no power to waive payment and the person whose shares have been forfeited ceases to be liable to the company when it has received payment in full of all moneys in respect of the shares.

See 58.27 below for cancellation of the shares forfeited in the case of a public company.

58.12 SHARE CAPITAL

Nominal capital. Every company limited by shares is required to have a nominal capital with which it is registered and this must be stated in the memorandum. See 35.2(*f*) MEMORANDUM OF ASSOCIATION. It is equal to the nominal value of the shares which the directors are authorised to issue and, in the case of a public company, must not be less than the 'authorised minimum'.

The '*authorised minimum*' is £50,000 or such other sum as the Secretary of State may by order specify. An order which increases the authorised minimum may require a public company with an allotted share capital of which the nominal value is less than the new amount to increase that value to not less than that amount or re-register as a private company (see 49.11 REGISTRATION AND RE-REGISTRATION).

[*Secs 11, 118*].

A company cannot issue shares beyond its nominal capital; if it does so the issue is void and the allottee may recover any money paid (*Bank of Hindustan, China and Japan Ltd v Alison (1871) LR 6 CP 222*).

The nominal capital may be increased or reduced by resolution of the company in general meeting. See 58.14 *et seq* below.

58.13 Shares and Share Capital

Issued capital represents the shares which have been taken up by shareholders who agree to pay for them either in cash or in kind, together with shares issued as fully paid bonus shares (see 13 BONUS ISSUES). The difference between the nominal and the issued capital is known as the unissued capital.

Equity share capital means a company's issued share capital excluding any part which, neither as respects dividends or capital, carries a right to participate beyond a specified amount in a distribution. [*Sec 744*].

Paid-up capital is the portion of the company's issued capital (which it cannot exceed) that has been paid up by the shareholders. Payment is made either by the company making a call (see 58.9 above) or by way of instalments fixed on the issue of the shares. Public companies must not allot shares unless they are paid up at least as to one-quarter of their nominal value and the whole of any premium. [*Sec 101*].

Any reference to share capital on the stationery or order forms of a company with share capital must be to paid-up share capital. [*Sec 351(2)*].

Called-up share capital. See 18.1 DEFINITIONS.

58.13 Reserve liability

A limited company may by special resolution determine that any part of its share capital not already called up can only be called up in the event, and for the purposes of, winding up. [*Sec 120*]. This reserve liability is also known as the reserve capital. Any mortgage of reserve capital is void, see Re *Mayfair Property Co [1898] 2 Ch 28*.

58.14 ALTERATION OF SHARE CAPITAL

A company limited by shares, or by guarantee and having a share capital, may, if authorised by its articles (see below), alter the conditions of its memorandum by

(*a*)   increasing its share capital by new shares;

(*b*)   consolidating and dividing all or any of its share capital into shares of larger amount than existing shares;

(*c*)   sub-dividing its shares, or any of them, into shares of a smaller amount than is fixed by the memorandum provided the proportion between the amount paid and the amount, if any, unpaid on each reduced share is the same as it was for the share from which the reduced share is derived; and

(*d*)   cancelling shares which, at the date of passing the resolution to cancel, have not been taken or agreed to be taken by any person and diminishing the amount of the company's share capital by the amount of the shares cancelled. Any such cancellation does not constitute a reduction of share capital (see 58.17 below).

The company must exercise the above powers in general meeting.

[*Sec 121*].

If a company has adopted *SI 1985 No 805, Table A, Art 32* (or *CA 1948, Table A, Arts 44 to 46*) the requirement of being authorised by the articles is complied with. If *SI 1985 No 805, Table A, Art 33* has also been adopted, where as a result of a consolidation under (*b*) above any member would be entitled to fractions of shares, the directors may sell the shares representing the fractions for the best price reasonably obtainable to any person (including the company) and distribute the net proceeds of sale in due proportion among those members. The directors may authorise some person to execute an instrument of transfer of the shares to, or in accordance with the directions of, the purchaser. The transferee's title is not affected by any irregularity in, or invalidity of, the sales procedure.

Examples of typical resolutions

Under (a) above
'That the capital of the company be and hereby is increased from £... to £... by the creation of an additional ... ordinary shares of 25p each.'

Under (b) above
'That the ... ordinary shares of 25p each be and hereby are consolidated and divided into ... ordinary shares of £1 each.'

Under (c) above
'That the ... ordinary shares of £1 each be and hereby are sub-divided into ... ordinary shares of 25p each.'

Under (d) above
'That the ... ordinary shares of £1 each in the authorised capital of the company which have not been taken or agreed to be taken by any person be and hereby are cancelled and that the authorised share capital of the company be diminished by £... accordingly.'

Conversion of shares into stock (and vice versa). A company, if authorised by its articles, may also alter the conditions of its memorandum by converting all or any of its paid-up shares into stock, and reconverting that stock into paid-up shares of any denomination. Such powers must be exercised by the company in general meeting. [*Sec 121*]. If a company has adopted *CA 1948, Table A, Art 40*, the requirement of being authorised by the articles is complied with and an ordinary resolution of the company is required. The holder of the stock may transfer the stock in a similar way to the shares from which it arose and has the same rights as regards dividends, voting etc. as if he held those shares. [*Arts 41, 42*]. There are no corresponding provisions in *Table A* in *SI 1985 No 805*.

Stock may not be issued directly, only by such conversion.

58.15 Notice to Registrar of Companies of alteration

If a company has

- consolidated and divided its share capital into shares of larger amount than its existing shares,
- converted any shares into stock or reconverted stock into shares,
- sub-divided its shares or any of them,
- redeemed any redeemable shares (see 8.2 ACQUISITION OF OWN SHARES), or
- cancelled any shares (otherwise than in connection with a reduction of share capital under *Sec 135*, see 58.17 below)

it must within one month of doing so give notice to the Registrar of Companies in the prescribed form (Form 122). In default, the company and every officer in default is guilty of an offence and liable to a fine up to the level in 40.1(*f*) PENALTIES. [*Sec 122, 24 Sch*].

58.16   Shares and Share Capital

58.16 Notice to Registrar of Companies of increase in share capital

If a company with a share capital (whether or not its shares have been converted into stock) increases its share capital beyond the registered capital, it must, within 15 days after passing the resolution authorising the increase, send to the Registrar of Companies

- notice of the particulars in the prescribed form (Form 123), and

- a copy of the resolution authorising the increase either printed or in some other form approved by the Registrar

and the Registrar must record the increase.

In default, the company and every officer in default is guilty of an offence and liable to a fine up to the level in 40.1(*f*) PENALTIES.

[*Sec 123, 24 Sch*].

58.17 REDUCTION OF SHARE CAPITAL

Subject to confirmation by the court (see 58.18 below), a company limited by shares (or limited by guarantee and having a share capital) may, if authorised by its articles, by special resolution reduce its share capital in any way. In particular, it may

(*a*)   extinguish or reduce the liability on any of its shares in respect of unpaid share capital (see *Re Doloswella Rubber Ltd [1917] 1 Ch 213*); or

(*b*)   either with or without extinguishing or reducing liability on any of its shares

- cancel any paid-up share capital which is lost or unrepresented by available assets; or

- pay off any paid-up share capital which is in excess of the company's wants.

See *Ex parte Westburn Sugar Refineries Ltd [1951] AC 625*; *Re Thomas de la Rue & Co Ltd [1911] 2 Ch 361*; and *Re Jupiter House Investments (Cambridge) Ltd [1985] 1 WLR 975*.

The company may, if and so far as necessary, alter its memorandum by reducing the amount of its share capital and shares accordingly.

[*Sec 135*].

If the company has adopted *SI 1985 No 805, Table A, Art 34* (or *CA 1948, Table A, Art 46*) the requirement of being authorised by the articles is complied with. An authority in the memorandum is insufficient (*Re Dexine Patent Packing and Rubber Co (1903) 88 LT 791*).

A special resolution for reducing share capital may be passed by a private company by written resolution (see 51.4 RESOLUTIONS). Otherwise although a resolution agreed to by all the members entitled to vote has been held to be effective without a meeting (*Re Pearce Duff & Co Ltd [1960] 1 WLR 1014*) the court normally requires the special resolution to be taken at a meeting (*Re Barry Artists Ltd [1985] 1 WLR 1305*).

Example of special resolution

'That the capital of the company be reduced from £... divided into ... ordinary shares of £1 each (which are all issued and paid in full) to £... divided into ... ordinary shares of 25p each and that such reduction be effected by returning to the holders of the said shares paid-up capital to the extent of 75p per share and by reducing the nominal amount of the said shares from £1 to 25p accordingly.'

58.18 **Confirmation by court order**

Where a company has passed a resolution for reducing share capital, it may apply to the court for an order confirming the reduction. [*Sec 136(1)*].

Where the proposed reduction of share capital involves

- diminution of liability in respect of unpaid share capital, or

- the payment to a shareholder of any paid-up share capital

and in any other case where the court directs, every creditor at a date fixed by the court can object to the reduction if his debt or claim would be admissible in a winding up commencing on that date. The court must settle a list of creditors entitled to object and publish notices fixing a day or days within which creditors not entered on the list must claim to be so entered or will be excluded from the right of objecting to the reduction.

If a creditor on the list does not consent to the reduction, the court may dispense with his consent if the company secures the payment of his debt by appropriating either

- the full amount of the debt or claim; or

- where the company does not admit, or is not willing to provide for, the full amount or the amount is contingent or not ascertained, an amount fixed by the court (after enquiry and adjudication as if the company were being wound up).

[*Sec 136(2)-(5)*].

The court may, however, if it thinks fit direct that *Sec 136(2)-(5)* is not to apply as regards any class or any classes of creditors. [*Sec 136(6)*]. (In most schemes for reduction of capital this power will be used because the company will either have agreed the capital reduction with creditors or secured its liabilities by means of a guarantee.)

See also *Re Lucania Temperance Billiard Halls (London) Ltd [1966] Ch 98* and *Re Antwerp Waterworks Co Ltd [1931] WN 186*.

If the court is satisfied that every creditor entitled to object has either consented to the reduction or had his debt or claim discharged or secured, it may make an order confirming the reduction on such terms and conditions as it thinks fit. It may direct that the company adds the words 'and reduced' at the end of its name for a set period (these words are then deemed to form part of the company's name). It may also order the company to publish information giving the reasons for the causes of the reduction. [*Sec 137*].

As well as the position of creditors the court must also consider present and future shareholders (see *Poole v National Bank of China Ltd [1907] AC 229*). See also *Ratners Group plc (1988) 4 BCC 293*. It must carefully scrutinise any scheme which does not provide for uniform treatment of shareholders with similar rights and must be satisfied that it is not unjust or inequitable, although this does not mean that it cannot sanction such a scheme (*British and American Trustee and Finance Corporation Ltd (and Reduced) v Couper [1894] AC 399*).

58.19 **Registration of order and minute of reduction**

The court must approve a minute showing, with respect to the altered share capital

- the amount of the share capital;

- the number of shares into which it is to be divided, and the amount of each share; and

- the amount (if any) deemed to be paid up on each share.

On production of the court order confirming the reduction, and delivery of a copy of the order and minute, the Registrar of Companies must register the order and minute (subject to 58.20 below) and certify the registration. Notice of the registration must be published in any way directed by the court.

The effects of registration and certification are as follows.

- The resolution for reduction of share capital takes effect from that date.

- The certification is conclusive evidence that all the requirements of *CA 1985* have been complied with and that the company's share capital is as stated in the minute.

- The minute is deemed to be substituted for the corresponding part of the company's memorandum and is valid and alterable as if it had been originally contained therein. Every copy of the memorandum issued thereafter must be in accordance with the alteration. If not, the company and every officer in default is guilty of an offence and liable to a fine up to the level in 40.1(*g*) PENALTIES for each occasion on which copies are incorrectly issued.

[*Secs 20, 138, 24 Sch*].

58.20 Public company reducing capital below authorised minimum

Where a court order confirming a reduction under 58.17 above brings the nominal value of a public company's allotted share capital below the authorised minimum (see 58.12 above) the Registrar of Companies must not register the order under 58.19 above unless the court directs or the company is first re-registered as a private company. The court may however authorise the company to be re-registered as a private company without passing the special resolution required under *Sec 53* (see 49.11 REGISTRATION AND RE-REGISTRATION) in which case it must specify in the order the alterations to be made to the company's memorandum and articles. The company may then be re-registered as a private company if an application in the prescribed form (Form 139), signed by a director or secretary, is delivered to the Registrar of Companies together with a printed copy of the memorandum and articles as altered. The Registrar must then retain the application and other documents delivered and issue the company with a certificate of incorporation stating that the company is a private company. On the issue of the certificate the company becomes a private company (the certificate being conclusive evidence of this fact) and any alterations in the memorandum and articles set out in the court order take effect. [*Sec 139*].

Where a public company reduces its share capital to less than £50,000 but immediately increases it again to more than £50,000 by a resolution which takes effect before, or at the same time as, the reduction resolution, the company is not obliged to re-register as a private company (*Re MB Group Ltd [1989] BCLC 672*).

58.21 Liability of members on reduced shares

Subject to below, following the reduction of a company's share capital, no member (past or present) is liable in respect of any call or contribution on a share in excess of the difference (if any) between the amount fixed by the minute under 58.19 above and the amount paid on the share or the reduced amount (if any) deemed to have been paid.

However, if

(*a*)   a creditor was not on the list of creditors because of ignorance of the reduction proceedings or their nature and effect with respect to his claim, and

(*b*)   after the reduction the company is unable (within the meaning of *IA 1986, s 123*) to pay his debt or claim

every member of the company at the date of registration of the court order for reduction and minute is then liable to contribute towards the payment of the debt etc. an amount up to the sum he would have been liable to contribute if the company had commenced winding up on the day before the date of registration. If the company is wound up, the court may, on the application of the creditor in question and proof of the ignorance under (a) above, settle a list of persons liable to contribute and make and enforce calls and orders on them as if they were ordinary contributories in a winding up.

Nothing in the above affects the rights of the contributories among themselves.

[Sec 140; IA 1986, 13 Sch Part I].

58.22 Liability of officers

An officer of the company who

- wilfully conceals the name of a creditor entitled to object to the reduction of capital,

- wilfully misrepresents the nature or amount of the debt or claim of any creditor, or

- aids, abets or is privy to any such concealment or misrepresentation

is guilty of an offence and liable to a fine up to the level in 40.1(d) PENALTIES. [Sec 141].

58.23 MAINTENANCE OF CAPITAL

There are a number of provisions in CA 1985 which seek to ensure that a company's capital is maintained other than by being lost in the ordinary course of business. This is because the issued share capital is the ultimate fund for payment of the company's creditors. See Flitcroft's Case (1882) 21 ChD 519. The provisions are considered in 58.24 to 58.30 below.

58.24 Allotment of shares at a discount

A company's shares must not be allotted at a discount. See 9.12 ALLOTMENT OF SHARES.

58.25 Company not to acquire own shares

Subject to certain exceptions, a company limited by shares (or limited by guarantee and having a share capital) must not acquire its own shares whether by purchase, subscription or otherwise. See 8.1 ACQUISITION OF OWN SHARES for details and exceptions.

58.26 Acquisition of shares by company's nominee

Subject to the exceptions below, where shares are issued to, or acquired from a third party as partly paid up by, a nominee of a company limited by shares (or limited by guarantee and having a share capital) then for all purposes

- the shares are to be treated as held by the nominee on his own account; and

- the company is to be regarded as having no 'beneficial interest' in them.

This does not apply in the case of a public company to shares acquired otherwise than by subscription by a nominee of the company with financial assistance given to him directly or indirectly by the company for the purpose of, or in connection with, the acquisition and where the company has a beneficial interest in the shares (in which case Sec 146 applies, see 58.27 below).

[Secs 144(1), 145(1)].

Again subject to the exceptions below, if the nominee is called upon to pay any amount (including any premium) on such shares and fails to do so within 21 days from the call, the following persons are jointly and severally liable to pay that amount.

- If the shares were issued to the nominee as subscriber to the memorandum by virtue of an undertaking of his in the memorandum, the other subscribers to the memorandum.

- If the shares were otherwise issued to or acquired by him, the directors of the company at the time of the issue or acquisition.

The court may, however, relieve a subscriber or director from liability, in whole or in part, in any proceedings for the recovery of any such amount if it is satisfied that he acted honestly and reasonably and ought fairly to be excused from liability to pay. A subscriber or director can apply for relief in advance of proceedings if he has reason to believe that a claim may be made for recovery.

[*Sec 144(2)-(4)*].

Exceptions. The above provisions do not apply to

- shares acquired by a nominee of a company when the company has no beneficial interest in those shares; or

- shares issued in consequence of an application made before 22 December 1980 or transferred in pursuance of an agreement to acquire them made before that date.

[*Sec 145(2)*].

In determining whether a company has a '*beneficial interest*' in shares, certain interests are disregarded (residual interests under pension and employee share schemes, company's right as trustee to expenses, remuneration, etc.). [*Sec 145(3); 2 Sch Part I*].

58.27   Cancellation of certain public company shares

In relation to a public company (but not an old public company, see 18.1 DEFINITIONS), where

(*a*)   shares in the company are, in pursuance of the articles, forfeited, or surrendered to the company in lieu, for non-payment of amounts owing on the shares (see 58.11 above), or

(*b*)   shares in the company are acquired by it otherwise than under 8.1(*b*)-(*e*) ACQUISITION OF OWN SHARES and the company has a 'beneficial interest' in those shares, or

(*c*)   the nominee of the company acquires shares in it from a third person without financial assistance being given directly or indirectly by the company and the company has a beneficial interest in the shares, or

(*d*)   a person acquires shares in the company with financial assistance given to him directly or indirectly by the company for the purpose of, or in connection with, the acquisition and the company has a beneficial interest in the shares

then unless the shares or any interest of the company in them are previously disposed of, the company must, not later than the end of the 'relevant period' from their forfeiture, surrender or acquisition

(i)   cancel the shares and diminish the share capital by the nominal amount of the shares cancelled; and

(ii)   where the effect of cancelling the shares takes the nominal value of the company's allotted share capital below the authorised minimum (see 58.12 above) apply for re-registration as a private company, stating the effect of the cancellation.

In determining whether a company has a *'beneficial interest'* in shares, certain interests are disregarded (residual interests under pension and employee share schemes, company's right as trustee to expenses, remuneration, etc.). [*Sec 145(3); 2 Sch Part I*].

The *'relevant period'* is three years where (*a*), (*b*) or (*c*) above applies and one year where (*d*) above applies.

[*Sec 146(1)-(3); CC(CP)A 1985, s 6(2)*].

Without having to comply with the requirements of *Secs 135* and *136* on reduction of share capital (see 58.17 and 58.18 above) the directors may take such steps as are necessary to carry out its obligation under (i) and (ii) above. This includes the passing of a resolution to alter the company's memorandum to state that the company is a public company and to make such other alterations as are requisite. A copy of the resolution must be forwarded to the Registrar of Companies within 15 days (see 51.9 RESOLUTIONS). The company may then be re-registered as a private company if an application in the prescribed form (Form 147), signed by a director or secretary, is delivered to the Registrar of Companies together with a printed copy of the memorandum and articles as altered. The Registrar must retain the application and other documents delivered and issue the company with a certificate of incorporation stating that the company is a private company. On the issue of the certificate the company becomes a private company (the certificate being conclusive evidence of this fact) and any alterations in the memorandum and articles set out in the court order take effect. [*Sec 147*].

Effect of non-compliance. If the company fails to cancel any shares before the end of the relevant period as required under (i) above, the company and every officer in default is guilty of an offence and liable to a fine up to the level in 40.1(*f*) PENALTIES.

If the company fails to apply to be re-registered before the end of the relevant period as required under (ii) above, similar penalties apply. In addition, the company continues to be treated as a public company until re-registered except that *Sec 81* (restriction on public offers by private companies, see 9.2 ALLOTMENT OF SHARES) applies to the company.

[*Sec 149, 24 Sch*].

Voting rights. The company, the company's nominee under (*c*) above and the other shareholder under (*d*) above must not exercise any voting rights in respect of the shares; any such purported exercise is void. [*Sec 146(4)*].

58.28 *Private company becoming a public company*

Where, after shares in a private company are forfeited, surrendered or acquired as under 58.27(*a*)-(*d*) above, the company is re-registered as a public company, the provisions of 58.27 above apply to the company as if it had been a public company at the time of the forfeiture etc. except that the 'relevant period' commences with the date of re-registration. [*Sec 148(1)-(3)*].

Where a public company or its nominee acquires shares in the company, or an interest in such shares, and those shares are shown in the balance sheet as an asset, an amount equal to the value of the shares or interest must be transferred out of profits available for dividend to a reserve fund and are not then available for distribution. [*Sec 148(4)*].

58.29 **Charges of public company on own shares**

A lien or charge of a public company on its own shares is void except in the following instances.

- Where the shares are not fully paid and the charge is for any amount payable in respect of the shares. See 58.10 above.

- Where the ordinary business of the company
    (i) includes the lending of money, or
    (ii) consists of the provision of credit or the bailment (in Scotland, hiring) of goods under a hire purchase agreement, or both

    and the charge arises in connection with a transaction entered into by the company in the ordinary course of its business.

- Where a company is re-registered as a public company (see 49.3 REGISTRATION AND RE-REGISTRATION) or registered as a public company under *Sec 680* (see 15.3 COMPANIES NOT FORMED UNDER CA 1985) and the charge was in existence immediately before the company's application for re-registration or registration.

- Where the company is an old public company (see 18.1 DEFINITIONS) which did not apply for re-registration as a public company before 22 March 1922 and the charge was in existence on or immediately before that date.

[*Sec 150; CC(CP)A 1985, s 6(3)*].

58.30 Duty of directors on serious loss of capital

Where the net assets of a public company are half or less of its called-up share capital, the directors must, within 28 days from the earliest date on which that fact is known to any director, convene an extraordinary meeting of the company, for a date not later than 56 days from that date, to consider what, if any, steps should be taken to deal with the situation. In default, each director who knowingly or wilfully authorises or permits the failure to convene such a meeting, or its continuance after the 56-day period, is guilty of an offence and liable to a fine up to the level in 40.1(*d*) PENALTIES. [*Sec 142, 24 Sch*].

59 Takeover Offers

Cross-references. See 44 RECONSTRUCTIONS AND MERGERS for schemes of arrangement, voluntary arrangements and merger references.

59.1 INTRODUCTION

There is currently very little legislation controlling takeovers other than the provisions in 59.19 to 59.27 below dealing with compulsory acquisitions. The conduct of most takeovers and mergers is governed by the City Code on Takeovers and Mergers (see 59.2 to 59.17 below) and the Listing Rules issued by The Stock Exchange (see 59.18 below).

59.2 THE CITY CODE ON TAKEOVERS AND MERGERS

The City Code on Takeovers and Mergers (the *'Code'*) is issued by the Panel on Takeovers and Mergers (the *'Panel'*). The Code and Panel operate to ensure fair and equal treatment of all shareholders in relation to takeovers.

The responsibilities described in the Code apply most directly to those actively engaged in the securities markets but they also apply to directors of companies which are the subject of the Code, persons who seek to gain or consolidate control of such companies through transactions to which the Code applies, and professional advisers in so far as they advise on the transactions in question.

Companies covered. The Code applies to offers for all listed and unlisted public companies (and, where appropriate, statutory and chartered companies) considered by the Panel to be resident in the UK, the Channel Islands or the Isle of Man. It also applies to an offer for a private company considered to be so resident but only where at any time during the ten years before the date of announcement of the offer or proposed offer

- its equity share capital has been listed on The Stock Exchange;

- dealings and/or prices at which persons were willing to deal in their equity share capital have been published on a regular basis for a continuous basis of at least six months, whether via a newspaper, electronic price quotation system or otherwise;

- the company has been afforded facilities for dealings in its shares to take place on a recognised investment exchange without prior permission for individual transactions and without limit as to the time during which those facilities are to be available (e.g. the shares have been dealt in on the Unlisted Securities Market); or

- it has filed a prospectus for the issue of equity share capital at Companies House.

The Code does not apply to open-ended investment companies.

The Panel normally consider a company to be resident only if it is incorporated in the UK, the Channel Islands or the Isle of Man and has its place of central management in one of those jurisdictions.

Transactions covered. The Code is concerned with takeover and merger transactions of all relevant companies including partial offers and offers by a parent company for shares in its subsidiary. It does not apply to offers for non-voting, non-equity capital (unless they are offers required by *Rule 15*, see 59.8 below).

59.3 Takeover Offers

Enforcement. The Code does not have the force of law but those who fail to conduct themselves in accordance with the Code may, by way of sanction, have the facilities of the securities markets withdrawn from them.

General principles and Rules. The Code is based on a number of general principles expressed in broad terms which are essentially statements of good standards of commercial behaviour (see 59.3 below) and a series of Rules (see 59.4 to 59.17 below). Although the Rules are expressed in more detailed language, they are not framed in technical language and regard should be had to their underlying purpose and spirit. The Rules are supported by substantial notes which are not generally considered in this chapter.

59.3 General principles

The ten general principles are as follows.

1. All shareholders of the same class of an offeree company must be treated similarly by the offeror.

2. During the course of an offer (or when one is contemplated) neither the offeror, offeree or any advisers of either party may furnish information to some shareholders which is not made available to all shareholders. This does not apply to furnishing information in confidence by the offeree company to a bona fide potential offeror (or vice versa).

3. An offeror should only announce an offer after careful consideration and the offeror and its financial adviser must have reason to believe that it can and will be able to implement the offer.

4. Shareholders must be given sufficient information, advice and time to arrive at an informed decision. No information should be withheld from them.

5. All documents or advertisements addressed to the shareholders containing information or advice from the offeror must be prepared to the highest standards of care and accuracy.

6. All parties must try to prevent the creation of a false market in the shares of the offeror or offeree company and must take care that statements are not made which may mislead shareholders or the market.

7. If a bona fide offer has been communicated to the offeree company, or the offeree board has reason to believe that an offer might be imminent, it must not take any action, without consulting the shareholders, which could effectively frustrate the offer or deny the shareholder the opportunity of considering it.

8. Rights of control must be exercised in good faith and the oppression of the minority is wholly unacceptable.

9. Directors of both companies, in advising their shareholders, must act only in their capacity as directors and not have regard to personal interests.

10. Where control of a company is acquired by a person or persons acting in concert, a general offer to all other shareholders is normally required. The offeror must, before making the acquisition, ensure that he can and will continue to be able to implement such an obligation.

59.4 The approach, announcement and independent advice

The approach. The offer must be put forward in the first instance to the board of the offeree company or to its advisers. The identity of the ultimate offeror or, in an approach with a view to an offer, the potential offeror must be disclosed at the outset. The board approached is entitled to be satisfied that the offeror will be able to implement the offer. (*Rule 1*).

Announcements. Secrecy before an announcement must be emphasised to all parties and advisers. An announcement is required

- when a firm intention to make an offer is notified to the board of the offeree company from a serious source;

- immediately upon the acquisition of shares which give rise to an obligation to make an offer under *Rule 9* (see 59.6 below);

- when, following an approach, the offeree company is the subject of rumour and speculation or there is untoward movement in its shares price;

- when, before an approach, the offeree company is the subject of rumour and speculation or there is untoward movement in its share price and a potential offeror's actions have led to the situation;

- when negotiations or discussions are about to be extended to include more than a very restricted number of people; or

- where a purchaser is being sought for 30% or more of the voting rights of a company or when the board of a company is seeking potential offers and

  (i) the company is the subject of rumour and speculation or there is untoward movement in its share price; or

  (ii) the number of potential purchasers or offerors approached is about to be increased to include more than a very restricted number of people.

Before the offeree company is approached, an announcement can only come from the offeror. Following the approach, the primary responsibility for an announcement will normally rest with the offeree company. An announcement of a possible offer may be made.

Any announcement of a firm intention to make an offer must contain

- the terms of the offer;

- the identity of the offeror;

- details of any existing holdings in the offeree company owned or controlled by the offeror (or by a person acting in concert) in respect of which the offeror has received an irrevocable commitment to accept the offer or in respect of which the offeror or a person acting in concert with him (as defined) holds an option to purchase;

- details of any outstanding derivative referenced to securities in the offeree company entered into by the offeror or any person acting in concert with it;

- all conditions to which the offer or the posting of it is subject; and

- details of any arrangements which may be an inducement to deal, or refrain from dealing, in the shares.

The offeror must then proceed with the offer unless the offer is subject to a prior condition which has not been met. Promptly after the start of the offer period, the offeree company must send a copy of the announcement (or summary of its terms) to its shareholders and the Panel.

A person making a statement that he does *not* intend to make an offer for a company will normally be bound by the terms of that statement for a period of six months. The statement should be as clear and unambiguous as possible.

59.5 Takeover Offers

(*Rule 2*).

Independent advice. The board of the offeree company must obtain competent independent advice on any offer and the substance of that advice must be made known to the shareholders. This is particularly important in cases where the offer is a management buy-out or is being made by the existing controlling shareholders. The board of the offeror company must take similar action when there is a reverse takeover or when the directors are faced with a conflict of interest.

The Panel do not regard as an appropriate person to give independent financial advice a person in the same group as the financial or other professional adviser to an offeror or who has a significant interest in, or financial connection with, either an offeror or the offeree company of such a kind as to create a conflict of interest.

(*Rule 3*).

59.5 Dealings and restrictions on the acquisitions of shares and rights over shares

Prohibited dealings by persons other than the offeror. In addition to the provisions relating to INSIDER DEALING (30) if any person other than the offeror is privy to confidential price-sensitive information concerning the offer he must not deal, or recommend another to deal, in securities of the offeree company between the time when there is reason to suppose that an approach or an offer is contemplated and the announcement of it or the termination of discussions. No such dealing may also take place in the offeror company unless the offer is not price-sensitive in relation to those securities. (*Rule 4.1*).

Restrictions on dealings by the offeror, etc. During the offer period, the offeror (and persons acting in concert) must not *sell* securities in the offeree company without the prior consent of the Panel and 24 hours' public notice. After any such consent and notice, the offeror etc. may not make any further *purchases*. (*Rule 4.2*).

Gathering of irrevocable commitments. Any person proposing to contact a private individual or small corporate shareholder with a view to seeking an irrevocable commitment to accept, or refrain from accepting, an offer or contemplated offer must consult the Panel in advance. (*Rule 4.3*).

Timing restrictions on acquisitions. Subject to the exceptions below, where a person (including a person acting in concert with him) holds shares or rights over shares carrying less than 30% of the voting rights of a company, he may not acquire further shares or rights over shares carrying voting rights in that company which, when aggregated with those he already holds, would carry 30% or more of the voting rights. A person holding 30% or more but 50% or less of the voting rights may only acquire a further 1% of the voting rights in any twelve-month period.

The above restrictions do not apply to acquisitions by a person

(*a*)   at any time from a single shareholder if it is the only acquisition within a seven-day period (unless the person has announced the intention to make a firm and unconditional offer);

(*b*)   immediately before the announcement of a firm intention to make an offer provided that offer will be publicly recommended by the board of the offeree company and the acquisition is conditional upon the announcement of the offer;

(*c*)   after the announcement of a firm intention to make an offer provided that the posting of the offer is not, at the time of acquisition, subject to a pre-condition and that either

   •   the acquisition is made with the approval of the offeree board; or

- the offer (or any competing offer) has been publicly recommended by that board; or

- the first closing date of the offer (or any competing offer) has passed and the Secretary of State has announced that no reference will be made to the Competition Commission; or

- the offer is unconditional in all respects; or

(*d*)   if the acquisition is by way of acceptance of the offer.

A person who makes an acquisition under (*a*) above must notify that acquisition and his consequent total holding to the company, The Stock Exchange and the Panel not later than 12 noon on the next business day. He is then subsequently restricted to making further acquisitions under (*b*) to (*d*) above until such time as he makes an offer for the company which lapses. He can then make a further acquisition under (*a*).

(*Rule 5*).

Purchases resulting in an obligation to offer a minimum level of consideration. Where an offeror (or person acting in concert) has purchased shares in the offeree company in the three months before the offer period, the offer to the shareholders of the same class must not be less favourable without the consent of the Panel. This period may be extended back further from the offer period if the Panel considers such a course necessary.

If, while the offer is open, the offeror (or person acting in concert) purchases shares at above the offer price (being the then current value of the offer) the offer price must be increased to not less than the highest price paid for the shares so acquired. A revised offer must then be immediately announced, stating the number of shares purchased and price paid, if practicable.

(*Rule 6*).

Immediate announcement required if the offer has to be amended. Purchases of offeree company shares by an offeror (or person acting in concert) may give rise to an obligation under *Rule 6*, *Rule 9* or *Rule 11*. Immediately after such a purchase, an appropriate announcement must be made, stating the number of shares purchased and the price paid, if practicable. (*Rule 7.1*).

Disclosure of dealings during the offer period. Dealings in relevant securities of the offeree and offeror (as defined) during the offer period by

(i)   the offeror, the offeree company, or by any associates, for their own account or for the account of discretionary investment clients,

(ii)   any such party for the account of non-discretionary investment clients, or

(iii)   any person who owns or controls (directly or indirectly) 1% or more of any class of relevant securities of the offeror or the offeree company, or as a result of any transaction will do so,

must be disclosed by 12 noon on the next business day to The Stock Exchange. In the case of (i) and (iii) above the information will then be made available to the Panel and the press and in the case of (ii) above to the Panel only. In both cases, specimen disclosure forms are available from the Panel.

(*Rule 8*).

59.6   **The mandatory offer and its terms**

Except with the consent of the Panel, where any person

- acquires shares which, together with shares held or acquired by persons acting in concert with him, carry 30% or more of the voting rights of a company, or

- holds, together with persons acting in concert with him, not less than 30% but not more than 50% of the voting rights and acquires, or such persons acquire, an additional 1% of the voting rights in any twelve-month period,

he must extend offers to the holders of all classes of equity share capital, voting or non-voting, and also to the holders of voting non-equity share capital in which he, or persons with whom he is acting in concert, hold shares. Offers for different classes of equity share capital must be comparable. Offers must, in respect of each class of share capital involved, be in cash or be accompanied by a cash alternative at not less than the highest price paid by the offeror, or persons acting in concert, for shares of that class within the preceding twelve months. The cash offer or alternative must remain open for not less than 14 days after the offer has become or is declared unconditional as to acceptances.

The offer must be conditional only upon the offeror having received acceptances resulting in the offeror, and any person acting in concert, holding more than 50% of the voting rights.

The offer must include, if appropriate, a term that if the offer is referred to the Competition Commission or there is an EC merger reference, the offer will lapse.

A director (or close relative or related trust) who sells shares as a result of which the purchaser is required to make an offer under these provisions must ensure, as a condition of sale, that the purchaser undertakes to comply with his obligations. Without the consent of the Panel, the director should not resign from the board until the first closing date of the offer or the date when the offer becomes or is declared wholly unconditional, whichever is the later.

(*Rule 9*).

59.7   **The voluntary offer and its terms**

The acceptance condition. It must be a condition of any offer for voting equity share capital which, if accepted in full, would result in the offeror holding over 50% of the voting rights in the offeree company that the offer will not become or be declared unconditional as to acceptances unless the offeror has acquired, or agreed to acquire, shares carrying over 50% of the voting rights attributable to

- equity share capital alone; and

- equity share capital and non-equity share capital combined.

(*Rule 10*).

Consideration to be offered. Except with the consent of the Panel, the offer for a particular class must be in cash or accompanied by a cash alternative where

(*a*)   the shares of any class under offer in the offeree company purchased for cash by an offeror (and any person acting in concert with it) during the offer period and within 12 months prior to its commencement carry 10% or more of the voting rights currently exercisable at a class meeting of that class (in which case the offer must be not less than the highest price paid by the offeror (or any person acting in concert with it) for shares of that class during the offer period and within 12 months prior to its commencement); or

(*b*)   subject to (*a*) above, shares of any class under offer in the offeree company are purchased for cash by an offeror or any person acting in concert with it during the offer period (in which case the offer must be not less than the highest price paid by the offeror (or any person acting in concert with it) for shares of that class during the offer period.

The Panel may grant exception to this but may also enforce the requirement where less than 10% of the voting rights have been purchased in order to give effect to General Principle 1 (see 59.3 above). (*Rule 11*).

Competition Commission, etc. If the offer is the possible subject of a reference to the Competition Commission, or the subject of proceedings or referral under EEC regulations, it must be a term of the offer that it will lapse if there is a reference etc. before the first closing date or the date when the offer is declared unconditional as to acceptances, whichever is the later. Except in the case of an offer under *Rule 9*, the offeror may, in addition, make the offer conditional on a decision being made that there will be no such reference, etc. (*Rule 12*).

Subjective conditions. Subject to consent by the Panel, an offer must not normally be subject to conditions which depend solely on subjective judgements by the directors of the offeror or the fulfilment of which is in their hands. (*Rule 13*).

59.8   Provisions applicable to all offers

Where there is more than one class of share capital. In such circumstances a comparable offer must be made for each class of equity share capital, whether having voting rights or not. An offer for non-voting equity should not be conditional on any particular level of acceptances for that class unless the offer for voting equity is also conditional on the success of the offer for the non-voting equity. Subject to certain exceptions, classes of non-equity share capital need not be the subject of an offer. Where an offer is made for more than one class of share, separate offers must be made for each class. (*Rule 14*).

Appropriate offer for convertibles, etc. Where the offeree company has outstanding convertible securities, the offeror must make an appropriate offer or proposal to the stockholders to ensure that their interests are safeguarded. The board of the offeree company must take competent independent advice on this and make the advice, and its opinion, known to the stockholders. Similar provisions apply *mutatis mutandis* if the offeree company has options or subscription rights outstanding. (*Rule 15*).

Special deals on favourable conditions. Except with the consent of the Panel, the offeror or person acting in concert may not make any arrangements with shareholders or deal in shares of the offeree company, either during an offer or when one is reasonably contemplated, if there are more favourable conditions attached than are extended to all shareholders. (*Rule 16*).

Announcement of acceptance levels. An offeror must make an appropriate announcement of acceptances, and simultaneously inform The Stock Exchange (if the shares are dealt in there), by 8.30a.m. at the latest on the business day following the day on which the offer

(*a*)   is due to expire; or

(*b*)   becomes or is declared unconditional as to acceptances; or

(*c*)   is revised or extended.

The announcement must state (as far as practicable) the total number of shares and rights over shares

•   for which acceptances of the offer have been received;

•   held before the offer period; and

•   acquired or agreed to be acquired during the offer period and must specify the percentages of the relevant classes of share capital represented by these figures.

In default, The Stock Exchange will consider a temporary suspension of listing of the offeree's and offeror's shares.

If the offeror fails to make the announcement under (*b*) above by 3.30p.m. on the relevant day, any acceptor will be entitled to withdraw his acceptance. This right may be terminated (but not earlier than eight days after the relevant event) by the offeror confirming that the offer is still unconditional and making the appropriate announcement.

(*Rule 17*).

Use of proxies, etc. The offeror must not require a shareholder, as a term of acceptance of the offer, to appoint a proxy to vote in respect of his shares or to exercise any other rights in relation to those shares unless the appointment is made on the terms that

- the proxy may not vote, or the rights be exercised, unless the offer is wholly unconditional (or, in the case of voting, will become wholly unconditional or lapse immediately upon the outcome of the resolution in question);

- the votes are to be cast to satisfy any outstanding condition of the offer;

- it ceases to be valid if the acceptance is withdrawn; and

- it applies only to shares assented to the offer.

Such terms must be set out in the offer document.

(*Rule 18*).

59.9 Conduct during the offer

Information. All documents and advertisements issued and statements made during the course of the offer must satisfy the highest standards of accuracy and must be adequately and fairly presented. Any document or advertisement must state that the directors accept responsibility for the contents which to the best of their belief is accurate and does not omit any material facts. There are restrictions on the use of advertisements (which in general should be cleared with the Panel in advance) and telephone campaigns (which may only be conducted by staff of the financial adviser who are fully conversant with the requirements of the Code). Certain statements are unacceptable (e.g. an indication of a possible improved offer without commitment or specification of the improvement). There are also rules for the conduct of radio and television interviews.

Copies of all documents and announcements bearing on an offer, and of all advertisements and material released to the press, must be lodged with the Panel and advisers to all other parties at the time of release (even if outside normal business hours).

(*Rule 19*).

Equality of information. Information about companies in an offer must be made equally available to all shareholders as nearly as possible at the same time and in the same manner. Where there is more than one offeror, any information given to one offeror must, on request, be given equally and promptly to another (even if a less welcome offeror). If the offer is a management buy-out or similar transaction, the offeror must, on request, promptly furnish the independent directors of the offeree company or its advisers with all information which has been furnished by the offeror to external providers or potential providers of finance for the buy-out. (*Rule 20*).

Restrictions on frustrating action. During the course of an offer, or earlier if it has reason to believe that an offer may be imminent, the board of the offeree company must not without approval of the shareholders in general meeting (unless in pursuance of a contract already entered into)

- issue any authorised but unissued shares;
- issue or grant options in respect of any unissued shares;
- create or issue any securities carrying the right of conversion into shares;
- sell or acquire assets of a material amount (or agree to do so); or
- enter into contracts otherwise than in the normal course of business.

(*Rule 21*).

Responsibilities of the offeree company regarding registration procedures. The board of the offeree company must ensure prompt registration of transfers during an offer and see that its registrar complies fully with various procedures set out in *Appendix 4* (e.g. counting, checking and certifying acceptances). (*Rule 22*).

59.10 **Documents from the offeror and offeree board**

Shareholders must be given sufficient information and advice to enable them to reach a properly informed decision on the offer. The offeror's obligation in this respect applies both to its own and the offeree's shareholders. (*Rule 23*).

Offeror documents. The offer document will normally be expected to cover the offeror's intentions regarding the continuation of the business of the offeree company (and any major changes therein) and the continued employment of the employees, together with the long-term commercial justification for the proposed offer. The offer document *must* contain *inter alia*

- certain financial and other information on the offeror and offeree company (profits or losses for the last three years; a statement of assets and liabilities as per the last published audited accounts; material changes since the last published audited accounts; names of directors, etc.);
- unless the Panel allows otherwise, a description of how the offer is to be financed and the source of the finance;
- if the value of the offer is compared with previous prices of the offeree's shares, a comparison between the current value of the offer and the price of the offeree's shares on the last day of business prior to the start of the offer period;
- details of shareholdings of the offeror in the offeree company;
- details of shareholdings in the offeror (in the case of a securities exchange only) and in the offeree company
  - (i)   in which the directors of the offeror are interested;
  - (ii)   which any person acting in concert with the offeror owns or controls;
  - (iii) owned or controlled by any persons who, prior to the posting of the offer document, have irrevocably accepted the offer (stating their names); and
  - (iv) owned or controlled by a person with whom the offeror (or any person acting in concert) has an arrangement;

  together with details of dealings in any such shareholdings in the twelve months before the offer period;

- a statement as to whether or not any agreement or arrangement exists between the offeror (or person acting in concert) and the directors or shareholders of the offeree company in connection with the offer and, if so, full particulars;

- where the offer is, or includes an element of cash, confirmation by a third party (e.g. bank or financial adviser) that resources are available to the offeror to satisfy full acceptance of the offer;

- a statement as to whether or not any securities acquired will be transferred to any other persons and, if so, details;

- if the offer involves the issue of unlisted securities, an estimate of their value; and

- in the case of a securities exchange offer only, whether and how the emoluments of the offeror directors will be affected by the acquisition of the offeree company or by any other associated transaction.

(*Rule 24*).

In addition to the above requirements in relation to the offer document, see also 59.18 below for requirements of The Stock Exchange.

Offeree board circulars. The board of the offeree company must circulate its views on the offer to its shareholders and make known the substance of the advice given to it by independent advisers under *Rule 3*. It should comment on the statements in the offer document regarding the offeror's intentions in respect of the offeree company and its employees. The first major circular from the board advising shareholders of the offer must contain *inter alia*

- details of the shareholdings of the offeree company in the offeror;

- details of the shareholdings in the offeree company and in the offeror

  (i)   in which directors of the offeree company are interested,

  (ii) owned or controlled by a subsidiary of the offeree company or a pension fund of the offeree company or its subsidiary,

  (iii) owned or controlled by a person who has an arrangement with the offeree company or an associate,

  although the details under (ii) and (iii) for shares in the offeror need only be given in the case of a securities exchange offer;

- whether the directors intend to accept or reject the offer in respect of their own beneficial holdings; and

- details of directors' service contracts with more than twelve months to run.

(*Rule 25*).

Display of documents. Various documents as specified in the offer document or offeree board circular must be available for inspection from the time of the offer document or circular until the end of the offer period. (*Rule 26*).

Material changes in information sent to shareholders, in particular in shareholdings and dealings, directors' emoluments and service contracts, special arrangements and profit forecasts, must be advised in subsequent documents. (*Rule 27*).

59.11 Profit forecasts

Profit forecasts (as widely defined) must be prepared to the highest standards of accuracy and are the sole responsibility of the directors. Any assumptions upon which they are based must be stated in the document and in any press announcement. If the offer is solely for cash, any forecast need not be reported on. In all other cases, the accounting policies and calculations for the forecast must be reported on by the auditors or consultant accountants and where income from land is a material element, that part of the forecast should be examined and reported on by an independent valuer. Any reports must be included in the document containing the profit forecast. Any subsequent documents sent out must contain a statement that the profit forecast remains valid and that the financial advisers who reported on the forecast have indicated that they have no objection to their reports continuing to apply. If a forecast of profit before tax appears in any document, there must also be included forecasts of taxation and, where material, extraordinary items and minority interests. Whenever a profit forecast is made in relation to a period in which trading has already commenced, any previously published profit figures for any expired part of that trading period must be stated (with prior year comparatives). (*Rule 28*).

59.12 Asset valuations

When a valuation of assets is given in connection with an offer, it must be supported by an opinion of an independent valuer. The basis of valuation must be clearly stated (normally open market value) and any potential tax liability which might arise if the asset were sold at the valuation. The effective date of valuation must also be given, together with a statement that the current valuation would not be materially different. (If this statement cannot be made, the valuation must be updated.) The opinion of the valuer, and the valuer's consent to publication of it, must be contained in the document containing the asset valuation. (*Rule 29*).

59.13 Timing and revision

Posting of documents. The offer document should normally be posted within 28 days of the announcement of a firm intention to make an offer. The board of the offeree company should advise its shareholders of its views as soon as practicable after publication of the offer document and normally within 14 days. (*Rule 30*).

Timing of the offer. An offer must initially be open for at least 21 days after it is posted. This may be extended by further notice. If the offer is unconditional as to acceptances, a statement may be made that the offer will remain open until further notice in which case at least 14 days' notice must be given before the offer is closed.

There is no obligation to extend an offer the conditions of which are not met by the first or any subsequent closing date.

Once an offer has become or is declared unconditional as to acceptances, the offer must remain open for not less than 14 days after the date on which it would otherwise have expired. This is not required if the offer was unconditional from the outset but, in such a case, the offer document must clearly and prominently set out the position.

If statements such as 'the offer will not be extended beyond a specified date unless it is unconditional as to acceptances' are included in documents sent to shareholders of the offeree company, or are made by the directors and not immediately withdrawn if incorrect, only in wholly exceptional circumstances will the offeror be allowed to extend its offer beyond the stated date.

Except with the consent of the Panel

(*a*)   an offer may not be declared unconditional as to acceptances after midnight on the 60th day after the day the initial offer document was posted (the Panel's consent will normally only be granted if a competing offer has been announced or the offeree board agree to an extension);

(*b*)   on the 60th day (or any other date beyond which the offeror has stated that its offer will not be extended) an announcement must be made by 5 p.m. as to whether the offer is unconditional as to acceptances or has lapsed;

(*c*)   all conditions must be fulfilled or the offer must lapse within 21 days of the first closing date or of the date the offer becomes or is declared unconditional as to acceptances, whichever is the later;

(*d*)   the consideration must be posted within 14 days of the later of the first closing date of the offer, the date the offer becomes or is declared wholly unconditional or the date of receipt of an acceptance complete in all respects.

(*e*)   the board of the offeree company should not announce trading results, profit or dividend forecasts, asset valuation or proposals for dividend payments after the 39th day following posting of the initial offer.

(*Rule 31*).

Revision. If statements such as 'the offer will not be further increased' are included in documents sent to the shareholders of the offeree company, or are made by the directors and not immediately withdrawn if incorrect, only in wholly exceptional circumstances will the offeror be allowed to amend the terms of its offer. Where an offer is revised, it must be kept open for at least 14 days following the date of posting and all shareholders who accepted the original offer must be entitled to the revised consideration. (*Rule 32*).

Alternative offers. In general, the provisions of *Rules 31* and *32* above also apply to alternative offers, including cash alternatives. However, where the value of a cash alternative is more than half the maximum value of the offer, an offeror is not obliged to keep that alternative open for 14 days after the offer has become unconditional if it has given notice to shareholders that it reserves the right to close the cash alternative on a stated date. (*Rule 33*).

Right of withdrawal. An acceptor must be entitled to withdraw his acceptance after 21 days from the first closing date of the initial offer provided that it has not been declared unconditional as to acceptances by that date. (*Rule 34*).

59.14   Restrictions following offers and possible offers

Except with the consent of the Panel, where an offer has been announced or posted but has not been declared wholly unconditional and has been withdrawn or lapsed, the offeror and any person who acted in concert with the offeror in the original offer, and any person who is subsequently acting in concert with any of them, cannot

- announce an offer or possible offer for the offeree company,

- acquire any shares in the offeree company if the offeror or any such person would then be obliged under *Rule 9* to make an offer, or

- acquire any shares in the offeree company if the offeror and any such person holds shares carrying over 49% but not over 50% of the voting rights in the offeree company

within the twelve months from the date on which the offer is withdrawn or lapses.

This restriction may apply where a person makes an announcement which, although not amounting to the announcement of an offer, raises or confirms the possibility that an offer might be made and then does not make a firm offer within a reasonable time.

Similar restrictions also apply following a partial offer which could result in a holding of not less than 30% and not more than 50% of the voting rights in the offeree company.

Except with the consent of the Panel, where a person, together with any person acting in concert, holds shares carrying more than 50% of the voting rights of a company, neither of those persons may, within six months of the closure of any previous offer which was declared wholly unconditional, make a second offer or acquire shares from any shareholder on better terms than the previous offer.

(*Rule 35*).

59.15 Partial offers

The Panel's consent is required for any partial offer. This will normally be given where the offer could not result in the offeror holding 30% or more of the voting rights in the company. It will not, however, normally be granted where the holding could exceed that percentage and the offeror, or any person acting in concert, has acquired shares in the offeree company

- selectively or in significant numbers during the twelve-month period before the application for consent; or

- at any time after the partial offer was reasonably in contemplation.

Buying during and after the offer. The offeror (and persons acting in concert) may not purchase shares in the offeree company during the offer period or, in the case of a successful partial offer, during the twelve months after the end of the offer period (except with the consent of the Panel). The latter restriction is also extended to purchases by any person who subsequently acts in concert either with the offeror or any person acting in concert in the partial offer.

Offers between 30% and 50%. When an offer is made which could result in the offeror holding shares carrying not less than 30% and not more than 50% of the voting rights, the precise number of shares offered for must be stated and the offer may not be declared unconditional as to acceptances unless acceptances are received for not less than that number.

Approval of offer for 30% or more by shareholders. Any offer which could result in the offeror holding shares carrying 30% or more of the voting rights of a company must normally be conditional on the approval of the offer being given by shareholders holding over 50% of the voting rights not held by the offeror and persons acting in concert with it. This is normally signified by a separate box on the form of acceptance. The requirement is occasionally waived if over 50% of the voting rights in the offeree company are held by one shareholder.

Warning about control. Where a partial offer could result in the offeror holding shares carrying over 49% of the voting rights of the offeree company, the offer document must contain specific and prominent reference to this and the fact that, if the offer succeeds, the offeror will be free, subject to the provisions above about buying during and after the offer, to acquire further shares without incurring an obligation to make a general offer under *Rule 9*.

Scaling down. Partial offers must be made to all shareholders of the class and arrangements must be made for those shareholders who wish to do so to accept in full for the relevant percentage of their holding. Shares tendered in excess of this percentage must be accepted by the offeror from each shareholder in the same proportion to the number tendered to the extent necessary to enable it to obtain the total number of shares for which it has offered.

Comparable offer. When an offer is made for a company with more than one class of equity share capital which could result in the offeror holding shares carrying 30% or more of the voting rights, a comparable offer must be made for each class.

(*Rule 36*).

59.16 Takeover Offers

59.16 Redemption or purchase by a company of its own securities

Where a company redeems or purchases its own voting shares, a resulting increase in the percentage of voting rights attaching to shareholdings of the directors and persons acting in concert with them will be treated as an acquisition for the purposes of *Rule 9*. However, subject to prior consultation, the Panel will normally waive any resulting obligation to make a general offer if there is a vote of independent shareholders.

During the course of an offer (or before the date of the offer if the offeree board has reason to believe that a bona fide offer might be imminent) no redemption or purchase by the offeree company of its own shares may be effected without the approval of the shareholders in general meeting (except in pursuance of a contract already entered into).

(Rule 37).

59.17 Dealings by connected exempt marketmakers

Where an exempt marketmaker is connected with an offeror or the offeree company

- the exempt marketmaker must not carry out any dealings with the purpose of assisting the offeror or the offeree company, as the case may be;
- the offeror (and any person acting in concert with him) must not deal as principal with the exempt marketmaker during the offer period. (It will generally be for the advisers to the offeror to ensure compliance rather than the marketmaker.)
- any securities which the marketmaker owns must not be voted in the context of the offer; and
- dealings in relevant securities of the offeror or offeree company by the marketmaker should be aggregated and disclosed to the Stock Exchange, the Panel and the press not later than 12 noon on the business day following the transactions.

Where an exempt marketmaker is connected with the offeror, he must not assent to the offer until it is unconditional as to acceptances.

(Rule 38).

59.18 THE STOCK EXCHANGE REQUIREMENTS ON TAKEOVERS AND MERGERS

In addition to the City Code on takeovers and mergers, there are also relevant provisions and requirements which apply to listed companies in the Listing Rules. These include the following.

- Where the consideration being offered consists of securities for which listing is being sought, listing particulars may be required either as a result of the original terms of the offer or as a result of a revision of the terms during the course of the offer. Where listing rules have already been published and the offer is revised, supplementary listing particulars may be required.
- The listing particulars must comply with the normal requirements (see 42.7 PROSPECTUSES AND PUBLIC ISSUES) subject to the following.
    - (i) References to the issuer's group does not, subject to (ii) and (iii) below, include the offeree company and its subsidiaries unless it has become a member of the issuer's group by the time the listing particulars are published.
    - (ii) Information regarding major interests in shares and directors' interests in

shares must be given in relation to the issuer's share capital both as existing and as enlarged by the shares for which listing is sought.

(iii) If the offer is recommended by the offeree board at the time of publication of the offer document, the issuer must publish working capital and indebtedness statements on the basis that the acquisition has taken place. If it is not, the issuer must publish its own working capital and indebtedness statements and the Exchange will allow the combined statements to be given later (in a circular or supplementary listing particulars published within 28 days of the offer being declared wholly unconditional).

- Listing particulars (or supplementary listing particulars) must be published subject to the normal rules (see 42.14 PROSPECTUSES AND PUBLIC ISSUES). Any revised or supplementary listing particulars must normally be published and circulated to shareholders at the time of despatch of the revised offer document.

  In certain circumstances, summary particulars may be despatched to the shareholders of the offeree company in place of listing particulars.

- Where listing particulars have been published in connection with an offer which involves the exchange of securities for securities of another company and the offer is revised to include a new class of debt security for which listing is to be obtained, it is not necessary to repeat the information contained in the original listing particulars but any additional information appropriate to the issue of those securities must be published in new listing particulars.

(The Listing Rules, Chapter 10.45-10.50).

59.19 COMPULSORY ACQUISITIONS

Where, following a successful takeover, the offeror has acquired at least 90% of the shares in the offeree company, subject to certain conditions there are provisions whereby

(*a*)   the offeror can compulsorily acquire the remaining shares; and

(*b*)   the remaining shareholders can require the offeror to acquire their shares.

See 59.20 to 59.27 below.

59.20 Definitions

Associates   in relation to an offeror means

- a nominee of the offeror;

- a holding company, subsidiary or fellow subsidiary of the offeror (or a nominee of such a company), see 18.1 DEFINITIONS;

- a body corporate in which the offeror is *'substantially interested'* i.e. where the body or its directors are accustomed to act in accordance with the offeror's instructions or the offeror is entitled to control one-third or more of the voting power at general meetings; or

- any person who is, or is the nominee of, a party to an agreement or arrangement with the offeror for the acquisition of shares subject to the takeover offer where the agreement etc. imposes obligations or restrictions on any of the parties with respect to their use, retention or disposal of the shares. The agreement etc. must be legally binding unless it involves mutuality in the undertakings, expectations or understandings of the parties to it.

Where the offeror is an individual, his associates also include his spouse and any minor child or step-child.

59.21 Takeover Offers

[Secs 203(3)(4), 204(2)(a)(5)(6), 430E(4)-(8); FSA 1986, 12 Sch; CA 1989, 18 Sch 35].

Offeror means, subject to 59.27 below, the person making the takeover offer. *[Sec 428(8); FSA 1986, 12 Sch]*.

Revised offers. Where the terms of an offer make provision for their revision and for acceptances on the previous terms to be treated as acceptances on the revised terms, the revision is not regarded as a fresh offer and references to the date of the offer are construed as to the date of the original offer. *[Sec 428(7); FSA 1986, 12 Sch]*.

Takeover offer means an offer to acquire all the 'shares', or all the shares of any class or classes, in a company other than 'shares already held by the offeror' at the date of the offer. This requirement is regarded as satisfied even though the offer does not extend to shares held by an 'associate' of the offeror. However, any such shares, whether held when the offer is made or subsequently acquired, are not regarded as shares to which the offer relates unless the offeror actually acquires those shares from the associate within the provisions of 59.21 below relating to *Other shares acquired during the offer period*.

The offer must be on the same terms for all the shares to which it relates or, where there are different classes, all shares of each class although a variation is permitted where

- the law of a country or territory outside the UK precludes an offer of consideration in any form specified in the offer or makes compliance impossible or unduly onerous; and

- the variation is such that the offeree receives consideration of substantially equivalent value.

'Shares' means shares allotted on the date of the offer although a takeover offer may include all or any shares subsequently allotted before a date specified under the terms of the offer. Shares include securities if they are convertible or entitle the holder to subscribe for shares.

'Shares already held by the offeror' includes shares he has contracted to acquire but that does not include shares the subject of a contract binding the holder to accept the offer when made and entered into by the holder either for no consideration and under seal in England and Wales or for no consideration other than a promise by the offeror to make the offer.

[Secs 428(1)-(6), 430(1)(2), 430E(1), 430F; FSA 1986, 12 Sch].

59.21 Right of offeror to buy out minority

Where, following a takeover offer which relates only to one class of shares, the offeror acquires at least 90% in value of the shares to which the offer relates, he may give notice to the remaining shareholders that he desires to acquire their shares. If the offer relates to different classes of shares, the provision similarly applies but to each class separately.

Notice cannot be given unless the necessary minimum has been acquired within four months of the offer date and must be given within two months of acquiring that minimum. It must be given on the prescribed form (Form 429(4)). See 59.25 below for the method of giving notice. On first giving such notice, the offeror must send a copy of it to the company, together with a statutory declaration in the prescribed form (Form 429(dec)) stating that the conditions for giving the notice are satisfied. Any person who fails to send a notice or statutory declaration, or makes a declaration knowing it to be false or possibly untrue, is liable to a penalty up to the level in 40.1(*b*) PENALTIES and for continued failure a daily default fine of one-fiftieth of the statutory maximum (see 40.1 PENALTIES). It is a defence for failing to send a copy of a notice that the person took all reasonable steps to comply with the provisions.

[*Sec 429(1)-(7); FSA 1986, 12 Sch*].

Other shares acquired during the offer period. Where the offeror acquires any shares to which the offer relates during the offer period but otherwise than by acceptance of the offer, then subject to the condition that the acquisition consideration does not exceed the consideration under the terms of the offer (as at that time or as subsequently increased), the offeror is treated for these purposes as having acquired the shares by virtue of acceptance of the offer. In any other case, shares so acquired are treated as excluded from those to which the offer relates. Subject to the same condition, where an associate of the offeror acquires or contracts to acquire shares to which the offer relates during the offer period, such shares are treated as shares to which the offer relates.

Example

A Ltd makes an offer for the 1 million issued shares in B Ltd at £1 per share which is subsequently increased to £1.20 per share. It receives acceptances from holders of 800,000 shares. During the offer period, A Ltd also buys 110,000 shares on the open market at £1.10 per share.

A Ltd will be treated as having acquired the 110,000 shares under the terms of the offer (£1.10 being less than the subsequently increased offer price). It has thus acquired 910,000 (800,000 + 110,000) shares (91%) under the offer and can buy out the minority. If, on the other hand, A Ltd had bought the 110,000 shares at £1.30 per share, these shares would have been excluded from the shares subject to the offer. A Ltd would be treated as having acquired 800,000 out of 890,000 (1,000,000 – 110,000) shares under the offer (i.e. 89.89%) and would not therefore be able to buy out the minority.

[*Secs 429(8), 430E(2); FSA 1986, 12 Sch*].

59.22 *Effect of notice*

Subject to 59.26 below, where notice is given, the offeror is *entitled and bound* to acquire the shares on the terms of the offer. If there is a choice of consideration, the notice must give the holder six weeks from the date of notice to indicate his choice which the offeror must then satisfy unless this is no longer possible; the notice must also indicate which consideration will apply in default of communication from the shareholder within the time limit.

At the end of the six weeks, the offeror must

(*a*)   send a copy of the notice to the company together with

- where the shares are registered, an instrument of transfer executed on behalf of the shareholder by a person appointed by the offeror, on receipt of which the company must register the offeror as holder; or

- where shares are transferable by delivery of warrants etc., a statement to that effect, on receipt of which the company must issue the offeror with warrants and those already in issue become void; and

(*b*)   pay or transfer to the company the consideration for the shares to which the notice relates (or, as the case may be, allot any shares or securities to the company) to be held on trust in a separate bank account for the original shareholder.

The company must pass over the consideration, together with any dividends or other sums accruing including bank interest, to the persons entitled. Where, following reasonable enquiries at reasonable intervals, such persons cannot be found within twelve years of receipt of the consideration or, if earlier, the company is wound up, the funds must be paid into court (in Scotland deposited in a bank account in the name of the Accountant of Court). The expenses of any enquiry may be defrayed out of property held on trust for the person to whom that enquiry relates.

[*Sec 430; FSA 1986, 12 Sch*].

59.23 Right of minority shareholder to be bought out by the offeror

Where, following a takeover offer which relates to all the shares of a company, the offeror, or any associate of his, holds at least 90% in value of the shares (whether acquired under the offer or otherwise as long as some shares are acquired under the offer) a shareholder may, in writing at any time within the offer period, require the offeror to acquire his shares. If the offer relates to shares of any class or classes, the provision similarly applies but to each class separately. See 59.20 above for the definition of '*associate*'. Unless the offeror has given notice to the shareholder under 59.21 above, he must, within one month, give that shareholder notice in the prescribed form (Form 430A) of his rights. The notice may specify a period during which the shareholder can exercise his rights under the provisions but such period cannot end before three months after the end of the offer period. See 59.25 below for the method of giving notice. If the offeror (or where the offeror is a company, any officer of that company) fails to send the required notice, he is liable to a penalty up to the level in 40.1(*d*) PENALTIES and for continued failure a daily default fine of one-fiftieth of the statutory maximum (see 40.1 PENALTIES). It is a defence for an individual to show that he took all reasonable steps to comply with the provisions.

[*Secs 430A, 430E(3); FSA 1986, 12 Sch*].

59.24 *Effect of notice*

Subject to 59.26 below, where notice is given, the offeror is *entitled and bound* to acquire the shares on the terms of the offer or on such other terms as are agreed. If there is a choice of consideration, the holder may indicate his choice when requiring the offeror to buy his shares and the offeror must then comply with this choice unless it is no longer possible. The notice from the offeror must, in any case, give details of the choice available and state which consideration would apply in default of the holder indicating his choice.

[*Sec 430B; FSA 1986, 12 Sch*].

59.25 Method of giving notice

The notice to shareholders by the offeror under 59.21 and 59.23 above must be given

(*a*)   personally; or

(*b*)   by recorded delivery post to

    (i)   his address in the UK registered in the company's books; or

    (ii)   if no such address is registered, the address (if any) in the UK given by him to the company for the giving of notices; or

(*c*)   if no address is registered under (*b*)(i) above or has been notified under (*b*)(ii) above, by air mail (if available) to the address outside the UK registered in the company's books.

Where notice cannot be given under (*a*) to (*c*) above because the holder of the shares is the holder of a share warrant to bearer, it must be given by advertisement as provided in the company's articles or, if no such provision is made, by advertisement in the *Gazette*.

[*SI 1987 No 752, Reg 4*].

59.26 **Application to the court**

Applications may be made to the court in the following circumstances.

(*a*)   Where notice is given by the offeror under 59.21 above, the shareholder may apply to the court within six months of the date of notice. The court may

   (i)   order that the offeror is not entitled and bound to acquire the shares; or

   (ii)   specify terms of acquisition different from those of the offer.

Where such application is pending at the end of the six-week period referred to in 59.22 above, the requirements of 59.22(*a*) and (*b*) need not be complied with until the application has been disposed of.

In the ordinary case of such an offer where the 90% who accepted the offer are unconnected with the offeror, the court will pay the greatest attention to the views of the majority. Where, however, as a matter of substance the persons putting forward the offer are the majority shareholders, the onus must fall on the majority shareholders to satisfy the court that the scheme is one with which the minority shareholders ought reasonably to be compelled to fall in with (*Re Bugle Press Ltd [1961] Ch 270*).

(*b*)   Where a shareholder exercises his rights under 59.23 above, the court may, on application by him or the offeror, vary as it thinks fit the terms on which the offeror is entitled and bound to acquire the shares.

(*c*)   Where a takeover offer has not been accepted by the necessary minimum under 59.21 above, the court may, on application by the offeror, nevertheless authorise him to give notice under those provisions if satisfied that

   (i)   the offeror has, after reasonable enquiry, been unable to trace one or more shareholders;

   (ii)   the shares which the offeror has acquired plus those within (i) above amount to at least the necessary minimum;

   (iii)   the consideration offered is fair and reasonable; and

   (iv)   it is just and equitable to do so having regard, in particular, to the number of shareholders who have been traced but who have not accepted the offer.

No order for costs must be made against a shareholder applying under (*a*) or (*b*) above unless the court considers that *either* the application is unnecessary, improper or vexatious *or* there has been unreasonable delay in making the application or unreasonable conduct on his part in conducting the proceedings on the application.

[*Sec 430C; FSA 1986, 12 Sch*].

In exercising its discretion under *Sec 430C* above, the court will consider the relevant provisions of the City Code on Takeovers and Mergers even though the Code does not have the force of law. Although a minor infringement would not necessarily lead the court to exercise its discretion in favour of the non-assenting shareholder, a substantial failure by the bidder to comply with the Code's provisions as to disclosure would be a major factor operating against compulsory acquisition of the non-assenting shareholder's shares (*Re Chez Nico (Restaurants) Ltd [1991] BCC 736*).

59.27 Takeover Offers

59.27 Joint offers

Where a takeover offer is made by two or more persons jointly, the conditions for the exercise of the rights conferred by 59.21 and 59.23 above are satisfied by the joint offerors acquiring the necessary shares jointly in the case of acceptances of offers and either jointly or separately in other cases. Subject to certain exceptions, the rights and obligations of the offeror under 59.21 to 59.25 above are joint rights and joint and several obligations of the joint offerors. [*Sec 430D; FSA 1986, 12 Sch*].

60   Unlimited Companies

Cross-references. See 49.8 to 49.10 REGISTRATION AND RE-REGISTRATION for an unlimited company re-registering as a public company, a limited company becoming unlimited and an unlimited company becoming limited.

60.1   DEFINITIONS

An unlimited company is a company having no limit on the liability of its members. Such a company can only be a private company not a public one. [*Sec 1(2)(c)(3)(b)*]. This liability arises only on the company being insolvent on winding up. Whilst the company is a going concern, liability is limited to the amount unpaid on shares.

60.2   MEMORANDUM AND ARTICLES

The memorandum and articles of an unlimited company with a share capital must be in the form set out in *SI 1985 No 805, Table E* or as near to that form as circumstances admit. [*Secs 3(1), 8(4)(c)*]. The articles must be registered with the memorandum and signed by the subscribers to the memorandum. They must state the amount of share capital with which the company proposes to be registered. [*Sec 7(1)(2)*]. Notice of any alteration or increase in the capital must be given to the Registrar of Companies. [*Secs 122, 123*]. See 58.15 and 58.16 SHARES AND SHARE CAPITAL.

60.3   DELIVERY OF ACCOUNTS TO THE REGISTRAR OF COMPANIES

Subject to below, the directors of an unlimited company are not required to deliver accounts to the Registrar of Companies in respect of a financial year provided that at no time during the accounting reference period

- has the company been, to its knowledge, the subsidiary of a limited company;

- have there been to its knowledge rights exercisable, by or on behalf of two or more limited companies which, if they had been exercisable by one of them, would have made the company its subsidiary; or

- has the company been the parent company of a limited company.

References to a limited company include a foreign limited company.

The exemption above does not apply to the following companies.

(*a*)   A company which is a banking or insurance company or the parent company of a banking or insurance group.

(*b*)   After 21 July 1993, the company is a '*qualifying unlimited company*' i.e. an unlimited company incorporated in Great Britain each of whose members is

    (i)   a limited company; or

    (ii)   another unlimited, or Scottish firm, each of whose members is a limited company.

References in (i) or (ii) to a limited company, another unlimited company and Scottish firm include references to any comparable undertaking incorporated or formed outside Great Britain.

(*c*)   A company which, at any time during the relevant accounting period, has carried on business as the promoter of a trading stamp scheme within *Trading Stamps Act 1964*.

[*Sec 254(1)-(3); CA 1989, s 17; SI 1991 No 2705, 2 Sch 1; SI 1993 No 1820, Regs 9, 10; SI 1993 No 3246, 2 Sch*].

61   Unregistered Companies

61.1   The provisions of *CA 1985* listed in the table below apply to 'unregistered companies' as if they were registered under that Act.

'Unregistered companies' means any body corporate, incorporated and having a principal place of business in Great Britain, other than

(*a*)   any body incorporated by or registered under any public general Act of Parliament;

(*b*)   any body not formed for the purpose of carrying on a business which has for its objects the acquisition of gain by the body or its individual members;

(*c*)   any body exempted by statutory instrument; and

(*d*)   any investment company with variable capital.

In addition to the specific modifications etc. in the table, the following general provisions apply.

•   The unregistered company is deemed to be registered in England and Wales if its principal office on 5 January 1976 or subsequent date of incorporation was in England or Wales (and similarly for Scotland).

•   References to the registered office of a company is construed as a reference to the principal office.

•   References to a public company and a private company are construed respectively as references to an unregistered company which does and does not have the power under the instrument constituting or regulating it to offer its shares or debentures to the public.

•   For references to the memorandum or articles of association of a company there should be substituted references to any instrument constituting or regulating it.

[*Sec 718(1)-(3), 22 Sch; CA 1989, ss 71, 106, 108(3), 109(2), 123(5), 127(7), 130(5), 142(2), 143(11), 10 Sch 23, 19 Sch 21, 24 Sch; FSA 1986, 16 Sch 26; SI 1985 No 680; SI 1990 No 438; SI 1990 No 1394; SI 1990 No 2571; SI 1991 No 2705; SI 1993 No 3246, 2 Sch; SI 1997 No 2827, 8 Sch 9*].

These provisions do not repeal or revoke any enactment, Royal Charter or other instrument constituting or regulating any unregistered company or restrict the power to grant a charter in lieu of, or supplementary to, any such charter. However, the operation of any enactment etc. which is inconsistent with any other provisions is suspended. [*Sec 718(5)*].

Provision	Modification, extensions etc.
Sec 18 (statutory and other amendments to memorandum and articles to be registered – see 35.9 MEMORANDUM OF ASSOCIATION)	A printed copy of any instrument constituting or regulating the company must be forwarded to the Registrar of Companies not later than 15 days after incorporation notwithstanding that the instrument has been altered. References to such an instrument should be substituted for references to the memorandum and any alteration should be construed accordingly

Provision	*Modification, extensions etc.*
Secs 35–35B (company's capacity: power of directors to bind it – see 16.1 DEALINGS WITH THIRD PARTIES)	*Sec 35* and *Sec 35B* are without prejudice to any rule of law which gives a person dealing with a company incorporated by letters patent or Royal Charter any greater protection than afforded by those *sections*
Secs 36–36C (contracts and execution of documents – see 16.4 to 16.8 DEALINGS WITH THIRD PARTIES)	In *Secs 36, 36A, 36B* references to common or other authorised seal should be substituted for common seal
Sec 40 (official seal for share certificates – see 54.3 SEALS)	References to common or other authorised seal should be substituted for common seal
Sec 42 (events affecting a company's status to be officially notified – see 16.13 DEALINGS WITH THIRD PARTIES)	
Secs 82, 86, 87 (allotments following issue of a prospectus and application for listing on stock exchange – see 42.32 and 42.34 PROSPECTUSES AND PUBLIC ISSUES)	These provisions are repealed by *FSA 1986* from appointed days, some of which are already in force
Sec 185(4) (exemption from duty to prepare certificates where shares etc. issued to stock exchange nominee – see 57.11 SHARE TRANSFERS ETC.)	
Sec 186 (certificate as evidence of title – see 57.13 SHARE TRANSFERS ETC.)	References to common or other authorised seal should be substituted for common seal
Secs 221–262A, 4–10, 10A Schs (with certain exceptions) (accounts and audit – see chapters on ACCOUNTS generally)	
Sec 287 (see 46 REGISTERED OFFICE)	
Secs 288–290 (register of directors and secretaries – see 47.3 REGISTERS)	
Sec 322A (invalidity of certain transactions involving directors – see 19.72 DIRECTORS)	
Secs 343–347 (register to be kept of certain transactions not disclosed in accounts – other related matters – see 19.93 and 19.94 DIRECTORS)	

61.2 Unregistered Companies

Provision	Modification, extensions etc.
Sec 351(1)(2)(5)(a) (particulars of company to be given in correspondence – see 16.17 DEALINGS WITH THIRD PARTIES)	For 16.17(*a*) to (*d*) there should be substituted (*a*) where the company has its principal office in England, Wales or Scotland and the number allocated to the company by the Registrar of Companies; (*b*) the address of the principal office; and (*c*) the manner in which it was incorporated and, if it is a limited company, that fact
Secs 363–365 (see 10 ANNUAL RETURNS)	
Secs 384–394A (see 12.1 to 12.10 to 12.17, 12.27 and 12.28 AUDITORS)	
Secs 431–445, 447–453 (see 31 INVESTIGATIONS other than 31.9)	
Secs 454–457 (effect of order imposing restrictions on shares – see 21.9 to 21.11 DISCLOSURE OF INTERESTS IN PUBLIC COMPANY SHARES)	To apply so far only as relates to orders under *Sec 445*
Sec 458 (punishment for fraudulent trading by company – see 16.14 DEALINGS WITH THIRD PARTIES)	
Secs 706–710A, 711, 713 and *715A* (see 48.2(*b*)–(*h*) REGISTRAR OF COMPANIES)	*Sec 711* is extended to cover any instrument constituting or regulating the company and any notice of the situation of the company's principal office
Sec 720 (insurance companies and deposit, provident and benefit societies to publish periodical statement – see 6.58 ACCOUNTS: INSURANCE AND BANKING COMPANIES)	
Secs 721–723A (see 45.5 and 45.6 RECORDS) and *Secs 725, 731, 732* (see 32.6, 32.2 and 32.3 LEGAL PROCEEDINGS respectively) and *Sec 730, 24 Sch* (see 40.1 PENALTIES)	To apply only so far as they have effect in relation to previous provisions in this table
Secs 735–744A (interpretation)	To apply so far as necessary for the interpretation of other provisions applied by *Sec 718* or this table

61.2 Certain unincorporated bodies

The provisions in 61.1 and the table above also apply in relation to an unincorporated body of persons

- entitled by virtue of letters patent to any of the privileges conferred by the *Chartered Companies Act 1837*; and

- not registered under any other Act of Parliament

except that 61.1(*a*) does not apply. [*Sec 718(4)*].

62 Wales

Cross-references. See 36.1 and 36.2 NAMES AND BUSINESS NAMES for use of Welsh equivalent of 'limited' etc.

62.1 DOCUMENTS RELATING TO WELSH COMPANIES

A company (whether registered or to be registered) whose memorandum states that its registered office is to be situated in Wales (as opposed to England and Wales) may prepare in Welsh any document which is delivered to the Registrar of Companies under *CA 1985* or *IA 1986*. Subject to the exceptions below, the document must be accompanied by a 'certified translation' into English. See 28.2 FORMS for the meaning of *'certified translation'*.

There is no obligation on such a company to deliver a certified translation (although it may if it so wishes) of

(*a*)   documents in a form prescribed in Welsh (or partly in Welsh and partly in English) by *Welsh Language Act 1993, s 26*;

(*b*)   the annual accounts, directors' report and audit report of a company; and

(*c*)   documents appended to the annual accounts of a company under *Sec 243(2)* (accounts of overseas or unincorporated subsidiary undertakings, see 3.7 ACCOUNTS: GENERAL) or *9 Sch Part II, para 7* (banking groups: information as to undertakings in which shares are held as a result of financial assistance operations, see 6.122 ACCOUNTS: INSURANCE AND BANKING COMPANIES).

The provisions of (*b*) and (*c*) above do not apply to public companies whose shares or debentures (or any class thereof) are listed on The Stock Exchange, which companies must send an accompanying certified translation.

Where there is no obligation to deliver a certified translation, if the document is to be available for inspection, the Registrar must obtain a certified translation and that translation is treated as delivered to him in accordance with the same provision as the original.

[*Sec 710B; Welsh Language Act 1993, s 30; SI 1994 No 115; SI 1994 No 117; SI 1994 No 727*].

63   Table of Cases

64 Table of Statutes

65   Table of Statutory Instruments

65 Table of Statutory Instruments

66   Index

contents of, 35.2
copies to members, 35.11
effect of, 11.5, 35.5
form of, 35.3
guarantee companies, 29.2
name of company, 35.2
objects clause, 35.2
—alteration of, 35.7
public company, 35.2
registration of, 49.1
share capital, amount to be stated in,
 35.2
subscribers to, 35.4
—to pay cash for shares, 9.22
variation of class rights, 14.2
Wales, companies registered in, 62.1
Merger references, 44.10–44.19
conditions for, 44.11
EC provisions, 44.19
interim orders, 44.15
Monopolies and Mergers Commission,
 44.10, 59.7
—duties of, 44.12
—report of, 44.14
references in anticipation of merger
—by Secretary of State, 44.16
—by others, 44.17
undertakings as alternative to, 44.18
variations of, 44.13
Mergers, *see* Reconstructions and mergers
Minority interests
alteration of objects, right to apply to
 court, 35.8
application to investigate company's
 affairs, 31
compulsory acquisition of shares,
 59.19–59.27
group accounts, 4.18
protection of, 34.5
public company re-registering as private,
 49.12
requisition of EGM, 33.4
variation of rights, 14
Minutes, 33.15
form of minute book, 45.5

N

NAMES, 36.1–36.8
See also Business names
change of name, 36.6
—direction to, 36.5
—on re-registration of company, 49.4
common seal, 54.1

details in correspondence, etc, 16.15
—Scottish charitable companies, 53.7
display outside premises, 36.7
guarantee companies
—exclusion of 'limited' from name, 29.4
improper use of, 36.8
index to be kept by Registrar of
 Companies, 48.2
memorandum of association, 35.2
names requiring approval, 36.3
oversea companies, 38.4, 38.16–38.19
public companies, 36.1
registration, 36.4
—fee for, 26.1
—prohibition of certain names, 36.2
re-use of, 19.47
Wales, companies with registered offices
 in, 36.1, 36.2, 49.4
Non-cumulative preference shares, 58.4
**Notes to the accounts, 4.23–4.25,
 5.15–5.54**
See also Accounts; Balance sheet; Profit
 and loss account
accounting policies, disclosure of, 5.6,
 5.15, 7.8, 7.17
acquisitions and mergers, 4.17
auditors' remuneration, 5.44, 7.31
capital expenditure, contracts for, 5.22,
 7.24
charges on assets, 5.22, 7.24
comparative figures, 5.15, 7.17
contingent liabilities, 5.22, 7.24
debentures, 5.17
deferred tax, 5.20
depreciation, 5.8, 5.18, 7.10, 7.20
development costs, 5.8, 7.10
directors' emoluments, 5.33–5.38, 7.30
—aggregate, 5.34
—compensation, 5.37
—highest paid, 5.35
—pensions, 5.36
—sums payable to third parties, 5.38
—waived, 5.35
directors' loans, etc., 5.39–5.42, 7.30
dividends, 5.23
—cumulative, 5.21
employees, 5.28
exceptional items, 5.29, 7.29
extraordinary items, 5.29, 7.29
fixed assets, 5.18, 7.20
foreign currency translation, 5.15, 7.17
general, 5.15
goodwill, 5.8, 7.10

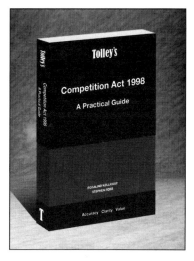

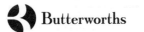

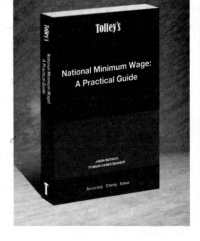

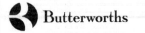